COLORADO CATHOLICISM

COLORADO CATHOLICISM
and
THE ARCHDIOCESE OF DENVER
1857–1989

Thomas J. Noel

INTRODUCTION BY J. FRANCIS STAFFORD,
ARCHBISHOP OF DENVER

UNIVERSITY PRESS OF COLORADO

First Edition

The University Press of Colorado is a cooperative publishing enterprise supported, in part, by Adams State College, Colorado State University, Fort Lewis College, Mesa State College, Metropolitan State College, University of Colorado, University of Northern Colorado, University of Southern Colorado, and Western State College.

The paper used in this publication meets the minimum requirements of the American National Standard for Information Sciences—Permanence of Paper for Printed Library Materials, ANSI Z39.48–1984.

Library of Congress Cataloging-in-Publication Data

Noel, Thomas J. (Thomas Jacob)
 Colorado Catholicism and the Archdiocese of Denver, 1857–1989 / Thomas J. Noel; introduction by J. Francis Stafford.—1st ed.
     p.   cm.
 Includes bibliographical references.
 ISBN 0-87081-179-7 (alk. paper)
 !. Catholic Church. Archdiocese of Denver (Colo.)—History. 2. Catholic Church—Colorado—History. 3. Colorado—Church history. I. Title.
BX1417.D35N64 1989
282'.788—dc20   89-27803

Manufactured in the United States of America

CONTENTS

PREFACE

The Roman Catholic Church has been Colorado's largest single denomination since 1857, yet it, unlike most other religions, has not received a detailed historical overview. At the request of the archdiocese of Denver, I have attempted to fill that gap with this book. Those wanting Colorado's Catholic experience tied to national and international trends will not find that here. My focus is on the Church's role in Colorado communities, on the interrelationship of the state's history and Catholicism.

Frederick Jackson Turner argued that the frontier transformed Americans. My investigation of one institution suggests the contrary: The wilder and more remote the frontier, the more some people—especially women—hungered for churches like those they had known "back home." True, the first churches, with their makeshift altars and pews, were shaped by frontier conditions; but even in primitive buildings, people prized statues and paintings, music and pageantry that were European in origin. Latin masses and Gregorian chant were heard in even the crudest churches, and in the saloons, public halls, and fraternal lodges that often sheltered pioneer religious services. The striking thing is not how the frontier affected the early Church, but how quickly Westerners installed the old traditions.

In one way, the frontier did shape Bishop Machebeuf, who learned its reckless optimism and borrowed money to the hilt—at breathtaking interest rates. As much as any miner or town promoter, Machebeuf never doubted that Colorado would pay off. Although he died on the edge of bankruptcy, he left his diocese rich in land and institutions.

As in other dioceses around the world, many of the priests and nuns who came to Colorado were foreign-born. The first religious were Spanish and French, soon reinforced by Germans, Italians, and Irish. Today, differences among European immigrant groups are minimal: The primary split is between Anglo and Hispanic cultures. To this day, some in New Mexico regard Machebeuf as Bishop Lamy's hatchet man, who drove out Hispanic priests with petty accusations and lack of sympathy for the Hispanic culture. That view is perhaps best explored in Fray Angelico Chávez's book, *But Time and Chance: The Story of Padre Martínez of Taos, 1793–1867.*

In 1887, Rome authorized creation of the Diocese of Denver from what had been the vicariate apostolic of the missionary era. Under bishops Matz, Tihen, and Vehr, the diocese struggled to build not only a church but also a school in every community. A good number of the churches, schools, hospitals, and foster care facilities in Colorado today were founded during the pioneer era of bishops Machebeuf and Matz, but most churches and schools during the long reign of Archbishop Vehr who tried to keep pace with Colorado's post–World War II boom. This parish building process and the traditional Catholic lifestyle were reversed during the post Vatican II era of Archbishop Casey. That postwar boom ended with the oil bust of 1983—a replay of Colorado's familiar boom and bust pattern in gold and silver, coal and gravel, uranium and molybdenum, farming and ranching, oil and water. Colorado lost population for the first time in decades, and Archbishop Stafford has seen his role as preserving rather than creating parishes. Although it is too early to tell, the era of Archbishop Stafford, since 1987, seems to be something of a return to traditionalism and conservatism. Critics have labeled the archbishop "ultramontane," but he is praised as one of the key leaders of the modern church in George Weigel's 1989 book, *Catholicism and the Renewal of American Democracy*. Especially when covering these recent decades, I have tried to provide only overviews of what happened, not to explain or assess. That task will fall to later historians.

As this manuscript goes to the publisher, I am aware of neglected sources, topics, and perspectives. Nevertheless, I hope you will find it a useful preliminary survey of Colorado Catholicism. As Father Howlett warned at the beginning of his 1911 manuscript history of the parishes of the Denver diocese: "No one is more painfully aware of the difficulties of writing a competent history of the parishes of Colorado. . . .There will necessarily be some inaccuracies in this account, which I leave subject to correction."

Concerning the inevitable errors and shortcomings of this book, please send corrections, additions, and complaints to the Archdiocesan Archives, 200 Josephine Street, Denver, Colorado 80206, where they can be kept on file. In the event that this book is reprinted, corrections will be made. If not, they will at least be saved for whoever writes the next history.

ACKNOWLEDGMENTS

Tom Weaver, Father John Anderson, and Monsignor Michael Chamberlain first proposed this book and have been patiently supportive as a one-year project turned into a three-year effort. Cathy Cancino of the Office of Major Giving helped type, retype, mail, sort, and proofread various drafts of the parish histories and bishops' biographies.

Many other people at the Archdiocesan Pastoral Center made the project possible, most notably archivist Sister Ann Walter, OSB. She not only provided access to her well-organized treasure trove but also made me and my students feel at home by her cheerful assistance. With her red pencil, Sister Ann, a former English teacher, greatly improved this manuscript by making it, as she puts it, "bleed."

Sister Jarlath McManus, CSJ, provided documents, information, and a review of much of the manuscript. Sister Mary Agnes McAuliffe, SC, historian for the Western Region of the Sisters of Charity, may have finally straightened me out on some confusing matters of "which order did what when." I leaned most heavily on Monsignor William H. Jones' book, *The History of Catholic Education in the State of Colorado*, and on interviews and manuscript reviews he graciously provided.

Monsignor Gregory Smith, who has one of the longest and sharpest memories I have encountered, provided critical as well as colorful detail, based on his key role in church matters ever since Tihen's time. Monsignor Thomas Barry, Father John Anderson, Sister Rosemary Wilcox, SL, and Sister Rosemary Keegan, SL, also provided unusually vivid recollections of things past.

Archbishop J. Francis Stafford generously granted interviews. His candor and support have been heartening. Fathers Edward Buelt and Edward Hoffmann provided interviews and most helpful reviews of the manuscript. Sister Mary Lucy Downey, SCL, gave me a tour of the Archdiocesan Housing Committee, Inc., projects, while James Mauck offered an interview, materials, and clarifications on the role of Catholic Community Services.

At the busy offices of the *Denver Catholic Register,* editor James E. Fiedler, managing editor Patricia Hillyer, staff writers Marty Moran, Harv Bishop, and Christine Capra-Kramer, as well as photo librarian Jacqueline Martinez were wonderfully helpful. Prize-winning *Register* photographer James Baca has graciously allowed use of his crackerjack work. Unless otherwise credited, the other illustrations are from the *Denver Catholic Register.* Zinaida "Sadie" Herrara saved me much time with her indispensible annual production, *The Official Directory of the Catholic Archdiocese of Denver.*

Thanks also for the skillful support of Eleanor Gehres and her staff at the Western History Department of the Denver Public Library, and Stan Oliner and the staff at the Colorado Historical Society Library. Fathers Harold Stansell, SJ, and Tom Steele, SJ, at Regis College, provided information and manuscript reviews. Many others, whose names appear in the text and in the sources, offered assistance for which I am grateful.

Luther Wilson and the crew at the University Press of Colorado transformed a troublesome, tattered, 850-page manuscript into this tome. Michael P. McKee, the amiable wizard who manages archdiocesan data processing, and June Callahan and Gerry Darr at the University of Colorado at Denver brought me into the computer age, rescued me from word processing nightmares, and helped with formatting and printing multiple drafts. Many CU-Denver students came to the rescue with parish histories, which supplemented my own research. They included Lynette Benson, Lien Bui, Dave Cole, Carole Hildebrant, Mary Judge, Randy Lichtenfield, Gwynne Ellen McFarland, Diana Miller, Ben Negrette, Hai Xuan Nguyen, Maggie O'Connor, Maureen Parish, Sarah Przekwas, Mike Rael, Steve Stamm, Betsy Stapp, Greg Thomas, Jill Thomas, and My Tran. Student histories of Catholic institutions and churchmen, which also augmented my research, were completed by Santa Adams, Mark Buchanan, Patrick J. Canavan, Andrew Coukous, Letitia Czartoryski, Denise Drvedahl, Patricia Halpine, and Gina Kastel. Three graduate students— Peg Ekstrand, Ben Negrette, and Vicki Rubin—helped in various ways, as did the indispensible graduate student assistant on this project, Sarah Przekwas. Fernie Baca, assistant vice-chancellor for research at CU-Denver, found graduate student research funding.

Outside reviewers, who improved this story, include the late Margaret Jacob, Philip Goodstein, Stephen J. Leonard, Duane A. Smith, and Ed J. Haley—the veteran cartographer, historian, and editor. Louise J. Noel, Dennis Gallagher, Lara Walchuk, and Vi—my wife— helped. To Vi, I dedicate this work. During its creation she joined the church and prayed this would be finished and acceptable.

Thomas J. Noel
April 1, 1989

INTRODUCTION

I lift up my eyes to the mountains;
whence shall help come to me.
My help is from the Lord,
Who made heaven and earth.
Psalm 121

Psalm 121, the song of Hebrew pilgrims journeying to Jerusalem to celebrate their faith, suits our homeland, Colorado. From the eastern plains, the central peaks, and the western plateaus, we join our voices with the men and women who have gone before us. With them we proclaim, "O Lord, you have been our refuge through all generations. Before the mountains were begotten and the earth and the world were brought forth, from everlasting to everlasting you are God" (Psalm 90:1–2).

When we celebrate anniversaries, our hearts and minds—almost without conscious effort or forethought—turn spontaneously to the people, the events, and even the places of those times. The 1987 celebration of the 100 years of the Catholic Church of the Rocky Mountain region was no exception. Part of that centennial was launching this book by Tom Noel of the University of Colorado at Denver. This is not just a history of the Archdiocese of Denver, it is a testament to that heritage we hold dear as Catholics in Colorado; to the faith of those early pilgrims and their children, who sacrificed to plant its seeds and nurture its growth.

Three centuries ago, Hispanic Catholic priests were singing their praises to God in the untamed, uncharted Colorado wilderness. And when the gold rush came, Bishop Jean Lamy of Santa Fe added the Pike's Peak region to his already vast vicariate of New Mexico, Arizona, and Utah. Lamy assigned his compatriate and right-hand man, Father Joseph Projectus Machebeuf, to the mission of Colorado and Utah in 1860. Machebeuf opened St. Mary Church in Denver for Christmas Eve mass that winter. The following spring, he began his missionary treks to establish churches in the mountain mining towns and the agricultural hamlets of the high plains. In a short time, Machebeuf established Catholicism as the largest and strongest Christian community in the Rocky Mountain West. For spiritual and financial support, Machebeuf appealed to the older churches of the San Luis Valley and New Mexico.

"Down among the Mexicans, who owned nothing but a mud house and a burro, he could always raise money. If they had anything at all, they gave," Willa Cather wrote in her great novel, *Death Comes for the Archbishop*. With such support, Machebeuf transformed the mission of Colorado into what became, in 1887, the Diocese of Denver.

When Father Machebeuf became the first bishop of Denver, he chose as the symbols of his newly established diocese the symbol of Christianity itself—the Holy Cross—and the sign of the sinless Mother of God—the crescent moon. The cross had been impressed upon the Colorado landscape even before the Crucifixion—in the granite sides of the Mount of the Holy Cross. This 14,005-foot-high peak in the Gore Range between Leadville and Vail has inspired the countless faithful who have witnessed its grandeur or heard about its wonder.

One popular legend tells of the first sighting of the Mount of the Holy Cross by two Spanish priests in the early 1700s: Crossing the Rocky Mountains, the two became hopelessly lost in a raging blizzard and were on the verge of death. Suddenly, the clouds parted, and the cross was revealed. Having thus been renewed in faith and hope, the pilgrims resumed their journey and found their way safely home.

Believing in the special care of the crucified and risen Christ for this newborn Church, the first pilgrims to this land would naturally seek the maternal protection of our Savior's Mother. As she had stood vigil at the foot of her Son's cross, so our ancestors sought her constant watchfulness for themselves and for those after them whose Catholic faith would be nurtured in the majesty of the Rockies and the simplicity of the plains. On the great seal of the archdiocese, against a red background, the two arms of her crescent moon embrace the cross, symbolic of two great geological regions of our archdiocese—the mountains and the plains.

It is my confident prayer that the cross of Christ will always reign over this land and in the hearts of those who make their home here. It is my further prayer that all who are blessed to call themselves Catholic will always and forever embrace that cross—the source of all fruitfulness. And it is my prayer that the cross of Jesus in eternity will be our glory whether we are farmers or ranchers, skiers or hikers, businessmen or businesswomen, homemakers and educators—our hearts and hands for God.

J. Francis Stafford
Archbishop of Denver

BOOK I

HISTORY OF THE ARCHDIOCESE

PROLOGUE: THE HISPANIC ROOTS OF COLORADO CATHOLICISM

European settlement of the Americas started with the Spanish. They were the first from the Old World to explore, write about, settle, and Christianize what has become the United States of America, a fact sometimes forgotten in what has become an English-speaking culture.

New Mexico and Florida—not Virginia and Massachusetts—boast the oldest Christian churches in the United States. When Anglicans in Virginia, and Pilgrims and Puritans in Massachusetts, discouraged Catholicism, Maryland was founded in 1632 as a haven for Catholics, and was the home of John Carroll, SJ, who in 1790 was appointed the first Catholic bishop in the United States. In 1808, he became archbishop of Baltimore with suffragans at Boston, New York, Philadelphia, and Bardstown, Kentucky.

By 1840, there were sixteen dioceses in the eastern United States. After that time, massive immigration of Irish, German, Italian, Slavic, and other Catholic peoples nourished a tremendous growth in the number of dioceses. The Denver diocese, however, also had roots in the much older Church of Mexico. The Diocese of Durango was created soon after that city was founded in 1562. By the time the English Pilgrims landed at Plymouth Rock, the Spanish had planted eleven churches in New Mexico. From these bases, priests ventured into Colorado.

Even before the Spanish and the Mexican priests came, Colorado's Native Americans had developed a culture that helped to shape Colorado Catholicism. At prehistoric settlements such as Mesa Verde, the Anasazi (Navajo for the Ancient Ones) had developed an advanced, urban civilization with religion at its heart. Kivas such as those at Mesa Verde are the oldest churches to be seen in Colorado today.

In these mud and masonry temples, the ancients worshipped their God and asked for mercy and for rain. The sophisticated religion of these Anasazi survives in the rites of the Pueblo people of the Rio Grande valley. The Catholic Church, with its 1,900-year-old talent for borrowing from other rituals, has used some of the ancient rites of the Anasazi and the Pueblo. The Eye of God (*Ojo de Dios*) and the gourd rattle, for instance, are often used in mariachi masses.

A few Franciscan friars may have wandered into what is now Colorado with early Spanish expeditions. Some say Fray Juan de Padilla, a member of Coronado's 1540 expedition, was the first priest to say mass and administer the sacraments in Colorado.

Colorado's oldest churches are probably the kivas in cliff dwellings such as these at Mesa Verde. (Photo by Jesse Nusbaum, Denver Public Library.)

Most modern scholars, however, find no evidence that Coronado actually entered Colorado on his pioneer probe, which got as far as present-day Kansas.

A Franciscan friar, Domingo de Anza, apparently established the first mission in Colorado in 1706. Colorado's misty Hispanic heritage may hide earlier missions, but this was the first to be well documented. Fray Domingo was with the expedition of Juan de Ulibarri, who documented his excursion in a diary and officially claimed what is now Colorado for King Philip V of Spain. Fray Domingo opened his mission at El Quartelejo, an Apache village thought to be near the junction of Horse Creek and the Arkansas River, about fifty miles east of the present city of Pueblo.

Fray Domingo and later missionaries began preaching among the Apache and converted some of them—with the help of chocolate and tobacco. In the summer of 1720, Don Pedro de Villasur journeyed with Spanish troops and a Franciscan friar north from El Quartelejo as far as the South Platte River, which he named Río de Jesús y María.

Various Spanish parties and priests probed Colorado in the subsequent years. Two Spanish Franciscan priests put this *terra incognita* on the maps of the Christian world:

Francisco Atanasio Dominguez, the Franciscan superior of the missionary Province of New Mexico, led the expedition; Fray Silvestre Vélez de Escalante, the Franciscan missionary at Zuñi Pueblo, compiled the diary that made the Dominguez-Escalante expedition famous. Among many other achievements, the expedition produced the first detailed map of Colorado.

Clad in the long brown or blue robes and broad-brimmed hats of the Franciscans, Dominguez and Vélez de Escalante set out from Santa Fe on July 29, 1776, in the same month that revolutionaries in the English colonies drew up a Declaration of Independence. The tiny, nine-man Spanish party pushed on through what is now Pagosa Springs, Durango, Mancos, and Dolores, sprinkling the rugged landscape with the gentle names of saints.

Spaniards, the first explorers and missionaries in Colorado, have been subjected to snide stereotyping, as this sketch by Frederic Remington suggests. (Denver Public Library.)

From a lookout that Vélez de Escalante called Nuestra Señora de Las Nieves, they surveyed the snow-capped San Juan Mountains. The San Juan River valley, Fray Silvestre scribbled in his diary, was "good land with prospects for irrigation and everything needed for three or four settlements, even if large ones."

Continuing westward, the priests and their tiny party crossed El Rio de Las Animas and El Río de Nuestra Señora de las Dolores. On the Dolores River, they encountered the Anasazi ghost village now famous as the Escalante Ruin. When the Spaniards became lost, they prayed. "After begging the intercession of our patron saints that God might direct us," Fray Silvestre reported, "we cast lots." God and the lots steered them westward over prickly terrain where they encountered a Ute village. The Spaniards used tobacco and white glass trade beads to recruit a guide. A short, friendly, dark-skinned Ute gave the Spaniards jerked deer meat and dried fruits and led them to the Uncompahgre River valley. At the headwaters of the Uncompahgre, Fray Silvestre marveled at "a spring of red-colored water, hot and ill-tasting." They followed the river northward past the future sites of Montrose and Delta to where it joined a much larger river that they christened El Río de San Francisco Xavier. (A century later, it would be renamed for another explorer, Captain John W. Gunnison.)

Ute Indians, Colorado natives for hundreds of years, welcomed the Franciscan padres Vélez de Escalante and Domínguez. (1873 photo by John Hillers. Denver Public Library.)

Continuing northward past what is now Grand Junction, the Spaniards encountered a Ute village of thirty tipis. Fearlessly, Fray Dominguez "went into the chieftain's tent and, after embracing him and his children, asked him to gather his people. When the Utes had assembled, he announced the Gospel to them through the interpreter. All listened with pleasure." When one Ute boasted of having two wives, Fray Dominguez "grasped the opportunity to instruct them on this point."

"God's glory and the good of souls," Fray Silvestre added in his diary, inspired the Spaniards "not to engage in trade . . . so that the infidels might understand that another motive higher than this one brought us through these parts." With the help of the Utes whom Vélez de Escalante described as "all of good features and very friendly," the Dominguez-Escalante party traveled on north. They found the Indian petroglyphs in Cañon Pintado near the future town of Rangely, killed and roasted a bison, and finally reached the Green River. There the Franciscans carved into a large cottonwood tree the cross of Christ, whom they trusted would lead them out of the primeval Colorado wilderness.

Despite reports of gold and silver from the Dominguez-Escalante party, the Spaniards would never plant a permanent settlement in what is now Colorado. Not until after the 1821 Mexican Revolution would Hispanics settle on the upper Rio Grande. By 1851, when San Luis became the first permanent settlement, in what is now Colorado, the Mexican American War was over; the land and the people were part of the United States. These new U.S. citizens were promised they could keep their own land, their culture, and their Catholicism by the Treaty of Guadalupe Hidalgo, the 1848 peace pact between the United States and Mexico. After the 1858 gold discovery near the confluence of Cherry Creek and the South Platte River, some 50,000 Americans threatened to overwhelm the culture of these earlier Coloradans. Spanish-surnamed pioneers of the upper Río Grande valley struggled to maintain their landholdings, their language, their culture, and their religion. In their isolation they clung to their religion and to each other, sharing what little they had.

To minister to these Hispanics and to Catholics among the mining hordes, the archbishop of Sante Fe selected a frail looking Frenchman; Joseph Projectus Machebeuf. In 1860, he was assigned a new parish—all of what is now Colorado and Utah. Father Machebeuf found an improbable ally in the famed mountain man, Kit Carson. This legendary explorer and Indian fighter converted to Catholicism in 1842 to win the hand of the beautiful Josefa Jaramillo, daughter of one of the most prominent clans in the Southwest. She was also the sister-in-law of Charles Bent.

After Charles Bent had been installed as the first U.S. territorial governor of New Mexico, Mexicans and Pueblo Indians revolted in Taos. On the morning of January 19, 1847, they murdered Governor Bent. Although this revolt was quickly surpressed, both Indians and Mexicans remained restless under Yankee governance. Carson, one of the most respected gringos in Taos, helped discourage revolutionary sentiment. Defending the prelates assigned to Americanize the Church in the southwest; he warned malcontents:

Kit Carson, the famed mountain man and commander of Fort Garland, was a defender of the faith. (Denver Public Library.)

> We shall not let them do as they did then in 1847 when they murdered and pillaged. I am a man of peace . . . but I can fight a little yet, and I know of no better cause to fight for than my family, my Church and my friend the Señor Vicario Machebeuf.

As the commander at Fort Garland in southern Colorado, Brigadier General Carson welcomed Father Machebeuf's services. When Father Machebeuf arrived at the fort in his buggy, he gave medals and holy pictures to the children, and catechism books to their parents. Machebeuf was surprised and pleased at his welcome at the fort, where Catholic soldiers prepared and decorated an improvised chapel and served mass "as well as the best altar boys."

Bishop Joseph Projectus Machebeuf.

CHAPTER 1

MACHEBEUF: THE APOSTLE OF COLORADO, 1860–1889

If Father Machebeuf ever complained about his American assignment, his letters and his biographer do not reveal it. Yet this harsh new frontier must have left him homesick for France, which he visited whenever the rare opportunity arose. He longed to see his cherished sister, who became a nun and took the religious name he chose for her, Sister Marie Philomene. He also missed his younger brother Marius and his father, a master baker. They lived in Riom, in the southeast central French province of Auvergne, where Machebeuf had been born August 11, 1812. Auvergne was a land not unlike Colorado with its hills and deep river gorges, hot springs, and the Auvergne Mountains. But Colorado farmers would never produce the fine wines and cheeses that made Auvergne famous. Memories of such delicacies left Machebeuf even more hungry and thirsty for his homeland.

Encouraged by a pious mother, who died when he was thirteen, young Joseph had attended the Christian Brothers School in Riom and then enrolled in the seminary at Mont Ferrand, which was conducted by the Sulpician fathers. He was ordained December 21, 1836. Auvergne Province was blessed with many more religious vocations than positions and sent its priests all over the world as missionaries. When John M. Odin, who later became bishop of Galveston and archbishop of New Orleans, came recruiting priests for the missions of America, young Machebeuf volunteered.

Father Machebeuf sailed from Le Havre on July 9, 1839. On board, he relished the salt air and the spirited company of a childhood friend and fellow seminarian, Jean Baptiste Lamy. Forty-four days after leaving France, they arrived in New York. The two young missionaries were delighted to be welcomed by other French priests, including the

Bishop Jean B. Lamy of Santa Fe, immortalized in Willa Cather's novel, *Death Comes for the Archbishop*, sent Father Machebeuf northward in 1860 to plant Catholicism in Colorado. (Denver Public Library.)

bishop of New York City. Machebeuf's first assignment was to the small town of Tiffin in northern Ohio. After a year as assistant pastor there, Machebeuf became the founding pastor of Holy Angels parish in Sandusky, where he served until 1849.

Father Machebeuf absorbed himself in learning English, American ways, and parish administration. He discovered that his new countrymen were fighting and winning a war far away in the Southwest. After Mexico's defeat, the United States acquired vast new territory that would become the states of New Mexico, Arizona, California, Nevada, Utah, and part of Colorado.

While the U.S. government tried to establish civil control over the Southwest, the American Church hierarchy grappled with the problem of Americanizing what had been Mexican parishes. In 1850, Father Lamy was named vicar apostolic in charge of New Mexico and Arizona, headquartered in Santa Fe. Father Machebeuf had just grown comfortable and even fond of "my dear Sandusky" when Father Lamy "grasped my hand and summoned me to keep my part of the agreement which we made never to separate." At the new vicar apostolic's insistence, Father Machebeuf became his vicar general in New Mexico. The two Frenchmen steamed down the Ohio and Mississippi to New Orleans, then procured an army escort across the plains of Texas, noted for hostile Comanches and desperados.

From El Paso, Lamy and Machebeuf followed the Rio Grande River route northward to Santa Fe. Machebeuf reported that "General Stephen W. Kearney, whose wife is a Catholic, gave us the privilege of drawing rations each week from the government supplies . . . and of paying for them at government prices." General Kearney also loaned the clergymen an army tent, but Machebeuf reported that "the nights were so calm and beautiful that we almost always slept out in open air." After a 400 mile trip across "a formidable desert" where "many human bones tell their tale of Indian slaughter,"

Machebeuf wrote that they received a cool reception from the Hispanics of Santa Fe. Over half the Mexican-American clergy eventually left New Mexico rather than serve under the new French-American hierarchy.

Upon their entry into Santa Fe on August 8, 1851, Lamy and Machebeuf were welcomed by the local Indians. Machebeuf reported that 8,000 to 9,000 Native Americans, wearing "gaudy and grotesque" costumes, built triumphal arches, "spread their shawls and cloaks on the ground for us to walk on," and welcomed them with "the docility of children." This riotous welcome, Machebeuf added, left Santa Fe's four Protestant ministers "filled with rage and envy."

The Mexican vicar of Santa Fe, Monsignor Juan Felipe Ortiz, had reservations about recognizing Lamy. Only after Lamy made a difficult 1,500 mile journey to see the bishop of Durango, José Antonio Laureano López de Zurbiria y Escalante, did Vicar Ortiz surrender the New Mexican church property. Padrés José Gallegos of Albuquerque, Antonio Martínez of Taos, and some other Mexican priests continued to challenge some of the reforms imposed by the new vicar apostolic. Lamy often sent his assistant, the loyal Machebeuf, out to the provinces to deal with these difficult cases, which ultimately were appealed to Rome. In a May 31, 1852, letter to his sister, Machebeuf reported that the Santa Fe vicariate, which included New Mexico, Arizona, and part of Colorado, was a vast "vineyard so overrun with thorns and thistles." Machebeuf courageously and persistently tried to discipline the rebellious Mexican priests. "Bishop Lamy is sure to send me where there is a bad case to be settled," Machebeuf once wrote to his sister. "I am always the one to whip the cats."

In 1853, Lamy's vicariate was made a diocese, and he a bishop. Machebeuf was appointed pastor first at Albuquerque (1853–1858) and then Santa Fe (1858–1860), while also tending missions throughout New Mexico, Arizona, and Southern Colorado. Rumors flew that Machebeuf would be appointed vicar apostolic of Arizona with headquarters at San Xavier del Bac mission in Tucson. The rumors did not end until Machebeuf's 1860 appointment as vicar apostolic of Colorado and Utah.

On his missionary travels throughout Colorado, New Mexico, Arizona, and Utah, Machebeuf logged over 100,000 miles. He traveled in a wagon outfitted with a square canvas top so he could sleep inside. This heavy carriage had side curtains, a half-curtain in front to be let down in case of storms, and a tailgate that could be lowered and used as an altar. Inside what he called his ambulance, Machebeuf had fixed up compartments for his Mass vestments and vessels as well as hay for the mules, and food, a frying pan, and a coffee pot for himself. He also kept close at hand his rosary, his breviary, and his copy

In Conejos, Our Lady of Guadalupe, the oldest church in Colorado, has evolved from the adobe fortress photographed by Timothy O'Sullivan in 1874 to a stately brick Romanesque landmark. (Museum of New Mexico.)

of Thomas à Kempis's *The Imitation of Christ*. This rolling church and rectory was pulled by two Mexican mules, which Machebeuf found more durable than American horses.

Whenever possible, Machebeuf preferred to sleep outside in his buffalo robe under the Southwestern stars. This short, wiry Frenchman became tough and tan after enduring sunstroke and blizzards, cactus and lice. Willa Cather—in her novel *Death Comes for the Archbishop*—created a vivid portrait of the man who toiled in that rough vineyard:

> Crimson from standing over an open fire, his rugged face was even homelier than usual—though one of the first things a stranger decided upon meeting Father Joseph was that the Lord had made few uglier men. He was short, skinny, bow-legged from a life on horseback, and his countenance had little to recommend it but kindliness and vivacity. He looked old, though he was then about forty. His skin was hardened and seamed by exposure to weather in a bitter climate . . . his eyes were near-sighted, and of such a pale watery blue as to be unimpressive. . . . [He was] homely, real, persistent, with the driving power of a dozen men in his poorly built body.

On one of his many cross-country treks, a fellow priest complained of the howling wolves at night. Those are only coyotes, Machebeuf reassured him and added, "You dreaded the monotony of the plains; you ought to be glad to have a free band to serenade you!" When spirits or health flagged seriously, Machebeuf might retreat to his wagon and bring out a bottle of French wine.

On Machebeuf's 1860 journey from Santa Fe to Denver to establish St. Mary parish, he and Father Jean Baptiste Raverdy stopped at the pioneer Catholic church in Colorado, Nuestra Señora de Guadalupe in Conejos. To get to Conejos, they had followed a tributary stream of the Rio Grande that flowed out of the San Juan Mountains into the broad valley of San Luis. Some said the tributary was called Conejos because it ran as swiftly as a rabbit; others said it was because of all the jackrabbits.

Nuestra Señora de Guadalupe, the patroness of Mexico, had guided Mexican settlers up the Conejos River, according to local folklore. A mule had refused to move on after the immigrants stopped at a cottonwood-shaded site on the Conejos nineteen miles west of the Rio Grande. The party had cajoled and cursed, pushed and pulled, but the beast would not budge. Then someone pointed out that this was the mule carrying the image of Our Lady of Guadalupe; surely this was a sign from heaven. On that spot, the village of Guadalupe was founded in 1854.

The Conejos River flooded the town that spring, and Indians ambushed shepherds as they headed out to the fields one morning. José María Jaques and other leaders decided to move the settlement to higher ground and rename it Conejos. There, these Mexican pioneers constructed a plaza rimmed with adobe buildings to keep in the sheep, goats, pigs, cattle, and mules and to keep out the Apaches and Utes.

Together, settlers dug the Conejos ditch to water corn and wheat, beans and peppers. To grind their corn and wheat, townsfolk started one of Colorado's first grist mills. They also decided to take up Bishop Lamy's offer: While visiting in 1854, the bishop had promised to send a priest if the people would build a church. With the communal energy that made Conejos one of the first successful colonies in Colorado, they went to work and, in 1857, celebrated completion of their church, which they called Nuestra Señora de Guadalupe.

In 1858, Father Machebeuf said his first Colorado mass at the little chapel at Conejos. It was a primitive *jacal* built of cedar posts stood on end and lashed together in stockade fashion. Adobe mud was plastered over to fill the cracks. This structure, though altered greatly over the years, is the oldest surviving Christian church in Colorado, but it is not, as is sometimes stated, the first. Louisa Ward Arps, in *Faith on the Frontier: Religion in Colorado before August 1876*, pointed out that the first non-Indian church in Colorado was apparently a Mormon log meeting house built in Pueblo in 1846 and in use for several years before an Arkansas River flood swept it away.

Initially, the Conejos church was tended as a mission by priests from Ojo Caliente, Arroyo Hondo, and Taos, three New Mexican parishes. In 1858, Bishop Lamy sent a resident pastor, José Vicente Montaño. Father Montaño founded a second Southern Colorado parish in 1860 at San Luis, the pioneer settlement on Culebra Creek. The San Luis church, Sangre de Cristo, became an independent parish with its own pastor, Joseph Percevault, in 1869. Sangre de Cristo parish helped establish and tend mission chapels at a dozen towns on the eastern side of the San Luis Valley, including Chama, San Acacio, San Francisco, San Pedro, Sierra Blanca, Trinchera, and Zapato.

Gabriel Ussel, who spent many years as a priest in the San Luis valley, recalled in his unpublished memoirs how he and Father Machebeuf traveled to the tiny villages for each town's feast day. Before dawn, by the light of pinon wood fires, priests and villagers met, for

> the morning chanted Mass, the procession, and that little world of people came from everywhere to participate in the religious festivity, and the usual innocent amusement of a happy people. The panorama of gaudy dress, the foot races, the horse races . . . short comedy all in the open air . . . enlivened by the musicians' band.

Guadalupe at Conejos became the mother church for at least twenty-five missions in the San Luis Valley and the San Juan Mountains to the west, including Alamosa, Antonito, Capulin, Cat Creek, Cerritos, Cumbres, La Jara, Mesitas, Osier, Pagosa Springs, and the mining camps on the headwaters of the Animas River. Some of these missions became churches, such as Sacred Heart parish in Alamosa. Others have disappeared, as have some of the towns. Many settlements that had oratorios, if not chapels, have vanished, leaving only forlorn little cemeteries and fragile folklore clues to now vanished Mexican villages.

While villages and missions came and went, the pioneer church at Conejos thrived. The Jesuits took over in 1871 with the arrival of Father Salvatore Persone. He soon was joined by three other Jesuit priests and, in 1877, Guadalupe parish built a convent and a school for the Sisters of Loretto, who opened Sacred Heart Academy as a private school and also taught in the public schools. The pioneer parish at Conejos spearheaded the Church's development in Southern Colorado with its academy and its many missions. Indeed, Our Lady of Guadalupe parish was second only in achievement to St. Mary's in Denver, where Father Machebeuf was also busy building firm foundations for what would become the Vicariate Apostolic of Colorado in 1868.

Joseph P. Machebeuf and his countryman, Father Raverdy, arrived in Denver on October 29, 1860. As Machebeuf wrote later, they were

> obliged to camp out on the 2 bare lots donated in Denver by the Express Co. and having no neighbors but squirrels [prairie dogs] and rattlesnakes. . . . We walked around to see, not the city, but the little village of Denver, made up of low frame stores, log cabins, tents and Indian wigwams on the banks of the Platte.

The handful of Catholics in Denver had acquired two lots at 15th and Stout streets and materials to build a fifty-by-thirty-foot chapel. This "pile of bricks and shingles was shown to us way out on the prairie," Machebeuf reminisced:

We all said, "what a folly to build a church so far from the town." Although in those days I was not lame, it tired me to walk to the spot. . . . We could not continue to camp in the big city of Denver . . . so I contracted to have a house built in eight days for $75 . . . in the rear of the church.

In the little shack tacked onto the rear of the church, Machebeuf and Raverdy used "our coats for a pillow" and a "mattress made

INDIAN VILLAGE IN DENVER, IN 1860.

Arapaho Indians camped in and around Denver "would not hurt me," Father Machebeuf reassured his family in France. When native Americans threatened to steal his food, Machebeuf served them pickles, glasses of vinegar, and a pile of black pepper. (Tom Noel Collection.)

up of our buffalo robe." Machebeuf begged, borrowed, and bought materials, then recruited volunteer labor to complete the church in time to say the first mass on Christmas Eve, 1860, in the windowless, unplastered church. On Christmas morning, Father Raverdy sang a second mass in Latin colored by his rich French accent. Father Machebeuf, who said the rosary daily, named the church for his special love, St. Mary.

"Our people," he noted, "were proud to have the first brick church in Denver." St. Mary's offered musical masses as Machebeuf had brought a melodeon with him from Santa Fe. Machebeuf acquired "a fine new Gothic case organ," according to the *Rocky Mountain News* of January 22, 1863, and St. Mary's began offering classical masses by composers such as Mozart. Yet, the church remained windowless and unfinished for several years until Father Machebeuf embarrassed parishioners by threatening to go south among the Mexicans "to ask them for some of their pesos to put windows in the church for the Catholics of Denver."

Slowly, the slender, cultivated French priest settled in at the raw frontier crossroads hundreds of miles from any city. He began to appreciate why Bishop John B. Miege, the first vicar apostolic of Kansas, had requested that the Denver parish be transferred to the Diocese of Santa Fe even though Colorado east of the Rockies, north of the Arkansas, and south of the fortieth parallel was part of Kansas until the creation of Colorado Territory in 1861. Miege, a Jesuit scholar turned bishop, had toured Denver in the spring of 1860 and, on May 27, said the city's first mass in Guirard's store at the corner of 15th and Market streets.

G. Guirard—a merchant from Paris, France, who was Denver's first lay leader—and Bishop Miege persuaded the Denver City Town Company and the Leavenworth and Pike's Peak Express Company to donate block 208 and much of block 139 to the Catholic Church. Block 208 (15th to 16th streets between Court and Tremont places) and block 139 (15th to 16th streets between California and Stout) were both on the outskirts of town but would become valuable as Denver grew.

After thus securing a toehold in Denver, Bishop Miege toured the mining regions—Central City, South Park, and Oro City. Of his Colorado tour, he wrote that "at least 100,000 men [are] bound for Pike's Peak. . . . I am doing all I can to dissuade the Catholics from going, firmly convinced as I am that danger for the soul and body is inevitable there, and for one who may succeed there will be at least fifty who will be ruined forever."

Miege wrote to the archbishop of St. Louis, Peter Richard Kenrick, requesting that he petition Rome to transfer the Pike's Peak region to the jurisdiction of the bishop of Santa Fe. Bishop Miege confided to his brother on July 15, 1860: "This will be my first and my last trip to the mountains, because Rome has seen fit, at my request, to confide the administration of that part of Kansas to the Bishop of New Mexico. My burden has thus been alleviated. May the Good God be blessed for it." Santa Fe, Meige pointed out, was only 350 miles from Denver while Leavenworth was over 500 miles away. Bishop Lamy, despite his severe shortage of priests, reluctantly accepted the responsibility for the Pike's Peak region. "I do not like to part with you," he told his lifelong friend and vicar general, Father Machebeuf. "But you are the only one I have to send, and you are the very man for Pike's Peak." Lamy could only smile and concede when Machebeuf agreed, on the condition that he be given an assistant—young Father Raverdy—and a little cash before embarking on this monumental mission.

From his headquarters in the wooden shed behind St. Mary Church in Denver, Father Machebeuf presided over his huge parish. Once St. Mary's was completed, he responded to urgent appeals to visit the new mining towns along Clear Creek. On this mountain stream, John H. Gregory had found a mother lode in Gregory Gulch in 1859. Almost overnight, Mountain City, Black Hawk, Central City, Nevadaville, Russell Gulch, and a dozen smaller gold camps sprang up in the area hastily organized as Gilpin County.

By the spring of 1861, Central City and its satellite mining towns had more people than had Denver. Machebeuf hitched up his mules and buggy and joined the throng streaming up Clear Creek Canyon. The masses were in search of gold, while the priest

Bishop Lamy toured Central City in 1861 and found "one street of crowded houses in the steepest gully you could imagine three or four miles in length." (1864 photo by George D. Wakely. Denver Public Library.)

was determined to establish the first mission of his Denver parish. Upon arriving in Central City, Machebeuf reported:

> The only place I could find to say Mass in was a kind of theatre and I had to put up the altar on the stage. A pretty good number of Catholics and others attended. At my second visit, Mass was said in a vacant billiard hall, and it required the work of two good men to clean and scrape the floor.

On Machebeuf's third visit, he said mass in a dance hall and on the fourth in an empty storefront: "Tired of looking at every visit for a new place, I posted a safe man at the door and told him . . . to lock the door and bring me the key." With his Central City parishioners thus corralled, Machebeuf announced, "Now my good men, none of you will go out until you contribute or subscribe for a church."

John B. Fitzpatrick, a mining man, laid $50 in gold dust on the altar, and others followed his example. A Central City parish was organized and named, at Machebeuf's urging, St. Mary's. By 1862, Machebeuf had purchased the house at 135 Pine Street and converted it to a church whose membership grew even more quickly than that of St. Mary's in Denver. A school and convent were added in the 1870s. Machebeuf sent Father Raverdy to be the first pastor in Central City. When he received a third priest for Colorado, Thomas M. Smith, he assigned him to Central City and returned Father Raverdy to Denver.

Bishop Lamy, on his way to the May 1861 Provincial Council of Bishops in St. Louis, visited Machebeuf for the first time. After spending two weeks with Machebeuf and Raverdy in Denver, the bishop and Machebeuf toured the mountain towns. The bishop marveled at booming Central City, a conglomeration of shacks, mines, mills, and shops perched over Gregory Gulch; he called it "the most curious sight I ever saw." In a May 10, 1861, report to Archbishop Kenrick of St. Louis, who oversaw the western half of America while the archbishop of Baltimore supervised the East, Lamy declared:

> If the mines continue to prove valuable, Colorado Territory cannot fail of becoming important. . . .The climate is rather mild and pleasant with the exception of some high winds in the spring. . . . Two or three more churches will probably be built this year in that new country.

Despite Lamy's optimism, Machebeuf's second mission was not founded until 1866 on the south fork of Clear Creek in Colorado's pioneer silver mining town, Georgetown. Our Lady of Lourdes parish thrived during the pastorate of one of the ablest of Machebeuf's priests, Nicholas C. Matz, who established a hospital as well as a school in the silver city that became the Clear Creek County seat. The other large town in the county, the gold mining and hot springs tourist town of Idaho Springs, gained its own parish, St. Paul's, in 1881.

Machebeuf and Raverdy spent much of their time traveling through the mountain mining camps, saying mass and offering the sacraments. "While among the highest mountains at California Gulch," Machebeuf wrote to his brother Marius in 1862, "I fell sick of the mountain fever, and I was two months without being able to say Mass." Concerned, Bishop Lamy ordered his Colorado pastor back to New Mexico to recuperate. The "care and good old wine of Father Paulet contributed not a little to the reestablishment of my strength," Machebeuf reassured his brother. The following year, Machebeuf suffered an even more serious mishap when his buggy overturned on the Big Hill Road to Central City. A physician hurriedly and inexpertly set the priest's broken leg, leaving him with a permanent and painful limp. The hardships he endured did not blind Machebeuf to the glory of the rugged peaks he labored among. Archbishop Salpointe of Santa Fe recalled, eulogizing his fellow priest, "Oh, how he loved these mountains! . . . I have

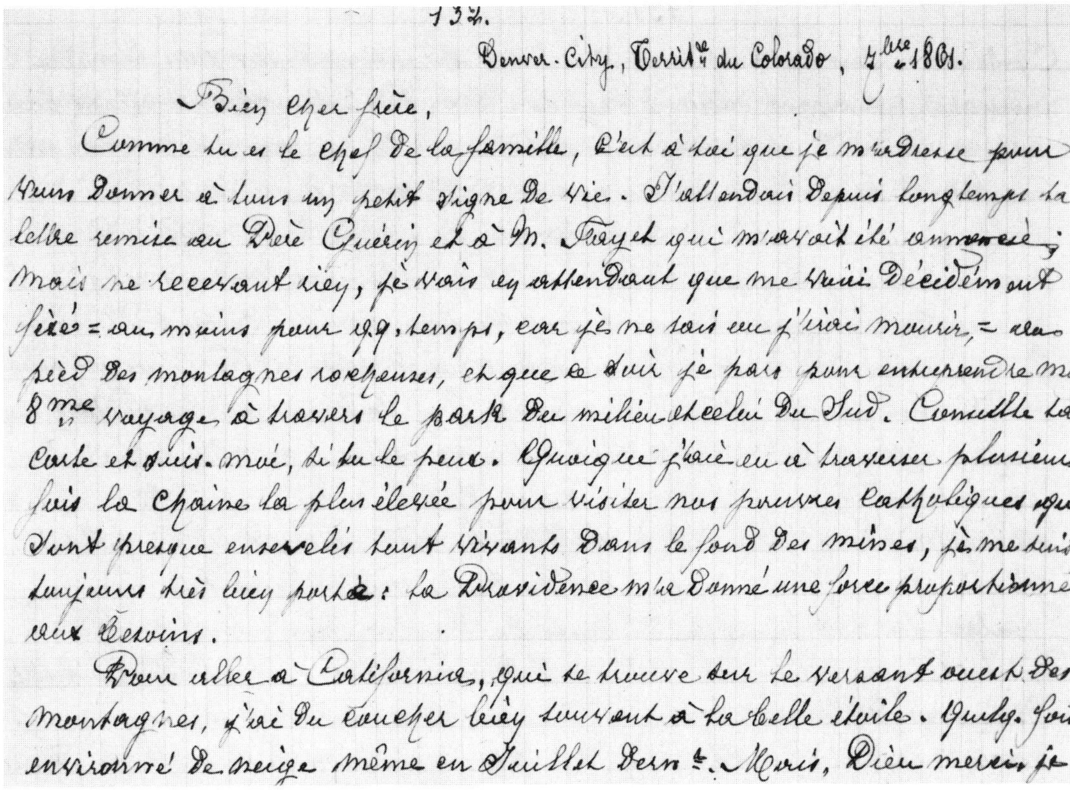

[handwritten letter in French]

Father Machebeuf's letters to his family in France are among the treasures in the Denver archdiocesan archives.

heard him tell of their beauty and their splendor, and how they seemed to him like great, strong, lonesome prayers reaching up to heaven."

Despite disabilities, Machebeuf traveled to Utah, the western half of his parish. He visited with Brigham Young, head of the Mormon Church in Salt Lake City, and made arrangements to send a priest. Father Raverdy and Father Smith took turns at trying to plant a church among the Mormons, with little success. Machebeuf did receive one bit of welcome mail from Salt Lake City, however, when Father Raverdy sent him a box of peaches. Machebeuf sold them for a dollar each in Denver to pay for desperately needed improvements at St. Mary's. The most audible improvements were lugged out from St. Louis—an organ and Denver's first church bell, an 800-pounder hauled by oxen across the plains at a cost of $305.90. It could be heard five miles away and became the town bell as well as the church bell. This bell blew over and broke during a windstorm in the fall of 1864. It was replaced in 1865 by a 2,000-pounder.

In 1867, Machebeuf established the fourth Denver mission, St. Joseph's in Golden City, seat of Jefferson County, and the fifth, Sacred Heart of Mary, in Boulder, seat of

By begging in pairs, nuns raised money to open hospitals. In Lake County, shown here in a June 7, 1879 *Frank Leslie's Illustrated Magazine* drawing, the sisters founded St. Vincent's Hospital of Leadville.

Boulder County. Boulder became the first town in Colorado with two Catholic churches when Machebeuf authorized creation of Sacred Heart of Jesus parish in south Boulder in 1875. St. Louis parish in the coal mining town of Louisville became the third Catholic church in the Boulder area in 1884.

During the late 1870s and 1880s, the brightest mineral boom in Colorado centered on the headwaters of the Arkansas River, where the silver city of Leadville sprouted up almost overnight in 1878. Two years later, it was the second largest city in Colorado. Machebeuf had opened a mission near there in 1860 at Oro City, a gold camp on California Gulch. Both the town and the mission, however, had faded before the silver boom attracted another, far larger swarm of miners.

Reverend Henry Robinson, who in 1874 had started a mountain parish in Fairplay, joined the rush to Leadville, where he founded Annunciation parish in 1879. Many of the miners pouring into Leadville were Catholics, particularly the Irish, Germans, Slavs, and Italians. Soon Leadville boasted St. Mary School, opened by the Sisters of Charity of Leavenworth in 1882, St. Joseph's Slovenian Catholic Church, St. Vincent Catholic Hospital, a Catholic Hall, Catholic club rooms, and St. Joseph Catholic Cemetery. When silver was found at Aspen, Machebeuf authorized establishment of St. Mary mission, which became an independent parish in 1881. Edward Downey, the pioneer priest at Aspen, also founded St. Stephen parish, in 1885, in Glenwood Springs.

Silver discoveries in the San Juan Mountains of southwestern Colorado triggered the rise of towns—and parishes. St. Columba Church, founded in Durango in 1882, was the first. During the 1880s, this parish opened a school, a convent, and the Sisters of Mercy Hospital, the only hospital in southwestern Colorado at the time. A second Durango parish, Sacred Heart, was opened by the Theatine fathers in 1906 for Italians and Mexicans who complained they had been slighted at St. Columba's.

Father Machebeuf created three more parishes during the 1880s in southwestern Colorado. Robert Servant started St. Mary's in Montrose in 1883. Shortly afterwards, he reported to Bishop Machebeuf that he had been doing missionary work in Montrose when a gang of ladies from Ouray more or less kidnapped him. In Ouray, the ladies had Father Servant start hearing confessions at 6 P.M. Saturday night. "I heard confessions until 12 o'clock that night," Father Servant reported and, at the 6 o'clock mass the next morning, "more than 100 received communion."

Ouray Catholics bought an old Protestant church and offered it to Bishop Machebeuf if he would only send a priest. In 1886, Machebeuf was able to oblige them by sending a resident priest, Lawrence M. Halton, to establish St. Patrick Parish. Two years later,

Bishop Joseph Projectus Machebeuf.

Halton was succeeded by the renowned James Joseph Gibbons, who left a classic account of the area, in his book, *In the San Juan, Colorado Sketches*.

Another mining town parish that survives to this day is St. Patrick's in Silverton. St. Patrick's became a full-fledged parish in 1884 with the appointment of Edmund Ley as the first resident pastor. A later pastor, Cornelius O'Rourke, drowned while circuit riding among missions in Eureka, Telluride, Marshall Basin, Howardsville, and Red Mountain. To the mineral-rich San Juan Mountains—Colorado's most rugged and remote range—Machebeuf sent missionaries and parish-builders on the heels of the mining rushes. Catholicism has a long, strong history in the silvery San Juan—an accomplishment symbolized by Silverton's huge marble shrine, Christ of the Mines.

While mining towns burst suddenly into brilliant prominence and then faded, Denver showed more stability. The town had stagnated, despite golden predictions, during the 1860s. The arrival of railroads in 1870 changed all that. Denver's population septupled, from 4,769 in 1870 to 35,629 in 1880. Colorado, whose population had grown from 34,277 in 1860 to 39,864 in 1870, likewise began to boom. The number of Coloradans quintupled during the 1870s, reaching 194,327 in 1880. The bonanza days of mining and railroading continued during the 1880s, bringing the state's population to 412,198 by 1890.

In 1870, a third of the forty-seven churches in Colorado Territory were Catholic. Their numbers mushroomed during the 1870s and 1880s: Many of the 372,334 newcomers were Catholics, most notably the Germans, Irish, and Italians.

Father Machebeuf and his handful of priests were swamped. At the urging of Bishop Lamy in Santa Fe, Church officials tried to help out. Despite his protests, Father Machebeuf was made bishop of Colorado and Utah. He traveled to Cincinnati that year to receive the purple robes. Archbishop John B. Purcell, with whom Machebeuf had come to America in 1839, consecrated him on August 16, 1868. The new bishop shared more apprehension than joy in a letter to his sister:

> I . . . tremble at the thought of such a position . . . my responsibility is already too heavy. . . . Pray always for the poor cripple. . . . Pray earnestly for me, and that the blessings of God may be on my future work [in] a diocese larger than the whole of France.

To Bishop Machebeuf's relief, his huge vicariate was cut in half in 1871 when Utah was transferred to the San Francisco archdiocese. The new bishop, in 1873, transformed Denver's tiny St. Mary church into a miniature cathedral, extending it in front to the Stout Street sidewalk and adding side chapels. The infectious boosterism of the Queen City of the Mountains and Plains animated Machebeuf's June 22, 1872, epistle back to France: "Denver has more than doubled its population in two years. We were obliged to transform and enlarge our church by additions to the front and both sides."

St. Mary's was enlarged as Denver was rapidly becoming a city. The rail age ushered in a new urbanity that included the 1871 introduction of streetcars and gas street lighting, followed in 1872 by a drinking water system. Bishop Machebeuf, who never lost his love of gardening, was particularly delighted with the Denver City Water Company, whose drinkable water now supplemented the old ditch-water system:

> Its iron pipes are buried three feet under the principal streets, with hydrants in case of fire, and the lawns, gardens, and houses upon every floor are furnished with water. Our walks, bordered with shrubs and flowers, are sprinkled by means of rubber tubes which a child can handle, and the force of the water is such that a stream can be sent to any part of the yard by merely directing the nozzle. The streets are lined with trees, and the houses with their lawns give beauty and healthfulness. . . . You see that our town is putting on the airs of a great city.

The once vacant prairie around St. Mary's blossomed with neat brick homes of prospering Denverites, including a small house Machebeuf built for himself next to the church. Bishop Machebeuf planted a white clover lawn and a garden where he grew onions and grapes, radishes and green chili.

The bishop's struggling vicariate also began to flourish. In 1875, Bishop Machebeuf awarded Colorado's first high school diploma to Jessie Forshee, who was graduating from St. Mary's Academy. (Jessie Forshee later became Sister Mary Vitalis, a Sister of Loretto who founded *The Loretto Magazine,* taught at Loretto Heights College in Denver, and became dean of studies at Webster College in St. Louis.)

The first confirmation class at St. Mary's Academy posed with the Sisters of Loretto and Bishop Machebeuf for photographer Alfred E. Rinehart. (Denver Public Library.)

For St. Mary's Academy, Machebeuf's pet project, he had purchased the home of George W. Clayton, a prominent pioneer businessman. This fine two-story frame house had cost Machebeuf $4,000 in 1864. The spacious yard stretched from 14th to 15th streets along California Street and was only a block from St. Mary's Church.

To staff the school, Machebeuf sought out the Sisters of Loretto. He was impressed with these nuns who had done so much good in New Mexico. Back in 1855, he had escorted the first contingent of sisters to Santa Fe from their motherhouse in Kentucky. Nine years later, three of the sisters in Santa Fe agreed to come to Denver. Sisters Beatrice Maes, Ignatia Mora, and Joanna Walsh slept little on the bouncy stagecoach ride from Santa Fe. Father Raverdy accompanied them and tried to assure them that they would not be scalped. That summer of 1864, Colorado was engaged in the bitter, bloody Indian war that would culminate in November with the massacre of Arapaho and Southern Cheyenne at Sand Creek.

St. Mary's Academy, founded on June 27, opened for business on August 1, 1864. Even Protestants, eager to have some refinement in the wild and woolly town, celebrated. Now, their daughters could learn French and be introduced to manners and to the liberal arts without going back East. Editor Byers of the *Rocky Mountain News* welcomed the "Sisters School" in his July 20, 1864, newspaper as a place where all Coloradans could "develop the charming qualities of modest intelligence, generosity of character and geniality of temper."

Reinforcements reached St. Mary's Academy by year's end with the arrival of sisters Ann Joseph Mattingly, Luisa Romero, and Agatha Wall. Machebeuf converted upstairs rooms of the Clayton house to a convent and helped the Sisters of Loretto transform one room into a chapel. He doted on these young women, who must have amazed the frontiersmen who stepped from Denver's rough wooden sidewalks into dirt streets to let them pass. In summer, Machebeuf proudly brought flowers and vegetables from his garden to the nuns. In winter, he chopped their wood. He looked forward to saying mass for them every day and teaching in their Sunday school. Five more sisters came to St. Mary's with Machebeuf when he returned to Denver in 1868 after being consecrated a bishop. By 1880, nineteen nuns taught forty boarding students as well as many day students, Catholic and non-Catholic.

St. Mary's initially accepted boys, but as the number of female students increased, it was converted to an all-girls' school. St. Mary's Academy, as the *Rocky Mountain News* noted on April 6, 1867, "flourished to a degree beyond the most sanguine hopes of its founders." Machebeuf began efforts to found a private boys' school but was unable to interest any of the orders until the 1880s. In the meantime, Denver lads could get a Catholic education at the parish school that Machebeuf launched at St. Mary's in Denver in 1871. Although overshadowed by St. Mary's Academy, this parish school survived to become the Cathedral School. Like St. Mary's, it was staffed by the Sisters of Loretto.

The first order of nuns to work in Colorado is still the state's largest sisterhood; at least, 1,000 of the black-robed sisters of Loretto have labored in the state since 1864. Their St. Mary's Academy is still the state's premier girls' school, and Loretto Heights for years was Colorado's only women's college. At first, Colorado seemed a wild and rugged land of godless gold seekers, a challenge to these civilizing sisters. Yet, Sister Joanna Walsh and the pioneer nuns at St. Mary's Academy found consolations—the climate and the scenery could be heavenly. On their journey from Santa Fe, Sister Joanna had persuaded Father Raverdy and the driver to stop for a picnic at the Garden of the Gods, where she found

> The ground was literally carpeted with flowers of various hue. There they had been for ages, spread out in a panoramic beauty and "born to blush unseen," till the speculators of the 19th century invaded their precincts. But still more affecting was the sight of the monuments, never touched by sculptor's chisel, yet they stand in their various forms of fantastic grandeur the gigantic labor of tertiary seas, hewn out of sedimentary rock. . . . One instinctively turns in admiration, praise, and adoration to consider the greatness and immutability of God.

These nuns brought not only religion, but also the arts and sciences to Colorado. The highest state would become a stronghold of the order that had originated in what is now Loretto, Kentucky, when, on April 25, 1812, Mary Rhodes, Christina Stuart, and Ann Havern had formed a religious community to educate the children of the Appalachian frontier. Charles Nerinckx, a Flemish priest, became the sisters' mentor and helped them draw up a simple rule to guide the order. Besides St. Mary's Academy, the sisters conducted sixteen other schools in Denver and throughout the state.

In 1864 and 1868, Machebeuf asked Bishop Miege to send a colony of the Sisters of Charity of Leavenworth to Denver to start a hospital. Machebeuf acquired a ninety-acre site, the St. Vincent's Addition in what would become the Globeville neighborhood, but his projected St. Vincent Hospital never progressed past its foundations, which stood forlorn on the prairie for decades. Machebeuf and Raverdy also raised hundreds of dollars for a Central City "Invalids Home," only to have their fund raiser, James T. "Rascal" Ritchie, run off with the proceeds.

In 1872, the first Sisters of Charity from Leavenworth arrived in Denver. After Mrs. William Perry donated a small home at 1421 Arapahoe Street, Sister Superior Joanna Brunner and sisters Theodora McDonald, Veronica O'Hara, and Mary Clare Bergen opened Denver's first private hospital there on September 22, 1873. Bishop Machebeuf announced at the opening that "the Sisters of Charity are now ready to receive patients without any distinction of nationality or creed."

The sisters did all the nursing, cooking, washing, and housekeeping, and a good deal of the doctoring. Their hospital filled rapidly, forcing the nuns to live in the attic and to use the kitchen as an operating room. Still, the sisters would not turn anyone away: They practiced their order's motto—"the greatest of these is charity."

In 1874, the sisters moved their hospital to a larger building at 26th and Market streets. Someone pointed out that Market Street was Denver's notorious red light district, filled with "*nymphs du pave*," "soiled doves," and "the brides of the multitude." When asked why they had chose such a questionable location, Sister Joanna replied, "We'll take the question out of the neighborhood."

Perhaps the sisters had second thoughts because shortly afterwards they moved their hospital into the Wentworth House (later the St. James Hotel) at 1528 Curtis Street. They moved for the last time, in 1873, to the northeast corner of East 18th Avenue and Humboldt Street, where former Territorial Governor William Gilpin donated the first lot of what would become a multiblock complex. On moving to the new site in 1876, the sisters renamed their hospital St. Joseph's. They were honoring not only the foster father of Jesus but also their own bishop, Joseph Machebeuf.

St. Joseph's completed, by 1878, a $40,000, eighty-bed hospital. Among its many supporters was John Evans, a staunch Methodist and Colorado's second territorial governor. He donated $1,000 in 1880, along with a note praising "the devoted attention and skillful care given to the sick by the ladies of your order." Dennis Sheedy, a wealthy banker and cattleman, donated money and beef from his Greenland Ranch. Another fan of St. Joseph's was Mrs. J.J. Brown, later lionized as the "Unsinkable Molly Brown." She chaired the group which staged a "gigantic city-wide bazaar," that raised $10,000 to expand St. Joseph's along Franklin and Humboldt streets.

The *Rocky Mountain News*, of August 31, 1891, praised St. Joseph's for turning "nobody from its doors. . . . The Sisters have hid themselves in the garret in order to make room for the increased number of sick." Such community support enabled the nuns to replace their 1879 building, during the 1890s, with the twin-towered landmark designed by two of Denver's more prominent architects, the Baerresen brothers. This eight-story brick hospital with 150 beds stood until the 1960s.

Surviving admissions books reveal that the first patient was twenty-six-year-old Dennis Morrow, who died a month later of one of the deadliest diseases in early Denver—typhoid. Other killers included acute alcoholism, consumption, diphtheria, dropsy, dyspepsia, erysipelas, insanity, mountain fever, nervous debility, pneumonia, and rheumatism. In one case, the sisters listed as the cause of a patient's death: "Was shot!! In a drunken row!!"

In a violent town accustomed to "lead poisoning" and "rope burn," these nursing sisters and the private physicians using their hospital offered the quaint treatments of nineteenth-century medicine. In 1899, four years after the discovery of X-rays, St. Joseph's introduced this magical diagnostic aid to Denver. While physicians offered new experimental treatments along with classical solutions—blood-letting, cupping, and purging—the nuns resigned themselves to making death as comfortable and dignified as possible, preparing patients for the next life. A fifth of the patients were nonpaying

St. Joseph's, Denver's first private hospital, started ambulance service shortly after opening at 1421 Arapahoe Street in 1873. (St. Joseph Hospital.)

indigents who received the same gentle care as the wealthiest Coloradans, who, by 1900, were paying $25 a week for a private room.

The Sisters of Charity were a welcome sight in early Colorado. They traveled the streets in pairs in their distinctive black and white habit, begging for funds to continue their work at St. Joseph's and, in 1879, to open their second hospital, St. Vincent's in Leadville. The good sisters, reported the *Leadville Chronicle* in its front-page welcome, "had heard that up here on the world's mountain top was sickness, sorrow and despair, and they came to comfort." At the sight of these sisters in the silver city, the *Chronicle* continued, "many a rough, long-bearded, coarsely appareled miner uncovered his head." Miners gladly paid a dollar a month to St. Vincent's—and other mining town hospitals—a fee that entitled them to full, free health care. St. Vincent's, which completed a new million-dollar hospital in 1964, still serves Leadville. Since 1895, the order has also owned and operated St. Mary Hospital in Grand Junction.

While the Sisters of Charity of Leavenworth founded and ran hospitals, another motherhouse of the Sisters of Charity concentrated on Catholic education. The Sisters of Charity of Cincinnati first came to Colorado at the invitation of Bishop Machebeuf in

1869, when five nuns opened Holy Trinity School in Trinidad on a site donated by Don Felipe Baca. The "Sisters' Academy" stood at the corner of Church and Convent streets until 1926, when it moved into a new facility and added a high school program.

The sisters from Cincinnati also opened Mt. San Rafael Hospital in Trinidad in 1889. This large, three-story stone building received many additions and improvements over the years, opening in 1893 what claimed to be the first Catholic nursing school west of the Mississippi River. Mt. San Rafael served as the only major hospital in Las Animas County. During the 1970s, the county replaced the old structure with a larger modern hospital. Somewhat to the embarrassment of the sisters it subsequently gained national fame for sex change operations. Located on the same site off East Main Street, the new hospital features a twelve-by-twenty-eight-foot ceramic tile mural in the lobby, created in 1982 by Sister Augusta Zimmer who made her three dimensional mural a spectacular, colorful overview of Trinidad's rich history.

The Sisters of Charity of Cincinnati were quite active in Pueblo also. There they established schools, beginning with St. Patrick's grade and high schools in 1885 and 1887 respectively, and St. Mary Hospital in 1882.

In Colorado Springs, the order took over the Albert Glockner Memorial Sanatorium in 1893. It was renamed Penrose Hospital after Julie Penrose, widow of Colorado Springs millionaire and *bon vivant* Spencer Penrose, who donated $5 million to build new facilities during the 1950s. The sisters also care for the beautiful Pauline Memorial Chapel behind the Broadmoor Hotel, and Divine Redeemer School established in 1955. Julie Penrose, in 1945, gave the Penrose mansion—El Pomar—to the Sisters of Charity, who converted it into the Julie Penrose Center, which houses a variety of programs for all religious denominations. Brockhurst, a center for chemically dependent adolescents, and Rigel Center for alcoholics have also been opened in the Springs by the sisters.

Since Vatican II, the Sisters of Charity have served in diverse ministries, ranging from Denver's Margery Reed Day Nursery to Trinidad's St. Joseph Home, an activity center for the underprivileged. The Sisters of Charity of Cincinnati have worked long and hard in Colorado, continuing the work Bishop Matz praised in his 1891 letter to the order's mother superior at Mount St. Joseph Motherhouse in Cincinnati:

> I come again to knock at your door, this time I hope and pray not in vain. Educated at St. Mary's of the West and having known your devoted Sisters, I have learned to love them and since my more intimate acquaintance with them in the Far West, in Denver and Trinidad, where I have been an eyewitness to their noble work, carried out most successfully, I am more anxious still to secure them.

While the Sisters of Charity opened many pioneer schools, the Sisters of Mercy introduced hospital care to many Colorado communities. In mining regions, the sisters found that the usual litany of diseases and accidents were compounded by the dangers of mining and smelting—high-risk occupations that regularly maimed, killed, or left survivors with chronic lung problems. The first four Sisters of Mercy came to Denver from St. Louis by train on February 11, 1882. They were warmly welcomed by Bishop Machebeuf and, at his request, went to Conejos to open a storefront hospital. A few months later, they moved on to build Mercy Hospital in Durango. As the Durango and San Juan mining region boomed, local miners, ranchers, and farmers donated land and helped the sisters build a three-story frame school.

The sisters' work led the *Durango Times* of April 30, 1882, to declare:

> The Catholic Society is always among the first in the field. Early last season it had completed in Durango . . . a church edifice of imposing proportions, the largest in the state west of the plains, and is just now completing a large three-story hospital and school building. . . . The Sisters of Mercy, that band of black-robed and devoted women whom we have all learned to reverence, have charge of the latter building and here-after no poor helpless wanderer need die uncared for in a strange land, however friendless, moneyless, or fallen.

Sisters of Mercy opened another hospital in Ouray—St. Joseph's—which they operated from 1887 to 1918. They provided loving care within this handsome, two-story granite hospital (now the Ouray County History Museum). Miners who had little use for religion came to appreciate the Catholic Church, as Reverend J.J. Gibbons observed in his book, *In The San Juan*, because of the gentle, skilled care of nursing sisters in rough-and-tumble mining towns. The sisters won many a convert to Catholicism as their patients prepared to face eternity.

In Cripple Creek, last and greatest of the Colorado gold cities, townsfolk implored the Sisters of Mercy in Denver to open a hospital. After Cripple Creekers donated a house on East Eaton Avenue, the sisters opened the first St. Nicholas Hospital there on January 4, 1894. In 1898, they moved into a much larger hospital across Third Street from St. Peter Catholic Church. Sister Veronica directed construction of this three-story brick and stone building, which boasted steam heat, electric lights, hot and cold water, and a surgery department. St. Nicholas Hospital also served as convent and school until 1924, when it was sold to Doctor W. Hassenplug. Still later, it became a city-owned and operated hospital before closing as Cripple Creek's population shrank to several hundred year-round residents.

Mercy Sanitarium and Water Cure Institute was the original name of Denver's Mercy Hospital, which opened this state-of-the-art hospital at 16th and Milwaukee in 1901. (Tom Noel Collection.)

Denver's Mercy Hospital traces its origins to Bishop Machebeuf's 1889 request that the Sisters of Mercy open a home for working girls. That September, the nuns opened the Mater Misericordiae Home in a rented frame building in the 1600 block of Lincoln Street. Shortly afterwards, they moved their home to 19th and Stout streets and changed the name to St. Catherine Home. In 1892, the Mercy nuns bought a three-story brick building in the 1400 block of California Street from the Sisters of Loretto for $105,000 and then remodeled it as St. Catherine Home for Working Girls. Besides cheap room and board and an employment bureau, St. Catherine's offered a night school with courses in cooking, dressmaking, needlework, music, painting, and sewing.

The Sisters of Mercy lost the St. Mary's site in the panic of 1893, but by renting two floors of a hotel at 1650 California Street, they kept the home alive until 1899. That year, they moved into a building at East 16th Avenue and Detroit Street, on the south side of City Park, where they operated St. Catherine Home. Shortly after 1900, the sisters closed St. Catherine Home to concentrate their efforts on building a hospital.

On August 27, 1900, the sisters bought six lots at 16th and Milwaukee streets for $4,650 and hired David Dryden, a Denver architect, to design the first building. This five-story, blond brick and red sandstone structure, executed in the Spanish colonial revival style, was dedicated on November 22, 1901, as the Mercy Sanitarium and Water

The Sisters of St. Francis of Perpetual Adoration opened a small Denver hospital for the Union Pacific Railroad in 1884 that has evolved into St. Anthony's Hospital Systems. (Photo by Bill Smythe.)

Cure Institute for lung and nervous diseases. In 1903, the sisters reorganized Mercy as a general hospital. As its fifty beds soon filled, a $60,000, eighty-five-bed addition was completed in 1905.

Newspapermen noted the hospital's bright decor, including "highly polished floors covered with bright-colored Navajo rugs" and "walls tinted in soft pastel shades. The doctor's consultation room is furnished in Flemish oak and carpeted in rich green velvet." Opening-day visitors marveled at the modern surgical and medical wards, at the private rooms with mahogany furniture and brass beds, and at "a modern elevator that operates automatically." To help staff this bright new hospital, the Sisters of Mercy established an in-hospital school of nursing in 1904. Further additions were built in 1916 and 1917.

In 1887, three Sisters of St. Francis of Perpetual Adoration arrived in Colorado Springs to staff the Colorado Midland Railway Hospital in a small adobe house. A year later, the sisters replaced it with a four-story structure, the still thriving St. Francis Hospital and Sanitarium. The Sisters of St. Francis, founded in Germany in 1863, had opened their first American motherhouse in Lafayette, Indiana, in 1875. They made Colorado Springs their western regional headquarters.

To help the Union Pacific railroad operate its new sixty-six-bed hospital at East 40th Avenue and Williams Street in Denver, Bishop Machebeuf enlisted the Franciscan sisters in 1884. These Franciscans had impressed railroad officials with their management of the main Union Pacific Hospital in the railroad's home town, Omaha, Nebraska, and the company probably gave Sister Beatrice, the superior, and sisters Haveria, Monica, Francisca, Columba, and Pauline a free ride to Denver.

The contract between the nuns and the Union Pacific specified that the railroad would pay $5.00 per day per patient to the sisters. Furthermore, the railroad promised to "furnish two horses, one ambulance, and two cows for hospital use." By 1889, fourteen sisters worked at the Union Pacific Hospital in Denver, where T.J. Fitzgerald served as chaplain.

Orphaned boys were housed, boarded, and taught marketable skills by the Sisters of Charity of Leavenworth at Mount St. Vincent, which has stood at 4159 Lowell Boulevard since 1883. (Colorado Historical Society.)

Eight years after they began work at Denver's Union Pacific Hospital, the Franciscans decided to open their own hospital where they could care for everyone and anyone. To fund this ambitious undertaking, the nuns began begging in pairs: "Bitte, canst du mich gelt gaben für das hospital? Danke!"

Particularly when they pleaded with German businessmen, and when they stationed themselves outside the Union Pacific paymaster's car on pay day, the sisters were successful beggars. With the proceeds, they purchased three blocks of land between the south side of Sloan's Lake and West Colfax Avenue. There, on June 14, 1892, Bishop Matz proudly dedicated the largest hospital in Colorado, a five-story, 180-bed, $175,000 haven for all colors, creeds, and ailments—St. Anthony's.

Bishop Machebeuf founded Colorado's first Catholic charity, the St. Vincent de Paul Society, on April 1, 1878, as a local unit of the worldwide charity founded in Paris by St. Vincent de Paul. By the 1880s, this society had raised and spent several thousand dollars a year on Colorado indigents, a mission it still pursues. Although the de Paul Society did what it could, the growing number of homeless children in the streets of Denver inspired Bishop Machebeuf to build the city's first substantial orphanage. The bishop persuaded the Denver & Rio Grande Railroad to donate a site on the west side of Lowell Boulevard between West 41st and 44th avenues. Then he enlisted the Sisters of Charity of Leavenworth to open the Mount St. Vincent Orphan Asylum on September 1, 1882, and it soon filled with 200 waifs.

After founding the asylum for boys, Bishop Machebeuf visited the Sisters of the Good Shepherd in St. Louis and persuaded them to open a Denver home for homeless and wayward girls on September 18, 1883. The mother superior of the Good Shepherd Home reported that Denver girls as young as ten were being exploited by pimps and began offering refuge to "penitents, magdalens, and preservates."

At first, the sisters cared for these girls in two frame houses on Galapago Street. In 1885, they moved to a larger Home of the Good Shepherd on Cherokee Street between Cedar and Byers avenues. Among the 300 girls there by 1900 were approximately fifty Sioux from North Dakota, for whom the sisters were remunerated by the Bureau of Indian Affairs. The Home of the Good Shepherd next moved to a twenty-acre site, donated by John Vail, at East Louisiana Avenue and South Colorado Boulevard. The new Good Shepherd home opened in 1912 with a four-story main building that sheltered 650 children and teenagers. Older girls, including child abuse victims, unwed mothers, and former prostitutes, were taught sewing, stenographic skills, and domestic science. In 1929, with the help of $60,000 donated by Mrs. J.A. Osner, the old building was remodeled and a new chapel and Magdalen Home erected, only to be destroyed by a spectacular fire forty years later.

Members of the various religious orders, who remain anonymous for the most part, played an overlooked role in early-day Colorado. These sisters opened hospitals, schools, and orphanages, which were desperately needed in Colorado's nineteenth-century. Raw, new towns filled with hardened miners, ranchers, sodbusters, and railroad workers severely tested these nuns.

Although the mountain mines attracted the first rush of population and the first efforts of Bishop Machebeuf, farming and ranching towns slowly took root on the dry, wind-swept, sun-blasted eastern plains. Seventy-five miles south of Denver, General William J. Palmer founded the town of Colorado Springs in 1871, beside the tracks of his Denver & Rio Grande Railroad. A little Catholic chapel, built in 1875, was sporadically visited by Bishop Machebeuf's missionary priests. Frederick Bender, one of the ablest priests in the diocese, transformed the struggling Colorado Springs mission into St. Mary's Church in 1877. The lovely red brick Romanesque church that Father Bender built boasted elegant furnishings, stained glass windows, pipe organ, and great bell. The Sisters of Loretto opened a parish school next door in 1885. St. Mary's Church, with its stately spire and impressive stone-step entry, remains a prominent landmark of old downtown Colorado Springs.

Forty miles south of Colorado Springs the Denver & Rio Grande Railroad revived Pueblo, an old town dating to the 1840s at the confluence of Fountain Creek and the Arkansas River. Pueblo had emerged as a trading fort and center for Spanish, French, and American mountain men. After the railroad arrived in the 1870s and the establishment of a steel mill, Pueblo quickly urbanized and requested parish status from Bishop Machebeuf, who remembered the place from his 1860 stop on the way up to Denver. Then, Pueblo had been an adobe hamlet occupied by a few trappers and traders and a sprinkling of miners and Mexicans. Father Machebeuf had stopped long enough to say mass, validate a few marriages, and baptize a number of children. Afterwards, Machebeuf or Raverdy had visited Pueblo on missionary trips.

In 1872, Machebeuf assigned Charles M. Pinto, SJ, as the first resident priest in Pueblo. A year later, Father Pinto had completed St. Ignatius Church, and the Sisters of Loretto from Denver opened Loretto Academy in 1875. The Sisters of Charity of Cincinnati were also active in Pueblo, where they conducted parochial schools, at one time or another, in St. Patrick, St. Francis Xavier, and St. Therese parishes, as well as Pueblo Catholic High School.

Trinidad, a city near the Colorado–New Mexico border, was made a mission in 1866, and the first Holy Trinity Church was completed shortly afterwards. Four years later, the Sisters of Charity of Cincinnati established a convent and school in Trinidad. Sister Fidelis wrote to the motherhouse that Trinidad looked like a "hiding place for thieves and murderers . . . and everybody speaks Spanish."

In hopes of taming this tough town, the Sisters of Charity also volunteered to teach in Trinidad's first public school, an old adobe house donated in 1870 by Don Felipe Baca. By 1887, Trinidad had a public school, a private day school, and a private boarding school—all conducted by the Sisters of Charity of Cincinnati. Trinidad's dirt-floored, adobe-walled, mud-and-pole-roofed chapel was replaced by the fine stone church of the Holy Trinity after the Jesuits took over in 1875. From Holy Trinity, the Jesuits tended twenty-seven different missions in the ranch and coal mining towns of Las Animas County. Bishop Machebeuf and, later, Bishop Matz made a practice of visiting the church every year for the feast of the Holy Trinity.

In northeastern Colorado, the rise of agricultural towns at Fort Collins, Longmont, Brighton, Yuma, and Platteville brought pleas to Bishop Machebeuf to send priests and open missions, if not parishes. Machebeuf had visited French Canadian trappers at Laporte on the Cache la Poudre River in 1861 and watched with interest the establishment of nearby Fort Collins. As the fort grew into a town, Bishop Machebeuf purchased the old schoolhouse for $400 in 1878 and refitted it as St. Joseph's, the first Catholic church in Larimer County.

Longmont, a Boulder County farm town established in 1871 by the Chicago–Colorado Colony, included several Irish Catholics. After first meeting for mass in the section house of railroad foreman Michael O'-Connor, Catholics donated a site on which St. John the Baptist Church was built in 1882.

Brighton had originally been a missionary stop for William J. Howlett, the historian and priest, who tended the towns northeast of Denver in the Platte valley. Father Howlett, in his manuscript history of Colorado parishes, reported that he built a small brick church in Brighton, in 1887, that he and parishioners named for St. Augustine. Fifteen miles farther down the South Platte River, Father Howlett also helped establish St. Nicholas parish in Platteville in 1889. Out on

In Longmont, as in many prairie parishes, Catholics held their first Mass in the home of an Irish railroad section boss. After the Longmont faithful completed this church in 1882, Bishop Machebeuf blessed it on June 24, the feast of the parish patron, St. John the Baptist. (Photo by Ed Tangen.)

the eastern plains, Bishop Machebeuf established another Catholic toehold in 1888—St. John's in Yuma.

Machebeuf, while struggling to gain a foothold in heavily Protestant Northern Colorado, did not neglect the south, where Catholicism prevailed. In those times of religious rivalry, Machebeuf was distressed to hear that Tom Tobin, a prominent pioneer rancher, had allowed John L. Dyer, a Methodist minister, to hold services at his ranch. Dyer recalled in his autobiography, *The Snow-Shoe Itinerant,* that Tobin was less hospitable on his second visit. Reverend Dyer discovered that Machebeuf had complained to Tobin's Catholic wife, who had her husband put a stop to any Protestant services on his ranch southwest of Fort Garland.

Dyer, one of the few Protestant ministers to undertake missionary work in Southern Colorado, complained that Machebeuf "taught that none but Catholic clergy could solemnize marriage, or do anything right." One of the most respected and successful missionaries in Colorado, he continued his work, adding that, unlike Machebeuf and his priests, "I have a wife to help me."

In *The Snow-Shoe Itinerant*, Dyer claimed "that the Roman Catholics were reformed more by Protestants than by any other means." He may have been right: Critical scrutiny by Protestants probably helped keep Colorado Catholics on their best behavior. At any rate, they avoided major scandals such as those with which Lamy and Machebeuf had wrestled in New Mexico.

Anti-Catholicism was relatively mild in Colorado but evident in such documents as the 1876 state constitution, which specified Protestant chaplains for the legislature. Admiration, rather than hostility, was expressed by the first Episcopal missionary bishop of Colorado, George M. Randall. In Bishop Randall's first report to the Board of Missions of the Protestant Espiscopal Church in 1866, he declared :

> We must . . . learn wisdom from the Romanists. Their priests are indeed ever in the vanguard of their missionary army, but their school teachers follow closely after. . . . They exhibit a tender solicitude for the lambs of other folds. . . . Episcopalians are sending their daughters to the Convent [St. Mary's Academy in Denver] because it is the best school in the territory.

Sectarian differences gave way to personal regard in many cases, and to admiration for accomplishments in the face of adversity. John Evans said of Machebeuf:

> He knew I was an earnest Protestant. But our friendship never faltered on that account. He was too wise and just and good. . . . Bishop Machebeuf was not only a good Christian, he was a good, patriotic and enterprising citizen. . . . He labored in all things to promote the ascendancy of the Catholic Church. . . . a motive that brings forth such works as these cannot be essentially bad. I have cooperated in a small way, in most of his charitable labors. . . . He not only aided the poor with a crust of bread and a cup of cold water, but he organized societies for their relief. He heard the orphan's cry and he founded asylums. . . . He early saw the importance of education and he founded schools, seminaries and colleges.

Bishop Machebeuf's strong defense of Catholic schools drew much criticism. At the 1876 Denver convention to draft a state constitution, he and other religious leaders fought successfully to exempt churches, religious schools, and charities from taxation. Machebeuf further argued that public education funds should be allotted to Catholic schools, but he failed to persuade the convention.

Machebeuf's championship of Catholic schools and advice to his flock to avoid public schools if at all possible led Aaron Gove, the able, long-time superintendent of Denver public schools, to declare that, acccording to the January 18, 1878, *Rocky Mountain News,* "The Catholic Church is an enemy of the Public School. It is an honest, conscientious and honorable opposition, but it is nonetheless an opposition and we must meet it by all honorable means."

Bishop Machebeuf's struggle to build and staff Colorado's pioneer parishes was compounded by the intense rivalry among immigrant groups. Machebeuf had dealt with ethnic factions in New Mexico, trying to reconcile sometimes violent differences among Indians, Hispanics, and other nationalities.

The Frenchman fully acknowledged the pioneer role of Hispanics in planting Catholicism in Colorado: "Everywhere," Machebeuf declared, "we have seen proof of the zeal and the devotion of the first Spanish missionaries who came to water with their sweat and their blood this earth."

On his arrival in Denver in 1860, Machebeuf had been greeted by a few Frenchmen, including G. Guirard. Although a few other Frenchmen, many of them old trappers and traders, also welcomed Machebeuf, he found Germans to be the most common foreign-born group in Colorado. At the urging of these Teutons, he authorized creation of Colorado's first national parish, St. Elizabeth German parish in Denver, in 1878. The national parish designation allowed a parish to incorporate the members' native tongue and culture into its liturgy and activities. Latin, of course, remained the official language of the mass. National parishes welcomed all members of their ethnic group regardless of where they resided.

French-born priests at St. Mary's and German-born priests at St. Elizabeth's prompted other ethnic groups to request their own parishes. Sacred Heart (1879), the third parish in Denver, was guided by an Italian; Machebeuf recruited John B. Guida, SJ, the first of a procession of Jesuits to preside over Sacred Heart.

The Irish, second in numbers only to the Germans among Colorado's foreign-born Catholic contingent, ballyhooed creation of St. Patrick's, the first North Denver parish in 1881. The Irish considered themselves "Americans," with the implication that they spoke English—unlike the "foreign" French, Italian, and German Americans. With the arrival of Father Joseph P. Carrigan, at St. Patrick's in 1885, the Irish had a parish to call their own.

Other Denver churches accommodated a jumble of ethnic groups. If friction arose, pastors sometimes steered ethnic factions to their own masses or reserved basement services for minorities struggling to raise money and membership for their own churches. Annunciation (1883), St. Joseph's (1883), Holy Family (1889), and St. Dominic's (1889) were all created during the Machebeuf era. These parishes in northwestern and northeastern Denver accommodated the thousands of new Catholics who arrived during the booming 1880s when Denver's population passed the 100,000 mark. By 1890, Denver was the second largest city in the West, second only to San Francisco and more populous than Los Angeles or any town in Texas.

Machebeuf tried to humor all the nationalities among his Colorado flock but did not hide his special fondness for the oldest and poorest group, the Mexican-Americans. He liked their custom of donating one day a week labor—or equivalent money—to the Church. He also admired their farming skill and the irrigation systems that they introduced to Colorado. "The American, the German and the Irish Catholic is really good," Machebeuf once told Reverend Gabriel Ussel, "but give me the childlike and incomparable faith of the good Mexican . . . the ardent faith that moves mountains." While favoring Hispanic parishioners, Machebeuf—and his successors—sought priests trained in North American or northern European seminaries. The diocese did not recruit Spanish or Mexican priests, perhaps because they balked at using English and allegedly lacked discipline and training. Justified or not, such cultural differences still haunt the Church in Colorado.

"My Irish Catholics," Machebeuf wrote to Archbishop John B. Purcell of Cincinnati on March 26, 1868, "have frequently manifested a strong dislike to my administration, caused first by my quick and passionate temper [and] by a scandalous Irish priest who I had to dismiss [and by my] opposition to the Fenian Brotherhood."

Father Raverdy, Machebeuf's first priest and his vicar after he became bishop, never really became comfortable with the English language and American ways, yet, Machebeuf wrote of Raverdy: "I thank God a thousand times for giving me such a co-laborer. What a comfort he has been to me in my loneliness and my troubles." On another occasion, Machebeuf revealed to his sister the pressure he felt:

> Everywhere it is churches and schools to build or repair, new parishes to start, money to borrow, and I must see to it all myself. . . . On Saturday and Sunday I am priest and bishop . . . on Monday and the rest of the week I am banker, contractor, architect, mason, collector, in a word, a little of everything.

Machebeuf's struggle to find priests and money led him to make begging trips to the eastern United States and to Europe. He apparently accepted any priest he could get, which helps to explain the high turnover among Colorado's nineteenth-century pastors. Alcoholism and other illnesses, mental and physical, were no doubt problems, though rarely mentioned in surviving records. During Machebeuf's time, a half dozen priests did most of the parish building. None of them launched more churches than Machebeuf's first home-grown priest, William J. Howlett.

Howlett, the tenth of twelve children, came to Denver with his family in 1865. In his unpublished recollections, Howlett recalled the trip to Denver along the Platte River road.

Jean B. Raverdy, Machebeuf's right-hand man, was French born and trained. He never really became comfortable with Coloradans and their strange English language.

Between Julesburg and Denver, "there were no settlements . . . but there was occasionally a fortified ranch house" and "buffaloes so numerous it was impossible to count them." The Howletts rented a house on Welton Street near St. Mary's and found Denver "filled with wagons, mostly heavy freight wagons, bringing in supplies of all kinds . . . and distributing them to the various mining camps."

The Howlett family tended Father Machebeuf's farm on Clear Creek, raising wheat and cabbages in what would become Mt. Olivet Cemetery. William became Machebeuf's first American-born protégé. He taught at St. Mary's Academy and accepted Machebeuf's invitation to go to the seminary. At St. Thomas's in Bardstown, Kentucky, and at Saint Sulpice's in Paris, Howlett was financially supported by Machebeuf. After being ordained by the archbishop of Paris on June 11, 1876, young Father Howlett returned to Denver and the service of his benefactor.

Machebeuf promptly assigned him to St. Mary's in Central City, where Father Howlett brought stability to a parish ravaged by fraud, fire, and ethnic rivalry. Howlett was adept at dealing with his fellow Irishmen, who insisted on calling St. Mary's "St. Patrick's" and resented being supervised by the little "French" parish of St. Mary's down in flatland Denver.

Howlett became a favorite with the Irish, who urged that he be made Machebeuf's coadjutor bishop. Machebeuf, in an 1886 letter to Cardinal Gibbons, acknowledged that Father Howlett had in Central City "succeeded completely in conciliating all parties, administered the parish for seven years, paid off all the debts, which were heavy, and was enjoying the esteem and confidence of all." Howlett, however, according to Machebeuf, "had taken the uncouth manners and languages of the miners," becoming "too full of confidence in himself," making him unsuitable as rector of Immaculate Conception

Cathedral; "still less would he be suited for coadjutor." If Howlett ever learned of his bishop's comments, he did not retaliate in his eulogistic biography of Machebeuf.

After stabilizing St. Mary's and its many mountain missions, Howlett's next assignment was Brighton. There he built the stone church that became St. Augustine's, and a string of missions at Fort Morgan, Brush, Akron, Sterling, and Julesburg, all of which ultimately became parishes. Father Howlett also handled assignments in Pueblo, Denver, Georgetown, Colorado City, and Loveland before his retirement in 1913.

Howlett retired to the motherhouse of the Sisters of Loretto in Kentucky, where he served as chaplain and devoted his last years to recording the history of the church in nineteenth-century Colorado. From Sister Marie Philomene Machebeuf, he acquired copies of her brother's letters. These letters, now in the Archdiocesan Archives at Denver, became the basis of Howlett's biography of the first bishop of Denver, published in Pueblo in 1908. Subsequent historians and the novelist Willa Cather, author of *Death Comes for the Archbishop,* are heavily indebted to Howlett, who also left three important unpublished manuscripts: his recollections; a history of many of the parishes in Colorado; and biographical sketches of some of the priests who had served in the state.

Monsignor Gregory Smith, who as a young priest visited Father Howlett at the Loretto motherhouse in Kentucky before the pioneer's death in 1936, recalled fifty years later:

> He was the grand old man down there and took special concern with the novices. He was rather short and stout of stature, at least in his old age, a plain-spoken and affable sort. He was not a scientific historian, but he knew his subject well.

Money, as well as manpower, was a constant problem for Bishop Machebeuf. While soliciting loans and gifts from his own family, he confided to his brother in an 1868 letter that he

> was thus obliged to borrow money from the banks and from private individuals at very high rates of interest . . . to secure at Denver favorable locations for churches, schools, convents, hospitals, cemeteries, etc. . . . and thus have increased my indebtedness to a considerable sum.

Colorado National Bank's surviving ledger books show Machebeuf to have been a frequent and heavy borrower at rates of interest ranging from 18 to 24 percent a year. As both loans and demands for new parishes, schools, convents, rectories, hospitals, and orphanages piled up, Machebeuf went East in search of money, priests, and nuns. Armed with a testimonial letter from James Cardinal Gibbons of Baltimore, Machebeuf solicited support in Baltimore, Philadelphia, New York, and other communities with Catholic capitalists.

Bishop Machebeuf finally found a financial angel in 1875, when Eastern prelates put him in touch with Eugene Kelly, a Catholic banker in New York City. Machebeuf, according to Howlett, had become an embarrassment to the Church because of his poverty and begging all over the country. Despite Machebeuf's rumored personal and episcopal bankruptcy, Kelly made two loans totaling $50,000 at 8 and 10 percent interest. This enabled the Colorado prelate to pay off his loans from Colorado National Bank and other Denver lenders. Kelly was a godsend to Machebeuf, who paid himself no salary and his priests only $400 a year, and faced interest payments of $5,000 a year by the end of the 1870s.

While churchmen found Machebeuf a financial embarrassment, some Coloradans saw him as a shrewd financier. It was no secret that he had accumulated property all over Colorado, including his 440-acre Clear Creek farm, part of which would become Mt. Olivet Cemetery. The bishop also acquired Denver parcels that, years after his death, would serve as sites for new parishes, schools, and hospitals.

Machebeuf, like Colorado capitalists such as John Evans, David H. Moffat, Jr., and Horace Tabor, mortgaged himself to the hilt, betting on Colorado's future. With the unshakeable optimism that characterized the great pioneers, he reasoned that land would only rise in value; it would be the best way to lay financial foundations for future church growth. Although accused of inept financial management, Machebeuf negotiated some rather sharp deals. In 1875, for instance, he sold to the county for $18,000 the block given to the church by the city in 1860. Eventually, the first county courthouse would be erected on that block, which was bounded by 15th and 16th streets and Court and Glenarm places.

Machebeuf, hounded and humiliated by debtors, wrote to Cardinal Gibbons on March 8, 1886: "It is surely hard for poor human nature after 47 years of hard missionary life in Ohio, New Mexico and Colorado in my old age of 74 to be under such a cloud . . . after having sacrificed myself and all I have for the church."

Bishop Machebeuf celebrated his fiftieth anniversary as a priest in Denver on December 16, 1886. It was a modest golden jubilee. Someone asked the bishop if he dreamed of a grand cathedral to replace small, homely, old St. Mary's. He replied: "A cathedral is a question of money, of stone and mortar, while my work was, and should have been, a question of souls." Unlike his friend Archbishop Lamy in Santa Fe, who built a grand French-style cathedral, Machebeuf never built anything architecturally grand.

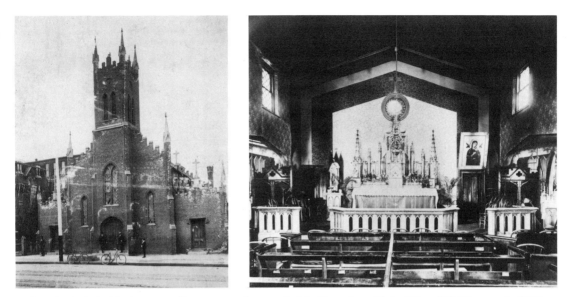

St. Mary's Cathedral in downtown Denver was photographed inside and outside by Edward N. Clements in 1900 on the eve of its demolition.

Machebeuf clung to the landholdings he had struggled to acquire for the future of his diocese. In 1878, he went to see his family in France and tried to organize a bond sale in Paris to pay off Denver diocesan debts. This scheme resulted in another embarrassing debt when the aging bishop was hoodwinked by Parisian con men. Machebeuf's growing financial headaches were increasingly shared by several priests and laymen who, in 1884, organized the Colorado Catholic Loan and Trust Association to sell bonds and handle church finances.

Notwithstanding growing concerns about his age and ability, Bishop Machebeuf negotiated a clever deal in 1887. He sold off twenty acres on the south side of Mt. Calvary Cemetery to Denver real estate developer Samuel B. Morgan for $20,000. Morgan transformed the tract along East 9th Avenue between Race and York streets into one of Denver's grandest residential neighborhoods, the Morgan Addition, designated a Denver Historic District in 1978.

After Omaha, Nebraska, was made a diocese in 1885, Bishop Machebeuf sought the same status for his vicariate apostolic. Besides recognizing Denver's importance and independence, such a promotion would aid fund raising. Rome concurred: On August 16, 1887, Pope Leo XIII elevated the Vicariate of Colorado to the Diocese of Denver. Machebeuf, because of his failing health and rising administrative and financial problems, was assigned a coadjutor. Nicholas C. Matz was appointed coadjutor with the right of succession, being consecrated bishop in St. Mary Cathedral on October 27, 1887.

This lessened Machebeuf's burden, but he did not retire from active work. Travel was made easier with the railroads extending throughout the state. Machebeuf sent his buggy ahead by rail to be waiting for him at the end of the line. This enabled him to continue his unending quest for Catholics in the mountains, plains, and canyonlands of Colorado.

Machebeuf became a familiar character around Denver, a simple gray-haired man, small of stature and limping painfully on his visits to churches, schools, and hospitals. His demeanor was described by Sister Blandina Seagale, S.C., in her autobiography, *At the End of the Santa Fe Trail* :

> I have often noticed his very kind eyes—eyes full of sympathy which show at a glance that his thought is for others. His lower lip has the expression of a good grandmother who fears she never does enough for all of us who belong to her.

He had survived many illnesses and accidents in his long lifetime, both on the streets of Denver and on craggy mountain trails. Of Machebeuf's stamina, Howlett wrote: "His indomitable will fortified his body, which was so accustomed to finding its 'rest in action' that it would not be strange if when death came it found him standing on his feet."

News of the death of his great life-long friend Archbishop Lamy, who had been like a brother, grieved Machebeuf. He hastened to Santa Fe in February 1888, to speak at Lamy's funeral. Machebeuf may have sensed in his great sorrow that his own call would come next. Later in 1888, he was present in Washington for the laying of the cornerstone of the Catholic University of America, but his strength was slipping.

The bishop reserved for himself a little room at St. Vincent Asylum, where it was his custom to retire for rest and quiet. On July 3, 1889, he went to this retreat. There, he calmly died on the morning of July 10, having received the last sacraments from the hands of Bishop Matz. His body lay in state in the chapel of St. Mary's Academy. Thousands came to pay their last respects. Nearly 100 priests were present at his funeral on July 16, 1889, when a temporary tomb was prepared beneath the sanctuary of the St. Mary's Academy chapel. In 1891, after Bishop Matz opened Mt. Olivet Cemetery, the remains of Bishop Machebeuf were reinterred there in an 800-pound casket of solid cast iron with a glass top. Each of the priests present took up a handful of dirt, blessed it, and threw it gently upon the casket.

Monsignor Raverdy, Machebeuf's close friend and vicar general, was returning from Chicago when news reached him of Machebeuf's death. Raverdy himself was ill with a fatal disease, but he hurried on to Denver, arriving on the arms of assistants during the funeral service. A chair was placed near the coffin, where Raverdy wept over the corpse of his dear friend and prepared for his own death. It came barely four months later.

The Colorado Catholic, Denver's first Catholic newspaper, mourned Machebeuf on July 13, 1889:

> In every hamlet, almost every home in this great state, his cheering words and patriarchal mien softened the hardened and quickened the thoughtless. His patient suffering of hardships incident to the establishment of religion where gold was god, his tiresome journeys—over the mountain passes which he, perhaps, more than any other fashioned to travel, his cheerful submission to conditions of life entailed by the newly opened country, his courage in dangers which appalled the bravest, and all inspired by zeal for God's honor alone—these touched every heart and made the name of Bishop Machebeuf revered, respected and beloved by all, without regard to creed or race. No man in the Rocky Mountain Country. . . has ever gone to his grave more universally respected for his sanctity of motive than the pioneer bishop of Colorado.

A century later, it is hard to disagree with the praise heaped on Machebeuf at the time of his death. He accomplished so much with so little, assuming frightening debts and running great risks. Certainly from a centennial perspective, his gambling paid off. Machebeuf—like other pioneer clergymen—did much not only for his Church but also for Colorado. The Church helped create a sense of community, a sense of caring and of permanence on the footloose frontier.

Bishop Machebeuf served as a moral authority at a time when gun-slinging sheriffs and primitive police departments were sometimes as lawless as their targets. The fragile frontier social order was reinforced by churchmen such as Machebeuf. Admittedly, some of the prejudices of the day were also reinforced by the bishop. For instance, he spoke sternly against women's suffrage. When Colorado's suffrage crusade began in the 1870s, Machebeuf blamed the agitation "on battalions of old maids disappointed in love" and on "women who, though married, wish to hold the reins of family government." Despite opposition from Machebeuf and many other churchmen, Colorado males voted to enfranchise women in 1893. While trying to establish a basic social order, Machebeuf displayed little interest in reform issues. His long sermons stuck to conventional and conservative themes, and their effectiveness may have been diminished by his frequent use of a spittoon.

Machebeuf and the Catholic Church played a large role in bringing refinement to Denver. In a city hungry for culture, the Church offered masses by Mozart and promoted cleanliness and better dress—at least on Sunday. It introduced and sustained the fine arts, fostering music, art, and architecture. Although the practice would later be discouraged by both Church and state, Catholic nuns served as the first public school teachers in Southern Colorado towns such as Antonito and Trinidad. All over Colorado, the Church founded schools and advanced education, bringing classical liberal arts, culture, and morals to remote frontier outposts.

Joseph Projectus Machebeuf's role may best be summed up by Howlett's words:

> When Father Machebeuf came to Colorado in 1860 he was alone with Father Raverdy, without a single church, or roof over his head; when he was made bishop he had but three priests within his jurisdiction; when he died the Diocese of Denver counted 64 priests, 102 churches and chapels, 9 academies, 1 college, 1 orphan asylum, 1 house of refuge, 10 hospitals and over 3,000 children in Catholic schools.
>
> This was primarily the work of one man, and that man was Bishop Machebeuf. In contemplating it we must concede that its author was a great priest, a great bishop, and merited well the title by which posterity shall know him—THE APOSTLE OF COLORADO.

Bishop Nicholas Chrysostom Matz. (Photo by Alfred E. Rinehart. Denver Public Library.)

CHAPTER 2

MATZ: THE BUILDER BISHOP, 1889–1917

In Nicholas Chrysostom Matz, Machebeuf had received just the man he wanted as his coadjutor. "I am getting old, and there is work for two," Machebeuf wrote early in 1887, adding that Matz

was my choice from the very first. He is well liked by priests and people—a man of study, and easily the peer of any priest in Colorado or New Mexico. . . . He has the advantage of knowing English, French, German and Italian, and sufficient Spanish to treat with the Mexicans. My poor Mexicans will have a father in Father Matz. . . . It is true that Father Matz is young, but a young man is best for this young diocese, for he will have more energy to push forward the work for more churches, more schools, and for a more early realization of the new cathedral.

Machebeuf's prophecy for his successor proved accurate during Matz's twenty-eight-year reign as bishop of Denver. Despite financial problems compounded by the depression of 1893, as well as troubles with his priests that led him four times to offer his resignation to Rome, Bishop Matz became Denver's builder bishop. He dedicated dozens of Catholic schools, thirty-four new parishes, a successful seminary, a grand cathedral, and a spacious cemetery that serves the diocese to this day.

Like so many of his parishioners, Matz was an immigrant, born April 6, 1850, in Münster, France. Nicholas was the son of Antoine and Marie-Anne Boul Matz, who with their children came to the United States in 1868. The Matz family joined relatives who had settled in Cincinnati, Ohio.

Eighteen-year old Nicholas, who had studied at church schools in Münster and for three years at the Petit Seminarie in Finstingen, France, continued his studies in Cincinnati at Mount St.-Mary-of-the West Seminary. This seminary was visited by Bishop Machebeuf on his 1869 eastern trip to recruit priests for Colorado. He found two volunteers: One was a young man who supposedly became horrified at stories that hungry Colorado Indians would scalp him, tie him to a tree, and treat him to a war dance before roasting him to death. That terrified young man subsequently left the seminary and became a farmer.

Machebeuf's other volunteer recruit was Nicholas Matz. He became Father Matz on a bright spring day, May 31, 1874, when Bishop Machebeuf ordained him at St. Mary Church in Denver. This capable young priest was Machebeuf's assistant pastor for the next three years.

In 1877, Bishop Machebeuf assigned Father Matz to one of his struggling mountain parishes, Our Lady of Lourdes at Georgetown. In Georgetown, an 8,519-foot high silver-mining city, Matz proved himself capable and popular. He built a $12,000 brick church, a rectory, a hospital, a convent, and a school, transforming what had been an impoverished, tiny chapel into a large and healthy parish plant.

In 1895, Matz was asked to deal with another problem parish—St. Ann's (Annunciation) in Denver, which had been destroyed by a fire. Matz served as pastor of Annunciation, living in humble quarters in the rear of the church until his consecration in St. Mary's Cathedral as bishop coadjutor, October 28, 1887, by Archbishop John Baptiste Salpointe, Lamy's successor in Santa Fe.

Matz looked and acted more like a bishop than had the scrawny, homely, Machebeuf. He stood 5 feet 11 inches tall, according to his passport. Photographs reveal a heavyset, erect carriage, ruddy complexion, and high forehead that gave him a benign appearance, which belied a steely inner determination to complete the work Machebeuf had begun.

Following the death of Machebeuf's vicar general, Jean Raverdy, Bishop Matz selected Henry Robinson as the second vicar general of the Denver diocese. Robinson, a second-generation Irish American, was one of the ablest priests to be recruited by Bishop Machebeuf. Machebeuf had persuaded Robinson to come to Colorado in 1869 while he was still a seminarian at Cape Giradeau, Missouri. After ordination in 1872, Father Robinson assisted at St. Mary's in Denver. Two years later, Machebeuf sent him to establish missions in Park, Chaffee, Summit, and Lake counties. In 1878, Robinson became the founding pastor of Leadville's large Annunciation Church. After his appointment as vicar general, Father Robinson moved from Leadville to Denver, where he followed Matz as pastor of St. Ann's (Annunciation) parish, building a beautiful church while simultaneously working as Bishop Matz's vicar general.

St. Mary's Academy moved in 1911 from its original site at 1340 California Street to this still-standing edifice at 1370 Pennsylvania Street on Capitol Hill. (Photo by Louis D. Regnier. Denver Public Library.)

Whereas Machebeuf had run the diocese loosely and informally—acting on suggestions from Archbishop Lamy and Cardinal Gibbons—Matz saw the need for tighter organization, for separation of the bishop's personal and diocesan finances, and for clarification of the rights and responsibilities of priests and parishes. Matz, who took an authoritarian stance on these issues, consequently attracted criticism from some leading priests and laymen.

In accordance with the decrees of the Third Plenary Baltimore Council of 1884, Bishop Matz asked every parish to open a parochial school. In these parish schools, religion was the principal subject and taught from the *Baltimore Catechism,* which had been drawn up at the 1884 council. At a time when many communities lacked adequate public schools, starting and maintaining a parochial school was no easy task for new and often struggling parishes. To staff these schools, Bishop Matz concentrated on bringing more nuns to Colorado.

Lying in the foreground of this Georgetown scene are the church, school, and hospital erected by Father Matz and the Sisters of St. Joseph of Carondelet. (Photo by George Dalgleish. Mazzulla Collection, Amon Carter Museum.)

Self-sacrifice and hardship characterized the lives of Colorado's pioneer nuns. Consider, for example, the Sisters of St. Joseph of Carondelet. This order, founded in 1650 at Le Puy, France, had sent sisters to Carondelet, a suburb of St. Louis, Missouri, in 1836 to do missionary work in the United States. In 1876, Bishop Machebeuf stopped at their Missouri motherhouse, imploring the sisters to help him with schools and hospitals in Central City, Georgetown, and Denver.

Three Sisters of St. Joseph reached the raucous mining town of Central City late in 1876. The high altitude left them gasping for breath as they climbed flights of rickety wooden stairs to the school and convent perched on a stony hillside. In winter, when the sun dropped behind the mountains by 4 o'clock in the afternoon, the sisters shivered. They had no salary, only what food and firewood people gave them. Yet somehow they persisted, eventually buying the school from the Diocese of Denver for $8,000. Despite all the hardships, and the grim specter of four sisters' graves in Central's Catholic cemetery, the nuns kept St. Aloysius Academy open until 1917.

Some of the Sisters of St. Joseph ventured even deeper into the Rockies to open St. Joseph Hospital in Georgetown in 1880. Miners voluntarily contributed a dollar a month from their paychecks to support this desperately needed facility. This practice soon became standard in other mining districts with Catholic hospitals, including Breckenridge, Durango, Leadville, and Ouray. Even with the dollar-a-month contributions from miners, however, the sisters inevitably nursed hospital deficits as well as miners.

"Everyone depended on those Sisters of St. Joseph," recalled Veronica Elliott of Georgetown, adding that:

> Those nifty nuns not only ran the Georgetown hospital but a parish school at Our Lady of Lourdes. After the 1893 silver crash, Georgetown was no longer a coming place. My father, Patrick Devaney, was a miner who took up collections to keep the hospital open. It was the only one in all of Clear Creek County. The sisters had to close the school in 1913 and the hospital in 1914, although Mother Lilly stayed on to teach piano and Sister Joseph kept the hospital open until it burned down in 1917.

Two tombstones in the tiny Silver Plume Cemetery above Georgetown commemorate the nuns' efforts to civilize the mining towns. The graves are of two Sisters of St. Joseph, close friends who both died young and were buried side by side. One aging stone reads, "Sweet Jesus Rest. Sister Mary Philomena, born March 1, 1848; died Aug. 10, 1891, in the 22nd year of her religious life"; the other, "Sister M. Bonaventure, born March 18, 1867; died Oct. 29, 1892, in the fifth year of her religious life." "Our order wanted to move those two to Mt. Olivet Cemetery where the other sisters who served in Colorado lie," Sister Jarlath McManus, CSJ, recalled in 1987. "But the people of Silver Plume objected and promised to take care of the graves of those sisters who had taken such good care of the mountain mining town people."

In 1883, the first Sisters of St. Joseph of Carondelet arrived in Denver at midnight. A freak snowstorm had delayed their Union Pacific Railroad trip for hours. Not until 3 A.M. did they finally arrive at St. Patrick Church, where they were given mattresses on the floor of a room without heat, light, or provisions. The next morning, women in the parish dropped by to greet them and to leave off children of all ages for "the Sisters' School," which was not yet built. Undaunted, the nuns opened classrooms in the church, where they slept in the basement. Seeming to thrive on such adversity, the sisters of St. Joseph, by 1900, had a convent and eleven sisters teaching 275 pupils at St. Patrick School.

The Sisters of Mercy from Omaha also responded to Bishop Matz's pleas for teaching nuns. This order had been founded in 1831 by Catherine McCauley, an Irish heiress, in Dublin, to care for the poor. Mother McCauley's fast growing order soon spread throughout the British Isles and to the United States. The Sisters of Mercy had initially been recruited by Bishop Machebeuf to build and staff Mercy hospitals in Denver and Durango, as well as St. Catherine Home in Denver. After seeing how cheerfully and capably they ran their hospitals, community leaders in Durango enlisted their efforts in education. They opened St. Columba (1882) and Sacred Heart (1903) schools in Durango; as well as tending to Catholic educational needs in Denver, Cripple Creek, and San Luis.

The Denver archdiocese has also relied on the Sisters of Charity of the Blessed Virgin Mary from Dubuque, Iowa, who came to Colorado in 1892. These sisters settled in Boulder to staff Mount St. Gertrude Academy until its closing in 1968 and have taught at Sacred Heart of Jesus School in Boulder since 1916.

Benedictine sisters from Chicago came to Colorado, also, opening St. Gertrude School (1886–1890) in Breckenridge, which closed when the nuns became discouraged by the harsh climate and the fluctuating mining fortunes. The Benedictines persisted a little longer in Aspen, where they opened St. Mary School (1892–1910).

Franciscan Daughters of the Sacred Hearts of Jesus and Mary from Wheaton, Illinois, first came to Denver in 1888 to teach at St. Elizabeth parish school until 1917, when another order of Franciscan nuns took over. Accidentally, the Wheaton Franciscans at St. Elizabeth's also got into the orphanage business. On Christmas Eve, 1890, a young father brought his four motherless daughters to the Franciscan Convent at 10th and Champa streets. The Franciscans could not say no, and this unplanned orphanage soon outgrew their convent. In 1907, they purchased sixteen acres between West 26th and West 29th avenues on Osceola Street and constructed St. Clara Orphanage. The old St. Clara Orphanage building at 10th and Champa was converted to St. Rose Home for Working Girls. The new orphanage, the largest in Colorado when it opened in 1908, housed as many as forty nuns caring for as many as 300 children under the age of fourteen.

During the great blizzard of 1913, St. Clara Orphanage was rescued by heaven-sent elephants. Ruth Wiberg tells the story in *Rediscovering Northwest Denver*:

> During what will always be called "Denver's Big Snow of 1913," St. Clara's Orphanage had run out of coal. With their usual knightly posture of rushing to the rescue, the *Denver Post* publishers sent wagonloads of coal. . . . Struggling up West 26th Avenue past the [*Denver Post*] circus grounds, the coal teams floundered in the deep drifts. The wagons would not move. The frustrated drivers plowed through the waist high snow to the circus and got permission to use the elephants.
>
> The mammoth animals trumpeted and bellowed at the cold wet drifts about their tropics-bred knees, but, one behind each wagon, they put their trunks around the rear axles, lifting the wagons off the ground. Rearing and plunging, the horses had to pull or be run over by their own wagons. St. Clara's received their coal and the orphans were saved from the cold.

St. Clara Orphanage was demolished in 1967, when it was replaced by Francis Heights, a senior high-rise residence. The Wheaton Franciscans also opened Sacred Heart Orphanage (1903–1981) in Pueblo with the help of donations and publicity from Captain John J. Lambert, editor of the *Pueblo Chieftan*.

Another order of Franciscans, the Sisters of St. Francis of Milwaukee, Wisconsin, operated St. Joseph Academy (1906–1920) and its successor, St. John the Baptist School, in Longmont, as well as other schools in various towns.

The Dominicans first came to Colorado to administer a new Denver parish named in honor of their founder—St. Dominic's at West 29th Avenue and Federal Boulevard. While Dominican fathers ran the church, the Dominican sisters of Sinsinawa, Wisconsin, opened St. Dominic's parish school in 1890. The Dominican sisters of Springfield, Illinois, in 1927, started Holy Rosary school in Denver's Globeville neighborhood, while the

Mother Frances Xavier Cabrini, who was canonized in 1946, inspired establishment of Queen of Heaven Orphanage and the Mother Cabrini Shrine. (Denver Public Library.)

Dominicans from Sinsinawa opened in 1955, Sts. Peter and Paul in Wheat Ridge.

Hundreds of now forgotten nuns did saintly work in the Denver archdiocese over the years, but only one of them would be canonized. Coloradans like to claim Francesca Maria Cabrini as their own. So do many of the other places where she founded schools, hospitals, and orphanages, from New York to Nicaragua, from Liverpool to Los Angeles, from Paris to Rio de Janeiro, from Chicago to Grenada, from New Orleans to her birthplace near Lodi, in Italy.

A flock of white doves came to rest on the home of Agostino and Stella Cabrini on July 15, 1850, the day their thirteenth and last child was born. Other legendary signs also suggested that the sickly little girl would become an energetic, world-traveling saint. As a child she created convents, dressing her dolls as nuns. She made little paper boats and filled them with violets, which she said were missionary flowers of faith. Locked church doors opened at her touch. At twenty-four, she began teaching orphans; at thirty, she founded the Missionary Sisters of the Sacred Heart. She so impressed Pope Leo XIII by

By accident, St. Joseph School was founded in 1906, when Mother Thecla and Sister Celestine mistook Longmont for Loveland and got off the train. Longmont townsfolk persuaded the sisters to stay and open a school, which used this horse-drawn bus. (Denver Public Library.)

setting up a school in Rome that the Holy Father officially blessed her next endeavor—comforting Italian immigrants who were flocking to America by the millions. She would take sixty-seven trips in America and found sixty-seven institutions.

Her first voyage came in 1889 when she visited New York City's Little Italy, where she started an orphanage, a hospital, and West Park, the first American novitiate for her Missionary Sisters. Mother Cabrini's reputation as a miracle worker brought her appeals from all over the United States. Two pleas came from Father Mariano LePore of Denver's Mount Carmel parish and from Bishop Matz, urging her to come and work her magic among the Italians, one of the largest and poorest immigrant enclaves in the Mile High City.

Mother Cabrini first came to Denver on October 24, 1902, blessing Mount Carmel parish with her gentle strength. Michael Notary, a leading Italian, loaned her his house at

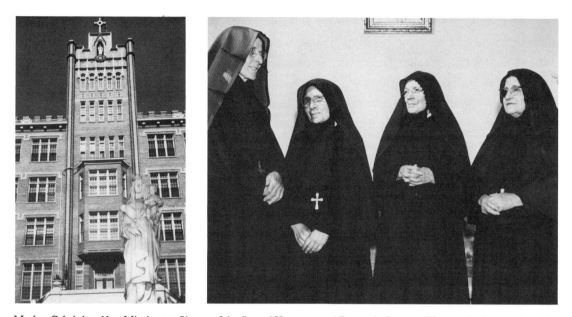

Mother Cabrini and her Missionary Sisters of the Sacred Heart opened Denver's Queen of Heaven Orphanage for girls at 4825 Federal Boulevard. Sisters Elizabeth, Giesumira, Gioconda, and Rosaria were among those conducting the orphanage until it was demolished in 1969. (Photo on right by Joseph C. Motta.)

34th and Navajo to use as a school, the first for Mount Carmel parish. (The large brick home is now a designated Denver landmark.) Notary's career typifies that of successful Italian immigrants. He came to Denver in 1889 as a produce peddler, opened successful grocery and liquor businesses, and died in 1935 a wealthy merchant and real estate man. The school opened on November 24, 1900, with the first floor converted to classrooms and the upstairs to a convent for the Missionary Sisters of the Sacred Heart.

In 1904, Mother Cabrini and the Missionary Sisters purchased a large farm house and several acres of land at West 48th Avenue and Federal Boulevard in North Denver. The recycled farm opened in 1905 as the Queen of Heaven Orphanage for girls aged two to fifteen. Queen of Heaven soon reached its capacity of 160 orphans, and in 1920 a magnificent new buff brick orphanage opened its doors. This large, neoclassical structure graced the Denver skyline with an electrically illuminated statue of the Queen of Heaven atop the lofty tower. The orphanage was reorganized in 1965 as a private elementary boarding school for girls and renamed the Saint Cabrini Memorial Private School. In January 1957, the Queen of Heaven Orphanage sold sixteen of its forty-three lots to the Colorado Highway Department for construction of interstate highway 70. Twelve years later, the home and school closed and were demolished.

Mother Cabrini became a naturalized citizen of the United States in 1909. While spending much of her time in Chicago and New York, she made several visits to Denver's Mount Carmel parish and Queen of Heaven Orphanage. She also toured mining towns, where many Italian immigrants worked ten or twelve hours a day underground. Defying superstitions against allowing women inside mines, she rode cage hoists down into the depths to bring a message of salvation: "My good brothers, we come down into the bowels of the earth to you in the name of Your Creator, He Who pines for your filial love."

On a 1912 visit to Denver, Mother Cabrini packed up her nuns for a picnic in the mountains. The captain at the firehouse on Tejon Street, if one of many North Denver folktales about Mother Cabrini is true, regularly took the sisters for such Sunday outings. When accused of using the fire department horses for these excursions, the chief supposedly replied, "As long as Mother Cabrini is with our fire horses, there never has been or never will be a fire in North Denver."

Upon reaching Mount Vernon Canyon, Mother Cabrini and some of the sisters climbed up the highest hill in sight. Overwhelmed with the splendid view of Denver and the Front Range, the sisters gathered white stones and arranged them in the shape of a heart to represent the Sacred Heart of Jesus. Inspired by the outing, Mother Cabrini somehow managed to buy the 900-acre hilltop site. She was warned there was no water but, according to legend, moved a rock to uncover a still-flowing stream of artesian water, which served the summer home for orphan girls that Mother Cabrini and the Missionary Sisters constructed.

In 1929, the spring was converted to a grotto, modeled after the Great Shrine of Lourdes in France, so all could come to sample the waters of Mother Cabrini. An anonymous donor contributed $1,000 for a life-sized marble statue of Mother Cabrini, a replica of her statue in St. Peter's in Rome. On July 11, 1954, the Missionary Sisters of the Sacred Heart erected a $15,000, Italian-made, twenty-two-foot-high statue of their patron, the Sacred Heart of Jesus, atop Mount Vernon. The flood-lit statue commemorates Mother Cabrini, whose faith could move mountains. Rock gardens, outdoor stations of the cross, a chapel, and a carillon that fills the hills with the sound of music attract thousands of pilgrims each year to the mountaintop shrine, which is maintained by a convent of Mother Cabrini's sisters.

Mother Cabrini died in Chicago on December 22, 1917, at Columbus Hospital, which she had founded. After a lengthy investigation verified her miraculous work, she was canonized by Pope Pius XII on July 7, 1946. Her body lies at her principal shrine, Mother Cabrini High School in New York City. At the time of her death, she had founded seventy-five convents and recruited 3,000 women to the Missionary Sisters of the Sacred

The 22-foot-high statue of the Sacred Heart of Jesus, patron of Mother Cabrini's Missionary Sisters, was erected in 1954 on the south shoulder of Lookout Mountain, where it is a prominent landmark for motorists whizzing through Mount Vernon Canyon on interstate 70.

Heart. In Colorado, this small, gentle nun with big, brown, unforgettable eyes is remembered in many parishes with an altar statue. Her shrine above Mount Vernon Canyon, now a favorite stop for travelers, also perpetuates the cherished memory of this world-famous saint who, at Bishop Matz's request, labored briefly but productively in the Denver diocese.

While Bishop Matz excelled at building parochial schools, his greatest achievement may have been persuading the Vincentian fathers to open a seminary in Denver. Like Machebeuf, Matz chronically lacked priests. He brought five new orders into the diocese: the Dominicans (1890), the Redemptorists (1894), the Servites (1898), the Theatines (1906), and the Vincentians (1907), but still had to pay Eastern seminaries to educate priests for his understaffed diocese.

A few of Matz's problems with priests came because he was forced to accept any priest willing to serve in Colorado, so he received some rejects from other dioceses as well as priests in poor health who came for the climate cure. These "TB priests" began arriving as early as the 1870s, when Bishop Machebeuf had written to his brother, "I am as thin as ever, yet more vigorous than half of my young priests [who] come to Colorado for their health."

Some TB priests became outstanding clergymen after recovering in the high, dry, salubrious Colorado air. Frederick Bender, for example, was a German-born priest who had worked in Cincinnati before coming to Colorado. After recovering some strength, he built St. Mary Church in Colorado Springs in 1877, St. Elizabeth's in Denver in 1878, and St. Ignatius's in Pueblo in 1887. Father Bender, who never fully regained his health, retired to tour the Holy Land but was called back to establish Our Lady of Perpetual Help parish in Manitou Springs. In 1905, he was called out of retirement once again, this time to establish Holy Ghost Church in Denver. This "lunger," with five churches to his credit, proved to be an extraordinary parish builder.

Percy A. Phillips, a French Canadian priest, also came to Colorado for his health. Although Father Phillips remained sickly much of the time, he served in Denver as founding pastor of St. Joseph Redemptorist parish, chaplain of the Good Shepherd Home, and first rector of Immaculate Conception Cathedral. Father Phillips, who had beautiful penmanship, was employed by both Machebeuf and Matz as their private secretary. Bishop Matz appointed him the third vicar general of the diocese after Monsignor Henry Robinson died in 1916.

Bishop Matz yearned for the day when his diocese would have its own seminary. The answer to his prayers arrived in the person of John M. Martin, a Congregation-of-the-Mission priest. This order, commonly known as the Vincentians, had been founded in

Paris in 1617 by St. Vincent de Paul. They had made St. Louis their headquarters in the United States and were looking, in 1906, for a Rocky Mountain region site for a seminary. Bishop Matz made various site suggestions to Father Martin and the Vincentians. The Miramount Castle in Manitou Springs was deemed too far from Denver, as was another possible location, the old home of the Jesuit College in Morrison. Finally, the Vincentians and the bishop agreed on a 59.5-acre tract of land on the outskirts of Southeast Denver, which the Vincentians bought for $15,218 on November 10, 1906. Temporary seminary offices and quarters were rented at 34 South Logan, 386 South Sherman, and 912 South Washington streets.

The Saint Thomas Theological Seminary of Denver, Colorado, was incorporated on September 4, 1905, with provision that "the Diocesan Seminary of St. Thomas Aquinas" would "be erected by the Priests of the Mission, at their own expense in the city of Denver." Appropriately, the seminary was named for the great Catholic philosopher and patron of higher education, St. Thomas Aquinas.

Groundbreaking was celebrated in the fall of 1907, and a four-story, $65,000, red brick building officially opened a year later on September 29, 1908. Old Red Brick, as the building designed by Denver architect John J. Huddart has been dubbed, now stands out amid newer blond brick buildings.

Father Thomas Levan, the first rector, and four faculty members welcomed twelve students that autumn. Only one of these twelve "apostles" did not remain through ordination, but all twelve may have been disillusioned when they arrived at the seminary, a bleak sixteen-block tract of prairie. To the south lay largely undeveloped land broken only by the first buildings of the University of Denver and a cluster of homes and shops in the adjacent University Park neighborhood. The site looked like the Great American Desert, not like the alpine garden of Eden described in the first St. Thomas catalog:

> The high, dry mountain air of Colorado, bracing and invigorating, [will be] a boon to the ecclesiastical student. . . . How very many young priests today enter their field of apostolic labor broken in health—not so much by undue application to the sufficiently arduous curriculum of studies as by reason of, possibly, the severe climate, and, generally, the uncongenial atmosphere in which they prosecuted their studies.

The single building housed students and faculty, chapel and classrooms, and a basement kitchen and dining room. St. Thomas offered a six-year program, divided into two years of philosophy and four of theology, with courses in philosophy, history of philosophy, canon law, church history, sacred scripture, Hebrew, theology, chant, ceremonies, liturgy, chemistry, and geology. Seminarians helped farm the huge site bounded by Steele and Monroe streets between Arizona and Florida avenues. They cultivated alfalfa and potatoes and tended to pigs and cattle as well as priestly studies. That the first major seminary of the region sprouted in Denver is significant. While Santa Fe was the initial archdiocese for the region, that city's failure to develop a major seminary, as well as Denver's rapid population growth, made Denver the hub for Rocky Mountain Catholicism.

Regis College, known as the College of the Sacred Heart until 1921, traces its roots back to the 1860s, when Colorado Territorial Governor William Gilpin and Bishop Machebeuf began trying to lure the Jesuits into Colorado, offering them land near Conejos in the San Luis Valley. Machebeuf's old friend and former supervisor, Archbishop Lamy of Santa Fe, likewise hoped to land the first Catholic college in the Southwest. Archbishop Lamy won this friendly rivalry when the Jesuits opened a college in Las Vegas, New Mexico, on November 5, 1877.

The Las Vegas college was founded and staffed by Italian Jesuits from Naples. By 1880, they had fifty men working in New Mexico and in three Colorado parishes: Our Lady of Guadalupe in Conejos; St. Ignatius in Pueblo; and Sacred Heart in Denver. Bishop Machebeuf continued to cajole the Jesuits about establishing a Colorado college. Toward that end, Machebeuf, in 1883, purchased the Swiss Cottage, which was also known as the Evergreen Hotel. The seller was former Territorial Governor John Evans, president of the narrow gauge railroad to Morrison, who had built the forty-two-room, two-story, stone resort hotel in the foothills village of Morrison, sixteen miles southwest of Denver. Machebeuf deeded the property to the Jesuits with the provision that they open a college there. Dominic Pantanella, SJ, president of Las Vegas College, persuaded the general of the Jesuits to approve this arrangement. Much to the dismay of Las Vegas, the Jesuits moved their young college to Morrison.

Father Pantanella christened the new institution the College of the Sacred Heart and opened it on September 15, 1884, with a nine-man faculty he had recruited largely in Europe. Twenty-four students, aged seven to eighteen, enrolled that first year. Many of them were locals who must have been curious to see what the Jesuits would do with the hotel's billiard room and dancing pavillion.

While the college catalog spoke of Latin and Greek, physics and philosophy, languages and the fine arts, the course work actually concentrated on basic bookkeeping, English, and penmanship. The school earned a good reputation and in its second year had sixty-seven applicants from thirteen states, but as the Jesuits no longer accepted elementary school pupils, they accepted only thirty-one. Academic achievement was rewarded with gold medals, including an annual prize from none other than James Cardinal Gibbons, archbishop of Baltimore and the great advocate of Catholic education.

Morrison, however, was thought to be too small and out of the way to serve as an adequate host city. If Sacred Heart were ever to become a real college, President Pantanella felt it must relocate in a sizable city. He made plans to move to Colorado Springs in 1887, only to be sharply reprimanded by Bishop Machebeuf. Machebeuf reminded the Jesuit that the Denver diocese had donated the Morrison property with certain stipulations. One of these was that Denver would have to be the next home for Sacred Heart, if it relocated.

The move to Denver was clinched on July 22, 1887. John Brisben Walker donated a forty-acre site at West 52nd Avenue and Lowell Boulevard. Walker, a real estate tycoon with two sons attending Sacred Heart in Morrison, reasoned that the Jesuit college would help him market residential lots owned by his Berkeley Farm and Cattle Company. Ten additional acres were donated by Lewis

With the pioneer building of Regis College looming in the background, four Jesuit faculty members cavort with the good ship St. James on the lake that used to grace the North Denver campus. (Denver Public Library.)

K. Perrin, a North Denver farmer and land developer. Although the Jesuits moved to the northwest Denver site in 1887, they continued to own and operate the Morrison property as a retreat villa until 1909, when they sold it for $7,500—to John Brisben Walker and his Colorado Resort Company.

Walker, who wanted a prestigious college building in his Berkeley town development, required that the Jesuits erect a structure "not less than 297 feet long, nor less than 60 feet in height, and to contain at least four floors, the walls of which shall be built of stone." President Pantanella borrowed $76,000 at 5 percent interest from Jesuit provinces in Ireland, Belgium, and elsewhere and broke ground on September 13, 1887. Edward Barry, a Jesuit scholastic trained in architecture, worked with Denver architects Alexander Cazin and Henry Dozier. They produced an impressive four-story mansard-roofed structure of pink sandstone and pinkish rhyolite, whose wooden trim was later painted pink. Although persistent legend has the structure completed in 100 days, it was not fully finished until a year later, when twenty Jesuits and one lay teacher took on 152 students.

The College of the Sacred Heart tried to protect its students from the evils in nearby Denver. Students were forbidden to leave the premises without "walking permits," a precaution continued until the 1930s. As both students and faculty, as well as all facilities were in the "Pink Palace," students had a hard time escaping "prison," as some of the more rebellious adolescents called the college.

Despite self-imposed isolation, the college made a favorable impression among judges called in to appraise student debates, and among audiences who saw the college drama club and chorus perform in downtown Denver at the Tabor Grand Opera House. Sacred Heart awarded its first four Bachelor of Arts degrees on June 23, 1890.

The Neapolitan Jesuits of New Mexico and Colorado weathered the depression of 1893, maintaining their hilltop campus on fees of $120 a semester for tuition, board, and lodging. The financial sacrifices of the Jesuit faculty and their devotion to learning enabled the College of the Sacred Heart to survive the 1890s depression and the lean first three decades of the twentieth century. These hard times undermined the nearby Presbyterian college, Westminster University, which had opened in 1892 with grand hopes of becoming the "Princeton of the West," but closed in 1917.

The Jesuits were determined that their college should survive all obstacles. One of the most bizarre ordeals was a 1913 court suit for $50,000 on the charge that former president Pantanella had "alienated the affections of the wife" of one Robert J. Lowery. Newspapers had a field day with these frivolous charges against the devout, eighty-three-year-old Jesuit, whose fine reputation was easily defended in Denver District Court.

In 1912, the college constructed its second building, a gymnasium used for student assemblies and elocution contests as well as athletics. By 1920, the college tightened its academic requirements to meet regional accreditation standards, requiring four years of high school and four years of college studies for a Bachelor of Arts degree. Physical education was also stressed by the Jesuits, who insisted that students rise at 5:30 A.M. and try to shine for calisthenics. On Sundays, both faculty and students were allowed to sleep late—until 6 A.M.

When football first became popular in America during the 1890s, Sacred Heart discouraged it as "rough and uncouth." Instead, the college encouraged tennis, baseball, handball, and billiards. Not until 1924 was coach Thomas A. McNamara hired to give "the Brown and Gold" a football team that he hoped would transform Denver's Jesuit college into the "Notre Dame of the West."

Athletics were not always followed by showers, because of the shortage of water. An artesian well supplied essential needs in the main building, which contained no bathtubs or showers. Finally, a small lake was dug out on the college's ninety-acre site. Although catalogs described it as a landscape feature and haven for boating, this lake served more prosaically for bathing.

After 1900, two prominent scholars brought acclaim to Sacred Heart. The college emerged as the regional center for seismographic studies after Armand W. Forstall, SJ, installed a seismographic machine in a basement room in 1909. Conrad Bilgery, SJ, put the college on the map for paleontological studies, attracting national attention in 1932, when he and some of his students excavated prehistoric bison and projectile points of the Clovis culture at the Dent site in Weld County.

Enhancing the worldwide reputation of the Jesuits as scholars who monitor earthquakes, professor Armand Forstall installed this seismographic tremor detector in the basement of Old Main. (Denver Public Library.)

In 1919, the Jesuit Province of Naples turned over its New Mexico–Colorado mission to the Jesuit Province of Missouri, who renamed Sacred Heart College as Regis College in 1921 in honor of St. John Francis Regis, a seventeenth-century French Jesuit. This name change may have been at least in part an attempt to defuse the rabid anti-Catholic sentiment of the 1920s: The name Regis, unlike Sacred Heart, was not obviously Catholic. Colorado's Catholic college, whose history is fully told by Harold L. Stansell, SJ, in his 1977 book, *Regis: On the Crest of the West,* had come of age.

Progress at Regis College and High School delighted Bishop Matz, a champion of Catholic schools. "Stand by your Catholic schools," the bishop urged in his May 19, 1892, pastoral letter on education:

Never begrudge the money you spend on the Catholic education of your children. It will all come back to you a hundred fold in countless blessings upon your children, who, reared in the faith of your fathers, will be your pride and glory on earth and your crown in heaven.

Hugh L. McMenamin, a crackerjack fund-raiser, promoter, and orator, spearheaded construction of the Cathedral of the Immaculate Conception, where he served as rector until his death in 1947.

Bishop Matz sternly promulgated the Council of Baltimore's decree that parents, under pain of mortal sin, must send their children to Catholic schools if they were available. Furthermore, parents could be deprived of the sacraments for such a sin. Matz's dedication to Catholic schools led him to make a cathedral school, rather than a cathedral, his first priority upon becoming bishop in 1889. By the spring of 1890, he had completed the $81,000, three-story, brick and sandstone school at 1824 Logan Street, which was designed by Colorado's leading architect, Frank E. Edbrooke. Shortly afterwards, Bishop Matz sold the old cathedral property at 15th and Stout streets to Winfield Scott Stratton, the Cripple Creek gold mining millionaire, for $175,000.

Cathedral School offered both an elementary and a high school curriculum, as well as a basement chapel that Matz designated as the procathedral. The Immaculate Conception Cathedral Association, which had been formed to build a new cathedral in 1880, would take thirty-two years to achieve its goal. After a 1901 visit to Rome and to his hometown of Münster, which boasted a splendid Gothic cathedral, Bishop Matz took a livelier interest in building. In 1902, a fifteen-day "Catholic Cathedral Building Fair" raised thousands of dollars that were sunk into Cripple Creek mining investments—and lost. Michael Callanan, rector of the procathedral and chief fund-raiser, lost still more by investing in glass-top caskets, a "sure fire" innovation in funeral rituals that failed to capture much of a market.

The turning point for cathedral construction came when Bishop Matz tapped an aggressive young priest, Hugh L. McMenamin, for the job. "I hereby appoint you Rector of Cathedral parish," Matz told McMenamin in his letter of July 25, 1908. "The time has come when the cathedral parish shall have to strain every nerve to build its grand cathedral. The people are willing and ready."

Bishop Matz showed wisdom in selecting Father McMenamin, a feisty, leprechaun-like go-getter. One of thirteen children of an Irish coal miner, Hugh McMenamin was born in Freeland, Pennsylvania, in 1872. On Sundays, as he later liked to tell his parishioners, his family had trudged three miles to hear mass, rain or shine, sleet or snow. Hugh spent his youth working in coal mines and lost his left thumb while sorting coal from slate. Afterwards, he turned to school work and became a teacher.

Young McMenamin entered Denver's Sacred Heart College in 1894 and graduated in 1897 with a Jesuit-instilled ambition for the priesthood. After three years at St. Mary Seminary in Baltimore, he was ordained by

The cathedral, minus its magnificent stained glass windows in this 1912 view, crowned Denver's Capitol Hill. Note the twin towers of St. Joseph Hospital in the background. (Photo by Louis C. McClure. Denver Public Library.)

James Cardinal Gibbons in 1900. His first assignment was to St. Mary's parish in Colorado Springs. There, he assisted Father Frederick Bender and then Godfrey Raber, two of Colorado's most distinguished pioneer priests.

"Father Mac," as McMenamin liked to be called (and as he signed his correspondence even after becoming a monsignor in 1933), was transferred to the cathedral in Denver in 1904. Bishop Matz, who had taken a special interest in this vigorous young Irishman and had arranged papal approval for his ordination despite the missing thumb, next asked him to establish a new parish in the east Denver neighborhood of Montclair. Although only a handful of Catholic families lived in the area, Father Mac founded and acquired expansion property for what became the stable parish of St. James.

Next, Bishop Matz gave Father Mac perhaps the toughest assignment in the diocese—raising money to build a long dreamed of grand cathedral. At the time, the cathedral project was stalled, as it had been for over a decade. The dream amounted to a huge hole in the ground with a fence around it at the corner of East Colfax Avenue and Logan Street. After throwing money into what seemed like a bottomless pit, Catholics had lost interest in Bishop Matz's dream of a Gothic masterpiece.

Father Mac did what no other priest or even the bishop had been able to do. After his appointment as rector of the procathedral in 1908, he built the cathedral. "The history of

Immaculate Conception Cathedral, under construction in 1911, and St. John's Episcopal Cathedral both took years to finish. Lightning knocked off a spire of Immaculate Conception while ground water plagued St. John's, leading its rector to chide Bishop Matz, "Well, at least our troubles do not come from above!" (Mile High Photo Company.)

the cathedral is his," Howlett wrote. By the end of 1921, Father Mac had paid off the debt and built a $190,000 cathedral high school and convent.

Father McMenamin had no doubt about the layman who should spearhead the cathedral campaign. John Kernan Mullen was born in Ballinasloe, County Galway, Ireland, on June 11, 1847. Fleeing the potato famine, his family sailed to New York when J.K. was nine. Joining the westward push of America's nineteenth-century frontier migrations, the Mullen family moved to Illinois and then to Kansas before arriving in Denver in 1871.

J.K. had little formal schooling; at age fourteen he started out as an apprentice flour miller. All his life, when asked about his early training, he held up his hands, which were scarred and embedded with pieces of millstones. In Denver, J.K. applied for work at Charles R. Davis's flour mill, located at 8th and Curtis streets. Young Mullen was told there was no work. "I am not asking for pay," he told Mr. Davis. "I am only asking for a chance to work." "Well, if you want to work that bad," Davis replied, "you may begin tomorrow morning. . . . If we get along all right I will pay you board and room."

J.K. soon earned a line on Davis's payroll as a journeyman miller. He was a hard worker and a cheerful volunteer who proved his worth on cold winter mornings by wading through the mill ditch from the South Platte River to break up the ice. Mullen became Davis's head miller but was saving his money for the day in 1875 when he bought his own Star Mill. The Star, which J.K. first leased and later bought from John W. Smith, was one of Denver's oldest mills. Under Mullen's control, it evolved into the largest and most modern milling operation in the Rockies—the multimillion dollar Colorado Milling and Elevator Company, whose products included the still familiar Hungarian High Altitude Flour. Mullen not only expanded milling operations, he purchased wheat fields and grain elevators. In Colorado, Kansas, Nebraska, Idaho, California, Utah, and Oregon, he

John Kernan Mullen, a poor Irishman who became a multimillionaire flour miller, emerged as the financial angel of the Denver diocese. (Denver Public Library.)

built up a $5-million empire of 800 employees and ninety-one mills, elevators, and warehouses.

Mullen became a major philanthropist. He was a devout Catholic and a teetotaler who organized the St. Joseph Total Abstinence Society to combat alcoholism, a disease that plagued many of his countrymen. Mullen gave generously and coordinated the campaign to construct St. Leo Church, at the corner of 9th Street and West Colfax Avenue. He donated the site of his old house as well as money to construct St. Cajetan Church at 9th and Lawrence streets. Thus, he made it possible for both the Irish and the Hispanics to have parishes of their own.

Mullen's generosity became legendary. He gave funds to help Denver Mayor Robert W. Speer develop the Civic Center. After silver king Horace Tabor fell on hard times and died in debt, Mullen bought the mortgage on his Matchless Mine in Leadville to allow Tabor's widow, Baby Doe, to live there without fear of foreclosure. (The Matchless remained in Mullen family ownership until J. Kernan Weckbaugh, J.K.'s grandson, helped establish it as a museum in 1953.) When Elitch Gardens floundered financially in 1916, Mullen bought the amusement park for $26,911 and later sold it to John Mulvihill with the proviso that Mrs. Elitch be allowed to live out her days there. Mullen's gifts enriched more than the Denver diocese. In 1925, he gave $500,000 to the Catholic University of America in Washington, D.C., to help build the J.K. Mullen Memorial Library. Mullen scholarships have for decades sent several promising Colorado students to the Catholic University every year.

As the first great leader of the Colorado laity, Mullen took a keen interest in church affairs. Many of his contributions to the Catholic Church were anonymous or unreported, but he probably gave the church at least $2 million during the course of his lifetime. As one of Colorado's shrewdest businessmen, he wanted a say in how his money was used.

The J.K. Mullen correspondence in Bishop Matz's papers at the archdiocesan archives preserves a vivid record of the emergence of lay leadership in what had been an authoritarian organization. At the request of Bishop Matz and Father McMenamin, Mullen became treasurer of the cathedral building committee. Furthermore, he helped persuade his fellow Catholic tycoons, mining men such as John F. Campion and J.J. Brown and bankers such as John C. Mitchell and Dennis Sheedy, to join the construction crusade.

Mullen tried to soften the ongoing hostility between the bishop and some of his Irish priests. As a layman with major business, social, and civic contacts with Protestants, Mullen also urged Bishop Matz to soften his militant Catholicism. For example, Bishop Matz, in his 1909 Easter Sunday sermon, made statements that led Mullen to send him a handwritten letter, saying in part:

> I was dreadfully grieved this morning to read in the news that you made the statement that not one Protestant minister in one hundred believes in the Divinity of Our Lord and Savior Jesus Christ. . . . God alone knows the innermost thoughts of a human mind and it is for the ministers themselves to say what their belief is. . . . Many of my best friends are among the Protestant clergy. . . . I could not in justice to myself and family stay on the Building Committee another day if I knew our Bishop was guilty of such intolerance and bigotry. So please deny it.

A crowd gathered at the corner of East Colfax Avenue and Logan Street on October 27, 1912, for the dedication of the Cathedral of the Immaculate Conception.

The bishop promptly and politely replied, refusing to retract his sermon. Mullen stayed with the cathedral project and maintained friendly relations with Matz as his May 17, 1914, letter reveals in its closing sentences and its final "Your sincere friend":

Thank you most heartedly for your great patience with me in the many years that has [sic] passed since you became a priest. . . . You it was that joined together in marriage myself and my wife in 1874 on Oct. 12. You baptized my children and have performed their marriage ceremonies.

J.K. and Catherine Smith Mullen had five daughters. The last, Anna, died at the age of four, but Ella, May, Katherine, and Edith grew to be young women who were enthusiastically courted. Mullen's daughters and sons-in-law—John Dower, Eugene Weckbaugh, James E. O'Connor, and Oscar Malo—followed his example and became generous patrons of the Denver diocese and its planned cathedral.

High above the dedication day crowds, John Cardinal Farley and Father Mac gave the cathedral spires a separate blessing.

Mullen was the treasurer of the Catholic Cathedral Building Committee; O'Connor served as secretary. The building committee paid $28,500 for eight lots at the northeast corner of East Colfax Avenue and Logan Street in Denver's wealthiest neighborhood, Capitol Hill. Leon Coquard, a Detroit architect, designed a Gothic cathedral somewhat similar to the one in Bishop Matz's hometown of Münster. After Coquard grew ill, Denver architects Aaron Gove and Thomas F. Walsh were retained to finish the job. J.K. Mullen regularly inspected the site and sent reports to Bishop Matz, including his distressed letter of July 14, 1911:

The firm of Gove and Walsh have caused you and the Cathedral Association more trouble. . . .They took Mr. Coquard's plans [and] did not put a scratch or a line on the plans . . . we had friction with Gove & Walsh from the very first day that work was begun under them as architects. . . . Walsh never once went on top of the building until the day he went up on the tower. I myself begged him to go up with me. . . . I climbed the ladder . . . and Mr. Walsh didn't . . . and he didn't hesitate to say . . . that it was dangerous.

Apparently, Mullen risked not only his money but also his life in overseeing construction of the Cathedral of the Immaculate Conception. No one, not even Matz or McMenamin, should have been prouder than Mullen on the day of dedication, October 27, 1912. This splendid piece of architecture, with its priceless stained glass and Carrara marble interior, is one of Denver's great monuments. Its twin Gothic spires rivaled the gold dome of the State Capitol for dominance of the city's skyline. Thanks in large part to J.K. Mullen and the laity he organized, Bishop Matz finally had an edifice to show the world that the Diocese of Denver had come of age. While Mullen shied away from publicity, Father Mac courted it. During World War I, he emerged as one of the great public promoters of the war effort. Speaking on behalf of the Liberty Loan drive, he gave a rousing speech that brought 15,000 cheering listeners to their feet at the Denver Municipal Auditorium. Father Mac also played a starring role on the executive committee of the Mile High Chapter of the American Red Cross. He was known well among even non-Catholics and converted an estimated 100 people a year to Catholicism.

Father Mac's interest in newspaper publicity led him to purchase the puny *Denver Catholic Register* in 1910. A few years later, he hired a youngster by the name of Matthew Smith to put some life into the sheet. With Father Mac always looming large offstage—and in newspaper stories—Smith transformed the *Register* into one of the greatest success stories in the history of religious journalism.

Father Mac emerged as a radio personality during the 1920s, when he began the Christmas Eve midnight mass broadcasts from Immaculate Conception Cathedral. Denver's "radio priest" regularly appeared on station KOA, where he attacked communism, fascism, and the Ku Klux Klan. He launched a war on pornography in 1937 by compiling and distributing a list of questionable magazines, then urging other clergymen, Catholic and non-Catholic, to put pressure on any place where these magazines were sold. Many Protestants joined McMenamin's holy war. In his zeal, the monsignor sometimes personally inspected drugstore magazine racks and confiscated the "dirty stuff."

This colorful and controversial monsignor initiated formation of an ecumenical censorship committee and a Police Board of Morals to ban "objectionable" movies, books, and magazines in Denver. By May 12, 1938, Monsignor McMenamin could write to Bishop Vehr: "I am now in a position to dictate to the Police Department what magazines may or may not be sold." Monsignor McMenamin's campaign evolved into part of the nationwide Legion of Decency program. During the 1940s, 1950s, and 1960s, Catholics were asked during Sunday masses to take a pledge to avoid objectionable movies and other materials.

During decades of depression, war, and rapid social change, McMenamin became a noted public champion of traditional values. One of his best-received and often given speeches lambasted divorce and birth control. With his long white hair and purple robes flowing, the monsignor condemned those who "severed hallowed bonds by divorce or prostituted its sacred privileges by birth control. . . . Let us drag from the hearts of our citizens that cancer of divorce and race suicide, which, like a blind Sampson, would tear down the majestic temple of civilization."

McMenamin was less successful in his attack on President Franklin D. Roosevelt, whom he came to regard as a wicked left-winger. McMenamin's open criticism of the president and letters urging votes against Roosevelt finally drew a rebuke from Archbishop Vehr. In a November 5, 1940, letter to the monsignor, the archbishop urged him to stop trying "even indirectly to influence the freedom of the votes of the Sisters, which is their own."

Even if he occasionally grew overzealous in pursuing devils as he saw them, Monsignor McMenamin generally drew high praise from both Catholics and Protestants. After his death on July 27, 1947, at St. Joseph Hospital, he was eulogized by the regional director of the National Conference of Christians and Jews: "In the passing of Monsignor McMenamin, American Brotherhood lost one of its staunchest leaders." Monsignor Matthew Smith praised McMenamin in the February 24, 1949, *Denver Catholic Register* as "a builder, orator, leader, and educator [who] did more than any priest . . . for awakening the Catholic clergy and people to a realization of their potential powers."

Most Catholics and many other Coloradans saw Immaculate Conception Cathedral not only as McMenamin's, but also as Bishop Matz's finest achievement. Some of his priests, however, found fault with Matz's priorities. Underlying friction between the French-born bishop and his Irish-American priests deepened the feud.

Foremost among the bishop's critics was Joseph P. Carrigan. Born November 7, 1859, as the seventh child in an Irish-American family, Carrigan was ordained at St. Joseph Provincial Seminary in Troy, New York, in 1882. When Carrigan caught tuberculosis, he came West for the salubrious climate often prescribed for what was then America's deadliest disease. After doing good work at St. Mary's in Breckenridge and Annunciation parish in Denver, Carrigan was assigned to the struggling new parish of St. Patrick's in North Denver. St. Patrick's had a history of sickly and/or unpopular pastors, and also suffered when an early, uninsured church building was destroyed by fire. When Carrigan took over in 1885, the little church at 3233 Osage faced foreclosure because of a $9,000 debt.

Father Carrigan transformed this problem parish into one of the strongest in the diocese. He built a parish school, established a parish library, and began a popular and successful effort to attract non-Catholics to the Church. His parishioners liked Father Carrigan and he liked them. Under his guidance, St. Patrick's not only flourished but also helped establish six other strong North Denver parishes.

Father Carrigan was an able, sincere, and attractive man, as was his bishop. Tragically, they did not always see eye to eye and were not shy about saying so publicly. A month after Matz succeeded to the bishopric of Denver, critical letters began appearing in the secular press. One critic declared in the August 12, 1889, *Rocky Mountain News:* "Irish priests have been ordered to outlying posts of the diocese, where a few jack rabbits can barely make a living." Even earlier, while Matz was coadjutor bishop, Father Michael J. Carmody, in a statement printed in the July 6, 1887, *Denver Republican*, declared: "I think Matz is unfitted by birth, training, and prejudice to be a proper spiritual director of the people of the vicariate."

Bishop Machebeuf had foreseen such criticism. In a June 14, 1887, letter to James Cardinal Gibbons, Machebeuf had confided: "Father Matz, although a very worthy man, may meet with some little opposition for not being an American or an Irishman, but I am confident that by his kindness, piety, prudence, and good sense he will overcome it and become very popular." Although ethnic tensions evidently underlay the conflict, the chronic economic difficulties following the depression of 1893 emerged as the major point of contention between the French bishop and a handful of Irish priests.

Bishop Matz became embroiled in a hot controversy with Father Carrigan in 1907, after Carrigan began building a new St. Patrick Church without consulting the bishop or the Diocesan Building Committee. Inspired by a tour of the Franciscan missions in California, Carrigan began erecting a mission-style church and rectory two blocks away from the old Romanesque structure. Bishop Matz ordered construction stopped, but Carrigan proceeded. The bishop, who was already at odds with Carrigan about diocesan financial affairs, retaliated by reassigning him to St. Ignatius parish in Pueblo.

Father Carrigan refused to leave St. Patrick's and enlisted the support of his parish board of trustees and the Ancient Order of Hibernians. The pastor of St. Patrick's refused even to respond to correspondence from the bishop, who on June 11, 1909, suspended him "from the exercise of all his sacerdotal faculties in the City of Denver, on account of grave disobedience." The case went before Denver district court judge Harry Carson

Riddle, who ultimately decided that the Church, not civil courts, should settle the squabble.

Carrigan, in July 1907, issued a pamphlet titled *Answer to Bishop Matz*. It accused the bishop of, among other things, theft, lying, simony, abuse of power, and forgery; and further publicized the scandal. Carrigan's overstated attack discouraged many sympathizers, including J.K. Mullen, who called the pamphlet "horrid" and damaging to the Catholic community.

Bishop Matz, on November 24, 1909, sent a letter to every parish and ordered that it be read at Sunday masses. This epistle declared that the "former pastor of St. Patrick's church in the city of Denver has incurred excommunication." Carrigan read the letter in his jammed church and then defended himself. The priest's defiance of his bishop attracted national press coverage, leading the apostolic delegate in Washington, Archbishop Diomede Falconio, to investigate.

Mullen, who discussed the situation with his friend Father Carrigan, with Bishop Matz, and with Archbishop Falconio, helped to work out a compromise. That November, Father Carrigan agreed to take a new assignment, St. Stephen parish in Glenwood Springs, and Matz's excommunication decree was rescinded.

The Carrigan–Matz feud probably exacerbated the attacks on Bishop Matz by two mentally unbalanced priests, Michael Culkin and John Hay Cushing. Both became obsessed with a paranoid conviction that Matz was out to get the Irish. Cushing physically attacked Matz in Rome; Culkin threatened to shoot him in Colorado. Both clerics tried to stir up the press and politicians against Bishop Matz who, at one point, requested police protection. Finally, both priests were steered into retreat houses where their mental problems, compounded by alcoholism, could be treated.

Pecuniary problems centered on the Colorado Catholic Loan and Trust Association (CCLTA), which had been incorporated by Bishop Machebeuf, Father Matz, and three other priests on March 24, 1885, as an alternative to bankruptcy. The CCLTA, according to its articles of incorporation, was formed to take possession of Machebeuf's real estate and to use mortgages, leases, or sales to pay off Machebeuf's staggering debts that amounted, in 1885, to $81,720. Machebeuf's considerable real estate holdings were then estimated to be worth $135,900. Subsequent events, most notably the depression of 1893 and dramatic drop in Colorado real estate values, left the CCLTA with considerably reduced assets but the same substantial debts and interest payments.

Machebeuf's will, which was contested by many creditors including his family in France, further clouded a complex and gloomy fiscal picture. One of Bishop Matz's first steps was to sell, for $80,000, St. Vincent's Addition, the proposed hospital site on the east bank of the South Platte River between 41st and 47th avenues. Matz sank much of that money into building the Cathedral School. Father Carrigan and others objected strenuously that the money should have gone, instead, to pay off various debts. Bishop Matz thought it wiser to invest in educating future generations. Despite ongoing protest, Bishop Matz continued to use the CCLTA to help fund his ambitious building projects on many fronts. Creditors, including Bishop Machebeuf's nephew Leo, the son of Marius Machebeuf, finally took their case to a civil court. Denver district court judge Robert Lewis, on August 25, 1913, dissolved the CCLTA, using its remaining assets to pay off Leo Machebeuf.

Even Father Carrigan, a founding incorporator of the CCLTA, joined Bishop Matz, and practically everyone concerned in a sigh of relief: "Thank God, the whole thing is over." Matz, who had only three more years to live, would find them relatively trouble-free. Thomas J. Feely, in his detailed study of the conflict between the bishop and some of his priests, portrayed it as a conflict between a European bishop with a paternalistic and authoritarian approach and independent-minded American clergy. After his exhaustive study of the Matz-Carrigan conflict and the role of the CCLTA, Feely concluded:

> Those in power almost feared that a clear victory by an underling would be a threat to the whole system of authority. The American concept in its real beauty would believe such a victory as a support to properly constituted authority.

Bishop Matz had troubles even with the dead. Denver's Catholic cemetery has, over the years, pitted the Church against the city, and critics such as Father Carrigan against the bishop. The story began in 1859, when General William H. Larimer, Jr., who had founded Denver a year earlier, established Mt. Prospect Cemetery on the hill now crowned by Cheesman Park and the Denver Botanic Gardens.

Undertaker John J. Walley took over this unkempt boot hill in 1863, when Larimer went back East. Bishop Machebeuf purchased forty acres of Mt. Prospect Cemetery from Walley for $200 on August 27, 1865, for use as a Catholic burial section. He named it Calvary Cemetery, but some called it Mt. Calvary. As Walley did not have clear title to the land, Machebeuf had to repurchase the forty acres from the city in 1873. When the city took over Mt. Prospect, renaming it City Cemetery. In deference to the well-kept Catholic section, the city sold the land to Machebeuf for the same price it had paid the federal government—$1.25 an acre. Thirteen years later, Bishop Machebeuf sold the southern half of his forty acres, for $1,000 an acre, to Samuel B. Morgan, a real estate developer who turned the site into one of the most expensive residential districts in the city, Morgan's Addition.

A Decoration Day flower wagon rolls into Colorado's first Catholic cemetery, Calvary, which once lay between York and Race streets along East Tenth Avenue. (Denver Public Library.)

After seeing Bishop Machebeuf make $20,000 on the site and then watching Morgan make even more on what had been municipal land, city officials brought suit against the bishop and the developer. Not until 1903, years after Machebeuf and Morgan were in their graves, did the U.S. Supreme Court uphold their transaction.

Mt. Calvary and the Jewish cemetery on the eastern edge of the Catholic section were well kept, but to the west, waterless and fenceless City Cemetery became a haven for pranksters and grazing animals, as well as for prairie dogs, owls, and rattlesnakes. This eyesore of a boneyard offered little comfort to mourners and became a fertile source of complaints to City Hall. Finally, the city announced a solution in 1890: Interested parties were told that City Cemetery was condemned, and they had ninety days to remove their dead from what was to become Cheesman Park.

Bishop Matz and many Catholics, who believed that graves should not be disturbed until the final resurrection, protested. At Bishop Matz's request, the city deferred its condemnation of the Calvary section of City Cemetery until 1891. Father Raverdy had administered Calvary until the 1880s when Edward P. McGovern, a leading Catholic undertaker, was made superintendent. McGovern installed irrigation and landscaping in 1887, and the diocese sold lots for $5 to $40 while maintaining a free section for paupers.

McGovern was also hired by the city to remove bodies from City Cemetery to Riverside Cemetery. As McGovern and his eighteen employees began exhuming bodies and placing them in new coffins, the macabre spectacle attracted curiosity seekers. This mass reburial came to resemble a "graveyard

After Mt. Olivet Cemetery opened near Golden in 1892, the old Calvary cemetery remained an informal playground until the city purchased it in 1950 as the site of the Denver Botanic Gardens. (Denver Public Library.)

party," according to the *Rocky Mountain News* of March 16, 1893: "Capitol Hill now has a new craze to kill the idle hours of the day, the old city cemetery has more visitors the past few days than ever before in its history." The sight, added the *Denver Republican*, on March 17, 1893, was "repulsive enough to please any ghoul. The old burying place looks like the scene of a premature resurrection."

As corpses were moved out of the area, the city put pressure on Bishop Matz. Despite advice from Father Carrigan and others, Matz decided to convert Bishop Machebeuf's ranch in Jefferson County into a new diocesan cemetery. Critics contended that the ranch should either be used for the industrial home and school planned by Machebeuf or sold to help settle Machebeuf's debts.

The 320-acre ranch had been purchased by Machebeuf for $1,365. He soon added another 120 acres that Father Raverdy had purchased in 1864 for $280. Machebeuf hoped someday to use the land for an industrial school and home for orphan boys. In the meantime, the bishop used it to raise wheat that he sold to the miller J.K. Mullen.

Plans for Machebeuf's ranch changed after the city condemned Calvary Cemetery. Bishop Matz and fathers Carrigan, Guida, Koch, Howlett, Malone, Murphy, and Robinson incorporated the "Mount Olivet Cemetery Association" on August 21, 1891. The site included all of the 440 acres that had been purchased from the Federal Land Office during the 1860s.

In a pastoral letter dated December 19, 1891, Bishop Matz announced that the old Calvary Cemetery had been condemned by the city. Catholics henceforward should bury their dead at Mt. Olivet, a cemetery on Bishop Machebeuf's "magnificent ranch eight miles from the city." Bishop Matz added that this new burial ground was so far outside Denver that the city "will never encroach upon the ground chosen" so "our dead could lie undisturbed until the Archangel's trumpet shall awaken them for judgment."

"The Union Pacific Railroad," Matz assured his flock,

> passes within fifty feet of our main entrance. The company agrees to build a funeral car and furnish up a special train for funerals. They will build a beautiful depot near the cemetery and take our funerals at the very reasonable rate of 50¢ for each person for the round trip.

After spending $23,000 to create a cemetery park, Bishop Matz consecrated Mt. Olivet on September 24, 1892: "We now solemnly declare Mount Olivet to be and remain the only cemetery for Catholics in Denver." Non-Catholics could also be buried at Mt. Olivet, but only Catholic religious services were permissible on the grounds. Five hundred folks, brought out by a special excursion train, celebrated the grand opening of the new graveyard park. In defiance of the bishop, some Catholics, including many Irish people, continued to use Calvary, where so many of their dead already lay. Though the bishop and the city officially closed it to further burials in 1892, Irish folklore has it that more bodies were nocturnally interred to join their relatives and friends there. The *Burial Journal* for Calvary confirms burials in the "closed" cemetery as late as 1908.

About 8,000 bodies slumbered in the silent city of the dead known as Calvary. However, a mass migration of the dead to Mt. Olivet began after July 4, 1892, when Elizabeth Kelly of Annunciation parish became the first burial at Mt. Olivet. Hundreds of corpses were transplanted in 1913 alone. In 1935, Horace A.W. Tabor was moved from Calvary to Mt. Olivet to join his beloved Baby Doe.

Mt. Olivet boomed over the years. Its subterranean population has now climbed to over 100,000. While Mt. Olivet grew, Calvary sank. Louisa Ward Arps, the late Denver historian, described its demise in *Cemetery to Conservatory*:

> The fence that once surrounded the sacred ground was broken and children would short-cut across the plots. Even without water, for years the lilacs and snowballs and iris would bloom for the children to take home to their mothers, and gradually the prairie flowers returned—the

Mt. Olivet, which Bishop Machebeuf acquired as his Clear Creek Farm during the 1860s, has evolved from the weedy boneyard shown in the 1892 view into today's beautifully manicured cemetery gardens, where over 100,000 await resurrection day. (Denver Public Library and Roger Whitacre.)

sand lilies and yuccas and cactus. As late as 1931 the two Kerr boys built an elaborate two-story house in one of the huge cottonwoods that graced the northwest corner of the cemetery. For their own uses, the children gathered bones, and hinges or handles or locks from coffins, and even, with great effort, took home some of the smaller headstones . . . on summer evenings, picnickers grilled steaks on pieces of iron fences that once surrounded family plots, laid between two tombstones.

Not until 1950 did Archbishop Vehr sell the old Calvary site to the city of Denver for $80,000, with the city agreeing to remove the 6,000 bodies estimated to remain. In subsequent years, the city converted the site to the Denver Botanic Gardens. Whenever new gardens and structures were installed there, groundbreakers frequently unearthed reminders that this was part of Denver's first cemetery. Meanwhile, Mt. Olivet has grown from a 100-acre cemetery to a beautifully landscaped and maintained 800-acre site. In 1981, the Archdiocese of Denver opened a mortuary at Mt. Olivet, despite the protests of some morticians, promising to provide complete and reasonably priced services.

Bishop Matz's administration of Mt. Olivet Cemetery and the rest of Machebeuf's estate raised the eyebrows of Thomas Malone, editor of the *Colorado Catholic*. This newspaper, the first Catholic journal in Colorado, had been started in November 1884 by John J. Quinn, rector of the procathedral. J.K. Mullen and Charles D. McPhee, a wealthy Catholic lumber baron, bankrolled this pioneer Catholic paper. When Father Quinn left Denver in 1886, the editorship passed to Patrick F. Carr, who replaced Quinn as rector of the procathedral.

In 1890, Father Carr turned the *Colorado Catholic* over to Thomas Malone, pastor of St. Joseph Redemptorist parish and William A. O'Ryan, pastor at St. Leo's. Shortly afterwards, Malone bought out his partner. O'Ryan, an erudite and prolific writer, launched another Denver Catholic newspaper in 1894, the *Celtic Cross*, but it died the following year.

Meanwhile, Malone ran into trouble when he fused the accounts of St. Joseph parish and the *Colorado Catholic* in 1892. After analyzing the parish financial statements, Bishop Matz determined that Malone still had not accounted for $12,000 owed to St. Joseph's. The dickering continued with Malone claiming he was being harassed, and Matz alleging that he wanted "justice, nothing more or less."

Ultimately, the bishop insisted that Malone choose between serving St. Joseph parish and editing the *Colorado Catholic*. Malone decided to retain the paper and resign his pastorship. Bishop Matz replaced Malone at St. Joseph's with the Redemptorist order who operate it to this day.

After leaving parish work, Malone resumed his criticism of Matz in editorials. As the attacks became more vicious concerning Matz's money management, Archbishop Francesco Satolli, the Vatican delegate, fired off a letter to Malone reminding him: "What is required for a Catholic newspaper is not only its conformity with the doctrine of the Holy See, but also uniform respect, deference, and submission to the bishops, and especially to one's own."

This apparently quieted Malone for a while, but he unsheathed his pen once again in 1895, prompting Matz to retaliate with a scathing pastoral letter to be read in all of Denver's parish churches. It said in part:

> We have . . . exposed the libelous insinuations of the editor of the Colorado Catholic, [which] proves furthermore, that a newspaper which does admit into its columns such vile slanders as the ones we have exposed . . . is not fit to enter a Catholic home.

While anything but an official diocesan paper, the *Colorado Catholic* made for lively reading. Malone, a well-educated, well-heeled sophisticate, had come to Colorado in 1886 for his health. He was chummy with the likes of J.K. Mullen and David Moffat, and maintained memberships in the exclusive Denver Club and Denver Country Club. Malone took on not only his own bishop but both major political parties by endorsing the Populist party during the 1890s.

Malone further riled Matz by using the *Colorado Catholic* to advocate a minority view within the Church—a view championed by Archbishop John Ireland of Minneapolis—that Catholic children should go to public schools, provided they attend mass before the school day began and receive Catholic religious lessons after the secular school day ended.

Malone became a public figure in Colorado whose views were sought and quoted. He wrote and published two books, *Colorado and Its Queenly Capital* (1900) and *The Idea Persistent* (1916). Father Malone continued to issue the *Colorado Catholic* as his personal, private newspaper until 1899, when he sold it for $8,000 to the *Inter-Mountain Catholic,* which was published in Salt Lake City. The *Inter-Mountain Catholic* thereafter devoted a section of stories and columns to Colorado. In 1939, it would become the *Inter-Mountain Register*, one of the many regional editions published by the national *Register* in Denver. Malone continued to be a public figure, a writer, and a speaker until his death in Denver, on January 12, 1935.

Malone's journalistic rebellion left Matz determined that the diocese must have an official newspaper. On August 11, 1905, he sanctioned the first issue of the *Denver Catholic Register.* Eight years later, this weekly emerged from relative obscurity after Matz recruited a new editor, a young, red-headed youngster from Altoona, Pennsylvania, named Matthew J. Smith. Bishop Matz, who once complained that the *Colorado Catholic* "well-nigh destroyed my authority in this diocese," was happier with the *Denver Catholic Register*. In his June 23, 1912, Lenten pastoral letter, "On the Catholic Press," Bishop Matz declared that:

> Our daily papers are reeking with scandal, murder, arson, marital infidelities, divorce suits, dynamite outrages, strikes and labor riots. . . . Invest in several good Catholic publications and thus assist in the creation of a first-class Catholic press. . . . Here in Colorado, we have an excellent paper, the Catholic Register, well edited, brimful of Catholic News from all over the country, and more especially Colorado.

Bishop Matz was a devout man given to study, meditation and writing out his thoughts. The archdiocesan archives contain two boxes of his handwritten notebooks, sermons, and meditations. The subjects of his reflections range widely, from "The Reasonableness of Faith" and "The Sorrowful & Mother" to "Christianity & Progress."

He thought about, prayed over, and put to paper his opinions about many things under the sun. In a time of dramatic social change and potential class conflict, Bishop Matz took strong, public stands along conservative, traditional lines. When wealthy and influential laymen such as J.K. Mullen and Dennis Sheedy asked Matz to sanction marriages of their daughters with non-Catholics, Matz firmly said, "No!" When militant labor leaders, struggling against dangerous working conditions and wages of $2 or $2.50 for a ten-or twelve-hour day, asked Matz for support, he had the same answer for them.

James Cardinal Gibbons, the archbishop of Baltimore, officially endorsed the Knights of Labor, a pioneer labor union, in his famous 1887 defense of the rights of labor. Pope

Leo XII, in his celebrated 1891 encyclical, *Rerum Novarum*, and other writings likewise defended the rights of working men, including their right to unionize. This liberal new view was slow to be accepted in the remote, conservative Diocese of Denver. Indeed, Bishop Matz joined the fight against Colorado's largest and most radical union, the Western Federation of Miners (WFM). Matz, like many other conservative churchmen, equated the labor movement with socialism, which the church had denounced.

The WFM, founded by striking miners in a Butte, Montana, jail cell in 1893, moved its headquarters to Denver in 1900. William D. "Big Bill" Haywood, a huge bulldog of a man, emerged as the WFM's treasurer, editor of its *Miners Magazine*, and star agitator. In the WFM's struggle to gain wages of no less than $3 for an eight-hour day, it made enemies that included the bishop of Denver.

Addressing the labor issue at the turn of the century, Bishop Matz declared:

> The church stands ready now to solve the later day problem of labor. . . . When labor oversteps the bounds of legitimate action, however, the church places the ban upon it. This also applies to organizations of capital combined to exercise unjust privileges.

The 1903 WFM strike against mine and smelter owners escalated into a bitter and murderous labor war. Big Bill Haywood declared that socialism was the only cure for a corrupt Colorado capitalism. Bishop Matz, in response, titled his 1903 Lenten pastoral letter "Socialism not the Solution of the Social Problem. Christianity alone can successfully solve it." The bishop reasoned:

> Labor organizations . . . not only have nothing to gain, but everything to lose by espousing the cause of socialism, which will make them the arm of the revolution socialism is contemplating. If they succeed, they will reduce labor to a condition of dependency equal to slavery; if they fail, they will abandon these poor unfortunate dupes to the civil power, while they themselves will try to escape, leaving the laborer in the lurch. . . . Idaho Springs and Globeville, Cripple Creek and Telluride, can furnish you with illustrations. If these are the fruits produced by socialism, you will have to agree with me that the tree is rotten.

In the towns Matz mentioned, the Colorado State Militia had successfully crushed the WFM, deporting strikers and ransacking union offices. Governor James H. Peabody and his adjutant general, Sherman Bell, announced they intended "to do up this damned anarchistic federation." They gained a major ally in Bishop Matz, who told his flock "to choose between the Western Federation and your church."

Haywood thereupon denounced the bishop as an "ecclesiastical parasite" and a "brazen and palpable liar." Opposed by both the Church and the state, the WFM lost the 1903–1904 strike, the bitterest in Colorado history, and died shortly afterwards. Once the radical WFM had faded, Bishop Matz seemed to soften his stand on the labor movement. Speaking in the coal mining town of Louisville, where he dedicated a parochial school in 1905, Matz assured a Boulder County gathering that "the church would always defend the rights of the laboring man."

Not until his final years did Bishop Matz begin to find some of the peace and respect sadly lacking during his first twenty years as bishop of Denver. The campaign begun by his sometimes fractious priests to build an episcopal residence reflected this happier turn of events. Matz for years had lived simply at the Home of the Good Shepherd, a residence he shared with an ever growing number of homeless and wayward girls.

In 1904, the diocese undertook a drive to build an episcopal residence. Opposition from a few priests and widespread complaints of parish poverty squelched the plan to assess each parish in Colorado 12 percent of its income. This embarrassing situation was ended by Verner Z. Reed, a wealthy Catholic layman enriched by Cripple Creek mining and Denver real estate. Reed donated the cost—about $12,000—of building an episcopal residence at 1536 Logan Street, just behind the new cathedral. The site had previously been occupied by the residence of David H. Coover. Coover, a physician who was not happy about having a cathedral built next door, had refused to sell his land to the Cathedral Building Committee. As a result, Immaculate Conception Cathedral had to be built out to the East Colfax Avenue sidewalk, with no room for landscaping at the entry. Once the cathedral construction began, however, Coover changed his mind and sold his site, which was purchased with parish contributions.

Mrs. J.K. Mullen and Mrs. John F. Campion hosted a reception for the bishop at his new home. The public was invited to this gala, which the *Rocky Mountain News* of September 25, 1904, called "the social function par excellence this week."

The bishop's maiden sister, Elizabeth, continued to serve him as a housekeeper, as she had for almost forty years. She saw him through the dark days and joined him for the joyous events of 1912. The day after the cathedral was dedicated, John Cardinal Farley of New York and Archbishop J.B. Pitival of Santa Fe stayed on to help the diocese celebrate Matz's twentieth-fifth anniversary as bishop. Matz was presented with a magnificent Carrara marble bishop's throne for the cathedral.

For Matz, who had struggled to build Catholic schools, the most meaningful part of the jubilee may have been the gift of Catholic school children. Dressed in their finest white suits and dresses, the youngsters presented him with flowers and a poem:

Dear Bishop, today while so many
Wait to greet you with eloquence rare,
We, the children, will claim just a moment
of this glorious feast, as our share.

We bring you this tribute of flowers.
Each one tells of reverence and love
And of fervent prayers offered for you
To our Heavenly Father above.

The troubles of the 1890s seemed far away during those glorious October celebrations. Then, overwhelmed by debts and criticism from his priests, Matz had repeatedly tried to resign. The beleaguered bishop was tortured by self-doubt, as well as by the doubts of some of his priests and laity. He had even stood in the pulpit of his own cathedral to announce his resignation. But Rome always said no. Rumors flew that Matz would be reassigned to Mexico or, in 1899, replace the resigning bishop of Fort Wayne, Indiana. To his credit, Matz endured, guiding the diocese through its worst financial ordeal and through priestly insurrections that no other Denver prelate would have to suffer.

In 1913, Bishop Matz prepared for a final visit to Rome. Aboard an ocean liner headed for Europe, he fell on a flight of deck stairs, breaking his knee cap. He never recovered fully and spent his time in Italy lying in a hospital, rather than making the hoped for visit with Pope Pius X. With the outbreak of World War I, Matz headed for home, arriving in Denver with his leg in a plaster cast.

While saying mass in his new cathedral on October 3, 1915, the bishop tripped over a rug, reinjuring his knee. Shortly afterwards, he suffered a nervous breakdown. He retreated to St. Elizabeth Hospital in Memphis, Tennessee, for treatment and rest, then returned to Denver grateful for the concern and prayers of his diocese.

In 1915, Bishop Matz suffered a series of strokes but continued his duties as long as possible. The bishop's chief aides, monsignors Richard Brady and Percy Phillips, his vicar general, handled many of his administrative tasks.

Matz, who had begun his administration as Machebeuf's coadjutor bishop, requested a coadjutor of his own in August 1916. He suggested to Rome the man he wanted—Bishop J. Henry Tihen of Lincoln, Nebraska—who had impressed many with his sermon at Immaculate Conception Cathedral in 1912. Rome would act favorably but too late to help Bishop Matz during his lifetime.

In 1917, the bishop became seriously ill and was taken to St. Anthony's Hospital. Elizabeth Matz was always with him. His other sister, Mary Mayers of Connersville,

Indiana, was also by Matz's side when he died, August 9, 1917, at 8:15 in the morning. During his last hours he told a visitor, "Tell the priests that I am the enemy of none."

Matz's unhappy, troubled reign left him a humble man. In his will, he expressed no grandiose plans, only simple directions for a modest funeral—but with the same authoritarian air that had alienated some of his priests: "I demand a plain wooden coffin, a plain, simple funeral (no funeral sermon shall be preached), a small stone or marble slab . . . bearing the inscription, 'Here repose the remains of N.C. Matz, Bishop of Denver. Pray for him'."

The great bells of Matz's beloved new cathedral tolled his death. At the solemn mass in the cathedral no funeral sermon was preached, but Bishop Tihen ascended the pulpit after the last gospel to announce the appointment of Monsignor Phillips, the vicar general, as administrator of the diocese. Then he read the brief burial request from Bishop Matz's will with the admonition, "Pray for him."

Over 150 motorists joined the funeral procession and hundreds of others took the train or streetcar to Mt. Olivet to honor their bishop. They may have been startled by the simplicity of the inscription on the granite cross at the head of the vault: "Rt. Rev. N.C. Matz, Bishop of Denver, Born April 6, 1850: Died August 9, 1917. Pray for me."

Even Matz's final wish was carried out not quite as he had ordered. That had been the story of his life. But despite all his troubles, St. Thomas Seminary and Immaculate Conception Cathedral stand today as perhaps the two most majestic architectural achievements of the Denver archdiocese. They are grand monuments to the builder bishop who insisted on the simplest of gravestones.

During his twenty-eight years as bishop, the number of Colorado Catholics tripled to an estimated 113,000 in 1917. The number of priests also tripled, to 179 by 1917. While Bishop Machebeuf had brought the Benedictines, the Franciscans, and Jesuits into the diocese, Bishop Matz greatly relieved the shortage of priests by introducing the Dominicans (1889), the Redemptorists (1894), the Servites (1898), the Theatines (1906), and the Vincentians (1907). The builder bishop was particularly interested in building Catholic schools. The Provincial Council of Baltimore, in 1884 had prescribed a parochial school for every parish—a goal Matz struggled to meet. The number of children in Catholic schools jumped from 3,000 in 1889 to 7,700. Eight new orders of nuns were introduced to Colorado during the Matz era to help operate schools, hospitals, and charitable endeavors.

Despite much dissent and even open rebellion, Matz had transformed a financially struggling diocese into a solid one. Although his hard-nosed crackdown on priests and his pecuniary problems made his administration uncomfortable for some, particularly himself, he was widely eulogized.

Gene Fowler, the noted author and *bon vivant* who ultimately converted to Catholicism, covered the funeral for *The Denver Post* of August 13, 1917:

> On his finger [was] the bishop's ring, symbol of the church of which he was a pillar. At his side a staff of gold. On his lips the smile of peace everlasting. . . . It was the funeral of a churchman, a service such as might well touch the hearts of the listeners no matter their creed or station. . . . Little children, garbed in white, black sashes extending from their shoulders to their waists . . . said good-by to the only father they have known since babyhood. For they are orphans, taken care of by the Catholic orphanges of the city. . . . [H]e gathered them to his bosom in the past and they remembered and loved him.

The *Denver Times* joined in the general praise for Bishop Matz after his death, expressing support he lacked during his lifetime:

> A man of determination, courage, and simplicity of life, Bishop Matz succeeded in all he undertook. Rising at 5 and retiring at 9, shunning all social festivities and attending to his office with the same zeal and piety with which he served as an altar boy in his native town of Muenster, he led an ideal life. Traveling almost constantly through his diocese. . . . he watched over his people.

Bishop John Henry Tihen. (Photo by Everett A. Stoffel. Denver Public Library.)

CHAPTER 3

VT·OMNES·VNVM·SINT·

TIHEN: TIME OF TRIAL, 1917–1931

Bishop J. Henry Tihen served the shortest term as bishop of Denver; yet this great orator guided the Church through two of its most severe trials—the challenge of the Ku Klux Klan and the beginning of America's Great Depression. These twin trials threatened to shred society into economic, ethnic, and religious factions.

While Bishop Matz had ignored the anti-Catholic crusade of the American Protective Association during the 1890s, Bishop Tihen felt that the Church had to defend itself against the Klan, an organization powerful enough to elect its members mayor of Denver, governor of Colorado, and U. S. senators. Through the resistance of the *Denver Catholic Register,* the diocese helped to end this nightmare of the 1920s.

The Great Depression that began in 1929 and the deeper problems of poverty and unequal distribution of wealth were also addressed by the Church during the Tihen years. Catholic Charities, subsequently reorganized as Catholic Community Services, became one of the largest and most effective arms of the diocese.

When John Henry Tihen was selected by Pope Benedict XV as the third bishop of Denver on August 6, 1917, few expected that the bishop "with a smile like the Colorado sunshine" would face a time of trial. The toughest times seemed to be over for the diocese: The rift between Bishop Matz and some of his priests was healing, and the fiscal chaos at the turn of the century had been resolved with the help of the laity. Colorado Catholics were learning to support their Church. J.K. Mullen and many other generous souls had enabled the diocese to complete a majestic cathedral as well as first-rate churches, schools, a home for nurses, and a home for the aged.

Tihen seemed just the man to bring Colorado Catholicism into its golden age. Unlike Machebeuf and Matz, he was American-born, the son of Herman B. and Angela (Bruns)

Tihen, immigrants from Hanover, Germany. Their son was born in a farmhouse in Oldenburg, Indiana, on July 14, 1861. Soon afterwards, Tihen's family moved to Jefferson City, Missouri, where he was raised on the family farm.

The Tihens soon realized that this personable, bright boy was destined for college. He packed his bags and boarded the train for St. Benedict College in Atchison, Kansas. After graduating with a liberal arts degree in 1881, he entered St. Francis Seminary in Milwaukee, Wisconsin, and was ordained April 26, 1886, for the Archdiocese of St. Louis. After three years as assistant pastor at St. John parish in St. Louis, Tihen went to work for the Diocese of Wichita, Kansas, where he was made chancellor and then vicar general. On July 6, 1911, he was consecrated bishop of Lincoln, Nebraska.

Colorado Catholics knew of Tihen as bishop of a neighboring diocese and as an orator. Tihen knew and loved the history of the Church and delighted in sharing it with Catholic and non-Catholic audiences, who welcomed his powerful pipe organ voice. After his initial 1907 tour, when he delivered sixty lectures in thirty days, he joined William Jennings Bryan and other distinguished Americans as a favorite attraction on the national Chautauqua lecture circuit.

Monsignor Thomas P. Barry, a young Irish priest brought to America to serve the Diocese of Denver, recalled in a 1986 interview:

> Bishop Tihen was a stately bishop, a walking example of kindness. He would take in any priest, give him work and play pinochle with him—Bishop Tihen was a great lover of pinochle. He was a German prince of the church who never forgot a face. He would tap us youngsters on the head and say, "Boy, you'll make it."

Unlike his predecessors, Tihen was noted as a broadminded socializer, a man who welcomed most modern contraptions such as automobiles and radios. Tihen loved many things in life, ranging from Notre Dame University football to motor tours of the Colorado Rockies. His musical taste, however, remained traditional. Of jazz, Tihen declared that the poet Dante would "undoubtedly have put the writers of it in his inferno and would have made their everlasting punishment the forcible listening of their own compositions."

Whereas European-born Machebeuf and Matz had been wary of liberal and secular trends in the American Church, Tihen was far more comfortable with non-Catholics, with secular society, and with liberal causes such as women's suffrage and the labor movement. By approaching even the touchiest problems with a smile and an open mind, Bishop Tihen gained many new friends for the Diocese of Denver.

Tihen's smile was especially radiant at his installation as bishop of Denver on November 28, 1917, according to an eyewitness, Monsignor Gregory Smith. Monsignor Smith recalled the bishop well:

Tihen was sent here to straighten out Matz's problems and did. His first priority was straightening out a fractious clergy. He was a young man's bishop who put his trust in the next generation—in the healthy classes of new seminarians he brought to St. Thomas Seminary. He ordered that any Denver diocesan student had to study at St. Thomas. If the man could not pay his way, Tihen would.

When you rang the doorbell at the chancery at 1536 Logan, Tihen often answered it himself. He was six feet tall, stocky and strong as a horse. He was always at home, always kind to his priests. If he chastised a priest, he kept it quiet.

Tihen was a grand master of ceremonies—he really knew the rituals and the liturgy. He and Monsignor McMenamin took pride in the cathedral's upon its pontifical high masses, with the wonderful choir of Monsignor Bosetti. Tihen knew we must have beautiful churches and grand, appealing ceremonies.

Tihen arrived in Denver in the middle of World War I. As the son of German immigrants who led a Church filled with many foreign-born people, Tihen headed off bigots who charged that Colorado Catholics were "un-American" and disloyal to the United States in its war on Germany and her allies. Bishop Tihen became an enthusiastic supporter of Liberty Loan bonds and of the National Catholic War Council, which was renamed the National Catholic Welfare Council after the war. Pupils in Catholic schools were organized as the U.S. Boys Working Reserve and the Children's Red Cross Campaign. He required every Catholic school to fly the American flag. In recognition of the Church's support for the U.S. war effort, Denver Mayor William F.R. Mills appointed Bishop Tihen a delegate to the Mid-Continent Congress for a League of Nations, which met in St. Louis in February 1919.

In 1921, Bishop Tihen made a pilgrimage to Rome, where some still remembered the embarrassing financial problems of bishops Machebeuf and Matz. To improve Denver's reputation, Bishop Tihen presented a $5,000 gift to Pope Benedict XV. Colorado Catholics vicariously shared Bishop Tihen's grand tour of Europe through his travel letters published in the *Denver Catholic Register*. Among American bishops, Tihen was one of the first—if not the first—to address his flock by radio, a practice he initiated with his August 29, 1922, sermon, "Love Your Neighbor."

An enthusiastic reception persuaded Tihen to begin radio broadcasts of solemn high masses from the cathedral. The bishop also considered establishing a diocesan radio

Monsignor Matthew Smith, editor of the *Denver Catholic Register*, personally supervised its lead type setting, making last minute changes that tested the patience of composing room foreman A. Wayne Kellerman.

station but decided to focus instead on the *Denver Catholic Register*, which was fast gaining readers and respectability during the 1920s.

Tihen healed the rift between Irish Catholics and the chancery by his strong support of Irish groups such as the St. Patrick's Catholic Mutual Benevolent Society of Denver, which had been organized on March 17, 1884. J.K. Mullen served as the founding president of this all-male lay group organized to do "works of charity and benevolence," to encourage "Christian education," and to "further elevate our social and moral standard in this community." In order to "bring out some of the latent Irish talent that is supposed to exist in Denver," reported the *Rocky Mountain News* on April 9, 1884, the society planned to sponsor literary meetings, reading rooms, debates, lectures, and band performances, as well as St. Patrick's Day festivities.

The late Most Reverend Hubert Michael Newell, retired bishop of Cheyenne, recalled after Tihen's death: "Bishop Tihen was a brilliant speaker who employed flawless English. He loved to hold a pontifical mass on St. Patrick's Day and preach on 'St. Patrick on St. Patrick's Day'."

Bishop Tihen also joined the Ancient Order of Hibernians (AOH), which had organized a Denver unit in 1889. Members of this Catholic fraternity supported Irish independence, aided the Queen of Heaven Orphanage, and tried to live up to their motto—Friendship, Unity, and Christian Fellowship. Tihen represented the Denver AOH at the 1919 national convention in San Francisco. "Though not of Irish birth," declared a grateful Hibernian, "he is a better Irishman than most of us Irish." (The AOH Denver membership peaked around 1900 with over 200 dues payers, before fading in the 1930s and dying. It was not reestablished in Denver until 1977.)

The bishop also worked ecumenically with Protestants and Jews. Setting an example for Catholics, among whom there were anti-semitic elements, he supported the National Jewish Consumptive Relief Society. Tihen endorsed construction of the B'nai Brith Infirmary in 1922, donated $100, served on a publicity committee, and spoke at the dedication of this hospital on the National Consumptive Relief Society grounds on West Colfax Avenue.

Bishop Tihen emerged as a convivial public figure. Upon his arrival in Colorado in 1917, the diocesan clergy gave him a black sedan, an 8-cylinder Cole. Tihen accepted the car, on the joking condition that he not be asked to leave Colorado in it, but relied on his horse, Black King. F.G. McCarthy, a Pueblo mortician, gave the horse and a buggy to Bishop Tihen in the spring of 1918 with the assurance, "I am sure automobiles will be plebeian after riding behind King."

Bishop Tihen kept Black King at the Denver Omnibus and Cab Company stables at East 18th Avenue and Pearl Street. Tihen delighted in buggy rides behind Black King until the magnificent creature died on January 15, 1923. The bishop wrote to the black-smith: "I have owned five horses in my life—all good ones but the best of these was easily King. I want no more because his equal cannot be found. If all men filled their part in life's drama as well as King did his part it would be a better world." Not learning to drive automobiles was a gentleman's privilege in those days, and the horse-loving bishop never did. Priests and seminarians drove him about in the car they had given him. For his visitations throughout the diocese, Tihen took the train.

Bishop Tihen's papers in the archdiocesan archives include numerous invitations to join or address non-Catholic organizations. In 1924, the peak year of Ku Klux Klan activity, he was recruited as a speaker by the Denver Chamber of Commerce. Tihen also

Ku Klux Klansmen convened in Golden on April 16, 1922, for this nocturnal ritual. Over 35,000 Coloradans joined the Klan during the 1920s and helped elect Kluxers as mayor of Denver, governor of Colorado, and U.S. congressmen. (Denver Public Library.)

took part in Colorado Education Week and in U.S. Constitution celebrations, joined the Colorado Historical Society, and encouraged formation of scout troops in Catholic parishes. His ecumenism helped defuse the rabid anti-Catholicism of the 1920s. This wave of bigotry culminated in the Immigration Act of 1924, which discriminated against Eastern and Southern Europeans, who were often Catholic peoples. To publicize the Church's stand on these matters, Bishop Tihen supported the Catholic press and enabled the *Denver Catholic Register* to emerge as a national system of newspapers, rivaled in popularity and prominence only by the *Our Sunday Visitor* magazine.

When launched on August 11, 1905, the *Catholic Register* neither hoped for nor received much attention. Although the Catholic population of Colorado had passed the 100,000 mark, Bishop Matz had complained in his 1912 pastoral letter, "On The Catholic Press," that the *Register* had only "five thousand bona fide subscribers who pay for their paper."

The obscurity and small circulation of the *Register* began to change in 1913 with the arrival of Matthew John Willfred Smith. One of six children of an Irish immigrant, he was born in Altoona, Pennsylvania, on June 9, 1892. At age twenty-one, Matthew was sent to Colorado by his father. "My father," Smith wrote in his memoirs, "had a dread of tuberculosis for his children because my mother had died at 41 of it." The widower, working as a shopman for the Pennsylvania Railroad, saved money to move his family one by one to Colorado.

To help with the expense of moving, Matt found work as telegraph editor on the *Pueblo Chieftan*, the leading newspaper of Southern Colorado but left a few months later for Denver, where he looked up another former Pennsylvanian, Monsignor Hugh L. McMenamin, the rector of the cathedral. The priest sent Matt to Aunt Sue Coughlin's boarding house at 1626 Washington Street and offered him work on the *Denver Catholic Register*.

At that time, the *Register* was privately owned, with the principle stockholder being Father McMenamin. Matt, who had four years' experience with the *Altoona Tribune* as well as the brief stint with the *Pueblo Chieftan,* jumped at the offer. McMenamin was struggling to keep the *Register* alive; the paper was $5,000 in debt. He gave Smith $20 a week and an old Oliver typewriter with a nonstandard keyboard. Matt became the entire editorial staff of the weekly as well as McMenamin's secretary. Only after the cub reporter proved himself did Father McMenamin promote him to editor in October 1913, buying him a secondhand $25 Underwood typewriter with a standard keyboard. The *Register* office consisted of a large room, shared with the *Daily Record-Stockman*, a livestock journal, in the Western Newspaper Union Building, 1824 Curtis Street.

As editor, Smith's first move was to ask Bishop Matz to make the *Register* the official organ of the diocese. Matz, still harboring painful memories of how Father Malone had used the *Colorado Catholic* to attack the bishop and his programs, agreed on the condition that Father McMenamin review everything that went into the "official organ."

Borrowing some ideas from Colorado's best-selling daily, *The Denver Post*, Smith transformed the *Register* with banner headlines, photos, and lively lead paragraphs that promptly explained who, what, when, where, why, and how. He set up a system whereby each parish had a correspondent, but he carefully edited their contributions. He abhorred wordiness and misspelling—and being scooped. He would exclude from the front page any correspondent who gave the story to another publication first.

Some of the rules for Catholic journalism in those days, Matthew Smith wrote later in his memoirs, were:

1. Be stodgy
2. Use language to conceal thought
3. Never say anything that will astonish anybody
4. Catholic papers should be as soporific as a phenolbarbitol tablet

"With a rip and a roar," Smith confessed, "I helped change all that. . . . Believe it or not there were both priests and laics in those days who did not think a Catholic paper was pious enough if people read it." Smith started saying no to priests who wanted him to print their sermons and theological treatises.

"The turning point in Catholic press history," according to Smith, was when the National Catholic News Service was formed in 1919. By then, Smith had moved the *Register* out of the one room office it shared with the *Record-Stockman* and set up his own presses and offices at 1929 Champa Street.

In 1921, Bishop Tihen bought the *Register* for $5,000 from the Catholic Publishing Company, whose principal owner was McMenamin. By that time, Smith had entered St. Thomas Seminary, but Bishop Tihen gave him free reign at the paper and arranged with his teachers to let him off each Tuesday to work on the diocesan weekly.

After Matt was ordained June 10, 1923, Bishop Tihen urged him to devote most of his time to the *Register*. He also served as chaplain for St. Rose Residence at 11th and Curtis streets, where he lived for the rest of his life. Smith was a small man, 5-feet-4-inches tall and never weighing more than 160 pounds. He always wore priestly garb—a high Roman collar, black sateen shirt, black trousers, and black Fedora. A long-time assistant, Paul H. Hallett, described Smith in *Witness to Permanence: Reflections of a Catholic Journalist* as an authoritarian editor who expected his *Register* stylebook to be followed as closely as the ten commandments. He had a "rock-ribbed Catholicity," revering the pope and clergy, not "contradicting ageless doctrine, celebrating heretics and dissidents, [and] sensationalizing the clowns of the clergy."

Father Smith recruited his younger brothers to help him transform the *Register* into a significant sheet. Seventy years later, Gregory Smith, who came west in 1914, recalled the adventure:

Denver was beautiful. Beautiful. So unlike industrial cities such as Altoona where there was little effort to build parks, boulevards and special lighting. I was sixteen when I came out and took the elevator—it was free then—to the top of the Daniels & Fisher Tower. From the top, I studied Denver with its tree lined parkways leading to parks. The air was so clear and the mountains stood out beautifully. Denver was a dream city to us.

"Matt helped put me through St. Thomas Seminary before he went himself," Greg Smith added, "paying my $250 a year tuition and also helped the rest of our miserably poor family rent a home at 817 East 17th Avenue." Young Hubert Smith also worked on the *Register*, acting as the business manager. Greg never held a formal position on the staff until he became vice president of the *Register* corporation in the late 1940s but says that he spent much time as an informal consultant. Thomas, the oldest brother, also worked in the business office and a sister, Julia, read proof.

In 1927, Matt launched a national edition and sent a star salesman, Leo "Team of Wild Horses" Connelly, on the road. Leo approached dioceses across the country with a deal they could not resist: Their local news would be "page one" with national news filling out the paper. The diocese could buy their special *Register* edition for a penny a copy and sell it for a nickel. While Father Smith and his crew in Denver did all the work, the dioceses and parishes would be making most of the money. In 1927, the *Register*, now a network of papers, moved into its new, custom-designed building at 938 Bannock Street. Smith equipped his new office and printing plant with the web press of the old *Denver Express*, a Scripps-Howard newspaper that had been acquired by the *Rocky Mountain News* in 1926.

The *Register* floated a $45,000 bond issue, backed by Bishop Tihen and the diocese, to pay for the elegant new plant. Behind the mission-style façade lay a two-story office building and factory-like press room, the proud showcase of the diocese which owned its own newspaper at a time when most diocesan organs were privately owned.

By 1928, editor Smith had boosted the newspaper's Colorado circulation to 7,000, while also building up a 15,000 circulation for the *National Register*. One of the paper's selling points was Father Smith's counterattack on the Ku Klux Klan.

The hooded nightmare for Colorado Catholics began in 1921 when William Joseph Simmons, imperial wizard of the Klan, visited Denver. Simmons had founded his reincarnation of the 1870s Southern organization in 1915; however, Simmons and his followers were less concerned about blacks than about Catholics and Jews. In secret sessions at the Brown Palace Hotel, Simmons recruited local leaders for what was first called the "Denver Doers Club."

The star Colorado recruit, the man who would make the "Kolorado Klan" second in power and per-capita membership only to the Indiana Klan, was John Galen Locke. A short, fat, 250-pounder, Locke had charismatic leadership qualities. Although he was a homeopathic physician spurned by both the Denver and the Colorado medical societies, Klansmen respected him as "Doctor." After his elevation to grand dragon of the Colorado Klan, membership climbed quickly; by 1924, an estimated 17,000 Denverites (25,000 across the state) had joined.

Governor Clarence F. Morley and cigar-chomping Denver City Councilman E.L. Mitchell, two KKK stalwarts, were captured in this June 14, 1925, *Denver Post* photo returning from a conference with Grand Dragon John Galen Locke. (Colorado Historical Society.)

According to historian Robert Alan Goldberg, in *Hooded Empire: The Ku Klux Klan in Colorado*, membership appealed to "joiners" seeking friends and status, and to the law-and-order element concerned about bootlegging and sexual promiscuity. The Klan even appealed to some progressives who believed its propaganda about improving the American way of life. Patriots were attracted by the Klan's cry of "100% Americanism." Locke used his powerful, clandestine organization to swing political elections. William E. Sweet, a progressive governor, had objected to the Klan's use of the Denver Municipal Auditorium. Bishop Tihen sent Governor Sweet a letter dated January 29, 1923, thanking him for protesting "the use of the Denver auditorium by an anti-Catholic and un-American Society, thus giving it civic recognition in Denver." Governor Sweet replied to "My Dear Bishop": "I appreciate more than I can tell you the action of the Catholic priests in approval of my protest."

Governor Sweet, in an August 8, 1924, address at the Denver Municipal Auditorium, declared himself "unreservedly opposed" to the Klan's efforts "to secure political power by capitalizing [on] religious prejudice and race hatred. . . . If we follow the advice of the Ku Klux Klan, we would soon emulate the merchant who hangs out the placard, 'I am 200 percent American. I hate everybody'." The governor further denounced the Klan, notorious for its burning crosses, for changing "the symbol of love, tolerance, good will and mercy" into "the symbol of hatred, intolerance and persecution."

While Bishop Tihen and the Catholic Church savored Sweet's attack on the Klan, the hooded empire sought revenge. In 1924, they backed the gubernatorial candidacy of an obscure Denver district judge, Clarence F. Morley, who was the "klokan"—chief investigator—of the Denver "klavern" or chapter. Morley received the Republican nomination and was elected; so was Rice Means, a Denver KKK member running for the U.S. Senate.

COLORADO SACRAMENTAL PERMIT

No. **450**

Rt. Rev. Joseph Bosetti,
Designated Agent

1536 Logan St.,   *Denver, Colo.,*
Street Address   Town

Catholic Episcopal Chapel
Name of Church

in accordance with the provisions of Chapter 98, Session Laws of Colorado, 1915, is authorized to purchase intoxicating liquors for the required use of said church or society in its religious services only, for one year.

Chas. M. Armstrong
Secretary of State.

Expires *May 16* 192 *8*   By _____
Deputy Secretary of State.

Coloradans rejected most of the Ku Klux Klan's political agenda, which included an effort to revoke all sacramental permits for the use of altar wines, such as this one issued to Monsignor Joseph J. Bosetti.

A year earlier, another Klan member, Benjamin F. Stapleton, had been elected mayor of Denver.

Before an audience of cheering Klansmen, Morley was sworn in on January 13, 1925. In his inaugural address, he proposed a state law outlawing use of sacramental wine (thereby prohibiting Catholic masses) and creation of a woman's reformatory as an alternative to the "sinister" Home of the Good Shepherd. Neither proposal materialized as law. The sacramental wine bill never left committee—the Episcopal bishop of Colorado, Protestants, Jews, Catholics, and even the Women's Christian Temperance Union testified against it. Only two Klan-sponsored proposals became law: the operation or ownership of a still became a felony; all schools were required to fly the American flag. Priests—or ministers—could continue the use of wine allowed by the "Sacramental Permit," a card issued each year by the Colorado secretary of state. Flustered Klan legislators killed their own bill to allow students to leave school every day for religion classes after Catholics and Jews endorsed the proposal. Morley was more successful in making Klan political appointments, including 200 additional prohibition agents, a move that enabled him to pay off political debts and give jobs to unemployed Klansmen.

Colorado's 126,000 Catholics became "public enemy number one" for the KKK. Whereas Jews and blacks were concentrated in Denver, "mackerel snappers" provided a

John Galen Locke, a plump physician from Denver, used his grand dragonship of the Colorado KKK to assert awesome political clout. (Denver Public Library.)

highly visible statewide target. The long-festering Catholic school issue, which pitted many champions of public schools against the strong Catholic school stance of the hierarchy, became a particularly heated issue. Klansmen attacked Catholic schools on the grounds that they taught loyalty to the pope rather than American patriotism and instilled in Catholic children a "paganistic creed with its worship of the Virgin Mary, dead saints, images, bones and other relics."

To counter Klan propaganda, Bishop Tihen issued a statement in March 1924 that explained that the Church, by educating 11,466 children in 1923, had saved Colorado taxpayers $957,754.98. Serious discussion of closing all Catholic schools led most to agree that this would put an impossible burden on tax-supported public schools.

The Protestant Herald, a short-lived Denver KKK newspaper, began to attack Catholic teachers in public schools: "If our public schools are not good enough for little Catholic kiddies to attend," declared the *Herald* on November 20, 1924, "then they are not good enough for Catholic teachers to teach in." In some school districts, Catholic teachers could not find a job.

The Klan attack on the Church was weakened by the ambivalent attitude of Grand Dragon Locke. By most accounts, he was not personally anti-Catholic but only used the bigotry of others to recruit members and increase his own power. Locke, it was widely noted, employed a Catholic nurse, housekeeper, and secretary, and treated Catholic patients. When KKK members suggested he discharge all Catholics employees, he told them it was his business, not theirs.

Nevertheless, many of Locke's followers did all they could to discredit the Church. They brought such alledged "ex-nuns" as Mary Angel to Denver, where she delivered sixty lectures, many in Protestant churches. Mary Angel's public confessions, according to Denver's *Register* of May 28, 1924, were "utter foulness. . . . It was the vomit not of the red light district, but of hell's depths." Her tales encouraged a few "pygmy-minded legislators," reported Monsignor Gregory Smith, to introduce a Convent Inspection Bill that allowed authorities to go in and inspect convents at any hour of the day or night.

In Canon City, the 1926 opening of Holy Cross Abbey by the Benedictines also aroused Klan attacks. By blasting the abbey as a proposed summer home for the pope and by denouncing Catholics as the "criminal element," Canon City Klansmen helped recruit members for what became one of the largest and strongest klaverns in Colorado.

When hot-headed Klansmen suggested that Immaculate Conception Cathedral be dynamited, Grand Dragon Locke restrained them, saying the Church would only spend the insurance to build a larger cathedral. Bishop Tihen, who never lost his composure and humor, heard this story and jokingly commented: "There are one or two churches we would like to get rid of. Why not recommend these architectural scarecrows to the Klan crowd."

The Knights of Columbus, however, took the Ku Klux Klan very seriously, particularly after Klansmen kidnapped one of their members, Patrick Walker. Walker was taken, on October 27, 1923, to a spot near Riverside Cemetery and pistol-whipped. Fort Collins–area Klansmen circulated fake copies of the Knights of Columbus's oath and condemned them as "the oily knights of the Pope's militia." Father Matthew Smith, who led the fight against the Klan in the pages of the *Register*, also attracted its wrath. Years later, Smith reported in his memoirs that he had been told the Klan had spied on him: "They can't find a single instance where you chased a woman. Neither can they prove you a boozer. They think you're too damn clean."

Father Smith, however, remained wary. On several occasions motorists yelled at him and tried to hit him on his daily walk from St. Rose Residence to the *Register* offices. Two other times, women summoned him to their rooms for spiritual guidance, hoping to trap him in a scandalous situation.

Gano Senter's popular restaurant at 1547 Champa Street posted a large sign in the window: "Fish served every day—except Friday." Senter's Kool Kozy Kafe and other KKK businesses sold cigars labeled "CYANA," an acronym for "Catholics, You Are Not Americans." More damage was done by Senter and his fellow Klansmen when they organized a boycott of Catholic businesses. Even this, however, was not very effective, according to Monsignor Smith. In the February 5, 1948, *Register*, he recalled:

We Catholics, on the whole, suffered little from the Klan, although great harm was planned against us. The Negroes of Denver, on the other hand, suffered much . . . because Klan committees went from door to door demanding that businessmen drop colored employees.

Although the damage, in retrospect, may appear minor, at the time the Klan terrified many Catholics, as well as Jews and blacks. Crosses were burned at Monday night rallies on South Table Mountain, on Ruby Hill, and on Pikes Peak on April 1, 1924. Unknown persons also ingnited a cross near Carroll Hall on the Regis College campus where, according to Judge John J. Dunn, "the Jesuits held the boys back inside or they would have torn those Kluxers apart." Crosses were also reportedly burned in front of St. Dominic Church, St. Ignatius Loyola Church, Loretto Heights College, and, if rumors can be believed, other Catholic churches in Denver.

In Durango, according to historian Duane A. Smith in *Rocky Mountain Boom Town*, William Kipp, pastor at St. Columba's, grew alarmed when the Klan threatened to burn down the church, school, and convent as well as Mercy Hospital across the street. Father Kipp bought a double-barreled shotgun, which he brandished during a Sunday sermon, saying that "if he needed to, he would use it." In Boulder, the *Rocky Mountain American*, a Klan newspaper, took frequent potshots at Catholics, including this poem in its April 24, 1925, edition:

> I would rather be a Klansman
> in robe of snowy white,
> Than to be a Catholic Priest
> in robe as black as night;
>
> For a Klansman is AMERICAN
> and AMERICA is his home,
> But a priest owes his allegiance
> to a Dago Pope in Rome.

The card parties, carnivals, and raffles with which many parishes supported their churches, schools, and social programs were attacked by the Klan as immoral gambling. One result was a letter from the Denver manager of safety and excise, a Klansman named Reuben Hershey, to Bishop Tihen, telling him that "congregations under your jurisdiction" must "absolutely discontinue in the future" all "raffles, enterprises or games of chance."

Catholics experienced a wide range of subtle discrimination. At the University of Denver, Catholic girls, finding themselves not welcome at existing sororities, established their own, Theta Phi Alpha, which, according to one member, soon developed a reputation for having the most beautiful girls on campus. This inspired fraternities to forget all about the KKK inspired boycott, and soon sororities also changed their discriminatory policies. Theta Phi Alpha disbanded.

Discrimination on many fronts, covert and overt, convinced the feisty, red-headed editor of the *Register* to take on the Klan. "A stock argument I heard over and over again," Smith recalled, "was 'Give them enough rope and they will hang themselves'. But they did not hang themselves. They had to be fought." Bishop Tihen concurred but told Smith that satire "is the most powerful sword that men can use."

Father Smith used both ridicule and exposés. Governor Morley was called a "pigmy Nero"; the April 9, 1925, edition questioned how much Locke "as grand dragon is making off each man or woman who saves the nation by buying a nightshirt for $16." On July 3, 1924, the *Register* published a list of over 2,400 alleged Denver Klansmen. Although not endorsing any candidates, the *Register* identified pro-KKK and anti-KKK candidates for its readers just before the 1925 spring city election.

Neither the fierce editorials of Father Smith nor the good humored patience of Bishop Tihen stopped the Klan, but they did hang themselves. Locke's greed for power and profits soon created rifts within the invisible empire. In 1925, only a few years after being elected as a Klan candidate, Mayor Stapleton denounced the KKK. Both Governor Morley and Senator Means failed to receive renominations by the Republican party, which abruptly ended its brief and embarrassing affair with the KKK. Morley left Denver for Indianapolis, where he and four partners formed a brokerage firm. In 1937, ex-governor Morley was accused of mail fraud, of taking money for securities he failed to deliver. He was sentenced to five years in the federal penitentiary at Leavenworth, Kansas.

John Galen Locke also found himself in trouble. The Internal Revenue Service, noting that he had failed to report any income between 1913 and 1924, began an investigation. Locke refused to produce his financial records, as ordered by U.S. district court judge J. Foster Symes, and was jailed in Denver for ten days. The national KKK was also curious about Locke's share of the Klan membership and uniform fees, which amounted to $300,000 in 1924. On June 30, 1925, Imperial Wizard Hiram W. Evans forced him to resign. Locke subsequently formed the Minute Men of America but never regained his following or his power. By 1926, the Ku Klux Klan nightmare in Colorado was largely over, though freelance bigots continue to invoke its name to this day.

Why so many Coloradans briefly accepted the Klan and its rabid anti-Catholicism remains a puzzle. However, the broadminded, ecumenical, and community-oriented administration of Bishop Tihen, epitomized by his support of the Charity Organization Society, probably won the Church many non-Catholic allies in the struggle with the "Invisible Empire."

Since its founding in 1887, Denver's premier welfare institution was the Charity Organization Society, (COS), a nondenominational umbrella organization attempting to coordinate charitable endeavors in the Mile High City. Monsignor William O'Ryan, one of the founders, apparently introduced the idea. O'Ryan, an Irishman who came to Colorado for the climate cure, had become interested in a novel approach to charities used in Liverpool, England. There, a loosely organized financial federation coordinated fund raising and distribution of funds to a variety of eleemosynary groups.

Under the COS plan, citizens would be approached only once a year by the one umbrella charity, whose professional and respected board would then decide how much should go to each institution. Although Denverites claim to have invented the idea of an umbrella charity, Buffalo, New York, had organized the first in the United States in 1877, and Indianapolis had followed suit before Denver joined the movement.

Monsignor O'Ryan, an intellectual who spearheaded the Catholic ecumenical movement in Colorado, discussed the idea of a single, interdenominational charity with Reverend Myron Reed, Denver's leading Congregational minister, and with Dean H. Martyn Hart, of St. John's Episcopal cathedral. Francis Wisehart Jacobs, a noted Jewish philanthropist, Rabbi William S. Freidman of Temple Emanuel, and Father Patrick F. Carr also helped establish the COS, which quickly came to dominate private charitable work. The society, as President James S. Pershing explained in the first annual report in 1889, was intended to save the general public and the business community from being "repeatedly and perhaps annoyingly solicited" and to spare the would-be giver the task of having to "determine for himself (often a difficult and embarrassing task) how he should apportion to the various charities."

Denver's COS raised $21,700 to fund ten charities in 1888; these included the Good Shepherd home and St. Vincent Orphan Asylum. Reverend Thomas Uzzell, a Methodist minister who operated the People's Tabernacle on Denver's skid row, congratulated the society at its 1889 meeting in the Tabor Grand Opera House:

> We have driven all the beggars off the street, all the organ grinders. You can hardly find one. The humbugs have been found out. Some of them arrested and imprisoned and you businessmen owe a credit to this association for what they have done in regard to this matter.

The silver panic and depression of 1893 led to reduced contributions while greatly increasing the number of indigents. In 1894, contributions fell to around $10,000 and would not pass the $30,000 mark until 1906. The COS survived by turning to less expensive projects, such as community gardens that were tended by and fed unemployed families.

Guy T. Justis, a social worker, was hired in 1917 to bring the Denver effort out of the doldrums. Justis proved to be an administrative dynamo who transformed an amateurish assortment of do-gooders into a professional outfit. Renamed the Denver Community Chest in 1923, it raised and distributed $649,000 to forty-five agencies. The Mile High United Way, as it would be called after 1957, remains the major charitable organization in Denver.

Bishop Tihen endorsed the Community Chest program, of which Monsignor O'Ryan continued to be a mainstay until his death in 1940. The bishop, in a characteristic show of support, wrote to the Community Chest in 1923: "We are greatly interested in the campaign and shall gladly extend our help to make it successful." Despite pressing needs of Catholic charitable groups, Bishop Tihen authorized Community Chest collections in each parish. Furthermore, he acted on the organization's complaints that Mother Cabrini's Missionary Sisters of the Sacred

The founding father of Colorado Catholic Charities, Monsignor John R. Mulroy, came West a thin, weak, health-seeker but became a robust giant who spearheaded expansion of social services both in the church and in the City and County of Denver. (Denver Public Library.)

Heart continued to beg in the streets despite generous allotments from the Community Chest for the Queen of Heaven Orphanage.

Borrowing an idea from the Community Chest program, Bishop Tihen decided to place all the Catholic charities under one central office. From the day Father Machebeuf arrived in Denver in 1860, the church had been involved in charitable endeavors, including the St. Vincent de Paul Society (1878), the Sacred Heart Aid Society (1881), and the Catholic Library Association (1884).

In 1927, Catholic Charities opened a two-room office in the Railroad Building at 1515 Larimer Street. To head this tiny office, Bishop Tihen appointed, on February 1, 1927, a young, tuberculosis-stricken priest, John R. Mulroy. Mulroy had come to Colorado as a scrawny health-seeker in 1917. He could devote only half time to Catholic Charities as he also served as pastor of St. Rose of Lima and then Holy Ghost parishes.

Father Mulroy described the early days in "Catholic Charities on the Wider Front, 1927–1951": "We began with six months paid rent, a borrowed social worker, a secretary paid each two weeks if we had the money, a volunteer Vincentian, some old clothes, some meal and lodging tickets and a part-time priest director." Few expected much of this part-time tubercular priest, but Father Mulroy fooled nearly everyone. He regained his health, became robust and energetic, and transformed the feeble Catholic Charities into one of the strongest programs of the diocese.

"Mulroy was a marvel," according to Monsignor Greg Smith:

He came here with a strange malady—tuberculosis of the eye—and never completely recovered. He was a quiet but determined crusader who pushed for public health reforms as well as public welfare, even if it meant inspecting toilets personally—which he did in Catholic schools. When he came here he found little in the way of welfare. Even the Community Chest program was feeble. He helped change all that. He interested the newly formed National Council of Catholic Women, who were casting about for a cause, in providing funding and volunteers for Catholic Charities. Mulroy was a thorough administrator and an easy smiler who worked well with Catholics and non-Catholics alike.

Father Mulroy knew where to look for help—to J.K. and Catherine Mullen. Catherine Smith Mullen was an active member and supporter of the Sacred Heart Aid Society, a founder of the Needlework Guild, and a founder of St. Joseph Hospital Baby Annex, which cared for homeless infants. The Mullens also contributed generously to the St. Vincent de Paul Society of Denver, which, under the zealous leadership of Edward A. Qualkenbush, operated a workingman's club and shelter homes, besides arranging foster homes for unwanted babies and children.

Other assistance came from the Knights of Columbus, who undertook an annual minstrel show at the Denver Municipal Auditorium to support Catholic Charities, which by 1931 was receiving $7,000 a year from them. This men's group also staged a "Silver Dollar Carnival" to raise money for the work of the St. Vincent de Paul Society.

Bishop Tihen and Catholic Charities gave strong support to the working class and the union movement. During the bitter, bloody Denver Tramway Company strike of 1920, Bishop Tihen spoke at the Denver Auditorium on behalf of the rights of labor. When a wealthy Catholic capitalist criticized the bishop for encouraging unions, Tihen responded that he would always be on the side of labor. Demonstrating his support for the working class, he often visited Denver's Catholic Workingmen's Club to chat and play pinochle. When J.K. Mullen announced his plans to erect a home "for the aged poor who of all are

The St. Vincent de Paul Society, oldest of the Catholic charities, opened this Workingman's Club at 1824 Larimer Street during the Great Depression of the 1930s. (Photo by Paul E. Norine.)

the most abandoned," Bishop Matz praised the plan as "an object lesson on the charity of Catholics."

In September 1913, Mullen bought a ten-acre tract between West 28th and 29th avenues, stretching from Lowell Boulevard to Newton Street, from Hiram G. Wolfe, a nursery man and realtor who lived on the site. Mullen called the location Denver's "most beautiful" hilltop, "with some of the finest trees in the city."

Mullen and Bishop Matz recruited the Little Sisters of the Poor from their Palatine, Illinois, motherhouse to run their home for the elderly. This order of nuns, founded by Jeanne Jugan in 1839 in France, strove to follow her admonition: "To have compassion is no longer to pay attention to self. To be attentive to others, and to look on them as one would on oneself. . . . Never forget, never forget, the poor are Our Lord."

Bishop Tihen, who told his flock to "begin in poverty to know how to serve the poor," celebrated St. Joseph's Day, 1931, serving meals to residents of the Mullen Home for Aged. (Colorado Historical Society.)

The Little Sisters of the Poor, who take joy in their mission of tending the sick and dying, worked with Mullen and Denver architect Harry James Manning to design a four-story complex for patients and nuns, with boarding rooms, health clinics, a dining room, library, recreation rooms, and a chapel.

Construction began in December 1916, and a year later four Little Sisters moved into the laundry building to supervise construction and prepare for the first residents, who were admitted in April 1918. Bishop Tihen formally dedicated the Mullen Home (also known as Sacred Heart Home) on September 1, 1918. This fine brick structure, executed in a neoclassical style, accommodated 150 indigent elderly men and women, regardless of their religious background. They received loving twenty-four-hour-a-day, seven-day-

The Little Sisters of the Poor, who opened the Mullen Home for Aged in North Denver in 1918, soon made it one of the finest nursing homes in Colorado.

a-week care from the Little Sisters, who aspired only to become the "Humble Servants of the Poor."

During Bishop Tihen's time, the diocese began establishing community centers, one of the Progressive era's prescriptions for poor inner city neighborhoods. These community centers offered diverse and varied assistance, which might include job training, education classes, recreational facilities, and counseling as well as food, shelter, clothing, and health clinics.

Denver's first Catholic community center was the Garfield Center at 1085 Yuma Street, which offered catechetical classes as well as welfare services. Garfield Center opened in 1923 and was replaced during the 1930s with the Vail Community Center. St. Cajetan Clinic and Community Center, one of many Catholic Charities financed by J.K. Mullen, opened in 1925 at 8th and Curtis streets, the site where Mullen had first found work fifty-four years earlier at the Excelsior Mill. In 1934, St. Cajetan Clinic was renamed the Ave Maria Clinic. It served as an outpatient department for Denver's three Catholic hospitals and soon outgrew its old storefront. It moved into the basement of St. Cajetan Church where 4,000 to 5,000 people a year received clinical attention.

Little Flower Community Center opened in 1928 in a house at 2809 Larimer Street that the Denver Diocesan Council of Catholic Women (DDCCW) transformed into a clinic, school, and library for the neighborhood. The DDCCW, a local council of the National Council of Catholic Women, was formed on September 25, 1925. Ella M. Weckbaugh, a daughter of J.K. Mullen, was the founding president, and Father Mulroy the spiritual director of this group that was to support Catholic Charities.

The DDCCW, which had its office in room 504 of the Railroad Building on Larimer Street, used its center to assist migrant laborers in Colorado. In its 1929 *Report on Mexican Welfare*, the DDCCW found that some 9,000 Spanish-speaking people wintered in Denver. "The beet workers' plight," according to the DDCCW, was commonly their failure "through no fault of their own to complete their contract" to work in Colorado's sugar beet fields. This "left many families destitute," and "many in addition to this, are in debt for their summer's provisions." Great Western and other sugar beet companies had given these people free rides to Colorado from Mexico or New Mexico in the spring but saw no need to take them back home after the beets were harvested. If migrants did not fulfill all terms of their contracts and stay on the job to the last day, they could lose all their pay.

For these poor migrants, the center offered classes in sewing, darning, music, folk dancing, and English, and served hot lunches. Sisters of Loretto taught catechism and other classes for girls, while Jesuits instructed boys. By 1940, the Little Flower Community Center had expanded its operations, moving into the two adjacent buildings. After landlords refused to make necessary improvements, the diocese purchased the buildings in the 1940s.

The center, by the 1950s, was offering over 6,000 lunches a year; classes in crafts, tap dancing, candle dipping, and woodcraft as well as baseball, football, and basketball programs; and day care for children. Neighborhood patrons of the center also used it for baptisms and weddings. The United Farm Workers, a group trying to organize and upgrade the lives of migrant workers, was given free office space upstairs at Little Flower, a center of hope for many peoples and causes ever since its opening.

St. Anthony Neighborhood House was established in 1930 along the lines of the settlement houses made famous by social workers such as Jane Addams, founder of Chicago's Hull House. This clinic and neighborhood house at 3638 Osage Street catered to the surrounding Italian neighborhood, offering health care, a library, and classes in

Mary Dean Reed, widow of a millionaire mining, oil, and real estate tycoon, established a $600,000 endowment in memory of her daughter Margery, in 1925, for the Margery Reed Mayo Day Nursery at 1128 28th Street in Denver. (Denver Public Library.)

catechism, music, art, and domestic science. It apparently merged, during the 1940s, with the Little Flower Community Center.

Vail Community Center opened in 1937 at 1904 West 12th Avenue in the South Platte River bottoms. John F. Vail, a wealthy Catholic businessman dealing in investments and real estate, and his wife financed the center, which served primarily a Hispanic population until it was washed away by the 1965 Platte River flood.

In 1906, Mrs. Verner Z. (Mary Dean) Reed had established a day nursery and social center in Denver's Five Points neighborhood with the idea of allowing poor mothers, including many blacks, Hispanics, and Orientals, to work or go to school. When her daughter, Margery, died in 1925, Mrs. Reed set up a $600,000 endowment to convert the old nursery into a model day care center at 1128 28th Street. The $450,000 Margery Reed

Rose Ann Bradford Taht, the smallest girl facing the camera in this 1948 ring-around-the-rosy, recalled life at the Margery Reed Mayo Nursery forty years later: "It was a loving, warm place where the Sisters of Charity gave us three meals a day, a nap, classes, and play." (Denver Public Library.)

Mayo Nursery, dedicated on January 4, 1944, by Archbishop Vehr and staffed by the Sisters of Charity of Cincinnati, still provides child day care for needy and working parents.

The Dominican Sisters of the Sick Poor opened, in 1923, a convent in a large old house at 2501 Gaylord Street. The order, founded in New York City by an Irish immigrant, Mary Walsh, sent sisters from their Mariandale headquarters in Ossining, New York, to Denver at the request of Bishop Tihen. After settling into the old boarding house at 25th and Gaylord, they began visiting the mentally and physically ill. By the 1930s, these Dominicans were making over 2,000 home visits a year.

"We are still making home visits," Sister Marie Therese McGath reported in 1987:

"Upon this rock I shall build my church," Jesus said, providing inspiration for Monsignor J.J. Bosetti to build St. Catherine Chapel on this crag at Camp St. Malo. (Photo by James Baca.)

Now we are a certified home health care agency. We still give priority to the poor, to those who cannot pay. Once we had six sisters here. Now we're down to four but have thirty to forty wonderful volunteers who help us to care for anyone who asks for our help, regardless of race, creed, color, class, or language. We've been doing that ever since 1923 when Mother Hyacinth McGuire started our order here in Denver.

In the years to come, other Catholic community centers would be established, including Denver's Holy Ghost Youth Center (1947–present) and the Fox Street Neighborhood Center, operated at 2930 Fox Street from 1948 to 1953.

Outdoor recreation and summer camping for children also became a goal of Catholic Charities. Back in 1916, Joseph J. Bosetti had established the first diocesan summer camp,

The original St. William Lodge, shown here during the 1950s, was demolished in 1986 to build the St. Malo Retreat and Conference Center on the southeast border of Rocky Mountain National Park.

on the eastern edge of Rocky Mountain National Park. Father Bosetti, who had spent much time mountaineering in the Alps of his native Italy, was camping on the spot when a fiery meteor fell from the sky one August night. Bosetti regarded this as a message from heaven and obtained permission from William McPhee, a wealthy Catholic lumberman who owned the site, to convert 160 acres into a summer camp and St. William's Lodge for his choir boys at Immaculate Conception Cathedral.

In 1934, Bosetti persuaded the Malos to donate $90,000 to build the main lodge and another $15,000 for the camp's beautiful stone chapel. It was christened St. Catherine Chapel in honor of Mrs. Malo's mother, Catherine Smith Mullen, and in honor of St. Catherine of Siena. With the Malo's generous donations—ultimately over $175,000—Bosetti also built a first-rate camp. Thousands of boys, aged ten to eighteen, have enjoyed

The John L. Dowers donated their summer resort at Cassells on the South Platte River in 1931 as the site of Camp Santa Maria. (Colorado Historical Society.)

the camp and expeditions into the adjacent park. Many seminarians from St. Thomas's have served as camp counselors at St. Malo, where Cathedral parish boys were admitted free while boys from other parishes were charged $7 a week.

Monsignor Bosetti was followed as director of Camp St. Malo by Monsignor Richard Heister (1952–1969), who reminisced in 1988: "Oh boy! It was a great camp. We often went hiking, including midnight hikes with flashlights up Twin Sisters Peak, trying to reach the summit in time for a sunrise mass." Monsignor Heister was succeeded by fathers John Anderson (1969–1970), Robert Jerrard (1970–1985), and Charles Scott (1986–1988).

Over the years, the camp came to include dormitories, stables, employees' housing, athletic fields, an archery range, and a swimming pond. In 1984, it closed for major renovation and additions, including a large new lodge and conference center, reopening in 1987 with over $5 million in improvements and a new name—the St. Malo Conference Center. The pioneer structure, St. William's Lodge, had been replaced by a larger, modern

Stonemasons polish the bust of Christ that has guarded Camp Santa Maria since 1933. This titanic statue is said to be second in size only to the *Cristo* overlooking Rio De Janeiro, Brazil. (Colorado Historical Society.)

complex, and at a spot where Monsignor Bosetti and his boys once had camped and cooked out sits an elegant new restaurant—Bosetti's.

Another Catholic summer camp originated with the old resort of Cassells on the South Platte River. The resort had been launched as a stop along the Denver, South Park & Pacific Railroad by David N. Cassells, the agent there, in the 1880s. In 1930, J.K. Mullen's son-in-law, John L. Dower, and his wife, purchased the place, located 8.3 miles west of Bailey, from Cassells' estate and gave it to Catholic Charities as a summer camp for underprivileged boys and girls between the ages of eight and fifteen. By 1931, the freshly rechristened Camp Santa Maria was offering three-week summer sessions, during which youngsters slept in the old Cassells hotel.

The landmark atop the hill behind the camp, a fifty-five-foot statue of Christ the King donated in 1933 by the Dowers, is supposedly second in height only to the famous statue of Christ in Rio de Janeiro, Brazil. Although the old hotel and Cassells–Dower summer house have been demolished, Camp Santa Maria still delights young summer visitors to this mountain retreat along the upper South Platte River. Since the 1950s, the Mary Mullen Dower Benevolent Corporation has leased Càmp Santa Maria to Catholic Community Services, which offers not only children's summer camping but also retreats and autumn camping for senior citizens.

Catholic Charities came to play a larger role after the stock market crash of 1929. At first, Coloradans thought themselves immune to the "eastern" economic collapse, but by 1933, Westerners too were experiencing 33 percent unemployment and the toughest times since 1893. Catholic Charities, which had begun receiving Community Chest funding in 1929, struggled to relieve poverty and suffering. Father Mulroy termed the new Community Chest funding of Catholic institutions good evidence that his two-year-old Catholic Charities had become "vigorous enough and had demonstrated a necessary and progressive social work program."

Bishop Vehr and retiring Bishop Tihen posed on July 18, 1931, with the Flag Drill Team at Camp Santa Maria. (Colorado Historical Society.)

Social justice emerged as an underlying goal of Catholic Charities in an economically troubled society. From 1928 to 1936, the diocese and Catholic Charities joined in the annual Catholic Conference on Industrial Problems and pushed concepts such as humane working conditions, living wage, profit sharing, credit unions, and curbs on child labor.

Father Mulroy was appointed in 1932 to the State Welfare Institutions Board by Governor William H. Adams. Mulroy could also take pride in the appointments of Herbert Fairall, a prominent Catholic businessman on the Catholic Charities Board, as chair of the Colorado Emergency Relief Association and first president of the newly created Colorado Department of Public Welfare. The Church was playing a larger role in improving the lives of all Coloradans.

Catholic Charities moved into a new home, the George C. Schleier mansion at the southwest corner of East 17th Avenue and Grant Street, in 1930. Rachael Schleier had donated the huge Queen Ann residence to Bishop Tihen for use as the office of Catholic Charities. As Father Mulroy's small office could scarcely fill even one floor of the three-story mansion, it also became the new office of the diocesan superintendent of Catholic schools. The Schleier mansion, Father Mulroy exulted, "is a far cry from the two rooms in the Railroad Building on Larimer Street" where Catholic Charities had opened on February 1, 1927.

Workmen took a break to join the Sisters of Loretto for this 1890 view of Loretto Heights Academy, the Southwest Denver landmark designed by architect Frank E. Edbrooke. (Denver Public Library.)

Meanwhile, Bishop Tihen was not forgetting that minds also need nourishment. Monsignor William H. Jones provides the best detailed documented account of Tihen's life and works in *The History of Catholic Education in the State of Colorado*, which includes this summary of Tihen's accomplishments:

> The number of parish schools was advanced from thirty-one to forty-nine. . . . Forty-four churches were dedicated; Loretto Heights College, three hospitals, an orphanage, and a home for the aged were established; the office of the Catholic Charities of Denver was organized; a most ambitious and effective Catholic press program was started; the number of priests was increased from 174 to 229; and the Catholic population of the State was strengthened by approximately 25,000.

The opening of Loretto Heights College was the greatest educational thrust of the Tihen years. The Sisters of Loretto had been pondering, ever since the 1880s, opening a college to complement their highly successful high school, St. Mary's Academy. In 1890, the sisters paid B.M. Morse $18,250 for a forty-five-acre hilltop in Southwest Denver,

In 1917, Loretto Heights Academy opened a college on its spacious campus. Shortly thereafter, the sisters and their students joined the World War I effort, transforming "the Heights" to a Red Cross camp and sewing bandages for the boys on the fighting front. (Colorado Historical Society.)

and on September 21, 1890, Mother Pancratia Bonfils and the sisters and pupils of St. Mary's Academy laid the cornerstone for Loretto Heights. The magnificent red sandstone school building, a $350,000 six-story structure, was designed by Denver's premier architect, Frank E. Edbrooke. The central tower, which rises ten stories above the five-foot-thick stone foundations, commands the skyline of Southwest Denver.

Loretto Heights opened its doors on November 2, 1891, to fifty-one secondary school students taught by twenty Sisters of Loretto. Two years later, the silver panic and prolonged depression almost closed the school. Both paying pupils and potential benefactors seemed to disappear, but Mother Praxedes Carty was able to persuade the mortgage holders, Northwestern Mutual and Penn Life insurance companies, not to foreclose.

Thomas H. Malone, editor of the *Colorado Catholic,* thought Loretto Heights' isolation was one problem, and in 1898 he, with some fellow investors, built a streetcar line from South Broadway west on Hampden Avenue to serve both the Heights and Fort

Logan. Three years later, the Fort Logan and Loretto Heights Street Railway Company was dissolved shortly after Father Malone ran a notice in the *Denver Times* of March 29, 1901, offering to donate, in order to get tax relief, the firm's entire rolling stock—two streetcars and four horses—to the Arapahoe County Commissioners.

Slowly, Loretto Heights established itself as an academy for young ladies. When prosperity returned in the 1910s, the nuns decided to expand the program. In September 1918, Loretto Heights College—the region's first Catholic women's college—opened its doors. Four students enrolled for courses taught by both the Sisters of Loretto and by priests from St. Thomas Seminary. In June 1921, Mary Hayden became the first graduate of the new college.

The college's role in the development of Southwest Denver inspired the Post Office, in 1986, to name its new station there Loretto. The college added a chapel and connecting arcade in 1911 and an auditorium in 1915, both handsome structures designed by the original architect, Frank Edbrooke.

The North Central Association recognized Loretto Heights as a degree-granting college in 1925. Bishop Tihen spearheaded a 1928 campaign to build Pancratia Hall, a new building devoted solely to the high school. Completed in 1930, the high school structure was named for Sister Mary Pancratia Bonfils, long-time principal of St. Mary's Academy and founding superior of Loretto Heights. The large, $950,000 library was named for a generous benefactor, May Bonfils Stanton, as was the $1,550,000 performing arts center. In 1941, the high school was closed and Pancratia Hall converted to a dormitory for what emerged as the only fully accredited senior college for women in Colorado, Wyoming, and New Mexico.

Loretto Heights, at last, had achieved the dream of its foundress—Mother Mary Pancratia Bonfils. She was the daughter of a prominent St. Louis physician, Francis S. Bonfils and a first cousin of Frederick G. Bonfils, the cofounder and long-time editor and publisher of *The Denver Post*. At age fifteen, she entered the novitiate of the Sisters of Loretto, the first order of nuns founded in the United States. After training at the Kentucky motherhouse, she was recruited by Bishop Machebeuf who brought her to St. Mary's Academy in Denver in 1868. After a thrilling stagecoach ride, the young nun first encountered Indians. Courageously, she offered them food, as she recalled later:

> Oh! How I trembled when I first walked out to those fierce looking fellows. But I swallowed my fears and showed them I was their friend. And don't you know I really believe some of those painted fellows began to love me. They often gave me presents made by their own hands.

Sister Pancratia was appointed mother superior at St. Mary's in 1882. She oversaw construction of a fine new brick structure on the old St. Mary's campus at 15th and California streets and made St. Mary's the rival of any of Denver's other private schools, including Miss Wolcott's School and Wolfe Hall. In the 1890s, Mother Pancratia purchased land and, in 1911, opened a new home for St. Mary's on Pennsylvania Street in Capitol Hill. With great vision and faith, she also bought a forty-five-acre hilltop in the southwestern outskirts of Denver, where, in 1891, she opened Loretto Heights Academy. Mother Pancratia dreamed of the day when the Sisters of Loretto would conduct a Catholic women's college. Before she could realize this goal, she died on October 12, 1915, in St. Joseph Hospital. She had told her sisters, "I am now on the threshold of eternity, but I would like to do God's will, to work for Denver still." Her sisters carried out her wishes. In 1941, Loretto Heights dedicated Pancratia Hall to the remarkable nun who had done more than anyone to bring Catholic education to the ladies of Colorado.

Mother Pancratia Bonfils, guiding light of Loretto Heights Academy and College, would be aghast at the events on the eve of its centennial year. The Jesuits at Regis College, after taking over the bankrupt school in 1988 to keep it open, sold it in 1989 for an estimated $6.5 million to Tokyo-based Teikyo University. (St. Mary's Academy.)

The KKK attack on Catholic schools helped to rally Catholics around the educational role of the Church. "You build churches in vain," Bishop Tihen declared, according to the *Denver Catholic Register* of September 2, 1920, "unless you build schools with them." In 1924, during the zenith of Klan power, Bishop Tihen dedicated five new parish schools—Presentation, St. John the Evangelist (later renamed Good Shepherd), and St. Philomena elementary schools, St. Francis de Sales High School in Denver, and Corpus Christi Elementary School in Colorado Springs.

In response to Klan criticism, patriotism was emphasized as part of the Catholic school curriculum. American flags were installed outside schools and also in each classroom, where the pledge of allegiance became a daily practice. Catholic schools strove to improve their academic offerings, introducing science courses and replacing the old Spencerian penmanship classes with the new Palmer method.

Athletics and physical fitness became a more important part of the school day during the 1920s. At the urging of Monsignor McMenamin of Cathedral parish, a high school parochial league athletic program was begun in 1926. The following year, the Oscar Malos donated $30,000 to build the Oscar L. Malo, Jr., Memorial Gym at Cathedral High School. This gym would be used by various Catholic high schools not only for gymnastics, basketball, and other indoor sports but also as a theater. The home team, the Cathedral "Blue Jays," led the way in parochial league athletics. Cathedral High School, which moved into a new $190,000 school and convent complex in the fall of 1920, attracted students from all over the city.

Monsignor McMenamin promoted not only scholarship and athletics but "Christian Conduct." In a letter to parents, he warned that, among other things, "Pupils of the Cathedral High School may not attend dances or parties of any kind without permission of the school authorities. The first offense of profane or indecent language by any pupil will be followed by dismissal."

While Colorado Springs, Denver, Boulder, Pueblo, Leadville, Trinidad, Canon City, Sterling, and Walsenburg had Catholic high schools by the 1920s, many smaller towns lacked even Catholic elementary schools. To help rectify this situation, Bishop Tihen, in 1930, asked the diocesan mission director, Father Gregory Smith, to organize religious vacation schools. Father Smith established a diocesan chapter of the Confraternity of Christian Doctrine and opened its prototype summer school program in his own parish, St. Mary's in Littleton.

In the Confraternity of Christian Doctrine summer school program, students attended four week-long sessions for four hours a day. Religion classes were complimented with recreation and lessons in history, health, and home economics. Within a year, twenty-two summer school programs were launched. Nuns, priests, and seminarians conducted the classes. Of the 846 nuns working in the diocese in 1930, 347 volunteered for summer school assignments. Most of them cheerfully accepted the work despite the fact that they received, if anything, only $25 to $40 a month (compared with the $190 a month paid at the time by Denver public schools). Two seminarians, Ray Newell and Walt Canavan, listed weekly expenses of $10.28 in their July 6, 1930 report to Monsignor Gregory Smith and added, "Tell the bishop we are first at the church every morning. This is due to various reasons, but principally because we sleep in the pews during the night!"

Despite the sacrifices Catholic education required of parents, as well as religious, enrollment in all Catholic educational institutions in Colorado had climbed to 12,633 by

1931. The number of parish schools increased from thirty-one to forty-nine between 1917, when Bishop Tihen was installed, and 1931, when he retired. Among the many new schools were Loretto Heights College, the Cathedral High School, and the Holy Cross Benedictine Abbey School in Canon City.

Bishop Tihen also concerned himself with Catholic students at non-Catholic colleges and universities. He arranged with Henry A. Buchtel, chancellor at the University of Denver, for Catholic Masses to be held in the chapel. Tihen helped found or strengthen Catholic Newman Clubs at the Colorado School of Mines in Golden, at the University of Colorado in Boulder, at the Colorado State Teachers College in Greeley, and at the Colorado State Agricultural College in Fort Collins.

The development of St. Thomas Seminary and of a native-born Colorado clergy

Soaring over St. Thomas Theological Seminary and the South Denver skyline since 1926, Tihen Tower commemorates the bishop's crusade to make the institution named for St. Thomas Aquinas the premier seminary of the Rocky Mountain West. (Photo by Roy E. Hyskell.)

was probably the goal closest to Bishop Tihen's heart. He spearheaded the evolution of St. Thomas's from a farm with one old red building, into a complex containing a chapel, a kitchen, a refrectory, a philosophy building, and living quarters. Between 1924 and 1926, Bishop Tihen raised $600,000 for the seminary.

Patrick Cardinal Hayes, archbishop of New York, dedicated the new philosophy building on October 17, 1926. This elegant Renaissance revival structure by Jacques Benedict featured the Tihen Memorial Tower, a 138-foot-high landmark. Sculptor Enrico Licari cast twelve-foot-high angels to adorn the four corners of the square tower. Along with other religious ornaments, the seals of great European and American seminaries were imbedded in the façade.

St. Thomas Seminary Chapel, one of the most exquisite ecclesiastical edifices in the Rockies, was constructed next to the Tihen Tower in 1930. Architect Jacques Benedict used over 200 different shapes, sizes, and colors of brick in this Renaissance revival masterpiece. Arabesque patterns in pearl, gold, and red enhance the terrazzo floor; eighty-five arched windows of various sizes including seventeen from the world-

Colorado master architect, Jules Jacques Benois Benedict, designed both Tihen Tower and the St. Thomas Seminary Chapel, which some consider Denver's finest religious edifice. (Photo by Roy E. Hyskell.)

renowned stained glass studios of Franz Meyer in Munich. The Botticino marble altar, a $15,000 gift of Paul Mayo, was hand-carved in Italy from eighth-century designs.

Seminary studies, as well as buildings, were upgraded. The seminary, which prided itself upon having Matt Smith as a graduate, claimed to be the first in the country to offer journalism courses. Courses were also added in church administration as well as in academic fields. From five priest professors and fifteen seminarians in 1917, the seminary grew to thirteen faculty and ninety-five students by 1931.

Bishop Tihen pleaded with every parish for seminary funding and used every resource at his command to promote what he called the "heavenly mission" of making St. Thomas's "an institution that shall do God's work in the West." Consequently, St. Thomas's emerged in the late 1920s as a degree-granting college, licensed to award Bachelor and Master of Arts degrees. Thanks to the seminary's work, Colorado began producing most of its own priests.

Bishop Tihen resigned at the age of 69 on January 2, 1931. In September, he quietly left Denver to take up residence at St. Francis Hospital in Wichita, where he once had worked as a young priest. He continued to use his wonderful voice for preaching until serious illness silenced him in March 1938. His death came on January 14, 1940. On a bitter cold but sunny January 18, he was interred in the Gallagher Memorial Chapel at Mt. Olivet Cemetery. Tihen's successor, Bishop Urban J. Vehr, was on hand as Tihen was laid to rest beside Machebeuf and Matz.

Vehr summarized the accomplishments of Denver's third bishop in his funeral mass sermon at Immaculate Conception Cathedral:

> The mitred figure of Bishop Tihen, cold and still in death, the third Bishop of Denver lying in state in his Cathedral church [deserves] public appreciation. Bishop Tihen viewed with considerable pride the building of St. Thomas' Seminary, without a doubt one of our most important diocesan assets . . . for the inspiration of native vocations. . . . The centralized Catholic Charities was organized by him and under his direction. . . . I prize highly the cordial relations and good will that have existed between officials of religion and civil government [established] by my revered predecessor [and his] development of projects of civic interest that promised well for the common good.

Bishop Urban John Vehr. (Photo by Peter Berkeley.)

CHAPTER 4

VEHR: THE FLOWERING OF CATHOLICISM, 1931–1967

Under Urban J. Vehr, the diocese planted by Machebeuf and nourished by Matz and Tihen came into full flower. Vehr, a handsome and debonair prelate, transformed a poor diocese into a thriving one. Recognizing this, Pope Pius XII in 1941 made Vehr an archbishop and Denver an archdiocese, with primacy over the Diocese of Cheyenne and the newly created Diocese of Pueblo.

At his 777 Pearl Street mansion, Vehr entertained mayors and governors, cardinals and a future pope. He transformed the old home used by bishops Matz and Tihen into the chancery office and converted the Schleier mansion at 1665 Grant Street into a home for Catholic Charities. He hired master architect Jacques Jules Benoit Benedict and, later, Benedict's assistant, John K. Monroe, to provide distinctive and consistent Renaissance revival design for many of the 404 new churches, schools, and archdiocesan structures built during his long reign. To administer this ecclesiastical empire, Vehr appointed an auxiliary bishop and a small army of monsignori.

While bringing style and prestige to the Denver archdiocese, Vehr never forgot the essentials. Trained as an educator, he made the training of priests and of every Catholic child his top priority. His dream was to endow every Colorado community with a thriving parish, complete with church and rectory, school and convent.

Vehr, like Machebeuf and Matz, spent formative years in the Archdiocese of Cincinnati. Born there on May 30, 1891, he was the first of six children for Anthony and Catherine Hamann. He was born and raised in Price Hill, a neighborhood noted for its prosperous Germans and for being almost 100 percent Catholic. Urban J. Vehr was one of four future bishops who grew up within a few blocks of the Vehr family home at 209

Born to a devout German family in Cincinnati, Vehr was bred to be a prince of the church, as his First Communion portrait may suggest. (Denver Archdiocesan Archives.)

State Street. His father, a mechanical engineer, sent his son to St. Gregory School and to Xavier, the Jesuit university in Cincinnati. After completing priestly studies at St. Mary of the West Seminary in Norwood, Ohio, Vehr was ordained on May 29, 1915, by Henry Moeller, the archbishop of Cincinnati.

Father Vehr's first assignment was as assistant pastor at Holy Trinity parish in Middleton, Ohio. Six years later, in 1921, he became chaplain of the motherhouse of the Sisters of Charity at Mt. St. Joseph on the Ohio. In this convent on the outskirts of Cincinnati, the handsome young priest learned how to work congenially with nuns, a talent that would benefit the Diocese of Denver.

Father Vehr became assistant superintendent of schools for the Archdiocese of Cincinnati in 1922, and, after earning a Master of Arts degree in education at the Catholic University of America, he was named superintendent. As superintendent between 1923 and 1926 of the first-rate Cincinnati schools, Vehr gained experience that enabled him to transform Colorado's Catholic schools into a better educational system.

Father Vehr's next position, as rector of St. Gregory Minor Seminary, likewise prepared him to manage and upgrade St. Thomas Seminary in Denver. In 1927, the young priest was elevated to monsignorial rank by Pope Pius XI. Following studies at the Collegio Angelico in Rome, Monsignor Vehr was consecrated a bishop in the Cathedral of St. Peter in Chains, Cincinnati, on June 10, 1931.

Archbishop John J. McNicholas handed Vehr the bishop's crook—symbolizing the leadership he must give his flock—and the bishop's miter—a helmet symbolizing divine protection. After consecrating this promising native son, the Cincinnati archbishop continued to counsel the young bishop, whose first assignment was to the small and distant Diocese of Denver.

Denverites were delighted with this charming gentleman who had the deep voice of a trained orator. At forty, he was the youngest bishop in the United States. Some feared that Denver was just the first step of a career that would lead him to larger cities and higher ranks. Bishop Vehr, however, fell in love with Colorado and lived out his life in the Highest State.

Vehr arrived in Denver on July 16, 1931, at 7:25 A.M., in the private coach of the president of the Rock Island Railroad. Three hours later at the Cathedral of the Immaculate Conception, he was installed as bishop of Denver by the archbishop of Santa Fe, Albert T. Daeger. Afterwards, the priests of the diocese staged a banquet for their new bishop at the Argonaut Hotel, where Monsignor O'Ryan gave a brief talk on the history of the Denver diocese, and the clerics presented Vehr with a check for $1,000 and a brand new black Studebaker automobile.

Bishop Vehr soon broke in his car; he visited every parish in his diocese. While a staff priest did the driving, Vehr used his car as a mobile office for briefings on the affairs of the parish that would be the next stop. He found Colorado to be a vast, depression-haunted state of soup lines and dust storms. As was the case throughout America during the 1930s, roughly a third of the work force was unemployed. The bishop could scarcely tell which were more depressed, the mining towns turning into ghosts or the farming villages blowing away in black blizzards.

To cheer up his flock and his priests, the bishop logged 30,000 miles a year during his first decade in Denver. Vehr used his ample sense of humor to win over priests, with whom he shared the latest jokes and news. He made a habit of staying in each parish rectory, no matter how humble, to share the lives of his priests, leaving a thoughtful gift behind when he drove on. Struggling parishes often received checks from Bishop Vehr, and some of them followed his suggestion that they help themselves by starting credit unions. He aspired to be a builder but actually lost parishes during the depression decade, when the number fell from 111 in 1930 to eighty-seven in 1940.

Vehr wisely sought the advice of his predecessor, Bishop Tihen. The two carried on a congenial correspondence, with Bishop Vehr sending Tihen $500 now and then "as a little compensation from the Diocese of Denver" and inviting him to visit the Denver chancery where "your rooms are always ready."

Vehr settled into the bishop's home and chancery at 1536 Logan behind the cathedral. As the depression worsened, the bishop found himself besieged by beggars.

"We couldn't get our work done," Vehr recalled years later. "Someone was running to answer the door every few minutes." The bishop did not want to turn indigents away empty-handed but eventually decided to try to get something in return for his handouts.

He began leaving a broom out on the front porch as a hint. "That worked for about one good sweeping," the bishop recalled. "Soon we noticed that before coming to the door the men would take a handkerchief out of their pocket, wrap it around their hand, and then complain of an injury which kept them from handling a broom."

Such inconveniences of combining a church office and a churchman's home ended for the new bishop in April 1932, when the John L. Dowers purchased the John Porter house at 777 Pearl Street from Porter's widow, Louise Coors Porter. The Dowers announced the gift with the explanation: "We feel we have a very fine bishop here and we want to see him comfortably housed for his great work."

This elegant home, a 1923 design by Denver architects Ernest and Lester Varian, was a large Jacobean place with formal gardens. The bishop moved his red easy chair into the living room and began lining the walls with his many books and art works, including nine Albrecht Dürer prints. Another room he converted into a private chapel. The elegant formality of this domestic scene was frequently shattered by the bishop's two Boston bull terriers, Patsy and Queenie, barking invitations to play ball.

Three Sisters of the Most Precious Blood came from Dayton, Ohio, to care for the bishop and his house as well as to help with the food service at St. Thomas Seminary. Bishop Vehr rewarded his secretary, housekeeper, and cook by taking them for strolls through the Capitol Hill neighborhood or escorting them to the Denver Symphony or to Monsignor Bosetti's operas. To avoid scandal, he always took all three nuns.

After daily mass in his private chapel, the bishop spent his mornings at the chancery office behind the cathedral. He brought to diocesan affairs some of the systematic Teutonic regimen he had learned in the Archdiocese of Cincinnati. Pastors were required to keep thorough records and send a complete copy each year to Vehr. These annual reports were then cataloged by seminarians at St. Thomas's and bound in heavy volumes for storage at the chancery.

To avoid the conflicts over church property that had plagued bishops Machebeuf and Matz, Vehr had all of it, including parish properties, put in the ownership of "Urban J. Vehr, Bishop of Denver." In his 1931 episcopal bulletin on this matter, Vehr asked each pastor to send to the chancery copies of the titles, mortgages, deeds, abstracts, and full legal descriptions of all parish properties. On his annual confirmation visits to each parish, Vehr would make sure its affairs were in order.

Thanks in part to such systematic precautions, Vehr's reign—even though it was longer than that of any other Denver prelate—would be the smoothest. He took every precaution to avoid even the appearance of impropriety. When someone gave him stock in a dog-racing track, for example, Vehr reported: "I disposed of those shares, as I do not care to be publicly identified in the event that their list of stockholders ever became public." Vehr's only "vice," apparently, was smoking Pall Mall cigarettes. He quickly dismissed any priest caught in a scandalous situation and pledged each new cleric to five years of total abstinence from alcohol. He required each to take an examination in the sacred sciences each year for five years following ordination. "Priests were told they only needed two black suits—one for summer and one for winter," Monsignor William Jones recollected in 1987, adding:

> And if you were going to have a car, he recommended that it be small and black. He told priests that their clothes, their Roman collar, their cars were symbols, speaking for the clergy and the church. If you followed the rules, Bishop Vehr oftentimes rewarded priests with a black Borsalino hat which he sent from Rome with your initials in it.

Mayor Benjamin F. Stapleton and Monsignor John R. Mulroy, director of Catholic Charities, share strategies for coping with the Great Depression.

Bishop Vehr's strict treatment of his priests earned him their respect, according to Monsignor Thomas P. Barry, who reminisced in a 1986 interview:

> Bishop Vehr was a German with an Irish sense of humor. He developed a folksy western American outlook that helped him get along with everybody. He never gave any priest a short deal. If he nailed you, it was your own fault. He had a complaint from some old bag that I wasn't taking care of my mission at Walden. Bishop Vehr gently but firmly rebuked me so I went back and built St. Ignatius Chapel out there.

In church pews on Sunday, Catholics were bombarded with pitches from the pulpit. Prompted by Bishop Vehr's episcopal bulletins, priests encouraged donations to the Denver Community Chest, to the American Red Cross, and to the World War II effort. Numerous Catholic charities were also promoted on specified Sundays. There was an annual collection for "the orphan homes of the diocese" and requests for "discarded

The George Schleier Mansion, 1665 Grant Street, housed Catholic Community Services from the 1930s to the 1980s. (Photo by Tom Noel.)

furniture, clothing and materials of all kinds" for the Catholic Benefit Shop at 1335 Lawrence Street, which was operated by the DDCCW. "Every Catholic home in this city," Bishop Vehr urged, should have and fill a donation bag for this shop whose proceeds helped finance the Church's community centers.

Community centers overflowed with needy people during the depression decade. Monsignor John R. Mulroy, director of Catholic Charities, incorporated the Denver Diocesan Community Centers in 1933, hoping to bolster their shoestring financing. This reorganization helped to secure Denver Community Chest funding. By 1933, Catholic Charities had recruited many volunteers, including twenty physicians, eighteen attorneys, eight dentists, eight optometrists, and the services of the National Catholic Federation of Nurses. In 1933, the worst year of the Great Depression, the three Denver clinics assisted around 7,000 people. In 1933, Catholic Charities was designated as a distributor of federal relief funds, and Monsignor Mulroy was chosen as chair of the Denver Council of Relief Agencies, a body overseeing distribution of federal relief. Monsignor Mulroy received, in 1939, an assistant, Reverend Elmer Kolka, who ultimately helped establish the Blue Cross Health Plan in Colorado, served as chairman of the Denver Housing Authority, and replaced Monsignor Mulroy when he retired as director of Catholic Charities in 1955.

Catholic Charities converted the Schleier mansion at 1665 Grant Street into its home base. The basement was made into a commissary from which to supply the hungry hordes who walked in the front door. Social worker Genevieve B. Short, then a fresh graduate of the University of Denver Social Work School, recalled in 1987 that she would interview walk-ins. After determining how many children and dependents they had, she would provide them with the allotted pounds of dried beans, cheese, flour, and whatever other foodstuffs had been donated. For clothing, indigents were sent to the St. Vincent de Paul Society.

Whenever possible, the diocese cooperated with President Roosevelt's New Deal depression-relief programs. For example, Bishop Vehr asked parish priests to offer weekly services at the two dozen Civilian Conservation Corps camps established in Colorado to provide youths with work. The $30-a-month federal check to cooperating clergymen also served as relief for priests, whose salaries then ranged from $400 to $600 a year.

Depression-era window shoppers looking for second-hand clothing found bargains galore at the Denver Deanery Benefit Shop at 1335 Lawrence Street. (Photo by Roy E. Hyskell.)

As the State of Colorado and the City of Denver balked at funding depression-relief programs, the burden fell on the federal government and private agencies such as Catholic Charities. Despite the shortage of revenues, Bishop Vehr supported an expanded charity program. "Charity and generosity of spirit," he said, "must be the guides of man's life because they can curb the damaging word and the hostile act."

A major depression-era accomplishment was the Mullen Home for Boys. Before his death on August 9, 1929, J.K. Mullen told his wife and daughters of his hope to build an industrial school for underprivileged lads. After his death, the John K. and Catherine S. Mullen Benevolent Corporation and a Mullen daughter, Mrs. John L. Dower, strove to

An antique hunter's paradise, the St. Vincent de Paul Salvage Bureau at 1615 Larimer epitomized the slogan, "One Person's Trash Is Another Person's Treasure." (Photo by Hal Kaminske.)

follow the wishes of the great philanthropist. In 1931, they acquired the 900-acre Shirley Farms Dairy on South Lowell Boulevard. The Christian Brothers were recruited to establish the home, which first opened temporarily on the Regis College campus.

Bishop Vehr blessed the new grounds at 3601 South Lowell Boulevard on April 14, 1932. By 1938, Mullen Home boasted a chapel, classrooms, dormitories, a gymnasium, cattle and poultry sheds, a tool house, a dairy house, and a greenhouse. Fifty boys lived at the Mullen Home, attending classes and helping the Christian Brothers produce annually around 500 tons of alfalfa and thousands of bushels of wheat, barley, oats, and corn, as well as operating the dairy. The Mullen Home accepted homeless teenagers and those from foster homes. The Mullen Benevolent Association constructed two new classroom buildings in 1950 and a $70,000 auditorium in 1952. The home began developing a championship athletic program. In 1966, the boarding school closed and was replaced by a foster home plan. Thus, what had begun as a training school for deprived lads during the depression evolved into one of Colorado's better prep schools.

The Church's counterattack on economic and social problems exacerbated by the depression led to good works on many fronts. Camp Santa Maria and Camp St. Malo continued to give youngsters summer experiences in the mountains, as well as exercise, wholesome food, and classes in catechism and crafts. The Catholic camp movement was furthered in 1938 when Martin Holland do-

Thanks to the John K. and Catherine S. Mullen Benevolent Corporation, the 900-acre Shirley Farms Dairy in Southwest Denver became a foster home and Mullen School for Boys in 1932. (Photo by Bill Smythe.)

nated to the diocese the Bendemeer Lodge and Resort. This summer camp for underprivileged children of all creeds was operated until 1947 by the Catholic Daughters of America of the Court of St. Rita, who also opened Camp Mont Rita in Nederland in 1932. These two pioneer girls' camps were closed in 1947, and the Catholic Daughters replaced them with Our Lady of the Rockies Camp at the old Wagon Wheel Ranch five miles west of Evergreen.

In the Northern Colorado city of Greeley, Father Bernard Froegel of St. Peter parish organized and supervised various mission stations for migrant laborers. Catholic Family Welfare, a bureau of Catholic Charities, maintained offices in Greeley, Colorado Springs, and Pueblo as well as five offices in the Denver area.

The Children's Department of Catholic Charities reported in 1934 that it was being overwhelmed by

an almost endless army of boys, young men, women and girls passing through Denver by auto, train and on foot in the quest of that elusive goal—employment. . . . [A] conservative estimate of over 1,500,000 boys and girls are stranded on the highways. . . . The Sisters conducting the five orphanages of the Diocese are supplying not only shelter, food and education but also reclaiming bodies and souls that had been broken by the Depression.

The Sacred Heart Aid Society, oldest of diocesan charities, was reinvigorated by the support of the Diocesan Council of Catholic Women. These ladies helped the society to continue offering a variety of services, ranging from telephone calls to flophouse rooms. The St. Vincent de Paul Society sprang into the "Catholic Action" recommended by one of its founders, Frederick Ozanam. The society sponsored a clothing program, institution-

Deprived city urchins were welcomed to Camp Santa
Maria by William J. Monahan, the first camp director.
(Colorado Historical Society.)

al and hospital visitations, a Big Brothers program, a foster home, and juvenile court pro-bation services. The Denver society, with around 150 members in nineteen parishes during the 1930s, opened a salvage bureau at 1615 Larimer Street. With the help of the Knights of Columbus, the St. Vincent de Paul Society operated a Denver Shelter House that, in 1932, provided 23,332 free meals and 9,962 nights' lodgings.

Denver's black community was another neglected population that attracted the attention of Catholic Charities. With Bishop Vehr's encouragement, St. Augustine's Colored Study Club was organized in the 1930s, with the idea that Denver's blacks would one day have their own parish.

The multifaceted programs of Catholic Charities during Vehr's years defy a complete survey. Monsignor John R. Mulroy, the director of Catholic Charities, concluded in his *Annual Report* for 1934 that "only the recording angel himself could give a complete account of the all but overwhelming volume of work carried on by the self-sacrificing workers of Catholic Charities."

Depression hardships and unemployment lingered until the United States entered World War II in 1941. With a humming wartime economy at home, Colorado Catholics began focusing on the suffering of war-torn countries abroad. Elmer Kolka supervised Colorado's War Relief Services for the National Catholic Welfare Conference. The Bishops' War Emergency Fund and the St. Vincent de Paul Society helped by collecting canned goods and clothing to be sent overseas. Rationing, including that of meats, and the emphasis on a healthy military and domestic work force led to a change in dietary laws. In a 1942 episcopal bulletin, Vehr announced that "Pope Pius XII, for the duration of the war, dispensed priests, religious and the faithful . . . from the Lenten obligation of fasting and of abstinence on Fridays except the Fridays of Lent."

Doing their part to alleviate the shortage of nurses, Mercy, St. Anthony, and St. Joseph hospitals in Denver all expanded their nursing school programs. Catholic school children chipped in by buying war bonds and stamps, even after they reached the archdiocesan goal of $100,000 in the spring of 1942.

Father Mulroy, showing his characteristic concern for underdogs, sought to help the German prisoners of war in Colorado. An estimated 600 POWs at camps in Fraser, Gould, and Kremmling were visited weekly by Monsignor Thomas Barry, then pastor of St. Peter's in Kremmling. Monsignor Barry recalled years' later: "Those Germans were very religious. They sang the Mass with me in Latin and at Christmas time they filled the air with their lovely German carols."

During the war, Catholic Charities closed the Workingman's Club on Larimer Street and St. Anthony Neighborhood House. These two institutions providing food and shelter for unemployed young men were not so badly needed as the war brought either jobs or military service to many of their former customers. Catholic Charities shifted to supporting USO centers in various Colorado cities to provide entertainment and sociability for military personnel. Catholic women rallied to the effort to bolster the morale of servicemen in many ways, including free dinners at Denver's Knights of Columbus Hall at 1575 Grant Street.

When the war ended in 1945, churches throughout Colorado celebrated with a Holy Hour of Thanksgiving and exposition of the Blessed Sacrament as well as the prolonged, joyous ringing of church bells. Catholic Charities established a Displaced Persons Service to help European victims of the war find new homes in Colorado. Elmer Kolka, assistant director of Catholic Charities, oversaw this effort, which by 1951 had resettled thousands of refugees. In subsequent years, the bureau turned its attention to helping immigrant workers, also. The annual Catholic Charities budget topped the $1-million mark in 1949, by which time the staff had grown to twenty-five. Newcomers included Reverend William J. Monahan, who had earned his Masters of social work degree at the Catholic University of America. After joining Catholic Charities in 1947, he promoted its increasing professionalization.

War's end enabled Vehr finally to receive the papal pallium he had been given by Pope Pius XII on November 21, 1941. That year, the pope had recognized the flowering of the Denver diocese by making it the twenty-first archdiocese in the United States. The Most Reverend Archbishop Amleto Giovanni Cicognani, the apostolic delegate to the United States, installed Vehr as archbishop on January 6, 1942. The sound of a trumpet and the voices of Monsignor Bosetti's magnificent choir opened the installation ceremonies at the Cathedral of the Immaculate Conception. The Most Reverend John McNicholas, who had consecrated Vehr as a bishop in Cincinnati and advised him on diocesan affairs, gave the sermon. Afterward, Mayor Benjamin F. Stapleton and Governor Ralph L. Carr honored the new archbishop in a civil ceremony at the Denver Municipal

Auditorium. Anyone missing the church or civil ceremonies could see them on the newsreel highlights at the Paramount Theater downtown.

Denver, which had previously been in the province of the Archdiocese of Santa Fe, was now its own archdiocese. This new status, Archbishop Vehr pointed out, achieved "a civic advantage for Denver and another recognition of the growing importance of this region." Vehr's installation attracted the greatest gathering of bishops ever assembled in the Rocky Mountain West. Visiting dignitaries included Monsignor Giovanni B. Montini, then Vatican secretary of state for internal affairs, who would be elected pope on June 21, 1963. The future Pope Paul VI stayed in Vehr's home on Pearl Street and toured the Mile High City.

Simultaneous with the creation of the Denver archdiocese, the Vatican split Colorado in half by creating the Diocese of Pueblo. Sacred Heart Church in Pueblo became the cathedral seat for the first bishop, Joseph Clement Willging, installed by Archbishop Vehr on March 12, 1942. Willging guided that diocese until his death in 1959. His administration and the early history of the Pueblo diocese are recaptured in Monsignor Patrick C. Stauter's book The Willging Years. The restructured Denver diocese included thirty-three counties in Northern Colorado with 87,907 Catholics, while the Pueblo diocese consisted of the thirty counties of Southern Colorado with a Catholic population of 78,373.

The new Metropolitan See of Denver included the Suffragan See of Cheyenne as well as that of Pueblo. The Diocese of Cheyenne, which had been created in 1887 as a part of the Archdiocese of Dubuque, Iowa, was placed within the new Denver archdiocese in 1941. Patrick A. McGovern, the bishop of Cheyenne since 1912, remained in that post until his death in 1951.

Archbishop Vehr, after traveling 30,000 miles a year to cover all of his Colorado parishes, was delighted with the reorganization. The symbol of his new office, the pallium made from the wool of Vatican City sheep, finally arrived in Denver on April 17, 1946. Samuel Cardinal Stritch, the archbishop of Chicago, bestowed the pallium on Vehr in ceremonies at the cathedral in Denver. As the only archdiocese between Dubuque, Iowa, and San Francisco, Denver dominated a Rocky Mountain hinterland of some 200,000 Catholics.

Between the depression of 1893 and the Great Depression of the 1930s, Coloradans had experienced relatively slow economic and population growth. Few anticipated that after World War II the state would undergo a boom comparable to that of the 1870s and 1880s. This postwar explosion was triggered by massive federal spending and the opening of many new federal jobs. Colorado's cool, dry, sunny climate and recreational outlets

Denver Post heiress Helen Bonfils, pictured here with Archbishop Vehr and Monsignor Mulroy at the dedication of Holy Ghost Church, emerged as the benefactress for many of Vehr's post–World War II building projects. (Denver Public Library.)

also made it a target for Americans on the move. Denver grew from a sleepy city of 322,412 in 1940 to a metropolis of over a million by the 1960s.

Many of these newcomers were young Catholic couples and soon parochial schools were overflowing. Archbishop Vehr began a campaign to raise $3.5 million to acquire school sites and build or add to schools. The archdiocese ambitiously acquired fifty sites, generally consisting of at least five acres. Vehr dreamed of building a complete parish plant—church and rectory, school and convent—within walking distance of everyone in the metropolitan area.

This grand dream grew ever more expensive as the number of Catholics in Colorado almost tripled during the Vehr era, climbing to 376,832 by 1967. The percentage of

Thanks to Archbishop Vehr's construction of seventy-two new schools and high schools, one out of every five Colorado scholars attended parochial schools by 1960, when schools such as St. Vincent de Paul overflowed with baby boomers. (Photo by James Baca.)

Catholics in the Denver metro area also climbed, from about 16 percent in 1941 to around 25 percent by 1970. To accommodate this tremendous growth, Archbishop Vehr launched, in 1965, the Archdiocesan Development Program, renamed the Archbishop's Annual Campaign for Progress in 1971.

Archbishop Vehr, who had been trained as an educator and administrator, made Catholic education his priority, using the slogan: "Every Catholic Child in a Catholic School." He insisted that a school rather than a church be the first building in new parishes. Vehr wisely let public school planners decide where growth justified new schools. Taking advantage of the extensive research, personnel, surveys, and projections of the public schools, he purchased land near new public schools. This plan worked, as the Catholic population was geographically well integrated within the general population. It also enabled Catholic schools to take advantage of the public school policy of building schools close to public parks and libraries.

Under Vehr, the parish building process typically began with acquisition of all or part of a block. The first construction would be a school with a large gym–cafeteria–assembly hall that also served as a church. As the parish grew and gained financial resources, it could strive to construct a separate church building. At the crucial early stages of such campaigns, a $1,000 check would arrive along with a letter of encouragement signed; "With every good wish and blessing, I am faithfully yours in Christ, Urban J. Vehr, Archbishop of Denver."

Vehr took a keen interest in each parish's building plans. The archbishop, according to superintendent of schools Monsignor William H. Jones, had pastors use archdiocesan approved architects and discouraged the use of such cheap materials as cinderblock, wood, and stucco. Consequently, the schools of the Vehr era became brick and stone lessons in the use of sound and attractive architecture. The World War II baby boom filled classrooms as quickly as they could be built. By 1956, 20 percent of Denver's school population was in Catholic classrooms. Catholic grade and high schools were overflowing and had to turn away hundreds of applicants for lack of space.

To remedy the shortcoming, the archdiocese initiated a $3.5-million Denver High School fund campaign that led to construction of Machebeuf High School and additions to Annunciation, Cathedral, Holy Family, and St. Francis de Sales high schools. Some of this funding also went to Mullen, Regis, and St. Mary's Academy. Vehr's long-range plan, which would never materialize, called for construction of four new Catholic high schools in the four suburban quadrants of the metro area.

Archbishop Vehr's commitment to Catholic schools led to a tremendous improvement not only in the number but also in the quality of Catholic schools. In 1934, Vehr created the position of diocesan superintendent of schools. The first superintendent, Father William D. McCarthy, worked with Vehr to improve and standardize textbooks, courses, extracurricular activities, and the school calendar. Vehr's keen interest in education was reflected in the fact that he personally passed out diplomas to graduates not only at Loretto Heights College and Regis College but also at joint graduations for Denver high schools at the Denver Municipal Auditorium. He continued to travel to outlying areas of the state each year to award other high school diplomas.

Vehr likewise concerned himself with Catholic children in public schools. For them, he relied on the Catholic summer school program, correspondence courses, and weekend and after-school classes sponsored by the Confraternity of Christian Doctrine (CCD). The Colorado efforts of the worldwide CCD program were directed by Monsignor Gregory

Monsignor Gregory Smith, who established the Confraternity of Christian Doctrine summer schools throughout Colorado, recalled almost fifty years later in a 1988 interview that "those were the golden days of Catholic education, when we offered religious instruction in even the smallest, most remote communities." (Photo by James Baca.)

Smith from their inception in the 1930s until the 1960s, when the program became a part of the Education Office. The Colorado CCD, according to Monsignor Smith, conducted as many as 161 summer school programs with over 14,000 students enrolled. It also sponsored two-day retreats each year for students in the Denver public schools. Monsignor Smith recalled in 1987:

We also had street preaching programs in the smaller towns. We'd get a loud speaker and play popular music on records to attract a crowd. Then Father Joseph Lilly, the scripture scholar at St. Thomas Seminary, would get up and introduce seminarian speakers. In small towns where they didn't have much to do on weekday summer nights, people would pile up to listen. We didn't make many converts, but we created some good will and got people to think about God.

Archbishop Vehr also encouraged formation of Junior Newman Clubs to help bring religous education to youngsters in non-Catholic high schools and endorsed extracurricular activities, which tied youth to schools and parishes. To encourage young interests in farming and ranching, 4-H Club projects were promoted in parochial schools. The archbishop was especially keen on establishing scout troops and dens at the parish level. Over 2,000 Catholic Boy Scouts earned the Ad Altare Dei award, which they received in the cathedral from the archbishop. Vehr, who had been a scoutmaster himself, received scouting's highest award to volunteers in 1967, the Silver Antelope medal.

While trying to give Catholic school children a full and well-rounded education, Archbishop Vehr never lost sight of the major reason for Catholic schools. "Religion," he told the *Rocky Mountain News* in a March 25, 1945, interview, "is a science and must be taught by capable religious leaders. It is both an intellectual and moral direction which makes for character building of the highest type."

Catholic nuns were the "capable religious leaders" recruited in the archdiocesan campaign for parochial schools. In 1947, Archbishop Vehr raised the annual salary of teaching sisters from $350 to $400 a year. For this, nuns were also expected to teach summer school and attend the refresher courses for teachers. Both nuns and priests were encouraged to pursue graduate degrees in education and in their special fields.

Despite poor pay, Colorado attracted new nuns. Like many other greenhorns flocking to "Cool Colorful Colorado," the sisters appreciated the salubrious climate and the spectacular Rocky Mountain setting. The Benedictine sisters of Atchison, Kansas, a branch of the order founded by St. Benedict in A.D. 529, first sent sisters to Colorado in 1913. They began teaching at St. Mary School in Walsenburg, a coal mining town with many immigrant Catholic families whose children poured into St. Mary's, where enrollment peaked at 831 in 1922. Even though the parish could not afford to pay them a salary, the Benedictine sisters stayed.

Sister Alcuin Seer described the classroom scene at St. Mary's for her colleague, Sister Alice Marie Hays, who recorded it in her book, *A Song in the Pines:*

> There were 128 on roll, ages five through ten, but I never had more than 105 present at one time. Eighty-five sat in desks; the others on radiators, window sills and floor. Even when I tied the short pencils, which I managed to collect, around their necks, they would come from recess pencilless. I soon learned to understand "Me falta un lápiz, no papel."

Thanks to the heroic efforts of the nuns, St. Mary's won accreditation by the North Central Association of Colleges and Schools in 1924. These Benedictines also labored in the poor villages of the San Luis Valley. In Antonito, they accepted the invitation of a struggling public school board to staff the public school, starting in 1933. Nearby, in Capulin, state and local officials offered to pay the sisters $75 a month to staff that village's dilapidated, condemned schoolhouse. Sisters Placida, Eulalia, Alphonsa, Julitta, and Vita arrived in the dusty hamlet of Capulin and were shown to their convent—a partially completed house of adobe. Undaunted, the sisters pinned up their long serge skirts and went to work. Monsignor Jones in *The History of Catholic Education in the State of Colorado* described the scene:

> There was no stove for cooking, and the nearest water was two or three blocks away in the public well. In a diary kept by one of the original band, a sister noted that nothing bothered them as much as the size and number of flies and mosquitoes and other sundry animals that flew in the open windows and cracks in the wall.

When the Walburga Benedictines fled Nazi Germany in 1935, they transplanted a 900-year old tradition of agrarian, contemplative life to Boulder, the univeristy town that has become a mecca for New Age religions. Mother Mary Thomas reads her prayerbook while Sister Angela visits the hen house. (Photos by James Baca.)

Eighty Benedictine nuns from Atchison formed an independent Colorado mother-house in 1965, converting Mrs. Potter's Riding Academy in Colorado Springs into the Benet Hill Priory (or monastery, as it has been called since 1987). In 1988, sixty-one Benet Hill sisters served in Colorado schools, parishes, hospitals, and other ministries, including the Benet Hill and Benet Pines retreat centers.

Persecution by Adolph Hitler and the Nazis led a venerable German order of Benedictine sisters to establish a motherhouse in Boulder. The Benedictine nuns bought 150 acres of the 160-acre site of Sacred Heart of Mary parish. Mother Abbess Bendicta sent Mother Augustina and sisters Boniface and Rita to open the the Boulder convent on St. Joseph's Day, 1935.

These hard-working German women astonished their Boulder neighbors by repairing dilapidated facilities next to the church. They repaired roofs and cracked walls, fixed up sheds and barns, and converted the old, unused 1872 Sacred Heart of Mary Church to a tool shed. Five more "Lilies of the Field" soon arrived from Bavaria—sisters Angela, Brigitta, Gertrude, Maria, and Mechtildis. Each sister had a special task, be it milking the cows, making butter, tending pigs, minding the beehives, driving the tractor, or being a "cowgirl."

The Walburga Benedictines thrived in Boulder, building a new convent in 1952 and running a model farm and ranch in rhythm with the seasons and their chapel bells. By 1986, the St. Walburga Convent had become financially independent of the Eichstaett Abbey in Bavaria. Mother Abbess Franziska Kloos journeyed from Eichstaett to Boulder to grant the Americans their independence. She found that the number of American-born nuns equaled that of the German-born, yet these women maintained monastic traditions, adorning their convent with homemade tapestries and their library with manuscripts that they illuminated in the medieval manner.

Denver novelist William A. Barrett's best-sellers included a tale about cloistered nuns, *The Lilies of the Field*, which was made into a popular movie.

Besides awarding independence to the American priory, Mother Franziska persuaded Pope John Paul II to raise its status to that of an abbey. St. Walburga's prioress, Mother Mary Thomas Beil, promised to keep sending "American nuns to Bavaria to expose them to the European monastic traditions" of the Eichstaett Abbey founded in 1035.

"It's very hard for Americans to comprehend something that old," Mother Mary Thomas observed. The late William E. Barrett, whom some consider to be Denver's most notable novelist to date, portrayed the life of German Benedictines in his best-selling novel, The Lilies of the Field, which also became a play and a movie. Mother Mary Thomas and her nineteen nuns opened a retreat house and convent at 6717 South Boulder Road, where they also continue to support themselves by raising cattle, chickens, horses, and llamas.

Dominican Sisters from Akron, Ohio, came into the archdiocese in 1963 to teach at Notre Dame Elementary School in Denver. Since then, these Dominicans have established a small convent in Lakewood at 8060 West Woodard Drive. Four Dominicans from the Akron motherhouse, founded in 1923, served the archdiocese in 1987 at St. Jude parish in Lakewood and at St. Elizabeth Ann Seton parish in Fort Collins. Still another branch of Dominicans, the Congregation of the Immaculate Conception, with a motherhouse in

Franciscan Sisters of Penance and Christian Charity converted the James B. Smith country estate at 5200 Federal Boulevard to the novitiate, retreat center, and school known as Marycrest.

Great Bend, Kansas, came to the archdiocese in 1966 to staff Holy Trinity School in Westminster.

The Sisters of St. Francis of Penance and Christian Charity first came to Colorado in 1917 to staff the school of St. Elizabeth parish in Denver. In 1938, these Franciscan women opened Colorado's first novitiate after purchasing for $25,000 the former James B. Smith residence at 5200 Federal Boulevard. They converted it into a motherhouse for their new midwestern province. Mother Lidwina Jacobs and her flock rechristened the three-story house and twenty-acre grounds Marycrest. On August 18, 1938, Bishop Vehr blessed the new chapel in the old house that had been refitted as a convent school.

Marycrest began, in 1949, offering credit courses for their own Franciscan sisters in conjunction with nearby Regis College. These classes proved popular and inspired Marycrest to construct a $100,000 three-story building with classrooms, as well as offices and a dormitory. Responding to the demand for Catholic education in the 1950s, the Franciscans transformed what had been a school for their novices into Marycrest High School in 1958. Beginning in 1962, Marycrest accepted girls for grades nine through twelve. By the 1970s, enrollment peaked the 200 mark as the school emerged as the female counterpart to nearby Regis High School. Marycrest, which crowns a spacious hilltop site, remained until its 1988 closure a tradition-minded all-girls school devoted to teaching religion and the liberal arts.

The Poor Sisters of St. Francis Seraph of Perpetual Adoration, who had founded St. Anthony Hospital in Denver in 1891, established a motherhouse at the hospital in 1932 when they formed a Western Province. On October 4, 1944, the order opened Mount St. Elizabeth Retreat in Morrison, in what had been the old Jesuit College of the Sacred Heart. Frank Kirchhof, a wealthy Catholic contractor and president of Denver's American National Bank, acquired the property, which had been reopened as the Hillcrest Inn after the Jesuits moved their college to Denver. Kirchhof donated the property, valued at about $50,000, to the Franciscan sisters to be used as a retirement home. In memory of his deceased wife, Elizabeth O'Connor Kirchhof, it was renamed Mount St. Elizabeth and housed thirty to forty elderly under the care of the sisters.

This Morrison retirement home closed in 1954 when the order moved St. Elizabeth's to the old Oakes Home property in Denver. The sisters purchased this site from the Episcopal Diocese of Colorado in 1943 for $67,500. The Oakes Home had been a tuberculosis sanatorium operated by the Episcopal Church at West 32nd Avenue and Eliot Street. Founded in 1894 by the Reverend Frederick W. Oakes, the property came to include architecturally exquisite buildings, most notably the charming Chapel of Our Merciful Savior. Fine landscaping also enhanced the ample grounds, which stretched from 32nd to 33rd streets and extended eastward a block and a half from Eliot Street.

Following Oake's death in 1934, the home closed, having treated at least 20,000 patients during the previous forty years. The Poor Sisters of St. Francis converted this landmark into a motherhouse. The chapel, an 1897 jewel by Denver architect Frederick J. Sterner, was renamed Christ the King Chapel. The Franciscans converted the historic tuberculosis sanatorium into their Western Province motherhouse in 1943. Between 1943 and 1954, the complex was called St. Joseph Convent.

In 1954, the Sisters of St. Francis of Perpetual Adoration moved their motherhouse from the Oakes Home–St. Joseph Convent in Denver to Colorado Springs. The fast growing convent and motherhouse had been given a 1,200-acre property, the former Woodmen of America Sanatorium, in 1954, by Mrs. Blevins Davis, the widow of a prosperous oil man. Since that time, the order has been based in Colorado Springs.

The exquisite Episcopal Chapel at 2825 West 32nd Avenue in North Denver became the centerpiece of St. Elizabeth's, the Western Province motherhouse and Old Age Home of the Poor Sisters of St. Francis Seraph of Perpetual Adoration. During the 1980s, the Gardens at St. Eliazbeth's emerged as a popular senior residence for independent living.

Meanwhile, back in Denver, the sisters converted the old convent complex into St. Elizabeth's retirement home. Despite protest, the sisters demolished much of the older complex in 1974, in order to build more functional modern housing for their elderly patients. In 1988, they completed a fourteen-story high-rise addition of 144 apartments. St. Elizabeth Gardens, as the home was renamed in 1987, endeavors to provide spiritual and physical care for approximately 300 senior citizens. Another group of Franciscan nuns, the Congregation of the Third Order of St. Francis of Mary Immaculate from Joliet, Illinois, came to Colorado in 1966, when they opened St. John the Evangelist School in Loveland.

The Sisters of the Most Precious Blood were founded by Mother Maria Anna Brunner in Castle Loewenberg, Switzerland, in 1834. They came to the United States in 1844,

In Greeley, the Our Lady of Victory Missionary Sisters converted this cottage at 306 14th Avenue into a center for Weld County's many migrant workers. (Photo by Roy E. Hyskell.)

establishing a motherhouse in Ohio. While the Sisters of the Most Precious Blood of Dayton came to Colorado in 1931 to manage Archbishop Vehr's household and work at St. Thomas Seminary, the Sisters of the Most Precious Blood of O'Fallon, Missouri, first came to Colorado in 1927 as teachers. They took charge of St. Charles School in Stratton when the Presentation sisters withdrew in 1927. In 1930, these nuns from Missouri adopted St. Louis parish school in Louisville, which had been opened in 1905 by Benedictines who had been followed by Franciscans. Three Sisters of the Most Precious Blood of Dayton, Ohio, opened Curé d'Ars School in Denver in 1954. The Sisters of the Most Precious Blood left St. Thomas Seminary in 1987, but about twenty remained in the archdiocese, serving in teaching, health care, the Hispanic ministry, and parish work.

Sisters of the Adorers of the Blood of Christ from Wichita, Kansas, moved into the Denver archdiocese in 1946, when they opened Sacred Heart School in Roggen. Sacred

Heart parish, which had dedicated a new church two years earlier, gave sisters Mary Lillian and Anita the old frame church built in 1920. The two nuns partitioned the old church so that Sister Mary Lillian could teach grades one to four in one half while her co-worker handled grades five to eight in the other.

Our Lady of Victory Missionary Sisters, an order founded in 1922 in Chicago by the Reverend John J. Sigstein, found a sponsor in Archbishop John Francis Noll of Fort Wayne, Indiana. The archbishop gave the Congregation of Our Lady of Victory the *Our Sunday Visitor* estate outside Huntington, Indiana, as a motherhouse. Subsequently, the nuns frequently called themselves the Victory Noll sisters. They came into the Denver archdiocese in 1944 at the invitation of Archbishop Vehr. The Victory Noll sisters, whose special mission is working with Hispanics, opened a youth center in 1948, in an old house on the corner of 22nd Street and Tremont Place in downtown Denver. They also started other catechetical centers in Greeley, at St. Augustine parish (1945) in Brighton, and at St. Mary parish (1952) in Montrose. This order was very active in teaching CCD summer school programs. In 1985, the Victory Noll sisters opened a small novitiate at 3311 Tejon Street in northwest Denver.

Discalced (Latin for shoeless) Carmelites established the Carmel of the Holy Spirit at 6138 South Gallup Street in Littleton in 1947. This branch of the cloistered order, which was founded by St. Theresa of Avila in 1562, moved into the country home and estate of Denver architect Jacques Benedict, who had been the favored architect of Archbishop Vehr. Benedict, a noted character and *bon vivant* who converted to Catholicism late in life, sold his elegant home one year before his death.

Four Carmelite nuns from the Carmel of Our Lady of Guadalupe in Grand Rapids, Michigan, opened the Denver Carmel at the invitation of Archbishop Vehr as the forty-eighth Carmelite convent in the United States. By 1956, the cloister had grown to fifteen nuns when Archbishop Vehr blessed a $118,000 addition. At the dedication ceremony, hundreds of visitors inspected the cloister's seven-by-eleven-foot cells furnished only with a straw mattress, a wooden stool, and a wash basin. "The whole reason for the Carmel, its prayer and its penance, its silence and its enclosure," Archbishop Vehr explained at the dedication, "is to allow the Carmelite nun to devote her entire energies to the worship, the contemplation, and the love of God." A new chapel and another wing with room for twenty-one sisters was added in 1963. The sixteen-acre site on Ketring Lake includes a small cemetery where Mother Theresa Ruoff—the founding prioress— and three other Carmelites are buried. In a 1987 interview, Mother Judith, the prioress, said, "Tell people that our sisters welcome messages and will pray for peoples' intentions."

The Daughters of Charity of St. Vincent de Paul, founded in Paris in 1633 by St. Vincent and St. Louise de Marillac came to the United States in 1854 to establish a motherhouse in Maryland. Daughters of Charity first came to the Denver archdiocese in 1959 from their Los Gatos Hills, California, motherhouse to staff the new Most Precious Blood parish school. The order, until 1964, wore a distinctive starched white sunbonnet habit with a "windmill" or "flying geese" coronet modeled after those of seventeenth-century peasant women in Normandy.

The Daughters of Charity withdrew from Most Precious Blood School in 1986, moving their operations to Immaculate Conception parish in Lafayette. "There are three of us left in Colorado," Sister Mary Elizabeth Reed said in 1987. "Here in Lafayette our work is the work St. Vincent envisioned. We visit the

Among the triumphs of Colorado's nuns is the 1964 Mercy Hospital on the south side of Denver's City Park, where the sisters celebrated the dedication with a little hardball. (Photo by Jim Peri.)

poor in their homes, bringing the Eucharist, praying with them, and taking them wherever they want to go. In 1976, we opened Lafayette's Carmen Center to provide food and clothing for the poor."

Only God, it has been said, knows how many orders of nuns there are. Over thirty different sisterhoods have worked in Colorado since the 1860s. As the nuns have concentrated on good works rather than on gaining recognition for themselves or their orders, entire orders as well as hundreds of individual sisters have escaped attention. Among the less well-known orders are the Sisters of St. Joseph of Stevens Point, Wisconsin, who came to Colorado in 1926 to staff St. Joseph Polish Catholic School in Denver. Servite sisters, who are also known as the Servants of Mary, came from Omaha, Nebraska, to Welby, a northeastern suburb of Denver, in 1920, to open the grade and high school of St. Mary of the Assumption parish. The Servite sisters closed this high school in 1950 to concentrate on the new Mount Carmel High School in Denver, which they ran until its 1968 closing.

Developing bodies as well as souls, Catholic schools launched parochial athletic leagues, in which St. Catherine of Siena's "Wildcats" regularly demolished volleyball opposition.

Declining numbers of vocations have forced some sisterhoods to withdraw from Colorado. The Sisters of the Holy Cross from South Bend, Indiana, for instance, opened a novitiate at Blessed Sacrament parish in Denver in 1977, only to close it six years later.

Archbishop Vehr presided over a golden age for Catholic nuns and parochial schools. Religious vocations flourished, and Vehr introduced to the archdiocese a dozen new sisterhoods, and several hundred new nuns. Nuns in traditional garb and their uniformed pupils filled burgeoning schools that earned reputations for good teaching, good manners, good sports, and good discipline.

Parish plants typically consisted of an impressive, traditional-style church, a rectory with a pastor and several assistant pastors, and a convent filled with teaching sisters. "Those were the days," recalled one Sister of Loretto, "of the proud and possessive pastor who could defy the superintendent of schools and declare St. Patrick's Day a holiday for everyone!"

To promote an *esprit de corps* among all the different orders, Archbishop Vehr staged two parties a year for the sisters. Practically all 400 nuns from all the orders—except the cloistered Carmelites and Walburga Benedictines—attended the archbishop's Labor Day party at Loretto Heights College and Christmas party at St. Thomas Seminary. Sister Rosemary Keegan, SL, recalled these galas with glee some thirty years later:

> After the party luncheon came the bingo game and some wonderful entertainment of songs and silliness by fathers Bernard Giblin, OFM, and Fabian Joyce, OFM, along with Monsignor Richard Heister. Then the archbishop handed out dollar bills with the admonition that no superior could take it away—each sister had to spend it herself. After the fun and games, there was a new, current movie—at a time when sisters were not allowed to go to theaters.

Introductions at these festivities led to committees and cooperation between the orders, to shared retreats and shared strategies on how to improve parochial schools. These two annual parties were a well-deserved treat for the sisters, whose work did not end when the school year closed in June.

Many teaching nuns sat on the other side of the teacher's desk during the summer, pursuing refresher courses and degree programs at various colleges and universities. Dozens of others prepared for new and more difficult teaching assignments—summer school sessions in rural areas lacking Catholic schools.

Nuns also played a starring role in bringing the federal Head Start program to Colorado. Head Start, one of the most successful War on Poverty programs initiated under President Lyndon B. Johnson, began its nationwide efforts in 1965. It was the first federal comprehensive preschool education program. Although open to all children, Head Start was most interested in giving children from lower socioeconomic backgrounds a head start on their education.

Mayor Thomas G. Currigan and War on Poverty director Corky Gonzales wanted a Head Start program for Denver. Monsignor William Jones, superintendent of schools of the Archdiocese of Denver, helped steer some of the first local programs into core city Catholic schools. Sister Rosemary Keegan, SL, a Denver nun specializing in early childhood education, did much of the groundwork to get the program rolling by the end of 1965.

Ladybird Johnson, wife of the president, came to Denver on September 11, 1965, to help launch the program. Three youngsters from Annunciation parish program, coached by Sister Keegan, presented the first lady with a bouquet of flowers and a St. Christopher medal blessed by their assistant pastor, C.B. Woodrich.

Ultimately, All Saints, Annunciation, Cathedral, Guardian Angels, Holy Rosary, Presentation, St. Anthony, St. Cajetan, St. Elizabeth, St. Joseph Redemptorist, and St. Patrick parish schools housed Head Start programs, as did many public schools. Head Start introduced children to reading, writing, and arithmetic, as well as to museums, music, dance, recreation, and other enrichments.

Tremendous growth characterized the Vehr years, with the creation of forty-three new parishes and expansion of many existing ones. The archbishop hoped to staff these parishes with St. Thomas Seminary graduates, a strategy that put a severe strain on the seminary, as the archbishop explained in a March 23, 1953, letter to his priests and people: "St. Thomas Seminary, where our priests are trained, is taxed beyond capacity. We have facilities for 140 students, but are forced to house 220. . . . The seminary is forced to turn away students each year owing to a lack of space." In this letter, Archbishop Vehr announced a campaign to expand the seminary and asked each of the 161 parishes to do its fair share. By June, $3,658,116 had been pledged to the Seminary Campaign, of which $2.6 million was actually collected during the next two years.

The seminary had flourished during the 1940s, reaching an enrollment of 200 students by 1950. Yet the only new building of the 1940s had been a small stone and wood canopy to shelter the old St. Mary Church bell. Initially hung at St. Mary's in 1865, this bell was installed in Holy Ghost Church in 1905. When replaced at Holy Ghost by an electric carrillon in 1942, the bell had been brought to St. Thomas Seminary and kept in storage until the World War II armistice, when seminarians hastily built the canopy one morning in order to ring the bell while President Harry S. Truman read the peace proclamation.

In 1947, this bell was moved into the memorial bell tower completed on the northeast corner of the grounds and dedicated to alumni who had served in World War II. The belfry, built of Boulder flagstone and Del Norte lava stone, is now illuminated and houses the bell, which is inscribed, "Cast by J.G. Stuckstede and Bro. St. Louis Mo 1865. SANCTA MARIA/SINE LABE ORIGINALIA CONCEPTA/ORA PRO NOBIS," and bears the names of donors John Felter and Amelia Guiraud. This one-ton bell is thought to be the city's oldest. Celebrated as "Old Faithful" or "Vox Dei," it still graces the seminary campus.

In 1950, St. Thomas's built an $80,000, two-story, red brick convent to house ten Sisters of the Most Precious Blood, who served the seminary. Architect John K. Monroe designed the convent with rooms for sixteen sisters, in harmony with Benedict's master plan for the seminary. In 1986, the Precious Blood nuns were replaced by the Sisters of

St. Joseph of Mexico (Hermanas Josefinas de México), who care for the Vincentian fathers and their seminarians.

Ground was broken for the seminary recreation center on Alumni Day, October 12, 1950. The lower level, completed in 1951 and named Bonfils Hall in honor of May Bonfils Stanton, contained a kitchenette, large meeting hall, and a stairway up to the gymnasium-auditorium. This $110,000 project designed by John F. Connell, a Denver architect, was finished in 1953.

Thanks to the 1953 Fair Share campaign, St. Thomas's opened, in 1956, a major new facility, which has been variously called the Theology Building, the St. Pius X Wing, and the Classroom Wing. The dedication ceremony for this three-story addition drew 4,000 people to the seminary grounds on June 10, 1956. They came for a dual celebration—the 25th anniversary of Vehr's installation as

During the 1950s and 1960s, Bishop Tihen and architect Jacques Benedict's dreams of a grand campus became reality at St. Thomas Theological Seminary. (Denver Archdiocesan Archives.)

bishop of Denver and the dedication of the St. Pius X Theology Building. James Francis Cardinal McIntyre, archbishop of Los Angeles, presided over the ceremonies, which attracted thirty-nine prelates.

Cardinal McIntyre blessed the $1.5 million Theology Building, which contained eighty-nine student rooms, eight classrooms, twelve faculty suites, guest rooms, lounges, and a chapel with five altars for instruction classes in liturgy. The new buildings were designed by John K. Monroe, long-time assistant and protégé of Jacques Benedict. They complimented Benedict's chapel and tower, creating a spacious campus of Renaissance and Romanesque revival buildings.

The library wing, completed in 1956 and designed by Monroe to match the rest of the campus, now houses nearly 150,000 volumes. It is one of the largest Catholic theological libraries in the country and is open to the community at large. The C. Blake Heister Periodical Room, completed in 1973 and named for a prominent Denver layman killed while climbing Long's Peak, contains a wealth of religious magazines and newspapers.

By 1965, enrollment at St. Thomas's reached its all-time peak, 274 seminarians. To promote vocations, Archbishop Vehr helped to establish the Serra Club, a lay organization to encourage and financially support religious vocations. "The priesthood," Vehr declared, "is the greatest fraternity in the world . . . the greatest gift God can bestow."

Theatine fathers established a second Catholic seminary in Denver in 1955. The Theatines, an order founded in Italy in 1524 by St. Cajetan, first came to the United States in 1906. They worked among Hispanic peoples and had established a novitiate in 1934 in the Southern Colorado town of Antonito. In 1951, the order purchased seven acres at East Mississippi Avenue and South Birch Street within walking distance of St. Thomas Seminary. There, the Theatines built St. Andrew Seminary for about $170,000, naming it for a Sicilian saint who forsook his law practice after he found that the profession led him to utter falsehoods in court.

Archbishop Vehr, on May 18, 1955, blessed this seminary, which has become the North American headquarters for the Theatine fathers. To accommodate growth, a high school preparatory seminary was built a few years later next to the original three-story, Spanish colonial revival seminary building. The Theatines, in 1986, celebrated the canonization of a seventeenth-century Theatine, Joseph Cardinal Tomasi. Reverend Mark Matson of St. Andrew's led an eighty-seven-member U.S. Theatine delegation that presented Pope John Paul II with a pair of K-2 skis engraved with his name, a ski pass to Aspen and Vail, a red Coors ski sweater, and two cases of Coors beer.

In guiding the Denver archdiocese through its golden age, Archbishop Vehr established the deanery system to provide leadership for outlying regions. He relied on the senior priests selected as deans as well as on two dozen monsignors. If Vehr's use of the monsignori strengthened church administration, it created some hard feelings. "When Archbishop Vehr made me a monsignor," reported Monsignor Thomas Barry, "he told me, 'Every time I give one of you priests the purple, I make the others blue'."

One of the most gifted of Archbishop Vehr's monsignors was an Italian priest who would not only develop a marvelous choir but also give Coloradans grand opera. Joseph Julius Bosetti was born in Milan on New Year's Day, 1886. Educated in Italy and in Switzerland, he became an avid skier and mountaineer as well as an enthusiastic student of both theology and the fine arts. An Alpine guide at the age of twenty, he was said to have once scaled the 14,780-foot Matterhorn in twenty-one hours.

After his ordination, Father Bosetti taught philosophy for three years at the Bethlehem Institute in Switzerland. Then, in 1911, he agreed to missionary work in the distant, mountainous, and semicivilized realm of Colorado. Bishop Matz first assigned him to organize a parish for the many Italian families in Welby, a small community of Italian farmers just north of Denver in Adams County. Bosetti bicycled around the area, enrolling parishioners and pleading for donations to establish Assumption parish.

Bishop Matz appointed Bosetti assistant pastor at the cathedral after its completion in 1912. The majestic cathedral needed more than a few feeble voices, lost in the grand Gothic interior, and Matz urged Bosetti to organize a large, male choir trained in classical music.

For his prized cathedral choir, Bosetti began writing his own music and masses, collaborating with McMenamin on an original operetta, "Bethlehem." After the operetta's success, the two priests formed the Denver Grand Opera Company. Bosetti served as the director and McMenamin as the business manager. Bosetti staged his first opera, an $800 production of *Cavalleria Rusticana,* in 1915, at the old Broadway Theater.

Monsignor Joseph Julius Bosetti, dubbed "Italy's Gift to Colorado," introduced better choir music and grand opera to the Archdiocese of Denver.

When this and other operas proved to be popular, the Denver Grand Opera Company began, in 1933, to stage more lavish productions at the Denver Municipal Auditorium. Proceeds were donated to Catholic Charities, giving patrons philanthropic as well as cultural motivation.

Maestro Bosetti imported star leads from New York and built his eras around them, using the best local talent he could find. His 1935 production of *La Traviata* featured two young Coloradans, Frank Dinhaupt and Jean Dickerson. Dinhaupt later became the New York Metropolitan Opera star Francesco Valentino, while Dickerson rose to celebrity status as radio's "Nightingale of the Airwaves." *La Traviata* would also be Bosetti's final production; in 1951, the opera company folded when his health failed.

The Denver Grand Opera Company shows became legendary annual galas, as Monsignor Gregory Smith recollected decades later:

Bosetti introduced the first successful opera in Colorado. Blocks of tickets went to each parish to sell. One way or another we filled that auditorium night after night. It was great sociability. Some of us went to the same opera six nights a week. Even if Denverites weren't ready for opera, they got it.

Monsignor Bosetti, a cultivated man who taught several foreign languages at Cathedral High School, became a prized figure in the local arts community and in Denver society. To honor his cultural contributions, the Italian government awarded him the Knight Commander of the Crown of Italy in 1938 and, in 1949, the Star of Italian Solidarity. This accomplished priest was likewise prized by the Diocese of Denver. Bishop Matz appointed him chancellor in 1917, and Bishop Tihen vested him as a monsignor in 1927; Bishop Vehr appointed him vicar general, a post Bosetti held until his death.

Camp St. Malo was another of Bosetti's legacies. This archdiocesan camp and conference center owes its existence to Bosetti's love of mountaineering. To reward his cathedral choir and altar boys, he took them camping at the mountain property of Cathedral parishioner William McPhee. Bosetti subsequently persuaded McPhee, a wealthy lumber baron, to donate the site as a Catholic camp and to erect St. William's Lodge in memory of his late son, William McPhee, Jr. Bosetti later induced the Malo family to fund what became Camp St. Malo. Beautifully located on the eastern edge of Rocky Mountain National Park near the base of Long's Peak, Camp St. Malo became a summer haven for young boys from throughout the archdiocese—and a favorite retreat for local and visiting clergy.

Monsignor Bosetti's work with boys as a choir and camp director, as well as a teacher, produced another major dividend for the archdiocese. "Bosetti loved working with boys and they idolized him," reported Monsignor Gregory Smith. "He fostered more vocations to the priesthood than anyone in the diocese. He made Camp St. Malo a breeding place for vocations."

Bosetti delighted in leading his boys into the outdoors. He treated many of them to ski expeditions, a sport he helped to promote in Colorado. Soon after his arrival in 1911,he took up skiing, to the astonishment of many Coloradans who had never dreamed of such a thing at that time. "Most people," Bosetti noted, "thought we were crazy to come down mountains on sticks."

To celebrate his twenty-fifth anniversary as a priest, Bosetti led a hiking party up the Mount of the Holy Cross for a mass on the summit. For his thirty-fifth anniversary, he orchestrated a similar hike up Twin Sisters Peak for an outdoor mass. Bosetti's active life came to an end on January 22, 1954, at Denver's St. Joseph Hospital.

One of Bosetti's former choirboys, Colorado Governor Stephen L.R. McNichols, remembered him fondly in a 1987 interview:

Monsignor Bosetti was a tremendous guy, a well-educated, cultivated old world gentleman. He cracked down on cigarettes and messing around with girls, offenses for which you could be kicked out of the choir. I was in his choir for eight or nine years and we sang both at the cathedral and in his annual opera at the Municipal Auditorium. He taught us to sing, and, at Camp St. Malo, he taught us to ski, to swim, and to look for the stars.

Another gifted administrator of the Vehr era was Hubert Michael Newell. Throughout his long career, Newell probably did as much as anyone to improve Catholic education in Colorado. Born in Denver on February 16, 1904, Hubert grew up in an Irish clan blessed with vocations. His identical twin Raymond became a parish priest, and another brother, John, became a Jesuit priest. Hubert's sister, Nora, married and produced three sons who became parish priests in the archdiocese of Denver—Monsignor William H. Jones, Father Raymond Jones, and Father Charles T. Jones.

Hubert Newell graduated from Annunciation Grade School, Sacred Heart High School, Regis College, and St. Thomas Seminary. After completing a master's degree in education at the Catholic University of America in 1937, Father Newell was appointed the second diocesan director of education by Bishop Vehr. In that post, Newell sought to standardize and upgrade Catholic schools, which varied frighteningly in quality, in courses offered, and in facilities. In his first year, Newell redesigned high school religious education as a four-year program consisting of five forty-five–minute periods each week devoted to doctrine, liturgy, Bible study, and church history. Superintendent Newell worked to establish harmonious relations with the public schools and with government officials and agencies. This led to such valuable contributions to Catholic schools as that of the Denver Visiting Nurse Association, which initiated regular sight, hearing, weight, and height checks, as well as immunization shots.

In collaboration with Bishop Vehr, who had established a Catholic Parent Teachers Association while superintending schools in Cincinnati, Father Newell started a PTA group for Denver in 1939. The DDCCW, which had been formed in 1926, played a major role in implementing the PTA program. The PTA helped school children to purchase textbooks, first communion outfits, athletic equipment, musical instruments, and playground apparatus. The PTA bolstered schools with everything from assistance in the cafeteria lunch lines to annual educational institutes. In 1941, Father Newell was honored for establishing a PTA program that the National Council of Catholic Women recommended as a national model. By September 24, 1947, when Newell was consecrated coadjutor bishop of Cheyenne, Wyoming, the PTA boasted more than 7,000 members in forty-two Catholic schools throughout Colorado.

Denver native Hubert Michael Newell was consecrated bishop of Cheyenne by Archbishop Vehr in this September 24, 1947, ceremony at the Catherdral of the Immaculate Conception.

In Wyoming, Bishop Newell assisted Patrick A. McGovern, who had been bishop of Cheyenne since 1912. Upon McGovern's death in 1951, Bishop Newell succeeded him until his retirement in 1978. "I had a wonderful, happy, and blessed time in Wyoming," he recalled in an interview shortly before his death at St. Joseph Hospital in Denver on September 8, 1987. His sister Nora died the same day in the same hospital.

Under Hubert Newell and his successors, Catholic schools kept expanding to accommodate the World War II baby boom. St. Mary's Academy, the oldest private school, moved to a spacious new home constructed on what had been the Hickerson estate at 4545 South University Boulevard in the affluent Denver suburb of Cherry Hills Village. After purchasing the estate for around $220,000, the Sisters of Loretto converted the Hickerson mansion into twelve classrooms, a chapel, and a convent for eighteen sisters.

St. Mary's Academy constructed a one-story, red brick classroom building in 1953, next to the old mansion, which was converted to a convent. The old St. Mary's at 1370 Pennsylvania Street in Capitol Hill was sold and has subsequently been renovated as a deluxe office building. In recent decades, St. Mary's added a new high school building—Bonfils Hall—and the Bishop Evans Sports Center. On their Cherry Hills campus, the Sisters of Loretto operate coeducational elementary and middle schools, as well as the high school for young ladies, which continues to be one of Colorado's premier prep schools.

During the late 1940s and the 1950s, parish schools were built at a terrific rate, particularly in the rapidly growing suburbs of Denver. Archbishop Vehr took a lively interest in the construction of each new school. As with new churches, he insisted on good architecture and good materials. Jacques Benedict continued to be the architect of record for many archdiocesan buildings, but his assistant, John K. Monroe, increasingly did more of the work. Monroe, like Benedict and Vehr, fancied a Mediterranean Romanesque style with red tile roofs, square bell towers, classical motifs in terra cotta trim, and Romanesque portals. Some of the loveliest parish structures in the archdiocese—Good Shepherd, Holy Ghost, St. Catherine of Siena, St. Vincent de Paul, Christ the King, and a now-demolished chapel in Evergreen—were built during the two decades. Schools, convents, and rectories as well as churches, reflected a design consciousness that produced inspiring buildings.

In 1931, shortly after his installation as the fourth bishop of Denver, Vehr received glum news from Regis College. The Jesuit school, which had been struggling for funds and students during the Great Depression, informed him that without financial assistance it would be forced to close in 1932. With Monsignor McMenamin, the bishop came to the rescue by initiating a five year, $125,000 campaign, christened "Save Regis—Regis Shall Not Close." Bishop Vehr made the first donation, followed by forty-six priests and

Regis College almost closed during the 1930s until Archbishop Vehr launched a Save Regis crusade to preserve and expand the campus, which consisted of Old Main, Carroll Hall, and a few outbuildings when the aerial shot was snapped around 1930. (Denver Public Library.)

innumerable lay people, Catholic and non-Catholic. Thanks to this campaign and to the willingness of the Jesuit faculty to work for little or no salary, Regis survived.

Not until 1945, however, did the college retire its $300,000 debt and begin to expand facilities for the first time since the 1923 construction of Carroll Hall. World War II veterans returning to college with the help of federal funding and loans began swamping American colleges. By 1948, enrollment at Regis soared beyond the 500 mark. By scrounging around, Regis acquired a small fortune in federal government surplus, including chairs, desks, file cabinets, and even surplus army barracks from Fort Logan, which were converted into classrooms and offices. In 1949, Archbishop Vehr dedicated the new, 500-seat St. John Francis Regis Chapel. The old chapel was remodeled as an addition to the rapidly expanding library.

Regis completed, in 1951, a $250,000 classroom building, Loyola Hall, which also became the main adminstrative offices and the language laboratory. During the 1950s, Regis began offering classes at Lowry Air Force Base and at an extended campus in downtown Denver. Under the presidency (1953–1968) of Father Richard F. Ryan, SJ, Regis College finally enjoyed prosperity. High school enrollment passed the 500 mark, while the college climbed to over 1,000. Full accreditation by the North Central Association of Colleges and Secondary Schools finally came in 1952.

The campus erupted with new buildings: a 1957 dormitory named O'Connell Hall; a 1960 fieldhouse containing classrooms, offices, lecture halls, and a swimming pool as well as a gym; a 1963 student center; a 1964 dormitory called DeSmet Hall; Dayton Memorial Library, and a science building in 1966. To make room for all these new developments, Jesuits in the on-campus cemetery were moved to a plot at Mt. Olivet

Cemetery. In 1968, Regis began admitting female students. Traditionalists were further mortified when the Jesuits, responding to student suggestions, lightened the college's stiff requirements for course work in Latin, theology, and philosophy.

Regis College produced some distinguished graduates, including the first Catholic governor of Colorado, Stephen L.R. McNichols. In office, McNichols proved to be exceptionally active and socially conscious. More than any other governor, he promoted health, education, and welfare. He created the Department of Institutions to handle health care and prisons and the Department of Resources to manage water, wildlife, and mineral resources. Furthermore, he left the state with a restructured financial system and a budget surplus. A long list of accomplishments during the McNichols administra-

Governor McNichols and his family were the first residents of the governor's mansion, where he often visited with his neighbor two doors away on Capitol Hill's East Eighth Avenue, Archbishop Vehr. (Stephen L.R. McNichols Collection.)

tion includes establishment of the State Parks and Recreation Department, a modernized highway department, and Colorado's green and white license plate with its mountainous horizon, which McNichols himself drew.

Like many others, the McNichols clan had come to Colorado as miners. "Grandfather McNichols left Ireland after the potato famine," Governor McNichols recalled in 1987:

> He settled in Iowa and as soon as his boys were old enough to pick up a shovel he sent 'em to Colorado to make some money in the mines. My dad, William H. McNichols, Sr., came to Aspen that way, liked Colorado and stayed. He was clerk and recorder up there and grand exalted ruler of the Elks. When Aspen faded he moved around 1910 down to Denver where he found work digging sewers.

W.H. McNichols, Sr., soon graduated from sewer digging to politics, serving as secretary of the state senate, secretary to the state land board, deputy Denver city auditor, and Denver city auditor, a post he held from 1933 until 1955. "Dad was known as the watchdog of the city," according to his son Stephen. "He knew that city charter like he

Governor Stephen L.R. McNichols (left), touring here with President John F. Kennedy and Lt. Governor Bob Knous, was the first Catholic governor of Colorado. (Stephen L.R. McNichols Collections.)

knew the Hail Mary. And he said his rosary every morning and always carried it with him."

The elder McNichols, who had only a seventh-grade education, insisted upon Catholic schools for his four children. Stephen, the youngest, graduated from Regis College and from the Catholic University of America Law School. After working for the Federal Bureau of Investigation, in a private Denver law firm, and as a federal attorney, Steve was elected state senator in 1948, lieutenant governor in 1954, and governor in 1957. Of his six years as governor, McNichols said in 1987:

Many people, especially Catholics, told me a Catholic could never be elected to statewide office in Colorado. So did my predecessor, Governor "Big Ed" Johnson. Critics said I would favor Catholic schools and neglect public schools. Well, I did more for public schools than any governor in fifty years. Our School Foundation Act redistributed funds to poorer rural schools. We consolidated about 900 school districts into 127 much stronger ones. We abolished those phony school districts set up by railroads and other big corporations to save them from having to pay significant taxes for a real district. These businesses reap the profits—well-trained students—from the educational system and ought to help pay for education.

We beefed up CU in Boulder and its Denver campus. We transformed the Colorado State Agricultural College in Fort Collins, which then had only about 3,000 students and pigs and cows in the center of the campus, into Colorado State University.

In office, my Catholicism guided me in many ways, particularly in setting up treatment programs for health care, both physical and mental. Mental hospitals and prisons can be distasteful and depressing institutions to look at, but I'm very proud of having augmented the Pueblo mental hospital with creation of the Fort Logan Mental Health Center and of my ongoing work to improve our penal system in Colorado.

Governor McNichols engaged as his secretary his older brother, William H. Mc-Nichols, Jr. After this taste of politics and government, Bill jumped into Denver politics, serving as manager of public works and deputy mayor, and then as mayor of Denver (1968–1982). Like his brother the governor, Mayor Bill (as he preferred to be called) presided over a golden age, marked by economic prosperity and governmental concern for the underprivileged, most notably in the form of public health, education, and welfare programs.

Whereas Governor McNichols maintained a cordial working relationship with Archbishop Vehr, Mayor McNichols established a similar relationship with Vehr's successor, Archbishop James V. Casey. After retiring from public office, both brothers remained active in the Church. Mayor Bill took a special interest in the Little Sisters of the Poor, cohosting their 1986 drive to raise $50,000 for improvements at the Mullen Home for the Aged. Mayor Bill chaired Archbishop Casey's Golf Tournament for Catholic Youth. Governor McNichols served as the chair of the 1987 Archdiocesan Centennial celebration. While exemplifying the growing role of the laity in archdiocesan affairs, the McNichols family has also facilitated a larger role for the church in providing community services to all Coloradans.

Monsignor Matthew Smith continued to make the *Catholic Register* the most spectacular, nationally noted accomplishment of the Archdiocese of Denver. Light shone all night long at the large *Register* plant on Bannock Street, where editor Smith often labored nocturnally, triple-checking copy and writing his Registorials. By the 1950s, the

Archbishop Vehr confers with Monsignor Matthew Smith, editor of the Register newspaper network, which Smith transformed from a feeble weekly into America's most popular Catholic periodical.

Denver staff had grown to thirty, and the *Register* system produced thirty-two editions for dioceses around the country. Total circulation was more than 800,000.

Some other dioceses followed the pattern established in Denver in 1939, when the *Register* began being distributed free to every registered parish family. Parishes conducted an annual free-will collection to help pay for this policy. Editor Smith and Archbishop Vehr used the newspaper to promote St. Thomas Seminary, construction of new parishes and other archdiocesan goals.

The National Catholic Press Association honored Smith in 1953, noting that his "prophetic vision, pioneer energy and devotion to Church and country have created the largest Catholic newspaper system in the country."

"Matt carried the cross of poor health all his life," according to his brother Gregory. "His living habits were irregular, although he did swim practically every day at the Denver Athletic Club." Monsignor Smith continued to live in his apartment at St. Rose Residence, where his workaholic nature began to strain his health. In the spring of 1960, he went into

St. Anthony Hospital, where death came on June 15, 1960. "Matt worked closely with the chancery all his life," recalled his brother. "Unlike some Catholic journalists, he did not regard himself as a divinely appointed scourge for bishops."

Although Archbishop Vehr's health began slipping in the 1960s, his able assistants and systematic administration kept the church on a steady course. The key man was David Monas Maloney, whom Pope John XXIII appointed the first auxiliary bishop of Denver on November 9, 1960. Bishop Maloney came from a prominent Catholic family. His father, James Maloney, was a civil engineer who came to Colorado as construc-

Archbishop Vehr and bishops, David M. Maloney (center) and Hubert Newell, led this 1961 procession into Immaculate Conception Catherdral.

tion engineer for Cheesman Dam. After the 1905 completion of this dam, now a National Civil Engineering Landmark, Maloney stayed on with the Denver Water Department as chief engineer and later became chief engineer of the Colorado Highway Department. James and his wife Margaret raised their six children in Littleton, where he served several terms as mayor.

Their son David graduated at the head of his class from Littleton High School. Unlike his brothers who all became engineers, David entered St. Thomas Seminary. His studies also took him to Rome, where he earned a doctorate in canon law and was ordained on December 8, 1936. In 1943, after several years of parish work, Archbishop Vehr asked Father Maloney to become full-time secretary and assistant chancellor. After Monsignor Bosetti's death, Maloney became chancellor in 1954 and was consecrated a bishop on January 4, 1961.

As auxiliary bishop of Denver, Maloney represented Archbishop Vehr at the Vatican II Council, helping to draft precedent-setting statements on the nature of the Church. Returning to Denver, Bishop Maloney shouldered more and more assignments for the aging archbishop. Although drastic changes were in the wind, Maloney worked closely with Vehr to provide smooth, traditional leadership. After Archbishop Vehr retired in 1967, and James V. Casey was appointed the fifth bishop of Denver, Bishop Maloney was appointed bishop of Wichita, Kansas, a post he held until his retirement in 1982.

In 1965, Archbishop Vehr underwent major heart surgery for an aortic aneurysm. Afterwards, he slowed down in his efforts to keep building for a booming Catholic population. He strove to continue his routine nine-to-noon hours at the chancery office but increasingly left day-to-day administration to Bishop Maloney. On February 22, 1967, Vehr retired in compliance with the new guidelines of Pope Paul VI, who suggested that bishops retire at age seventy-five.

Archbishop Vehr continued to serve as administrator of the archdiocese until he could help to install his successor, James Vincent Casey, the bishop of Lincoln, Nebraska, as archbishop of Denver. Then Vehr retired to his home at 777 Pearl Street. The three loyal Sisters of the Most Precious Blood continued to live on the third floor of the house and serve him as secretary, housekeeper, and cook. The archbishop summered in a Bear Creek Canyon home a few miles above Evergreen. Various priests took turns chauffeuring him about with his beloved Patsy (the name he gave to a succession of pet Boston bull terriers). Priests and monsignori also took turns staying with the grand old churchman during his declining years. The end—pneumonia—came September 19, 1973, at St. Joseph Hospital.

Archbishop Casey and Auxiliary Bishop George Evans, whom Vehr had named executors of his estate, read the will: "Kindly bury me in Mount Olivet with the priests and the people I love. . . . Give $300 each to the devoted Sisters of the Most Precious Blood [who] have made my home life most enjoyable, prayerful and peaceful." At Vehr's request, "my stamp collection of American commemorative stamps, first day covers and Vatican stamps" went to sisters Mary, Damien, and Naomi, who "have been with me more than 20 years." His household furnishings, at his request, were split up among numerous priests and friends. His library of 1,442 books went to St. Thomas Seminary. Everything else, "I bequeath to the Archdiocese of Denver."

On September 24, 1973, the archbishop was laid to rest next to bishops Machebeuf, Matz, and Tihen in the Gallagher Memorial at Mt. Olivet Cemetery, with his hands clasped around the rosary his mother had given him. After his death, Catholics and non-Catholics showered the prelate with praise. State Senator Will F. Nicholson, a former Denver mayor, cosponsored a resolution of the Colorado General Assembly that, in part, read:

From 1931 to 1967, Archbishop Urban J. Vehr has zealously promoted the cause of religion and good citizenship within the State of Colorado. There is not an area of the State of Colorado where he has not traveled and become a friend of all. . . . He blessed and dedicated a total of 404 buildings, which include 43 new parishes, 121 churches and additions, 72 schools and additions, 56 convents and additions, 44 rectories, [and] 71 hospitals, youth centers, recreation centers and other allied buildings . . . for the welfare of all citizens of this state. . . . Under the guidance of Archbishop Vehr the Catholic Archdiocese has become a great and creative force within the State of Colorado.

The *Rocky Mountain News*, in a February 24, 1967, editorial upon his retirement, had praised Denver's fourth bishop and first archbishop as "a man of urbanity, gentleness and great humor," who had provided "a brilliant stewardship for the Catholic faith in Colorado." The *Denver Catholic Register* of September 20, 1973, judged Vehr "the ablest business administrator the diocese has ever known. . . . unafraid to act, always ready to listen to advice, fully capable of making his own decisions, and never unduly postponing an important problem."

Upon his installation in 1931, Bishop Vehr had asked, "How could the Holy Father send a priest from Price Hill in Cincinnati to be a Bishop in the rugged Rockies of Colorado?" At Vehr's funeral, Archbishop Casey recalled those words and declared that "the priest from Price Hill measured up fully to the highest of our mountains."

Archbishop Casey, principal celebrant at the funeral mass in Immaculate Conception Cathedral on September 23, 1973, described his predecessor as "a gentleman in the classical tradition of Cardinal Newman . . . carefully avoiding whatever might jar or jolt, any collision of feelings. His great concern was to make everyone at ease."

Monsignor William Jones, who had served Vehr as a chauffeur, chancery official, and school superintendent, included a 168-page chapter on the Vehr era in *The History of Catholic Education in the State of Colorado*. Jones pointed out that Vehr "was a financial maestro, a tremendous administrator." Vehr had worked closely with John Sullivan of Bosworth, Sullivan & Company, a leading brokerage firm, to put the church on a solid financial foundation with ample property holdings and an enviable stock portfolio. "Vehr left the archdiocese in good shape," Monsignor Jones added in a 1987 interview. "He insisted that the *Register* and other church organizations pay for themselves. He modeled the Denver archdiocese after the Cincinnati archdiocese, one of the most prosperous and progressive in the country."

During his thirty-six-year reign, Colorado Catholicism had flourished. Church membership had tripled, reaching 275,000 by 1967, and Vehr had ordained 202 priests, including 162 for the Denver archdiocese. To promote unity, *esprit de corps,* and discipline among his priests, Vehr had held annual retreats at St. Thomas Seminary, and had organized the annual Forty Hours Devotion in part as a get-together for priests in each area of the state. Every parish held this eucharistic rite, a time of continual exposition of the Blessed Sacrament and around-the-clock-prayer, at a different date, so that neighboring priests could participate.

"For isolated priests in rural areas, those forty hours were wonderful," reported Monsignor Patrick Stauter in 1987. "They provided a chance for sociability, for a little bit of card playing and beer drinking. Some of those priests were great characters to meet, like the priest up in Ouray, who arrived in his Ford coupe with at least a dozen cats."

Bishop Newell, in a 1987 interview, said of his fellow administrator: "He had the ability to get along with all groups. He gave Catholic Charities and Catholic schools a tremendous boost by involving Catholic women. He had a great talent for organizing people, for getting the laity concerned and working on a volunteer basis."

Governor McNichols, a Capitol Hill neighbor and fellow executive, appraised Vehr's contribution in a 1987 interview:

> The community fell in love with him. He would entertain with luncheons at his home, followed by a walk and a talk in his rose garden, where he lobbied me and many others on behalf of the Church. He was a discreet, tough, conservative German, a strictly business guy who bought a lot of property cheap ahead of expansion for Church purposes. He was a prince of the Church who brought Colorado Catholicism into full flower.

Archbishop James Vincent Casey. (Photo by Joseph Motta.)

CHAPTER 5

NISI DOMINUS

CASEY: THE GENTLE SHEPHERD, 1967–1986

After Archbishop James V. Casey first came to Denver, protesters camped on the cathedral lawn. Every group under the sun, including some priests and nuns, seemed to be demanding something during the 1960s. Antidemonstrators were protesting demonstrators: Everyone seemed to have a chip on her or his shoulder. Some said the Church must reform; others thought that Satan was on the loose.

The United States' war in Southeast Asia attracted the most protest. Bob Dylan, a popular singer who accompanied himself on guitar and harmonica, led youngsters in songs such as "Masters of War," which struck back at militarists who "play with my world like it's your toy." During the spring that Casey came to Denver, millions of demonstrators all across America marched, spoke, and used civil disobedience to denounce what the veteran journalist Walter Lippmann called "the most unpopular war in American history." Archbishop Casey would become a leader of the American hierarchy in calling for an end to the Vietnam war.

During the sizzling summer of 1967, Afro-Americans rioted in Detroit, Newark, and other cities, leaving almost 100 dead, several thousand injured, and estimated property damage of $500,000,000. Steel-grated storefronts subsequently became standard fixtures in America's core cities. Denver's black militant Lauren Watson and Chicano radical Rodolfo "Corky" Gonzales warned that the same thing could happen in Colorado unless whites began to accept darker-skinned peoples as equals.

The numbers of Spanish-surnamed people had soared from 8.7 percent of Denver's population in 1960 to 16.8 percent in 1970. Corky Gonzales, a Denver native, poet, and former professional boxer, emerged as a spokesman for the most militant Chicanos.

Opposition to the Vietnam War, typified by this 1971 march on Denver's East Colfax Avenue, sparked questioning of all authority, including that of the Church. (Photo by Glenn Cuerden.)

Gonzales wrote an epic poem for his Mexican-American people, "I Am Joaquín," which included the lines:

> As Christian church took its place
>   in God's good name,
> to take and use my virgin strength and trusting faith,
> the priests,
>   both good and bad,
>   took—
> but
>   gave a lasting truth that
>   Spaniard
>   Indian
>   Mestizo
> were all God's children.

Dealing with militant Hispanics would become the touchiest of Archbishop Casey's troubles. On the evening of March 23, 1976, a special command action team of the Denver Police Department defied the pastor and picked the lock to enter Our Lady of Guadalupe Church in North Denver. Police expected to find dynamite and weapons but found only sacks of pinto beans. The parish and its activist pastor José Lara, CR, had been stockpiling not weapons but food for the poor. Archbishop Casey, though he had not granted permission personally, accepted the blame for allowing the church to be raided. In an astonishing demonstration of his humility and efforts to reach out to critical militants, the archbishop apologized for the incident from the pulpit of Guadalupe Church.

"The times they are a-changing," as Bob Dylan's raspy voice put it. Times were changing in the Church as well, with the revolutionary recommendations of Pope John XXIII's Vatican Council, held in Rome during the early 1960s. As with any revolution, the changes horrified some and struck others as only token concessions designed to preserve the status quo. Malcontents on both sides left the Church, as did priests and nuns in record numbers. Priests, after centuries of using Latin and facing the altar, had to face their congregations, use English, and endure amateur guitar masses. Nuns shed their traditional habits for lay attire. Implementing the recommendations of Vatican II became the greatest challenge of Archbishop Casey's episcopacy.

Nothing in the background of this shy farm boy prepared him for the chaotic 1960s and 1970s. Jimmy Casey was born September 22, 1914, in Osage, Iowa, a corn-belt village 120 miles northeast of Des Moines. He was the second of two children of Nina (Nims) and James Casey, a farm machinery dealer, state senator, and postmaster of the town of 3,500 people. Despite Jimmy's antics—such as sawing the handles off a neighbor's wheelbarrow—his father never yelled at him or lost his temper. He set an example of patience perpetuated by the future archbishop.

At Osage High School, Jimmy began to shine. He was elected senior class president and captain of the football team. He played clarinet in the band and made the basketball, debate, drama, and track teams. "He was a terrific athlete, an over-achiever who loved competition," recalled Jimmy's high school coach. "He made up for his small stature by his scrappiness." Despite his passion for competitive sports and his natural leadership, Jimmy Casey also had a shy, solitary side reflected in the poetry he began writing at the age of eight. After some of his poems were published in the *Des Moines Sunday Register*, townsfolk dubbed him "the child poet laureate of Osage."

Casey majored in philosophy at Loras College, a Catholic institution in Dubuque, Iowa. After graduating in 1936, he entered the seminary, spending four years at the North American College in Rome before ordination on December 8, 1939. Father Casey said his first mass in one of the chapels of St. Peter's Basilica. In 1940, Father Casey sailed home to America. From the glory and grandeur of Rome, he went to the assistant pastorate at St. John parish in Independence, Iowa, where he taught in the high school and coached boys' and girls' basketball. Interviewed forty-two years later, a member of his championship girls' basketball team remembered Coach Casey fondly:

> He used to come over to the gym after supper to shoot baskets with us and give us some pointers. . . . He was so proud of us that he set up games in other towns with teams who were not on our regular schedule just so he could show us off. . . . He had this wonderful way of bringing out the best in everybody.

In 1944, the young priest joined the World War II effort as a chaplain in the Navy. He spent two and a half years in the South Pacific, reaching the rank of lieutenant. From 1946 to 1949, he studied canon law at the Catholic University of America, receiving his doctorate in 1949. Doctor Casey quipped that his dissertation, *A Study of Canon 2222, Paragraph One,* had more footnotes (421) than pages (127).

Archbishop Henry P. Rohlman of Dubuque recruited Casey in 1949 as his secretary. Father Casey served as president of the Canon Law Society of America, directed the Family Life Bureau of the Dubuque diocese, was chaplain of the Mount Carmel house of the Sisters of Charity of the Blessed Virgin Mary, and was moderator of the Catholic Lawyers Guild. Pope Pius XII, whom Casey had met in Rome, named him a monsignor in 1952. By his own admission, Casey was "playing hooky" on the golf course in April

1957, when Archbishop Leo Binz tried to reach him with the news that Pope John XXIII had appointed him auxiliary bishop of Lincoln, Nebraska.

"When we were told to lie prostrate on the floor," Casey recalled later of his consecration ceremony on April 24, 1957, "I could hear someone asking, 'Are they dead?'" Nebraskans found their new bishop all too lively. "Most of us just shook our heads," recalled Monsignor Clarence Crowley of Lincoln in an interview with the *Denver Catholic Register* of April 28, 1982. "And while we were shaking our heads, [Casey's] projects not only were accomplished in short order, but were so successful that we were all in a state of amazement." Lincoln's builder bishop erected a new chancery building and an ultramodern, sleek Cathedral of the Risen Christ. He completed a school for retarded youngsters, a retreat house, high schools, grade schools, and a Newman Center. He also undertook the painful task of closing and combining some Catholic schools, a process he would continue in Denver.

Bishop Casey, concluded the *Southern Nebraska Register*, "accomplished more for the Diocese of Lincoln in 10 years than any other comparable period in our history." After establishing his reputation as a doer in Lincoln, Bishop Casey was appointed on February 22, 1967, by Pope Paul VI, to succeed Archbishop Urban J. Vehr in Denver.

The sound of trumpets and the prayers of 1,600 Coloradans welcomed Casey to his installation ceremony as archbishop of Denver; a pageant that included white-clad Dominicans, Jesuits in black, Franciscans in brown, and monsignori in purple. Rabbis in yarmulkes, Orthodox bishops in their beards and black robes, and Protestant clergymen added an ecumenical note to the solemn two-hour installation. Retiring Archbishop Vehr led his fifty-two-year old successor across the sanctuary to the episcopal chair, where he was installed by Archbishop Egidio Vagnozzi, the apostolic delegate. Casey's eyes glistened with tears as he was handed the shepherd's staff, a symbol of his care for a new flock—the 261,944 Catholics in the Denver archdiocese.

Television crews from channels 2 and 7 captured Casey's humble words that day: "I do not come to you as one thinking he has all the answers. I do not even know all the questions. I come among you poor and weak but with a special role to fill as your archbishop and your shepherd. Please pray for me." Afterwards, prominent Coloradans of all faiths joined the installation banquet in the Onyx Room of the Brown Palace Hotel, where cigars and the cordial wagon were circulated after the meal.

At his first Denver press conference, Casey squinted into a battery of cameras, microphones and television lights. Asked about a new Colorado law permitting abortions, Casey quipped, "It happened before I got here." Then he added seriously, "I have moral convictions about this, but also, as a good citizen, I recognize the authority of civil law, and I respect the good faith and conviction of others."

In his first year, Denver's new archbishop appointed a full-time director of religious vocations, sanctioned masses in private homes and started an archdiocesan census and school study. He gave nuns and priests greater control over their assignments by establishing the archdiocese's first Sisters Council and Priestly Personnel Board. The "fresh air" promised by Vatican II flowed into the Archdiocese of Denver, where the new archbishop's office was dominated by a large oil painting of Pope John XXIII.

Archbishop Casey's sense of humor and mature spirituality were part of the change. Virginia Culver of *The Denver Post* noted:

> His candor could be refreshing. He was a priest who readily confessed that he disliked hearing confessions—"Sometimes a priest can be helpful, but there are an awful lot of scrupulous people. And it's hard to talk them out of their scrupulosity. Staying cooped up in that little confession box and hearing piddling sins is really uncomfortable for me." Returning from a national bishops' conference on human sexuality, he once joked, "If God had spoken to me in the beginning, I would have advised some other means of procreation than sex. Sex creates a lot of problems."

Whereas Archbishop Vehr had lived as a prince of the Church, Casey chose a different lifestyle. The archdiocese had purchased for him a large home at 869 Vine Street near Cheesman Park. Casey, who often said he came to serve, not to be served, declined the offered services of the Sisters of the Most Precious Blood who had cared for Archbishop Vehr. He moved into the large house with his housekeeper from Lincoln, Emily Marstradoir, and his handyman, Leonard Biskup, the brother of Archbishop George J. Biskup of Indianapolis.

In 1972, Casey moved out of the Cheesman Park mansion and into a penthouse at the Park Lane Apartments on the northern edge of Washington Park. Emily and Leonard, his faithful servants, moved into private residences in Littleton, commuting to work for the archbishop. Casey, who preferred to cook his own meals and read while eating, was delighted with his new-found freedom.

One of Archbishop Casey's first moves in Denver was to invade Mile High Stadium, the corral of the Denver Broncos. Since this professional football club's formation in 1960, they had inspired a major cult that the archbishop joined. Casey joked that the 75,000-seat stadium was the largest church in Colorado and cleared his schedule for the Sunday rituals there. In 1967, he announced a rally at the stadium to launch his "Year of Faith" for the archdiocese. Despite freezing weather, 30,000 Catholics joined him for the services. Coloradans needed faith. Not only were the world, the country, and the Church experiencing trying times: That fall the Oakland Raiders demoralized the Broncos, 51 to 0. Casey's Year of Faith proved to be a successful recharging of Colorado Catholicism, and that fall the Broncos went to the Super Bowl.

Archbishop Casey's faith must have been bolstered by the glorious day in August 1967, when he created four new parishes. The Church of the Risen Christ in Southeast Denver took the name and used the same dramatic contemporary architecture as Casey's cathedral back in Lincoln. The other three churches served Denver's booming suburbs, which outgrew the city's core during the 1960s. Aurora emerged as the third largest city in Colorado and Lakewood the fourth largest by 1980. Both of these suburbs, as well as the flourishing neighboring towns of Arvada and Littleton, received two new churches during the Casey years. On the outskirts of the metro area, new parishes were founded in Boulder, Conifer, and Wattenberg.

Four thriving ski-resort towns—Dillon, Eagle, Snowmass, and Winter Park—earned new parishes, as did the fast growing Northern Colorado towns of Fort Collins, Longmont, and Windsor. Of the twenty-four parishes Archbishop Casey dedicated, all but seven were in the booming Front Range urban corridor between Littleton and Fort Collins.

Reflecting Casey's commitment to Vatican II, these new churches were dramatically different from earlier ones. Not only did modern architecture distinguish them; they were built and operated with considerable input from the laity. Not one had the traditional Catholic school so important to Casey's predecessors. Rather, they had classrooms for after–public school and weekend religion classes, business offices, and reconciliation rooms instead of confessionals.

Whereas Archbishop Vehr strove to create a parish within walking distance of every Denver Catholic, Archbishop Casey felt that in the age of automobiles and freeways larger parish boundaries were possible; huge suburban parishes were also a way to deal with the declining number of nuns and priests. Perhaps they were also something of a reaction to the many struggling core city parishes: Denver's ten suburban parishes averaged over 2,000 registered families while the average core city parish had less than 400.

From the day Casey took over, his chancery seemed under siege by protesters. The Church, like the local, state, and federal governments, was picketed by militants demanding more for the poor and for minorites. Between 1968 and 1970, reformers camped in front of the chancery and the cathedral. Julia "Julie" Boggs, the archbishop's long-time secretary, said she will never forget the day a protester burst into the chancery carrying a cross to dramatize his demands. In a 1987 interview, she recalled the scene:

Here was this new archbishop from nice, quiet Lincoln, Nebraska and those [expletive deleted] camped out in two pup tents in front of the chancery. Two of their leaders were renegade priests. Because of all the threats we had to take the archbishop out the back door. To make matters worse, his first chancellor ran off with his first secretary. That's when George Evans recruited me. They knew I wouldn't run off with a priest. They're too damn spoiled!

Despite all the picketing and the protesters, Archbishop Casey absolutely would not say anything bad about them. He was the most compassionate, caring man. A lot of very troubled people came to see him and I can't remember one who didn't leave his office looking relieved.

Inside the besieged chancery, Archbishop Casey began working to expand archdiocesan services, many of which accommodated groups who were protesting his inaction. Between 1967 and 1986, Casey transformed a tiny office where three priests often did their own typing to a bureaucracy of 170 employees. Often using lay personnel, the archbishop created many new offices: Aging; Campus Ministry; Catholic Youth Services; Chicano Concerns; Data Processing; Family Life Services; Handicapped Services; Housing, Justice, and Peace; Major Giving; Parish Services; Priestly Personnel; Prison Ministry; Pro-Life; Single Adults; and the Renew Program. With this battery of new programs, Archbishop Casey set about implementing the reforms of Vatican II and transforming the Denver archdiocese.

The new archbishop critically scrutinized the main claim to fame of the Mile High archdiocese—the *Register* system of newspapers. After Monsignor Matthew Smith's death in 1960, Monsignor John B. Cavanagh became editor. Cavanagh had worked on the paper ever since his ordination in 1936, first in the editorial department, then in circulation. As editor, he installed modern, high-speed Goss Headliner presses and, in 1960, added typesetting machines.

Monsignor Cavanagh suffered a heart attack in 1965 and retired on October 10, 1966. Daniel Flaherty, who had been with the *Register* since his ordination in 1954 and had launched the paper's military edition, assumed the editorship. Despite the efforts of the organization Smith had built up, the *Register's* circulation dwindled after his death. Many of the diocesan editions became independent, and new publications began eating away at the empire. When Archbishop Casey arrived in 1967, the *Register* was losing $728,000 a year. To plug this financial drain, Casey sold the national network to Twin Circle Publishing Company of Culver City, California, which printed the paper in Texas. For a few months, the Texans even printed the home edition of the *Register* before Archbishop Casey brought it back to Denver.

After several short terms by lay editors, Archbishop Casey selected one of his most colorful and outspoken priests for the job— Father Charles Bert "Woody" Woodrich. This Buffalo, New York, native had worked for a New York City advertising agency be-fore coming to Denver's St. Thomas Seminary. Archbishop Casey appointed Woodrich archdiocesan information director on June 12, 1968, acting editor of the *Register* in 1972, and editor in 1977. Editor Woodrich soon transformed the paper:

Cigar-chomping James Fiedler, who began as cub reporter with Monsignor Smith at the *Denver Catholic Register*, became that newpaper's first lay editor in 1983.

I asked Casey for directions but he told me that I was the editor and should know what to do. One thing we did agree on was that we didn't need a newspaper to compete with the *Post* and the *News*, but more of a specialized Catholic news- and feature-oriented publication. I decided to be absolutely open with the press. When Casey's chancellor ran off with his secretary, we didn't hide it. We let out everything and it blew over in twenty-four hours. You only get in trouble when you're hiding things.

I couldn't type, write, or spell but tried to make the *Register* exciting and readable. I never did a column but made the paper a forum for readers' opinions. I emphasized headlines, graphics, and introduced color photographs. And under Jim Pierson we jumped from $80,000 a year to $800,000 a year in advertising income. And we went from 14,000 to 82,000 in circulation. I wasn't a Monsignor Matthew Smith poring over words—over the minutiae—I just wanted the paper to look good, to have sex appeal.

In 1983, Father Woody turned over the editorship to a long-time staff member, James Fiedler. By 1987, when Woodrich retired as executive editor and was replaced by Robert H. Feeney, the *Register* had evolved into a 30 to 40 page-tabloid. Circulation climbed to more than 85,000 by 1988, making it the most popular weekly newspaper in Colorado.

Sale of the newspaper left Casey with the large plant in the 900 block of Bannock Street. In 1971, he moved the chancery from the crowded old Matz home at 1536 Logan Street into the *Register* building, where he also found room for various archdiocesan offices that had been scattered around the city. The old chancery was demolished to build a new rectory for the cathedral. For four years, Casey supervised the archdiocese from the old newspaper building before buying the Bankers Union Life Building for $2.25

Archbishop Casey moved his office in 1971 to the Register building, which occupied much of the 900 block of Bannock Street. (Photo by Pat Coffey.)

million. This modern, granite-clad, six-story office building at 200 Josephine Street has been the home of the archdiocese ever since. When the archdiocese first moved in in 1975, critics protested the move as extravagant and fussed about the other major tenant—the Central Intelligence Agency.

To orchestrate the multiplying archdiocesan programs, Casey recruited the executive director of the National Council of the Catholic Laity in Washington, D.C., Martin Work. Work began in Denver in 1970 as director of administration and planning. Besides being a skillful administrator, Work also exemplified Casey's plan to bring lay people into church administration. Work and Casey had met at Vatican II, where they had labored together on recommendations for expanding the role of the laity. Together, the two men began promoting the idea of lay councils and business managers for parishes. For priests accustomed to full control of their parishes, this was not always easy.

John V. Anderson, shown here at a fund raiser with comedian Bob Hope, was appoined first director of the Archbishop's Annual Campaign for Progress in 1978, and by 1989 was collecting $2.8 million a year.

In 1972, Work began issuing public financial reports. In the September 20, 1973, *Register*, the archdiocese announced that it was finally operating in the black. Instead of relying on high-interest, short-term bank loans, as in the past, Casey used bond issues. After tabulating income and expenditures for all the parishes, schools, institutions, agencies, and the chancery, the archdiocese ended the 1973 fiscal year with a surplus of $1,061,900. The $19,124,600 budget that year included $14 million for parishes and parish schools, $1.1 million for community services, $1 million for high schools, and $1.2 for general operations. By 1985, Casey's last full year of life, the budget had climbed to over $45 million.

Archbishop Casey and Martin Work tightened central administrative control, consolidating all parish and institutional debt. In 1978, they opened the Office of Major Giving under the direction of Reverend John V. Anderson, who subsequently raised about $2 million a year. By the 1980s, the archdiocese had a top bond rating—AAA—and enough investments and assets to cover its $10-million bonded indebtedness, according to archdiocesan director of real estate and investments, Bill McCook. Reverend Michael J. Chamberlain, who served Casey in the chancery office in various positions before succeeding Bishop Evans as vicar general in 1985, reported:

Before Casey and Work set up the business office, pastors had much more discretion, could squirrel away funds in Altar and Rosary Society treasuries or wherever. Consequently, the archdiocese did not know what its resources were and what it could do. Casey's idea was to make the chancery a resource center for all the parishes. He also used this consolidation to establish better employee salaries, health care, and retirement benefits.

Reverend Edward M. Hoffmann, who served Casey as secretary and chancellor, described the archbishop as "a careful administrator who assigned responsibilities and then put great confidence in his assistants. He delegated much responsibility and gave much freedom to his subordinates. That made him wonderful to work for."

"He would talk to anybody," recalled Julie Boggs, "so I became his watchdog."

People were constantly interrupting him. Finally, we installed a secret buzzer system so he could push the button hidden under his desk and I would dash in to say his next appointment was waiting. I had to shoo people out so he could lunch on the clam chowder and corned beef on rye sandwiches I made for him.

Father Edward Hoffmann recollected in a 1987 interview that Casey wanted work done on the most appropriate level of the bureaucracy. If a decision had to be made at the top, Casey would discuss it in staff meeting, solicit advice, and then make the decision. After Martin Work retired in 1984, Casey came to rely most heavily on Bishop Evans. Other members of Casey's inner circle jokingly called Evans the "vicar for everything."

Born in Denver on September 25, 1922, Evans attended St. Vincent de Paul grade school, where the parish center now is named in his honor. Afterwards, the lanky youth sailed through Regis High School, Notre Dame University, and St. Thomas Seminary before his ordination on May 31, 1947. Evans earned a doctorate in canon law at the Lateran University in Rome in 1950. Upon his return to Denver, Archbishop Vehr appointed him vice-chancellor. Named a monsignor in 1960, Evans succeeded Monsignor Gregory Smith as vicar general in 1968. On April 23, 1969, Evans was installed as the auxiliary bishop of Denver.

In 1971, Bishop Evans amazed some observers by moving into a one-bedroom unit of archdiocesan housing at 1300 South Irving Street. The bishop felt it took "first hand,

Bishop George Evans, a Denver native who became Archbishop Casey's right-hand man, committed the archdiocese to social action on many fronts.

living-in experience to make one sensitive to the problems of the people who live in our projects" and "that even a bishop can be happy in the kind of housing we're running."

Bishop Evans maintained that "the role of the church should be that of the conscience of our society, alerting it to the problems and providing examples for their solution." Although Archbishop Casey shied away from public demonstrations, he encouraged Evans to represent the Church at antiwar and social justice rallies. With singing stars Judy Collins and John Denver, Evans addressed 30,000 anti-Vietnam war demonstrators gathered at the Colorado State Capitol on June 15, 1972, for an "Evening of Peace." When several Sisters of Loretto were charged with trespassing at the Rocky Flats nuclear weapons plant, Bishop Evans went to court with them. He took a public stand against the death penalty; he lobbied the state legislature on behalf of the poor, the elderly, and the homeless. When Southeast Asian refugees sought a home in Colorado, Evans spearheaded the archdiocesan placement efforts and personally adopted one family.

This tall, wiry bishop seemed to be everywhere. After Martin Luther King's assassination, Evans rode through Five Points with black militant Lauren Watson "to show a justifiably angry black community that some in the white community were listening." He marched with César Chávez and the United Farm Workers in California, trying to unionize migrant laborers. He conducted a protest prayer in 1984 on a railroad track over which nuclear weapons were scheduled to pass and joined Governor Richard D. Lamm in condemning deployment of MX missiles in the Rocky Mountain West.

When giving Bishop Evans the 1984 B'nai Brith Humanitarian Award, the regional director of the Jewish Anti-Defamation League called him "the most energetic person I've ever worked with." Evans served as a board member and chair of the AMC Cancer Research Center, as a board member of the Auraria Higher Education Center, and as the president of the Colorado Council of Churches. Evans further championed ecumenism as president of the Denver Area Interfaith Clergy, a group he helped found. He also startled some Catholics by publicly sharing a Passover meal with Rabbi Daniel Goldberger of Temple Emanuel.

The bishop's private as well as his public life exemplified charity. Evans' federal income tax forms in the archdiocesan archives reveal a total 1983 income of $11,612, of which he gave away $7,070, including $1,420 to the Colorado Women's Employment and Education Fund and $2,600 to the Sisters of the New Covenant, an ecumenical sisterhood that had settled in Commerce City in 1981.

"Bishop Evans was super special," reported Sister Rosemary Keegan, SL, in a 1986 interview. "He was especially good to sisters and to the Sisters Council. After Vatican II he helped sisters move up and into all sorts of jobs." As a defender of women's rights,

Sister Rosemary Keegan, SL, one of Bishop Evans' many admirers, cherished his support in her efforts to bring Head Start programs to Catholic schools. In honor of her work and her spirited recovery from a brutal hammer attack and robbery, Sister Rosie was feted at this 1985 dedication of the Sister Rosemary Keegan Head Start Center. In her little red van with a customized wheelchair lift she continues to be a fountain of hope and good humor. (Photo by James Baca.)

Evans spoke out in favor of the Equal Rights Amendment to give women equal protection under the federal constitution. Outlaw women also had Evans' ear; for years he heard confessions and said masses for them in the Denver County Jail.

Bishop Evans attended countless meetings and once quipped: "If I get to purgatory and find out that all these meetings don't count, that'll be hell." Evans had to go to many more meetings after October 1984, when Archbishop Casey was hospitalized for months. Thanks in part to his noon matches at the Denver Tennis Club, Evans never exceeded his high school weight of 155. Despite his physical fitness, friends saw him age rapidly trying to fill in for the ailing archbishop. He died on Friday, September 13, 1985, at St. Joseph Hospital, after a painful four-month battle against cancer of the colon.

Ignoring his own illness, Archbishop Casey insisted upon saying the funeral mass at the cathedral for his beloved colleague. Governor Lamm eulogized Evans as "always on the cutting edge of life and——in my mind—that is the highest expression of religious conviction. He brought a tremendous vitality to his faith and to his community." Bishop

Bishop Richard C. Hanifen was put in charge of the Colorado Springs diocese after its creation in 1984.

William C. Frey, shepherd of Colorado's Episcopalians, noted that he hesitated to pray that Evans rest in peace because "resting in peace was the last thing George wanted in life."

Archbishop Casey's second auxiliary bishop was, like Evans, a Denver native. Richard C. Hanifen came from a clan with deep roots in Colorado. His grandfather, Edward Anselm Hanifen, Sr., immigrated from Canada to Leadville during the 1880s silver boom, ultimately becoming a successful mine owner whose properties poured forth not only silver but also lead and zinc. The bishop's father, Edward A. Hanifen, Jr., cofounded a leading Colorado investment firm—Hanifen, Imhoff, Inc. Richard, the third of four children, was born June 15, 1931. He attended St. Philomena School in the parish where his family was active and prominent. His mother, Dorothy Ranous Hanifen, recalled that the future bishop as a boy sat in the front pew at daily mass so that if one of the altar boys did not show up, "he'd get that extra chance to serve Mass."

After graduating from Regis High School and College, Hanifen entered St. Thomas Seminary. He was ordained in 1959 by Archbishop Vehr, who encouraged the young priest to pursue a masters degree in guidance and counseling at Catholic University and a degree in canon law at the Lateran College in Rome. Following stints at Our Lady of the Mountains in Estes Park and at Immaculate Conception Cathedral, Hanifen was chosen by Archbishop Casey as his chancellor in 1970.

Impressed by Hanifen's pastoral abilities, Casey worked with Rome to elevate him to the rank of auxiliary bishop in 1974. A year later, Casey created the vicariate of Colorado Springs in that rapidly growing city and put Hanifen in charge as the vicar. When Colorado Springs was made a diocese on January 30, 1984, Hanifen was selected as its first bishop by Pope John Paul II.

Archbishop Pio Laghi, the papal nuncio, assisted by Archbishop Casey and Bishop Arthur Tafoya of the Diocese of Pueblo, installed Hanifen as the crosier carrier of

Colorado Springs in a ceremony at the Pike's Peak Center. Hanifen, an easy-going and friendly leader, transformed this long-time stepchild of the Denver archdiocese into a proud and independent diocese. In 1984, the baby diocese contained ten counties—Chaffee, Cheyenne, Douglas, Elbert, El Paso, Kit Carson, Lake, Lincoln, Park, and Teller—with a combined population of approximately 65,000 Catholics.

St. Mary's Church in downtown Colorado Springs became the cathedral of the new diocese, which encompassed 15,560 square miles, twenty-four parishes, ten missions, fifty priests, 230 sisters, five grade schools, and one high school. Of his plans for the new diocese, Hanifen told the *Colorado Springs Gazette-Telegraph* on January 21, 1984: "A bishop should not be a glaring watch dog of orthodoxy but a good shepherd of his flock." On September 5, 1984, Hanifen launched *The Catholic Herald*, a monthly diocesan newspaper.

Archbishop Casey gave the new diocese a $3-million "dowry," enabling Colorado's third diocese to make a sound, debt-free debut. Bishop Hanifen graciously accepted what he called "a Christmas present of memorable proportions." Years later, Hanifen would express his appreciation for less tangible gifts from the archbishop. "He was a man of gentleness but also courage. It was his vision which eventully brought about the formation of the Diocese of Colorado Springs. Catholics of the Colorado Springs diocese will always be grateful for his love and leadership."

All in the archdiocese was not growth, however. While his predecessors, particularly Archbishop Vehr, had gloried in opening Catholic schools, Casey undertook the thankless task of closing and consolidating them. Initially, Casey hoped to solve the financial crunch in Catholic education by enlisting state support, advocating the voucher system whereby parents could direct that their educational taxes go to a school of their choice. But in 1971, the state legislature voted down this proposal to help nonpublic schools. Monsignor William H. Jones, the superintendent of Catholic schools, remembered school-closing and consolidation as one of the toughest issues bedeviling Archbishop Casey:

> We had to tackle the consolidation question. The numbers of teaching nuns, teaching priests, and pupils were all declining. If we ever hoped to have new schools in new parishes, we had to consolidate the many Catholic schools of the core city. We tried to look at every alternative. Notre Dame University did a school study for us. Our appointed Catholic School Board looked at the question in detail, we held public meetings. Every parish was given a vote on whether or not it would support keeping those high schools open. The majority felt they could not afford to. We decided that consolidation was the answer.

St. Vincent de Paul School in Denver was one of the survivors during the Casey era school closings, which eliminated seventeen high and thirty-three elementary schools.

By closing some of the more poorly attended schools, the archdiocese hoped to pump limited personnel and resources into the survivors. Although this rationale seemed painfully obvious to the chancery office, implementation generally provoked controversy and criticism. Such was the case in 1973 when the archdiocese announced, in the *Denver Catholic Register*: "To improve the facilities for the Catholic high school students of Denver, it was decided to establish a new Central Catholic High School by consolidating Cathedral, St. Francis de Sales, and St. Joseph High Schools."

As Sacred Heart had closed in 1939 and Annunciation and Mount Carmel during the 1960s, the core city was left with only one Catholic high school. Critics, of whom there was no shortage in the 1970s, charged that Casey was abandoning the poor in the inner city. This uproar had hardly subsided when the decision came in 1982 to close Central Catholic High School nine years after its opening. Casey had never attended Catholic schools until college, and some felt this explained his apparent lack of commitment to Catholic education. Denver, which once had eleven Catholic high schools, now had only two archdiocesan high schools (Holy Family and Machebeuf) and four private ones (Mullen, Regis, St. Mary's Academy, and Marycrest, which would close in 1988). Of the twenty-three Catholic high schools in Colorado during the 1950s, only six remained open as of 1989.

Regis High School, which became a separate entity from Regis College in 1923, broke ground in 1988 for a new, twenty-seven-acre campus at the northeast corner of Parker and Arapahoe roads. This suburban, Arapahoe County site was donated by Richard Campbell, a trustee of the school. Plans were laid to sell the old high school site at 5232 Lowell Boulevard to Regis College to help finance the new high school, estimated to cost more than $5 million, according to high school president Ralph Houlihan, SJ. Mullen High School, which had opened in 1931 as a boys' orphanage and dairy, evolved into a boarding school ten years later. In 1965 Mullen became a day-student–only high school and in 1989 began admitting girls.

Catholic elementary schools, which continued to be supported primarily by the parishes, survived the 1960s and 1970s in greater numbers than did high schools. When Archbishop Casey came to Denver in 1967, the archdiocese boasted seventy elementary schools with 21,365 students. When he died in 1985, thirty-seven elementary schools hosted 10,247 students.

In the city of Pueblo, all Catholic schools were closed by Bishop Buswell in 1971. Five Catholic elementary schools survived in the Colorado Springs diocese: St. Joseph's in Salida; and Corpus Christi, Divine Redeemer, Holy Trinity, and Pauline Memorial in Colorado Springs. The only new Catholic school to be opened in Colorado since the 1960s is St. Stephen elementary in Glenwood Springs.

Why this decline in the number of Catholic schools during an era of growth and prosperity? At least four factors can be identified.

1. The drastic decline in the number of sisters, whose self-sacrifice had made Catholic schools possible, was the key factor. The number of teaching sisters in the Denver archdiocese fell from 492 in 1962, to 385 in 1972, to 147 in 1982. Whereas religious, both men and women, taught for $1,500 a year or less, the average salary of lay Catholic school teachers was $13,461. Father Lawrence St. Peter, who helped Monsignor Jones administer Catholic schools during the 1960s and 1970s, explained the problem in a 1987 interview:

Without nuns, it is very difficult to keep Catholic schools open. That's not only because lay teachers salaries are much higher but also because parents are less willing to make the extra financial sacrifices to send their children to lay teachers. They equate Catholic education with nuns.

2. The number of children per Catholic family declined. This demographic phenomenon initially escaped the attention of educators trying to cope with the World War II baby boomers who began flooding schools in the 1950s. Between 1948–1949 and 1958–1959, Catholic elementary and high school enrollment in the archdiocese climbed from 13,951 to 24,640. Enrollment stabilized during the 1960s, reaching 25,282 in 1968–1969. The 1950s and 1960s were the golden age for Catholic schools, but between 1968 and 1978, the elementary and high school population fell to 15,719.

3. Catholics developed a greater acceptance of public schools. Whereas sending children to public schools when Catholic schools were available was once considered a serious—if not mortal—sin, both the hierarchy and laity grew much more tolerant of public schools after World War II. As Catholic immigrant groups became better integrated into the American mainstream, the differences between Catholics and other denominations narrowed during the ecumenical 1960s. The 1960 election of a Catholic, John F. Kennedy, as president, was one of the most obvious signs that ill will between Catholics and non-Catholics was waning. Growing tolerance as well as the growing numbers and quality of public schools led a majority of Catholics to use non-Catholic schools.

4. The cost of education soared. In 1941–1942, the archdiocesan superintendent of schools calculated the cost per pupil per year at $113.72. By 1949–1950, the average cost had risen to $213 a year. Since then, the costs of teachers' salaries, of equipment in a science-minded age of computers, and of everything from textbooks to utilities to building materials have soared. By 1983–1984, according to the Denver Archdiocesan Education Office, the average cost per student per year had climbed to $1,067. As of 1986–1987, Catholic elementary schools in the archdiocese were a $10-million program supported 61 percent by tuition, 25 percent by parish subsidies, and 14 percent by other fund raising. By 1988 the cost per pupil had climbed to $1,400 a year. As tuition averaged only about $707 a year, the parishes used bingo and other revenue to keep schools open, with archdiocesan support from the Archbishop Annual Campaign for Progress (AACP). Eighty percent of the school expenses went for salaries, which averaged $13,461 in 1986–1987, only half what the public schools offer.

Countering criticism that the archdiocese ignored core city schools, the Archdiocesan Education Department spearheaded creation of an urban school coalition in the 1980s.

By giving youngsters special attention from their earliest years, as in this play day scene at Denver's Margery Reed Mayo Day Nursery, Catholic schools are doing a better job of educating minorities than are public schools, according to the studies of James S. Coleman. (Denver Public Library.)

Annunciation, Guardian Angels, Loyola, Presentation, St. Francis de Sales, St. Joseph, and St. Rose of Lima elementary schools united to form Denver's Schools in Urban Neighborhoods (SUN), a coalition to cope with core city school issues. Sister Jean Anne Panisko, SCL, principal of Annunciation since 1981, reported that SUN addresses the special problems of "at risk" students likely to fail or drop out. SUN has stressed that all ethnic groups succeed. As of 1986–1987, Catholic schools in the archdiocese were 16.4 percent Hispanic, 4 percent black, and 1.3 percent Asian.

Catholic schools now usually out perform public schools, if national standardized tests are a valid criterion. James S. Coleman, a professor of education and sociology at the University of Chicago, noted for his educational studies, analyzed the successes of Catholic schools in *Public and Private High Schools* and *High School Achievement:*

Sister Jarlath McManus, CSJ, associate secretary for Catholic education, pointed out in 1988, "After a decade of declining enrollments, we are now enjoying a renaissance, with both enrollments and test scores rising as of 1987."

Public, Catholic, and Private Schools Compared. In both works, Coleman found that Catholic school students are better educated and that Catholic schools did better at training black and Hispanic students. This national finding was locally verified in a study of Denver archdiocesan elementary school children taking the California Test of Basic Skills between 1983 and 1985. They scored from 8 to 28 percent above the national average. Catholic school pupils excelled in English language arts, math, reading, and spelling, in that order. Moreover, they tended to exceed the national norm by growing percentages each year. Composite test scores show third graders 15 percent above the average and seventh graders 28 percent above the national norm.

During Archbishop Casey's administration, various superintendents dealt with the rapidly changing school situation, including Monsignor William H. Jones, and fathers Lawrence St. Peter, Tom Woerth, and Joseph M. O'Malley. In 1983, Archbishop Casey picked a layman, Michael J. Franken, former principal of an inner city school in Chicago and of Sacred Heart grade school in Boulder, as superintendent and secretary of archdiocesan schools. Franken reflected in 1988:

> We must rekindle the spirit of support for Catholic Schools by focusing on their mission, their quality, their accessibility, their affordability. I believe we can do this but it will necessitate a strength of conviction, magnitude, and breadth we have lacked in the recent past.

Archbishop Casey gave schools, as well as parishes, greater flexibility. The tight guidelines imposed upon schools during the Vehr era were relaxed. Each school was given much greater freedom to select its textbooks, to structure its program, and to tailor courses to its particular student body. Subsequently, some abandoned the use of student uniforms, adopted non-Catholic texts for secular subjects, and began curriculum experimentation.

Sister Jarlath McManus, CSJ, the associate secretary for Catholic education, explained in 1987 that, despite the low pay, many teachers accept Catholic school positions:

> Catholic schools allow more creativity and confront teachers with less bureaucracy. We also pride ourselves on having fewer alcohol, drug, and disciplinary problems. We've maintained our reputation for concentrating on traditional, basic education—the four Rs—reading, 'riting, 'rithmetic, and religion.

The education office's 1988 profile of archdiocesan elementary school teachers found that of the 510 teachers, 472 (93 percent) are lay. Of the lay teachers, 74 percent are married and 60 percent are parents, with an average teaching experience of 10.7 years.

"Catholic schools are experiencing something of a renaissance," Sister Jarlath reported in 1988.

> Catholics, and Americans in general, are returning to the idea that religion and morality are basic to education. We've gone back to emphasizing religion courses every year in every grade. We're trying to regain some of the old values that Catholics took for granted before teaching nuns and Catholic schools began disappearing. About 14 percent of our students are non-Catholics. After declining enrollments and school closings of the 1970s, enrollment in all archdiocesan schools during the 1980s seems to have stabilized at about 13,000 students each year.

While providing secular education, Catholic schools also continue to emphasize religious education. The Religious Education Department of the Archdiocesan Education Office, headed by Cris Villapando since 1987, oversees adult and family religious education programs. Reverend Lawrence M. Freeman directs a Special Religious Education office that, by 1988, had programs for the developmentally disabled in twenty parishes. With the closing of many Catholic schools, the majority of Catholics, children as well as adults, now receive training from Religious Education Programs. Fred L. Eyerman, director of the media center and adult faith formation, noted in 1989:

> Religious Education is responsible for the development of about 90 percent of our people. During Archbishop Casey's time, Denver became a national leader in religious education programs which replaced traditional Catholic schooling. Many programs and processes developed here have been adopted in other parts of the country. Our Christians in Search program had write-ups in *America* magazine and our Mile Hi Congress for Religious Education, which is now in its twentieth year, is known nationally.

Following tumultuous times in the 1970s, Loretto Heights College became nonsectarian, then a part of Regis College, and then the Denver branch of a Tokyo university, depriving Coloradans of what had been a prominent school for drama and the fine arts. (Photo by Roger Whitacre.)

One of the most successful adult religious education programs has been the Catholic Biblical School, which has been operating since 1982. The Biblical School, a pet project of Archbishop Casey, grew out of awareness that many Catholics hungry for scriptural understanding were joining Protestant Bible study groups. Sister Macrina Scott, OSF, who had just finished graduate studies in scripture at the University of California at Berkeley, was enlisted to start the Catholic Biblical School. She set up a four-year course, with weekly sessions. Graduates, of whom there are about 100 a year, were prepared to go back to their own parish and launch further Bible study programs.

Beginning in the 1950s, the rapid expansion of inexpensive public higher education threatened Catholic colleges. Faced with declining enrollments and the necessity of raising tuition to hire lay teachers, Loretto Heights College fell upon hard times. In 1968, the Sisters of Loretto sold the college for $1 to a coalition of alumni, teachers, and supporters who endeavored to operate the school as a nonsectarian private college. Twenty years later, in 1988, Loretto Heights was again financially strapped and threatened to close its doors for good until a merger with Regis College was negotiated to save the school.

Regis College fared much better. Indeed, during the 1970s and 1980s when many private schools declined or died, Regis thrived. Credit should be given, according to college historian Harold L. Stansell, SJ, to David M. Clarke, SJ, who became the twenty-second president of Regis on August 1, 1972. Clarke, who held a doctorate in physical chemistry from Northwestern University, had served as academic vice-president at Gonzaga University in Spokane and at the College of St. Francis in Joliet, Illinois.

President Clarke gave Regis a more effective board of trustees, bringing in laymen such as Peter Coors of the brewery clan, Max Brooks, president of Central Bank of Denver, and Walter F. Imhoff of Hanifen, Imhoff, Inc. Subsequently, Regis renovated Old Main and added new buildings such as the Coors Life Directions Center (with the help of $1 million from the Coors Foundation).

Enrollments since the 1970s have stabilized at around 1,000 on-campus students. Off-campus programs, however, have mushroomed, attracting 3,000 to 4,000 part-time students a year. Regis has reached out into other Front Range communities, offering programs in Colorado Springs, Longmont, Southeast Denver, and Sterling.

When Regis celebrated its centennial in 1987, the college really could celebrate. Instead of the twenty-four students of 1887, Regis could claim 5,500 full- and part-time students. Over the course of a century, the college had evolved into a fully accredited institution offering twenty-seven undergraduate degrees and masters degrees in business administration and adult Christian development. A student–faculty ratio of fifteen-to-one enabled Regis to provide a seminar format in many classes. Of the full time faculty, 75 percent hold a Ph.D. or the highest degree available in their field. "The Regis spirit," as President Clarke declared in a special Regis centennial issue of the *Denver Catholic Register*, September 30, 1987, "allowed us to survive the trying times and celebrate the richest."

More attention has been given to Catholic students on non-Catholic campuses since the 1930s when George Cardinal Mundelein, the archbishop of Chicago, roared that if students "choose to go to a state university, they can go to hell!"

To augment the Newman Club movement active on Colorado campuses since the Boulder club opened in 1906, Archbishop Casey created an archdiocesan campus ministry office in the early 1970s. The term "campus ministry" came into vogue after Vatican II to describe what had been known as the Newman Club or Melvin Club movement. Both clubs were founded by a student, Timothy Harrington. While an undergraduate at the University of Wisconsin, Harrington encountered anti-Catholic faculty and discussed this with his Thanksgiving dinner hosts, the family of Professor Melvin.

Before you challenge a professor, Melvin urged Harrington, know what you are talking about. This inspired Harrington to organize the Melvin Club at the University of Wisconsin in 1883. Later, while a medical student at the University of Pennsylvania, Harrington read John Henry Cardinal Newman's "The Idea of a University" and founded the Newman Club movement on that campus in 1893. Both clubs fostered religious reading, study, and prayer as well as sociability with other Catholics.

Following World War II, hundreds of thousands of veterans—among them many Catholics—armed with new federal student loans and grants, had flooded colleges. In the spirit of Vatican II, campus Catholic communities tried a more positive approach, viewing

Dennis Gallagher, a veteran state legislator, epitomizes the growing role of the laity. He serves as a lector at St. Dominic's Church, teaches at Regis College, and welcomes rubberneckers to his celebrated tours of the gold-domed statehouse. (Photo by Tom Noel.)

college years as a time when idealism is high and permanent value systems are formed. By 1989, more than 2,000 Catholics worked among students in campus ministry programs throughout the United States. In the Archdiocese of Denver, campus ministries have been established on all college and university campuses, Catholic and non-Catholic, targeting an estimated 46,000 Catholic students and 4,000 Catholic faculty and staff.

The Office of Campus Ministry also sponsors a theologian-in-residence program at the University of Colorado, Colorado State University, and the University of Northern Colorado. The AACP has provided roughly $100,000 a year to support the Campus Ministry program, which by the 1980s had seventeen full-time employees as well as several part-timers and volunteers. The Office of Campus Ministry, which is part of the Education Secretariat, has been directed since 1982 by Reverend George Schroeder, who reported in 1988:

Catholics are now attending colleges and universities in numbers that far exceed their percentage of the general population. Our Campus Ministry goal is to promote theological study and reflection on the religious nature of human beings so that spiritual and moral growth may keep pace with intellectual growth.

Archbishop Casey's greatest effort was to elevate the laity to a much more instrumental role. He issued a brief and eloquent statement on May 5, 1976: "To Consider Prayerfully the Work of the Coming Day." In this four-page document Casey prescribed a much greater role for the laity in parish administration. Parishes that once had from two to four priests began to notice a shortage in the 1960s. To fight the decline in religious vocations, Archbishop Casey appointed the archdiocese's first full-time director of vocations in 1967. Thanks to rigorous recruitment, the number of priests in the archdiocese increased from 327 in 1967 to 356 in 1986. This increase, however, did not

Archbishop Casey became a nationally prominent leader in implementing the reforms suggested by the Vatican II Council, notably Pope John XXIII's call for greater reliance on the laity. (Photo by John Gordon. Denver Public Library.)

meet the demand in an archdiocese that had grown from 261,844 Catholics in 1967 to 330,270 in 1986. The shortage was exacerbated by the resignations of at least forty-five priests during the 1960s and 1970s. "I was crushed by their leaving," Archbishop Casey told the *Denver Catholic Register* of April 28, 1982. It was, he added, the most difficult task he faced as archbishop.

Sorrow for the loss of priests could only be partially eased by the joy Casey took in elevating lay persons to positions of responsibility. "I believe," the archbishop declared, "that all baptized people are to share equally in the work of the church. I do not see the clergy on an exalted level."

"The role of bishops and priests," Casey added in 1969, "is to recognize the talents of lay people and call them out to take positions of leadership." Parishes began to use lay men and women as religious education directors, youth ministers, liturgists, business managers, and senior citizens' coordinators. Women religious and lay people began to minister side by side with the clergy, distributing communion, reading, and guiding their fellow parishioners. Sanctuaries once occupied exclusively by a priest and altar boys were crowded during mass with lay men, women, and children who were all given roles in the revised liturgy.

In unprecedented moves, Casey selected laymen for key chancery positions. Besides Martin Work as director of administration and planning, he appointed James H. Mauck the first lay director of Catholic Charities and Michael J. Franken as the first lay secretary for education and superintendent of Catholic schools. Richard J. Bowles, a permament deacon, was named the first lay director of the Liturgy Office, and Cyndi Thero became director of pastoral process and, later, of the Parish Council Services.

Following Vatican II recommendations, Archbishop Casey started the permanent diaconate as the heart of the lay revolution. A two-year training program was launched at St. Thomas Seminary under the direction of Reverend Leo Horrigan. Archbishop Casey ordained the first class of ten permanent deacons on April 6, 1974. Another thirteen deacons, many of them married men, were ordained in 1975. By 1985, eighty-five deacons had completed the two-year training and gone to work in the parishes of the archdiocese. Deacon Bowles reflected on Archbishop Casey's role in promoting the laity to prominence in a 1987 interview:

> Despite the reluctance of some clergy and lay people, Casey never lost his conviction that Vatican II was essential. While attending the Vatican II Council in Rome, he really caught the infectious enthusiasm of Pope John XXIII. In an archdiocese used to a stern father, as Vehr and other previous bishops had been, Casey insisted that the laity take adult responsibilities, not just follow directions of priests and nuns.

By opening up many positions to nuns, Archbishop Casey attracted many to the archdiocese, where they were given freedom to experiment with a wide variety of ministries. As Vicar General Michael J. Chamberlain put it in 1988:

> Casey created an atmosphere, complimented by bishops Evans and Hanifen, of openness, of tolerance for experimentation. He would listen to any proposal. But you had to have done your homework, to have a rationale, a game plan, and a way to pay for it. He would pin you down on the why and the how.

Casey, who had been chaplain of the motherhouse of the Sisters of Charity of the Blessed Virgin Mary in Dubuque, Iowa, encouraged nuns to expand their horizons. He raised sisters' annual salaries, in 1974, from $3,100 to $4,600. The same year, he appointed Sister Helen Flaherty associate vicar for women religious and two years later named her vicar; she may have been the first woman religious in the nation elevated to that rank.

The archbishop's efforts were deeply appreciated. He became remembered, in the words of Sister Loretto Anne Madden, as "a man who in a quiet way was deeply committed to justice. . . . [H]e was one of the most outstanding church leaders in the United States in promoting women to leadership positions in archdiocesan offices."

Casey established a Commission on the Status of Women to explore expanding roles for women in the Church. Real change came on March 9, 1970, when the archbishop au-

Sister Cecilia Linenbrink exemplified the novel missions of women religious after Vatican II. In 1964, she started a literacy and adult education program that has reached thousands. (Photo by Ralph Morgan.)

thorized distribution of communion by not only nuns but also lay women. At the same time, Casey made mass attendance easier by allowing Saturday afternoon and evening services to fulfill the obligation for Sunday masses.

Archbishop Casey raised eyebrows even higher when presenting his quinquennial report in Rome in 1983. He told Pope John Paul II, according to *The Denver Post* of November 8, 1983: "American sisters feel alienated and some anger, because they are treated in a paternalistic way by the church. They aren't treated as co-workers and with the dignity they deserve."

Denver's archbishop appointed Sister Loretto Anne Madden, SL, director of the Colorado Catholic Conference, which lobbies for the archdiocese at the state legislature. He named Sister Rosemary Wilcox assistant director of administration and planning, the first of many administrative posts she would hold in years to come.

Many nuns took advantage of the new worlds opened to them to accomplish much on many fronts. Sister Cecilia Linenbrink, OSF, at St. Elizabeth's in Denver, decided in 1964 to "take a new look at my own involvement with people in poverty areas—not so much to see what I could do, but what they needed." This Franciscan found that many Spanish-speaking people needed and wanted a high school education and English lessons. So Sister Cecilia founded the Adult Learning Source to prepare people to take the high school equivalency exam and earn a diploma. Hundreds took her course, and, by 1974, other churches, community centers, and schools had adopted it, using volunteer teachers to train 5,000 students in the first decade of Sister Cecilia's popular program.

The Dominican Sisters of the Sick Poor, who deal daily with depression, disease, and death, ham it up at their annual carnival. Amid the clowns raising money for their convent and health care center at 2501 Gaylord Street are sisters Joseph, Naomi, Marie, Therese, and Mary Grace.

In 1989, Sister Cecilia's program celebrated its twenty-fifth anniversary, having touched the lives of 27,000 students taught by more than 6,000 volunteers. Sister Cecilia, who holds a Ph.D. in education, is now executive director of the first and foremost Colorado group combating illiteracy, which she says afflicts one in five adults in the United States. "Most of these people just want to read," she told the *Denver Catholic Register* of December 23, 1987. "Some want to be able to read to their children and grandchildren. Others just want to read the newspaper."

Sister Julia Benjamin, OSF, took on one of the most difficult of tasks, reaching out to women who had fallen into prostitution. She became a "streetwalker" herself, passing out her card, with its butterfly logo and message of hope: "If you want to get off the street and out of prostitution, call Sister Julia at 455-9705 8 A.M. to 9 P.M." When women called, she offered them refuge at the Magdalen Damen House, formerly part of the Marycrest Convent at West 52nd Avenue and Decatur Street. Sister Julia, who earned a psychiatric social work M.A. at the University of Denver, has made working with street women and women in or out of jails and prisons her mission. "We've just received $92,000 in grants from the U.S. Department of Housing and Urban Development," she reported in 1988. "This will enable us to remodel facilities and expand our program so we can offer not just a shelter but extended treatment programs."

Sister Helen Falvo, OP, came to Denver in 1975 to coordinate the SUN program. Archbishop Casey was so impressed with her work that he appointed her vicar for women religious in 1979. The Colorado Council of Churches was likewise impressed with the work of this Dominican nun and in 1982 elected her its president; she spearheaded efforts at ecumenical cooperation until her untimely death in 1983.

Sister Ann Walter, OSB, archdiocesan archivist since 1981, opens to all comers that treasure chest of documents, manuscripts, photos, and publications, including these baptismal records, at the Pastoral Center. (Photo by James Baca.)

Sister Anna Koop, SL, founded the Catholic Worker House at 2420 Welton Street in 1979, offering housing, a soup line, and employment to the down and out. The Catholic Worker House put the unemployed into business making coffins in the Catholic Worker woodworking shop, which sells coffins for $210 to $225, "cremain" boxes for $30 to $84, and prayer benches for $15. Nicole Santisteven, a teenage correspondent for the *Denver Catholic Register*, reported in her October 28, 1987, column on volunteering at the Catholic Worker House Soup Kitchen, "I found it difficult to see Jesus in those people. . . . I smelled alcohol and dirt and it scared me." But, Nicole concluded, "we have to remember that Jesus is in the person who walks through the soup line as much as He is in the person who distributes the food."

Hundreds of nuns took on new projects. For most it was slow, hard work with little reward. But they made schools, parishes, hospitals, the chancery, and other institutions work. Sister Elizabeth Skiff, SC, for example, turned rooms filled with scattered boxes of documents into a usable repository after Archbishop Casey reorganized the archdiocesan archives in 1973. When Sister Elizabeth retired to the Sisters of Charity motherhouse in Cincinnati in 1981, Sister Ann Walter, OSB, stepped in to continue the archival mission of organizing, preserving, and providing public access to the priceless historical documents, photographs, manuscripts, records, and memorabilia beginning with Father Machebeuf's letters from 1860s Denver.

"Come in and see this fascinating corner of the chancery office," Sister Ann smiled in 1989. "Practically every day we get a new and unusual request and find some new jewel of information here, like the photo of the Münster Cathedral from Bishop Matz's cousin. It suggests that Matz had our basilica designed along the lines of his hometown cathedral."

When Archbishop Casey arrived in Denver in 1967, sisters served primarily as either teachers or nurses. By the 1980s, however, they filled a maze of different ministries. Sister Rosemary Wilcox recalled in a 1988 interview:

> During the 1970s, we sisters were first allowed to start making our own choices about what we would be trained for and what work we wanted to do. Archbishop Casey supported this idea. He was a shy but strong Irishman. He would listen to all the pros and cons, then make a decision "in the best long-run interests of the Church." He was willing to take the flack for his decisions and didn't get defensive when people attacked him.

Shortly before his death, Archbishop Casey declared, according to the *Denver Catholic Register* of March 14, 1986:

> I am sensitive to the fact that the changing role of women is hard for some to accept. Still, I hope that we can grow in our appreciation for the need and the beauty of their contribution. . . . I encourage all our people. . . to consider more seriously the tremendous possibilities for ministry in the Church by women and especially women religious. Their professional training, personal spirituality and unique talents contribute substantially to the church's vitality.

Perhaps the most dramatic achievement of a nun was a Herculean effort at housing the needy. This $25-million success story began after Martin Luther King was shot and killed at a Memphis motel on April 4, 1968. Archbishop Casey vowed to continue King's work, to do more for minorities and the poor. He set aside $1 million for this purpose and authorized his vicar general, Monsignor George Evans, to set up a housing program.

Evans had someone in mind. He had a talk with Sister Mary Lucy Downey, who had taken vows as a Sister of Charity of Leavenworth in 1954 and was teaching language arts and music to second graders at Annunciation School. This rosy-cheeked, twinkle-eyed daughter of a Butte, Montana, copper miner recalled in 1987:

Sister Mary Lucy Downey, SCL, founding director of the Archdiocesan Housing Committee, Inc., in 1968, oversaw a $30-million empire of HUD subsidized senior housing units by 1988.

> After creation of the Archdiocesan Housing Committee, Inc. [AHCI] on December 16, 1968, I was the first staff person. Everyone thought housing for the poor and elderly was a great idea—but not in their neighborhood. We lost seventeen court battles trying to build our first housing project.
>
> If only you could hear the stories of where some of our people were living—it would break your heart. Many of them are middle class people, widows who could be your own mom. They don't want or expect charity. They get stuck on the third story of a walkup and can barely get out. Or they are shuffled back and forth among relatives. Many live in substandard apartments with a shared bathroom down the hall or on another floor.

AHCI and Sister Mary Lucy completed the first project, a thirty-unit family complex at 801 South Monaco Parkway, in 1970, with the help of a $1,143,352 loan from the Metropolitan Life Insurance Company. This southeast Denver townhouse proved to be a successful prototype, a reasonably attractive development that blended into the neighborhood. By the end of 1970, three other low-income family housing sites were completed: twenty-six units at 3700 Humboldt; thirty units at 1900 South Raritan; and thirty units at 1300 South Irving. A second loan from Metropolitan Life in 1971 enabled AHCI to construct Glen Willow townhomes, a thirty-four-unit family project in Boulder.

Archdiocesan family housing achieved a turnover rate of about 25 percent. Most families moved out into private housing or became homeowners after finding or recovering their economic and social equilibrium. This track record encouraged the U.S. Department of Housing and Urban Development (HUD) to fund Sister Mary Lucy's next project, a senior citizen high-rise. This was the first church-sponsored project in America to be funded by HUD, according to Sister Mary Lucy, who noted:

With the hearty support of Pastor Jan Mucha, Globeville's St. Joseph Polish School has been converted to a senior residence. Some graduates, Father Mucha reports, have been tickled pink to find their old classrooms are now roomy apartments. (Photo by John Manos.)

Before we began planning Cathedral Plaza, we visited every high-rise—including the luxury residences—and every senior center in Denver to see what worked best. We discovered that it's best not to hide the laundry room in the basement but to put it on the top floor with a sunny view because it's prime socialization space.

We learned to color code each floor of a high-rise so residents don't become disoriented and embarrassed. Within the high-rises, we found it was important to have a beauty parlor, a lounge, recreation areas, and a clinic.

But the most important thing is to provide a sense of family, of belonging and of loving. HUD's idea of senior housing is just bricks and mortar—no emotional or social support. They prescribe only one person, a manager, but we've snuck in a staff of eight people to do programs at Cathedral Plaza, to make sure that our residents enjoy the highest possible quality of life.

Cathedral Plaza, located at 1575 Pennsylvania Street behind Immaculate Conception Cathedral, is a $4.5-million, eleven-story, 154-unit home that opened July 1, 1980. The elderly living there pay no more than a quarter of their monthly income for rent. Residents know each other because of the "buddy system" used in archdiocesan senior housing. If residents have not removed a crocheted ring from their door knobs by 10 A.M., their buddies investigate. Much of the work at Cathedral Plaza, the sister explained, is done by forty to fifty resident volunteers who handle such tasks as manning the front desk, setting table, cleaning up, and housekeeping. Sister Mary Lury elaborated:

> This enables the nun whom HUD pays as our "janitor" to spend her time arranging social programs, classes, tours, and other activities. On birthdays we have a special celebration of life and interview the celebrity. We have so many wonderful people here with so many fascinating life stories. We're afraid we'll lose them before we really get to know them.

Cathedral Plaza soon had a long waiting list of would-be residents, which Sister Mary Lucy used to sell HUD on the next project. On April 23, 1981, AHCI completed a second HUD-sponsored senior high rise, Holy Family Plaza in the Holy Family church and school complex at 4300 Vrain Street in North Denver. This five-story, $4.5-million, 120-unit home has become an integral part of the two-block parish complex. Father Lawrence St. Peter, who as pastor of Holy Family welcomed the senior residence, told the story in "The Great Intergenerational Get-Together," in the February 1985 issue of *Today's Parish*. "The most exciting part of the Holy Family story," he wrote, "concerns parish efforts to integrate the Plaza residents into the total life of the parish." The seniors are urged to become "grandparents" for preschoolers, to supervise them on the playground, tell them stories, show them how to do crafts, and give them one-on-one attention. In Holy Family Grade School, Plaza residents serve as tutors for spelling, penmanship, reading, and other subjects. High schoolers learn oral history by interviewing residents and then staging "This Is Your Life" parties.

Sister Marie de Lourdes Falk, SCL, the director of Holy Family Plaza, also directs daily dances. "We dance with anybody," she boasted: "We dance alone, with each other, with the eighth graders and high schoolers. We've even gone out on the road to show other senior residents how to dance. It's splendid sociability and great exercise."

Before the dances, Mae Padilla is swamped in "Mae's Angel Fingers Beauty Salon," the Plaza's "Place to Get a Faith Lift." Photographs of residents adorn the walls by the elevators to promote sociability; exercycles on each floor foster dance-floor mobility. The parquet oak dance-floor in Holy Family Plaza looks well-used, as do the walking trails outside. High school students in Holy Family's "Understanding the Elderly" class take residents for walks and talks. "Those high schoolers," Sister Marie de Lourdes reported, "have been able to get people up and out of here who thought they would never walk again. In exchange, our residents teach high schoolers how to play bridge, do crafts, and—of course—how to dance!"

Sister Theresa Madden, SL, of Denver's famous Madden clan of politicians, policemen, priests, saloonkeepers, and Sisters of Loretto, administered the third AHCI-HUD high-rise, Marian Plaza, a $4.2-million, eleven-story, 120-unit senior residence at 1818 Marion Street. "Marian Plaza is a beautiful building," Sister Theresa bragged during our 1987 interview.

> We have a roof deck for sunning and mountain viewing behind our crenelated roofline, a whirlpool bath and a beauty shop, but most beautiful of all are the people here. We have both residents and senior day care clients, who for $15 a day get health monitoring, physical exercise classes, physical therapy, educational programs, nutritional meals, recreation, and socialization.

AHCI's successes in Denver led the Diocese of Cheyenne to enlist its aid in constructing St. Anthony Manor, a $3-million, sixty-four–unit senior residence in Casper, which opened in July 1984. Another Wyoming senior residence, the $1.4-million Holy Trinity Manor scheduled to open in 1989 in Cheyenne, will be managed by AHCI. Other AHCI-HUD projects have included St. Martin's Plaza, a $2.4 million, eight-story senior residence opened in 1988 at Marion Street and Bruce Randolph Avenue. The city of Denver provided the land, giving AHCI a ninety-nine–year lease for $1, and Mayor Federico Peña joined Sister Mary Lucy at the groundbreaking on August 13, 1987, when he praised her "faith and commitment." Madonna Plaza, a three-story, fifty-unit residence, is scheduled to open in 1989 at East 62nd Avenue and Kearney Street in Commerce City. In East Denver at East 14th Avenue and Detroit Street, Higgins Plaza—with ninety independent living and eighteen assisted living units—is projected to open in 1990 on the site of the demolished St. Philomena Church.

Thus, Sister Mary Lucy became landlord of a $30-million housing operation and a certified property manager and real estate broker, who was elected the 1988 president of the Colorado Association of Homes and Services for the Aging. Besides being executive director of AHCI and Housing Management Services, Inc., for the Archdiocese of Denver, she served in 1987–1988 as president of the association of HUD Managing Agents for Region VIII and as a national representative of the American Association of Homes for the Aging.

"Just before he died," Sister Mary Lucy confided in 1987, "Archbishop Casey urged us to pursue our housing mission and talked about the need for nursing homes. I have been blessed to continue the work that he and Bishop Evans began in 1968."

Founded as an orphanage in 1883 by the Sisters of Charity of Leavenworth, Mount St. Vincent Home in North Denver remains a refuge for troubled youths, who can wash away their troubles there.

In 1967, the Franciscan sisters closed St. Clara's Orphanage between West 26th and 29th avenues on Osceola Street. With the support of long-time benefactors such as Ernie Capillupo, proprietor of Ernie's Restaurant & Lounge, the sisters converted the orphanage to the John XXIII Center for retreats and meetings as well as a coffeehouse for youth. In 1972, the old orphanage was demolished and replaced by Francis Heights and Clare Gardens. Francis Heights is two high-rise residences for the elderly on what had been the orphanage athletic field. Residents of its 400 independent living units benefit from the Federal Rent Supplement Assistance funding of the 1968 Housing Act. Next door, Clare Gardens opened in 1973 as 128 subsidized family townhouses. The old orphanage gym is still used as a recreation center, and the two-story St. Clara's Orphanage bell tower was likewise preserved as a link with the past.

Together with the new housing facilities built by AHCI during the 1970s and 1980s, Clare Gardens, Francis Heights, St. Elizabeth Center, Mullen Home, and St. Joseph Home made the archdiocese a leader in housing the increasing percentage of the population who find themselves old and poor.

For homeless and troubled children, Mount St. Vincent Home has been a haven ever since February 15, 1883, when the Sisters of Charity of Leavenworth opened the orphanage at 4159 Lowell Boulevard. Sister Daniel Stefani, SCL, director of Mount St. Vincent's, reported in 1988 that

> since 1969 we have specialized in treating children with emotional, social, and academic difficulties. Over the course of the last 105 years, we have adapted our program to the changing needs of child care. Today the six sisters working here care for forty-five children in a resident program and sixteen in day treatment. We have a school and recreation program aimed at preparing children to return to their families or to foster homes and to community schools.

To celebrate their 105th anniversary in 1988, the Sisters of Charity opened another home, the Ryan Residence at 11485 West Exposition Avenue in Lakewood, for boys aged eleven to eighteen. A married couple supervise this operation in a conventional suburban ranch house, from which youngsters attend community schools and recreational facilities.

Archbishop Casey's last great project was housing for the homeless. Back in 1959, Monsignor Mulroy had suggested converting the Welcome Hotel at 1830 Larimer Street into a shelter for homeless men but dropped the idea after Archbishop Vehr and the St. Vincent de Paul Society showed little financial interest. Archbishop Casey proved to be more sympathetic; he earned his reputation as a gentle and good shepherd when unusually cold, snowy winters and the oil bust of 1983 exacerbated the situation in Denver. An estimated 1,750 were homeless and as many as 200 slept overnight on the pews in Holy Ghost Church. Hundreds more slept on office tower ventilation exhaust grates, in alley dumpsters and doorways, and in cardboard and newspaper nests under the Cherry Creek and South Platte River bridges.

The desperate plight of the homeless led Archbishop Casey to initiate a $50,000 crusade to convert Central Catholic High School to a shelter. The old basement cafeteria, which ninety years earlier had been the procathedral, was converted to a food line and 122-bed dormitory for men. A former classroom became a thirty-one-bed women's dormitory. Several second-floor classrooms were converted into quarters for families, with a nearby classroom recycled as a playroom.

On the night it opened in the old Cathedral High School, the Samaritan Shelter was swamped with homeless men, women, and children. (Photo by James Baca.)

Two other classrooms became storage areas for used clothing while another became a "store" where shelter residents could select secondhand clothing from racks and shelves marked small, medium, and large. In another former classroom, a resource center was launched to provide classes and materials and volunteer counseling on how to cope with poverty, alcoholism, drugs, and finding a job.

On Samaritan Shelter's opening night, November 8, 1983, it quickly reached maximum capacity of 175 men, women, and children and had to turn away more than 100 persons. In exchange for serving food with other volunteers, Samaritan Shelter supervisor Dorothy Leonard gave me a tour one night. This tall, trim young woman explained that the line outside on Logan Street consisted of applicants for the "first come, first served" numbered beds. The large number of applicants allowed the "Samaritan Sheraton" to turn down drunks and troublemakers. Applicants were screened for weapons, drugs, and liquor. Rejects were pointed in the direction of the Denver Rescue Mission at 23rd and Lawrence streets and the Salvation Army's "shelter of last resort" at 2141 Larimer Street.

Multimillion dollar negotiations with the developers of 1999 Broadway behind Holy Ghost Chruch, enabled the archdiocese to undertake projects such as the Samaritan House. (Photo by Glenn Cuerden.)

Once admitted to the "Samaritan Sheraton," homeless men, women, and children were allowed to stay up to twenty-eight days, provided they returned by 7 o'clock every evening for the free dinner. "If they're not here by then," Dorothy Leonard said, "their bed is given to someone else." After a free breakfast, guests were required to leave by 8 A.M. to look for work, while the staff and volunteers prepared the inn for the next evening.

"Our goal," Leonard said,

> is to get people back into jobs and their own living quarters. Many of our people have drug or mental problems. The main thing is just to talk to them, help them get over their difficulties and the shock of being here. We try to get them out and into happier situations but about 50 percent of our people ask for an extension—a second twenty-eight-day stay.

Although Dorothy must have been disappointed to see former residents return, she greeted several by their names, using both Spanish and English, with a hug for the children.

While showing me the free "store" piled high with old clothes and shoes, Dorothy explained, "We sort this out using the criteria of keeping only what we would wear ourselves. We get so many clothes here that we ship some to other shelters, to Indian reservations, and to Mexico."

Following its 1983 opening, the Samaritan Shelter captured local and national media attention in *People Magazine*, *The Wall Street Journal*, and on ABC television's "Nightline." Reverend Charles B. Woodrich, who had accepted homeless in his Holy Ghost Church and helped open Samaritan Shelter, became a public champion of the poor. Both local and national media broadcast his message, as quoted in *The Denver Post*, November 14, 1984:

> A city is more than new soaring skyscrapers filled in the day and emptied by evening. It is people, a milling mix of diversity, that give a city its soul, that bring life to the architecture and the commerce. The rich and the poor are all part of the landscape although the poor are too often unfairly and summarily dismissed as useless, bereft of ambition and content with the minimum needed to sustain life. Our Samaritan Shelter has a different bottom line—one that stresses a caring, human dimension to restore the personal dignity of those who have been denied a sense of self-worth.

Samaritan Shelter, which was overcrowded and inadequate from the night it opened but still the "Sheraton" of homes for the homeless, concerned Casey. Federal, state, and local governments, which once had made the homeless a concern, all backed away from the problem. When the archdiocese received a windfall—$8.5 million for the air rights

Father Woody, champion of the homeless, received an honorary doctorate from University of Colorado's president E. Gordon Gee in 1986 and appointment as a monsignor in 1988. (Photo by James Baca.)

and land next to Holy Ghost Church—Casey knew what to do with it. With $2.4 million from the developers of the Holy Ghost property, he purchased the block of land bounded by Larimer, Lawrence, 23rd, and 24th streets.

Despite his fragile health, Casey made his last major public appearance at the July 31, 1985, groundbreaking for Samaritan House, wearing a sombrero for the festivities. The ailing archbishop declared: "The thing I'm proudest about is the fact that Samaritan House is . . . welcoming every person who comes through that door with the dignity of a child of God."

Barker, Rinker, Seacat & Associates, the Denver architects who had designed several archdiocesan housing projects, were asked to create a dignified, elegant home that would, by its quality, refresh its residents. Samaritan House opened November 22, 1986, at 2301 Lawrence. The red brick structure with a landscaped courtyard contained 125 beds for men, forty-five for women, and eighty for families, as well as a chapel, recreation rooms, and offices. Father William Kraus, a young Kansas farmboy who had joined the Capuchins, became the first full-time director, in 1984, of the old Samaritan Shelter and also directed the new Samaritan House. During a 1988 tour and interview, he told me:

> This time, for a change, the poor get to go first class! Usually shelters are recycled old buildings unwanted for anything else so they become human warehouses. This is the first home in the U.S. to be designed as a shelter. San Diego began work on a new shelter before we did but didn't complete their $11 million, 400-bed mission-style shelter until 1987.
>
> Here we have an attractive building with a roomy outdoor deck occupying much of the second floor. Our Chapel of St. Francis is open twenty-four hours every day for quiet prayer, meditation, or just getting away from it all.
>
> Samaritan House shows that the Denver archdiocese is serious about preferential options for the poor. And Isaiah reminds us that when we shelter the homeless our own wounds are healed, our prayers are heard, and our light shines. Therefore our new home not only ministers to the needy but also enriches all who care for the poor.

During 1987, its first full year, Samaritan House relied heavily on 300 volunteers to achieve a remarkable record:

- 14,020 persons housed
- 778,200 meals served
- 2,986 medical clinic visits
- 364 dental clinic visits
- 47 families helped to self-sufficiency
- 1,165 enrolled in jobs program
- 411 full-time work placements

"The worst thing about operating Samaritan House," said Father Kraus, "is having to turn people away on nights when it's blizzarding outside. Fortunately, Central Presbyterian and Central Baptist churches have also now opened their basements to the homeless on the worst nights."

"The best thing," Father Kraus added,

> is that we are able to place almost a third of our residents in full-time jobs that enable them to return to a normal living situation. About a third of our residents are mentally ill, and we work with Catholic Community Services, the Denver Department of Social Services, and the Veterans Administration—half of our men are veterans—to get them treatment. We've

never had any real trouble here, although we have to kick someone out about once a week for disturbances. People are really appreciative of this shelter. They form a good, caring community that will come to the rescue of our staff when we get into trouble.

The new Samaritan House incorporates many of the rules and procedures worked out earlier at Samaritan Shelter. If they pass entry screening, new residents are registered, given a bed, a locker, and a cosmetic case with tooth brush, tooth paste, and shaving gear. They are asked to shower each morning. On their first day as residents, newcomers are required to work in the kitchen or on maintenance at Samaritan House. After thus getting acquainted with their new "family," they are given job counseling and sent out to look for employment.

Father Kraus adds, "If you need snow shoveling, grass mowing, house painting, leaf raking, or whatever, give us a call at Samaritan House. We suggest you pay at least $5 an hour. Even better, we hope to get our people into full-time permanent jobs. Samaritan House is just trying to get people back onto their feet."

Samaritan House was only the best-known of many projects launched during the Casey years. The archbishop elaborated on his concerns in the *Denver Catholic Register* of April 28, 1982: "We discover Our Lord in other people, and we love Him and help Him in serving the poor and afflicted. . . . Christ walks on every street and He expects us to recognize him. He is found in our nursing homes, in our prisons, in our hospitals, in our schools, among our neighbors."

Casey's commitment to the poorest of his flock led to the mushrooming of the small Catholic Charities office that Monsignor Mulroy had launched in 1927. Following the death of Monsignor Elmer Kolka, the second director of Catholic Charities, Archbishop Casey appointed William J. Monahan the third director in 1969. Monahan, the first trained master of social work to head Catholic Charities, closed Ave Maria Clinic and dropped the neighborhood health clinic approach. Instead, the sick poor were steered to the updated outpatient facilities in the three Catholic hospitals as well as to the neighborhood clinics opened in the 1960s by Denver's Department of Health and Hospitals.

Catholic Community Services was restructured in 1971 to create offices in Colorado Springs and Northern Colorado as well as Denver. Donald Dunn, Monsignor Monahan's assistant director, replaced him at the helm in 1974. Father Dunn found his office swamped with indigent needy. "The needs are so immense we are barely able to keep up," he told *The Denver Post* of January 24, 1975. "We give about $1,500 a month in direct aid to persons for food, shelter, clothing, help with back rent and utility payments."

With encouragement from Archbishop Casey and Bishop Evans, Dunn, in 1976, set up the Office of Justice and Peace. Inspired by Pope Paul VI's declaration, "If you want peace first you must seek justice," this office tackled issues ranging from discrimination to renter's rights, from protesting the toxic waste and nuclear weapons produced at Rocky Flats to the high drop-out rate among Hispanic students.

Father Dunn also served as a national director of Catholic Charities, U.S.A., before leaving CCS in 1974, when he turned the agency over to James H. Mauck, the first lay director. Mauck, after earning his masters in social work at St. Louis University in 1965, went to work for Catholic Charities in his hometown of Wheeling, West Virginia, where he served as director from 1968 to 1974.

"I applied for the Denver job," Mauck explained in a 1987 interview, "because Father Dunn and his predecessors had made Denver a nationally noted leader in Catholic Charity work. Dunn had pioneered a model parish outreach system and expanded the immigration program set up by Monsignor Monahan."

With the help of Father Dunn, who stayed with CCS until he left for the Monteria Mission in 1983, Mauck undertook to maintain and refine the ambitious CCS agenda. The Social Concerns Office, an outgrowth of the social activism of the 1960s and 1970s, strove to empower community and neighborhood groups to meet their own needs through community organizing, the parish social ministries, and an emergency assistance program. The last supplied food, clothing, housing, and friendship through various parish, outreach, and neighborhood assistance centers. It included programs such as the Food Bank Coalition and Operation Rice Bowl, which attempted to collect food and funds at the parish level. As of 1988, the archdiocese operated eight Emergency Assistance Centers.

Family and Children Services of CCS consisted of Youth Ministry Services, Senior Centers, Marriage Preparation, and the Separated/Widowed/Divorced Ministry. With the closing of many Catholic schools, the archdiocese inaugurated several youth programs during the 1970s, including Catholic Youth Services, Hispanic Youth Ministry, Original Scene Theater program, and youth programs in each parish, while Camp St. Malo and Camp Santa Maria continued to be used as archdiocesan summer camps. Marriage preparation instruction at the parish level was also launched during the 1970s, as were ministries to counsel and comfort separated, divorced, widowed, and single Catholics.

The CCS Senior Centers program is directed by Ralph Lowder, who first went to work for the archdiocese in 1956 as a counselor at Vail Center. Senior Centers work with existing facilities (the Mullen Home, Clare Gardens, St. Elizabeth Center, and the new AHCI residences). Senior Centers also had a contract with the Denver Housing Authority (DHA) to operate Mulroy Senior Center at 3550 West 13th Avenue, a residence that the DHA erected in 1969 and named for one of its founding fathers—

Monsignor Mulroy. Senior Services also operates the Alcott Senior Center at 3850 Alcott Street in a five-story senior home built by the DHA in 1980. Senior Centers opened the old St. Joseph School at 4626 Pennsylvania Street in the 1970s as St. Joseph Home for active and independent living. A senior camp was established at Camp Santa Maria in the autumn, after school began for youngsters. CCS Senior Services encouraged John Q. O'Connell, CM, who since 1969 has been offering a television mass for the sick and shut-in. Channel 2 carries this 7 A.M. Sunday mass for Father O'Connell's flock, which numbered around 30,000 viewers by 1988.

Ralph Lowder reported in 1987 that the senior services include pot-luck suppers, health screening, counseling, transportation, exercise classes, arts and crafts, friendly visiting, telephone reassurance, recreation, and information and referral services. Lowder observed that "Catholic Commmunity Services has been providing senior services ever since the 1930s at centers such as Little Flower, St. Anthony's, and Vail, long before senior centers became common in the 1960s."

As the man behind the mushrooming of Catholic Community Services, Archbishop Casey gave much time to thinking about social concerns and putting them into eloquent homilies and written statements. As he once said, "I must speak out, to remain silent would go against everything I believe." Mrs. Frank McGlone, a neighbor and close friend, confided, in a 1987 interview:

> The archbishop was a brilliant, shy, considerate man, really concerned more than most people realized. He loved learning, always surrounded himself with books. Thomas Merton was one of his favorite authors. He got up early and worked late in his home office, putting deep thinking and concern into his homilies and his pastoral letters. He would meditate for five to ten minutes on a homily even if it were only a mass in his home for us and our children and grandchildren.

The McGlones and Archbishop Casey built neighboring homes on South Columbine Lane in the Columbine Valley neighborhood on the western edge of Littleton. Casey paid for the house with money he had inherited from his family, refusing to use archdiocesan funding. "The archbishop largely designed the house himself," recalls Doctor McGlone. "He built in a small swimming pool for lap swimming. He called me his 'athletic director' and framed my prescription for him—morning and evening swimming and twice-a-week golfing. This helped him cope with the pressures of his job," McGlone added. "He said he loved golf because people didn't treat him like an archbishop on the course."

Casey also enjoyed driving around his archdiocese, relishing the anonymity of the open road on drives to visit outlying parishes. He brought a black Lincoln with him from

Nebraska but swapped it in 1973 for a new dark blue Lincoln Continental Mark III, which he drove until 1981. Then he purchased a black Buick Rivera, followed in 1985 by his last car, a white Lincoln Continental. There were times when he could not drive those cars through the streets of Denver, when at the urging of police he traveled in unmarked cars to avoid radical confrontations. No matter how bad things got, Casey always reserved Wednesdays for golf with his cronies—McGlone, Jim Lannon, and Pete Smythe.

Smythe, a popular radio and television personality, recalled later:

He was a good man and so good to me and for me. It didn't matter that I was a non-Catholic. He called me the agnostic and we called him the Arch. He always had a twinkle in his eye and could figure out a situation and relate to all kinds of people better than anyone I've known.

Casey learned from and appreciated Smythe as a consummate media man and began a series of KLDR talk radio appearances. Casey also continued and expanded televison coverage of the midnight Christmas mass at Immaculate Conception. He welcomed media coverage, declaring, "Too often the Good News of Jesus Christ has been drowned out by the sheer volume of the consumer gospel."

Archbishop Casey eloquently addressed the issues of his time. Of Vatican II, he said, according to the *Register* of May 11, 1967:

There will be many changes in the church and changes bring confusion. But confusion, we must realize, is an unhappy but necessary by-product of any revolution; and the church is in the midst of a revolution. This is the early dawn of a new day with its chilly mists and grey skies, but noon-day will bring the warm, clear rays of sunlight.

In a 1970 letter to Richard M. Nixon, Casey respectfully urged the president "to set a definite date for the withdrawal of our American military personnel from Vietnam at the earliest possible moment." President Nixon replied in a friendly letter, saying he was negotiating a peace treaty. Denver's archbishop became one of the first American bishops to take a strong and controversial stance against America's intervention in the Vietnamese civil war. A year before the U.S. Conference of Bishops denounced militarism, Casey condemned nuclear war in his statement, *Human Life and War*:

Life is what our religious faith is all about; and war remains the greatest threat to human life. The Divine imperative: "thou shalt not kill" lies at the heart of the dialogue on human life.

Let us all join our voices with Pope Paul VI and cry out to the world: "No more war; war never again."

On another occasion, the archbishop declared that:

This nuclear madness drains precious human resources and captivates our society in an endless maintenance of illusory "balance of terror." Quite simply, the people of the world are crying for food and health care, not for sophisticated, expensive weapon systems; they are crying for justice, not for a phony "security" based on the threat of international violence; they are begging for peace, not for endless displays of diplomatic brinksmanship.

The federal government eventually heeded the protests of its citizens and of such outspoken leaders as Archibishop Casey, withdrawing troops from Vietnam in 1973. When peace came, Archbishop Casey created the Immigration and Resettlement Office to help find homes for hundreds of war babies, and homes and jobs for refugees. Thus, Casey not only fought against an unjust war, he helped heal wounds and resettle victims when peace came.

To the end, Casey was a protestor. In the spring of 1978, he issued a pastoral letter calling for the conversion of the nuclear weapons plant at Rocky Flats to peaceful purposes. When President Ronald Reagan proposed his MX missile building program, Casey, according to the *Rocky Mountain News* of September 20, 1983, condemned it as "an escalation of the arms race which is unwise, unjustified and will be counterproductive."

Casey was not without his detractors. Widely publicized attacks by militant Hispanics included persistent criticism from Joseph Lara, pastor of Denver's Our Lady of Guadalupe Church until he left the priesthood. Some members of the United Mexican American Students, August 1969, demanded Casey's resignation after he rejected their demand for $100,000 in scholarships. When Casey agreed to administer a $40,000 grant from the National Catholic Campaign for Human Development to Corky Gonzales' Crusade for Justice, he was criticized for catering to radicals. Archbishop Casey, it seemed, was "damned if he did and damned if he didn't."

Despite much painful publicity and embarrassing personal attacks, Casey continued to meet with Chicanos, agonized over their complaints, and tried to establish helpful agencies. In 1968, he created the Archdiocesan Office of Hispanic Concerns and in 1981 raised that office to the vicariate level. Eugenio Cañas was appointed the first vicar for Hispanics, who made up roughly a third of Colorado's Catholic population.

Archbishop Casey, here fishing Black Lake, guided Colorado Catholics through troubled times. He wrote "The voice from the pew is asking church leaders for commitment to the human person, to the poor and afflicted, to the oppressed and the deprived and the disadvantaged."

Casey's dogged efforts were rewarded, as Celia Vigil, archdiocesan director of Hispanic concerns, later recalled:

I saw the archbishop grow from a person who feared the Chicano community to a real shepherd who was concerned about all of his flock. . . . He was very concerned about the exodus of Hispanics from the Catholic Church. The people loved having the archbishop as the celebrant at their annual mass for the feast of Our Lady of Guadalupe. . . . The moment I will treasure is when he asked me for a hug.

The civil rights movement found an early supporter in Archbishop Casey, who wrote in 1966:

In the midst of unparalleled prosperity, American Negro people [suffer] degrading poverty [and] are denied equality in seeking jobs and housing for their families as well as the use of educational and recreational facilities. . . . Catholics[who] were themselves descendants of immigrants are today beneficiaries of the equality and opportunity enjoyed in this country. Yet their cup of hate ran over as they sought to deny this same freedom and opportunity to the Negro American. These suffering, disadvantaged minority people are the real challenge of our day.

Acting against the advice of some who felt Denver had too many small, struggling parishes, Casey allowed blacks to operate their own parish, Curé D'Ars on Martin Luther King Boulevard, smiling on the "soul" masses which used black musical traditions. Despite some protests from traditionalists, the lively Curé D'Ars choir is now in demand at many other parishes. In 1972, Archbishop Casey authorized the creation of Ascension parish in the new northeast neighborhood of Montbello. Thus, he supported the only neighborhood in Colorado that was conceived, planned, and developed to be fully integrated, open to blacks, browns, whites, and anyone else.

Archbishop Casey often spoke of the Christian, rather than just the Catholic community, emphasizing the commonality, not the differences, among Christians. Under Casey, the archdiocese first joined the ecumenical alliance known as the Colorado Council of Churches. In 1969, the Colorado Conference of the United Church of America named Casey its "Churchman of the Year," giving its award to a Catholic for the first time.

Shortly before his death, Casey startled some Catholics by allowing participation in the Reverend Billy Graham's 1987 Denver Crusade. The preaching of this famous Southern Baptist, Casey explained, helped focus attention on problems of concern to all

Christians. At a joint Protestant–Catholic Prayer Service, Casey spoke on "the scandal of Christian disunity":

> Christ desires unity in His Church. . . . What we must do now is to make ourselves worthy of the gift of unity. The success of ecumenism is measured by the depth of self-renewal it inspires in us. The road ahead to unity is long and difficult, but we are unafraid.

Stephen Singular, a star Denver scribe, interviewed Casey for the December 1981 *Denver Magazine*. Singular reported that the archbishop's "face is sober and shows a long life of sacrifice and service. His mouth is downturned and sad and there is a perpetual strain around his eyes." Casey told Singular, "I see the problems of the church . . . all the money and personnel problems . . . much more than the joys of the Catholic Community. . . . I may not have done a very good job at times, but at least my life was centered on eternal and spiritual values."

The archbishop then presented the central theme of his Denver years:

> As a Catholic in the 1940s and '50s, you could feel that if you didn't eat meat on Friday and went to Mass on Sunday and took the sacraments once a year, then you were a saint. . . . People loved to be dependent and just let the priests be responsible for them. Today, it has become much more complex. Each person must look inside himself and make moral and religious decisions in every aspect of his life. This takes maturity and a sense of responsibility and a growing up on the part of the laity.

While golfing on October 27, 1984, Casey burst a major blood vessel in his abdomen. Recovering from this near-fatal blow, he contracted hepatitis in the hospital. When he returned to work on April 18, 1985, his baggy black suit, loose clerical collar, and wizened visage suggested he would never really recover. Yet, the archbishop began planning for the 1987 centennial of the archdiocese. He suggested that a history of each parish be written for the centennial, which he described as "an opportunity to reflect on our faith, and particularly on the history of the faith as it has grown and flourished in Colorado."

Archbishop Casey did not live to see the centennial year. On March 1, 1986, the seventy-one-year-old archbishop was found unconscious in his bedroom. A blood clot the size of a lemon was removed from his brain the next day during a four-hour operation at St. Joseph Hospital. The stricken prelate received hundreds of prayers and letters, including one from David Beaudoin, a third-grader at Risen Christ Parish in Denver:

O my God. Pleas make bishop Casey better. Care for him. With all your hart. If he dies, put him in hevin.

Casey would have chuckled over that, but he never regained consciousness. After receiving the last rites from Father Lawrence St. Peter, the gentle shepherd died at 11:47 A.M., March 14, 1986. His last letter was to the state legislature, urging passage of a bill to provide potable water and portable toilets for migrant workers.

Banks of yellow and white flowers against a backdrop of Lenten purple did little to cheer mourners squeezing into the cathedral, where Casey's body lay in state for three days. On the third day—Friday, March 21, 1986—Archbishop Pio Laghi, apostolic nuncio to the United States, officiated at the mass of Christian Burial. Protestant clergy, rabbis, and Orthodox bishops joined thirty-two of Casey's fellow bishops for the rite. Reverend Edward Hoffmann, Casey's former chauffeur, secretary, and chancellor, flew home from Rome to deliver the homily:

Archibshop Casey was patient and compassionate, even when I lost his Bronco season tickets—which is a mortal sin worthy of special condemnations. He invited others to be involved in the programs he began. How much easier it would have been to select a small group, a chosen few, to perform and thus avoid the uncertainties and difficulties that inevitably rise when breaking new ground. Archbishop Casey's programs are not just his—they are ours because of his confidence in us.

A chorus of Coloradans, clerics and laity alike, shared their thoughts. Denver's mayor, Federico Peña, said, "As Archbishop Casey lived, so he died, with dignity, grace and courage. . . .The archbishop was a true and natural leader who fought for the causes of justice, humanity and goodness. The city of Denver mourns him."

Vicar General Michael Chamberlain reflected on his experiences of working closely with the archbishop. "He was always around when you needed him. If you had something personal to talk about he'd be there. He was just an incredibly understanding person. . . . He wasn't a person who took himself too seriously. . . . He knew when to be a boss and when not to be."

William C. Frey, Episcopal bishop of Colorado added that:

The whole Christian community has lost a great friend and a great leader. . . . I think he was the most unassuming archbishop I've ever known. There was a deep simplicity and spirituality to him which was very winsome and impressive. . . . The monuments to him are not etched in bronze and stone, but they are alive in the poor and the hope for justice and peace.

Governor Richard D. Lamm of Colorado concluded:

There aren't many people I would call inspired or inspiring, but I've watched Archbishop Casey's career and seen the impressive way he joined people of all faiths in working towards common goals. What he believed was the wellspring of everything he did. He didn't just talk about the relevance of religious belief, he lived it.

Archbishop James Francis Stafford. (Photo by Larkin.)

CHAPTER 6

IN THE BEGINNING THE WORD

STAFFORD: SCHOLAR AND SOCIAL WORKER, 1986–

Denver's sixth bishop and third archbishop came from Baltimore, the hometown of Catholicism in the United States. Maryland, one of the few English colonies to welcome Catholics, became the first Catholic community. After the American Revolution, Baltimore became the seat of the first bishop and, later, of the second cardinal in the United States.

Archbishop Stafford's grandfather, an immigrant from Dungannon in Northern Ireland, opened a furniture store in 1902. The archbishop's father, Emmett, worked in this family business until his retirement in 1980, five years before his death. Stafford & Brothers is still in business in West Baltimore, operated by the archbishop's uncle and cousins.

James Francis Stafford was born July 26, 1932, the only child of Emmett and Mary Dorothy (Stanton) Stafford. The youngster excelled at St. Joseph Monastery Grade School, where his third-grade teacher, Sister Mary Pacifica, SSND, recalled in 1986 that Frank was "responsible and studious . . . a natural leader. . . always trying very, very hard . . . he always wanted to do things perfectly."

Raised in the West Baltimore suburb of Catonsville, Stafford attended Loyola High School, where friends remembered him for his loyalty. Once, when a chum was hospitalized with polio in an isolation ward, Frank "borrowed" two cassocks from his parish church so he and another friend could visit the hospital without interference. Boyhood pals, reported the *Denver Catholic Register* on July 30, 1986, said that Stafford's face "has always been a barometer. The redder it gets the more intense his feelings."

After high school, Frank Stafford entered Loyola College in Baltimore as a premedical student. The death of a close friend in a car crash and the guidance of his Jesuit teachers, however, led him to rethink his life. Subsequently, he entered St. Mary's Seminary in Baltimore in 1952, going to Rome two years later to complete a bachelor's degree in sacred theology at the North American College. He was ordained by Bishop Martin J. O'Connor in Rome on December 15, 1957, at the age of twenty-five.

Father Stafford returned to Baltimore where he began parish work. In 1964, his concern for social justice led the young priest to complete a master's degree in social work at the Catholic University of America, writing his thesis on foster care of children. To learn more about the poor, the 5-foot-8-inch, 170-pound priest lived and worked in core city parishes, also serving as the chaplain for the Villa Maria home for disturbed children. Even after his elevation to the rank of auxiliary bishop, which entitled him to live in a large home with a housekeeping staff, Stafford chose to live in a rectory in one of Baltimore's poorest neighborhoods.

When Baltimore businessmen pressured him to move a soup kitchen to another neighborhood, saying it drove their customers away, Stafford stood his ground. "This is where these people are," he told protesters, "and we have to come to where they are to serve them." In his native archdiocese, Stafford served as the associate director (1964–1966) and then as the director (1966–1976) of Associated Catholic Charities, and on numerous church and civil boards.

Father Stafford became Monsignor Stafford on September 8, 1970, and was consecrated an auxiliary bishop of Baltimore on February 29, 1976, in the Cathedral of Mary Our Queen. On January 17, 1983, he was installed as the second bishop of the diocese of Memphis in Tennessee. When Stafford was tapped to become archbishop of Denver, the *Tennessee Catholic Register* of August 4, 1986, praised him for giving "direction, strength, piety and trust to the 45,000 Catholics in the state's 21 western counties." In this southern Bible Belt city with many poor blacks, the *Tennessee Register* complimented Bishop Stafford on

> forthright policies asserting the dignity, and demanding justice for all . . . with the unique ingredient of his own gifted, compassionate, and gentle personality. . . . Together with the Bishop of Nashville, he urged state officials to recognize and rectify—Tennessee's wretchedly deficient progress in aiding poor families with dependent children.

After Archbishop Casey's death in March 1986, six priest consultors were appointed to elect an administrator to guide the archdiocese until Pope John Paul II selected a new

archbishop. This team of priests chose Lawrence St. Peter, the archdiocesan vicar for
priests and pastor of Mother of God Church.

"I was honored and surprised to be
elected administrator," Father St. Peter said in
a December 29, 1987, interview:

Father Lawrence St. Peter administered the archdiocese between the time of Casey's death and
Stafford's arrival. (Photo by James Baca.)

> I tried to keep things going, not to make any
> great changes and prepare the way for a new
> archbishop while fifteen cardinals in Rome
> made the final decision for Denver. We were
> delighted with how quickly Rome acted and
> with their choice of Archbishop Stafford. I
> helped the new archbishop move in. We un-
> packed three solid walls of books. I opened some of them and found they were underlined,
> with notes scribbled in the margins. The archbishop's library is extensive and very well used.
> He is a scholar.

Soon after his June 3, 1986 appointment to Denver, the new archbishop visited the
Gallagher Memorial at Mt. Olivet Cemetery to pay his respects to his predecessors,
bishops Machebeuf, Matz, and Tihen and archbishops Vehr and Casey. At their tombs,
archbishop Stafford meditated on his own career, then turned to Father St. Peter to ask,
"Which niche have you reserved for me?"

"As for my plans for Denver," Archbishop Stafford told the *Denver Catholic Register*
of June 11, 1986, "I do not carry a suitcase full of pastoral blueprints. Usually I strive for
two hallmarks in my ministry: compassion and fidelity. Compassion means among other
things to listen attentively to the priests and the people of the church, to learn about your
history, current vision and mission."

On July 30, 1986, 1,200 people squeezed into the Cathedral of the Immaculate
Conception for the canonical installation of the new archbishop of Denver. Mary Dorothy
Stafford sat in a front pew, tears of joy streaming down her face as her son formally
accepted the care of the 310,000 Catholics of the Archdiocese of Denver.

The next day, in order to accommodate all who wanted to honor the new archbishop,
an installation mass was celebrated at the Currigan Convention Center. One plane load
of Stafford's friends had flown from Baltimore; another from Memphis. Nearly 12,000
people joined the pope's personal representative, Archbishop Laghi, and numerous

More than thirty bishops joined Archbishop Stafford for the archdiocesan centennial mass at the Basilica of the Immaculate Conception on August 9, 1987. (Photo by James Baca.)

cardinals, archbishops, bishops, and religious in prayer and thanksgiving for Denver's new spiritual shepherd.

"Although I did not know the late Archbishop Casey," Stafford told the crowd, "I am mightily impressed with his catholic sense of the Church's mission, especially to the poor. . . . I am very impressed with what I've seen of the City of Denver. Its citizens appear to have achieved a level of civility especially evident in the well-placed and flower-decked parks. At the same time, tensions between the deprived and well-to-do cannot be absent," he added, noting "the omnipresent 'neighborhood watch' signs."

On August 9, 1987, Archbishop Stafford celebrated the centennial of the establishment of the Archdiocese of Denver with a solemn mass at the Cathedral of the Immaculate Conception, jammed with a capacity crowd of 1,200, including thirty visiting bishops and archbishops and the papal pronuncio to the United States, Archbishop Pio Laghi. Archbishop Stafford shared his reflections in his pastoral letter of May 28, 1987, "This Home of Freedom":

> We of the Church of Denver mark a pair of anniversaries, the centennial of our diocese and the bicentennial of the United States Constitution. . . . As we enter our second century as the Church of Denver, may we each contribute to the building of the public community of virtue without which there cannot be liberty and justice for any, much less for all.

After settling into a house on South Eudora Street, within walking distance of the chancery, the archbishop began exploring his new neighborhood. Walking is one of Stafford's favorite pastimes; in Baltimore he regularly donned street clothes to explore the poor inner city neighborhoods and become better acquainted with the people. Leaving his Roman collar and episcopal garb at home, he took a walk on his first Sunday in Denver. Stafford, a national leader in the effort to reconcile Catholics and Lutherans, wandered into Augustana Lutheran Church at 5000 East Alameda Avenue.

"There's no way they could have known who I was," he told religion reporter Terry Mattingly of the *Rocky Mountain News* on August 1, 1986. "Of course I sat, like a good Catholic, in the last pew." To the astonishment of the incognito archbishop, Reverend Ron Swensen of Augustana Lutheran asked his flock to pray for the new Roman Catholic archbishop. "That," Stafford smiled, "was a very warm and hospitable greeting."

"I also went incognito to the Samaritan Shelter for dinner," the archbishop confessed in a December 5, 1986, interview. "I found that two-thirds of the people I ate with were willing and able to work. I'm amazed Colorado doesn't have a work program for them."

The archbishop described his day, in a 1988 interview, as beginning with meditation in his home chapel from 6:15 to 7:15, followed by a home mass. Over a breakfast of high-fiber cereal and fruit juice, the archbishop reads both Denver dailies, weekly magazines, and theological journals before heading for his office around nine o'clock. He frequently hosts business lunches in his home with various guests, including Denver's Mayor Federico Fabian Peña.

Daily, the archbishop does the Royal Canadian Air Force exercises and takes frequent walks. "In town, I walk three times a week to Cranmer Park. Weekends, I love to get to the mountains for hikes, at places like Wild Basin in Rocky Mountain National Park. Or when I'm retreating to Snowmass Monastery, I enjoy hiking around Independence Pass." Besides walking, the archbishop is fond of tennis and skiing, which he tries to do several times each winter. In his younger days, Stafford was one of the priest–ski bums who slept in the basement of St. Mary Church in Aspen in order to try out that resort's celebrated champagne powder snow. The archbishop is an intermediate skier, says Father Lawrence St. Peter, who welcomed him to Colorado with a ski trip to Keystone.

Archbishop Stafford has long shown a keen interest in the ecumenical movement to further understanding and work for unity among religions. He has cochaired the national Oriental Orthodox–Roman Catholic Consultation, the international Roman Catholic–World Methodist Council Bilateral Dialogue, and the national Roman Catholic–Lutheran Dialogue as well as serving on the Ecumenical and Interreligious Affairs Committee. In 1987, he was elected to a three-year term as chair of the Catholic Bishops Committee on Ecumenical and Interfaith Affairs. In Denver, Archbishop Stafford pursued his ecumenical efforts, joining in Orthodox, Protestant, and Jewish activities. "Healing the divisions between religious people has been a major concern for me ever since I became a bishop," Stafford explained in an August 25, 1988, interview. "The division of the Christian community is a scandal to the faith."

Stafford likewise took a lively interest in the Lutheran Anglican Roman Catholic Dialogue, which was founded by Bishop Evans during the 1970s. With his counterparts in the other two churches, Archbishop Stafford launched an annual three day joint retreat for Anglican, Lutheran, and Roman Catholic clergy. During a January 1989 retreat, Stafford became the first Catholic archbishop to preach in St. John's Episcopal Cathedral, where he joined Episcopal Bishop William C. Frey and Evangelical Lutheran Bishop Wayne Weissenbuehler for an ecumenical service. The three men agreed that it was painful and very difficult to try to negotiate agreement on divisive issues; best to focus on, as Stafford put it, "working together in areas of justice, helping the poor, building programs to help those with AIDS, and trying to find ways to worship together."

Jewish–Catholic relations also interested Stafford, who became the first archbishop to appear in a Denver synagogue, where he helped to open an exhibit at the Mizel Museum of Judaica in Denver's BMH Congregation synagogue. This 1986 exhibit, "It Shall be a Crown Upon Your Head: Headwear Symbolism in Judaism, Christianity and Islam," emphasized common roots of the three religions. Stafford noted that the Vatican, in 1965, had issued the *Nostra Aetate* (*In Our Times*), which officially struck down the charge of deicide against Jews. "The prayer hat worn by Jews," Stafford added, was adopted by Catholic bishops because "of the cold churches of Europe and bishops wanting to protect their bald heads."

Asked about his biggest disappointment since coming to Denver, the archbishop, after several minutes of thought, replied:

> It has been my own lack of familiarity with the richness and traditions of the church here. This is a different world for me. The Civil War, for instance, which is so important back East, played little role here. People seem to think not in terms of North and South, but of East and West.
>
> The fierce, immense Colorado landscape has shaped people here, making them more independent. Coloradans show a greater respect for climate and environment. When I go hiking in these awesome, solitary mountains, I sometimes think of Bishop Machebeuf, who first faced them. They provide a marvelous opportunity for reflection.
>
> My impression of Northern Colorado, after two years here, is very positive. It's a young society of many newcomers, searching in new ways to discover the truth. People are more independent, less institution-minded. For example, I was surprised to find that the cathedraticum tax on each parish here is only 3.4 percent of ordinary collections. It was 12.5 in Baltimore, 16 percent in Memphis. But we must live within our means.

Six months later, after the archdiocese faced a projected 1989 budget deficit of $624,000, Father Leonard Alimena, vicar for administration and planning, announced a

1.5 percent increase in the cathedraticum, the assessment parishes pay for the general operations of the archdiocese.

Asked in our August 25, 1988, interview if he planned to stay in Colorado, the archbishop smiled and said, "I have just changed my will. I added a codicil specifying that I am to be buried in the Gallagher Memorial at Mt. Olivet, with my predecessors Machebeuf, Matz, Tihen, Vehr, and Casey."

The archbishop's slow, thoughtful style, his love of books, and his bright, blue eyes sparkling behind his spectacles are not deceiving—he is a scholar. He frequently astonishes religious and laity alike with his references to and quotations from early churchmen. He began our first interview in 1986 by showing me some musty, leather-bound books in Latin. In subsequent interviews, he made it clear that he feels answers to current church problems may lie in thousand-year-old writings: "I make a priority of reading. We must draw upon the riches of Catholic tradition, on the church fathers. They can help us with our own problems."

Stafford is a writer as well as a reader. Besides numerous public addresses and the weekly columns he has contributed to the Memphis diocesan newspaper and to the *Denver Catholic Register*, he has published a dozen articles and book reviews for such journals as *Origins*, *Our Sunday Visitor*, and *America*. Most frequently, he has written on the church and family policy but occasionally tackles new ground, as he did in "Options for Those on Society's Margins" in *Origins* and "The Compassionate and Faithful High Priest" for *The Priest Magazine*.

Stafford's many articles on family life have made him a nationally recognized scholar on the topic. In 1980, he was one of four U.S. bishops to participate in the General Synod of Bishops on Marriage and Family Life, in Rome. His fellow prelates of the National Council of Catholic Bishops (NCCB) chose Stafford, in 1986, for the NCCB Ad Hoc Committee on Biblical Fundamentalism; a year later, Stafford also took on the chairmanship of the NCCB's Ad Hoc Committee to assess the Catholic Telecommunications Network; and in 1988, he was elected to the standing committee overseeing the North American College in Rome.

In the April 19, 1987, *National Catholic Register*, Archbishop Stafford's review of George Weigel's book, *Tranquillitas Ordinis: The Present Failure and Future Promise of American Catholic Thought on War and Peace*, provides an answer to those who have condemned him for not denouncing nuclear weapons and war. Stafford concurred with Weigel's defense of St. Augustine's argument for the "just war," suggesting that "the liberal Catholic establishment" has dealt with only one of "modernity's twin horrors: the destructive capabilities of weapons and totalitarianism." Stafford defends what he calls "the use of power, even coercive power, by the state to pursue the public order necessary for creating the conditions for the possibility of virtue."

Referring to the controversial 1983 letter of America's Catholic bishops, "The Challenge of Peace: God's Promise and Our Response," Stafford wrote:

> As one bishop who took part in the deliberations preceding the publication of the letter, I believe that it is legitimate to question whether our discussions focused too much on the casuistry of weaponry. This raises several further questions in my mind. Does this emphasis lead to a latent pessimism in the letter about the affirmation of peace as a human possibility? Does the "terror" over the nuclear threat in the letter's opening paragraphs create subtle survivalist distortions about the meaning of peace?

Stafford agreed with Weigel that "new left" thought swept many Catholics off the traditional track during the 1960s and 1970s. He, like Weigel, suggested a more rational, less emotional look at war and peace. Among other things, Stafford cited Pope John XXIII's encyclical, *Pacem in Terris*, which emphasized international political solutions such as the United Nations.

In 1986, while bishop of Memphis, Stafford published a two-part booklet, *In Christ Jesus*, which discussed various topics including racial and ethnic justice. He concluded his study of racism with initiatives "to lessen racial and cultural hostilities," including his order that "no Catholic parish or organization is to make any use of facilities or services of a segregated club or group."

With the bishop of Nashville, Bishop Stafford of Memphis conducted hearings on capital punishment. Crime victims, criminals, criminologists, theologians, and concerned citizens were asked to focus on the death penalty as a public policy issue. Subsequently, James D. Neidergess, bishop of Nashville, and Bishop Stafford published "But I Say to You . . . : A Pastoral Letter on Capital Punishment, May 14, 1984," concluding: "It is painful to develop 'an entirely new attitude' toward violence. It can be done through the transforming grace of Christ. We, too, pray that capital punishment will not happen again in the State of Tennessee. It is unworthy of us."

While bishop of Memphis, Stafford also issued "In the Person of Christ: A Letter on the Ministerial Priesthood," in which he took a strong traditional stance on the nature of the priesthood, including a defense of male, celibate priests. Stafford further elaborated on the priesthood in his pastoral letter of September 27, 1988, "In the Person of Christ, the Head of the Body: The Mystery of the Priestly Vocation." Here, he emphasized the mystical nature of the church and of the clergy, declaring that celibate, male, ordained priesthood is characteristic of Catholicism. While all Catholics are called to the universal

Father Edward Buelt, secretary to the archbishop, and his boss led this Walk for Peace on the Auraria Higher Education Center Campus on the feast of St. Francis of Assisi in 1987. (Photo by James Baca.)

priesthood of the baptized, this should not be confused, Stafford contended, with the ordained priesthood.

While some have expressed disappointment with Stafford's traditionalism, others point out that he has pursued liberal change within the traditional framework of the Church. "I realize tradition is living and changing," Stafford said in our 1988 interview, indicating he will listen with an open mind even to his critics. In Memphis, he said "he felt the pressure of Christian fundamentalists"; in Denver, he has experienced more criticism from the liberal wing of the Church.

For Stafford the scholar, answers lie in the Church's 2,000-year-old tradition, in the classics of Church Fathers such as Tertullian, St. Augustine, and St. Thomas Aquinas, and in the best modern Catholic thinkers such as the late Jesuit philosopher John Courtney Murray, whom Stafford called "the finest public theologian produced by the Catholic Church in the United States."

Sister Loretto Anne Madden noted upon the archbishop's arrival, "He is an ideal person for the position in Denver . . . with his degree in social work from the Catholic

University and his work in Baltimore and Memphis towards eradicating racism." Two years later, Sister Mary Lucy Downey, SCL, gave the archbishop high marks for his concern about housing the elderly poor: "We were only able to start Higgins Plaza, which we hope to open as a combination senior residence and nursing home, because the archbishop loaned the Archdiocesan Housing Committee, Inc., start-up money of $150,000."

Reaching out to one of the most stigmatized groups in society, Archbishop Stafford set up an Archdiocesan AIDS [acquired immune deficiency syndrome] Task Force soon after his arrival. He conducted a special mass at the cathedral on October 23, 1987, for AIDS victims and asked all Catholics to pray for them. "Many people are afflicted with the AIDS virus," the archbishop noted, "and seek the healing which only the Lord can give. . . . Christians are not to judge one another, for God calls us all to a deeper conversion and healing."

A Denver spokesperson for Dignity, a national organization for gay and lesbian Catholics, told the *Rocky Mountain News*, of October 14, 1987, that Stafford "should be applauded for making a courageous statement, especially in the current national atmosphere." A year later, Archbishop Stafford repeated what he promised will be an annual AIDS mass. More than 150 people gathered for the AIDS mass, some of them weeping as the archbishop anointed the foreheads and palms of AIDS victims with the holy oil of the sick.

As a former social worker and director of Catholic Charities in Baltimore, Archbishop Stafford took a special interest in Catholic Community Services, whose capabilities were stretched by the depression that began in 1982 with the international collapse in crude oil prices. Stafford, who was honored in 1988 by the Catholic University of America Alumni Association as one of its outstanding social work graduates, acknowledged the frustration of social services: "The needs of hungry, homeless and hurting people far outrun our resources."

James H. Mauck, secretary for Catholic Charities, reported in 1987 that CCS served nearly 400,000 persons in a variety of programs. "There is not a person in the archdiocese who at one time or another might not need our services," Mauck added. Sponsoring adoption as an alternative to abortion has been a major thrust of the CCS Adoption/Foster Care/Pregnancy Counseling office, which traces its origins to the Infant of Prague Nursery opened in 1946 in the old St. Clara's Orphanage next to St. Elizabeth Church. This nursery took care of unwanted babies from Catholic hospitals. In 1954, Infant of Prague Nursery moved to West 33rd Avenue and Eliot Street, where the Franciscan sisters have established their new complex of social services at St. Elizabeth Gardens.

St. Clara's Orphanage, which once cared for homeless children such as these, evolved into an adoption and foster home care placement center. (Photo by Paul E. Norine.)

Queen of Heaven Home for Girls closed its doors in 1966, in keeping with a national trend away from institutionalization and toward foster homes. Subsequently, Infant of Prague Nursery pioneered archdiocesan efforts to place unwanted babies with foster families. This program has grown over the years, with foster parents now adopting babies two or three weeks after birth. In 1987, according to Family and Children Services director Gail Shattuck, "We counseled 203 birth mothers, fifty-two birth fathers, made 449 contacts with other family members, and placed forty-one children in foster homes."

Cam Krysko, a social worker who did her graduate work at the Catholic University of America, has served as an adoption counselor for CCS since 1962. "We have a long waiting list for babies," she reported in 1988,

Many of J.K. Mullen's descendants, including (left to right) Mr. and Mrs. Frank Tettmer, Melvin and Edith Malo Roberts, and Eleanor M. Weckbaugh, attended this 1964 groundbreaking for the new V-shaped south entry wing of the Mullen Home. (Photos by Joseph Motta and James Baca.)

so we can select a foster home even before a baby is born. The societal stigma of being an unwed mother is lessening, and more and more pregnant girls are keeping their infants. In 1986, our department counseled 257 pregnant women but only fifty-two relinquished their infants for adoption. Since 1985, mothers read profiles on adoptive couples so they can help pick the home. It's reassuring to them.

To serve all populations in the community, CCS created counseling services in the 1970s, augmenting the program in 1976 by creation of Peer-Counseling, a volunteer program that works primarily through the parishes. The CCS counseling staff offers a fifty-hour training session to volunteers. Upon successful completion of training, the volunteers work in their parishes and at branch offices in Aurora, Boulder, Denver, and Lakewood.

By 1987, CCS was spending $3.2 million a year on social services and operating twenty major programs. Program fees covered 34 percent of the budget, according to Mauck, while United Way contributed another 26 percent. Other revenues are donations from individuals, parishes, and the AACP. Mauck reported in 1987 that about 85 percent of the budget goes for programs and only 15 percent for administration; his staff of 120 is assisted by over 1,200 volunteers. "Our CCS budget has increased fivefold since 1974," Mauck said in a 1988 interview, "and this growth is due largely to the imput of the laity and of volunteers."

CCS has been devoting more time to senior citizens, who, with improved modern health care, are now the fastest-growing age group in the United States. Sister Mary Lucy Downey and the HCI continued to plan new HUD-financed senior low-income housing.

In 1986, the Sisters of Charity Health Care Systems formed a corporate partnership with Sunny Acres that, by 1987, cared for approximately 1,000 seniors in four retirement communities: Sunny Acres Villa in Denver; Medallion and Medallion West in Colorado Springs; and Villa Pueblo Towers in Pueblo.

Shortly after he came to Denver, Archbishop Stafford helped his mother move into the Mullen Home for the Aged, where he paid frequent visits. Mrs. Stafford was delighted with Mullen Home, the first Catholic home for the elderly in the archdiocese, where the Little Sisters of the Poor, since 1918, have operated what many consider the finest nursing home in Colorado.

Mullen's spacious, elegantly landscaped two-block site at West 29th Avenue and Lowell Boulevard is impressive, as is the interior with its glistening linoleum floors, freshly vacuumed carpets, and bright, homey decor. Mother Agnes Bernard, LSP, administrator of Mullen Home since 1986, reported in 1987:

The lavish, loving care that the Little Sisters of the Poor give residents of Mullen Home inspired one nursing home inspector to say, "We send all new inspectors to Mullen Home first so they can see how good nursing homes can be."

Since December 22, 1917, when the first five sisters arrived from France to open the Mullen Home, we have grown to our current staff of twelve Little Sisters of the Poor. We care for both the physical and spiritual needs of our residents. We reach out to them in their last days, to see them through their death. When someone dies all of us try to be with them. Last week, when someone died suddenly, we were all there with them and comforted them with songs. If it's a slow death, someone is with them all the time, twenty-four hours a day, seven days a week.

The hardest part of our job is having to turn people away. We have hundreds of people on our waiting list.

As Social Security and Medicare provide only a small fraction of Mullen Home's expenses, Mother Agnes Bernard said that the home depends on "our beautiful benefactors who give us hundreds of thousands every year." The Little Sisters rely on St. Joseph, their patron, to take care of the deficit. Each sister carries a figure of the saint in the pocket of her habit, and they have many stories of how he has responded to a cry for help, such as that of Sister Patrick, Mullen's public relations director and second-floor supervisor: While she was taking a tour group through the kitchen in 1983, one tourist spotted an empty beer can in front of a statue of St. Joseph.

"A beer can?" he asked.

"Yes," a sister told him. "At lunch time—the big meal of the day here—we give our residents a can of beer if they want it. The trouble now is that we're out of beer, and we're asking St. Joseph to find some for us."

"Do you mind a rival brand?" asked the visitor, who turned out to be a Coors Brewery executive.

"Indeed not. The residents here would drink any kind of beer."

The next day, eighteen cases of Coors were delivered to the Mullen Home, along with word to telephone the warehouse whenever the supply was running low.

Mullen Home, one of thirty-four nursing homes operated by the Little Sisters of the Poor in the United States, seeks out the poor—two thirds of its residents are on welfare. The sisters are assisted by a paid staff of almost 100 and by hundreds of volunteers. In 1975, a $3.1 million expansion included remodeling the older facilities and construction of a three-story south wing on 29th Avenue, which became the main entrance. As of 1988, the Mullen Home had eighty-eight residents, as well as those in the Jeanne Jugan Apartments (fourteen self-care units), and a day care program for seniors.

During the 1970s, CCS started the Hospice of Peace to offer support and home health care programs for those wishing to die at home. Once persons, their families, and their doctors agree on a hospice death, the Hospice of Peace provides nurses, social workers, volunteer hospice friends, and pastoral care counselors, regardless of religion or ability to pay.

The Archdiocese also concerns itself with new Americans. The Immigration and Resettlement Office grew out of the Displaced Persons program established after World War II by monsignors Kolka and Monahan. While resettling Cuban refugees was the major undertaking of the 1960s, during the 1970s and 1980s the office helped hundreds of Southeast Asians resettle in Colorado. In 1975, the Immigration and Resettlement Office set up shop at 3417 West 38th Avenue in Denver to provide sponsors, translation services, legal aid, assistance with citizenship applications, visas, alien cards, and affidavits of support. Barbara Carr, the supervisor in 1988, had a staff attorney, receptionist, secretary, and two counselors.

The 1987 Federal Immigration Act, which offered amnesty to undocumented workers who had been in the United States for a long time, put a heavy burden on the office. Counselor David Moore told *The Denver Post* of November 20, 1988, that he had talked to several thousand undocumented workers. Moore reported that of the 40,000 undocumented aliens living in metro Denver in 1987, about 15,000 had been granted amnesty and citizenship, another 10,000 had been deported, and about 15,000 remained. As the 1987 law provided stiff fines for employing undocumented workers, they were having a very tough time finding jobs. But many of them told CCS that they would stay because, as Moore reported, "they still believe that life in Colorado as an undocumented worker is superior to life in their own country."

Archbishop Stafford, who had served on the governor's Committee on Migrant Labor in Maryland, beefed up the Denver Archdiocesan Migrant Labor Ministry. Directed since 1982 by Father Thomas More Janeck, OFM Cap., the migrant ministry had grown by 1988 into a team of two priests, two sisters, and fourteen lay persons.

Father Janeck asked for the migrant ministry at an age when some priests retire. When his request was granted in 1982, he left the pastorship of Denver's Annunciation parish for a roving pastorship. His altar was the folding card table he carried in the back of his car, and his church was often a parking lot or the fields where he celebrated a Spanish mass, wrapped in his multicolored serape-chasuble. Father Janeck ended each mass with cookies and small talk in fluent Spanish.

Father Janeck was chosen in 1988 to be president of the Colorado Rural Migrant Coalition, an umbrella group of forty public and private agencies concerned with migrant laborers. In 1988, he logged over 200,000 driving miles, saying masses, baptizing babies, blessing cars, helping his people to celebrate and to mourn.

"These people have none of the comforts that we take for granted, like running water or privacy or a chair to sit in," Father Janeck told the *Rocky Mountain News*, of October 12, 1987. Migrant laborers in Colorado earn about $5,000 to $6,000 a year: "They show us the value of poverty. They show us the value of work. They show us the value of simplicity."

Providing religious education to migrants is particularly difficult, noted Sister Ann Lucia Apodoca, SCL, a native of Windsor, Colorado, where she and her family once worked beside migrant laborers. Since the children of migrant laborers toil in the fields, Sister Apodoca explained, "there are very few hours left for education. Sadly, in most cases, the migrant kids have dropped out of school because of their tough work schedule."

The first program in the archdiocese specifically designed for developmentally disabled persons was established in Longmont in 1941. That October, five Sisters of St.

Francis of Assisi from Milwaukee, Wisconsin, opened St. Coletta School for atypical children in conjunction with their parochial school at St. John the Baptist. This school, opened in the old St. Joseph Academy at 6th and Atwood streets, welcomed mentally handicapped children from throughout the Midwest, who were given religious, academic, and vocational training. In 1948, the Franciscans moved the school to Chicago, leaving Colorado without a Catholic center for the developmentally disabled.

That void inspired Cary Carron to establish a Ministry for the Handicapped in Denver in 1960, working at Notre Dame parish with William Joseph Koontz. After Father Koontz died in 1969, Archbishop Casey asked Carron to establish an Archdiocesan Ministry to the Handicapped. From 1969 to 1975, she supervised the ministry out of the former St. Philomena Convent. In 1975, the archdiocese leased the old Notre Dame parish convent for the Ministry to the Handicapped until its 1981 move to 1050 South Birch Street, where the archdiocese leased the former conference center of St. Andrew's Seminary from the Theatine fathers.

Carron, founding supervisor of the program, relied heavily upon volunteers to provide services not available through government agencies. CCS handicapped programs include a coffeehouse, a college for living, respite care, a group home, service for the hearing impaired, and a metro Denver youth group. A Follow-Along plan developed in 1985 dispatches friend–counselors to accompany clients, helping them with such everyday ordeals as check-writing, telephone-dialing, and teeth-brushing.

The Knights of Columbus have adopted the developmentally disabled among their many causes, bankrolling the coffeehouse at 1050 South Birch. The Knights also undertook, in 1987, official sponsorship of the Colorado Special Olympics Basketball Tournament. "Since 1960," Cary Carron said in a 1989 interview,

> we have evolved from a small special religious education program to a $300,000-a-year program of many support services for the handicapped and their families. We now offer many programs with the help of generous funding from the State of Colorado, the City and County of Denver and private donors. Our mission, however, remains the same—to further, regardless of their race, religion, and financial status, the spiritual, intellectual, emotional, and physical well-being of our disabled brothers and sisters.

"Cary Carron really established handicapped services in this archdiocese," noted Sister Mary Catherine Widger, SL, in a 1989 interview, adding:

> Father Larry Freeman and I started the Office of Special Religious Education and Pastoral Care in 1976 and now have two additional staff members. We have tried to create a family

community for the disabled by offering weekends at Camp Santa Maria and annual trips to Disneyland. We now have three programs for the developmentally disabled. First, we sponsor weekly parish programs with one religious education teacher for each student. As of 1989, we have over 200 students and 130 volunteer teachers in twenty parishes throughout Northern Colorado.

Secondly, in 1979 we established at the state's Wheat Ridge Regional Center an interdenominational "religious nurture" program for the severely retarded people there. We use music, puppets, singing, dancing, prayer, and talk about Jesus. Lynne Thier of our staff coordinates this program, and two of us spend four nights a week at Ridge Home.

Thirdly, in 1985 we started Bridge Home, a community for eight developmentally disabled women in the old convent of All Saints parish. Three of our staff, Sister Sue Rogers, SL, Lynne Thier, and myself, live there and provide twenty-four-hour-a-day companionship in this unique program. The ladies there all work in sheltered workshops, such as those of Goodwill Industries and Laradon Hall. At the Bridge Home and in our other programs, our aim is to give the developmentally disabled opportunities to grow by structuring a safe environment that gives them a maximum amount of freedom.

The St. Vincent de Paul Society, the oldest charitable arm of the Church in Colorado, has been active ever since its 1876 establishment by Bishop Machebeuf. Santos C. Vega, executive director, noted that the society receives no money from the government or the archdiocese. "Our lifeline," Vega told the *Denver Catholic Register* of February 11, 1987, "is the annual St. Nicholas appeal and people who contribute generously throughout the year."

The society has a small basement office at St. Thomas Seminary, 3434 East Arizona Avenue, and a store at 10829 East Colfax Avenue. Sixteen parishes of the archdiocese maintain St. Vincent de Paul ministries with about 100 volunteers handling calls for everything from rent money to automobile repairs. The society continues to ask the fortunate to help the unfortunate with the slogan, "We Give to Others What You Give to Us."

"If You Seek Peace, Work for Justice" is one of the bumper sticker slogans of the Justice and Peace Office, which was created by Archbishop Casey during the 1970s. Archbishop Stafford, who for years has spent Christmas and Easter celebrating mass in jails and visiting with prisoners, reorganized the office in 1988. Dennis Kennedy, CM, an assistant professor of liturgy and education at St. Thomas Seminary, was appointed director of the office.

One of Father Kennedy's first efforts was a "Way of the Cross" march through downtown Denver on Good Friday. Starting at St. Elizabeth Church on the Auraria Campus, the marchers stopped at twelve sites, including the United States Mint, the

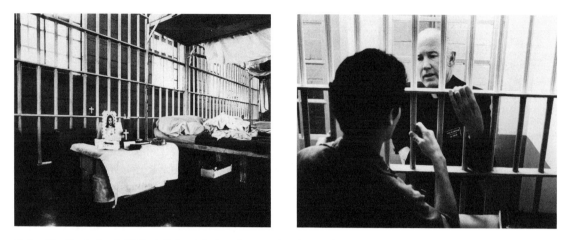

Father Jim Sunderland, SJ, the jail chaplain, has also spearheaded the Colorado Coalition to Abolish the Death Penalty. (Photos by James Baca.)

Denver Police Headquarters, and the Market Street Station shopping area. "At Market Square," Father Kennedy told the *Rocky Mountain News* of March 19, 1988, "we'll be talking about the sin of consumerism, something I believe we all need to pray about." At the police headquarters and jail, the marchers prayed for improvements in the nation's justice system and for officers killed in the line of duty.

The Justice and Peace Office has joined protests against violations of human rights in Central America, including U.S. interference in Nicaragua. Father Kennedy says his office focuses on "Gospel values—living with others in peace, helping the needy and speaking out for those who do not have a voice."

Peace and justice is likewise the preoccupation of James C. Sunderland, SJ, chaplain for the Adams, Arapahoe, Denver, and Jefferson county jails. To tend his flock, Father Sunderland spends much time behind bars, where, he confessed, "I do not put a Bible in their hands and preach. I find out what they need."

Father Sunderland founded the Coaliton to Abolish the Death Penalty in 1984 because

life is sacred, even when a person has done the worst possible thing—take a life. The death penalty just perpetuates a cycle of violence. You have to make a distinction between the sin and the sinner. Nobody else is going to speak for them. Sometimes they're the lowest of the low, but if they can be given a spark for something better, that's my role.

In 1987, Father Sunderland spent his birthday—December 25—in the Adams County Detention Center in Brighton. There, he and the inmates were visited by Archbishop Stafford. After celebrating Christmas mass for twenty-nine inmates, the archbishop visited with the prisoners, showing, with the help of a volunteer prisoner, how his crosier can be used to capture lost sheep. The archbishop urged inmates to "pray for me and I'll pray for you." Then he joined them in singing happy birthday to Father Sunderland.

Father Jim, as some prisoners call him, frequently appears in court on their behalf, urging juries to recognize the sanctity of human life and spare one of his flock the death penalty. His unpopular position has earned him many critics, within and without the Church. "One lady called me to tell me what a disgrace I was to the Catholic Church," he reported in 1988. "I told her, 'I know, but how did you find out?' She didn't see the humor."

The Justice and Peace Office and Archbishop Stafford have announced support for Amnesty International in its campaign for worldwide human rights. Masses and prayers were held throughout the archdiocese to call attention to the work of the Vicariate of Solidarity, a Catholic order internationally noted for its human rights work. Members have suffered death threats, abduction, torture, and murder at the hands of some Central and South American governments.

The Missions Office set up by Archbishop Casey was enlarged by Archbishop Stafford, who placed Reverend Edward M. Hoffmann in charge of collecting and distributing funds. Among the programs supported are the Society for Propagation of the Faith, the Society of St. Peter the Apostle, the Holy Childhood Association, and the Catholic Relief Services Rice Bowl Project.

The archdiocese also maintains its own mission at Monteria, Columbia. Archbishop Casey adopted the Monteria Mission in 1979, after spending a week there. He assigned a priest, lay missionaries, and funding to the mission, where the archdiocese works in partnership with the Bethlehem fathers of Inmensee, Switzerland, who founded the mission to minister to an estimated 100,000 *barrio* dwellers.

The Bethlehem fathers withdrew from the mission in 1988, whereupon Archbishop Stafford committed the Archdiocese of Denver to sole sponsorship. He doubled the staffing to two priest-led teams. Reverend Bert Chilson, a St. Thomas Seminary graduate who took Spanish lessons before taking over one of the archdiocesan teams, told the *Denver Catholic Register* of February 1, 1989:

The population of Monteria is 300,000 and the archdiocese has two parishes in the poorest parts of the barrio, which lack running water, electricity, telephones and automobiles. It is important to know other people of our faith, to know other cultures so we can know what it means to be Catholic. The mission experience expands our vision and faith and it gives us the opportunity to learn other cultures. I receive much more than I give.

The old St. Joseph Hospital stood for over half a century at 1800 Humboldt Street in East Denver before falling in 1964 to the wrecking ball, and its high-rise replacement facing Franklin Street.

Catholic hospitals, like American health care institutions in general, underwent growth and consolidations during the 1980s. St. Joseph Hospital, the largest and oldest private hospital in Colorado, has expanded considerably since its 1873 founding. The Sisters of Charity of Leavenworth financed early expansions by traveling in pairs to beg for support.

The original hospital at East 18th Avenue and Humboldt Street in Denver was replaced at the turn of the century by a much larger twin-towered structure. An east wing was added in 1905 and a north wing in 1911. After the dedication of the fifty-bed, $100,000 north wing, Sister Mary Irene McGrath received a gentleman caller who insisted upon seeing the superior. When Mother Irene entered the parlor, he exclaimed, "I just wanted to look at you. I heard a woman ran this establishment, and I wanted to see her for myself."

St. Joseph's celebrated the 1933 opening of the $115,000 Catherine Smith Mullen Memorial Home for Nurses on the north side of the hospital. This elegant art-deco building, donated by Ella Mullen Weckbaugh and designed by Denver architect Temple Buell, remains a functional, ornate part of St. Joseph's to this day. St. Joseph's opened in 1917 an Infants Home that has evolved into its widely acclaimed birthing center, where, by the 1980s, approximately one in every ten Colorado babies was born.

The 1940 Dower Surgical Pavilion, with its modern equipment and air conditioning, was donated by May Mullen Dower (another daughter of J.K. Mullen who had received kind attentions at St. Joseph during his final illness). After the opening of an air-conditioned, sixty-five-bed north wing in 1952, St. Joseph's bed capacity reached 400 patients.

Sister Mary Asella, director from 1936 to 1963, oversaw completion of the Weckbaugh Chapel in 1940 and undertook the hospital's most ambitious expansion. The old twin-towered main building was demolished and replaced by a $9-million, twelve-story structure, dedicated in 1964. Although decidedly modern in style, the new main building incorporated the twin-towers motif of the old building: Circular towers contain wedge-shaped patient rooms, which all open to a core nurses' station. This "health care in the round" solved the usual hospital problem of

Trimmed in art deco fantasy, the 1933 landmark designed by Denver architect Temple H. Buell still stands as the Catherine Smith Mullen Memorial Home for Nurses at St. Joseph Hospital. (Photo by Glenn Cuerden.)

long hallways separating nurses from their patients. Sister Asella retired in 1963; she was succeeded as hospital administrator by Sister Mary Andrew Talle. Sister Mary Andrew emerged as a civic leader at the same time she made St. Joseph's a pacesetter in hospital care. While serving on the boards of the Denver Chamber of Commerce, Great West Life Insurance Company, and United Banks of Colorado, Sister Mary Andrew also joined efforts to revitalize the north Capitol Hill neighborhood. As part of its 1973 centennial, St. Joseph's sponsored a community health fair for employees and neighbors.

In 1974, St. Joseph's opened a $5-million surgical wing where Colorado's first open-heart surgery was performed. Since the 1970s, the hospital has continually expanded and updated its facilities, including, in 1973, a three-floor radiology–cardiovascular wing, a Day Surgery Wing in 1983, a Senior Care Center in 1986, a Women's Pavilion in 1984, and a $6-million expansion of the surgical facilities in 1988. When Kaiser Permanente—a pioneer health maintenance organization—opened a Colorado program in the 1970s, it chose St. Joseph's as its hospital. Willingness to work with Kaiser personnel and patients has helped keep St. Joseph's successful at a time when many hospitals are faltering.

Sister Mary Andrew Talle, chosen as the Woman of the Year in 1982 by the Denver Chapter of the National Federation of Business and Professional Women, shared her management philosophy in a 1986 interview:

St. Anthony Hospital in West Denver undertook this ambitious expansion program during the late 1960s.

We're as much a university as a hospital. We have the largest private hospital teaching program for interns and residents in the region. Education and growth are the ways in which we become *better* people, and my whole job in management is to aid the growth of people.

In 1988, Sister Mary Andrew resigned as chief executive officer of St. Joseph Hospital, to be replaced by David Reeb, the first lay administrator. "I'm leaving the hospital where patients are getting what they deserve, and they're getting it in a short period of time. Patients used to stay an average of three weeks, now the average patient stays three to five days," Sister Mary Andrew told the *Rocky Mountain News* of November 11, 1988. St. Joseph's had grown into a 565-bed hospital with over 2,000 employees, over 1,000 physicians, and over 300 volunteers. "We are still owned and operated, as in the beginning, by the Sisters of Charity of Leavenworth," Sister Mary Andrew pointed out; "we still have nine sisters working full time." Sister Mary Andrew plans to continue working at the hospital in fund raising and gerontology.

St. Anthony Hospital in west Denver has evolved from the 180-bed hospital dedicated by Bishop Matz on June 13, 1893, into a vast health care system embracing six hospitals.

St. Anthony answered so many of the prayers of Sister Mary Huberta and the Poor Sisters of St. Francis Seraph that they named the hospital, opened in 1892, for him.

In 1972, St. Anthony's became the first hospital in the Rockies with a whirlybird ambulance.

This hospital on the south shore of Sloan's Lake added a chapel and a laundry in 1901. The facility at West 16th Avenue and Quitman Street was enlarged in 1918; its new west wing increased its bed capacity to 200 patients. In 1921, a convent was erected to house forty Franciscan sisters. St. Anthony's nursing school opened in 1919 and became a full four-year program in 1948. By 1960, St. Anthony's was overflowing, with an occupancy rate of 115 percent; patient beds lined the hallways. That year, the hospital launched a fund-raising campaign that led to completion of a new south wing (1962) and west wing (1964), which became the new main building. The old main hospital was demolished in 1965 to make way for a new east wing.

Ellsworth V. Kuhlman became the first lay administrator of St. Anthony's in 1969. Two years later, St. Anthony North, a 194-bed satellite hospital, was opened in the Denver suburb of Thornton. As of 1988, St. Anthony's also operated two emergency room outreach programs on Colorado's Western Slope: the Summit Medical Center in Frisco and the Emergency Medical Center in Granby.

St. Anthony's pioneered same-day surgery, a Neuro Trauma Unit, and a helicopter ambulance service in the Denver area. The helicopter Flight for Life program, launched in 1972, provides an airborne emergency room as well as rapid transportation to St. Anthony Central. The whirlybirds carry emergency equipment and staff to the sites to stabilize victims before transporting them. Since St. Anthony's pioneered Flight for Life, other cities have adopted similar programs.

A giant step forward for St. Anthony Hospital came on March 16, 1987—merger with the Sisters of Charity of Cincinnati Health Care Systems. The combination created a $1-billion operation that was the fifth largest health care system in the nation, according to the *Denver Catholic Register* of March 25, 1987. St. Anthony's parent organization, the Franciscan Healthcare Corporation of Colorado Springs, operated six hospitals, and a retirement home and centers in Colorado, Nebraska, and New Mexico. The Sisters of Charity Health Care Systems consisted of eleven hospitals, three nursing homes, and retirement centers in Colorado, Kentucky, Michigan, New Mexico, and Ohio, including Penrose Hospital in Colorado Springs, St. Mary-Corwin Hospital in Pueblo, St. Joseph Hospital and Manor in Florence, and four Sunny Acres retirement communities.

St. Anthony Hospital Systems, as the new outfit was called, continued to expand. In 1987, it purchased Mercy Medical Center in East Denver and Beth Israel Hospital, a Jewish hospital founded in 1923, in West Denver. St. Anthony's thus emerged as the largest Colorado-based hospital system. With over 4,700 employees by 1989, St. Anthony's is ranked by the Greater Denver Chamber of Commerce as the thirteenth largest employer in metro Denver.

Mercy Hospital of Denver, after its 1901 establishment by the Sisters of Mercy on the south side of City Park, initially specialized in treating nervous and lung disorders. As it soon evolved into a general hospital, the name was changed from Mercy Sanitarium to Mercy Hospital in 1903. Further expansion came for the hospital and nursing school in 1932, when a $350,000 addition increased the hospital's capacity to 275 beds and added new surgical, X-ray, and laboratory facilities. Thirty years later, a ten-story addition designed by Linder, Wright, and White Architects cost $8.6 million. Subsequently, the fine 1901 building—the only Spanish-style building in the hospital complex—was demolished, and the 1932 wing became an administrative, educational, and residence center for the Sisters of Mercy.

Mercy opened the first combined intensive care/coronary care unit in Denver in 1966, building a special wing for that program in 1975—where open-heart surgery was first performed a year later. During the 1970s, the physical medicine program was expanded to encompass speech and occupational therapy, and social service. A year later, Mercy became a pioneer center for microsurgical procedures of the eye and ear and, in 1974, made local medical history with its first cochlear implant. During the 1970s, Mercy also set the pace for regional hospitals by opening a drug and alcohol abuse treatment center.

Mercy Medical Plaza opened in 1976, providing parking and office space for physicians. To serve Denver's far-flung suburbs, Mercy also started a twenty-four-hour emergency center, clinic, and pharmacy at Highlands Ranch during the 1980s, as well as a similar facility for northeast metro suburbs—the Green Valley Family Health Center. Mercy Hospital had come a long way since that cold day in February 1882 when Sister Mary Baptist and a little band of nuns arrived in Colorado in response to Bishop Machebeuf's plea to tend the sick.

Education, as well as health care, remained a major thrust of Colorado Catholicism under Archbishop Stafford. During a 1988 conference at the Loretto Heights Campus of Regis College, Stafford unveiled initiatives to preserve Catholic schools. These included establishment of an endowment fund, which would provide tuition assistance for poorer families and boost teacher salaries by 25 percent within three years in the thirty-eight Catholic schools of the archdiocese. To aid in guiding schools, the archbishop announced that St. Thomas Seminary would provide education courses and have seminarians do field work in parish schools.

The archbishop told the 300 principals, teachers, administrators, and parents at the Loretto Heights conference that he did not foresee establishing any new schools "in the immediate future" but would "focus on stabilizing the schools we have at present." Stafford added that he once felt Catholic schools should be phased out and replaced by religious education programs. He had changed his mind after seeing Catholic schools out-perform public schools, especially in educating minority and disadvantaged youth. He also noted that in Northern Colorado, parochial school enrollment actually increased for the first time in years during the fall of 1988, when enrollment was 4 percent higher than in 1987. Yet, the archbishop noted, only 48 percent of Catholic children were receiving religious education, and only 15 percent attended Catholic schools. Catholics, Stafford concluded, must find a way to keep their schools open to preserve "our Judeo-Christian value system" and help young people tempted to seek "escape through drugs, cults, various kinds of self-indulgence or self-abuse, fantasy, materialism or the ultimate escape of suicide."

Although only about 13,000 students were enrolled in Catholic schools—half the number enrolled in the peak year of 1965—the Archdiocesan Education Office could point to some bright spots in 1988. Denver's Schools in Urban Neighborhoods was working, according to Sister Jean Anne Panisko, SCL, principal of Annunciation School. Sister LaVonne Guidonni, SCL, had worked with seven core city schools to form SUN in 1987; enrollment had climbed from 1,167 to 1,243 a year later. By pooling resources, these schools have strived to make sure that no child is turned away for lack of tuition.

SUN schools received a boost from the Paroke Alumni Association formed in 1986. The Parokes, graduates of Denver's Catholic high schools and members of the old Parochial Sports League, contributed to a half-million-dollar endowment in conjunction with the Elementary Education Fund, which, by 1987, was awarding $35,000 in tuition grants for 162 children. And the Parokes were having fun fund raising with an annual Old Parokes Round Robin Basketball Tournament launched in 1986. This was followed by a match between the All Star Old Parokes and a team of Denver Broncos stars, including Randy Gradishar, Haven Moses, Dennis Smith, Norris Weese, and Louis Wright. While reviving the glory days of parochial league basketball games, the Parokes raised money for SUN schools with the help of paying spectators. SUN schools are now up to snuff

Spirited scholars and staff of Annunciation School have made it a sparkplug of Denver's Schools in Urban Neighborhoods revitalization program. (Photo by James Baca.)

Peppy alums have come to the rescue of struggling parochial schools with the Old Parokes athletic contest fund-raisers inaugurated in 1986. (Photo by James Baca.)

with the other thirty-six elementary schools and two high schools in the archdiocese, according to Sister Patricia Beckman, who was appointed superintendant of Catholic Schools in 1989.

Although Regis College prospered during the 1980s, Loretto Heights College succumbed to the many problems besetting Catholic education. After World War II, the college had flourished, adding 160 acres and seven new buildings. Enrollments peaked during the 1960s, reaching some 900 students. The fine craftsmanship and loving care given the building are reflected in the original, unmarred tile floors. Next to the main building, the Chapel of Our Lady of Loretto, completed in 1911, glories in twenty-three stained glass windows from the renowned Meyer studios in Munich, Germany. On December 12, 1968, the Sisters of Loretto sold the college for $1 to the board of trustees, which continued to operate it as a nondenominational school until 1988, when Regis College took over to prevent closure threatened by dwindling finances and enrollment.

"One of Bishop Machebeuf's problems with the pioneer church in Colorado is also one of mine—finding enough priests," Archbishop Stafford noted in 1988, a year after he was elected to a three-year term as chair of the seminary's board of directors.

During the past fifty years, St. Thomas Theological Seminary has witnessed a slow start, a boom, and a slow decline in enrollments, making the current shortage of vocations and of priests a major headache for Archbishop Stafford. (Photo by Roy Hyskell.)

Enrollment had fallen to thirteen that year, with another thirty-three seminarians of the archdiocese studying in other seminaries or assigned to parishes. The local decline in the number of new priests was part of a national trend. By 1988, the nationwide numbers had dropped to 8,921—a 5.2 percent decline from 1987 and half the number of seminary students twenty years ago. As enrollments shrank, the seminary welcomed the general public as tuition-paying students. The public was also welcomed in the three-floor, 120,000-volume library. Marguerite Travis, librarian since 1966, says, "Just show us your driver's license and you can check out a book."

Lawrence St. Peter, a St. Thomas graduate who served as vicar for priests from 1982 to 1988, reported in 1987 that "so far we don't have any priestless parishes in this archdiocese. We do have business managers, pastoral assistants, professional counselors, permanent deacons, and lay volunteers doing much of what priests used to do." Father St. Peter added:

The vocations are out there but we no longer have so many Catholic high schools to nourish them. And although we desperately need more priests, we will not drop the standards. We accept about 70 percent of the applicants each year. In 1987, only twelve of eighteen applicants made it. A beginning priest's salary is only $850. Although they receive free housing, health insurance, and retirement benefits, men don't join the seminary to get rich.

Reverend Reinhold B. Weissbeck, archdiocesan vocation director, told the *Denver Catholic Register* of February 24, 1988, that the greatest number of vocations now come from men in their late 20s or 30s embarking on a second career:

Some were very successful in business with homes and cars and great incomes, but they found the fulfillment wasn't there. Many had the seed of a vocation sown years ago, a seed which would never go away. To experience God in himself and in other people, the priest needs to be a man of interior silence so he can hear and act on the word of God. . . . The whole idea of the priesthood and religious life has changed. It used to be a status symbol. Now a priest is part of the counterculture.

The Permanent Diaconate program established by Archbishop Casey in 1974 continued to play a major role in archdiocesan parish staffing. "I am thoroughly committed to the diaconate ministry in the United States," Archbishop Stafford commented in the May 6, 1987, *Denver Catholic Register*. "The more I meet the men and their wives, the more I'm impressed by their quality." In 1987, Archbishop Stafford inaugurated a Deacon's Day celebration on August 10—the feast of St. Lawrence, a third-century deacon and martyr. In the evening ceremony at the cathedral, sixty-five deacons renewed their vows, and fifteen candidates were initiated as acolytes. The archbishop presented the first outstanding deacon award to Lewis Barbato, a psychiatrist who had served as vicar for family life.

"There is a deep lay tradition in the church," Archbishop Stafford noted in a 1988 interview.

Relying on the laity has been done since the early centuries of the church. And we are fortunate to have burgeoning lay ministries to do what priests and sisters once did. To help train lay people for church responsibilities, I'm hoping to open a catechetical center at St. Thomas Seminary in the next year or two.

By 1988, Archbishop Stafford had put together his team at the Pastoral Center. Monsignor Michael J. Chamberlain, who remained as vicar general, noted:

Sister Rosemary Wilcox's smile grew even wider than usual in 1988 when Archbishop Stafford appointed her to the rank of chancellor, a new high for women religious. (Photo by James Baca.)

The archbishop doesn't shoot from the hip. He's very thoughtful and cautious about the church and very sensitive to people. He consults very broadly and will listen to ideas on how to try a new track. He's been very careful about how to build up a team to replace the one built by Archbishop Casey.

In 1986, J. Anthony McDaid was confirmed as judicial vicar, and the following year Leonard S. Alimena was appointed episcopal vicar for administration and planning with primary responsiblity for archdiocesan finances. During 1988, Edward M. Hoffmann was appointed moderator of the curia, and R. Walker Nickless episcopal vicar for priests and seminarians. Sister Rosemary Wilcox, SL, became, in 1988, the first woman chancellor.

Marcian T. O'Meara was reappointed episcopal vicar for religious, vicar and director of the permanent diaconate, and the archbishop's liaison for Catholic health. Lorenzo Ruiz, OFM, was appointed episcopal vicar for Hispanic affairs, and Edward L. Buelt was named secretary to the archbishop, master of ceremonies to the archbishop, and ecumenical officer of the archdiocese.

Three laymen served in key secretariates: Michael J. Franken as secretary for education and superintendent of Catholic schools; Robert H. Feeney as secretary of communications and executive editor of the *Denver Catholic Register*; and James H. Mauck as secretary of Catholic Community Services.

Upon his arrival in Denver, Archbishop Stafford had observed, according to the *Denver Catholic Register* of June 11, 1986, "I would like to see a greater role for women with particular gifts in this Church. I believe in absolute equality of the sexes." Two years later, he appointed Sister Rosemary Wilcox chancellor of the archdiocese. Sister Rosemary became the sixth sister to be elevated to such a high rank in the Catholic Church in the United States. Upon her appointment, Sister Rosemary, a former English teacher and principal, fetched her dictionary and read the old definition for "chancellor" with a twinkle in her eye: "A Roman Catholic priest heading the office in which diocesan business is transacted and recorded."

Sister Loretto Anne Madden, SL, the popular and effective legislative lobbyist for the archdiocese, was given this 1986 award for promoting social justice by Dottie Sheridan of the Archdiocesan Council of Catholic Women.

A native of St. Louis, Missouri, Sister Rosemary entered the Sisters of Loretto novitiate at their motherhouse in Kentucky in 1944. She professed first vows in 1947 and came to Denver to teach at St. Philomena's school, pronouncing her final vows in 1950. After earning an English degree from Loretto Heights College, she went to Marquette University to complete a masters degree in education. In 1958, she became the founding principal of Machebeuf High School.

In 1984, Archbishop Casey named her vice chancellor, the first woman to hold the post. Four years later, when Chancellor Edward M. Hoffmann was named vicar general, Archbishop Stafford selected Sister Rosemary as chancellor, with responsibility for the archdiocesan archives, records, and statistical data, for maintenance and operations of the Pastoral Center, and for coordinating the Office of Financial Management. Sitting behind a spotless desk, piled high with computer printouts and a relentlessly ringing telephone,

Sister Rosemary is known for a smiling disposition that matches her wall plaque: "Peace to All Who Enter Here."

Another Sister of Loretto, Sister Loretto Anne Madden, received the CCS's Hospice of Peace 1988 Tribute for Caring. Born in Denver in 1923, Sister Loretto Anne is the daughter of Captain Edward Madden of the Denver Police Department and sister of Edward Madden, pastor of St. Bernadette parish in Lakewood. Her sister, Sister Theresa Anne Madden, works at St. Mary's Academy. Another of the Madden girls, Sister Karen Madden, SL, works with Sister Loretto Anne as an administrative assistant.

In 1974, Sister Loretto Anne, after teaching sociology at Loretto Heights and chairing the Social Concerns Committee of the Sisters Council, became executive director of the Colorado Catholic Conference, the public policy office of the archdiocese. A champion of the elderly, homeless, and poor, she was honored at the state capitol in 1988 as an advocate for better handicapped services, health care, housing, minority relations, prison reform, and welfare systems.

Since 1974, Sister Loretto Anne has been the only nun registered as a lobbyist with the state legislature. Although she has neither the desire nor the funds to wine and dine legislators, she has earned their respect because of her diligence and compassion, according to State Senator Dennis Gallagher. She has likewise endeared herself to the press corps by sharing her copious notes on the legislative agenda with reporters. Representative Wilma Webb has christened her "the conscience of the legislature."

On May 20, 1988, hundreds of friends and admirers gathered at St. Mary's Academy to honor another Sister of Loretto, Sister Mary Luke Tobin. A Denver native, she served for twelve years as national president of her order and as president of the National Leadership Conference of Women Religious. A nationally noted peace activist, Sister Mary Luke has led antiwar demonstrations and joined protestors at Denver's Rocky Mountain Arsenal and the Martin Marietta Aerospace plant. At age eighty, Sister Mary Luke Tobin still traveled widely as a speaker and demonstrator, directed the Thomas Merton Center for Creative Exchange, swam daily, and taught at the Iliff School of Theology in Denver.

Sister Helen Flaherty, SC, member of Cathedral High School's state championship debating team in 1938, made news when she was chosen as the national president of her order. Sister Susanna Kennedy, another Sister of Charity, converted the old Sacred Heart Convent at 2844 Lawrence Street into Sacred Heart House in 1987. This is a short-term shelter for families and single women, annually housing about 800 of the 7,000 homeless women wandering around Denver. Sister Susanna reported in 1987, "Women with no

Sister Mary Luke Tobin, SL, former national president of the Sisters of Loretto and of the National Leadership Conference of Women Religious, remains a staunch social activist. (Photo by James Baca.)

place to go are a serious, ongoing problem. It's not getting any better. About 35 percent of the homeless are women. They could be our mothers, our sisters—even ourselves."

Sister Bernadette Teasdale, SCL, has done as much as anyone to make the archdiocese prayerful. She was a sparkplug for the Renew program, and, in 1987, Archbishop Stafford appointed her the Liaison for Contemplative Outreach. According to Father Edward Buelt, the archbishop's secretary, "Sister Bernadette is fulfilling a role of inestimable value, teaching people how to center their prayer and achieve a contemplative life."

In Fort Collins, Victory Noll Sister Mary Alice Murphy opened her $776,000, two-story, 8,600-square-foot "impossible dream" in 1989—the Mission. This shelter for the homeless at Linden Court and Linden Street is a complex for the homeless, hungry, jobless, and elderly. Sister Mary Alice is the director of the Northern Colorado Catholic Community Services, which was established in 1972 with headquarters in Fort Collins.

To complete her long-time dream, she worked with the four Fort Collins parishes, six non-Catholic churches, and over 200 volunteers. As a result, the Mission opened its doors to forty overnight guests and 100 diners every day of the year, while simultaneously offering the community a Hostel of Hospitality, a Job Bank, a Hospitality Kitchen, and an Elderly Outreach Program.

Several new orders of women religious have been welcomed to the archdiocese by Archbishop Stafford. In September 1987, the Spirit of Life Monastery was established in Lakewood as an independent Benedictine monastery. The Benedictines, who first came to the archdiocese in 1984, run the Spirit of Life Holistic Spirituality Center. The tiny, five-sister monastery, says the prioress, Sister Charlotte Redpath, hopes to recruit more members and expand its programs.

Sadly, the Sisters of St. Francis of Penance and Christian Charity closed their Marycrest High School in Denver in 1988. This ending of an era inspired Sister Julia Benjamin, OSF, to undertake an ambitious oral history project, "Sharing Hearth and Home: The Daily Life of Sisters." With funding from the Colorado Endowment for the Humanities, younger sisters interviewed the order's old timers for a series of public programs, exhibits, publications, and oral history transcripts donated to the Western History Department of the Denver Public Library.

"Sharing Hearth and Home" revealed to the general public a handful of biographical sketches from among over a thousand sisters who worked and died in Colorado. A typical story is that of Sister Julia Schneider, OSF, as recorded in the 1988 interview by Sister Rosie Drey, OSF. Sister Julia, a farm girl from South Dakota, was one of the pioneers to open Marycrest in 1938.

After arriving by train in Denver, Sister Julia recalled taking a street car—"they let sisters ride free in those days"—to 50th and Federal, which

was all farm land then. . . . We wore long blue aprons that covered us completely, you know, to keep us clean. We had a white veil, stiff white veiling. . . . You had your jaws tied up with this guimpe pinned on the top of your head and tight around your face. . . . We had the big habits, our arms were folded in our sleeves. . . . We weren't allowed to dangle our arms. So I have a hard time, even now, when I go walking even to let my arms hang loose.

In the early days at Marycrest, the sisters . . . were very work oriented. It was easy to know what God wanted you to do 'cause all you had to do was look at the schedule. . . . The Superior just made all your decisions for you.

In the olden days . . . someone would go through the house, and rap at everyone's door and say, "Arise you who sleep, let Jesus Christ be your light." And we all answered, "Deo Gratias" and jumped out of bed . . . at 4:30 in the morning.

"A spiritual powerhouse" was brought to Colorado in 1989 by Archbishop Stafford when he recruited ten Capuchin Poor Clare Nuns from Mexico to bless the archdiocese with their six hours a day of cloistered prayer. (Photo by James Baca.)

In the olden days, there was so much penance and so much suffering that was offered to God. . . . When I first entered [the convent] we were not allowed to run. And I thought to myself, "I'll never be able to run again." I really liked to jump around and not just walk stately, you know. But then, after . . . after years, things got where you could do a little more, you know, jump and run around and have fun. You know. Play.

I don't remember having to make very many decisions, even after Vatican II. I still wore the veil until 1972 . . . without it you felt sort of naked. We started wearing shorter habits, and when you go out in the cold, your legs get so cold. When you took your veil off, you were two colors . . . reddish, and then white up on your forehead. Then, you know, you had to allow for your hair to grow.

After recounting a long, hard life of doing laundry, gardening, teaching, and working in hospitals, Sister Julia concluded her interview: "Although I am eighty years old, I could still be useful. I could still be able to do a little something around, you know, to be of service."

Transformation of the fading St. Patrick's in North Denver into the Our Lady of Light Monastery for the Poor Clares from Mexico delighted the Hispanic North Denver neighborhood. It also cheered the entire Archdiocese of Denver, for whom Mother Josefina Vargas and her sisters promised to pray night and day. (Photo by James Baca.)

In 1988, ten Capuchin Poor Clare nuns in Mexico were invited by Archbishop Stafford and the Capuchin fathers of the Mid-America Province to open a monastery in North Denver at the former St. Patrick parish house. The old St. Patrick's church, a National Register and Denver landmark, was converted to a cloister for these Spanish-speaking nuns. They come from an order established by St. Francis of Assisi and St. Clare in thirteenth-century Italy. In the 1500s, this particular Franciscan order initiated a reform to return to a stricter observance of the rules of St. Clare and St. Francis. They adopted habits with long cowls, or hoods, which led children on the streets to call them Capuchins ("hooded ones").

Sister María Inez Cacho, president of the Federation of Poor Clares in Mexico, escorted the ten sisters to Denver. She told the *Denver Catholic Register* of December 7, 1988, that "the order does not advertise for vocations but interested women between the ages of 17 and 25 may come on their own. Six years of training is required before final vows and applicants can leave at anytime during the six years if they decide a vocation is not for them."

They came to Denver from their home convent of Our Lady of Guadalupe in Irapuato, 165 miles northwest of Mexico City. Dressed in traditional black and white garb, the sisters arrived to be greeted in Spanish by the archbishop. "What a fiesta," he observed, praising the sisters as a "source of great strength" who "will make the evangelization of the Hispanic people of the archdiocese one of the chief concerns of your intercessory prayer and community life."

The Capuchin abbess, Sister Josefina Vargas, smiled silently and led her sisters out to the monastery they named Our Lady of Light. There, the nuns adhere to rigid cloister, have no possessions, sleep on hard wooden planks, and pray around the clock. Visitors are admitted to the waiting room at 3325 Pecos Street, where one nun is designated to accept prayer requests.

Catholic lay women, like religious women, have made tremendous but largely undocumented contributions to the archdiocese. For instance, a small, back-page article in the *Denver Catholic Register* of October 7, 1986, reported that the Theresians are an organization of Catholic women dedicated to a deeper appreciation of the vocation of Christian women. Four Denver-area ladies—Josephine Taylor, Shirley Moriarity, Agnes Pino, and Laura Salvato—have been elected to the national presidency of this 2,000-member organization in recent years. Maesel Yelenick of Denver, vice-president of the board of directors of the Theresian World Ministry, traveled, in 1987, to lecture and facilitate workshops and seminars in Australia, Ghana, Hong Kong, the Philippines, Thailand, and West Africa.

The Archdiocesan Council of Catholic Women (ACCW), founded in 1926, has supported foreign missions, aided Colorado's migrant laborers, and visited Denver's needy in homes, hospitals, and nursing homes. In 1986, ACCW president Marie Jennings declared that the council was revising its priorities "to concentrate on areas of social justice." Among those new goals, she listed bringing minority women into ACCW, supporting literacy programs, finding financial support for retired religious, promoting a women's auxiliary for the Samaritan Shelter, and pursuing areas of "social justice that are not being worked on."

In his March 18, 1988, pastoral letter Archbishop Stafford declared that "a top priority" should be ministry to "thousands of Hispanics who have been drawn to other Christian denominations, notably the Jehovah's Witnesses and fundamentalist Christian groups." He estimated that 100,000 Northern Colorado Hispanics are not registered in any parish.

To underline his commitment to Hispanics, Stafford began taking Spanish lessons soon after his arrival in Denver. Publicly defending Spanish and other non-English-speaking cultures, the archbishop condemned the English-only language campaign of the 1980s. Inspired by passage of constitutional amendments in California and twelve other states, some Coloradans launched a referendum to make English the official language of Colorado. Calling this campaign "a lightning rod for the evils of mindless prejudice," the archbishop denounced it as "pointlessly provocative" because it could "encourage discrimination and division in our society." Despite the early, vocal opposition of the archbishop and most political leaders, the amendment passed in the 1988 fall general election.

Shortly after his arrival in 1986, Archbishop Stafford began using his grey Nissan automobile to visit the 112 parishes and thirty-eight missions in the twenty-four counties of Northern Colorado. He started with the farming and ranching communities of the eastern high plains. The economic plight of many farmers attracted his attention in his first Denver pastoral letter, "The Crisis of Rural Colorado," which was issued January 14, 1987. In 1988, the archbishop commemorated St. Isidore's feast day by visiting the rural, ranching community of Eagle and its Catholic parish, St. Mary's. There, the pastor and parishioners gave the archbishop a white hat and a horse named Hammerhead for a cattle round-up. Although many of the beeves proved to be "Protestant," the archbishop managed to give about fifty head a St. Isidore's Day blessing.

Not only ranching towns on the Western Slope but also farming communities on the eastern plains welcomed the archbishop's interest. "I'm very pleased," Reverend James Morgan of St. John's parish in Yuma told the *Denver Catholic Register* of September 10, 1986, upon the archbishop's arrival in this little town near the Kansas border. "I know there are several large parishes in Denver he hasn't visited yet."

At St. Anthony's in Julesburg, Reverend Thomas S. Fryar said he and his congregation were "tickled to hear he's coming. It's kind of a rarity to have a bishop coming this far out. A lot of the young have never had a chance to meet or hear an archbishop." On his tours of prairie parishes, the archbishop blesses farms and ranches, crops and livestock. On his St. Isidore's Day visit to Roggen, he pointed out to the congregation at Sacred Heart that St. Isidore, the patron of horticulturalists, "did not even own his own farm but like all good farmers was a man of profound faith."

By 1988, the archbishop had visited every parish in his archdiocese. "We're building new churches in Aurora, Basalt, and Carbondale," he revealed in 1988, "but need new parishes in Aurora, north of Northglenn, and south of Fort Collins. And the Vietnamese are pushing hard for a national parish. But we have limited funds and Camp St. Malo and Samaritan House are draining them."

Archbishop Stafford began his tenure in Denver by asking the priests and the Presbyteral Council (an advisory board overseeing archdiocesan ministry) to recommend priorities for his administration. One of the most pressing needs, according to priests, was to establish orderly, uniform guidelines for pastors and parish councils. Archbishop Stafford responded by issuing new "Norms for Parish Pastoral Councils and Finance Councils" in December 1988. These norms attempted to standardize the work of parish councils, which wielded great power in some parishes and did not even exist in others. The guidelines specified that parish pastoral councils were to advise and assist the pastor, not usurp his power. And parishes without pastoral and finance councils were instructed to establish them.

"The Catholic Church," Stafford reflected in 1989,

is an institution that is working on interpersonal levels. I see its basic strength in its ability to bring about conversations between people, especially in the neighborhoods and at the parish level. The strength of the Catholic Church is also its greatest challenge—to open up areas of communication between husbands and wives, rich and poor, Hispanics and Anglos. That's no easy task in this very privatized world. To see what the church is doing for the 310,000 Catholics in northern Colorado, we must look to the parishes.

BISHOP MACHEBEUF'S COLORADO

1857   Our Lady of Guadalupe, Conejos, first church in Colorado

1858   Gold discovered; Denver founded

1860   Machebeuf and Raverdy arrive in Denver, first Denver Mass in St. Mary Church, Christmas Eve

1861   St. Mary of the Assumption, Central City

1864   Sisters of Loretto open St. Mary's Academy, Denver

1865   Civil War ends; President Lincoln assassinated

1866   Our Lady of Lourdes, Georgetown

1867   St. Joseph, Golden City, and Sacred Heart of Mary, Boulder

1868   Bishop Machebeuf made vicar apostolic for Colorado and Utah

1870   Railroads reach Denver

1871   Utah transferred to Diocese of California

1873   St. Joseph Hospital, Denver, opened by Sisters of Charity

1875   Sacred Heart of Jesus, Boulder; St. Mary's Academy grants Colorado's first high school diploma

1876   Colorado becomes the thirty-eighth state

1878   St. Joseph, Fort Collins; and St. Elizabeth, Denver

1879   Sacred Heart, Denver

1881   St. Patrick, Denver; and St. Paul, Idaho Springs

1882   St. Vincent Orphanage, Denver; and St. John the Baptist, Longmont

1883   St. Joseph, Denver; St. Ann (Annunciation), Denver; and House of the Good Shepherd, Denver

1884   St. Louis, Louisville; Jesuits open College of Sacred Heart, Morrison

1885   St. Mary, Breckenridge; and St. Stephen, Glenwood Springs

1887   Vicariate of Colorado elevated to Diocese of Denver; Reverend Nicholas Matz consecrated coadjutor; St. Augustine, Brighton

1888   St. John, Yuma; Sacred Heart College (later named Regis) moves to Denver; Loretto Academy opened (later Loretto Heights College)

1889   Fathers Malone and O'Ryan help found Denver's Charity Organization Society (United Way); St. Nicholas, Platteville; Holy Family, Denver; and St. Dominic, Denver; Death of Bishop Machebeuf

BISHOP MATZ'S COLORADO

1889 Nicholas Chrysostom Matz becomes second bishop of Colorado
1890 Precious Blood, Newcastle
1891 Mt. Olivet Cemetery, Golden
1892 St. Francis de Sales, Denver; St. Anthony Hospital, Denver, and St. Mary, Aspen
1893 St. Patrick, Holyoke
1894 Holy Name, Fort Logan; and Our Lady of Mount Carmel, Denver
1901 Mercy Hospital, Denver; and St. Mary, Littleton
1902 St. Joseph (Polish), Denver; Mother Frances Xavier Cabrini opens Queen of Heaven Orphanage in Denver; St. John the Evangelist, Loveland
1903 St. Peter, Greeley
1904 St. James, Denver
1905 St. Thomas Seminary; Holy Family, Meeker; Holy Ghost, Denver
1907 Immaculate Conception, Lafayette; St. Mary Magdalene, Denver; and Holy Name, Steamboat Springs
1908 St. Anthony, Sterling; St. Anthony, Julesburg
1909 St. William, Fort Lupton
1910 St. John, Stoneham; St. Helena, Fort Morgan; St. Mary, Rifle
1911 St. Louis, Englewood; Assumption, Welby; St. Mary Church, Brush; Guardian Angels, Mead
1912 St. Catherine of Siena, Denver; Presentation of Our Lady, Denver; Blessed Sacrament, Denver; Dedication of Cathedral of the Immaculate Conception
1913 Matthew Smith takes over the *Denver Catholic Register*; St. Peter, Fleming; St. Patrick, Minturn; Mt. Carmel, Redcliff
1914 Sacred Heart, Peetz
1915 Our Lady of the Mountains, Estes Park
1916 Camp St. Malo, Allens Park
1917 Mullen Home for the Aged, Denver; St. Joseph, Akron; death of Bishop Matz

BISHOP TIHEN'S COLORADO

1917   J. Henry Tihen becomes third bishop of Colorado; United States involved in
          World War I
1918   St. Rita, Nederland; Holy Rosary, Denver; St. Andrew, Wray
1919   St. Francis, Weldona
1920   Shrine of St. Anne, Arvada; St. Michael, Craig; Holy Family, Keenesburg
1921   College of Sacred Heart renamed Regis College; Loretto Heights grants first
          Bachelor of Arts degree; Cathedral of the Immaculate Conception con-
          secrated; Cathedral High School dedicated
1922   St. Cajetan, Denver
1923   St. Theresa, Frederick
1924   Sacred Heart, Roggen; St. Ignatius Loyola, Denver; St. Rose of Lima, Denver;
          St. Peter, Crook; Holy Family, Fort Collins
1926   St. Thomas Seminary dedicates new buildings and grants Bachelor and Master
          of Arts degrees; St. Vincent de Paul, Denver; St. Therese, Aurora
1927   St. Catherine of Siena, Iliff; Catholic Charities formed
1928   J. K. Mullen Memorial Library, Catholic University of America; Little Flower
          Center, Denver
1930   Camp Santa Maria opened west of Bailey; Sacred Heart, Gilcrest
1931   J. K. Mullen Home for Boys, Denver, St. Ignatius, Rangely; Bishop Tihen
          resigns in poor health; dies 1940

ARCHBISHOP VEHR'S COLORADO

1931   Urban John Vehr installed as the fourth Bishop of Denver 1932; Christ the King, Evergreen

1933   Christ the King, Haxtun

1936   Our Lady of Guadalupe, Denver

1937   St. John the Baptist, Johnstown

1940   St. Martin, Oak Creek

1941   Our Lady of Peace, Greeley; Denver becomes an archdiocese and Pueblo a separate diocese; United States in World War II

1944   St. Anne, Grand Lake; St. Peter, Kremmling

1947   Our Lady of Lourdes, Denver; St. Anthony of Padua, Denver; St. Bernadette, Lakewood; Christ the King, Denver

1948   Holy Trinity, Westminister; Sacred Heart, Silt

1949   Mother of God, Denver; Sts. Peter and Paul, Wheat Ridge

1950   Our Lady of Visitation, Westminster; All Saints, Denver; St. Thomas Aquinas, Boulder; St. Ignatius, Walden

1951   St. Elizabeth, Buffalo Creek; Our Lady of Grace, Denver

1952   Curé d'Ars, Denver; Most Precious Blood, Denver

1953   Mt. Carmel, Redcliff; St. Mary, Ault; Guardian Angels, Denver

1954   St. Pius Tenth, Aurora; All Souls, Englewood

1955   St. Benedict Monastery, Snowmass

1957   Holy Cross, Thornton; Notre Dame, Denver

1958   Our Lady of Fatima, Denver; Nativity of Our Lord, Broomfield

1960   David Monas Mahoney named first auxiliary bishop of Denver

1962   Vatican II Council opens

1963   John XXIII, Fort Collins

1965   St. Mary, Greeley

1967   Archbishop Vehr retires; dies 1973

ARCHBISHOP CASEY'S COLORADO

1967 James Vincent Casey installed as the fifth bishop and second archbishop of Denver; Immaculate Heart of Mary, Northglenn; Risen Christ, Denver; St. Joan of Arc, Arvada; St. Jude, Lakewood

1968 Queen of Peace, Aurora; Assassination of Martin Luther King; St. Martin de Porres, Boulder

1969 George R. Evans named auxiliary bishop of Denver; Our Lady of the Snow, Granby; Our Lady of the Valley, Windsor

1970 Our Lady Mother of the Church, Commerce City

1972 Montbello Catholic, Denver; St. Thomas More, Englewood; Our Lady of the Plains, Byers

1973 Columbine Church, Littleton; St. Mark, Westminster; Spirit of Christ Catholic Community, Arvada,

1974 Richard C. Hanifen named auxiliary bishop of Denver; Christ on the Mountain, Lakewood

1975 Our Lady of Peace, Dillon Valley

1978 Our Lady of Grace, Wattenberg

1979 Light of the World, Littleton; St. Michael the Archangel, Aurora; Our Lady of the Pines Catholic Community, Conifer

1980 St. Bernard, Winter Park; St. Mary of the Crown, Carbondale

1981 Church of the Good Shepherd, Denver; St. Elizabeth Ann Seton, Fort Collins

1982 Spirit of Peace, Longmont

1983 Oil bust and recession

1984 Colorado Springs diocese created

1985 St. Mary, Eagle; Death of Bishop Evans

1986 Death of Archbishop Casey

BOOK II

HISTORY OF THE PARISHES

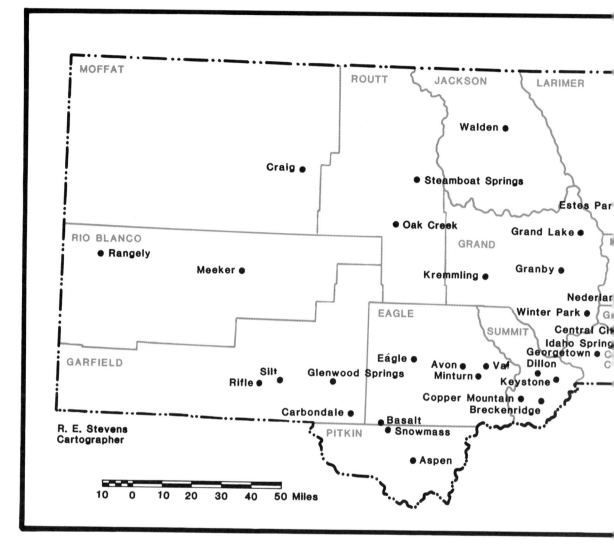

MOFFAT

ROUTT   JACKSON   LARIMER

Walden ●

Craig ●

● Steamboat Springs

Estes Par

RIO BLANCO   ● Oak Creek   Grand Lake ●

● Rangely   GRAND

Meeker ●   Granby ●
Kremmling ●

Nederlar

EAGLE   Winter Park ●   G

SUMMIT   Central Ci

Idaho Spring

Eágle ●   Georgetown ●   C

GARFIELD   Avon ●   ● Va   Dillon   C
Silt   Minturn ●   Keystone ●
Rifle ●   Glenwood Springs ●

Copper Mountain ●   Breckenridge
Carbondale ●   ● Basalt
PITKIN   ● Snowmass

R. E. Stevens
Cartographer

● Aspen

10 0 10 20 30 40 50 Miles

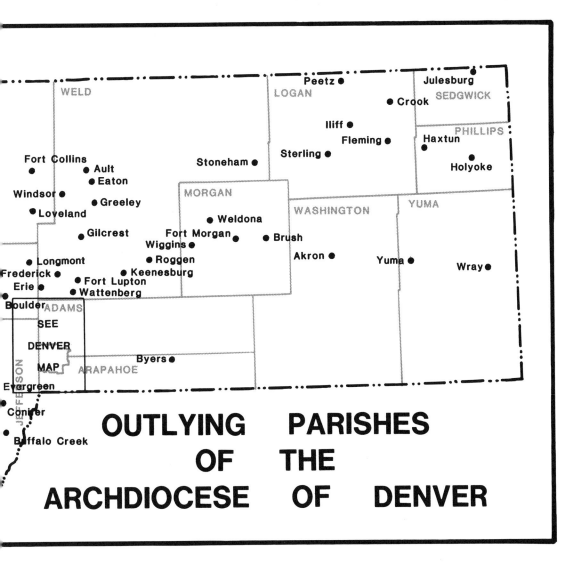

OUTLYING PARISHES
OF THE
ARCHDIOCESE OF DENVER

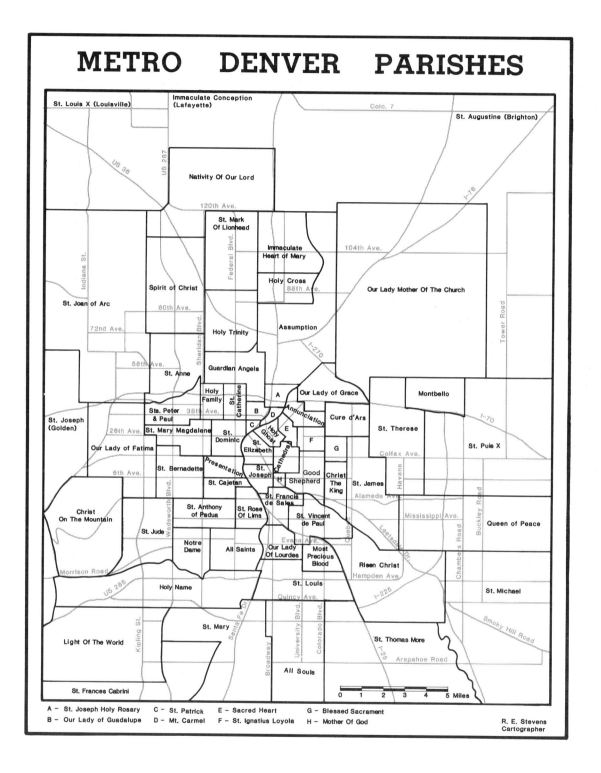

METRO DENVER PARISHES

St. Louis X (Louisville)

Immaculate Conception (Lafayette)

St. Augustine (Brighton)

Colo. 7

US 36

US 287

I-76

Nativity Of Our Lord

120th Ave.

Indiana St.

St. Mark Of Lionhead

Federal Blvd.

104th Ave.

Immaculate Heart of Mary

Holy Cross

88th Ave.

Spirit of Christ

Our Lady Mother Of The Church

St. Joan of Arc

80th Ave.

Tower Road

72nd Ave.

Sheridan Blvd.

Holy Trinity

Assumption

I-270

58th Ave.

St. Anne

Guardian Angels

Holy Family

St. Catherine

A

Our Lady of Grace

Montbello

Sts. Peter & Paul

38th Ave.

B

D

Annunciation

Cure d'Ars

I-70

St. Joseph (Golden)

St. Mary Magdalene

26th Ave.

C

Holy Ghost

E

St. Therese

St. Dominic

F

Our Lady of Fatima

St. Elizabeth

Cathedral

G

St. Puis X

Colfax Ave.

6th Ave.

St. Bernadette

Presentation

St. Joseph

Good Shepherd

Christ The King

St. James

Havana

St. Cajetan

H

Wadsworth Blvd.

Christ On The Mountain

St. Anthony of Padua

St. Rose Of Lima

St. Francis de Sales

Alameda Ave.

Buckley Road

St. Jude

St. Vincent de Paul

Mississippi Ave.

Chambers Road

Queen of Peace

Notre Dame

All Saints

Our Lady Of Lourdes

Most Precious Blood

Evans Ave.

Cherry Creek Dr.

Leetsdale Dr.

Risen Christ

Morrison Road

Hampden Ave.

St. Michael

US 285

Holy Name

St. Louis

Quincy Ave.

I-225

Kipling St.

Santa Fe Dr.

Broadway

University Blvd.

Colorado Blvd.

St. Mary

St. Thomas More

Smoky Hill Road

Light Of The World

Arapahoe Road

I-25

All Souls

St. Frances Cabrini

0 1 2 3 4 5 Miles

A – St. Joseph Holy Rosary C – St. Patrick   E – Sacred Heart   G – Blessed Sacrament
B – Our Lady of Guadalupe   D – Mt. Carmel   F – St. Ignatius Loyola H – Mother Of God

R. E. Stevens
Cartographer

Akron

ST. JOSEPH (1917)
551 West 5th Street

Sun-baked, wind-swept Akron needed a saint. Ethnic squabbles plagued the founding pastor and the dark days of the depression drove another to beg for reassignment. Then Akron was blessed with an unlikely hero—stern-faced, big-eared William J. Coyne.

Before Father Coyne arrived, St. Joseph parish had had twenty-four short-term pastors. William J. Howlett first said Mass in Akron, the seat of Washington County, five years after the Burlington Railroad had arrived and laid out the town in 1882. A railroad official's wife named it for her hometown in Ohio. Terry McAloon, a railroad worker, stayed in the division point and opened a flour and feed store. As founding chairman (with trustees John J. Gebauer, Dan Diamond, Dick Meenan, Herman Gebauer, and E. W. Morand) of the Catholic Church in Akron, McAloon hosted Father Howlett and other early missionaries.

"Every 'church' day Terry would be seen going down the street carrying a pail of coal and a bundle of kindling wood to start the fire in the stove," his daughter Margaret Hall related in *The Pioneer Book of Washington County, Colorado*. McAloon's wife, Mima, rigged up an altar with an old table and cracker boxes.

In 1898, the fledgling congregation bought a Main Street store and converted it to a church. When Bishop Matz paid his first confirmation visit on September 28, 1907, the *Akron Pioneer Press* reported:

> The crowd was so great that the front doors of the church were left open and many stood outside holding up umbrellas to protect them from the sun. . . . This was the first time a bishop ever visited Akron and when his lordship came from the sacristy dressed in royal purple, wearing his miter and carrying his golden crosier, the greatest silence prevailed. . . . The unusual ceremony brought out many Protestants whose pardonable curiosity helped to swell the attendance. Before the services in the church began, Bishop Matz dedicated the building by sprinkling it with holy water and pro-

nouncing the words that dedicate the house to the Lord's use. A choir composed of Misses Edna and Elma Yeamans, Nellie Jones and Josephine Ballard tendered appropriate music. . . . The church on this visit of the bishop received the name of St. Joseph and hereafter it will be known by that name.

Rev. J.L. Juily, who became the missionary pastor in 1911, bought three lots on Bent Street. To build a new church there, the Catholic Church Extension Society of Chicago contributed cash, as did Akronites of various denominations. With labor and materials contributed by parishioners, St. Joseph's was completed and dedicated on May 17, 1914.

The following year, Bishop Matz received a long letter in German complaining about Father Juily. It was followed by a letter from Terry McAloon, which read in part:

> I have seen priests come here when they did not have money to get home on; when there were only two or three persons at church. I often had to give them money to go home on. Now we have a nice little congregation but unfortunately [some German parishioners are] transferring the European war over here. I am Irish, cannot help it, would not if I could. Father Juily is French and seems proud of it. . . . We have never had a priest who went to more trouble and inconvenience to accommodate the people than Father Juily. He is clean, respectable and a credit to the church.

Father Juily, who had four brothers fighting the Germans back in France, stayed on and, apparently, achieved peace. In 1918, he was replaced by Louis J. Grohman, a World War I chaplain who became the first resident pastor. A year later, Father Grohman and Bishop Tihen blessed each room of a $25,000, two-story brick school. That September 1919, six Sisters of the Presentation of the Blessed Virgin Mary welcomed twenty-four boarders, and sixty-five day students.

While joyously celebrating this achievement, the parish had no idea of the ordeals ahead. Poor health forced Father Grohman to resign in 1920, leaving $35.89 for the next pastor's expenses. The next year, the Farmers' Bank of Akron failed, and the parish lost all its savings. St. Joseph's had thirteen different pastors in ten years, before Joseph Fleck arrived in 1930. Three years later, Father Fleck wrote to Bishop Vehr from the dry, depressed, dusty town:

> If optimism ever miscarried it did so here and many victims of it here have left. . . . We have reached the zero mark in our bank account and I can see no prospects whatever to raise the $360.00 due in October. We are out of candles and Altar Wine and soon need coal and, oh, how the church needs painting and a new roof . . . the school building cannot be disposed of. . . . I am a nervous wreck, can get no sleep for nights in succession and . . . would therefore appreciate it if Your Excellency could reassign me to another charge.

Father Fleck wrote this letter in 1933—the worst year of the Great Depression—and the year when William J. Coyne arrived. Parishioner Avis Willeke recalled in the parish's 1976 history that Father Coyne came by train and walked over to the rectory where he shook the dust out of his bedding. That first Sunday, he told penniless parishioners just to put eggs in the collection basket and he would trade them for whatever else he needed. "I'm no spring-chicken," Father Coyne added, "and I won't put up with any bickering. I'm a hard-nosed businessman and we need to put this parish on a paying basis!" He rallied the men of the parish to redecorate the church interior, paint and landscape the exterior, dig out a basement, install restrooms, and spruce up the cemetery.

Father Coyne leased half of the school to the Washington County School District for $65 a month, procured a monthly $20 subsidy from the Catholic Extension Society in 1936, and sold $13,000 in parish bonds. In 1937, he shocked Bishop Vehr—who had grown accustomed to complaints and financial requests from Akron—by sending him $25, as "a little offering for your confirmation services."

A decade later, Archbishop Vehr received a letter from St. Joseph's 210 parishioners, asking him to relieve the popular priest of some of his many mission assignments:

> He is continually on the go from six o'clock in the morning until nine or ten o'clock at night, and many nights until twelve o'clock. The strain is telling on him to a greater extent than he will admit. . . . In the last ten years he has brought our parish out of a $13,000 debt, besides making many substantial improvements. . . . We have never had a priest who is as well thought of by Catholic and non-Catholic alike or who has done so much to unite this parish into a progressive unit. We are proud to say there has never been a complaint against him.

Although this request was futile, Father Coyne and his parishioners went to work, beginning a new church on the northwestern outskirts of Akron. Thanks to generous contributions of money, labor, and materials, Father Coyne expanded his plans, constructing a handsome, red brick edifice with a full basement. Architect John F. Connell designed this $107,000 neo-Gothic structure, which Archbishop Vehr dedicated on March 24, 1953. Two years later, the 350-seat church overflowed for Father Coyne's silver jubilee, as forty-two priests and 300 Akronites gathered to thank the one-time Casper, Wyoming, businessman who had switched careers at age forty-three to enter St. Thomas Seminary.

In 1963, St. Joseph's buried its long-time, beloved pastor in the parish cemetery, eulogizing him as "the light that guided them through the depression [and] through the war." The small but reinvigorated parish Father Coyne left behind was subsequently guided by Clement V. Gallagher (1962–1970), Andrew E. Gottschalk (1970–1975) and V. Leo Smith, who has written of his enduring parishioners:

> These people have come many miles each week to faithfully worship their God in good times and in bad. . . . Regardless of the difficulties which the people of St. Joseph's have encountered over the years, they have tried to imitate the faith of their patron. Like St. Joseph, they have believed, worked, and prayed—even when they did not understand how God could be working in this way.

Arvada

ST. JOAN OF ARC (1967)
12705 West 58th Avenue

Arvada's second parish was created by Archbishop Casey on August 22, 1967, with the appointment of James W. Rasby as the pioneer pastor. "I was in the right place at the right time. I was at St. Anne's in Arvada and knew the territory," recalled Father Rasby, who named St. Joan's for the French martyr because of his special devotion to her.

Parish organizational meetings were held in the Arvada Square Shopping Center on Wednesday evenings, and charter members of the parish met for mass in the gymnasium at Arvada West High School. Father Rasby struggled not to laugh every time the congregation stood up or sat down—and the bleacher seats either groaned or breathed a loud sigh of relief. For Easter, Christmas, and other special services, the baby parish borrowed the King of Glory Lutheran Church, whose five-sided sanctuary inspired a similar floor plan for St. Joan of Arc Church.

St. Joan's celebrated the first mass in the new church on Thanksgiving, 1968. The 900-seat church contained oak pews wrapped around a semicircular altar. Despite the decidedly modern architecture, the interior artwork included some traditional elements, such as the peacocks symbolizing the Holy Eucharist.

Father Rasby was named rector of Immaculate Conception Cathedral on March 26, 1969, and was succeeded at Arvada by Robert I. Durrie. Father Durrie replaced the old $22,000 rectory at West 58th Avenue and Independence Street with a new one next to the church. A youth center, a convent on Vivian Street, landscaping, and a paved parking lot were completed during his time.

"Many of the youth of Arvada come here," Father Durrie remarked after the St. Joan's Youth Ministry began sponsoring weekly dances. Some 250 youngsters, aged five to eighteen, also attended the religious education classes launched at Campbell Elementary School in 1968 and continued in the parish center after its construction. Sisters Andrea, Rita, and Ricardis began the program, assisted by lay teachers, to be followed over the years by Sisters Louise Skoch, OSF, Mary Cohara, SC, and others.

When Father Durrie was transferred in 1982, he was followed by a hearty Irishman, Michael A. Walsh. In 1988, Father Walsh officiated at the dedication of Orleans Community Center for a parish that had grown to over 2,200 households.

"I want people to look on the parish as something more than a place to go on Sunday," Father Walsh commented. "Our goals are evangelization, education programs, and better Sunday attendance.

Whereas the first decade at St. Joan of Arc's was organization and the second was consolidation, the third decade will be expansion."

SHRINE OF ST. ANNE (1920)
7555 Grant Place

"The most impressive small church in America," crowed the *Arvada Enterprise* on December 1, 1921, was being built in that Jefferson County town and would house "the largest relic of St. Anne in the United States."

St. Anne's site in downtown Arvada was purchased by Bishop Tihen from William Gunther for $1,000. Harry James Manning, a leading Denver architect, designed the $125,000 beauty, inspired by Quebec's Basilica of Ste-Anne-de-Beaupré. Parishioners had excavated the site before the J. K. Mullen Construction Company went to work.

Bishop Tihen, who had brought St. Anne's wrist bone back from Europe for the shrine, dedicated the church on June 25, 1922. Arvada Catholics, who had been organized as a mission of Holy Family parish since 1914, left the little upstairs hall where they had been meeting above the First National Bank for their magnificent new home.

Shrine of St. Anne, Arvada. (Photo by Tom Noel.)

"The church is a gem," proclaimed the *Denver Catholic Register*. "Its architectural lines are unusual, and while in one or two of its features, like the terra cotta work, the edifice almost approaches the bizarre, yet there is around it such an air of piety and true Catholic conservatism." Some called the style Renaissance revival, others fancied it Lombardic Romanesque. Few remained unimpressed with the hulking, vertical shape, looming skyward in red pressed brick, glazed blue and white terra cotta trim, and variegated roof tiles. Inside, the church was surprisingly small and cozy, with rosy, translucent Romanesque windows rising into the barrel-arch ceiling.

The soaring single bell tower housed the shrine. At night, a light shone on top of the church tower, then Jefferson County's tallest building. Soon, this pilgrimage church was attracting the sick and the handicapped and became the reason, according to the *Arvada Enterprise*, that the road from Denver was paved.

The Shrine of St. Anne also attracted the hooded eyes of the Ku Klux Klan, which met on nearby Hackberry Hill. These spooks burned crosses in front of the shrine and harrassed Walter Grace, the first pastor. The Klan and its sympathizers took glee in charging Father Grace with forging an altar wine permit and serving wine socially during the prohibition era, for which he served two years in prison.

In August 1925, several thousand Klansmen marched through the streets of Arvada. In reply, thousands of Catholics led by the Knights of Columbus and Holy Name societies from throughout Denver countermarched from Regis College to St. Anne's for an outdoor mass. Shortly afterwards, the Klan collapsed. The shrine survived, though its small congregation wrestled with a large debt, particularly during the depression.

Over twenty-five different pastors and copastors followed Father Grace, including Jesuits, Benedictines, and Claretians, all of whom struggled at the beautiful but impoverished church. Until 1948, when the parish finally could afford to build a rectory, its priests lived in the church basement.

Not until the 1950s did Arvada begin to boom, becoming the third largest and one of the most progressive of Denver's suburbs, with its own historical society, well-preserved downtown historic district, and an outstanding arts and humanities center. Between 1955 and 1960, the number of registered parish households climbed from 550 to 1,200, necessitating additions to the church. Even after the creation of two other Arvada parishes in 1967 and 1973, the Shrine of St. Anne retained over 2,000 households. It is the dominant landmark of the Olde Town, and, in 1960, built a sixteen-room, $329,000, boxy, buff brick school at 7320 Grant Place was built.

In 1987, when many parochial schools had closed or were declining in enrollment, St. Anne's had 400 students, nineteen lay teachers, and kindergarten through eighth grades. That year, the parish undertook a $1-million expansion to add a new library, science laboratory, gym, kindergarten, and computer classroom. Walker Nickless, the pastor, told the *Denver Catholic Register*, "There's nothing greater than being able to help parents with the religious and academic life of their children."

SPIRIT OF CHRIST CATHOLIC COMMUNITY (1973)
7400 West 80th Avenue

"This parish is being developed from the grassroots with as much lay input as possible," the founding pastor declared. And from the beginning, a vibrant community spirit enlivened Spirit of Christ.

"Our Catholic community," parishioner Kathy Galiffa wrote in 1989,

> emerged from the warmth and caring of St. Anne's Parish in Olde Town Arvada. During the early 1970s, St. Anne's became so large that it took 13 Masses a weekend to accommodate everyone. Even after St. Anne's established mini-parishes which met in people's homes, the liturgies became so crowded it was apparent that a new parish was needed.

Archbishop Casey saw the need and authorized a parish to serve the northern part of Arvada. Emil Schneider, Sr., donated a large parcel of land, St. Anne's donated $50,000 in seed money, and John Martens went to work as the first pastor. This Claretian father gathered with 200 parishioners for Sunday masses at the Weber Elementary School gym, and, on July 1, 1974, for an outdoor candlelight mass on the church site.

Parishioners voted to name themselves the Spirit of Christ Catholic Community. Bishop Richard Hanifen, in his first official action after consecration as auxiliary bishop, presided at the groundbreaking. David M. Sobieszczyk, who would become pastor a year later, was also there. Parish volunteers did much of the finish work inside, where Sister Martha Clare Bond, CPPS, created the liturgical design. Seracuse Lawler & Partners, a Denver architectural firm, was responsible for the stark, low-slung, red brick and grey metal church with its raw brick and redwood interior, which Archbishop Casey dedicated on July 1, 1975.

Kenneth Leone, a Denver native, had always wanted to be a priest. As a grade schooler, he said pretend masses at a small make-believe altar in his basement. After graduating from St. Catherine Grade School, Regis High School, and St. Thomas Seminary, he became the third pastor in 1981. Building on the lay-minded styles of his predecessors, Father Leone turned Spirit of Christ into what Archbishop Stafford has called a "church of the 21st century."

Father Leone celebrated his twentieth anniversary as a priest in 1987 by ascending over the church in a hot air balloon to shower children below with candy from heaven. Father Leone, a former archdiocesan director of Catholic Youth Services, has been nicknamed the "McDonald's Priest." That, he explained, is because he goes to wherever teenagers feel comfortable to talk with them, to arrange reconciliations and marriages. Father Leone adds, "I've heard more than 1,000 confessions at McDonald's."

Spirit of Christ is unusual in having a permanent deacon, Michael J. Howard, who serves as associate pastor, and in having Sue McNulty standing next to the tabernacle during Mass to sign for the deaf. Masses are also amplified with video cameras, a sound board, and an electronic screen that flashes song lyrics.

Although the 1974 structure held 750 worshippers, it seemed to grow smaller every Sunday, as the parish zoomed past the 1,000-family-memberships mark by 1979. On September 28, 1986, Archbishop Stafford dedicated a $1 million addition and renovation for a congregation of over 3,500 registered families.

Father Leone remarked in 1988 that:

> As a community we tithe 10 percent of our offertory collection to assist not only our parish families in crisis, but crisis situations in the larger community—such as shelters for battered women, peace and justice here and abroad. We help missions in Sudan, Mexico, China, and El Salvador, sending some of our members all over the globe to do missionary work, while others stay in Arvada

and donate time to Meals on Wheels and the Arvada Food Bank.

Spirit of Christ is a stewardship community, striving to return to God a fitting portion of our time, talent, and treasure. Spirit of Christ's goal is to make every person entering our community feel welcomed, accepted, loved; and an abundance of Christ's peace.

Aspen

ST. MARY (1882)
104 South Galena Street

Aspen's "Sky Pilot" since 1882 has been St. Mary's. Weathering economic peaks and valleys as steep as that of the surrounding mountains, St. Mary's has served Pitkin County continuously from the silver boom to the ski boom.

Father Edward Downey, the founding pastor, celebrated Christmas, 1885, at St. Mary's in Aspen. (Denver Public Library.)

Prospectors poked into the upper Roaring Fork River valley as early as the late 1870s. Where the Roaring Fork of the Colorado River is joined by Castle, Hunter, and Maroon creeks, silver seekers founded Aspen in 1880. The new camp attracted hundreds, then thousands of prospectors swarming in each year over Independence Pass.

Aspen, a part of Gunnison County until the creation of Pitkin County in 1881, was first a mission tended by priests from Gunnison. Luke Harney said the first mass on Sunday, July 3, 1881, in the *Aspen Times* building at Hyman Avenue and Mill Street. Father Harney's assistant in Gunnison, M. McCarthy, OSB, also traveled over Pearl Pass to say Sunday masses until Bishop Machebeuf appointed Edward Downey the first resident pastor in June 1883.

Father Downey, who had been born, raised, and educated in New York, endeared himself to Aspenites by riding with troops policing the Utes. He and his flock used bazaars, dinners, and dances to raise money to build St. Stephen's mission on Main Street between Galena and Hunter streets. This plain, frame church was dedicated in June 1883. Next door, at the corner of Main and Galena, the parish constructed, in 1888, the $6,000, two-story brick rectory still in use.

Miners' candlesticks were used to light the church and to pin paper flowers to the walls. Soon, the congregation outgrew this small, simple church, as Aspen became the third largest city in Colorado. On the eve of the 1893 silver crash, Aspen's population reached 5,108 and its silver production surpassed even that of Leadville.

During these flush times, Father Downey used St. Patrick's Day dinner balls and other extravaganzas to help raise $22,000 to build a new, debt-free church, St. Mary's. This sturdy two-story brick church, brightened by numerous Gothic windows, was dedicated on March 13, 1892. The seventy-five-by-forty-five-foot structure on a stone foundation contained an elevated chair box and a pipe organ. That fall, Benedictine nuns from Chicago opened a parish elementary school on the first floor, while the church room above doubled as an assembly hall.

As St. Mary's had become one of the largest parishes in the diocese, Bishop Machebeuf, in 1890, sent John Baptist Pitival to Aspen to assist Father Downey. Father Pitival was a French-born priest who had been ordained by and worked under Archbishop Lamy in Santa Fe. The hard work of building a new church, school, and rectory, as well as Aspen's rugged 7,908-foot-high climate, wore down Father Downey's health. He was reassigned to relatively balmy Brighton in 1891. Father Pitival, an able administrator who would become the archbishop of Santa Fe, became St. Mary's second pastor and made the church a mainstay of the community, which fell on hard times after the silver crash.

The Benedictines left the school in 1900, but Bishop Matz persuaded the Sisters of Mercy to reopen it in 1904. The nuns were given the old St. Stephen's mission as a convent home. *The Aspen Courier* of September 12, 1905, voiced the town's joy at regaining St. Mary School:

> The church and school in Aspen are both in a flourishing condition. Both buildings have been thoroughly renovated. New sidewalks have been put in, and beautiful shade trees planted. . . . The school has a very high standard and quite a number of non-Catholics.

Aspen's silver mines continued to close as the metal's price fell from over $1.32 an ounce to fifty-nine cents. The town's population slid to 1,834 in 1910 and tumbled to under 700 during the 1930s. St. Mary's School, so joyously reopened in 1904, closed permanently in 1910. Seven short-term pastors struggled to keep the church open. Aspenites, whose town hall shared the same block as St. Mary's and whose county courthouse was just across Main Street, feared for the day that the church would shut its doors.

The once shiny silver city became a semi-ghost town. Townsfolk turned to raising cattle, sheep, and hay, or tried living on the spectacular scenery. Old prospectors dozed in front of the Hotel Jerome, one of the few places to remain open.

"Pop," a visitor asked one of these old timers during the 1930s, "what makes Aspen so slow?"

The old codger squinted at the questioner and mumbled, "The people's mineralized, that's what. They got silver in their hair and lead in their pants."

Over at St. Mary's, Reverend Felix Dilly wrote to Bishop Matz suggesting St. Mary's be closed because "the support of the pastor is now becoming very meager in every respect." Instead, Bishop Matz replaced Dilly with Patrick J. McSweeney in 1914. Father McSweeney stayed with the parish until his death in 1941. Returning the loyalty of his small, poor flock, he stuck it out through a mining bust that closed many other parishes. "I regret that I am unable to meet the Diocesan dues this year," he wrote to Bishop Tihen on December 29, 1930. "The mining situation is deplorable. The people are poor and cannot find work. They are certainly striving to keep a resident priest here."

Father McSweeney was also assigned, in 1932, the missions at Basalt and Marble, which had been tended from St. Stephen Church in Glenwood Springs. By the time Father McSweeney died, Aspen's renaissance had begun. In 1938, André Roch, a Swiss skier, laid out Roch Run on Aspen Mountain. In 1942, the U.S. Army opened Camp Hale to train ski troops, some of whom would start the Aspen Skiing Corporation in 1946. A few years later, Walter Paepcke, a wealthy Chicago industrialist, founded the Aspen Institute for Humanistic Studies.

By the 1950s, Aspen had emerged as a skiing, cultural, and resort haven for an international jet set. By the 1970s, Pitkin was, per capita, the wealthiest county in Colorado and the ninth richest in the United States. As the population climbed to over 3,000, St. Mary's, with a seating capacity of 200, began to overflow, as it had in the 1880s. Clergymen as well as laity vacationed in Aspen and the basement of St. Mary's became a dormitory for visitors, including one young priest from Baltimore, Frank Stafford, who liked to ski.

St. Vincent's, the mission church in Basalt, received its own pastor in 1970 and, in 1973, opened a mission at Snowmass Village. Phenomenal population growth prompted Archbishop Casey to establish St. Mary of the Crown in Carbondale in 1980. Pitkin County Catholics and tourists were also served by a summer vacation school, operated at St. Mary's by the Sisters of Charity of Leavenworth.

The good sisters liked to retell the legend of the quaking aspen tree. Supposedly, Christ was crucified on an aspen, and after that the trees were banished from the Holy Land to cold, mountainous regions. The aspen's trunk and branches would never again grow straight enough to form a cross, and the heart-shaped leaves would never stop trembling.

Thomas A. Bradtke, the pastor of St. Mary's since 1981, provides unique "therapy" for parishioners and tourists—raft tours down the Roaring Fork River with "Father Tom's Rafting Academy." Father Tom, who says he fell in love with the area while on sick leave from Chicago in 1970, guided St. Mary's through its centennial celebration in 1982. Following a pontifical high mass by Archbishop Casey, students and faculty from the Aspen Music Festival provided a series of free concerts of ecclesiastical and secular classics. In November, after winter brought "white silver" to Aspen's ski slopes, St. Mary's staged a banquet for the "old timers," the persistent parishioners who had never lost faith.

At the banquet, St. Mary's honored the likes of Elizabeth Callahan, who was born in Aspen in 1896 and now lives across the street from St. Mary's. She recollected how the priests used to read students' report cards in front of all the pupils. "The whole east end was full of Slovenians," she added, "while other Catholics—Irish, Italians, French, and Germans—lived all over." And she recollected the scariest times of all, the blizzards "when you couldn't see across the street to the strength that is St. Mary's."

Ault

ST. MARY (1953)

Ault is a town of around 1,000 people, located in western Weld County ten miles north of Greeley. Founded in 1898, it was named for Alexander Ault, the principal grain buyer in the area.

Although Dominic Morera, SF, pastor of Our Lady of Peace in Greeley, was tending sixteen other missions, he showed special concern for Ault. He established St. Mary mission there in 1953 and wrote to Archbishop Vehr in 1955:

> Ault is the heart of the sugar beet district of Northern Colorado. There is a great percentage of Spanish-speaking people in the area. . . . The people are poor, many of them employed only during the summer months. Yet they spend $6,000 on the church.

Rewarding the generosity of the thirty-eight families of the Ault Mission, the Catholic Extension Society of Chicago donated $2,970 to help them acquire a one-room schoolhouse from the Ault School District. Father Morera and his flock then bought two lots of J.C. Romero's cornfield in northeastern Ault and moved the frame schoolhouse there before remodeling it into a 100-seat chapel, furnished with secondhand fixtures from other churches.

Over the years, that humble little frame chapel has evolved into a small but handsome brick-fronted church with almost 100 member families in 1988. Parishioners from Ault, Nuhn, Pierce, and surrounding areas welcome the missionary ministry from Greeley's Hispanic oriented parish, Our Lady of Peace.

Aurora

QUEEN OF PEACE (1968)
13120 East Kentucky Avenue

The mansard-roofed fortress of Queen of Peace with its large central tower and Celtic cross on top traces its origins to 1968 when Archbishop Casey asked the Oblates of Mary Immaculate to start a new parish in the proliferating subdivisions of Aurora.

Frank McCullough, OMI, the pioneer pastor, oversaw groundbreaking on September 4, 1968, for the first parish building. This structure contained a forty-seat chapel, offices, and a rectory, which were blessed by Archbishop Casey on February 4, 1969. Architect Keith Ames of Longmont planned the second edifice to be built on the 9.9-acre site—a 25,000–square-foot, pyramidical church seating 1,200, with four large classrooms, a gym, and a counseling center on the perimeter. Parishioners gathered around the strange new structure in July 1975 to watch a giant construction crane top off the church with a fifty-eight-foot-high precast tower surmounted by a twelve-foot cross. A life-sized Queen of Peace statue was installed at the porte cochère entrance.

Under the guidance of William Breslin, pastor since 1987, Queen of Peace sponsors the St. Andrews House, a day hospitality center at 1536 Dallas Street, which provides physical and spiritual assistance to the needy. In 1989 this large, modern church was overflowing with about 3,200 family memberships and anticipated expansion.

ST. MICHAEL THE ARCHANGEL (1979)
19099 East Floyd Avenue

Archbishop Casey asked Robert M. Syrianey, in 1978, to start a new parish in southeastern Aurora. Land had already been acquired for a new church to relieve overcrowding at Queen of Peace, Risen Christ, and St. Thomas More.

Father Syrianey celebrated the first mass on March 12, 1978, at the Meadowood Recreation Center. About 300 persons attended those early masses and meetings and expressed interest in building a new church. Potlucks, picnics, and meet-the-pastor nights were used to muster support.

By the summer of 1978, St. Michael's had grown so large that Sunday masses had to be shifted to the auditorium of Smoky Hill High School. The Gold Rush (a parish carnival) was launched to raise money, as were St. Patrick's Day and November-fest dances, enabling Father Syrianey and his parishioners to break ground in June 1980.

The new parish center was completed in time for a Valentine's Day mass in 1981 and blessed by Archbishop Casey on March 21. As St. Michael's passed the 1,000-families-registration mark in 1981, Sister Marie C. Fitzpatrick, BVM, took charge of the religious education and sacramental preparation programs.

In June 1985, Bernard A. Schmitz, an Aurora native, became the second pastor of St. Michael's. The parish family membership reached 2,300 that year but has since stabilized, after the oil bust of 1983 and leaner years. Because the 2,180 parish families in 1988 had many children, Father Schmitz says the parish continues to emphasize its preschool and youth ministry. The daily preschool program is one of the few in Colorado to earn accreditation from the National Academy of Early Childhood Programs.

Sister Marie Fitzpatrick reported in a 1988 interview:

> Our parish, like its building, is contemporary and informal. We were one of the first Catholic communities to enact Vatican II reforms and liturgy. St. Michael's is a wonderful place where we have

high expectations of parishioners. Hundreds of them are involved in parish and social justice programs. At our tenth anniversary dinner, for example, we reminded people of the misfortunes of others by serving a homeless shelter type of meal—chicken neck soup. And there were no seconds.

ST. PIUS X (1954)
13670 East 13th Place

On June 14, 1954—two weeks after the canonization of Pope Pius X—Archbishop Vehr created St. Pius X parish in Aurora. The first masses were held in the banquet room of the Town House Supper Club at Peoria Street and East Colfax Avenue by Francis J. Syrianey, the pioneer pastor.

Following a 1954 door-to-door census of the area bounded by Smith Road on the north and Sixth Avenue on the south between Peoria and Picadilly streets, Father Syrianey counted approximately 400 Catholic families in the new parish.

In June 1955, the congregation broke ground for a sixty-eight-by-one-hundred-foot church on a five-acre site bought in 1954 for $40,000. This $161,172 church was constructed with the help of volunteers who laid the asphalt tile, hung the acoustical tile ceiling, and painted the interior. Local artists designed and executed the liturgical appointments and art.

Pews for the 400-seat church cost $12,000, and another $12,360 was expended to buy an adjoining Hoffman Heights home as a rectory for Father Syrianey, who converted the attached garage into a chapel. After the church was completed in June 1956, parishioners began a school construction fund, and the St. Pius X Federal Credit Union made loans that enabled parishioners to pay their school construction pledges.

Work began April 24, 1960, on the split-level, twelve-classroom, $286,000 school. Three lay teachers and two Sisters of Charity of Cincinnati opened the school that September, with the Aurora Public Library providing bookmobile service. In 1964, four new classrooms, a library, and a multipurpose room were added to the school, allowing it to double classes in all eight grades.

To reach out more effectively to the community, husband and wife teams organized "little parishes" in 1962 for home meetings and masses. In 1967,

Father Syrianey received an assistant pastor, John C. Kelley, who took responsibility for Sunday and holy day services at the mission churches in Strasburg and Deer Trail.

St. Pius X had grown to approximately 1,200 families by 1968, when Queen of Peace parish was formed for Catholics living in southeast Aurora. Another 250 parishioners were lost in 1972, when the Montbello Catholic Community was formed for those living in northwestern Aurora and northeastern Denver.

Despite financial hardships and the loss of members to newer parishes, St. Pius X struggled to keep up its church and school. Bingo games were begun in 1976, despite objections from some parishioners, while other fund-raisers included potluck dinners, dances, roller skating parties, garage sales, Country Dinner Playhouse socials, raffles, and Gold C coupon book sales.

James E. Kane became pastor in 1982 and oversaw burning of the mortgage in 1985, when the parish celebrated its financial independence as a debt-free, $1,250,000 plant with an eight-grade school, day care, and a "little lambs" preschool.

ST. THERESE (1926)
1243 Kingston Street & East 13th Avenue

Although it is the third largest city in 1980's Colorado, Aurora was for decades a small, stagnant farm town on the eastern outskirts of Denver. Franciscan friars from St. Elizabeth's in Denver began saying mass in Aurora's Sable Schoolhouse in 1903.

After the Sisters of Mercy established a novitiate in 1915 at East 14th Avenue and Dayton Street, mass was offered there daily. When the novitiate closed in 1922, East Denver's St. James' was the nearest Catholic church, and Aurorans began agitating for a parish of their own.

Bishop Tihen obliged them, asking Henry A. Geisert to establish Aurora's first parish in 1926. It was named St. Therese of Lisieux in honor of the Little Flower who had been canonized on May 17, 1925. Father Geisert bought the two-story frame house, which had served as the Sisters of Mercy novitiate, and six adjacent lots for $15,000.

The home's parlor was converted to a chapel for the sixty or so Catholic families in Aurora, who supported the church by holding dinners and ba-

Like many other parishes, St. Therese's started out in an old house, making a church out of this two-story frame residence at East 14th Avenue and Dayton Street. (Denver Archdiocesan Archives.)

zaars in Murphy's Garage. These popular fifty-cent dinner carnivals raised as much as $500 a night. Daniel A. Barry, who succeeded Father Geisert in 1932, was a handyman who built confessionals into the church and remodeled much of the rest of the old house. During the 1930s depression, St. Therese's survived, though Sunday collections rarely brought in as much as $50.

Aurora boomed during and after World War II. Louis J. Mertz, pastor from 1946 to 1954, saw the town's population skyrocket from 3,437 in 1940 to over 50,000. Rapid growth around Stapleton, Lowry, and Buckley airfields led St. Therese's to offer five Sunday masses for an estimated 500 parishioners by 1949. That year, the parish purchased forty-eight lots on Kingston Street. John K. Monroe planned a $95,000 church, which was dedicated on July 2, 1951. A $310,000 grade school and convent came next. School children squealed with delight as four F-80s of the Colorado National

Guard buzzed the school as part of the dedication ceremony on September 23, 1955.

The Sisters of Charity of Leavenworth were teaching 663 pupils by 1960, when a $176,698 addition gave the school a new library and brought the number of classrooms to fifteen. In 1966, the parish received a new pastor, James B. Hamblin, better known nationwide to the readers of the *Junior Catholic Messenger* as "Father Jim." He added a $209,318 gymnasium to the flourishing school.

With the construction of three new Aurora parishes between 1954 and 1979, St. Therese's membership stabilized at around 900 households. The parish has maintained the kindergarten-through-eighth-grade school, plus an extended day care program, a credit union, a blood bank, scout troops, and a broad spectrum of programs in what has grown to be a two-block parish complex.

Avon

ST. MARY'S UPPER EAGLE VALLEY COMMUNITY (1985)

Avon, a tiny railroad and ranching town established in the 1880s, was transformed a century later by development of the Beaver Creek Resort and Ski Area.

Not only the homes and condos of the wealthy but also trailer-camp housing for construction and service workers mushroomed, inspiring Edward J. Poehlmann, pastor of St. Patrick's in Minturn, to open an Avon mission.

"In many ways," Father Poehlmann reported in 1988,

ski town people are like migrant laborers for whom we completed a magnificent chapel on November 6, 1988. Former President Gerald Ford spearheaded the campaign to raise $950,000 for this new Beaver Creek interdenominational chapel designed by Zehren & Associates of Vail and Scottsdale. This will be a tremendous improvement over our cramped services in the old Avon Town Hall, where I started saying Mass in 1984.

Basalt

ST. VINCENT (1970)
240 Midland Avenue

When the Colorado Midland Railroad construction crews reached the junction of the Frying Pan and Roaring Fork rivers in 1886, they established a town first called Aspen Junction. It was incorporated in 1901 as Basalt, a name inspired by the nearby mountain of basaltic lava.

Joseph P. Carrigan, pastor of St. Stephen's in Glenwood Springs, reported to Bishop Tihen in the 1920s that the faithful in Basalt had completed "an attractive little church with a steeple and a bell and a cement sidewalk in front of the lots on the main street." This church was a renovated three-room house, which was dedicated by Bishop Tihen in June 1924.

Father Carrigan, Patrick McSweeney, and other visiting priests said mass for Catholic families in this haying, ranching, and resort area. In 1954, Joseph Bosch, pastor of St. Mary's in nearby Aspen, began saying evening mass daily. Particularly on Sunday, Father Bosch found that all his Basalt parishioners could not squeeze into the church.

In 1956, parishioners raised $1,781 to build an addition that doubled the size of their chapel. In 1970, St. Vincent's was elevated to parish status by Archbishop Casey, who appointed Thomas Bradtke the first pastor. Father Bradtke also established and tended missions in Carbondale, Snowmass Village, and, until it closed in 1985, the Sacred Heart mission in Redstone.

Robert E. Hehn, the current pastor, tends these missions as well as St. Vincent's, which in 1989 has about seventy registered families. Since 1981, Sisters Clare Ahler and Janet Dielen, two Franciscans, have directed parish education, liturgy, and music programs. The growing parish built a new church and parish hall, which was first used for mass in 1988, when the old church bell rang out the glad news.

Boulder

SACRED HEART OF JESUS (1875)
14th and Mapleton

The sixth church and second Catholic church to be built in Boulder, Sacred Heart of Jesus, was the largest Catholic church in town by 1890 with over 1,300 registered households. The school, church, and parish complex began with the creation of the parish on July 19, 1875. Bishop Machebeuf, in an 1876 letter, expressed pleasure at its growth:

Last year I organized another parish at Boulder with an excellent young German priest, ordained at Baltimore. He is poor but satisfied with his place. . . . I was surprised last week to find a neat church and residence at Boulder, due partly to the generosity of a pious lady convert, who also directs the choir and plays the organ.

In an ultramodern church underneath a novel baldachino, Archbishop Casey celebrated the centennial mass of Sacred Heart of Jesus in 1975.

Vincent Reitmayr was the young German priest who served from 1875 to 1877 and built the first church on two lots at the northwest corner of 14th and Mapleton, which had been purchased by Bishop Machebeuf in 1875, for $600. The first mass was celebrated on Christmas Day, 1877, in the new $1,600 brick church with its distinctive square bell tower.

Anthony J. Abel succeeded Father Reitmayr as pastor in 1877, followed by numerous brief pastorates until the Boulder County parishes were placed under the Benedictine fathers of St. Vincent's Abbey in Westmorland, Pennsylvania, in 1887. Father Chrystosom Lochschmidt, OSB, pastor from 1889 to 1902, launched the parish school that thrives to this day.

Sacred Heart was not the first Catholic school in Boulder County. That distinction belongs to Mount St. Gertrude Academy, which opened in 1892 in the meadow beneath Chatauqua in what was known as the University Place Addition. Mount St. Gertrude was operated by four Sisters of Charity of the Blessed Virgin Mary from Dubuque, Iowa, who located in Boulder in 1890 at the invitation of Bishop Matz. Initially, Sisters Mary Theodore, Thecla, Faustina, and Luminia rented the Mallon residence at 14th and Walnut as their convent, then moved to Martha Decker's home at 13th and Mapleton to be next to Sacred Heart Church.

The sisters opened their academy, a grand $30,000 Victorian two-story schoolhouse, at what is today 970 Aurora Street. At first, St. Gertrude's accepted both boys and girls, Catholics and non-Catholics. Within a few years, the enrollment was so large that the sisters began accepting girls only. Sister Mary Luminia, the principal, advertised the academy for "girls who desire health as well as primary education," hoping to attract to this dry, sunny foothills boarding school girls suffering from or exposed to tuberculosis.

Mount St. Gertrude offered elementary, secondary, and music education. In 1919, the original 1892 school was expanded with the addition of two large wings costing $90,000, as well as two more stories for the main building, and a chapel. Much of the funding was donated by Boulder residents, Catholic and non-Catholic. Townsfolk remembered that after the 1893 silver crash, the sisters at St. Gertrude's had staged a carnival to benefit the whole community. Mount St. Gertrude continued to be Boulder's leading private school until 1969, when it closed.

The building was sold to the University of Colorado, whose Continuing Education Department used it until the fire of October 26, 1980. The charred shell still sits on the hillside where Mount St. Gertrude first opened its doors—a dormant, brick and stone landmark awaiting restoration.

The Sisters of Charity of the Blessed Virgin Mary also volunteered to open a parochial school for Sacred Heart of Jesus parish. Sisters Mary Marcelliana, Anthony, Augustina, Hilarita, and Cypriana opened Sacred Heart of Jesus School on September 4, 1900, in the two-story frame rectory that the Benedictines had built at 14th and Mapleton in 1891. The parish purchased this building for $3,500 and remodeled it as a coeducational elementary school. The sisters lived upstairs until, in 1909, the parish bought the J. H. Decker home, 1321 Mapleton, as a parish convent. In 1917–1918, the old convent was torn down and replaced by a large, three-story school and convent at 13th and Mapleton.

Livingston Ferrand, president of the University of Colorado, was a guest speaker at the dedication of the sleek new Lyons sandstone and manganese white brick school. William O'Ryan, the orator priest from Denver, added that Sacred Heart School graduates should go to the University of Colorado, which "would become the greatest institution of public education in the nation."

Agatho Strittmatter, OSB, pastor from 1902 until his death in 1938, began planning a larger parish in 1903. Architect Frederick W. Paroth of Denver was commissioned to build the second church of the Sacred Heart of Jesus on the original site. Paroth designed a two-story Romanesque church of rusticated Lyons sandstone with a roof of Pennsylvania slate. This church, with its 108-foot-high bell tower capped by a gold-leafed copper cross, with its Romanesque arch windows and doors and huge rose window, was, according to the *Boulder Camera* of May 4, 1908, "considered by many the finest in the city."

Bishop Matz dedicated the new $30,000 church, illuminated by 500 candles as well as electric globe lights shedding light on a magnificent $2,000 marble altar. Walter P. Chrysler, the automobile tycoon, donated the twenty-tube chime tower, in honor of his friend, Father Agatho, in 1927. Throughout his later life, Father Agatho drove Chrysler automobiles, reportedly gifts from his friend in Detroit.

This magnificent church and the large school served the parish well until the postwar boom, when Boulder's population soared from 19,999 in 1950 to 76,685 in 1980. By the 1950s, the school overflowed, with more than 300 children in grades one through eight. Plans to expand began with Paul Fife, OSB, pastor from 1943 to 1957, and were carried out by Edward J. Vollmer, OSB, pastor from 1957 to 1966. For the Sisters of Charity of the Blessed Virgin Mary, who had served the parish since the 1890s, a new $175,000 convent was constructed on the northeast corner of 14th and Mapleton. A dozen Sisters of Charity and nuns from several other orders moved into the modern convent in 1966.

The school was demolished and replaced in 1959 by a $300,000 classroom building designed by architects Langhart and McGuire of Boulder. During the 1960s, over 700 students broke attendance records year after year, quickly filling the new school, a four-classroom annex, and a new gymnasium. Consequently, Sacred Heart invested $320,000 in a junior high school, a contemporary design by Rogers-Nagel-Langhart, which opened in September 1967.

During the 1970s, Sacred Heart School and its twenty-two teachers worked closely with the Boulder Valley public schools to give Sacred Heart students the best possible education, which entailed dual enrollment with Casey Junior High School across the street.

Sacred Heart's tuition is no longer $1.50 a month as it was in 1900, and a decline in the number of nuns led the parish to convert the convent to a parish center in 1983. Yet, Sacred Heart School, especially since the closing of the Mount St. Gertrude Academy, remains a major parish commitment.

Hoping to match the new schools with a new church, Father Vollmer began a tithing campaign in 1960 that raised the entire cost of a new $500,000 church. Houses on the northwest corner of 14th and Mapleton as well as the old church were demolished for a new design by Langhart, McGuire, and Hastings. The cornerstone was laid in subfreezing weather on December 23, 1962, and afterwards the chocolate-colored Norman brick walls began to rise in a cruciform shape, with all four wings facing a central altar beneath a soaring copper and bronze spire. Limestone trim, a light blue terra cotta tile roof, and six cast bronze doors distinguished the exterior of the new church. It was dedicated by Archbishop Vehr on November 21, 1963, when Father Vollmer sang the solemn high mass, celebrating both completion of the church and his silver jubilee as a priest.

Inside, Sacred Heart of Jesus is strikingly contemporary. Large exposed wood ribs lift the ceiling to a central skylight over the altar while fifty-three windows of imported mouth-blown antique stained glass help illuminate the 792 seats.

This dramatically modern church contains reassuringly traditional symbols. Next to the bronzed doors depicting Old Testament scenes stand seven-foot-high bronze statues of the Sacred Heart of Jesus and St. Benedict. Inside, the communion symbols—wheat and grapes—appear on the ceiling, corona, and chandeliers. Such liturgical symbols, as well as the communion of saints itself, link today's Sacred Heart of Jesus parishioners to the handful of Catholics who met in 1875 to create this parish.

Father Tom Woerth, pastor since 1985, declared in 1987, "My hope is to make this a twenty-first-century parish, to meet the needs of all our parishioners from the womb to the tomb."

SACRED HEART OF MARY (1867)
6739 South Boulder Road

Sacred Heart of Mary, the oldest Colorado Catholic church north of Denver, and the Benedictine monastery next door, introduced not only Catholicism but also Old World culture to the gold mining town on Boulder Creek.

After its founding by the Boulder City Town Company on February 10, 1859, the settlement remained small for years. Isabella Bird, the English world traveler and author, described it in *A Lady's Life in the Rocky Mountains*: "Boulder is a hideous collection of frame houses on the burning plain, but it aspires to be a 'city' in virtue of being a 'distributing point' for the settlements up the Boulder Canyon, and of the discovery of a coal seam."

Like other rough-hewn frontier towns, Boulder lusted after a veneer of civilization, seeking churches and schools as prized ornaments of culture during the rush to respectability that followed successful mining rushes. Boulder claimed the first schoolhouse in Colorado Territory, and the state university. The town, striving to become Colorado's cultural capital, welcomed the first visit of Joseph P. Machebeuf in January 1861. Afterwards, it was visited from time to time by Father Machebeuf or his assistant, Father Raverdy. Catholic ser-

In 1910, parishioners still worshipped in the 1875 carpenter Gothic church perched on a South Boulder hilltop, where since the 1930s the Benedictine Walburga nuns have pursued the contemplative, agrarian life prescribed by St. Benedict. (University of Colorado Western Historical Collections and James Baca.)

vices, according to the *Boulder County News*, were held in a hall above the City Drug Store at 14th and Pearl streets "every first and third sunday at 10 o'clock A.M. and Christian instruction at 2 o'clock, P.M."

Father Machebeuf purchased 160 acres in south Boulder from Daniel Delehant for $500 on December 9, 1867, and a small frame church was built on this prairie hilltop under the supervision of Thomas McGrath, pastor of St. Joseph's in Golden. A pioneer parishioner, John DeBaker, made the pews, and Bishop Machebeuf donated vestments, sacred vessels, and twin pictures of the Sacred Heart of Mary and the Sacred Heart of Jesus to decorate the wall behind the altar. Machebeuf named this $600

white frame church Sacred Heart of Mary and asked priests from Golden to conduct Sunday services there.

In 1886, Bishop Machebeuf transferred the church and its site to the Benedictines from St. Vincent Abbey in Latrobe, Pennsylvania. These Benedictines agreed to care for all the souls in Boulder County. Their missions included flourishing new coal-mining towns such as Erie, Lafayette, and Marshall, as well as missions in the silver-mining town of Caribou, and St. Joseph Chapel in Ward (the building survives today as a county garage). St. James mission, which the Benedictines opened in Gold Hill, is now a private home. In Superior, a saloon was remodeled with a steeple and bell tower to become a chapel.

South of Sacred Heart of Mary Church, the Benedictines constructed a five-room frame house ambitiously christened St. Bernard Monastery. They built a barn and a few outbuildings and began growing wheat and oats. The monastery, by 1889, had three Benedictines who, besides tending the farm, the monastery, and Sacred Heart of Mary, staffed Sacred Heart of Jesus Church in downtown Boulder and missions scattered around Boulder County.

In 1896, the Benedictines closed St. Bernard's to concentrate on their new monastery school in Pueblo. While Pueblo had mushroomed into the second largest city in Colorado, Boulder remained a small town of 3,330, according to the 1890 census. At that time, Sacred Heart of Mary had thirty-five member familys, primarily German, French, Belgian, and Irish.

Services were conducted twice a month by priests from Sacred Heart of Jesus Church until 1909, when Suitbert Rickert, OSB, became the resident pastor of Marian parish. Therese Stengel Westermeier recalled Father Rickert's Sunday services and catechism lessons in her 1973 parish history, *Centennial of a Country Church*. She reported that Father Rickert strove to civilize as well as Catholicize, telling parishioners that it was *not* correct to:

1. Make the Sign of the Cross as if fanning off flies.

2. Give a little bobbing curtsy instead of a proper genuflection.

3. Deliberately turn around to stare up at the choir or at those entering church.

4. Go to sleep or read the prayer book during the sermon.

5. Be in an ecstatic condition of devotion when the collection box approaches.

Therese also recalled the outdoor Corpus Christi celebration, when sawhorse and plank altars were draped with her family's "best white sheets." Catechism lessons were suspended in order to teach children "to walk properly" in the procession:

> The boys were warned not to start any monkey-shines, such as poking a partner in the ribs to get him off balance. The girls were admonished not to giggle or gossip and to walk "gracefully" trying to balance a tissue covered shoe box, filled with flowers, dangling from our necks with one hand, and a wreath of smilax on our heads with the other.

Antoine Hintenach, OSB, the next pastor, arrived in 1911. To the delight of little Therese and her friends, he was "riding a motorcycle—something new to us country kids!" Father Hintenach gave sermons in both English and German, or sometimes skipped the sermon to conduct a pop quiz on the *Baltimore Catechism*. In 1913, he began building a new church next to the original 1872 frame structure. Parishioners hauled bricks and lumber from Boulder to build the $8,000 Romanesque landmark. Next door to the church, the old Benedictine monastery found a new use in 1934, when it became St. Walburga Benedictine priory.

Sacred Heart of Mary Church struggled over the years to pay off the new church debt with old-fashioned barn dances, hoedowns, sewing circles, and basket socials featuring homemade candy, cakes, and pies. Children such as Therese Westermeier made novelties to sell at the annual parish carnival at Valmont Lakes and at the summer suppers under the trees in the churchyard. During the 1920s, Father Antoine and his parishioners dug water ditches to the parish cemetery so that it could be something more than a weed patch. Men of the parish cleaned it twice a year, on Memorial Day and on All Soul's Day. On May 25, 1930, the big cross was unveiled in the center of the reborn cemetery.

Benedictine priests Robert Murray (1938–1945), Kevin Clark (1945–1955), Francis Hornung (1955–1957), Baldwin Haydock (1957–1966), Joseph Hannan (1966–1971), and Edward J. Vollmer guided the parish. "Once we had eighteen Benedictine priests here in Boulder County," Father Vollmer, the former abbot of Holy Cross Abbey in Canon City, noted sadly in 1987. "Now, I'm the only one left."

Father Vollmer reported in 1989 that the parish is doing well, thanks in part to a tithing program introduced in 1972:

> All fund-raising gimmicks have been eliminated. Yet we have added a large activity room to the parish hall in 1977 and an adult education center in 1979, with more classrooms and a youth center in 1982. The rectory was remodeled in 1985 with additional office space, a conference room, a reconciliation room, and we became the first computerized parish.
>
> For social activities we have potluck suppers, an annual golf tournament, parish picnics and cookouts, a St. Patrick's Day dinner dance, Mother's Day Breakfasts, a Spirits, Ribs and Parables Dinner Club, a Ladies Bowling Club calling themselves the "Holy Rollers," and a Double Nickel Club for all parishioners over fifty-five years old.
>
> In 1973, Gene and Toni Crabtree and I started a clothing, bedding, and food drive for American Indians. That year, we hauled a truckload of these things to the Winnabago Indian Reservation near Omaha. The next year another truckload went to the Navajo Reservation in Arizona. Other parishes, both Catholic and Protestant, have joined the drive and we now deliver over five large truckloads to St. Michael's Indian Mission each fall. In 1986, the Crabtrees and our parish continued the program for the poor in Juarez, Mexico. We are also working with the Sister Carmen Center in Lafayette.
>
> The tithing program at Sacred Heart of Mary has made it a far more loving, sharing, and involved parish, which now sends at least $100,000 a year to the missions, especially the Indian missions.

Abbot Edward, as Father Vollmer is also called, celebrated his fiftieth anniverary as a priest and his eightieth birthday in 1988. Among his presents was the first assistant pastor that Sacred Heart of Mary parish ever had. "Father Andrew Kemberling and I were both ordained on June 11th," Father Vollmer noted of his associate, "but fifty years apart!"

ST. MARTIN DE PORRES (1968)
3300 Table Mesa Drive

Much of Boulder's recent growth·has been on the south side, where the federal government, after World War II, established offices of the National Center for Atmospheric Research, the Rocky Flats Weapons Plant, the U.S. Bureau of Standards, and the National Oceanic and Atmospheric Administration. Thousands of newcomers, including hundreds of Catholics, moved to Boulder to work for these installations.

Boulder's St. Martin de Porres has been likened to a big sombrero. (Photo by Tom Noel.)

One of the largest new subdivisions on the south side is Martin Acres. William Martin, after striking paydirt in a Caribou silver mine, established a dairy and cattle ranch along the Denver to Boulder wagon road in 1872. His children sold the family ranch in the 1950s when it was platted as Martin Acres and annexed to Boulder. Foreseeing the need for a fourth Catholic church in Boulder, Archbishop Vehr, in 1956, paid the Martins $23,940 for 7.98 acres.

On May 23, 1968, Archbishop Casey appointed John Rae, assistant pastor at Immaculate Conception Cathedral, the founding pastor. Father Rae and his parishioners selected the name St. Martin de Porres, which seemed doubly appropriate as it commemorates both the original settler and the patron saint of interracial justice, a cause revived with the civil rights movement of the 1960s.

St. Martin de Porres was the illegitimate son of a Spanish grandee and an Indian woman. Born in Lima, Peru, on December 9, 1579, Martin had the dark complexion of his mother and was disowned by his father. At fifteen, he joined the Dominican Priory of the Holy Rosary in Lima, where he cheerfully served as a janitor, a profession commemorated by his attributes as a saint—a broom and a feather duster.

Martin also taught himself medicine and became a barber, nurse, and surgeon. When his daily tasks were completed at the priory, he went into the barrios of Lima to minister to the sick and poor. After becoming a Dominican brother, he founded a hospital and an orphanage that is still in existence. To help Martin serve the poor and needy, God blessed him with miraculous powers of bilocation, of being able to pass through closed doors, and of levitation, according to Butler's *Lives of the Saints*. Martin died on November 3, 1639, but the poor of Lima never forgot his work. In 1962, Pope John XXIII canonized this once scorned, half-breed, illegitimate Peruvian as the patron saint of worldwide interracial and social justice.

The 350 families initially registered in St. Martin de Porres parish held their first services in St. Paul Methodist Church and at Southern Hills Junior High School. Meanwhile, architect Keith J. Ames, a parishioner, was commissioned to design a multifunctional building. When fully opened up, this dramatic contemporary round structure seats as many as 650.

After Father Rae resigned in 1969, he was replaced by Leonard Alimena, who completed the $250,000 church, dedicated on June 6, 1971, by Archbishop Casey. After Father Alimena's appointment as pastor of St. Mary Church in Littleton, St. Martin's was guided by John Holloway (1975–1976), and Carl Longwill (1976–1978). Father Carl, an Irish-born priest, was cherished for his hospitality and his booming Irish brogue.

Since 1979, the pastor of St. Martin's has been Albert E. Puhl, former pastor of Christ the King in Denver and of Holy Trinity and St. Mark's parishes in Westminster. Father Puhl noted in 1989 that:

> St. Martin was a gentleman who cared for animals as well as people and, like St. Francis of Assisi, he is often portrayed with animals. So children are especially drawn to him. We now have over 500 families in the parish. But as St. Martin always felt, there's always room for more people.

ST. THOMAS AQUINAS (1956)
904 14th Street

A Newman Club was established at the University of Colorado by Father Agatho Strittmatter, OSB, pastor of Boulder's Sacred Heart of Jesus parish. Out of that club founded for university students, staff, and faculty on October 25, 1908, evolved St. Thomas Aquinas University parish.

Fire, which has destroyed at least a dozen Catholic churches in Colorado, gutted St. Thomas Aquinas in October 1985. Determined parishioners rebuilt, restored, and enlarged the church in 1988. (Photo by James Baca.)

At first, Newman Club Catholics met in private homes and held social functions in the Boulder Knights of Columbus Hall in the Sullivan Building at 14th and Pearl streets. Beginning in 1940, university Catholics convened in the lovely chapel of the Mount St. Gertrude Academy. In 1946, Father Charles Forsythe, OSB, was appointed the first full-time Newman Club chaplain. Father Forsythe had been educated at Sacred Heart of Jesus parish in Boulder, at Fordham and St. Louis universities, and at Holy Cross Abbey in Canon City. As an army chaplain, he had been awarded the Silver Star and the Purple Heart after losing a leg in the 1945 Easter

Sunday battle of Luzon in the Philippines. Over the next twenty-seven years, he would transform a small Newman Club into a parish.

University students and faculty, neither of whom were noted for their financial resources, found an angel in the John H. Phelans, a Beaumont, Texas, couple who summered in Boulder. In 1946, the Phelans donated their summer home at 1609 15th Street as a Newman Club center. In 1950, the club built a chapel nearby at 898 14th Street and converted the house at 904 14th Street to a rectory for Father Forsythe. The Phelans donated $30,000 to this project, while Julie Penrose, the Colorado Springs philanthropist, gave $3,000. Archbishop Vehr blessed this chapel on May 19, 1950. Fortunately, architect John K. Monroe had designed the chapel with possible expansion in mind, for the university Catholic community soon outgrew this little garden level church.

The Phelans donated another $27,000 to convert the chapel to a handsome church made of the same Lyons sandstone, Italian Renaissance style architecture that distinguished the University of Colorado campus. A red tile roof, Romanesque entries, and a single, stocky, corner tower adorned with a seven-foot statue of St. Thomas Aquinas enhanced the new church. St. Thomas, the great medieval theologian, is the patron of scholars, and the stained glass windows commemorated various academic pursuits from music to medicine, from chemistry to drama, from law to the military arts. Behind the altar a thirty-five-foot mosaic served as the backdrop for a life-sized crucifix, which, like the altar reredos, was carved by artists of Bolzano, Italy. The old basement chapel was converted to a kitchen, lounge, game area, and meeting rooms.

After the new church was dedicated in 1956, it welcomed students—no matter how badly they needed haircuts. Guitar masses were initiated in 1967, leading one elderly parishioner to groan, "I should have died while this was still a Catholic church." The University of Colorado, which started with twenty Newman Club members in 1908, had attracted about 1,800 Catholic faculty and students by the 1960s. Recognizing this tremendous growth, Archbishop Casey changed the university chapel to the university parish in 1968.

The Paulist fathers took over the parish in 1977 and found an ally in Sister Sheila Carroll, OSF, who became a full-time campus chaplain in 1985 and announced that she was engaged in "hand-to-hand combat on campus," wrestling with students to make them "feel a part of this parish." Since the 1960s, St. Thomas has sponsored a theologian-in-residence who, among other duties, teaches classes for the university's Religious Studies program.

Under the leadership of David W. O'Brien, CSP, the first Paulist pastor, several changes were made. Women associates were added to the staff, and made valuable contributions. Through the voluntary labor and contributions of many parishioners, the house owned by the parish at 889 15th Street was transformed into a residence for the Paulist priest. This freed the rectory for parish offices and activities.

On October 9, 1985, an arsonist set fire to the interior of the church. Fire fighters saved the exterior but the interior was gutted. Father John J. Kenny, CSP, pastor since 1984, and the other priests and sisters of the parish began holding services on campus.

Finding good even in the tragic fire, Father Kenny reported that by "moving into student territory," the staff at St. Thomas increased mass attendance by several hundred a week. "For weddings, funerals, and large meetings, all the Boulder Catholic parishes, as well as First United Methodist Church and Trinity Lutheran Church have lent us their facilities."

In 1986, St. Thomas received permission from Archbishop Stafford to spend up to $850,000 rebuilding and enlarging the charred church. After meeting in campus buildings, student dormitories, at Protestant churches, and at Baseline Junior High School, St. Thomas Aquinas parishioners cheered the news. They raised over $300,000 to reconstruct the church, which was rededicated on April 16, 1988, by Archbishop Stafford.

Breckenridge

ST. MARY (1885)
115 South French Street

"I have to cross the highest range of mountains to visit our poor Catholics, who are almost buried alive in the depths of the mines," Father Machebeuf

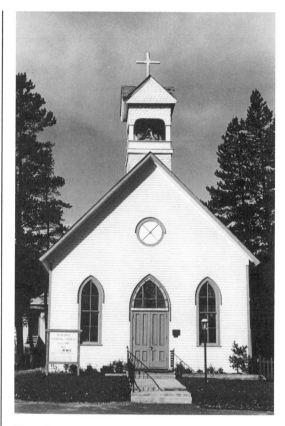

Elegantly restored, the 1880s original still stands next to St. Mary's slick, new $500,000 church. (Photo by Tom Noel.)

wrote after his first visit to Breckenridge in 1861. Father Machebeuf himself was in danger of being buried alive in blizzards on his solitary horse and buggy treks to Summit County over 11,481-foot-high Boreas Pass.

In 1874, probably to his relief, Bishop Machebeuf assigned Summit, Lake, and Chaffee counties to one of his ablest young priests, Henry Robinson. Father Robinson also tended other mountain mining towns and when the discovery of million-dollar silver mines gave birth to Leadville in the late 1870s, he concentrated on building Annunciation Church in that instant city.

Although outshone by Leadville, Breckenridge had over 1,000 residents in 1880. Bishop Machebeuf and Thomas M. Cahill visited the growing county seat in 1881 and acquired a church site at the southeast corner of High Street and Washington Avenue. Within twelve days, Father Cahill had completed a frame shell. Bishop Machebeuf christened it St. Mary's, as he named so many pioneer Catholic parishes in honor of his beloved patroness.

In 1882, Father Cahill left the demanding mountainous parish for gentler, greener Ireland. Bishop Machebeuf replaced him with an energetic Swiss priest, James E. Chapius. Father Chapius completed the interior of St. Mary's and also helped to establish mission churches: Our Lady of the Snows at Robinson; St. Benedict's at Como; St. Edward's at Montezuma; St. Joseph's at Fairplay; and St. Patrick's at Alma.

In 1886, Father Chapius added a Breckenridge hospital to his rapidly growing Summit and Park county facilities. Three Benedictine nuns arrived to help staff the small Summit County Hospital built jointly by the Miners Protective Association and the county. In gratitude for the sisters' work, the small frame building at the northwest corner of Harris Street and Washington Avenue was renamed St. Joseph's Hospital. After several more Benedictine nuns arrived, the order opened St. Gertrude Academy and Convent at the northeast corner of French Street and Lincoln Avenue in 1887.

Father Chapius's ambitious plans for Summit County were doomed by declining mineral production and population. The Benedictines, to whom Bishop Machebeuf gave the parish in 1886, sent Rhabanus Gutmann, OSB, to Breckenridge. The new pastor was shocked to find a crude church with makeshift plank pews and a soap box tabernacle. He called it "a disgrace to the name of St. Mary."

The community as well as the church horrified Father Rhabanus, who reported that "all the roustabouts, rascals, loose women, adulterers, etc., etc., find their way to Breckenridge." At least St. Mary's escaped the fate of the Methodist church. The minister there, Florida Passamore, not only preached against "Demon Rum" but personally inspected saloons to enforce the midnight and Sunday closing laws. This probably explains why, on the night of August 17, 1891, his church bell and belfry were dynamited to smithereens. The good reverend was hanged in effigy.

St. Mary's, located on the outskirts of a boom town expecting to become a city, soon found itself at the end of a long uphill walk outside a shrinking community. In 1890, the little frame church was dragged downhill to its present location. The Benedictines, who had spent much of their time in their own hospital recovering from Summit County's

weather, retreated from the high country parish in 1892. Bishop Matz replaced them with a series of priests who lasted only a year or so at most. One of them, J. C. McCourt, was the brother of the beautiful Elizabeth McCourt, better known as Baby Doe, the second wife of H.A.W. Tabor. Father McCourt ran away from blizzard-blasted, debt-ridden St. Mary's only to be ordered back by Bishop Matz.

Not until the 1910 arrival of Aloysius Hilbig did St. Mary parish find stability. Father Hilbig's letters to Bishop Matz shed light on a real mining town hero—one of those persistent people who struggled to keep towns alive after the mining hordes departed, leaving a shambles behind them.

Father Hilbig subsisted on "my own money . . . on account of the parish being so poor. . . . During the last few years I have lost over half of the people in my missions." Only by bumming free passes from the Colorado & Southern Railway was Father Hilbig able to take Mass and the sacraments to the five missions and fifteen station stops among the dying mining camps of Summit and Park counties. Of St. Patrick's in Alma, a typical doomed parish, Father Hilbig wrote to Bishop Matz on February 15, 1915:

> A few days ago the little chapel at Alma burned down when the big hotel next door caught fire. There was not an inch of space between these two buildings and no water close by it. . . . The chapel was in bad condition, being about 35 years old and not worthwhile to be repaired. . . . I did not say Mass in it on account of it being too dangerous. The roof leaked all over, the floor was caved in on one side, and one side towards the front was badly crashed in.

Father Hilbig left St. Mary's at the end of 1918. Breckenridge became just another Sunday mission stop for the priests of Annunciation parish in Leadville. After 1930, when the population of all of Summit County fell to 987, the pot-bellied stove in St. Mary's was fired up only once a month for fifteen families clinging to their faith.

That faith was rewarded during the 1960s and 1970s. Construction of interstate 70 with its Eisenhower and Johnson tunnels, of the Dillon Reservoir, and of three major ski areas resurrected the once dying county. During the 1970s, Summit emerged as the fastest growing county in Colorado, soaring to a 1980 population of 8,848. Foreseeing the boom,

Archbishop Vehr sent John J. Slattery up to Breckenridge in 1966 to reopen St. Mary's as a full-time parish. The decrepit, leaky-roofed, cobweb-filled church was rehabilitated, and the old ceiling stenciling restored as a precious example of "primitive Italian baroque" folk art. Father Slattery was followed by Leo Kennedy, Donald Frawley, and Edward J. Poehlmann, who arrived in 1973. As newcomers flooded into the tiny frame church, Father Poehlmann dashed back and forth from the organ to the altar, where he led parishioners in hymns.

John G. Kauffman joined Father Poehlmann as assistant pastor in 1978. In his spare time, Father John prospected for gold, a traditional Summit County art he mastered and taught to others in classes and in his *Handbook for Placer Mining*. Writer Mary Ellen Gilliland used Father Slattery's research and reminiscences and, with the help of many parish old timers, produced a history, *Century of Faith*, for St. Mary's centennial in 1981.

Once a skeleton church called "a disgrace to the name of St. Mary," this resilient high country parish began an expansion program. A mission parish, Our Lady of Peace, was opened in Dillon in 1975. The priests at St. Mary's also began offering Sunday Masses at two Summit County ski areas—in the lodge at Keystone Lodge and in the Copper Mountain Chapel. St. Joseph Church in Fairplay remained a mission of St. Mary's until the 1984 establishment of the Diocese of Colorado Springs in which St. Joseph's became a mission of Buena Vista.

In the early 1980s, the priests of St. Mary's donned hard hats and worked side-by-side with parishioners to construct a spacious modern church. Like Father Cahill a century earlier, they begged, borrowed, and bought materials to complete an ambitious project. Their $500,000 frame structure was completed in 1985 with a high cathedral ceiling and a stained glass window, depicting St. Mary, behind the altar. In the distance loom the shimmering peaks of the Ten Mile Range, sporting ski slopes and lavish new resorts, shopping areas and condominiums that now eclipse old mining ruins. Since 1986, St. Mary's and its Summit County satellite missions at Dillon, Keystone, and Copper Mountain have been the bailiwick of Father Thomas Mosher.

Brighton

ST. AUGUSTINE (1887)
6th Avenue & Egbert Street

Brighton began in 1870 as Hughes Station on the Denver Pacific Railway. Not until 1882 was it platted as Brighton by Daniel F. Carmichael, who named it for his wife's hometown in New York.

Mary Stieber, in her 114-page centennial history of St. Augustine's, says the first masses "were said in the Higgins Bar, with planks placed across beer kegs to make seats." The saloon belonged to John P. Higgins, a pioneer rancher and tavernkeeper who became the first sheriff of Adams County in 1902 and later served as mayor of Brighton.

Youngsters pose with Father Emile Verschraeghen, who could tell them in six languages to smile, in front of the second (1930) of three Brighton churches.

Under the auspices of Bishop Machebeuf, William J. Howlett and twelve Catholic families organized the parish in 1887. D.F. Carmichael donated a church site. John Stieber, a homesteader, farmer, and dairy man, gave $100 toward building a church, with the stipulation that it be brick. This quaint church—which looked like a brick house with a little wooden steeple—had a pump organ and rose window given by the Higgins family. It was completed in 1888 for $1,500 at 139 North Division (now Main) Street (a site now occupied by the *Brighton Blade* newspaper).

Father Howlett, historian of the early Colorado Church and biographer of Bishop Machebeuf, proved to be an energetic pastor. Besides building St. Augustine's, he constructed a series of mission churches along the Platte at railroad towns. In 1888, he moved to Sterling, where he built St. Anthony Church. James G. Hickey took over at Brighton.

By 1890, Brighton had grown to a town of 306 souls, and Carmichael donated a new church site at the southeast corner of 3rd Avenue and Bush Street. St. Augustine Church was moved to the new site, where a small house next door became the rectory. A series of short-term pastors followed Father Hickey. One of them, D.C. Robertson, wrote to Bishop Matz on August 2, 1902:

> The church was in dilapidated state—almost gone to ruin. The same might be said of the house; it needed renovating, costing me almost $300.00 for the repair of the church and house.

Bernard J. Froegel, a German immigrant sponsored in Eastern seminaries by Bishop Matz, became St. Augustine's ninth pastor in 1904. This energetic clergyman built a new, two-story brick, $2,500 rectory and also helped found the Brighton Public Library. Subsequently, Father Froegel built mission churches in Akron (1907), Julesburg (1908), Fort Lupton (1909), Welby (1912), Keenesburg, (1918) and Hudson (1918). Besides these missions, the "Mother Church of Northeastern Colorado" also sponsored services at Barr Lake, Dacono, the Denver Poor Farm at Henderson, Frederick, Gilcrist, Hardin, Hudson, Masters, Orchard, Platteville, Roggen, and Weldona until other parishes could be created to help with the churching of northeastern Colorado.

Father Froegel also planned a Catholic hospital for Brighton, for which D.F. Carmichael once again donated a site. The hospital was never built, but the site served the community well anyway; the Brighton Volunteer Fire Department flooded it in winter to create a public skating rink.

Emile J. Verschraeghen succeeded Father Froegel in 1929. This fiery red-haired priest from Belgium, generally accompanied by a halo of pipe smoke, set about building a new church. Brighton had grown to a town of 3,394 by 1930, thanks in part to the thriving Great Western sugar beet refinery and the Kuner canning, food-processing, and pickle plants. The new church site, occupying an entire block, was purchased in 1929 for $10,000,

the same price for which the old parish plant was sold to T.A. Allen. He converted the church to a mortuary and the rectory to a private residence. A new $49,000 rectory and church with a basement parish hall were completed in 1930, with the old church's rose window and two Gothic windows installed over the altar.

Howell B. Baber, who surveyed the church for the Works Progress Administration Historical Records project in 1939, left a detailed description:

> Modernized Romanesque type of red pressed brick, semi-tower containing two bells which harmonize. One half of church inside completed, altar installed temporarily until completion of church which will take on the form of a cross. Plastered walls. Altar of white painted wood, communion rail of wood, wooden pews. Two small, sacred art colored windows to left and right of Altar. All other windows colored but with no religious significance. Organ and choir balcony in rear of church. Father Weakland has taken an unusually enthusiastic interest in his Spanish charges and during the past two years has, instead of seeing them spend their earnings on luxuries, imbued in them a spirit of thrift.

Bernard Weakland, who became pastor in 1938, arranged for sisters from Denver to teach catechism classes two hours each week. In 1944, he collaborated with the Archbishops' Guild, an organization of Catholic women pursuing missionary work under the direction of Monsignor Gregory Smith, to purchase a house at 6th Avenue and Egbert Street for $6,000. By September 1945, it had been converted to a catechetical center operated by the Missionary Sisters of Victory Noll. The sisters also traveled from their Brighton headquarters, which was christened Saint Augustine Convent, to teach religion in Barr Lake, Fort Lupton, Lafayette, and Wattenberg. Father Weakland, a much loved pastor, died in 1948. Catholics and non-Catholics alike flooded St. Augustine's for the solemn funeral mass with Archbishop Vehr presiding.

Roy Figlino, the next pastor, immediately endeared himself by adopting Father Weakland's distraught pet Pekingese, Zookie. Father Figlino, as assistant pastor at St. Augustine's, had shown his compassion during World War II by ministering to the German and Italian prisoners of war sent to work farms in Brighton and Fort Lupton. These

POWs joyously joined their voices in Latin masses, singing and praying with special earnestness for war's end.

Father Figlino delighted the many agriculturalists in his parish by leading church processions out to bless surrounding farms and ranches. Hispanic farmers and field workers fancied the parish's 1958 construction of the Shrine of St. Isidore, a Spanish saint revered as the patron of farmers.

In 1955, Father Figlino joined Archbishop Vehr and the Victory Noll nuns in dedicating St. Augustine School, a modern, $50,000 brick structure at 7th Avenue and Egbert Street. Before the order withdrew from Brighton in 1969, thirty-seven sisters had lived and worked at St. Augustine's over the course of twenty-four years.

Father Figlino tended Our Lady of Sorrows mission in Eastlake until its closing in 1970 and Our Lady of Grace Mission in Wattenberg. St. Augustine's started a Knights of Columbus Council (1950), opened a credit union (1960), and contributed generously to town enterprises, notably scholarships for Brighton High School graduates and improvements in the City Park.

In 1966, the parish broke ground for its third church, on the twelve lots that had been donated sixty years earlier for a Catholic hospital. This emphatically modern church, dedicated by Archbishop Casey on September 24, 1968, was built of native wood and stone to replicate a sacred tent where a pilgrim people might gather for worship. A detached cement and steel streamlined bell tower soars over the front yard.

Father Figlino was transferred to St. Mary Magdalene parish in Denver in 1969, when Patrick J. Kennedy became the new pastor at St. Augustine's. In the new church, Father Kennedy soon encountered some of the turbulence of the 1970s, including an arsonist's work in 1971. In 1973, armed protestors seized the church, demanding that Brighton build a youth center. Father Kennedy worked with local authorities to defuse this clash, then donated the old church building as the Ricardo Falcón Memorial Community Center.

Tensions between Hispanics and Anglos were eased with the help of Sam Trujillo, a parishioner who became one of the first permanent deacons in the archdiocese. Trujillo served as president of the first parish council and as Adams County Jail chaplain, and helped establish the Crusillo movement in the archdiocese. Father James Purfield, a Spanish-speaking priest who established a mariachi choir, served as pastor from 1977 until taking a missionary assignment in 1981. By that time, the parish had grown to include over 800 families, many of whom were Hispanic. Jude Geilenkirchen became the pastor who presided over St. Augustine's centennial celebration, followed in 1988 by Stephen V. Padilla.

Broomfield

NATIVITY OF OUR LORD (1958)
900 West Midway Boulevard

Although a post office and railroad stop since the 1880s, Broomfield consisted of little more than broom corn farms until its incorporation in 1961. Between 1950 and 1980, the Boulder County farm town grew from a hamlet of 176 people to a Denver suburb numbering 20,739 that sprawled into neighboring Adams and Jefferson counties.

A Broomfield Welcome Wagon hostess, whose business it was to visit and greet newcomers to the community, happened to be a Catholic. After she had counted almost 200 Catholic families in the area, she helped organize a new parish, which held organizational meetings at the Turnpike Lumber Company.

These Catholics met for the first parish mass on September 7, 1958, in the basement of the Broomfield branch of Empire Savings Bank. On August 29, 1958, Archbishop Vehr established the Nativity of Our Lord Church and appointed George Weibel as the first pastor. Land for a parish had been acquired in 1955, and construction began in January, 1959.

A local architectural firm, Langhart and McGuire, designed a flexible modern red brick building. Its first stage was a gym, but the fast growing congregation soon tested the architects' idea of an expandable building. In 1979, the altar was moved from the south to the west side of the gym and additional pews were built in a fan shape around it, leaving no seat further than forty feet from the altar. Under the expanded wood-beam ceiling, the church contained a large mahogany crucifix with a corpus of hand-carved oak. This crucifix as well as the stations of the cross were carved in Italy.

Nativity of Our Lord has had three pastors and four rectories over the years. Father Weibel (1958–1969) was followed by Arthur Dresen (1969–1978) and William P. Murphy (1978–present). Originally, the pastor lived in a rented apartment at 357 Laurel, then at 580 West 3rd Avenue in a building that is now the parish center, next at 590 West 3rd Avenue in what is now the parish convent, and then at 105 Midway.

The Sisters of Mercy opened the parish school in 1963 for grades three through eight. A school gym was built in 1966, and first and second grades were added in 1973. In 1981, the Sisters of Mercy were replaced by Dominican and Franciscan sisters.

Thirty years after the Broomfield Welcome Wagon hostess helped organize local Catholics for a mass in a bank basement, Nativity of Our Lord has become a congregation of about 1,300 families with an eight-grade school. Built and maintained with the help of over $200,000 raised by bingo games, this two-story, modern glass and brick school is the pride of the parish.

Brush

ST. MARY (1911)
340 Stanford Street

Jared L. Brush, a pioneer cattleman who became lieutenant governor of Colorado, ran longhorns across the South Platte River as early as the 1870s. Brush, who later settled down on a ranch and began raising purebred cattle, lent his name to the town founded on the Burlington Railroad in 1881. After the Great Western Sugar Company built a factory in Brush in 1906, it grew into a town of several thousand souls.

J.L. Juily, the pastor at St. Andrew's in Wray, was the first Catholic priest to proselytize in this cattle and beet town. He celebrated mass in 1909 in the cafe of the Desky Hotel (now the Cattleman's Inn). With encouragement from Father Juily, St. Mary's was organized on April 11, 1911. Nellie (Grady) Wittwer and Clara (Lawless) Brubaker borrowed a horse and buggy from Grady's Livery and canvassed the countryside for donations to build a house of worship.

Nellie's husband, Charles Wittwer, and Bill Chandler constructed the church, which was so small that the big drum stove took up a fourth of the pew space. The white frame structure at the corner of Custer and Eaton had an open bell-less belfry when Bishop Matz dedicated it on April 11, 1912.

Missionary priests said mass in Brush on the first, third, and fifth Sundays of every month until 1927, when John C. Erger became the resident pastor. Father Erger lived with the Brubakers, whose house was just across the street from the church. When Leo Patrick succeeded Erger in 1939, he remodeled the church, adding twenty feet. This $10,000 project modernized the once quaint interior and brought seating capacity to 250. A former Nazarene Church, acquired by St. Mary's in 1960, was refitted as a parish hall.

Building lots in the new Sunset subdivision on the outskirts of Brush were offered to St. Mary's in 1966, with the stipulation that a new church and rectory be started in three months. James L. Ahern, pastor from 1958 until his death on February 25, 1969, jumped at the opportunity. A new $163,000 church, dedicated on June 19, 1967, by Archbishop Casey, consisted of a modern brick and concrete façade and a freestanding, skeletal bell tower.

Leo M. Blach, pastor of St. Mary's from 1976 to 1988, also tended the mission of St. John in Stoneham and, until it was closed, the mission in Grover. Father Blach introduced Archbishop Stafford to the rural parishes of northeastern Colorado in September 1986. Even with the patience of Job, as the archbishop noted, it was difficult not to despair when the price of a bushel of wheat fell below that of a box of breakfast cereal.

Despite poor wheat prices, poor beef prices, and the closing of its sugar beet plant, Brush has grown in recent decades, reaching a 1980 population of 4,082. St. Mary's, with its modern red brick church and rectory, also kept growing, boasting 202 registered families in 1988.

Buffalo Creek

ST. ELIZABETH (1951)

Two years before Buffalo Creek was platted in 1881 as a town on the Denver, South Park & Pacific Railroad, John W. Green opened the general store his descendants still operate. The Greens, along with other Buffalo Creek residents and summer visitors, hoped for a church in their tiny community.

Not until July 17, 1943, however, did Monsignor Elmer J. Kolka begin saying summer Sunday masses in the community chapel. Monsignor Kolka, who grew fond of the quaint little mountain town, soon established a summer home there. He and the Greens dreamed of a Catholic church, a dream made possible by Bal F. Swan, a wealthy Denver banker and developer. Swan, who owned a large ranch just upstream from Buffalo Creek, donated the former Buffalo Hotel site. Don Green, who still runs his father's 1879 general store, headed a construction committee. The Fred Fisher Construction Company completed a rustic log church, dedicated by Archibshop Vehr on June 21, 1952.

The Franciscan friars at St. Elizabeth's in Denver agreed to staff the new mission, which was named in honor of their church. Archbishop Vehr donated the 500-pound statue of St. Elizabeth for the entry niche as a Christmas present. When as many as 150 worshippers squeezed into the knotty pine interior for Sunday mass, the 10 o'clock service had to be supplemented with an 8 o'clock mass. Construction of the $35,000 chapel left the parish heavily in debt, but Bal Swan paid it all off, saying, "I don't like to have any debt between God and myself."

Byers

OUR LADY OF THE PLAINS (1972)

Byers was founded in 1870 when the Kansas Pacific Railroad reached that point near West Bijou Creek. It was named for *Rocky Mountain News* editor William N. Byers, who helped coax the rail-road and settlers onto this high plains stretch of Arapahoe County.

Byers was incorporated in 1889 but, though Alphonse C. Keiffer occasionally offered mass at the Curry home, it did not become a mission of St. Pius X parish in Aurora until the 1960s. In 1972, John C. Kelley of St. Pius's consolidated the Deer Trail and Byers missions as Our Lady of the Plains parish.

A little church was constructed in the 1970s and received a resident pastor with the arrival of Andrew E. Gottschalk. Father Gottschalk, who was reared on a Kansas farm, took a lively interest in the declining fortunes of his farmer parishioners. He joined the American Agricultural Movement, a protest group organized by long-suffering eastern Colorado farmers, and declared that "next to my Roman collar, the AAM cap is the proudest thing I've ever worn."

Father Gottschalk and his flock forgot, at least for a while, their tractor motorcade protests, after the birth of the Miller quintuplets in St. Joseph Hospital in Denver. Parishioners Greg and Kathy Miller were the proud and astonished parents. Father Gottschalk visited them in the hospital to present $500 donated by parishioners and subsequently kept his congregation posted on the famous Miller quints in weekly church bulletins. Our Lady of the Plains rejoiced in its five new members. At their September 8, 1985, baptisms, beaming parishioners watched as Father Gottschalk showed up with four blue roses and one pink one for Mallory, Joseph, Timothy, Michael, and Tyler.

Carbondale

ST. MARY OF THE CROWN (1980)
395 101 Road

Carbondale was incorporated as a town in 1888 and named by one of its founders, John Mankin, for his hometown in Pennsylvania. This ranching and rail-road town lies near the confluence of the Crystal and Roaring Fork rivers, thirteen miles southeast of Glenwood Springs.

Between 1970 and 1980, the population jumped from 726 to 2,084, inspiring local Catholics to pray for a parish of their own. Thomas A. Bradtke, pastor of St. Vincent's in Basalt, began offering masses during the 1970s in the Carbondale American Legion Hall. As the congregation grew, services were moved into the Carbondale Methodist Church, where Reverend Lynn Sparks and his wife made the Catholics welcome. Meanwhile, parishioners began building a small house of worship, where the first pastor, Robert E. Hehn of St. Vincent's, celebrated the first mass on September 3, 1978.

Archbishop Casey dedicated the new church on May 13, 1979, and a year later St. Mary of the Crown was established as a parish, staffed by the pastor of St. Vincent's in Basalt. Sisters Clare Ahler and Janet Dielen, two Franciscans, have directed the liturgy, music, and religious education in the parish since 1981. By 1988, Father Hehn, the founding pastor, was offering a mass each Sunday at St. Mary's, which was overflowing with 100 registered families. A new addition was completed and used for mass on December 4, 1988, with a formal dedication on February 5, 1989, by Archbishop Stafford.

Central City

ST. MARY OF THE ASSUMPTION (1861)
135 Pine Street

Central City sprang up almost overnight after John H. Gregory struck paydirt in the spring of 1859, becoming the largest town in Colorado Territory during the 1860s. Argonauts swarmed up Clear Creek and soon satellite gold camps mushroomed around Central City—Apex, Black Hawk, Eureka, Gold Dirt, Missouri City, Mountain City, Nevadaville, Nugget, Russell Gulch, and Tip Top.

Father Machebeuf visited in 1860, celebrating the first mass in the Sons of Malta Hall on Main Street. Mary York, the first white woman to settle in Gilpin County, was overjoyed that her church had come to the hell-bent mining town. Father Machebeuf presided over the first Catholic wedding in northern Colorado, when, on December 30, 1860, Mary York became the wife of Central City's

This turn-of-the-century bird's eye view shows St. Aloysius Academy on Gunnell Hill behind St. Mary's church, rectory, and convent.

fearless first sheriff, William Z. Cozens, who converted to Catholicism in order to win her hand. On their wedding night, if local folklore is true, the sheriff kept a prisoner chained to their honeymoon bed.

St. Mary's started as a mission of St. Mary's in Denver in 1861. After renting theaters, billiard saloons, and even a dance hall for Father Machebeuf's monthly masses, Mary and William Cozens helped the pioneer priest acquire a two-story frame house. Bishop Jean B. Lamy of Santa Fe came to Central City in 1861 to bless the new church, the first for any denomination in the Colorado mountain mining regions. Bishop Lamy reported to his superior, the archbishop of St. Louis:

> The most prosperous place I saw is what is called Gregory Diggings, still further up there is another place called Nevada. All these places form one street of crowded houses in the steepest gully you could imagine, three or four miles in length. Quartz mills, stores, shops, dwelling houses all mixed up. New mines are discovered every day. I saw a number of mills at work.... It is certainly the most curious sight I ever saw.

The booming Central City mission received Thomas A. Smith as the first resident pastor in 1863, followed in 1866 by Father Raverdy. Honoratus Burion, the third pastor, was an energetic fellow, after whom a Central City street leading to the church is named. He planned a cathedral-sized church seating 800 with twin 150-foot spires, a bold plan for which Bishop Machebeuf laid the cornerstone in 1872.

After the fire of May 21, 1874, destroyed the rectory, convent, and the old wooden church, parishioners moved into the basement of the partially completed new church. Under Father Burion's enthusiastic direction, they staged a lottery to build the $75,000 edifice, only to have the fund-raiser abscond with the proceeds.

Not only the fire and the embezzlement, but mining doldrums doomed Burion's plans. After the flush times, Central City's population stabilized at around 2,500, and about 3,000 more people remained in the rest of the 149 square miles of Gilpin County. Despite these setbacks, Irish miners donated a life-sized statue of St. Patrick and began calling the basement church "St. Patrick's Cathedral," but at Bishop Machebeuf's insistence the name officially remained St. Mary of the Assumption.

Bishop Machebeuf and Father Burion brought the Sisters of Charity of Leavenworth to Central City in 1873. On Gunnell Hill behind the church, the nuns opened the St. Aloysius Select and Boarding School. This $30,000, two-story, Gothic revival stone academy was crowned by a bell tower and a Celtic cross. The sisters and their students staged annual fund-raising performances in the Central City Opera House, using drapery and stage props borrowed from a local undertaker.

William J. Howlett guided the Gilpin County parish from 1879 to 1886, constructing a handsome mansard-roofed house for the sisters and connecting the growing parish complex with an elevated wooden staircase. On weekdays, a hundred school children trudged up Gunnell Hill on the 150 rickety stairs to St. Aloysius. On Sundays, as many as 700 Gilpin County Catholics squeezed into St. Mary's for masses.

After 1880, Leadville, Aspen, Cripple Creek, and other mining towns eclipsed Central City, undermining its proud boast of being the "Richest Square Mile on Earth." The mining bust crushed St. Mary's ambitious hopes, and the basement of the never completed church was roofed over as a "dug-out" church. Not until 1892 was the present St. Mary's built on the site.

Although not the grand church Father Burion dreamed of, St. Mary's was—and is—Central City's largest church. Contractor-architect Fred W. Paroth of Denver built a native granite and red brick church, ninety by forty-two feet, with Gothic

stained glass windows. It seated almost 400 people under a thirty-one-foot-high circular frescoed ceiling. Bishop Nicholas Matz presided at the dedication of the $10,000 brick and stone church with its distinctive corner belfry.

The Central City Weekly Register-Call for November 25, 1892, called the three-story church "an ornament to the city" and "a monument to the liberality of the citizens of Gilpin County." Central City's generosity was also praised by Godfrey Raber, the tall, ascetic-looking Swiss pastor from 1892 to 1898. Father Raber reflected: "Beneath the miner's rough exterior you so very often find a real nobility of soul—a clear mind—a warm heart—just as gold normally lies deep in the earth and the surface indications are mostly deceptive."

Central City's population peaked at 3,114 in 1900. St. Aloysius Academy and the convent, which had been taken over by the Sisters of St. Joseph of Carondelet in 1877, once had six sisters teaching 120 students but closed in 1917 for lack of paying pupils. Ten pastors struggled with the dwindling population between 1899 and 1929, when St. Mary's became a mission, attended first from Our Lady of Lourdes in Georgetown and then from St. Thomas Seminary in Denver.

During these trying times, pastors wrote to the bishop in Denver of leaking roofs and broken furnaces in the church, and of the delapidated academy on the hill, which was not torn down until 1936. "The parish is going down hill very fast, hardly a handful of parishioners left," Michael J. Webber reported in a May 28, 1918, letter. A year later, after Father Webber was taken ill to St. Joseph Hospital in Denver, thirty surviving parishioners sent a petition to Bishop Tihen begging him to "try and send a Priest to officiate for the Holy Season of Christmas."

Pioneer parishioners were buried in the large Catholic Cemetery at the head of Eureka Gulch, and few newcomers took their pews in the church that sat deathly quiet. The *Central City Catholic Cemetery Records, 1879–1928* in the archdiocesan archives reflect life and death in a mining town. In 1879, for instance, there were thirty-eight burials—eleven of the dead were under one year old, thirty were under thirty-five years of age, and four were "killed in a mine."

Since 1944, St. Mary's has been a mission church with Sunday masses celebrated by the pastor of St.

Paul Church of Idaho Springs. During the 1950s, Helen Bonfils had St. Mary's carefully restored, and Mrs. Spencer Penrose rehabilitated the old rectory as a private residence. The basement foundations of St. Aloysius School have been converted to an overlook. Set into its stone wall is the school's old iron Celtic cross, a monument to Ida Kruse McFarland, a graduate of the school who spearheaded Central City's restoration.

This sturdy church, a monument to Central City's golden age and the archdiocese's first mission and second parish, still overlooks Gregory Gulch, cradle of Colorado's gold rush. Tourists and townsfolk alike still trek up the hill on Sundays to worship in the church called "Central City's Guardian Angel."

Commerce City

OUR LADY MOTHER OF THE CHURCH (1954)
6690 East 72nd Avenue

This parish's history begins with the humble mission of St. Catherine in Derby, a truck-farming area in the eastern part of Commerce City. John Giambastiani, OSM, the pastor of Assumption parish in nearby Welby, acquired five acres for a Derby mission in the 1940s.

After counting a parish base of sixty families, another Servite priest, Dominic Albino, served as the first pastor and designed and supervised construction of a $17,500 chapel, dedicated by Archbishop Vehr on August 19, 1949. Parishioners donated much of the labor and materials and helped pay for the rest by launching the annual Derby Fair in 1950.

The mission was given parish status in 1954 by Archbishop Vehr. By 1955, 835 families belonged to St. Catherine's, and the sanctuary was moved back to squeeze in ten more pews. Surplus government barracks were purchased and converted to a parish hall and six classrooms, where as many as 1,033 children a year attended Confraternity of Christian Doctrine classes.

Augustine M. Holloway, OSM, became pastor in 1967 and campaigned to build a new church. It was completed in 1970 and dedicated by Archbishop Casey as Our Lady Mother of the Church. Four years later, on March 21, 1974, this church burned in a $228,000 fire, thought to be arson. Members moved back into the old church and began rebuilding. By December 8, 1974, a new church had risen from the ashes and was rededicated by Archbishop Casey.

Gilbert Hayden, pastor from 1976–1982, replaced the old confessional with the Pieta Shrine, and the Knights of Columbus added their hall to the parish complex. The Servites turned over the parish to the archdiocese in July 1982. F. Bernard Schmitz was the first archdiocesan pastor, followed in 1985 by Thomas L. McCormick, who became a civic as well as a spiritual leader in Commerce City. When toxic wastes stored at Rocky Mountain Arsenal, which is only a few blocks east of the church, contaminated South Adams County Water District wells, Father McCormick and his parishioners helped organize the Citizens Against Contamination. Spurred in part by the concerned pastor and parishioners, the Shell Oil Company and the U.S. Army began a multimillion-dollar cleanup of the Rocky Mountain Arsenal.

Today, Our Lady Mother of the Church occupies almost two full blocks; next to the religious education building and rectory–office, the elegant new brick church rises in an A-frame of massive wooden beams that look like modern buttresses. The humble little St. Catherine Chapel, resurfaced with bricks and converted to a multipurpose hall, is now part of a parish serving over 700 registered families.

Conifer

OUR LADY OF THE PINES CATHOLIC COMMUNITY (1979)
U.S. 285 and Eagle Cliff Road

Conifer was first called Bradford Junction after the 1860s stage stop built there by Robert Bradford. Not until 1894 was Conifer established and named for the surrounding evergreen trees or, according to some, for a George Conifer who kept a roadhouse nearby.

This little hamlet, which remains unincorporated, began to boom during the 1970s. Our Lady of the Pines was established in 1979 as a mission of Christ the King parish in Evergreen. John J. Murphy, pastor of Christ the King and Our Lady of the Pines, reported in 1988 that some 300 families worshipped in the multifunctional parish building.

"As no resident priest serves Park County," Father Murphy added,

> we take care of many Park County families, as well as the people of Aspen Park, Bailey, Conifer, Pine, and Shaffers Crossing. Today we have 300 registered families and only 430 seats. Some day the parish hopes to build a church, but in the meantime we use the upstairs of our building for worship services and the bottom for meetings and classrooms.

Craig

ST. MICHAEL (1920)
678 School Street

Craig, at the end of the Moffat Railroad, became the seat of Moffat County. It is one of the largest and emptiest of Colorado's sixty-three counties, from which Mary E. Lewis wrote in 1986:

> Father Joseph H. Meyers, a most saintly man, of Steamboat Springs came to Craig and various ranches around the community to say Mass. My father, Joseph Biskup, would help him get to wherever he needed to visit or say Mass. Yost's pool hall was used a few times for Mass, as was the old courthouse.... Our first church was a small white frame building, first used to house the 1st and 2nd grades.... It was sold to the city for a library when the new school building was built.
>
> Father Michael O'Beirne was the first pastor of St. Michael's and he had living quarters in the back of the church. Father was a large man and kept a big white horse in a shed behind the church.... to ride to nearby ranches to visit parishioners and to say Mass.
>
> The church has a small steeple with a bell in it. My father would ring the bell one half hour before Mass time and again five minutes before.... In 1923, Father Francis J. Brady came from Rifle and supervised the building of the new church. It was

dedicated in 1925. Many of the parishioners dedicated their time and various talents in helping build the church.... Money making projects included ... the annual Harvest Dinner of fried chicken, mashed potatoes (how many hundreds I peeled!) and gravy, corn on the cob, coleslaw and pie.

Father Slats, as Mary Lewis and other parishioners called Paul Slattery, became the first resident pastor of St. Michael's in 1935. He stayed sixteen years in the small isolated parish where most pastors remained only a year or two. Father Slattery persuaded the Denver & Rio Grande Railroad, which took over the Moffat Road, to give him a free pass enabling him to minister to the faithful all along the line in private homes and section houses as well as at St. Brendan's in Grand Valley (now Parachute), at St. Mary's in Rifle, and at the Community Hall in Silt.

John V. Anderson, assigned to St. Michael's in 1958, felt it was still a frontier region. "I have found that there are at least fifteen Catholic families living in an oil camp 63 miles northwest of Craig," he wrote to Archbishop Vehr, seeking permission to take a portable altar out to the oil field workers at Powder Wash. "That was wild country," he recalled twenty years later, "with wild cats, wild mustangs, and wild people. I said Mass outdoors and heard confessions in the can—that was the only private place!"

In 1953, Craig erected a $25,000 rectory and basement parish hall. Robert Syrianey and his parishioners also spent $10,000 to remodel the 1920s brick church.

During the 1973–1983 boom in coal, oil, and oil shale, St. Michael's grew into a parish of almost 400 households, thriving with Sister Mary Ann Flax, CSJ, as the pastoral assistant and Cathal Longwill as pastor.

Crook

ST. PETER (1924)

General George Crook, a U.S. Army Indian fighter, was the eponym of the town platted in 1909 near the South Platte River and the Union Pacific Railroad. Charles H. Hagus, pastor of St. Anthony's in Sterling, acquired a block of land in Crook in 1924 and with a $1,000 donation from the Catholic Extension Society built St. Peter Church.

This little frame mission was attended from Sterling and then from Iliff until 1947, when Joseph E. Bosch became the first resident pastor. Father Bosch moved the church to a better site along the highway (U.S. 138) and built a $15,000 rectory next to the church.

Charles J. Salmon became the second resident pastor in 1951 and worked with parishioners to support the church with steer auctions, dances, and bazaars. In 1962, Father Salmon enlarged the 1924 frame church with a $4,500, twenty-four-by-twenty-four-foot addition. Subsequently, Crook's Catholic church with its stalwart membership of about twenty families became a mission tended by priests from St. Anthony's in Julesburg.

Denver

ALL SAINTS (1950)
2559 South Federal Boulevard

Major Arthur "Tex" Harvey bought a 320-acre farm and built his home at 2277 South Tennyson Street in 1948. As Southwest Denver began to boom, Harvey subdivided his spread between Federal and Sheridan boulevards on the south side of West Jewell Avenue.

By 1950, 221 Catholics lived in the Harvey Park and Brentwood areas, leading Archbishop Vehr to buy five acres on South Federal Boulevard on January 5 for a new parish. John Harley Schmitt, the pioneer pastor, first held masses and catechism classes at nearby Loretto Heights College. On August 13, 1951, Archbishop Vehr and many other clergymen attended the dedication ceremony of the first, $44,240 building. A barn donated by Safeway, the grocery chain, was remodeled and stuccoed by volunteers as a serviceable meeting hall, and a small house was found for Father Schmitt on Federal Boulevard.

On January 8, 1953, All Saints Church burned to the ground, the work of a mentally retarded man playing with the votive lights amid sere Christmas greens. All that was salvaged was the Blessed Sacrament and the Infant of Prague statue. The *Denver Catholic Register* of January 15, 1953, called it "the worst fire in Denver Catholic history."

The struggling, shocked congregation received condolences from many, including Pope Pius XII, who sent a blessed piece of mortar and his apostolic blessing. Many sympathetic souls contributed more than $11,000 to begin rebuilding. Meanwhile, a parish that had grown to 550 families resumed meeting at Loretto Heights.

The congregation conducted a Bonanza Night until it was found in violation of the state's antigambling law and hastily reorganized its fund-raiser as an annual bazaar. Denver architect Henry J. de Nicola of the John K. Monroe firm helped design the new $145,000 church; parishioners donated much of the labor, even constructing the communion rail and altar, before dedication on August 15, 1954.

A parish elementary school was opened in 1959 in a new catechetical building. A few grades were added each year until 1960, when All Saints became an eight-grade school conducted by the Sisters of the Most Precious Blood. Although the school closed in 1978, the facilites are still used for religious education classes.

All Saints parish had grown to over 1,600 households by 1957, when parishioners west of Stuart Street joined in the formation of the new Notre Dame Parish. By 1967, the congregation was finally free of debt and decided to build a new church, which incorporated the old church's altar, stations of the cross, and other furnishings.

This 1,100-seat, modern structure designed by Henry de Nicola had a rusticated stone exterior and a free-standing bell tower, and was crowned by stainless steel crosses. On the east side fronting Federal Boulevard, de Nicola designed a thirty-foot-high mosaic glass and plaster mural of Christ the Saviour. The cornerstone reads: "TO THE HONOR AND GLORY OF GOD ALL SAINTS CHURCH ERECTED IN THE YEAR OF FAITH A.D. 1967–1968." On Thanksgiving Day, 1968, the third church built during Father Schmitt's time at All Saints was dedicated by Archbishop Casey.

After nineteen years at All Saints, Father Schmitt was transferred to Our Lady of Fatima parish in 1970. He left behind a thriving parish plant that occupies the full block between Federal Boulevard and Grove Street, with a church, school, convent, parish hall and rectory wrapped around a central playground and parking area.

Following the pastorates of Fathers Daniel Kelleher, Paul Wicker, and Dorino DeLazzer, James R. Purfield took charge in 1985, assisted by Thomas P. Stone and Deacon Arthur A. Vigil. As a third of the congregation are over age sixty, caring for the elderly and the shut-ins has become a major part of the parish ministry. The ethnic composition has also changed: More than a third are now Spanish-surnamed; many Hmong refugees also attend All Saints, which since 1984 has housed the Hmong Catholic Community. The convent has been turned into the Bridge Community, a home for developmentally disabled women.

All Saints parish has relied on the help of all the saints, according to its pastor, in its heroic efforts to build despite a relatively poor congregation and a disastrous fire. These struggles of the past are hidden from motorists whizzing by on Federal Boulevard; they see a large, modern parish plant and a dramatic church with its inspirational mosaic of Christ.

ANNUNCIATION (1883)
3601 Humboldt Street

To some, Annunciation might seem a dreadfully old-fashioned church and school in what the 1980 federal census found to be the poorest neighborhood in Denver: 51.1 percent of the residents lived in poverty. Amid tiny, antique Queen Anne houses painted pink and turquoise, a cock crowed to celebrate the core city sunrise on the mornings I visited in 1988.

"Actually," explained business manager Della García, "we're the richest parish in the diocese. We have more nuns than any other school. Seven Sisters of Charity of Leavenworth live over there in the old Bissell mansion."

Sister Therese Klepac gave me a tour of the Italianate mansion at the corner of East 36th Avenue and Lafayette Street. "Once," she explained, "it housed Amos Bissell, a pioneer banker. Since 1907 it has housed over 100 Sisters of Charity of Leavenworth who gave their lives to this parish, this school, this neighborhood."

In a tough core city neighborhood, Annunciation parish and the Police Athletic League channel youthful aggression into sports such as boxing.

The old home, with its twelve-foot ceilings, saints, and statues, and cross country skis behind the refrigerator, holds stories:

> On Halloween we have 100 to 200 trick or treaters. They've heard our convent is a haunted house, spooked by the spirit of Amos Bissell's widow. She was declared insane by Judge Ben Lindsey and dragged out. And cars of kids also pile up here on Halloween because we keep the lights on and have plenty of goodies. Besides, these kids know we're safe and that we love them.

"When the Capuchins first came here in 1970," Sister Therese said softly,

> the church and the neighborhood were dying. Then the Capuchins and the parishioners worked together to restore the church. European immigrants built this parish, but the Hispanic and Afro-American parishioners restored it. Once we fixed up the church, people began fixing up homes and businesses around here. Folks began to feel that the whole neighborhood was worth saving. And people started to look at the history of this area and this parish.

Annunciation parish started in 1883 as St. Ann's, a small brick church at 38th and Delgany streets. Bishop Machebeuf donated the site on a ninety-acre farm he had purchased in the 1860s in what became known as Denver's St. Vincent's Addition, a tract between the South Platte River and the railroad tracks. The bishop sent Michael J. Carmody, his assistant at the cathedral, to serve as the first pastor of St. Ann's. At the dedication, Bishop Machebeuf led a procession of parishioners around the exterior and interior of the church, which he sprinkled with Holy Water.

The bishop's Holy Water did not prevent the fire that completely consumed the little church in 1885. A freight train parked across an intersection prevented the fire department from reaching the inferno. Nicholas C. Matz, the second pastor, rebuilt. Matz was succeeded at St. Ann's by Godfrey Raber, who started a parochial school. This school quickly filled with the children of immigrants who had settled in the Platte River bottoms.

In 1889, Father Raber swapped parishes with Henry Robinson, the capable cleric who had founded the first parish in Leadville. Upon his arrival at St. Ann's, Father Robinson found that his flock was moving out of the increasingly industrialized bottom land. As parishioners moved eastward, they found it difficult and dangerous to cross the growing maze of railroad tracks to get to the church. Father Robinson sold the church, school, and grounds for $7,300, constructing a new church in 1890 in rapidly developing northeast Denver. He renamed the parish Annunciation, the same name he had given his pioneer Leadville parish.

The partially completed church and a new school opened in October 1890. Ultimately expanded to become a large, three-story brick structure at the northwest corner of 37th and Humboldt, Annunciation School housed elementary grades on the first floor, a second-story junior high, and, as of 1913, a third-story high school. The Sisters of Charity of Leavenworth operated this complex as the largest Catholic school in Denver with enrollment as high as 675 students.

After Father Robinson and his parishioners completed the church, it was consecrated in September 1907. Plans to build a large bell tower and steeple on the corner of 36th and Humboldt never materialized, but this massive red brick Romanesque structure with its glorious rose window over a triple Roman arch entry is still a magnificent sight. The Most Reverend Hubert Michael Newell, the late bishop of Cheyenne, grew up in Annunciation parish and helped to resurrect its past in a 1987 interview:

When I attended Annunciation church and school, it was a bastion of immigrant Irish, Italians, Germans, and Slavs. Father Robinson was a tall, gaunt, U.S.–born Irishman, a pious pastor who also served as vicar general for Bishop Matz. Toward the end of his life, Father Robinson was very hard of hearing and used an ear trumpet. We had to shout out our sins during confessions which became all too public. When Father Robinson died in 1913, a procession of school children escorted his body from St. Joseph Hospital back to Annunciation for the funeral services and burial at Mt. Olivet.

Michael Francis Callanan, a County Galway, Ireland, native ordained by Bishop Matz, served as pastor from 1916 to 1934. Father Callanan remodeled and embellished the interior with stained glass windows from Munich, golden oak pews, and ornate scagliola columns that burst into florid capitals and ornate arches carrying the ribs of the high vaulted ceiling. Annunciation is an old-fashioned, traditional church, jammed with neoclassical architectural detail and with paintings and statues. A pair of life-sized angels (if angels are about the size of humans) with folded four-foot-long wings perch atop the twenty-five-foot-high marble altar.

As the Annunciation year books in the archdiocesan archives indicate, Father Callanan was a traditional, hard-nosed priest capable of fire-and-brimstone rhetoric:

> Our free parochial school deprives parents of any excuse for the non attendance of their children.

> Satan never spat up from his burning, broiling lungs a thing fouler than [Martin] Luther.

> At no slight inconvenience to themselves, the ushers are always in their place, rain, sunshine or storm. Our parishioners should show a fitting appreciation ... by not giving them the glassy stare as a substitute for a dime when they modestly extend their gentle palms in humble supplication for the seat money.

Trying to support a magnificent church and one of the largest grade- and high-school complexes in the archdiocese was never an easy task. Annunciation served three of Denver's poorest neighborhoods: Swansea with its blue collar stockyards and smelter workers as well as Cole and Five Points, which have come to house many of the city's poorest Afro-American and Hispanic families. During the 1930s Denver Fire and Safety Department inspectors condemned the school three times for numerous undesirable and hazardous conditions.

"Then, miraculously, the Good Lord and Father Callanan came to the rescue," recalls Monsignor Thomas Patrick Barry, pastor from 1955 to 1970.

> When Mike Callanan died in 1934, they found a little black box he left to the parish. Inside was gold mining stock he had bought at fifty a share. I think it was in the Mary McKinney Mine at Cripple Creek. Joseph Craven, the archdiocesan attorney, and John J. Sullivan of Bosworth Sullivan Investment Company sold the stock for $80,000. With the proceeds, the parish built a new high school [now the grade school] in the 3500 block of Lafayette.

Archbishop Vehr dedicated the new high school in the fall of 1951. Annunciation parishioners rejoiced in the brand new brick building. Before, the parish had educated its children in the old Bissell house and in the decrepit Irontown School, an abandoned public school the parish had leased for $50 a month.

Charles H. Hagus, pastor from 1934 to 1954, kept the church and school healthy with the help of the mining stock. Father Callanan, who had spent an estimated $100,000 on the church and school, had also left his estate of $3,112.95 to his beloved parish. Father Hagus, the son of a pioneer Colorado Catholic clan, had been baptized by Monsignor Robinson and had received his first Holy Communion from Father Callanan. To support the parish, Father Hagus launched bingo, after a statewide vote in the 1950s legalized charity bingo. Bingo buffs gathered in the the old Greek Orthodox Church at 3690 Lafayette, which Annunciation bought and renamed Hagus Hall. Hagus Hall has since been demolished and, in 1986, became the site of new HUD townhomes.

Some very capable assistant pastors made Annunciation a vibrant core city parish. Charles B. Woodrich, a former New York City advertising man, made the Sunday night $1,500 bingo games popular and profitable. "I went to Las Vegas," Father Woodrich elaborated in a 1987 interview,

"to learn how to professionally stage bingo extravaganzas."

James Moynihan, a Denver native, worked with youngsters in the tough eastside neighborhood, bailing them out of jail, counseling them as parolees, and pushing sports instead of drugs and crime. Unwilling to give up on boys others called "rotten" and "hopeless," Father Jim befriended two national heavyweight boxing champions, Rocky Marciano and Sonny Liston, and brought them to the parish to promote athletics. Assistant pastor Donald A. McMahon wrote and directed musicals for the school's drama program and introduced youngsters to the fine arts.

Monsignor Barry, who followed Father Hagus as pastor, worked with assistant pastor Moynihan to build a $240,000 addition to the high school and replace the miserable little gym, equipped with one cold shower. When high schoolers reported for football practice one afternoon, Father Moynihan handed them sledges, crowbars, and hammers instead of footballs. Gleefully, they demolished the old gym. Students worked with plumbers, carpenters, and bricklayers in the parish to build the new gym, which was dedicated by Archbishop Vehr on March 1, 1961.

Archbishop Casey, on May 1, 1970, assigned Annunciation parish to the Capuchins, the Franciscan Order of Friars Minor (OFM Cap.), who have been in charge ever since. By the 1980s, 90 percent of the 519 families in the parish were Spanish-surnamed. This rich Hispanic heritage is celebrated with mariachi masses and a procession and potluck feast on December 12, the feast of Nuestra Señora de Guadalupe. As of 1987, 190 pupils were enrolled in the kindergarten and elementary school. The high school was closed in 1968, and the old 1890 school was demolished and replaced, in 1970, by the Humboldt Apartments, a joint effort of the Archdiocesan Housing Committee, Inc., and HUD.

The Capuchins, the congregation, and their friends gave Annunciation Church a $50,000 facelift between 1976 and 1982. Wall paintings and stations of the cross, almost invisible behind decades of dust, were restored by parish artisans working with preservation experts. Thomas More Janeck, pastor at the time, oversaw and fully documented a first class restoration. "The poor," said this brown-robed pastor, "need art and beauty, too." Street trees, flower gardens, and a grape arbor were planted, and the stone grotto of Our Lady on the north side of the church was spruced up.

In 1976, the parish acquired a venerable grocery store at the southwest corner of Humboldt and 37th, which parishioners brightened with an Aztec-style mural and reopened as the Twin Parishes Center, a joint venture of Annunciation parish and the large, suburban Shrine of St. Anne parish in Arvada. Twin Parishes Center offers employment counseling, a food bank, and emergency assistance.

Janeck, Annunciation pastor from 1976 to 1981, remains at the Humboldt Street friary but, since 1981, has devoted himself to a migrant labor ministry. In 1989, he also became chaplain to the Capuchin Poor Clare Sisters. Julian Haas, who became the fourth Capuchin pastor in 1986, and five other Capuchins in various ministries, now live at the Annunciation Friary at 3621 Humboldt. Sister Marie Michael Mollis, SCL, the pastoral assistant, and the other Sisters of Charity of Leavenworth live in the Bissell house.

Hollywood came to this historic parish in 1988, choosing Annunciation as the site of the television movie series, "Father Dowling Mysteries." Viacom Productions of Universal City, California, hired Father Haas as technical advisor for this Friday night prime time show. "What a great way to start our centennial!" Father Haas exulted in 1989. "For in 1990 we celebrate 100 years of Good News, the 100 years of Annunciation Parish on this site."

Summarizing the Franciscans' role, he concluded: "As sisters and priests, we are always listening to the Hispanic, black, and white voices of this neighborhood, trying to deal with their needs." Father Janeck, the former pastor, chimed in: "At Annunciation, we begin with faith to get things done when we do not have the wherewithal."

ASCENSION (1972)
14050 Maxwell Place

Montbello was created by Perl-Mack Homes in 1965 when a cattle ranch was converted to a neighborhood combining residential, commercial, and industrial uses. Montbello welcomed many black, brown, and white residents, becoming notable as the first Colorado community planned from the beginning to foster the ideal of racial, economic, and social integration.

This dream of an integrated community, born during the racial troubles and civil rights movements of the 1960s, was welcomed by Archbishop Casey. On January 19, 1972, he created the Montbello Catholic Community. The Paulist fathers, who focus on urban areas and minority groups, accepted an invitation to staff the new parish. Thomas F. Stransky, CSP, president of the Paulist fathers, walked the neighborhood to help in the planning process.

While awaiting the arrival of a Paulist pastor, Leo R. Horrigan served as an ad hoc pastor and established an ad hoc parish council. At first, the newly formed flock met in the Montbello Elementary School, later sharing facilities with St. Andrew's Lutheran Church and subsequently with the United Church of Montebello.

After Paul M. Aselin, CSP, arrived as the first Paulist pastor, he bought a large four-level home at the corner of East 48th Avenue and Andrews Drive. The two-car garage was converted to a chapel and the lower basement into parish offices, while the Paulists established a rectory upstairs. The parish house also welcomed community groups, including Boy Scout Troop 750. Ground was broken for the present brick parish center on October 18, 1975, and the first mass was celebrated June 5, 1976.

After establishing the parish, Father Aselin moved on in 1977 to another assignment, and Montbello was returned to the archdiocese by the Paulists. Various priests guided the church over the years, and on October 22, 1981, the Montbello Catholic parish became the Montbello Catholic parish under the Patronage of the Ascension of Our Lord. Parishioner Peter Varisano painted the mural of the Ascension over the altar, where it was dedicated during the parish pastoral feast of the Ascension of Our Lord on May 8, 1986.

Lawrence B. Kaiser, pastor since 1984, and his parishioners joined with other neighborhood churches in 1986 to form the Montbello Cooperative Ministries. With the assistance of Catholic Community Services staff member Mary Ebner and Sister Michael Mary Egan, SC, this ecumenical cooperative established a food bank, employment assistance, and other programs.

Mary Smith, one of many Ascension volunteers working at the Montbello Cooperative Ministries at 4690 Peoria Street, reported in the Catholic Community Services newsletter for the spring of 1988 that the office had become a popular refuge for many of the hungry and homeless. Responding to a tearful couple asking for assistance for the first time in their lives, she told them, "You have given so much to others. Let the Lord help you now. Let others reach out and give to you."

ASSUMPTION OF THE BLESSED VIRGIN MARY (1911)
2361 East 78th Avenue

Welby is a small town on the northern outskirts of Denver in Adams County, where many Italians planted vegetable farms along the South Platte River. Joseph Bosetti, a young priest just arrived from Italy, bicycled out to Welby in 1911 to say the first mass in Rotolo's Grocery Store.

Dominic Rotolo, the grocer, spearheaded fund raising for a church on an acre of ground bought from the Denver, Laramie & Northwestern Railway, which had platted Welby in 1910. A handsome, simple red brick church was completed for $1,300 and dedicated on May 12, 1912.

The Servites, an Italian order, took charge of the Assumption church, which they have served ever since. Father Stanislaus "John" Giambastiani, the first Servite pastor, lived in the tiny sacristy behind the altar. Weekdays, he traveled about the parish, blessing homes and fields and welcoming dinner invitations.

The many Catholic children in Welby led Father John to open a school in 1920. Mother Mary Veronica and three other Sisters Servants of Mary handled thirty-one grade school students and four high schoolers the first year. The sisters offered not only reading, writing, arithmetic, and religion but also classes in ballet, music, rural life, sports, and swimming. In 1950, a $40,000 gymnasium was added to the parish plant for assemblies, athletics, and the popular spaghetti dinners. Although the high school closed in 1952, and the nuns left in the 1970s, Assumption School remains open as a kindergarten and grade school. Bingo games, begun in 1963, became a winning way to finance education.

In winter, the brick church was heated by a feeble coal stove, next to which the elderly and children were given the pews. After the 1933 South Platte River flood almost swept away the church, parishioners helped to persuade the Army Corps of Engineers to build a dike along the South Platte River. This dike, now part of the Platte River Greenway hike–bike trail, would delight Father Bosetti, who once toured his parish on a two-wheeler.

Father John started Our Lady of Sorrows in Eastlake in 1917. Although this mission was closed after the 1950s, Holy Trinity mission in Westminister and Our Lady Mother of the Church in Commerce City have become independent parishes. At Assumption parish, a handsome brick rectory (1916) and convent (1922) were built by Henry Kline on land he donated. Father John, who had left Assumption in 1924, returned as pastor in 1945. Finding his little church jampacked on Sundays, he enlarged the structure. In the process, he carefully preserved the old bell tower, vestibule, sanctuary, and windows, while adding a second matching bell tower and installing a new Hammond organ.

Mrs. Raymond (Agnes Porreco) Domenico, who compiled the seventy-five-year history of Assumption parish in 1987, reported that the annual bazaar and spaghetti dinners date back to the 1920s when "outdoor feasts were held during the summer months on Saturday and Sunday evenings to celebrate the feasts of Saint Anthony, Saint Rocco and the Assumption." Another traditional gala came after the Christmas holidays when, as Agnes Domenico recalled,

> four or five families would get together to butcher their hogs, render the lard and make the Italian sausage that was either canned or dried for winter meals. In the middle of all this activity was Father John, to give his blessing on the work and then to join with everyone at dinner followed by card games of "Tresette," "Briscola" and "Scopa" and a keg of beer.

Four-day-long bazaars, as Agnes Domenico recorded, were also "held in November after the farmers had finished their harvests and had more time. . . . The bazaars were held in the upstairs of the school and the spaghetti dinner was cooked in the classrooms. The school children enjoyed this as they were given two days off from school."

Joseph M. Carbone, OSM, pastor since 1988, reported in 1989 that Assumption parish now has over 1,100 families of whom 40 percent are Italian and 30 percent are Hispanics, along with Irish, Germans, and many other groups. The grade school enrolls 140 students taught by eight lay teachers. Rotollo's old grocery store—now a garage—is still next door. And like Rotollo and those old timers who met with Monsignor Bosetti in 1911, we're still preparing for the future. We've only just begun!

BLESSED SACRAMENT (1912)
4930 Montview Boulevard

"I hear lots of babies crying at Mass—and that's a good sign in a seventy-five-year-old parish," Leo R. Horrigan noted in 1987. Father Horrigan, pastor of Blessed Sacrament since 1976, added that many second and third generation families stay with the parish.

Blessed Sacrament parish helped to build Machebeuf School to serve all of East Denver and Aurora in what proved to be the last Catholic secondary school constructed in the archdiocese. (Photo by Bill Smythe.)

"Maybe I shouldn't be saying this," Father Horrigan added,

but our ghost has also stuck with the parish. He lives in the third floor of the rectory. We call the ghost Fred—Monsignor J. Frederick Mc-Donough, who put his heart and soul into this parish for twenty-four years, dying here in the rectory in 1936. Fred doesn't bother me anymore but he's spooked a lot of assistant pastors.

Father Fred is said to ride a bicycle around Denver's Park Hill neighborhood, as he did in June 1912, while organizing thirty-four families into a parish. Although the Baron Eugene A. von

Winckler platted Park Hill in 1887, development was slowed by the 1893 Depression. Not until after Mayor Robert W. Speer began building the tree-shaded streets, boulevard, and parkways for which Park Hill is still famous did the neighborhood begin to flourish.

Initially, Park Hill Catholics attended the chapel at Mercy Hospital, the procathedral in the basement of Cathedral School at 1842 Logan, or St. James's after that church opened at 13th and Newport in 1904. Bishop Matz and Monsignor Hugh Mc-Menamin, rector of the cathedral, sent McMenamin's assistant pastor, Father Mc-Donough, to establish the new parish requested by Park Hillians. By 1913, the first parish census listed forty-five families.

The neighborhood welcomed Father Mc-Donough, a rosy cheeked, shy young priest. The youngest of thirteen children, McDonough had been educated by Jesuits at Boston College in his native Massachusetts. After three years at St. Mary's Seminary in Baltimore, he was ordained by James Cardinal Gibbons on June 19, 1907. Like so many other early Colorado priests, Father Mc-Donough came west because of failing health, hoping to recover in high, dry, sunny Colorado.

Father McDonough, thanks to the kindness of Park Hill Methodist Church, held the first Catholic meetings and services in the Methodists' large building at East 23rd Avenue and Dexter Street (the structure still stands as an apartment building with storefronts that include Park Hill Drug). Respecting Father McDonough's special devotion to the Blessed Sacrament, parishioners chose that name. In 1912, the parish purchased six lots at Elm Street and Montview Boulevard—at a reduced price—from parishioner Lawrence Purcell. Later, Robert Sullivan donated two adjoining lots.

Following a whirlwind of bazaars, card parties, and socials to pay for construction, Bishop Matz dedicated a $25,000, neoclassical, two-and-a-half-story building of grey pressed brick on June 29, 1913. The basement served as a parish center and the first floor as a church; Father McDonough lived on the second floor. In 1915, Blessed Sacrament launched its famous Easter Monday Ball at the Brown Palace Hotel, a fund-raiser that helped pay for a school staffed by the Sisters of Loretto and for constructing, in 1923, a $23,000 three-story brick rectory next door.

During the prosperous 1920s, when Park Hill emerged as one of Denver's most prestigious neighborhoods, Blessed Sacrament had Denver architect Harry James Manning design a $250,000 neo-Gothic cruciform church with twin spires soaring over Montview Boulevard. This cathedral-sized fantasy, frosted with Art Deco and Tudor elements, was to remain only a beautiful drawing in the parish files. The crash of 1929 and depression decade of the 1930s shattered the dreams of Blessed Sacrament parish. Manning died in 1933, and his associate, William E. Andress, was asked to scale down the project. The basement and ground floor of the church were completed on September 15, 1935, and consecrated by Bishop Vehr.

Father Fred, the person most responsible for the new structure, lay ill that day, but on Christmas Eve, he was cheered by the news that he had been made a monsignor. He died the following year on December 23, 1936.

One of the pallbearers at Monsignor McDonough's funeral, Harold V. Campbell, succeeded him as pastor in 1936. Campbell, a native of Providence, Rhode Island, had studied at St. Thomas Seminary in Denver where he was ordained in 1924. After his first assignment as an assistant at Holy Family parish in North Denver, Father Campbell served as a founding organizer of Catholic Charities, as a chaplain at the Mullen Home for Aged, and as pastor of the Shrine of St. Anne in Arvada.

Although never completed, Blessed Sacrament remains an interesting example of perpendicular Gothic, a phase of the English Gothic style. Despite several remodelings, including two updatings of the sanctuary for liturgical purposes, surviving original elements include the Gothic grand entry (which was to be crowned with a glorious rose window and two spires), a narthex, and exquisite stained glass windows from the studios of Franz Mayer of Munich. The $60,000 Indiana limestone church seats 400. Instead of being 164 feet long with eighty-six-foot-wide transepts and eighty-nine-foot-high towers, it measures 122 feet by fifty feet and is thirty-two feet tall.

Rather than pour more money into finishing the church, Father Campbell concentrated on expanding the school. In 1942, the parish completed a convent at 1901 Eudora to house the ten Sisters of Loretto teaching in the grade school. In 1944, Father Campbell and his parishioners celebrated retirement of the entire parish debt of $115,500. Five years later Father Campbell's work was acknowledged by Pope Pius XII, who promoted him to the rank of monsignor. Monsignor Campbell dedicated the Our Lady of Fatima Shrine at the corner of Montview and Elm later that year.

Meanwhile, Monsignor Campbell and Archbishop Vehr began planning a new Catholic high school to serve all of East Denver. With the post World War II population boom, Park Hill, Montclair, and Aurora attracted thousands of newcomers, many of them Catholic. To meet the growing demand for a Catholic secondary school, Blessed Sacrament and the archdiocese undertook to build the first unit of a secondary school, named in honor of Colorado's first missionary priest and bishop, Joseph Projectus Machebeuf. Construction began in November 1949. When completed and opened to students in September 1951, the $255,000 junior high school contained seven classrooms, offices, a cafeteria, and a full-sized gym that doubled as an auditorium. Blessed Sacrament, which ultimately gave a half million dollars to build Machebeuf, helped complete the second stage in 1958, expanding it from a junior to a senior high school. The original 1949 structure is now Blessed Sacrament Middle School for grades six, seven, and eight.

The convent was expanded in 1959, making room for forty sisters. Machebeuf quickly became one of the largest Catholic high schools and hired famed football coach Pat Panek, upon his retirement from East High in 1966, to develop an athletic program.

In 1971, the congregation bought the old Lawrence Higgins family house, a bungalow at 1912 Eudora Street, as a parish center. To further accommodate growth, Campbell Hall was erected on the south side of the church in 1979. It was named for Monsignor Campbell, long-time pastor, who had written to Archbishop Vehr in 1964 requesting retirement: "I am suddenly old and the parish needs youth." Monsignor Campbell subsequently became auxiliary chaplain at St. Joseph Hospital, Denver, where he died December 21, 1967. Monsignor Edward A. Leyden served as pastor of Blessed Sacrament from 1964 to 1970, guiding the parish through the difficult years of integrating Park Hill and its schools.

After Afro-Americans began moving east of Colorado Boulevard in the 1950s, the Denver public schools built a new elementary school, Barret, at 2900 Jackson Street, to keep blacks from attending Park Hill Elementary School. Black families, who were moving into Park Hill in search of better neighborhoods and better schools for their children, brought suit. The result, in the U.S. Supreme Court case *Keyes v. School District No.1*, was a 1973 order that Denver public schools be integrated. While many white families moved out of Park Hill, others stayed, and Monsignor Leyden at Blessed Sacrament joined with ministers of St. Thomas Episcopal, Park Hill Methodist, Montview Presbyterian, and other neighborhood churches to pursue peaceful integration. These churches spearheaded creation of the Greater Park Hill Community Association, which staged block parties to introduce new black neighbors to the older white residents. On a block by block basis, Park Hillians came to accept the fact that blacks and whites could live in the same place and work toward common goals of a safe, attractive neighborhood with good schools and churches.

Blessed Sacrament welcomed blacks under Monsignor Leyden and his successor as pastor, Michael A. Walsh, (1970–1976). Many blacks also attended Curé d'Ars, a second Park Hill parish that had been formed in 1952.

During the 1970s, the parish sold the former Loretto convent to the Jesuits, who use it as a Western Province novitiate. Sister Ellen Kerr, BVM has served as principal of Blessed Sacrament School since the 1970s with help from Sister Sheila Dougherty, BVM, while Sister Mary Bernard, CPPS, serves as pastoral assistant and bookkeeper. Sister Mary Paraclete, SLG, a black nun, handles parish outreach.

Leo R. Horrigan succeeded Father Walsh as pastor in 1976. Father Horrigan, a native of Imogene, Iowa, was reared in Denver and studied at St. Thomas Seminary before going to the North American College in Rome, where he was ordained in 1959. After earning an M.A. in education at the Catholic University of America and working for six years in the Denver archdiocesan chancery, Father Horrigan moved to Blessed Sacrament and into the old rectory with the ghost of Father Fred.

"Blessed Sacrament," Father Horrigan reported in 1987,

> continues to be a vibrant social and spiritual center for Park Hill. We're still working closely with other churches and Temple Micah, Park Hill's Jewish synagogue, to preserve the neighborhood and make integration work.

Blessed Sacrament's location across the street from a masonic temple and only a few blocks away from five Protestant churches, typifies the diversity of Park Hill, a neighborhood that has become nationally prominent for its relatively smooth integration of blacks and whites, of elegant mansions and modest bungalows. Father Horrigan pointed out in 1987:

> Blessed Sacrament School, which is preschool through eighth grade, and Machebeuf High School are healthy examples of how ecumenism and racial integration can work. Our student population is one-third minority and one-third non-Catholic. We've grown from thirty-four families in 1912 to 582 families today. Father Fred's ghost, who still inhabits the third floor of the rectory, seems to be satisfied that we are continuing the work he started out to do on his bicycle seventy-five years ago.

CATHEDRAL OF THE IMMACULATE CONCEPTION (1860)
1530 Logan Street

The magnificent Gothic cathedral at East Colfax Avenue and Logan Street traces its origins to a tiny, brick church completed in 1860 by Joseph P. Machebeuf. After the Denver City Town Company donated a site at 15th and Stout streets, then on the outskirts of town, Machebeuf and the pioneer Catholics of Denver erected a little chapel, which Machebeuf called St. Mary's. City fathers rejoiced, confident that churches would help civilize their raw frontier town, which had only one other church building—the Methodist church at 14th and Arapahoe streets—but thirty-five saloons.

With mountain pine boughs, Father Machebeuf decorated the still unfinished, thirty-by-sixty-four-foot church for the first mass on Christmas Eve, 1860. Canvas was nailed over the panel-less windows to shut out the cold and snow so that Father

Machebeuf and his sidekick, Jean B. Raverdy, could start the ceremony.

These two French missionaries built, a year later, a twelve-by-thirteen-foot wooden shed behind the church as a rectory. "In this miserable shanty," Machebeuf wrote to his sister back in France, "our beds are sacks of straw."

How well Father Machebeuf would care for his vast new parish was suggested by how well he cultivated the soil at St. Mary's. There, he dug a well, put up a fence, and planted flowers, vines, lettuce, radishes, onions, and something he had come to fancy during his seven years in New Mexico: *chile verde.*

Father Machebeuf added a sturdy wooden derrick to his garden for the first church bell in Colorado, an 800-pound monster lugged out from St. Louis. The same ox-drawn freight wagon brought to St. Mary's Denver's first church organ. "The Catholic Church is in the lead of all denominations," Machebeuf boasted in 1864.

Exquisite Carrara marble altar furniture, stained glass from the Royal Bavarian Art Institute, and fifteen thunderous bells in the east spire are among many details gracing the cathedral. (Photos by Tom Noel.)

At St. Mary's parish, the Sisters of Loretto opened St. Mary's Academy in 1864. To house the sisters and their school, Father Machebeuf paid George W. Clayton $4,000 for his two-story, frame house near the church at 1430 California Street. During an Indian scare that summer, Machebeuf and Raverdy and Sisters Joanna Walsh, Beatrice Maes, and Ignatia Mora were defended by the parish's stout Irish housekeeper, Sarah Morahan. Standing watch with an antique musket, she found no Indians to massacre but did chase off a gang of soldiers raiding the parish henhouse.

Humble St. Mary's became a cathedral in 1868, when Machebeuf was consecrated the vicar apostolic of Colorado. The vicar began dressing up his diminutive cathedral—the roof was raised nine feet and the front extended sixteen feet in 1870–1871. By the time of Bishop Machebeuf's death in 1889, St. Mary's had Gothic stained glass windows beneath a crenelated roof line bristling with crosses and minarets.

Bishop Nicholas C. Matz, Machebeuf's successor, made the erection of a grand new cathedral one of his top priorities. In 1890, Bishop Matz erected a $51,000 brick and red sandstone structure at 1842 Logan Street. Denver's foremost architect, Frank Edbrooke, designed this handsome structure in the Romanesque style. The upper four stories served as the Cathedral School, while the basement was converted to the pro-cathedral. This temporary cathedral served for a long time as the 1893 depression postponed Bishop Matz's hopes for a cathedral that looked like a cathedral.

Four prominent and wealthy members of the parish mining magnates—J.J. Brown and John F. Campion, miller John K. Mullen, and entrepreneur Dennis Sheedy—paid $28,000 for eight lots within walking distance of their Capitol Hill mansions. In 1900, the old St. Mary's Church was sold for $24,000 to Cripple Creek gold mining tycoon Winfield Scott Stratton, who had the pioneer church demolished (the site at 1500 Stout has been, since the 1960s, a multi-story parking garage). Proceeds from the sale were used to stage a cathedral groundbreaking ceremony in 1902 and to complete the basement excavations and foundation. Shortly afterwards, work came to a halt with the discovery that Michael Callanan, the rector of the procathedral, had sunk the building fund into some dubious Cripple Creek mining properties, losing $52,794.70. Callanan also invested heavily in a glass casket company, convinced that viewable corpses would become standard burial practice. Although Father Callanan repaid the fund with almost $20,000 of his own money, Catholics became chary of cathedral building.

Into this distressing state of affairs strolled one of the most colorful and commanding characters in the history of Colorado Catholicism—Hugh L. McMenamin, known as Father Mac. Soon after he came to Immaculate Conception as an assistant in 1905, he organized fund-raising efforts, including a "Carnival of Nations" that netted $4,000, enabling construction to resume with the laying of the cornerstone on July 15, 1906. After Father Mac was appointed rector of Immaculate Conception in 1908, the construction pace quickened.

Architect Leon Coquard of Detroit produced a French Gothic design, borrowing ideas from Bishop Matz's native cathedral at Münster and other great churches of Europe. After the famed Michigan architect became ill, Denver architects Aaron Gove and Thomas Walsh, whose work included Denver's Union Station, supervised completion of the cathedral. Slowly and with great effort, the building fund and walls were raised.

Father McMenamin begged constantly for funds to complete what was becoming a $500,000 cathedral with a $26,000 bank account. To the rescue came John K. Mullen and his son-in-law, James E. O'Conner, as well as John F. Campion. J.J. McGinnity and Charles D. McPhee of the McPhee and McGinnity Lumber Company contributed money, as well as a good price on all the interior woodwork and golden oak pews.

Frank Damascio, a leading Denver stonemason, laid the $30,000 foundation of Gunnison granite for this cruciform cathedral measuring 195 by 116 feet. Indiana Bedford limestone was used for the exterior walls, and the two slender Gothic bell spires, towering 210 feet above East Colfax, were capped in 1911.

On August 7, 1912, a lightning bolt knocked twenty-five feet off the west spire, setting back completion in what had become a race between Immaculate Conception and St. John Episcopal Cathedral five blocks away at 14th and Washington. St. John's was plagued with ground water and financial difficulties. Bishop Matz and Dean Martyn Hart met and commiserated about their respective financial and construction problems. "At least," Dean Hart told Bishop Matz, "our troubles do not come from above!"

Marble from the world's most famous quarry—Carrara, Italy— was used for the altars, pedestals, statues, pulpit, bishop's throne, and communion rail. Leonardo da Vinci's *Last Supper* inspired the altar table bas relief, while Murillo's *Immaculate Conception* served as the model for the statue of the ecstatic virgin at the thirty-foot-high main altar. Colorado Yule marble was used for the confessional, vestibules, steps, risers, baseboards, balustrades, and pillar bases. At the top of each interior column, a trinity of ribs spring from a cluster of marble wheat and grapes. These ribs support the Gothic vaulted ceiling, soaring sixty-eight feet over the slightly sloping nave with its seating for 1,500.

Art and artifacts, including a relic of the True Cross, fill the cathedral, which has side altars for the Blessed Mother, St. Joseph, and the Sacred Heart, as well as St. Paul Chapel and the Children's Chapel with its Guardian Angel Shrine beneath the Nativity window. School children saved enough pennies, nickels, and dimes to dedicate one small stained glass window to a nun who was their favorite teacher.

Grandest of all the art treasures are the seventy-five stained glass windows from F.X. Zetter's Royal Bavarian Art Institute in Munich (the firm and its secrets for exquisite stained glass were destroyed during World War II). Dry powder paint and sparkling silver were used for the cathedral's astonishing and ageless art. Handcrafted details as delicate as pencil-stroke-thin eyelashes individualize the large cast of stained glass characters used to dramatize the New Testament story of Christ's life. Both east and west transept windows are fashioned with more than 20,000 pieces of colored glass. At the rear of the cathedral facing Colfax Avenue, the large rose window over the choir loft features seven "musical angels." They accompany the magnificent Kimball pipe organ whose thirty-one speaking registers include a hauntingly realistic *vox humana*.

"To really appreciate this basilica," says caretaker Alphonse Riedo, a former Swiss Guard with hair-raising tales of patrolling the Vatican during World War II, "you need to come in with field glasses. We're open daily 6 A.M. to 6 P.M., so you can see the special glory of each of these windows at its own special time of day."

Father Mac and Bishop Matz staged a memorable dedication ceremony on October 27, 1912, which included a parade of some 20,000 people down Broadway and up Colfax. "The completion of Denver's most beautiful church, and the spectacle of ten thousand souls kneeling outdoors to receive the Benediction of the Blessed Sacrament," reported the *Denver Republican*, "was one never surpassed in the ecclesiastical history of the West."

Behind its traditional Gothic façade, the cathedral featured 1912 state-of-the-art technology. Telephones connected all parts of the structure, which used the latest fireproof, steel frame construction, and subtle tungsten lighting built into the walls and ceiling. An up-to-date ventilation system filtered, washed, and warmed fresh air while pushing old air out of louvers built into the roof. The John F. Campion family donated the fifteen bells,

which range in size from a 3,500-pound D flat to a 525-pound G flat, housed in the east tower.

In the 1913 parish census, Father Mac reported a cathedral flock of "about 3,500" of whom "the majority are Irish Americans." One such Irish-born American, the millionaire miller John K. Mullen, wrote a check for $110,000 in 1921 to retire the cathedral mortgage. Mullen did this, according to his barber—and he reportedly went to the barber daily—after raising the price of his flour a penny a pound, thus passing the cost along to consumers.

Father Mac was promoted to Monsignor Mac in 1933. A small, dignified man rushing about in his flowing purple robes and long white hair, he became a favorite Denver character, noted for pornography raids, powerful sermons, raids on the nearby State Capitol to denounce the Ku Klux Klan, avid support of the Denver Symphony Orchestra, and hard-nosed fund raising.

Immaculate Conception charged pew rent of twenty-five cents per adult and ten cents per child until Monsignor Mac's death in 1947. Collecting pew rent was no problem at the eleven o'clock Sunday mass, which was a favorite of Denver's high society and one of the best fashion shows in town. Ushers wearing morning coats, pin-striped trousers, and white gloves unhooked the purple velvet drapes for prominent parishioners who "owned" purple pillowed pews. A chauffeur, driving a Pierce Arrow with Colorado license #1, would often drop Helen Bonfils off at the front door. Mrs. J.J. Brown (whose house, a block and half away at 1340 Pennsylvania, is now the Unsinkable Molly Brown House Museum) would come thudding up the center aisle to pew #6 with her huge walking staff, which she decorated with ribbons and flowers.

Monsignor Bosetti, assistant at the cathedral from 1912 until his death in 1954, founded the choir and made it one of the best in the city. After Bosetti's passing, Monsignor Richard Heister took his place and ably directed the choir and another of Bosetti's projects, Camp St. Malo.

Father Walter J. Canavan became the second rector in 1947. He had been ordained in the cathedral in 1934 by Bishop Vehr and was an associate editor of the *Denver Catholic Register* and a director of the Denver Press Club. Canavan, who called himself "a journalist by day and a priest by night," charmed Catholics and non-Catholics alike with his sense of humor. He accomplished much for the cathedral, including renovation of the high school and construction of a new grade school and a new gym, which was christened Canavan Hall. In recognition of his fine work, Rome made him a monsignor in 1959. In 1969, Monsignor Canavan was followed by Monsignor James W. Rasby.

The old rectory at 1854 Grant, and the nearby barn, were transformed in 1921 by architect Harry J. Manning into Cathedral High School, a prize-winning Spanish Renaissance building wrapped around a courtyard. Between the new high school and the old grade school, Oscar and Edith Mullen Malo constructed the Oscar Malo, Jr. Memorial Hall at 1835 Logan, in 1928. This elegant structure housed a gym equipped for theater as well as athletics.

The cathedral's Blue Jays excelled at both drama and sports before the grade school closed in 1960 and the high school in 1982. The old school building at 1842 Logan reopened November 8, 1982, as the Samaritan Shelter.

Ministering to Denver's down and out is a long and cherished tradition at Immaculate Conception, according to Monsignor Rasby. In the 1870s, the cathedral first brought the St. Vincent de Paul Society to Denver to tend to the poor, and, in 1979, Cathedral Plaza, was built at 1575 Pennsylvania Street to house the indigent elderly.

Immaculate Conception, adds Monsignor Rasby, welcomes the full range of humanity found in its Capitol Hill neighborhood, ranging from the Dignity group for homosexuals to the parish's Young at Heart senior citizens' group. The cathedral offers everything from contemporary guitar masses for young people to pontifical high masses enriched by the celebrated Basilica Vested Choir. With a staff of two priests, two permanent deacons, and two sisters, the basilica offers five weekday masses and seven Sunday masses. "I.C." parishioners enjoy extended "coffee hours" after mass on Sundays, when the library and credit union are also open. The cathedral's midnight mass on Christmas Eve—a tradition ever since Father Machebeuf's first mass at St. Mary's—is now televised for viewers throughout the Rocky Mountain region.

A 1974 modernization of the cathedral interior brought a lawsuit from J.K. Mullen's grand-daughter, Eleanor Weckbaugh. She, like hundreds of other traditionalists, opposed any tampering with this National Register and Denver Landmark. Despite these "improvements," Immaculate Conception remains a good example of French Gothic architecture. In recognition of its outstanding architecture, history, and social concerns, Pope John Paul II designated Immaculate Conception in 1979 as one of twenty-nine churches in the United States to be honored with the title of basilica.

Archbishop James V. Casey, as the official pastor of the cathedral, presided at the Christmas high mass celebrating Immaculate Conception's elevation from cathedral to minor basilica, a process begun three years earlier by Monsignor Rasby. The history of the cathedral was reviewed, from the origins of humble St. Mary's to dedication of the magnificent cathedral in 1912, when the *Rocky Mountain News* spoke for many Coloradans:

> May the Cathedral of the Immaculate Conception long stand, its spires an expression of the questioning, upturned face of humanity, its chimes an eternal call to the spirituality that stirs within us, and its doors a haven to the weary-hearted in search of hope and rest!

CHRIST THE KING (1947)
845 Fairfax Street

When World War II ended, Denver's boom began. Newcomers included many military personnel stationed at Lowry Air Force Base and other area installations. Quite a few of the new residents chose to live in quiet, tree-shaded East Denver.

This population explosion inspired Archbishop Vehr to create a new parish east of Colorado Boulevard. In 1946, he paid $25,000 for a block of land, and Christ the King parish was born on July 3, 1947, with the appointment of John R. Scannell as the first pastor.

With a committee of parishioners, Father Scannell planned a traditional parish plant with a church, school, rectory, convent, and gymnasium–auditorium. The first step in achieving this ambitious goal was the purchase of a $24,000 residence at 700 Fairfax, which served as the first rectory and chapel for daily mass, then as a convent for the Sisters of the Most Precious Blood.

A combination church–school building, designed by John K. Monroe in buff brick with

Christ the King Church in Denver. (Photo by Tom Noel.)

cream-colored terra cotta trim was dedicated on August 18, 1949. Church services were conducted in the upper level of this $303,633 structure, while the lower housed the parish school. A rectory and $110,000 convent were completed in 1954. Under Edward Leyden, the second pastor, the parish raised $265,000 to begin building a splendid new church. Ultimately, this edifice, which architect John K. Monroe described as eleventh-century Lombardic, was erected for $763,000. The 900-seat church, whose interior is dominated by a twenty-five-foot-high stained glass window of Christ the King behind the altar, was dedicated on April 2, 1963.

Donald A. McMahon, the third pastor, finished the final component of the parish dream, a gymnasium–auditorium complex. Built in the same buff brick and style as the church, the gym was graced by fine landscaping—a Japanese garden, pool, and fountain fill the courtyard at the center of the parish block.

The twelve sisters living in the convent taught over 400 children at Christ the King and also helped out at Curé d'Ars School in Park Hill. To this day, the parish emphasizes children, and its school offers kindergarten through eighth-grade education in the well-equipped building at 860 Elm Street.

Since 1979, Robert L. "Father Bob" Amundsen has directed Christ the King, which in 1988 numbered more than 600 households. The stately church bell tower graces the neighborhood skyline, which it shares with many nearby hospital buildings and high rise apartment houses. To help care for the many sick and elderly within the parish, Sister Marilyn Carpenter, OSB, serves as a pastoral associate and in hospital ministry.

"Christ the King has a long history of ministry to the sick and shut-in," Father Amundsen noted in 1989. "And we also feature annual mission masses and two annual masses for those celebrating their twenty-fifth and fiftieth-plus wedding anniveraries. Recently, we also have formed the Korean Catholic Community in our parish, coordinated by Sister Laetitia Choi, OSF, and Doo Sung Lee."

CURÉ d'ARS PARISH (1952)
3201 Dahlia Street and Martin Luther King Boulevard

Curé d'Ars is a multi-ethnic parish with a strong black Catholic focus. Charlotte Newell, a member of the parish's gospel choir, noted in 1982 that once "we had to suppress our blackness. How much rhythm can you have in Latin? Now, after Vatican II, it's a beautiful thing to rejoice, to be black, and to be Catholic."

Church-hopping Catholics fancy the soul masses and swinging choir at Curé d'Ars.

Originally Curé d'Ars—like the surrounding north Park Hill neighborhood—was primarily white. After World War II, thousands of new homes were built in this part of northeast Denver. Many Catholic families moved in, flooding Blessed Sacrament, the parish that had served Park Hill since 1912.

To relieve overcrowding at Blessed Sacrament, Archbishop Vehr created Cure d'Ars parish in 1952. William Mulcahy, an assistant at Blessed Sacrament, became the first pastor. Mulcahy's World War II experiences prepared him well for the struggle to establish a parish in a rapidly changing neighborhood. He had been one of the first chaplains to land on the beaches of Normandy, lived in trenches for the next five weeks, and developed trenchmouth that left him toothless.

Father Mulcahy was the kind of obscure but heroic pastor commemorated by the parish's namesake, a nineteenth-century French pastor (curé), John Baptist Vianney, who spent forty years as the pastor of a poor parish in the little town of Ars and was canonized as the patron saint of parish priests.

Father Mulcahy borrowed the Tower Theater at 2245 Kearney Street for the first mass of his new-born parish in November 1952. Soon the theater–church hosted two Sunday masses, as well as religion classes taught by the Sisters of Loretto from Blessed Sacrament School. By 1953, over 800 families had enrolled in the new parish bounded by East 28th and 46th avenues between Colorado Boulevard and Syracuse Street. Ground was broken, August 9, 1953, for a church–school building on a one-block site that had previously been part of Thomas Keefe's brickyard. It stood between East 32nd Avenue (as Martin Luther King Boulevard was called until the 1970s) and Thrill Place, Dahlia Street, and Elm Street. Father Mulcahy died that year of exhaustion and overwork at the age of forty-six. Nicholas Haley, a Canon City native, became the second pastor, serving until 1961, when Frank G. Morfeld, VF, took charge.

John Connell, a Denver architect and member of Blessed Sacrament Church, designed the initial Curé d'Ars at 3200 Dahlia. Although a modern, low-slung building of brick and concrete, it contained ornamental hints of late Gothic architecture. William Joseph, designer of the Beaumont Fountain at 18th and Broadway and the statue of Christopher Columbus in the Civic Center, worked with Connell to make Curé d'Ars a harmonious blend of traditional and modern church elements.

Archbishop Vehr dedicated the $350,000 parish plant on June 14, 1954. That fall, the three-grade school opened with 200 students taught by three Sisters of the Most Precious Blood, for whom a convent was built on Eudora Street. By 1958, over 1,500 families belonged to the parish, which enlarged the school to handle grades one to eight.

Two developments of the 1960s, however, undermined what appeared to be a large and successful parish. In 1963, Continental Airlines moved its headquarters from Denver to Los Angeles. Many Curé d'Ars parishioners worked for Continental at nearby Stapleton Airport and either lost their jobs or moved. At the same time, black families began moving across Colorado Boulevard into Park Hill. Afro-Americans, who were primarily Protestant, replaced whites who moved southward. The exodus of one-time Curé d'Ars members included two future Denver mayors: Thomas Guida Currigan moved from 2915 Ivy to 444 South Oneida Way while William H. McNichols, Jr., relocated from 3395 Grape to 754 Krameria.

Curé d'Ars School enrollments tumbled. A block to the north the King Soopers grocery closed, triggering a decline in the Dahlia Shopping Center. Suddenly, Curé d'Ars found itself with a facility far too large for its needs, as well as costs and debts too heavy for the 200 families still with the parish by the early 1970s. On May 1, 1974, the parish plant was sold to Union Missionary Baptist Church, whose home at 3148 Humboldt Street had been razed by the Denver Urban Renewal Authority.

John A. Canjar, who replaced Father Morfeld as pastor of Curé d'Ars in 1969, declared that "the parish is not physical buildings but where the parishioners congregate for services and meetings." Father Canjar moved his flock into the Park Hill Congregational Church at East 26th Avenue and Leyden Street, which also leased its facilities to Temple Micah for Jewish Sabbath observances.

Although Father Canjar and his flock appreciated this unusual ecumenical arrangement, many missed not having a church to call their own. In 1978, the parish used $180,000 from the sale of its original home to begin construction on church-owned property across the street from its original building. Architect Paul Maybury incorporated the stations of the cross and the altar from the original church into the new, smaller, $250,000 structure. The post–Vatican II design featured a square church with wedge shaped banks of pews. A knotty pine wood ceiling and small stained glass window slits gave the church an intimate feeling.

Archbishop Casey blessed the modern stone, brick, and cinderblock structure on December 2, 1978. Under the leadership of pastors Robert Kinkel (1975–1981) and Martin Lally (1981–1986), Curé d'Ars began growing again. From a nadir of 179 families, membership climbed above the 300 family level during the 1980s.

Flush times continued after the Capuchin–Franciscans of the Mid-American Province accepted leadership of Curé d'Ars in 1986 and sent the current pastor, Lloyd Schmeidler, OFM Cap. On a visit to the church in February 1988, we found Father Schmeidler and Clarence G. McDavid, a black deacon, at the doorway welcoming both regulars and newcomers. A standing-room-only crowd of families, perhaps a quarter of them white, squeezed into the 250-seat church as a full choir, resplendent in green robes, opened the mass with a hand-clapping, drum-thumping, piano-popping hymn. Father Lloyd joined enthusiastically in the spirituals and then welcomed all "our brothers and sisters." His homily emphasized Black Awareness and Black History month, to be celebrated with a special excursion to Denver's Black American West Museum.

At the Prayer of the Faithful, the congregation publicly shared their joys and sorrows, eliciting pious exclamations. Holding hands and singing the "Our Father" took close to five minutes, while the extended visiting during the sign of peace lasted almost ten. Mass ended with a rousing spiritual, applause, and hallelujahs.

One elderly black gentleman, hearing a "soul" mass for the first time, hugged a choir member and exulted: "This is the first time in thirty years I haven't looked at my watch during mass!"

GOOD SHEPHERD (1981)
2626 East 7th Avenue Parkway

"Although Good Shepherd is one of the newest parishes in the archdiocese of Denver," founding pastor John V. Anderson reported that "it is actually a continuation of two dearly departed parishes—St. John's and St. Philomena's."

St. John the Evangelist was started in 1891 by Thomas H. Malone, a prominent cleric-journalist who coauthored the 1889 *History of the Catholic Church in Colorado*. The first masses were offered in the old Harman School House at East 4th Avenue and Columbine Street. James Motley was the mayor of Harman, then a country town, which later became annexed to Denver and is better known today as the Cherry Creek neighborhood. Mayor Motley worked with Father Malone to build a small, twenty-five-by-forty-foot church in the 300 block of Detroit Street.

Timothy O'Brien, who succeeded Father Malone as pastor of St. John's, found the original church too crowded and built the traditional red brick church at the northeast corner of East 5th Avenue and Josephine Street and a rectory next door. The $9,000 church was dedicated by Bishop Matz on May 10, 1903. As the surrounding Cheesman Park, Cherry Creek, and Country Club neighborhoods developed, the parish flourished, prompting construction of a $50,000 parish school at East 6th Avenue and Elizabeth Street in 1924. Charles J. Carr, pastor from 1907 until his death in 1932, was followed by Monsignor Gregory Smith. The monsignor reported in a 1987 interview that this "little toy church" had many prominent parishioners, some of whom lived in the adjacent Country Club neighborhood.

Patrick R. "Reddy" Gallagher was among the most colorful of St. John's parishioners. He was called "Reddy" because of his red hair and readiness for fisticuffs. As Denver's prime proponent of the sport of boxing, he was a pugilist himself, coached others, staged many fights, and, in the 1920s, began a long career as a sports writer for *The Denver Post*. Although he supposedly could neither read nor write, Reddy could dictate and knew more about boxing than anyone else around. After his death, his wife donated the Gallagher Memorial as a mausoleum for the bishops and archbishops of Denver at Mt. Olivet Cemetery.

Monsignor John Moran followed Smith as pastor at St. John's in 1940 and remained until his retirement in 1968. Monsignor Moran acquired a house at 2611 East 7th Avenue Parkway, in 1949, as a convent for the Sisters of Loretto who taught at St. John's School. Archbishop Vehr, in 1961, blessed a $280,000 addition to the school, which included six more classrooms and a gymnasium–auditorium.

The old St. John's overflowed with parishioners by the 1950s, when Monsignor Moran began planning a new church with architect John K. Monroe. They decided upon a beautiful Lombardic church, with a matching rectory next door to the east. Designed in buff brick and terra cotta, it is a low, warm structure that compliments rather than overshadows the neighboring residences.

Archbishop Vehr dedicated the church on December 2, 1953, and St. John's moved into its elegant home on one of Denver's loveliest parkways. The old organ was incorporated into the new church choir gallery. The old St. John's was partitioned for use as classrooms until the new school was completed at East 6th Avenue and Elizabeth Street. Then it was remodeled as a recreation center and basketball court, with hoops where an altar and a choir loft once stood. The old landmark church continued to be used by St. John's for recreational purposes until 1981, when it was sold to Ramón Kelley, the celebrated Southwestern artist and Good Shepherd parishioner, who converted the old church to his studio.

At the other end of the consolidated parish, the Archdiocesan Housing Committee, Inc., broke ground in 1989 for Higgins Plaza on the site of St. Philomena's. "Higgins Plaza," explained housing administrator Sister Mary Lucy Downey in 1986, "will be low-income, elderly housing named for the long-time pastor of St. Phil's—Monsignor William Higgins."

St. Philomena's, established on June 21, 1911, by Bishop Matz, completed a Romanesque church in 1912 at the southeast corner of East 14th Avenue and Detroit Street. A fine, $2,600 marble memorial altar was donated by members on September 25, 1932, the 20th anniversary of the church's dedication. Michael Donovan, the founding pastor, served the parish until marching off to World War I service as a chaplain. In 1919, he came home to St. Phil's full of patriotism and built a parade ground at the corner of 14th and Detroit.

After Father Donovan's death in 1922, Monsignor Higgins was pastor at St. Philomena's until his death in 1967. Monsignor Higgins was "God with a terrible temper," according to one plump nun who taught in the parish school. "But after he blew up he always sent peace offerings—candy, ice cream, or pastries."

Leonard Urban, a long-time assistant at St. Phil's, memorialized the monsignor in his weekly column for the *Denver Catholic Register*, December 10, 1986:

> Monsignor Higgins was able to preach at length on any subject, holding interest by sheer force of vocabulary and intonation. He strode through life with a flourish, hurrying along with cape and red trimmed cassock floating gracefully behind him. . . .

Subsequent pastors were Monsignor Elmer Kolka, Frank G. Morfeld, Leo Horrigan, Raymond Jones, and Dennis Dwyer. During the 1970s, membership declined in both parishes, leading Archbishop Casey to announce on January 9, 1981, that the two neighboring and shrinking congregations would be merged. The consolidated parish was christened the Church of the Good Shepherd and used St. John the Evangelist Church for services. Both the old St. John School at 620 Elizabeth Street and the old St. Philomena School at 940 Fillmore Street were used for the new school program.

For the challenge of uniting two fiercely proud and quite different parishes, Archbishop Casey chose John V. Anderson, who had been pastor of St. John's since 1978. "That was a difficult and painful assignment," Father Anderson recalled years later, "but for the future of our archdiocese we have to use parishes and priests in the best way possible."

Father Anderson is a Denver native active in church and community affairs, serving twice as president of St. Thomas Seminary Alumni Association, secretary of the Priest's Retirement Board, and as a trustee of the Denver Center for the Performing Arts and the Helen G. Bonfils Foundation, as well as being a board member and treasurer of the Bonfils Theater.

Good Shepherd maintains a preschool (ages three–five), a Montessori School (age 2 to fourth grade) and a middle school (grades five–eight). The middle school offers a full academic curriculum, including calligraphy, spelling bees, dance, and computer classes. An enrichment program provides before- and after-school activities.

Today, Good Shepherd Church boasts not only a comprehensive school program but also is noted for its classical and contemporary music and Tridentine Latin Masses. Because of his fine voice, knowledge of Latin, and sensitivity to tradition, Father Anderson was selected by Archbishop Stafford in 1989 to offer monthly Tridentine Masses, which had been requested by tradionalists. "We try," Father Anderson reflected in 1988, "to perpetuate here at Good Shepherd the history and traditions of two great old parishes."

GUARDIAN ANGELS (1953)
1843 West 52nd Avenue

After a census-taker found 147 Catholic families in the flourishing Chaffee Park, Chaffee Heights, and Berkeley Hills areas of Northwest Denver, lay activist Fred R. Van Valkenburg wrote to Archbishop Vehr in 1951, asking that a new parish be created.

Even before this request reached the chancery, the archbishop had begun negotiating: In 1953, he paid $13,400 for a 3.8-acre church site. Leonard A. Redelberger was appointed the first pastor, and John K. Monroe was commissioned to plan the new church.

Father Redelberger began saying masses on July 12, 1953, in the North Denver Knights of Columbus Hall, while church construction progressed. Father Redelberger, a young product of St. Thomas Seminary, was an amateur carpenter who worked side by side with parishioners to assemble the pews, make furniture, and install the oak paneling. An $80,000 loan from Bosworth, Sullivan & Company and a $15,000 loan from the archdiocese helped to complete the brick church for approximately $155,000. Archbishop Vehr solemnly blessed the newborn church of the Guardian Angels on December 15, 1954.

Funds have been raised over the years with Christmas card and boutique sales, bake sales, teas, an annual summer bazaar, father–son breakfasts, and Friday and Saturday evening games at the Pot of Gold Bingo Hall. After the church construction debt was reduced satisfactorily, Father Redelberger and his congregation undertook construction of a school. Denver architect Henry J. de Nicola designed the $160,000 brick school, which was dedicated April 2, 1962. Franciscan sisters from nearby Marycrest Convent, who had been conducting parish catechism lessons, agreed to staff the school, which opened in the fall of 1962 with kindergarten through sixth-grade classes. Seventh and eighth-grade classes were added later, as were the 1969 gym and 1984 library.

A shortage of sisters later forced the Franciscans to withdraw from the school, where twenty lay teachers are now led by Principal Mary Gold. Sister Evangeline Spenner, OSF, remained as pastoral assistant, while sisters from various other orders have handled religious education. These sisters and lay teachers have developed an Individual Guided Education Program which allows each student to advance according to his or her academic abilities and energies.

The founding pastor was forced to retire in 1966 because of a heart condition. He died six years later and was succeeded by John J. McGinn, who oversaw construction of a new rectory and formation of a parish council. Subsequent pastors have been Monsignor William V. Powers, Joseph Sullivan, and Samuel J. Aquila, who left to pursue studies in Rome in 1987, when he was replaced by Robert J. Reycraft. Father Reycraft and his flock still find strength in the theme of the parish's 1954 church dedication:

> Every church has its patron saint, but no church will have so many people in heaven directly interested in its welfare as does this one dedicated to the Guardian Angels. This parish will have as many patrons as there are souls of parishioners, for every person has a Guardian Angel.

HOLY FAMILY (1889)
4377 Utica Street

"This is an extraordinary parish," noted Rev. Robert J. Greenslade, the pastor who guided Holy Family through its 1989 centennial.

> We are fortunately old-fashioned in having preschool through high school Catholic education. Yet, we are a national model, thanks to Holy Family Plaza, of the intergenerational parish of the future. By serving the needs of all ages, we enrich the lives of young and old through parish relationships that bridge the generation gap.

"Holy Family parish reeks of history," according to Father Greenslade. It began in 1888 when Sacred Heart (now Regis) College moved to West 50th Avenue and Lowell Boulevard. The following year, Bishop Machebeuf asked the Jesuits at the college to tend to Catholics living between Olivet [Cemetery] Road (now Ward Road) on the west, Meade Street on the east, West 38th Avenue on the south, and Arvada on the north.

In 1891, Bishop Matz officially christened the parish Holy Family. It served the Berkeley neighborhood, which started out in the 1880s as an incorporated farm town but was annexed to Denver in

1902. Now, the neighborhood and parish, bounded by Federal and Sheridan boulevards between West 38th and 52nd avenues, form the northwest corner of the City and County of Denver.

From 1889 to 1905, members of the new parish attended mass at Regis College Chapel. Lawrence Fede, SJ, who became pastor in 1901, thought that the growing parish needed its own church. Edward L. Johnson donated lots at the southeast corner of West 44th Avenue and Utica Street for a nominal $10 consideration. A small, pressed brick hall, designed to serve as both church and school, was completed for $5,849.34 and blessed by Bishop Matz on June 3, 1905.

Father Fede, a native of Naples who was the first prefect of discipline and a professor of Spanish at Regis College, reported in 1916 that his congregation consisted of 115 "English" families, forty Italian families, five German ones, and one French family, of whom all but seven had made their Easter duty. Holy Family acquired more lots and built a rectory for Father Fede before this gentle, scholarly pastor retired in 1918. Subsequently, Bishop Tihen made Holy Family a diocesan parish.

Cornelius F. O'Farrell, pastor from 1919 until he died in a 1923 automobile crash, set about building a school on the south side of the church. Parish volunteers began excavating on February 14, 1920, and the $60,000 grade school was opened that September by five Sisters of Loretto. The basement auditorium of this fast growing school was partitioned in 1922 to create a ninth-grade classroom. Thirty students enrolled at once, inaugurating what has become Holy Family High School.

The next pastor, Mark W. Lappen, purchased the house south of the school for $4,950 and converted it into a convent in 1923. To pay for the convent and other parish projects, Holy Family began staging the first of many annual galas at Elitch Gardens. This famous amusement park, located four blocks from Holy Family at West 38th and Tennyson, has continued to donate its grounds to the parish yearly, thanks to the generosity of owners Mr. and Mrs. T.J. Mulvihill and, later, their son-in-law, Arnold Guertler. The first Elitch's social of 1923 helped Holy Family School to establish a library and a chemistry laboratory in the high school, where the first twelve graduates received diplomas in 1926. During the off-season, Holy Family dramatists were allowed to stage their productions in Elitch's Summer Stock Theater.

By 1929, Holy Family grade and high schools overflowed with almost 400 students. The next year, the parish bought John P. O'Connor's corner grocery at 4379 Tennyson for $5,000 and converted it to first- and second-grade classrooms. Still, Holy Family School bulged with students, including ninety-four first graders. In the fall of 1931, four rooms were added to the rear of the school at a cost of $6,500. The parish's heavy investment in education was rewarded in 1933, when the high school was accredited by the North Central Association of Colleges and Schools.

Jobs, as well as academic credentials, became a focus of Holy Family High School during the Great Depression, when vocational training was begun in 1933. To support the parish and its ambitious education program, Holy Family held bazaars and also smokers for menfolk, where Holy Family boxers—the terrors of Denver's Parochial League Boxing Tournament—provided the entertainment. Leo M. Flynn succeeded Father Lappen as pastor in 1937. A 1941 addition to the convent was followed by construction of more classrooms, with parish volunteers providing much of the labor. Father Flynn, who died shortly after becoming Monsignor Flynn in 1951, was followed by Forrest Allen.

Monsignor Allen purchased the house south of the convent and incorporated it in an addition for the sisters. A bungalow behind the convent on Tennyson Street was purchased and converted to the home economics department, where students could practice the domestic sciences. Additional classrooms were built on top of and behind the original church–school hall, whose entry was remodeled. As supports for the upper story classrooms blocked views of the altar, pew rent was lowered for those behind the columns, though some found them a welcome screen for catching a few extra winks on Sunday mornings.

After decades of adding classrooms here and there, Holy Family constructed a modern high school, cafeteria, and gym in 1958. Lawrence St. Peter, pastor from 1972 to 1983, oversaw complete remodeling of the parish plant and publication of the *Holy Family Diamond Jubilee*. This substantial, generously illustrated parish history captures many memories of old timers, which ranged from seeing

Grace Kelly at mass when she was starring at Elitch Theater to having Elvis Presley sing in the church at a funeral mass for a Denver policeman. Among celebrities graduating from Holy Family High School are Walter "Dusty" Saunders, ace media columnist for the *Rocky Mountain News* and Regis College professor and state legislator, Dennis Gallagher.

Holy Family's top priority, now as then, has been education. This explains why a large parish (1,300 families by the late 1980s) has never moved out of its original, homely church. Indeed, the "temporary" 1905 building is still the parish church, with multiple additions.

Instead of spending a million dollars to build a new church, Father St. Peter explained in a February 1985 article in *Today's Parish* magazine, "after much discussion and consultation, the parish council and staff decided to invest in a total renovation of the existing facility." In cooperation with the City of Denver, Utica Street was closed off on the south side of West 44th Avenue and a cul-de-sac park created to provide "a safe and pleasant place for the school children to play and for people to mingle after Mass."

As in the beginning, its schools are the pride of the parish. Over 150 sisters have taught there since 1920 and a few of them still do, though most of the sisters residing in the large convent pursue other ministries. An active Holy Family Booster Club supports the "Tigers."

Motorcycle riding Richard Haber, the young principal, explained in 1988 that Holy Family High School has three diploma programs. The most popular is college prep, as 80 percent of the students go on to college. For high achievers there is an honors program, while a general diploma program provides vocational education in cooperation with Denver and Jefferson counties public schools.

"We promote Christian values," stated Sister Fran Maher, CSJ, associate principal, in a March 2, 1988, *Denver Catholic Register* supplement featuring Holy Family High School. The school offers daily mass, religion classes, overnight student retreats, community Halloween and Christmas parties, and a Mission Club, which emphasizes contact with society's down and out. A model Holy Family program sends high schoolers out to nursing homes to help feed, entertain, and interview elders. Jim Hunt, a Holy Family senior, explained the idea in

the *Rocky Mountain News* of December 12, 1986: "It's hard to be old today. We're trying to make these senior citizens happy. In these days when things move so fast, technology and stuff, people forget about the older people."

The elderly have also been physically adopted by the parish, which in 1981 welcomed a $4.5-million, five-story, senior high-rise constructed at 4300 Vrain Street. Sister Marie de Lourdes Falk, SCL, administrator of the Holy Family Plaza residence, reported in a 1987 interview that Holy Family preschool, elementary, and high-school students have all welcomed senior citizens to the parish. Our seniors, she added, benefit from intergenerational activities, such as dancing, story telling, oral history projects, bridge lessons, and the high school's Understanding the Elderly class. The seventy-nine units filled up quickly and there is now a waiting list of over 100.

Father St. Peter, the pastor who worked for Holy Family Plaza despite some neighborhood opposition, also transformed the parish into what has been rechristened Holy Family Center. Exemplifying the spirit of the parish, this family center demonstrates how a parish can accomodate everyone from the cradle to the grave.

HOLY GHOST CHURCH (1905)
633 19th Street

Holy Ghost parish was created by Bishop Matz in 1905. Frederick Bender, who had established Denver's second parish—St. Elizabeth's— was called out of California retirement to be its pastor. Father Bender used his own money to buy two lots at 1950 Curtis Street and build the first Holy Ghost Church in 1905. He furnished this small church with fixtures saved when the old St. Mary's Church was demolished in 1900, including the main altar, the pews, the altar rail, and the church bell that had been lugged across the plains in 1865.

Father Bender retired for a second time in 1911 and died three years later. Garrett J. Burke, the second pastor at Holy Ghost, started the parish tradition of making the poor a top priority. Father Burke recruited musical and operatic stars for performances at the Denver Municipal Auditorium, using the proceeds to open a Catholic Workingman's Club that provided food, clothing, shelter,

Helen Bonfils, who spent $1 million to make Holy Ghost perhaps the finest architectural masterpiece of the archdiocese,, celebrated the July 8, 1943, dedication with Archbishop Vehr and Monsignor Mulroy.

and jobs for the needy. In 1918, William S. Neenan became the third pastor. He soon found his 450-seat church filled to capacity and, in 1923, acquired six lots for $70,000 as a site for a larger church.

Jacques Jules Benoit Benedict, a leading Denver architect trained at the Ecole des Beaux Arts in Paris, told a *Denver Catholic Register* reporter, in 1924, why he chose the "Lombard-Romanesque style" for Holy Ghost. For "a downtown church, hemmed in by business buildings, hotels, garages and the like," Benedict noted, he wanted "directness and simplicity." Bishop Tihen dedicated the $170,000 basement church on December 14, 1924, calling for "Brotherly Love," at a time when the church was under attack from the Ku Klux Klan, which in 1923–1924 elected members as mayor of Denver, governor of Colorado, and U.S. congressmen.

Father Neenan died on August 25, 1930, and was followed by John Raymond Mulroy. Father Mulroy, like many other priests, had come to Colorado after being stricken with tuberculosis. Bishop Tihen gave him an easy task, heading the small Catholic Charities office started in 1919. As Colorado's salubrious climate reinvigorated Father Mulroy, he transformed Catholic Charities into one of the largest and most powerful arms of the diocese. He found many of Denver's needy in his home parish, which included the demimonde and skid row within its boundaries—Broadway to the railyards, between 14th and 23rd streets. Several "brides of the multitude" were among the parishioners, and

Father Mulroy purchased the ancient Urban Hotel—a former brothel at 621 19th Street—and converted it to a rectory and the Denver Catholic Library. In recognition of Mulroy's outstanding work with the poor, the Holy See raised him, in 1936, to the rank of papal chamberlain, with the title of very reverend monsignor.

In 1948, Monsignor Mulroy bought an old house at 22nd Street and Tremont Place, which he converted to the Holy Ghost Youth Center. Missionary Sisters of Our Lady of Victory have been there ever since, conducting classes in English, religion, crafts, and skills, providing recreation, and making home visits to the sick, needy, and lonely.

Monsignor Mulroy sympathized with the indigent dead, as well as the living. He and some of his parishioners began making caskets for paupers in the basement of the rectory. As the poor person's church, Holy Ghost offered masses for unclaimed corpses before their internment in Mt. Olivet Cemetery. Monsignor Mulroy crusaded for the poor on many fronts, setting up other community and assistance centers within the church and also working with the city to promote public housing and welfare programs. He found some powerful allies in his work, most notably Helen Bonfils, who inherited *The Denver Post*.

"Miss Helen" frequently left her suite at *The Denver Post* to find solace in nearby Holy Ghost Church. She, like Monsignor Mulroy, began to dream of the day when Benedict's grand dream church would be completed, would rise from the basement foundation under a temporary tar roof that had to be sprinkled with water to keep the hot, stuffy, subterranean worship hall bearable. On April 23, 1941, Bonfils gave $300,000 to fund completion of Holy Ghost as a memorial to her parents. Her father, Frederick G. Bonfils, had been baptized on his deathbed by Monsignor Mc-Menamin. Her mother, Belle Barton Bonfils, had died in 1933 on her way to visit the Margery Reed Mayo Day Nursery, another of Monsignor Mulroy's many projects for the poor. Belle Bonfils had received instructions and was preparing to join the Church at the time of her sudden death.

Architect John K. Monroe, who had been Benedict's assistant, began work anew on the 1924 foundation. The dignified Renaissance exterior featured blond bricks and cream-colored trim designed and cast by the Denver Terra Cotta Company for the exquisite doorways, windows, and trim underneath a green, Mediterranean tile roof. Inside, almost 300 tons of travertine marble from Salida, Colorado, were used for the columns, piers, and walls. This creamy travertine contrasted with the rich, dark hardwood used for the pews, coffered ceiling, and exquisitely carved pulpit and baldachino (altar canopy). This elaborate hood over the main altar celebrated the special role of Holy Ghost Church, since 1933, as the designated Denver shrine for daily exposition of the Blessed Sacrament.

Helen Bonfils, whose generosity enabled Holy Ghost to come out of the basement and become one of Colorado's most beautiful houses of God, ultimately donated an estimated $1 million to the church. She had seen people faint in the old basement, so she donated air conditioning—then a novelty—that made Holy Ghost one of the most comfortable places of worship in Denver. She also provided a large lounge room with a "fainting couch," now known as the Bride's Room, and the thirteen wrought iron and opaque glass chandeliers—huge cross-shaped lamps that conceal loudspeakers. Postal workers at the Main Post Office a block away at 19th and Stout streets donated the missal and missal stand.

On July 8, 1943, Archbishop Vehr dedicated the 800-seat downtown church with its commanding Renaissance campanile. Among the 1,500 spectators were Denver's mayor, Benjamin F. Stapleton, Colorado Governor John Vivian, and hundreds of downtown workers who relished having this spiritual haven nearby. "While bombs . . . are leveling the Christian monuments of the ages in the Old World," Archbishop Vehr declared at the dedication ceremony, the Church was building "in the cities and towns of the New World in ever increasing dignity and beauty. . . . The beauty of this house of God will stimulate piety and love of the creator and bring consolation and peace of soul."

Monsignor Mulroy died in 1965 and was succeeded by Bishop David M. Maloney (1965–1967) and Monsignor Richard Heister (1967). Even after the transformation of the liturgy in the 1960s, Holy Ghost kept a Latin high mass at 10 o'clock on Sunday mornings. Hundreds of tradition-loving Catholics jam this mass. The Holy Ghost Choir enriches and colors the masses with Gregorian chant and classical ecclesiastical selections that thrill music lovers of all denominations.

Monsignor Heister was called to Vietnam war duty as a military chaplain in 1968, and John V. Anderson began his decade as pastor of Holy Ghost parish. Father Anderson and Charley, his pet basset hound, moved into the rectory with Jerome L. Weinert, the assistant pastor at Holy Ghost since April 24, 1934, who ably handled many of the daily operations of the church while the pastors, from the time of Monsignor Mulroy, ministered to archdiocesan affairs. "Charley and I," Father Anderson reminisced with a wink, "quickly discovered that Father Weinert had converted the rectory basement to a sauerkraut factory. Rectory residents had to tolerate these olfactory offenses rising from those huge basement vats, however, because Father Weinert supplied the stuff to Archbishop Vehr, who loved it."

Father Anderson soon found himself in the booming business of supplying sandwiches to Denver's street and alley people. "When the Wazee Center for the hungry and homeless closed in 1974," Father Anderson recalled,

Erma Kattau, my secretary, and I set up a sandwich line. We bought Rainbow sandwich bread, French's Salad Mustard, baloney, and Velveeta Cheese. The first day we had fifteen customers. By the time I left Holy Ghost in 1978, it was more like 350. "For the street people, we also set up a free health clinic in our parish hall in 1975, which was tended by Doctor Frank Seydel, Jr., and two nurses from Denver General Hospital. When the homeless asked for lodging, we would send them down to the Larimer Street hotels and pay for their rooms there.

In 1978, Father Anderson became pastor of St. John the Evangelist parish and was replaced by a former New York City ad man. Charles Bert Woodrich had spent three years as an account executive with a large advertising agency before being ordained in Denver in 1953, after training at St. Thomas Seminary. "Father Woody," as he liked to be called, had worked for fourteen years in Annunciation parish, as chaplain at St. Joseph Hospital, and as editor of the *Denver Catholic Register* since 1972, the same year he began living at the Holy Ghost rectory. Father Woody built on the work of his predecessors to make Holy Ghost an example of Christian charity that attracted national press and television coverage.

The Christmas blizzard of 1982 dumped over two feet of snow on the metro area in twenty-four hours, paralyzing the city. It was a storm that came within a few inches of erasing the 1913 blizzard as the Mile High City's worst. Weeks of unusually cold, snowy weather followed, compounding the nationwide economic chill that left Colorado in a recession with hundreds of homeless and hopeless.

"I would say Mass and see those poor people hiding in the corner of the church," Father Woody recalled. "To me that was Christ pleading for help. I didn't hold a meeting. Those old-time giants of the church, characters like Monsignor Mulroy, didn't hold meetings. They did what they had to do and held a meeting about it later."

On the afternoon of February 3, 1982, Denver hoped for relief from a subzero cold spell. Instead, the forecast called for more snow, a wind chill factor of 30 below and "a high tomorrow of 3 to 7 below zero." After the 5:10 afternoon mass, Father Woody ordered that the doors be left open. That evening, about eighty-five indigents who normally slept in doorways, trash dumpsters, and on heating grates, slept on the oak pews of Holy Ghost.

The next night it was 8 below zero and the word was out. Over 400 people slept in the church. "My staff thought I was insane," Father Woody reported. "People were lying down two or three to a pew and on the floor." The national press and all the major television networks broadcast the story of the Denver church's radical solution to a growing national problem of homelessness.

"Some parishioners objected, so I took to the pulpit," said Father Woody. "I told them they couldn't pray to the Lord and reject the ones he loved most; that if they wanted sterilized people sitting next to them, to go to another church. We burned a lot of incense to cover the smell." Holy Ghost Church continued to welcome the homeless for three months, until spring finally came, and Archbishop Casey announced that the former Cathedral High School would be opened as the Samaritan Shelter.

While caring for the poor, Father Woody was also negotiating with the rich—developers eager to build a high-rise office building on the Holy Ghost triangle bounded by California, 19th, and Broadway. "This was a miraculous deal," exulted Father Woody in a 1987 interview.

> The developers of 1999 Broadway gave the church $1.5 million in improvements and paid the archdiocese around $5 million cash and a $6 million note for the site. Then they built a forty-story, semicircular high rise around the church, using a dark green glass that matched the church roof and reflected the architectural jewel it frames. When the oil bust of 1983 knocked the bottom out of the office building market, the developers wanted out. We settled for the return of the church title. So what really happened is that we sold the old rectory and garage for $9.5 million. The Louisiana Purchase, the Alaska Purchase, and the nonsale of Holy Ghost are deals that will never be duplicated. Now Holy Ghost Church can continue to help the needy and offer weekly services that draw about 4,000 a week in a parish with fewer than fifty resident Catholics.

In 1988, in recognition of Father Woody's outstanding contributions, Pope John Paul II, acting on the advice of Archbishop Stafford, awarded the pastor of Holy Ghost the title of reverend monsignor.

HOLY ROSARY (1918)
4695 Pearl Street

This handsome, twin towered church, only a half-block from St. Joseph Polish Catholic Church and three blocks from Holy Transfiguration Russian Orthodox Church, is a monument to the religious devotion and ethnic pride of Denver's Slavic peoples.

In 1918, after World War I, the old Austrian empire was broken up, freeing Slavic peoples, including those of Bosnia, Croatia, Dalmatia, Hercegovina, Macedonia, Montenegro, Serbia, and Slavonia. These countries claimed that they—not their neighbors the Greeks—first developed truly democratic government. Democracy and independence have subsequently been burning issues because Balkan peoples have been conquered and oppressed for much of their long history; Romans, Franks under Charlemagne, Turks, Hapsburg emperors of Austria, Napoleon, Nazis, and most recently, Soviets, all aggrandized their empires at Eastern Europe's expense.

Holy Rosary Church, Denver. (Denver Public Library.)

In search of greater economic and politcal freedom, many Slavs immigrated to the United States; Slovenians, Croatians, and others began settling in Denver during the 1880s. Many found work in the Globeville area with its smelters, stockyards, packing houses, railyards, and other industries. Sunday masses and religious festivals in their own language were among the precious few things these poor, hard working immigrants possessed. Ignatius Burgar, chaplain of Sacred Heart Orphanage in Pueblo, said masses in St. Jacob Hall, 4485 Logan Street, a Slavic tavern and clubhouse. After Father Burgar's death in 1904, Cyril Zupan, OSB, traveled to Denver from Pueblo to offer spiritual guidance, mass, and the sacraments.

Bishop Matz tried to steer all the Slavs into the small, struggling St. Joseph's Polish parish established in Globeville in 1902. Slovenians formed a substantial minority group within St. Joseph parish, but the Polish priest, Theodore Francis Jarzynski, and Polish parishioners controlled the church.

Slovenians complained that they paid $10-a-year pew rentals and fifty-cents-a-month confession fees, yet still had to sit in back of the church and be poked in the stomach with the collection basket by Polish ushers. After Bishop Matz died in 1917, Slovenians began crusading for their own parish with the new bishop, J. Henry Tihen.

Peter Grabian (a driver), Joseph Horvat (a shoemaker), Frank Jancan (a butcher), Joseph Lesser (a cabinet maker), laborers Louis Silk, John Starr, and George Pavlakovich, John Peketz, (a bartender), grocers Jacob Pavela, Joseph Videtich, and John Yelenick, and others met with the pastor of St. Mary Slovenian Church in Pueblo, Cyril

Zupan, OSB, to establish Holy Rosary parish. At an organizational meeting in St. Jacob Hall on December 10, 1917, they drafted a letter to Bishop Tihen declaring that the "Slovenian and Croatian people of Globeville . . . will regard . . . permission to build their church . . . as the best Christmas gift they have ever received or expect to receive."

Accompanying this letter was a petition signed by 108 families with 213 children under the age of twelve. This evidence of a large and growing ethnic community helped convince Bishop Tihen to create Holy Rosary parish in 1918. Father Zupan served as the first pastor from 1918 to 1921, commuting by train from his regular parish in Pueblo.

Southern Slavs were overjoyed with their new parish and bought thirteen lots for $1,680; parishioners Nick Shaball and John J. Yelenick donated three additional lots. The Desjardins family, Denver contractors and architects, designed a $35,000 brick church with twin bell towers. These fifty-foot-high towers looked down on St. Joseph's single spire and everything else in Globeville except for the smelter smokestacks. Inside, the ninety-six-by-forty-six-foot church had three altars and a wealth of Slavic Catholic symbols and statues. Parishioners donated or made these religious art treasures, but none outshone their electric light-bulb rosary.

A spring blizzard postponed dedication of the church until July 4, 1920, when members celebrated both their political and religious independence. John J. Judnic, a Slovenian-born diocesan priest trained at St. Thomas Seminary, came to Holy Rosary from St. Joseph parish in Leadville on February 27, 1921, to become the first resident pastor.

For their new pastor, Holy Rosary parishioners built a large $10,352 rectory at 4670 Pearl. Father Judnic moved out of the rectory into tiny rooms in the back of the church in 1927, turning over his house to four Sisters of the Third Order of St. Dominic of Springfield, Illinois. They came to teach in the Holy Rosary School, a $26,714 building designed by Colorado Springs architect Thomas McClaren, which opened its doors to 152 squirming young scholars in September 1928.

Father Judnic, who was ultimately made a monsignor, guided the parish until his death on July 12, 1959. Among the many accomplishments during his pastorate were erection of the present rectory and the complete renovation and redecoration of the church in 1957. He was followed by John Canjar, a native son of the parish, who guided it from 1959 to 1969, working with parishioners such as David Williams to restore and repaint the church after the devastating South Platte River flood of 1965.

Leopold Mihelich, a Croatian survivor of a Nazi concentration camp, came to Denver in 1955 in search of religious freedom. Father Mihelich served as assistant pastor at Holy Rosary from 1955 to 1959, then as pastor from 1969 to 1977, presiding over a major refurbishing of the church, including repair of the large rose window and restoration of the original liturgical symbols with twenty-three-carat gold leaf. Father Mihelich spent four days cleaning the chandeliers.

The parish school closed May 28, 1969, but reopened in 1974, revamped as a traditional "Four R's" school offering reading, 'riting, 'rithmetic and religion. A rigid demerit system, tough dress code, required daily attendance at mass, flag ceremonies, and even use of the old McGuffey's readers attracted pupils from throughout the city. After this school closed, the building was converted to senior housing. Subsequent pastors have been Monsignor Edward A. Leyden (1977–1982) and the current pastor, Joseph A. Meznar.

Father Meznar, a Slavic-American whose parents were married in Holy Rosary parish, was baptized there along with his brother, Robert P. Meznar, the associate pastor at St. Catherine of Siena parish. Father Joseph wrote in 1989:

> Holy Rosary welcomes all nationalities and has established a satellite parish for former parishioners forced out of the Globeville area by the construction of [highways] I-70 and I-25. Recent parish "facelifting" has included extensive plumbing repairs, repainting and recarpeting, replacement of electrical wiring and broken and cracked windows. A new sound system was installed and the church grounds were landscaped. Lightning rods were installed to protect the thrice-struck church.
>
> The spirit of the parish is reflected in the fact that all of this work has been donated by volunteers, without whose devotion and assistance the parish would not be able to remain open. Indeed, Holy Rosary has been and is an example of community pride and spiritual commitment.

MOST PRECIOUS BLOOD (1952)
2250 South Harrison Street

"To have the services of the Church available as soon as the need arises," Archbishop Vehr told the *Denver Catholic Register* of January 2, 1947, he had purchased forty-six lots at South Colorado Boulevard and Iliff Avenue, from the University of Denver, for $24,000.

The need for a new parish arose sooner than most expected, as Southeast Denver exploded with residential and commercial developments after World War II. The sparsely settled 1880s neighborhood of University Park, next to the University of Denver, boomed, with development spilling over into the newer neighborhoods of University Hills and Wellshire. The block between Colorado Boulevard and Harrison Street, East Iliff and Warren avenues, which had been Joseph Weid's bee, wheat, and chicken "ranch," was soon to become a new parish plant.

On July 10, 1952, Archbishop Vehr authorized creation of Most Precious Blood parish and appointed a Vincentian priest, John Donohoe, CM, the founding pastor. Father Donohoe held the initial mass and organizational meeting August 10, 1952, in the large outdoor grotto at Our Lady of Lourdes Church. Several hundred people attended and were given census and donation forms. Subsequent masses of the baby parish were held in the eighth-grade classroom at Our Lady of Lourdes School. By December, the young parish had outgrown that room and began meeting in the basement chapel at St. Vincent de Paul School. Meanwhile, Most Precious Blood parishioners began raising money for a church of their own, using socials at Observatory Park, bazaars, Levi Blue Jeans dances, swimming parties, hay rides, bake sales, spaghetti dinners, "Country Cousins" square dances, and festivities featuring filmed highlights of Notre Dame football games.

John K. Monroe designed a rectory, meeting hall, and temporary church completed in March 1953, on South Colorado Boulevard. Father Donohoe, who had been living with his fellow Vincentians at nearby St. Thomas Seminary, moved into the one-story beige brick complex dedicated by Archbishop Vehr on May 13, 1954.

As many parish families were looking for loans to build homes in the area, one of the first services offered by Most Precious Blood was a parish credit union, established in the fall of 1956. After persuading many members to donate or pledge 2 per cent of their income to build a school, the parish hired the Roland Johnson architectural firm to design six classrooms. This modern one-story brick structure, which included a library, audiovisual room, health room, business office, and kitchen, was built for $241,011. The school opened in the fall of 1960, and was staffed by four Daughters of Charity. At first, the nuns wore their order's quaint starched white coronet with a blue habit; pupils had no uniform. But in 1961, students were asked to wear uniforms, and in 1964 the nuns shed their 300-year-old headgear—the coronets also called "windmills" and "sunbonnets."

To house the Daughters of Charity, a home across the street from the school was purchased for $33,200 and remodeled in 1959. Four years later, this home was replaced by a large two-story convent, built for $127,384. Over the main entrance was a life-sized bas relief of a Daughter of Charity in the old costume. Rumor had it that many shuffleboard tournaments enlivened the basement after the convent was completed and blessed on November 19, 1963.

By 1962, the parish had grown to 1,000 families, and Bernard P. Degan, CM, became the second pastor. During Father Degan's time, the school was expanded to eight grades, and the church was enlarged. Even with the enlargement, parish historian Pamela Jill Thomas recalled that "if you were late for mass, you sat *way* back in the church or even out the door!"

Maurice P. Kane, CM, who became the third pastor in 1968, began working on a new church. Architect Roland Johnson designed the spectacular modern structure, a low, circular, red brick church rising to a glistening white concrete central tower. This edifice, which included a library and shrine, cry and meeting rooms, was dedicated by Archbishop Casey on May 21, 1971.

Parishioners were shocked on the night of January 19, 1978, when Father Kane died in his sleep. His plans for the parish were pursued by the next pastor, Oscar Lukefahr, CM, who, with parishioners, completed a parish center on September 17, 1979, as a memorial to Father Kane. Father Lukefahr was an avid runner who began using marathons as fund-raisers. He believed in spiritual

as well as physical exercise and made Most Precious Blood the first parish in the western states to inaugurate a Renew program.

David A. Darling, CM, followed Father Lukefahr in 1982. Although the Daughters of Charity withdrew from the school, preschool through eighth-grade education is still offered. Despite creation of new parishes from its territory, Most Precious Blood maintained a family membership of over 1,560 as of 1988.

John F. Clark, CM, the pastor since 1988, focused on building up a Counseling Center and a fully accredited Day Care Center. "M.P.B. certainly is a very active, concerned and caring parish," Father Clark reported in 1988. "The promotion of Gospel values is at the center of our activities and programs, indeed at the center of our life as a parish."

MOTHER OF GOD (1949)
475 Logan Street at Speer Boulevard

The handy little church at Speer and Logan was built around 1900 and housed various Protestant sects over the years. During the 1920s, it was acquired by the Reorganized Church of Jesus Christ of the Latter Day Saints. This Mormon splinter sect, founded by the widow of Joseph Smith after a dispute as to who would succeed him, used the church until the 1940s when it moved to a larger building at 480 Marion Street.

When the Catholic population of Denver's Capitol Hill neighborhood mushroomed during and after World War II, Archbishop Vehr paid $27,000 for the tiny church with its twin crenelated turrets fronting Speer Boulevard. To relieve crowding in neighboring parishes, Mother of God was created for the faithful living between Broadway and Downing Street, between East 1st and 8th avenues.

Upon discovering the basement pool dug for total immersion baptisms, Archbishop Vehr declared Mother of God "the only Catholic Church in Colorado with a swimming pool." A $16,000 remodeling filled in the "swimming pool" and added two sacristies. Margie Setvin donated the grand stained glass window on Speer, which portrays the Joyous Mysteries surrounding the Mother of God.

The parish prospered during the pastorates of John Regan (1949–1954), Paul Reed (1954–1960) and John V. Anderson (1960–1969). Generous

Mother of God Church, Denver. (Photo by Mike O'Meara.)

church members retired the parish debt by the mid-1950s and enabled the church to acquire the entire triangle of land bounded by Speer, Logan, and East 5th Avenue. Helen Bonfils, a parishioner then living at 707 Washington Street, donated air conditioning, a rectory, and a wedge-shaped addition on the west side of the church. A niche outside the addition was filled with a life-sized statue of the Mother of God, which keeps a vigil over passing Speer Boulevard motorists.

Parishioner Marcella Tangney, who directed the choir for the parish's dedication mass on August 16, 1949, still leads the singers. Besides playing the organ for as many as seven masses on a weekend, she sometimes sings solos. "Marcella is an outstanding example of how parishioners sustain a parish," said Father Lawrence St. Peter, pastor since 1985.

Marcella's husband, Leonard, was a journalist who spent ten years with the *Denver Catholic Register* and thirty-six with the *Rocky Mountain News*. He compiled the congregation's silver jubilee history. Among many other active parishioners have been Colorado Governor Stephen L.R. McNichols, who brought his wife and five children from the governor's mansion at East 8th Avenue and Logan Street. "The McNichols family usually sat in the middle of the church," recalled Father Anderson, "unless one of the boys was serving mass. Then they would all sit in a front pew."

Monsignor Walter Canavan guided Mother of God from 1969 to 1980, celebrating there his fiftieth anniversary as a priest. "We've been blessed with such fine pastors," observed one long-time member. "They have used a traditional, caring litur-gy that helps give this church its special intimate feeling. Come see for yourself, but you'll have to squeeze in. We only have seats for 150 and practically every mass is a sell-out!"

Monsignor Canavan was succeeded by his assistant pastor, Charles Jones, who had taken loving care of the monsignor and sustained him as pastor for as long as possible. The next pastor, Lawrence St. Peter, was chosen to head the archdiocese during the interregnum following Archbishop Casey's death in 1985. "That was a humbling and exciting time," Monsignor St. Peter recalled in 1988. "Now we're in good hands with Archbishop Stafford, and I'm relieved to be able to spend more time in my parish, which is a special, small urban church."

NOTRE DAME (1957)
5100 West Evans Avenue at Sheridan Boulevard

Southwest Denver grew rapidly during the 1950s and only ten years after All Saints parish was founded, Archbishop Vehr paid $30,000 for another new church site. He authorized the new parish on August 14, 1957, and selected Father William Joseph Koontz, chaplain of the Englewood Federal Correctional Center, as the founding pastor. Father Koontz, an Indiana native trained at Regis College and St. Thomas Seminary, prayerfully buried some religious medals on the vacant site and went to work. He teamed up with architect John K. Monroe to plan a modern brick church with an

Monsignor Richard Hiester, the second pastor at Notre Dame, also directed Camp St. Malo, where he taught youngsters to shoot straight. (Photo by C.B. Woodrich.)

L-shaped design. It included seating for 650 in the main church hall, a 275-seat adjoining hall, and three classrooms and a cafeteria designed to be the first part of a school wing.

While this $325,000, one-story parish plant was under construction, the first mass was held on October 13, 1957, in the auditorium of Dorothea Kunsmiller Junior High School. Parishioners acquired a tri-level home at 2207 South Zenobia Street and made the upstairs into a rectory for Father Koontz, converting the basement into a chapel for daily masses, beginning on December 18, 1957.

Parishioners celebrated their first service in the new church at midnight, on Christmas Eve of 1958. The faithful came not only for the mass but also for the unveiling of their impressive, modern house of God. Stig Gusterman, a Colorado craftsman, had made the tabernacle, candlesticks, candelabrum, ciboria, and sanctuary appointments. Giacumo Mussers' Sculpture Studios in Bologna, Italy, provided the statues, crucifixes, and stations of the cross. Dark, dramatic stained glass windows depict Old and New Testament scenes.

Over the main entrance, facing west, a statue of Our Lady of the Universe greeted churchgoers. Another tribute to Notre Dame was the shrine on the north side of the building, featuring a marble Pieta. The shrine was lit every night until vandals shot off Mary's nose.

Notre Dame School thrived under the Dominican Sisters from Our Lady of the Elms Motherhouse in Akron, Ohio. Before expanding the school, the parish helped the sisters construct a convent at 2141 South Zenobia Street, which was finished and blessed by Archbishop Casey on June 22, 1967. The following year, more classroom space was created to provide two classrooms for each of the school's six grades.

At the suggestion of Father Koontz, Notre Dame launched a special education program in 1963 for slow learners and physically handicapped children. This pioneer program evolved into an archdiocesen wide program, the Ministry to the Handicapped directed by Cary Carron, who had worked with Father Koontz to set up the program at Notre Dame.

The third major construction project was a new rectory–parish center, an imposing column-and-portico structure at the northeast corner of South Sheridan and West Evans. Architect Joseph Pahl, who had created the Pieta shrine for the parish,

designed the rectory–administration building. Father Koontz, who had built Notre Dame despite health problems, died of a heart attack as the rectory was being completed.

Monsignor Richard C. Heister, director of the Cathedral choir and of Camp St. Malo, became the second pastor of Notre Dame. A Denver native educated at Regis College and St. Thomas Seminary, he had also attended the Gregorian University in Rome, where he was ordained on July 25, 1937. During World War II, he served in the U.S. Chaplain's Corps, earning a Silver Star, a Purple Heart, and a Bronze Star.

Monsignor Heister and the Holy Name Society transformed the vacant land south of the parish center into an athletic field in 1971. That year, the Altar and Rosary Society installed the church's fine stained glass windows and a new organ. A new family center, designed by Ames and Thorpe Architects, Inc., opened in 1974.

The white-robed Dominicans left the parish, and their convent was converted into a kindergarten and preschool christened Koontz Hall. Seventh and eighth-grade classrooms were built in the basement of the Family Center. Musically, the church and school excelled, thanks to the talents of banjo-playing Monsignor Heister and children's choir director, Leo Frazier. Notre Dame School produced a national champion in 1982, when Molly Dieveney went to Washington, D.C. to win the National Spelling Bee.

In 1982, Notre Dame celebrated its twenty-fifth anniversary by publishing a full-color parish history. After Monsignor Heister retired in 1983, the family center was renamed for him. Father Joseph O'Malley, who had been assistant pastor at Notre Dame from 1959 to 1962, returned in 1983 as pastor. Under Father O'Malley, the parish continues to operate a kindergarten and an eight-grade school, as well as religious education and a youth center for a stable parish of about 1,800 households.

Monsignor Heister, who remains in residence at Notre Dame, reflected on its relatively short but distinguished history:

From the moment Father Koontz was given permission to start a parish on empty acres of ground, the parish has built, increased, and improved. We have this singular and unequaled parish because Notre Dame people started with a spirit of wanting to build the best and most religious parish in the archdiocese.

OUR LADY OF GRACE (1951)
2645 East 48th Avenue

James F. Moynihan, a.k.a. "Father Jim," the "Putting Padre," and the "Father Flanagan of Denver," fathered Our Lady of Grace after persuading Archbishop Vehr to sanction the new parish on September 1, 1951.

Father Moynihan, a product of Denver's St. Patrick Grade School, North High School, Regis College, and St. Thomas Seminary, was assistant pastor at Annunciation when he saw the need for a new parish in Northeast Denver's Swansea neighborhood. This blue-collar area was named for the smelter that once dominated the triangle bounded by the South Platte River, Colorado Boulevard, and East 40th Avenue.

Father Moynihan began offering mission masses in the Johnson Community Center, while awaiting completion of the church at East 48th Avenue and Josephine Street. He took a special interest in the children of his working-class families, learning Spanish and a smattering of other languages in order to reach them. He once told the *Denver Catholic Register* that "the greatest times of my life were spent helping troubled youths."

For youngsters, Father Jim pushed sports as an alternative to crime and drugs. Known for his efforts with troubled boys, he would bail youths out of jail, accompany them to court, accept them as parolees, and work with them in athletic programs he instigated.

In a novel partnership, Our Lady of Grace deeded some of its property to the City and County of Denver in April 1971, enabling the city to build a desperately needed community center. As a result, the neighborhood as a whole—as well as the parish—has benefitted from the Swansea Community Center with its spacious gym, exercise and craft rooms, and game areas.

A widely known public speaker, Father Jim was noted for his ability to motivate people, as well as his stories and jokes. He received many awards, including "Man of the Year" from the Denver Juvenile Court and the Denver Jaycees. "He got along with the big shots, from President John F. Kennedy on down, as well as the ditchdiggers," said his brother, John, of Denver.

Father Jim was not only a coach but also an avid golfer. As the late Archbishop Vehr frowned on golf for priests, he would enter tournaments under such monikers as J. Beam and I.W. Harper. Father Jim also befriended ex-priests, inviting any and all of them to his rectory for Monday night football games and sociability.

Capitalizing on their pastor's popularity and fund-raising abilities, Our Lady of Grace parish quickly retired its debt by using banquets, bingo, and bazaars. In 1966, the parish initiated a 10,000-square-foot addition that doubled the church seating to 540. The enlarged and remodeled church, including landscaping and freshly paved parking lots, was dedicated on March 9, 1967, by Archbishop Casey, in one of his first official acts.

"I told Archbishop Casey," Father Jim revealed later, "let me stay here—the people like me and I like them. If that ever changes, I'll gladly go." That arrangement lasted, as he stayed with his parish until illness forced his retirement in December 1986. Father Jim died March 31, 1988. His many fans, friends, and parishioners flocked to Our Lady of Grace for the rosary and memorial services. Among the many eulogizing Father Moynihan was his friend, Reverend Tom Kelly of Holy Ghost Church: "Jim was a friend to all those no one else would touch. He was open, absolutely himself, and always available. He was always cheerful. I only saw him sore a couple of times, and then for good reason."

OUR LADY OF GUADALUPE (1936)
3565 Kalamath Street

When the Reverend Jesse Jackson brought his presidential campaign to Colorado in 1988, he chose the humble church of Our Lady of Guadalupe as a Sunday stop. Two years earlier, Nicaragua's president, Daniel Ortega, likewise had selected it as the place to meet with area religious leaders regarding his country's efforts to rebuild following decades of repressive dictatorship.

Few were surprised, as Our Lady of Guadalupe Church has been a center of both social and religious activism for years, as its Theatine pastors pursued the Gospel mandate: "Seek first the

An unknown employee of the Federal Writers Project of the Works Progress Administration took this 1930s view of the original Guadalupe chapel. (Denver Public Library.)

kingdom of God and his justice." For years, the parish motorbus and the basketball backboard carried the logo of the United Farm Workers (UFW), a union led by César Chávez of California to organize agricultural laborers. For Hispanics and especially for newly arrived Mexicans, Our Lady of Guadalupe has been a refuge and a center of hope since its founding.

The Theatine fathers first came to Denver in 1925 to establish St. Cajetan Church and opened Guadalupe, in 1936, as a mission. To emphasize the church's special ministry to Mexican-Americans, it was named for the patroness of Mexico, whose dark-complexioned, life-sized statue occupies the niche over the doorway.

Starting on a shoestring, the Theatines acquired Slavin's corner store at 1201 West 36th Avenue in 1935, and remodeled it for services. Spanish-speaking priests from St. Cajetan's tended to the little mission in the South Platte River bottoms. As the Hispanic percentage of Denver's population grew from less than 1 percent in 1920 to the largest single ethnic minority in recent decades, Our Lady of Guadalupe outgrew its storefront church.

Under the leadership of Andres Burguera, CR, a new, Spanish mission–style church was completed and dedicated by Archbishop Vehr on August 12, 1948. This $66,500 church featured a specially cast bell from San Luis Potosí, Mexico. Guadalupe Hall, at 3632 Lipan Street, was completed in 1974, and a three-day fiesta inaugurated its use for classes in boxing, dancing, karate, language, and religion, as well as community and parish gatherings. A rectory

and parish offices at 1209 West 36th Avenue were constructed during the 1970s.

Parish expansion began with the 1969 arrival of a new pastor, José María Lara, CR. This Theatine priest, born and bred in the Basque region of Spain, transformed the parish into a center of Chicano activism. To the dismay of some traditionalists, Father Lara even celebrated mass with the United Farm Workers' eagle emblazoned on the back of his bright red sackcloth chasuble. The UFW, La Raza political party, Rodolfo "Corky" Gonzales' Crusade for Justice, and other militant Hispanic groups found themselves welcome at Guadalupe. Among parishioners rising to political prominence were city councilman Sal Carpio, Federico Peña—Denver's first Spanish-surnamed mayor—and Paul Sandoval, a state legislator and Denver School Board member.

To reflect the faith and culture of the congregation, Guadalupe Church adopted mariachi masses, Hispanic fiestas, and folkways. These included the Christmas-time street drama of Las Posadas, with processioners accompanying Mary and Joseph from house to house in a reenactment of the search for a shelter where Christ could be born. Those welcoming the Holy Family invited processioners into their homes for song, prayer, and refreshments, including *menudo, empanaditas, buñuelos,* and *bizcochitos.*

Hispanic artists were invited by Father Lara to redecorate the parish plant. Andrew and Jesse Mendoza and James Romero, teenagers who lived next to the church and served as altar boys, painted a mural of a fifteenth-century Aztec sundial on the church office entrance wall. Its black-light florescent paint in hues of blue, red-pink, and yellow glows at night, as do a variety of pre-Columbian gods painted in the multipurpose room. Father Lara wanted to emphasize the Indian, as well as the Spanish, roots of his people.

Carlota Espinoza painted the ceiling of the church with La Nuestra Señora de Guadalupe, who appeared to the Indian Juan Diego on a hill outside Mexico City in 1531. This 1977 mural portrays a lovely lady and angels floating in an azure sky with snowcapped mountains in the background. In 1982, Carlos Sandoval painted the Sagrada Familia (Holy Family) mural on the west wall of the parish hall, using the Sangre de Cristo Mountains and the San Luis Valley as the backdrop.

Father Lara's political activism led Denver police to raid the church on March 23, 1976. Despite Father Lara's protests, officers picked the lock to search the church. As the handcuffed priest watched, over thirty members of the Special Command Action Team looked for rumored explosives, which turned out to be sacks of pinto beans the parish was stockpiling for its cooperative grocery.

Although Archbishop Casey had been out of town at the time, the police had obtained permission from other archidocesan officials to raid the church. After Father Lara publicly criticized him, Archbishop Casey attempted to heal the wounds on Easter Sunday, April 18, 1976. He concelebrated mass with Father Lara at Our Lady of Guadalupe, apologizing from the pulpit for the incident and elevating Our Lady of Guadalupe to formal parish status.

Father Lara left the parish in 1979 and subsequently left the priesthood. Pat Valdez, the first U.S.-born pastor, subsequently guided the parish, continuing to make it a refuge and center of hope. Marshall Gourley, CR, pastor since 1982, continued activist traditions. He was arrested in March 1983 while protesting a nuclear weapons "Death Train" passing through Denver, using his censor and incense to exorcise the tracks of "nuclear devils." In April 1988, as gang violence escalated in Denver, Father Gourley started an antiweapons campaign. Parishioners and others were asked to turn in their guns and sign a personal and international disarmament pledge. When praised for his courageous social activism, Father Gourley told *The Denver Post* of March 5, 1989, that his parishioners inspired him to act on Christian principle: "Priests are like leaves, they come and go. The people are the branches. They are always here."

Since 1980, the parish has sponsored an annual pilgrimage to the Basilica of Our Lady of Guadalupe in Mexico City. In 1987, one of the pilgrims was Denver's new archbishop, J. Francis Stafford, who declared that a major goal of his administration would be reconciling Hispanics to the church they first introduced to Colorado.

OUR LADY OF LOURDES (1947)
2200 South Logan Street

Old timers still remember the folding chairs, hard floors, and communion counts for the first parish masses of Our Lady of Lourdes, celebrated in the gymnasium of the State Home for Children at East Iliff Avenue and South Logan Street. After the parish had acquired a spacious one-block site in February 1947, its first construction project was an outdoor shrine to Our Lady of Lourdes. Father Damen L. McCaddon, the first pastor, and men of the parish organized the "Rocks of Lourdes"—220 volunteers who built the massive, fifty-two-foot-high stone shrine and outdoor altar.

The Rocks also served as parish builders, raising money through picnics, bazaars, bingo, Sunday breakfasts, harvest parties, St. Patrick's Day dances, and Mardi Gras galas. The first Mardi Gras netted $5,000, which was the price of the house at 2218 South Logan purchased for a temporary rectory and meeting place.

Groundbreaking began on a $150,000 church and school combination building on June 3, 1948. The first four classrooms were ready on September 27. Sisters Angelita, Dorothy, Helen Ann, and Loretta of the Sisters of St. Francis of Perpetual Adoration persuaded the 101 pupils to attend Saturday classes to make up for the late start. By December 16, 1948, the library, offices, and basement church were completed for Archbishop Vehr's dedication ceremony. That Christmas, over 1,650 people attended mass in the new subterranean church.

A new school wing was completed on the north side of the church in 1952 and by 1954, seven nuns were teaching 384 pupils in the school's eight grades. After being chauffered in each day, the sisters finally moved into their own Our Lady of Lourdes convent following its completion in 1955. Father McCaddon lived in an old house that formed the core of the 1952 school wing.

Father McCaddon and his dog Mike loved the great outdoors and frequently took parish youngsters camping, both on the church property and at his summer cabin near Empire. Father McCaddon, an admirer of Colorado's great naturalist Enos Mills, also loved to use nature themes in his sermons. And he worked with the Rocks to transform the spacious parish grounds into a tree-shaded retreat, complete with outdoor stations of the cross.

Most kids appreciated the fresh air life espoused by Father McCaddon. An exception was little Stephen J. Leonard, who subsequently became a famous Denver historian, writer, and long-time chair of the history department at Metropolitan State College..Leonard recalled in 1987:

> Father McCaddon had been an army chaplain and loved the great outdoors. He had us school kids camping on the church property during the 1950s in a stockade-like area. Most kids liked it. I hated it. Green eggs full of sand in the morning. It's stupid to leave a comfortable bed to sleep on the ground, even if we did get to watch Hopalong Cassidy movies.

Father McCaddon retired in 1966, a year after the parish completed its church building and finally moved masses out of the basement hall of the school. Archbishop Vehr presided at that long-awaited church dedication on May 16, 1965, blessing a buff brick, neo-Romanesque structure designed by John K. Monroe. Subsequent pastors were Robert E. Kekeisen, Robert M. Harrington, Joseph Lievens, and, since 1985, George L. Weibel.

As of 1988, Our Lady of Lourdes is a parish of 386 households with a school offering kindergarten through eighth-grade education. Despite its setting in a now developed part of Denver, the well-landscaped parish plant includes not only the impressive grotto, but also woodsy nooks, outdoor picnic pavilions, and Maryhaven—a two-story brick home for the elderly on the northern edge of the parish campus along Warren Avenue. The 1947 dream of Father McCaddon and the Rocks of Lourdes has materialized in this peaceful, green, parish plant.

OUR LADY OF MOUNT CARMEL (1894)
3549 Navajo Street

"Seated in a comfortable carriage of the Santa Fe Railway, my glance swept across those immense plains which, around Denver, are dotted with the cottages of our Italian agriculturalists," reported Frances Xavier Cabrini, the Italian-born foundress of the Missionary Sisters of the Sacred Heart. The first U.S. citizen to be canonized a saint, she first came to Denver as a missionary in 1902.

Touring Colorado, Mother Cabrini found that:

> here the hardest work is reserved for the Italian worker. There are few who regard him with a sympathetic eye, who care for him or remember

Mother Frances Cabrini, an Italian immigrant, came to Denver and other American cities to establish churches, schools, hospitals, and orphanages.

> that he has a heart and soul: they merely look upon him as an ingenious machine for work. . . . I saw these dear fellows of ours engaged on construction of railways in the most intricate mountain gorges.

Mother Cabrini further lamented that Colorado's many Italian miners spent most of their waking lives underground, "until old age and incapacity creep over them, or . . . a landslide or explosion or an accident of some kind ends the life of the poor worker, who does not even need a grave, being buried in the one in which he has lived all his life."

At the request of Bishop Matz, Mother Cabrini came to Colorado to bring "the holy joys" to "our poor emigrants." In North Denver's "Little Italy," Mother Cabrini joined a handsome young priest who made building a parish for his countrymen his life's work—Mariano Felice Lepore. It was Father Lepore who had first invited Mother Cabrini to

Colorado, after hearing of her miraculous ability to do God's work with meager resources.

Initially, Italians had settled in the South Platte River bottoms where they found cheap rent, good soil, and water for their vegetable patches. As these hard-working people prospered, they moved up to North Denver and began attending St. Patrick Church, a heavily Irish parish. Italians wanted their own national parish, and the roots were planted in 1891 with the arrival of Father Lepore and the founding of the Mt. Carmel Society by Michael Notary, a leading merchant and real estate man, who also spearheaded the campaign to make Colorado the first state to declare Columbus Day a legal holiday.

Father Lepore became a champion of the poor Italian immigrants, who were mocked as WOPS (without passports), and founded a newspaper, *La Nazione*, to advance their cause. Father Lepore and the Mt. Carmel Society purchased seven lots, where, on Palm Sunday, March 18, 1894, Bishop Matz dedicated the original Our Lady of Mount Carmel, a small frame church.

A fire, possibly arson, destroyed this little church, according to *The Denver Times* of August 17, 1898, which reported that the blaze left all of Little Italy mourning, "Santo Rocco mio; Madonna mia; disgrazia." The Mt. Carmel Society immediately began planning a grand new church. A rival Italian group, the St. Rocco Society, also entered what became a bitter race to construct a new Italian national church. Bishop Matz, caught in the middle of another of the lively ethnic squabbles of the early Denver Church, refused to consecrate the Chapel of Saint Rocco or send a priest there.

Father Lepore, who had helped lay the cornerstone in 1899, was not there to see the dedication of the 109-by-fifty-nine-foot Romanesque church, which he had worked so hard to complete. On November 18, 1903, the thirty-five-year-old priest was fatally shot under still mysterious circumstances. His assassin, a laborer named Guieseppe Sarvice, was killed at the same time.

For the dedication, a procession of hundreds of singing, flag-waving, flower-carrying Italians led Bishop Matz up Navajo Street on December 18, 1904, a bright, sunny "Italian" day. Bishop Matz followed the suggestion of Mother Cabrini and invited the Servite fathers to tend the new church. The Servites, an Italian-American order based in

Chicago, sent Thomas M. Moreschini, OSM to guide the parish. Father Moreschini, with the help of Mother Cabrini, set about uniting the fractious Italian community. He achieved a reconciliation with the St. Rocco Society and bought their chapel at 3601 Osage as a parish school.

Mother Cabrini, who had set up a grade school in the fall of 1902 in the home of Michael Notary, moved her flock of children and four nuns to the new school with relief. In the Notary house at 3357 Navajo Street, the first Mt. Carmel School had overflowed with students. For lack of tablets and blackboards, Mother Cabrini's teaching nuns had students blow on chilled window panes and use their fingers in the condensation to do their lessons.

Besides using the Milnew arithmetic, Lawlor history, Atwood geography, Benziger Brothers Bible history, and the *Baltimore Catechism*, Mother Cabrini and her sisters used Columbus readers and Mother Tongue English textbooks to teach first and second-generation immigrant children how to use English properly. Although the grateful parish could not afford to pay the nuns regular salaries, they held monthly food showers to assure that the teachers at least ate well.

Father Moreschini, Mother Cabrini, and Frank Damascio, a prominent Denver contractor and parish member who was the architect of the church, set about making it an elegant house of the Lord. Marble statues were brought from Italy and fine Italian frescoes painted on the ceiling and walls. The exterior was transformed into one of Denver's finest examples of "Roman" architecture with its twin, four-sided copper domes and a 1,000-pound bell that the parish proudly baptized "Maria del Carmelina." Former Denver councilman Ernie Marranzino, whose family has lived in the house behind the church since the 1890s, calls Maria the "heartbeat" of North Denver: "That bell regulates life here the way church bells did in the old country."

When Father Moreschini was transferred to Chicago, he was replaced by his assistant, Julius M. Piccoli, OSM. Father Piccoli put the parish in financial order. "He ate only bread and onions," noted Mt. Carmel's seventy-five-anniversary history, "because he was sacrificing that much for the poor Italians of the parish." Father Piccoli also helped make Mt. Carmel the hub of North Denver's "Little Italy." By 1930, the parish served a population of almost 3,000 Italians, who had become the Mile High City's fourth largest foreign-born group.

The parish's grandest festival is the Feast of St. Rocco on August 16. Parishioners carry the statue of the saint and his little dog through the streets of North Denver, celebrating gloriously afterwards with music, food, and a carnival.

After Father Piccoli died in 1938, he was succeeded by Gaetano M. Del Brusco (1938–1946), Tom LoCascio (1946–1958), Alphonse Mattucci (1958–1966), Robert Volk (1966–1968), Hugh M. Moffett (1968–1974), Gabriel M. Weber (1974–1977), Donald Duplessis (1977–1978), Joseph M. Carbone (1978–1988), and Gabriel M. Ramacciotti. These Servite fathers transformed the struggling parish they adopted in 1904 into one of the staunchest bulwarks of the archdiocese.

In the fall of 1926, the Servite Sisters of Omaha replaced the Missionary Sisters of the Sacred Heart at the grade school. A large, modern, $400,000 Mt. Carmel High School at 3600 Zuni Street was dedicated on September 23, 1951, by Archbishop Vehr. Three years later, the thriving parish built a new grade school at West 36th Avenue and Pecos Street.

After World War II, Denver's flourishing Italian community spread out into the north metro suburbs in Adams, Boulder, and Jefferson counties. Servite priests established new Italian-oriented parishes, continuing the work begun at Mt. Carmel, at Assumption Church in Welby, Our Lady Mother of the Church in Commerce City, and Holy Trinity Church and School in Westminster. As many Italian families moved into these new parishes, enrollments dropped at both Mt. Carmel High School and Grade School. Both were closed in 1968, and the grade school was sold to the City and County of Denver to become the Northside Community Center.

Father Joseph Carbone, a scion of the pioneer family famous for their bakery, sausage shop, and pizza palace, was modest about his role as pastor at Mt. Carmel. "I never got into making dough," he quipped during a 1985 interview. "And I haven't gone very far in life. I was born across the street from this church." But Father Carbone and Denver's Italian community have come a long way from the days when Italian immigrants were among the city's poorest people, squatting in the Platte River bottoms and peddling vegetables. They worked hard, prospered, and built Mt. Carmel,

whose colorful history and architecture led to its designation by both the Denver Landmark Preservation Commission and the National Register of Historic Places.

Backsides of churches are a good clue to the love and craftsmanship invested in them. The rear of Mt. Carmel is fine stone masonry work with an ancient red brick chimney carrying a blonde brick cross. Only alley people will see this, but all of North Denver and downtown can appreciate the twin front spires, with their copper domes and white crosses, restored in 1986 to shimmer above Denver's "Little Italy."

PRESENTATION OF OUR LADY (1912)
665 Irving Street

In November 1912, a black-robed man in a buggy headed southwest out of Denver. On the bleak, open prairie, the priest sometimes had to jump out of his vehicle to tug his horse through the mud. James Joseph Gibbons was surveying the newly created parish of the Presentation of Our Lady, bounded on the north by West Colfax Avenue, on the east and south by the South Platte River and stretching west "halfway to Golden." This new parish on the southwestern outskirts of Denver served Barnum, an area subdivided by circus czar Phineas T. Barnum. Barnum's wonderful, fresh air, boasted Phineas, would bring even the sickest souls "back from the verge of the tomb."

On November 21, 1912—the Feast of the Presentation—seventeen families gathered in Redmen's Hall at West 7th Avenue and Knox Court as Father Gibbons said the first mass. In the coming months, the congregation built a small church at West 8th Avenue and Knox Court. Members handmade the pews, and Father Gibbons used sawhorses and planks for an altar. Bottles served as candlesticks and Mason jars as flower vases when Bishop Matz dedicated this tiny frame church that autumn. Not until eleven years later did the small, struggling parish complete a three-room schoolhouse at 659 Julian Street, where the Sisters of Mercy opened Presentation School for neighborhood scholars.

Father Gibbons served as pastor of Presentation until his death on December 2, 1931. This priest, according to a banner headline in the *Denver Catholic Register*, was "a pioneer noted for hard

Father James J. Gibbons, founder of Presentation parish, wrote two books about his adventures as a pioneer Colorado sky pilot. (Rebecca Waugh Collection.)

work" during his forty-five years in Colorado and the "oldest priest among the diocesan clergy." After his ordination in Chicago, this "giant in physical strength and mental stature" served in Denver, Georgetown, Leadville, and Ouray. Father Gibbons wrote two books about his missionary work on the Colorado mining frontier, *Notes of a Missionary Priest* (1898) and *In the San Juan, Colorado: Sketches*, an 1898 classic reprinted in 1972 by one of his old missions, St. Patrick's in Telluride.

Presentation parish attracted another literary pastor in 1934: Henry Amand Geisert, a noted criminologist and author of the textbook, *The Criminal*. Father Geisert served at Presentation until his death on December 2, 1944, when Father Matthias J. Blenkush took over. The parish grew rapidly with Denver's post–World War II population boom, and in 1950, Father Blenkush oversaw construction of a new brick church–school. The four classrooms and 400-seat church, with a Carrara marble altar and a mosaic donated by Helen Bonfils, were dedicated on February 16, 1950, by Archbishop Vehr. Architects John K. Monroe, William H. Monroe, and Robert G. Durham designed this sturdy modern complex and, in 1963, added ten more classrooms.

A parish credit union had been started in 1946, and by the 1960s claimed to be the largest individual parish credit union in Colorado. Besides helping members to acquire their own homes, the credit union has also helped finance parish expansion—at a savings to all concerned. John M. Gibbons, the pastor since 1980, established an endowment fund that enables the school to provide many scholarships.

A long-time dream came true for Presentation parish on May 5, 1984, with the dedication of a new church—a striking, large contemporary structure that incorporates two walls of the old church. The parish, already a spiritual home for many Hispanic families, has also welcomed hundreds of Vietnamese who began pouring into this Southwest Denver neighborhood during the 1970s.

Presentation now houses the Vietnamese Catholic Community offices, staffed in 1989 by Jude Ban, CMC, and Francis Do Cao Tung, CMC, and offers special Vietnamese masses. The Sunday afternoon children's Vietnamese mass is one of the most moving services in the archdiocese. Several hundred children jam the church, sitting by grade with older children as monitors. A teenager directs the sweet, soft children's voices of the choir. Youngsters take much responsibility for this service, with duties ranging from reading at the altar to taking up the collection. Under the skylight's shafts of sunlight spotlighting the altar, Vietnamese priests say traditional Vietnamese masses, perpetuating the language and culture of their distant homeland. Like the Irish, Germans, Italians, and Hispanics who came to Presentation parish before them, the Vietnamese are finding that the church accommodates not only their spirituality, but also their heritage.

RISEN CHRIST (1967)
3060 South Monaco Parkway

Archbishop Casey gave to the first parish he created in Denver, Risen Christ, the same name he had given the cathedral he built as bishop of Lincoln,

Nebraska. He paid Hutchinson Homes, the developer of the surrounding residential neighborhood, $43,805 for the 5.15-acre site. Adjoining parishes were asked to contribute $10,000 each to help establish the new congregation.

Archbishop Casey created the parish on August 22, 1967, and authorized construction of a $386,000 showcase church for all of rapidly growing southeast Denver south of Jewell Avenue and east of interstate highway 25. James Sudler, a leading Denver architect, was commissioned to do the "ski jump" church.

This dramatic structure, glistening in its white rusticated stucco skin wrapped about a steel frame skeleton, is a curved-sided triangle. The third side rises on the northwest to a peak seventy-six feet above the altar, with vertical panels of stained glass, whose abstract designs splash the interior with color. A landscaped circular walkway surrounds the triangular church, geometrically combining the Christian symbol of unity with the symbol of the Triune God.

The cylindrical, forty-foot-high baptistry was placed at the main (south) entrance of the church, symbolizing baptism as the doorway to the faith. It is connected to the church by a ruby red translucent plastic arch. The church is illuminated not only by the chancel stained glass behind the oval sanctuary but by skylights and slit openings in the three-foot-thick cavity walls.

The 1,250-seat church was completed in 1970 and blessed by Archbishop Casey. To complement the church, a parish center was constructed in the fall of 1974 to house the parish office, conference space, and rooms for activities ranging from instructions in the Creighton Model Ovulation Method of Natural Family Planning to the Mt. Tabor Support Group for divorced and separated Catholics.

Joseph M. O'Malley, the founding pastor, was a Massachusetts native, a former tight end for the Holy Cross College football team, and a newspaper reporter who also served as chaplain for the Denver Fire Department. Father O'Malley was followed by Monsignor William H. Jones, who became the second pastor at Risen Christ on July 15, 1980.

Monsignor Jones, a Denver native whose uncle, Hubert Newell, was the bishop of Cheyenne and who had brothers and uncles in the Colorado clergy, has been a leading administrator and historian of the Archdiocese of Denver. For his Ph.D. disserta-

tion in history at the Catholic University of America, he compiled *The History of Catholic Education in the State of Colorado*. After a stint as chancellor and superintendent of Catholic schools, Monsignor Jones took over at Risen Christ, then and now one of the largest Catholic congregations, with over 2,000 registered families.

On a 1986 visit, we found the church jammed with red-coated ushers squeezing people in for the 11 A.M. mass. The organist and choir loft vocalists were not hidden in back but were up front in the raised sanctuary. This strikingly different church contains not only a cry room but also a playroom with hobbyhorses and toys, as well as a book and religious goods store, the Book Nook.

In the summer of 1987, members of the congregation donated a 6.5-ton, twelve-foot-high statue of the Risen Christ for the church's prayer garden. Mario Benassi of Florence, Italy, sculpted the statue from Carrara marble, using as a model a twenty-four-inch bronze by Denver artist Dee Toscano.

SACRED HEART (1879)
2760 Larimer Street

Sacred Heart is Denver's oldest still-used church. St. Mary's, the pioneer 1860 church, was demolished in 1900, and St. Elizabeth's—the second Denver parish—outgrew its original 1879 church, which was torn down in 1898 to build the current St. Elizabeth's.

Episcopalians can claim the oldest surviving church building in Denver—the 1876 Emmanuel Chapel at 10th and Lawrence streets. This charming, stone landmark was converted to a synagogue by Congregation Sherith Israel in 1902 and, in the 1970s, was recycled again, becoming an art gallery for the Auraria Higher Education Center.

Sacred Heart parishioners have allowed the city's senior functioning church to be designated officially as both a Denver Landmark and as a National Register of Historic Places Landmark. Sacred Heart parish's history may be begun with the arrival of the railroads in 1870. That year, the Denver Pacific and the Kansas Pacific tied the remote frontier crossroads of Denver into a growing national rail network. Denver had stagnated during the 1860s, starting the decade with a census population of

As the oldest church in Denver still using the original structure, Sacred Heart has been elevated to the National Register of Historic Places. (Interior from Denver Public Library; exterior photo by Roger Whitacre.)

4,749 and ending it with an 1870 population of 4,759. After the railroads arrived, the self-proclaimed boom town did begin to boom, reaching an 1880 population of 35,629.

Many of the immigrants pouring into Denver were Irish and Italian Catholics. These newcomers squeezed into pews at St. Mary's and St. Elizabeth's and strained to follow Bishop Machebeuf's French or Father Bender's German accent. They were overjoyed when Bishop Machebeuf authorized a new parish. The bishop bought five lots for $2,500 in 1879, in the Curtis Park neighborhood, nestled between the railroad tracks and new streetcar lines on Larimer and Champa, and then the fastest growing part of the city. Many of the Irish and Italian immigrants settled there to be near their jobs with the railroad and, in the case of many of

the Italians, their vegetable farms along the South Platte River bottoms.

Emmet Anthony, one of Denver's first architects, designed a brick church in the traditional cruciform shape, placing the solitary steeple over the Larimer Street entrance. Anthony used carpenter Gothic woodwork to dress up his brick shell. McPhee and McGinnity provided the woodwork, glass, and finishing, while many parishioners donated other materials as well as money, labor, and prayers. Even the altar was made of wood and bathed in light from the large, wood frame Gothic windows of colored glass.

As his young diocese was too poor to support the new parish, Bishop Machebeuf placed it in the hands of the Jesuit order, who were eager to establish a toehold in the mushrooming Queen City of the Plains. John Baptiste Guida, SJ, a philosophy professor from Georgetown University, became the first pastor. On September 12, 1879, he celebrated the first mass, a Mass of the Sacred Heart.

Father Guida was soon saying three masses each Sunday in the tiny frame rectory. On the crisp, sunny morning of April 25, 1880, parishioners celebrated completion of their church with Vicar General Raverdy singing the high mass. It was a bittersweet celebration for the Irish, who had hoped that Sacred Heart would be given an Irish, not an Italian pastor.

By fall, the church basement had been partitioned into classrooms for a free school taught by four lay women. Six Sisters of Charity of Cincinnati (sisters Pelagia, Charles Regina, Marcelline, Carlotta, Flavia, and Anne de Sales) began teaching in the fall of 1882—at salaries of $25 a month. The nuns taught the *Baltimore Catechism*, Gregorian chant, and ecclesiastical history, as well as calligraphy and secular subjects. Not until February 2, 1890, would Bishop Matz dedicate the large, two-story brick Sacred Heart School building at 2840 Lawrence Street. Some 250 students flocked to the new school, which in 1890 added a high school curriculum. Father Guida borrowed money from his Jesuit confreres in Europe to build the school and a convent next door at a cost of $52,000.

Both church and school were jammed. Sacred Heart was then one of the fastest growing parishes in the booming city of Denver, which reached a population of 106,713 in 1890. To relieve overcrowding, lots were purchased for $8,000 at East

26th Avenue and Ogden Street, where the Loyola Oratory and Chapel were built in 1909 for $5,000. About 500 Catholics in the eastern portion of Sacred Heart parish used the Loyola Chapel.

In 1912, Sacred Heart parishioners finally paid off their debts and began to think about a new church. The eastern half of the overcrowded parish was designated as St. Ignatius Loyola parish, which constructed a large, impressive Gothic church in 1924. The Jesuit order operated both the old Sacred Heart parish and the newer one named for its founder.

As many parishioners moved east away from the older area bordering the railroad tracks, Sacred Heart became a poorer, core city church. To help the neighborhood's needier souls, the parish launched, in 1892, the Sacred Heart Aid Society. This was one of the pioneer Catholic charities that gave clothing and cash (usually $5 a month) to indigents. In 1925, the society helped establish the Little Flower Social Center at 2809 Larimer, which offered food, clothing, shelter, and sociability to the down and out, who flocked to Larimer Street, once Denver's main street but its skid row by the time the Great Depression struck in 1929. The parish struggled through the trying times of the 1930s, closing the high school in 1939.

Sacred Heart claims some saints, such as Julia Greeley, an ex-slave who was baptized at Sacred Heart in 1880. She displayed heroic charity by begging for others and giving all she had to the poor and needy. After her death in 1918, she continued to help those who prayed to her, even curing a cancer patient, an incident witnessed and reported by Doctor Martin Currigan.

Sacred Heart's best known parishioner, Elizabeth "Baby Doe" Tabor attended Sacred Heart Church. Her husband Horace, the fabled silver king, was baptized on his deathbed at the Windsor Hotel by Father Barry from Sacred Heart, where a solemn Requiem Mass was held for him on April 14, 1899.

Sacred Heart has been served by many Jesuit pastors, but John E. Casey, SJ, holds a special distinction. Besides growing up in the parish, Father Casey was pastor for the longest period of time—a quarter of a century. John Casey, a wide-awake altar boy and Sacred Heart School graduate, returned to his old parish in 1948 as pastor. From his office, he could see the old terrace across 28th

Street where he was born and raised by County Galway immigrants. His old neighborhood had changed dramatically over the years. Irish and Italian parishioners had been largely replaced by Mexican-Americans, and the once solid residential neighborhood now housed struggling small businesses, factories, warehouses, and public housing.

Along with the rest of the neighborhood, the church had deteriorated. Structural engineers warned Father Casey that the rotting belfry, struggling to support the massive bell, might collapse at any time and come crashing down on Larimer Street. Casey, who had grown up to the rhythm of those bells, reluctantly took down the old tower and replaced it with a wooden steeple.

Father Casey began making rounds in the neighborhood, calling on parishioners where they lived and worked. He was determined to revitalize the parish and was convinced that "you can't know your people by sitting in your office." His Mexican-American parishioners responded to the congenial Irish pastor. Whole families donated time, labor, and materials, helping Father Casey spruce up the church. Priest and parishioners replaced the old pump organ; they remodeled the church with secondhand confessionals, stations of the cross, and other furnishings Father Casey picked up when the old Sacred Heart Church in Boulder was razed. Some of the congregation and Father Casey spent their evenings lying on their backs atop a scaffolding to restore the venerable ceiling, and repainted the whole church. "I've spent more time with a paint brush in my hand during the past twenty years than I have with religious objects," Father Casey quipped.

He was followed as pastor by Father Robert A. Hagan, SJ (1973–1980), Father Mark McKenzie, SJ (1980–1984), and Father Eugene Renard, SJ (1985–1988). Sadly, the parish closed its grade school in 1979. That loss was partially compensated when the parish acquired the vacant lot next to the church and transformed it from an eyesore into a park and outdoor shrine. The old fence along 28th Street, which Baby Doe Tabor had long ago donated to her church, was repaired and repainted. Sacred Heart Church, once considered ripe for demolition, began to sparkle with a new spirit. When the skylight over the main altar collapsed, knocking down and shattering a huge crucifix, Carlota Espinoza replaced it with her huge, colorful mural of the death and resurrection of Jesus Christ. Proud parishioners celebrated their centennial in 1979, when Sacred Heart became the first parish in the Denver archdiocese to spend a century in the same church.

In 1980, the old convent next to the school at 2844 Lawrence Street was converted to the Sacred Heart House. There, the Sisters of Charity of Leavenworth care for as many as eighteen women and children at a time, perpetuating the charitable endeavors begun in 1892 by the Sacred Heart Aid Society.

Father Renard, the last Jesuit pastor before the parish was turned over to archdiocesan priests in 1988, continued to make Sacred Heart a spiritual center in tune with the renaissance of the neighborhood. "It is a constant struggle," Father Renard remarked in 1987, "but parishioners and others help, like Carlota Espinoza who lovingly put Christ back together again."

Marcus M. Medrano, an archdiocesan priest, took charge on July 1, 1988, saying, "The oldness of the parish plant creates many challenges. My people and I, poor though we are, will continue the struggle to keep Sacred Heart a great parish."

ST. ANTHONY OF PADUA (1947)
3801 West Ohio Avenue

St. Anthony parish was formed on February 24, 1947, by Archbishop Vehr, to serve 175 families in fast growing West Denver. Michael A. Maher, the founding pastor, held the first mass on August 3, 1947, in the Westwood Skating Rink. Subsequent services were held in the banquet room of a historic West Alameda Avenue tavern, the Aeroplane Club. Another local business, Westwood Cleaners, housed early meetings of the Holy Name Society and also made room for Father Maher's Saturday confessions, which inspired the slogan, "Cleaning Clothes as Well as Cleaning Souls."

By Christmas of 1947, when mass was celebrated with the debut of the parish choir at the Aeroplane Club, Father Maher was saying three Sunday masses. On September 29, 1948, the parish finally moved into its brand new church.

Since an estimated 1,200 Catholic school children lived within the parish boundaries, Father Maher's flock also undertook to build a school.

Sisters from Presentation parish conducted religious education classes until November 8, 1954, when Archbishop Vehr dedicated a three-classroom school, built as a $72,000 annex to the church. A Junior Newman Club was founded to promote religious education and vocations, as well as parish activities such as the first St. Patrick's Day dance and the first bazaar, both held in 1948. In this young parish teeming with children, religious education was conducted with the help of the Sisters of Loretto and the Missionary Sisters of Our Lady of Victory, as well as the Sisters of Charity.

Father Maher traveled to Rome in 1950 and returned with a special papal blessing from Pope Pius XII for St. Anthony parish. Eight years later, Robert E. Kekeisen became the second pastor and launched an $80,000-a-year campaign that led to construction of a new school auditorium and classrooms.

In the fall of 1959, St. Anthony's began work on a larger, new church, designed by Langhart and McGuire of Denver and built by the Frank J. Kirchoff Construction Company. The handsome new edifice, made of burnt-orange brick, was ready for Christmas services in 1960.

The same year, Father Kekeisen undertook a unique Confraternity of Christian Doctrine program—Operation Door Knock. This effort to interest any and all Westwood neighborhood children and adults in religious instruction added 150 families to the parish rolls and brought the number of children receiving religious instruction to over 1,400. A parish convent was completed in 1964, and the School Sisters of St. Francis were recruited to live there while they expanded St. Anthony of Padua's school to a full eight grades. For its youth, the parish also launched a softball program that, as of 1988, has fielded fourteen teams.

Patrick V. Sullivan, pastor from 1976 to 1987, was confronted by declining enrollments and closed the school in 1979. Sister Gloria Fews, SSSF, softened the loss by opening the Southwest Montessori Preschool in St. Anthony Convent. The school uses the system developed by Maria Montessori, an Italian physician and educator who died in 1952. This school for students aged two to six had ninety students and a waiting list in 1988.

Father Sullivan became an activist advocate for the neighborhood, which includes many low-income Hispanics. Among the many programs he offered were sessions with César Chávez, the heroic founder and long-time leader of the United Farm Workers. Chávez, crusading for an end to pesticides, which he claims endanger as many as 300,000 farm workers, thanked "Father Pat who brings us in, feeds us and gives us a special Mass."

Father Sullivan launched an Hispanic studies and a health program at the parish, a food bank, and Christmas basket operations. His work on many fronts earned him Denver's 1986 Minoru Yasui Community Volunteer Award for his leadership and dedication as a volunteer with Options, Inc., Shalom House, Denver Family Corporation, Metropolitan Organization for People, Denver Family Housing, and Denver Catholic Community Services. Poor health forced Father Sullivan to retire in 1987, when he was succeeded by Joseph Sullivan.

ST. CAJETAN (1922)
99 South Raleigh Street

Two St. Cajetan churches are cornerstones of Denver's Hispanic heritage. The old St. Cajetan, the peach and gray–painted landmark now used as an auditorium for the Auraria Campus at 9th and Lawrence streets, was the first Hispanic parish in Denver. The second St. Cajetan's, a striking contemporary design by Denver architect Ramón F. Martínez on West Alameda Avenue between Raleigh and Stuart streets, symbolizes the ability of Hispanics to move up and out of the core city. Like the parent church, it continues to serve as the Spanish national church of Denver.

Auraria, the oldest continually occupied neighborhood in what is now Denver, began attracting Hispanics from Southern Colorado, New Mexico, and Old Mexico in the early 1900s. They attended either St. Elizabeth's (a German national parish) or St. Leo's (a heavily Irish church at 10th Street and West Colfax Avenue). During the 1920s, leading Hispanic ladies presented Bishop Tihen with a petition asking for their own church and for the Theatine fathers, an order active in the American Southwest. The Theatines had been founded in 1524 by St. Cajetan of Vicenza, and from the beginning Hispanics wanted their parish to be named St. Cajetan. This Italian saint trusted in Divine

Denver's pioneer Hispanic church, St. Cajetan, initially occupied this Spanish colonial revival gem, which is now recycled as an auditorium for the Auraria Higher Education Center. (Denver Public Library. Photo by Sandra Dallas Atchison.)

Providence to care for the lilies of the field, the birds of the air, and the poor and humble of this world.

In 1922, Bartolomew Caldentey began saying masses for Hispanics in the basement of St. Leo's. As Denver's Hispanic population swelled, this congregation became larger than that of some parishes. The Spanish-speaking people began to aspire to their own parish and recalled a proud heritage; they had built the first churches and offered the first masses in Colorado. Fathers Dominguez and Escalante, after their path-breaking 1776 exploration of the Southwest, had given the world its first published account of the mountainous realm that would become the State of Colorado a century later.

Despite this proud past and despite the fact that many of Father Caldentey's flock at St. Leo's were not "Mexicans" but third-, fourth-, and fifth-generation Colorado natives, Hispanics found themselves often treated as second-class citizens. They wanted their own church, and Father Caldentey knew just the man to ask.

John Kernan Mullen, a poor, uneducated Irishman turned millionaire flour miller, had grown up in Auraria and had helped build St. Leo Church. Mullen had left his old home at 9th and Lawrence streets to build a Capitol Hill mansion. Father Caldentey approached Mullen, the most generous philanthropist in town, about using his old home in

Auraria as a church site. In 1923, after repeated conversations among Father Caldentey, William O'Brien of St. Leo's, and Bishop Tihen, the Mullens donated their old home as a new home for St. Cajetan's.

Joyously, the Theatines and their Hispanic parishioners moved out of St. Leo's basement and into the small house, which soon resounded with masses, classes, and meetings. The parish borrowed $15,000 for a new church and broke ground on October 1, 1924. By January 1925, the basement was finished, the borrowed money exhausted, and Father Caldentey had been called to Rome to become the superior general of the Theatine order. Once again, J. K. Mullen came to the rescue, donating $65,708 of the $89,000 needed to complete St. Cajetan's on March 21, 1926. Celebrating their heritage, parishioners had Robert Willison (who was also the architect for the Denver Municipal Auditorium and St. Dominic Catholic Church), design a 700-seat Spanish colonial revival gem.

Bishop Tihen appointed Father Humphrey Martorell to replace Father Caldentey. As Denver's Hispanic population soared from 1,390 in 1920 to 12,345 in 1940 and to 43,147 in 1960, St. Cajetan parish flourished. Magdalena Gallegos, who was born in the small rental house at 943 10th Street, eloquently recorded the life of her Auraria neighborhood and of her parish in Issue 2 of the 1985 *Colorado Heritage* magazine:

> Discrimination from the outside brought the Hispanic community closer together. There was a sense of belonging in the neighborhood. The permanence of the community was established in 1926 when St. Cajetan's Catholic Church was built.... The lives of the Spanish speaking people in Auraria revolved around their church.... where they met weekly, made friends, and watched the children grow. . . .The Hispanic people did not have [any other] public institution where they could mix and feel important.

Festive weddings kept the parish young. Magdalena's father said of his wedding at St. Cajetan's, "I saved $200 and paid for the wedding gown, the flowers, my suit, and all the food and drinks for the wedding dinner at 943 10th Street. I rented a brand new white Chrysler and for the honeymoon, we drove to Greeley just for the heck of it."

Music filled the lives of the people and their church. "Every girl sang in the choir," recalled Magdalena Gallegos,

> and the men played in the band. The basement of the church was always filled with music as people practiced for operettas and plays. A magnificent organ was donated to the church from the old Tabor Grand Opera House complete with cowbells and cymbals. Billy Bernard, the organist, would nearly blast the praying parishioners out of their pews when he played his elaborate renditions of rumbas, sambas, and boleros before the 10:30 Masses on Sundays.

Six Sisters of St. Benedict from Atchison, Kansas, opened the St. Cajetan School and convent in the fall of 1935. This new brick, two-story school soon overflowed with students in all eight grades. The parish's Ave Maria clinic dispensed not only health care but also free lunches, and every day the black-clad Benedictine nuns marched a parade of children from the school at 9th and Lawrence to lunch at the clinic at 8th and Curtis streets.

To help Hispanic families buy cars and homes and meet life's emergencies, the St. Cajetan Credit Union opened on January 10, 1939. Many successful Colorado Hispanics, to this day, trace their rise to the spiritual, cultural, physical, and economic assistance that St. Cajetan's offered. Trying to reach out to even the poorest people squatting in the South Platte River bottoms, St. Cajetan's established Our Lady of Victory Mission, a tiny chapel at West 12th Avenue and Umatilla Street that was washed away by the flood of 1965.

When rumors swept the Auraria neighborhood in the 1960s that the Denver Urban Renewal Authority was going to demolish the neighborhood to make way for the 169-acre Auraria Higher Education Center, neighbors met in the basement of the church. Some prayed, some decided to fight the project, and some resigned themselves to the blow. Father James Prohens, who in 1970 had succeeded Father John Ordinas as the fourth Theatine pastor, recalls that sad time:

> We watched them knock down the school, the clinic, and the credit union. We had to build a new church. Practically the whole community moved out to Southwest Denver with us in the new St. Cajetan, which opened in 1975. We also found ourselves strengthened in the new church by a

largely Hispanic, Catholic community that was already living out there.

Parishioners worked with preservationists to at least save the handsome old church building that had been the center of so many activities. As a monument of Hispanic architecture, culture, history, and religion, St. Cajetan's was declared both a National Register and a Denver Landmark Preservation Commission landmark. This forced the Denver Urban Renewal Authority to spare it and allowed the Auraria campus to recycle the church as the largest and most elegant hall on campus. It is used for everything from theater to the annual storytelling conference, where Hispanic students have reminisced about St. Cajetan's past as the heart and soul of the now vanished community of Auraria.

ST. CATHERINE OF SIENA (1912)
4200 Federal Boulevard

Catholics in the northwest Denver neighborhood of Berkeley built one of the loveliest churches in the archdiocese and had a glorious time doing so in what they nicknamed "the carnival parish."

Even the Ku Klux Klan could not stop St. Catherine's from holding its lavish and lucrative bingo parties, according to Judge John J. Dunn. Judge Dunn's mother, before her marriage, was John Galen Locke's nurse, and his father happened to be a long time patient of Doctor Locke, the KKK grand dragon. It was Locke who arranged bingo permits for St. Catherine's with Denver's anti-Catholic chief-of-police, William Clandish.

The "carnival parish" was born and raised in the Bungalow Theater, a large home with a basement theater still operating at 4201 Hooker Street. Bishop Matz created St. Catherine of Siena parish in the spring of 1912, in a letter responding to "a petition signed by many Catholics who live in the vicinity of Harkness Heights, North Denver."

Bishop Matz appointed as first pastor William W. Ryan, assistant pastor at Annunciation parish. Father Ryan, a graduate of Denver's Sacred Heart School and St. Thomas Seminary, was a devotee of St. Catherine of Siena. St. Catherine, a fourteenth-century Dominican mystic, did historically memorable work, not only with the poor, but also

St. Catherine of Siena Church in Denver.

helping Pope Gregory XI end the captivity of the papacy at Avignon, and promoting peace between Rome and Florence. In a May 21, 1952, letter in the archdiocesan archives, written a month before his death, Father Ryan says he named the parish "after my mother and (of course) St. Catherine of Siena in the year 1912."

For the first masses, Father Ryan rented the theater on Hooker Street. On Friday and Saturday nights, this space was used for live theater, and during the week it housed the George S. Swartz Shakespearean School of Drama. Beginning on Sunday, May 19, 1912, about fifty families attended the little theater services for which a big wooden packing box was converted to an altar. Some, according to Judge Dunn, worried about falling off gangplanks over the orchestra pit on their way up to the stage to receive communion.

In 1913, St. Catherine's completed its first church, a Romanesque $7,000 brick structure with a large rose window facing Federal Boulevard. Construction had begun on January 5, 1913, and the first mass was said in June, though the interior was not fully completed and not dedicated by Bishop Matz until February 21, 1915.

Poor health forced Father Ryan to retire in 1921, and Bishop Tihen replaced him with John Raymond Mulroy. A year later, Edward John Mannix was appointed pastor, and Father Mulroy stayed on as associate pastor. Father Mulroy persuaded the Sisters of St. Joseph of Carondelet at St. Patrick's to open a school in the fall of 1921 in the basement of the small church. The sisters rode the streetcar each day to school, where each of them taught two grades in the four basement classrooms. When St. Catherine Hall and Gymnasium was completed for $40,000 at the southeast corner of Federal Boulevard and West 43rd Avenue in 1923, cardboard partitions were used to create additional classrooms for the overcrowded school.

Father Mannix launched St. Catherine's famous carnival with a modest August gala in 1921, featuring spaghetti dinners under a big tent on the tennis courts. By 1924, the carnival had become a three-day event on the last weekend in August, and St. Catherine Hall was converted to a banquet hall. Among the numerous attractions were raffles of bicycles, Shetland ponies, automobiles, and even the two lots of land south of the church. Entertainment included the forty-four-piece Denver & Rio Grande Western Railroad band, tightrope walks by Ivy Baldwin, and the Denver Police Department sharpshooters—who blasted cigarettes out of the mouths, ears, and fingers of brave volunteer targets.

The climax came when a specially built tower was set afire. Just in time, according to Father Mannix in his 1933 booklet, "Carnivaling for God," three crack companies of the Denver Fire Department "roared into the Carnival grounds with sirens screaming and red lights gleaming." Chief John F. Healy's smoke eaters would quickly put out the fire and then demonstrate their rope work, pontoon drilling, and net jumping. Such sensational attractions helped lure over 5,000 to the carnivals, which by 1933 had raised $150,000 for St. Catherine's.

The "carnival parish" used its earnings to purchase lots on West 42nd and 43rd avenues in 1926 and build a $12,737 convent and a $39,000 parish school dedicated on May 29, 1929. Now the nuns, freed from daily commuting, could spend more time with the eight grades, which filled rapidly.

Father Mannix was a large man and a fine orator who proved to be as aggressive about building up parish athletics as he was about fund raising. Father Mannix would urge the whole parish to turn out for the Sunday afternoon baseball games in which St. Catherine's often trounced other parishes. Father Mannix also coached the St. Catherine's girls' basketball team, the Red Sox. You could always find Father Mannix, be he visiting the school, promoting the carnival, or coaching basketball in the gym, by the perfume of his perpetual cigar.

Father Mannix remained pastor until his death on December 16, 1934. Delisle A. Lemieux, JCD, the next pastor, launched a building program to replace the overcrowded old church, which was demolished. Architect John K. Monroe designed a Lombardic Italian Renaissance church of blonde brick that matched the school and convent. The basement phase was completed in 1935, but the Great Depression and then World War II helped delay completion of the grand superstructure. Not until November 27, 1952, did Archbishop Vehr dedicate the gorgeous, $390,000 church. A handsome exterior features a massive single square bell tower, and a large rose window faces Federal Boulevard, depicting St. Catherine as the Protectress of Rome. The blind arches or tympanum over the main entrances are done in gold foil. They feature in bas relief the attributes of St. Catherine—the Papal Keys, her writings, and the cross and thorns of her mystical stigmata.

The breathtakingly beautiful interior features stately brick and stone under massive, exposed ceiling beams. Stained glass windows honor several popes and Mother Francis Cabrini, a favorite of the many Italian parishioners. "St. Catherine's had many Italians," recalled former assistant pastor Father John V. Anderson, "and they tried on several occasions to persuade the city to rename Federal Boulevard as Francesca Cabrini Boulevard."

Among the many colorful assistant pastors at St. Catherine's during these years was Bartalo Paolazzi, who directed the choir and favored the parish with his musical abilities. Father Paolazzi was a priest of the Archdiocese of Venice, Italy, and Cardinal Roncalli was his ordinary. When Cardinal Roncalli was elected Pope John XXIII, he had Father Paolazzi come to the Vatican as one of his assistants.

St. Catherine's, with its architecturally harmonious church, school, gym, and convent wrapped around an interior courtyard, now occupies the block across from McDonough Park. Under the pastorate of Monsignor Lemieux, who was known for his excellent administrative ability and foresight, St. Catherine's parish and school flourished and became one of the outstanding parishes of the archdiocese.

Monsignor Lemieux resigned as pastor in 1966 and was followed by Theodore Haas (1966–1974),

Matthias Blenkush (1974–1977), and Raymond N. Jones. During his first decade as pastor of St. Catherine's, Father Jones raised $500,000 to endow parish educational programs, a feat in the best tradition of the "carnival parish."

"We celebrated our seventy-fifth anniversary on April 26, 1987," Father Jones noted,

> with the archbishop and many former parishioners. We are blessed as a parish. We have 1,023 families and a healthy school, K–8, with about 190 students and extended day care from 6 A.M. to 8:20 A.M. and from 3 P.M. to 6 P.M. Thanks to our generous parishioners, we have been able to roll back our tuition, perpetuating the key role our school has played ever since 1921. At St. Catherine's, we have much to be thankful for, and a beautiful, strong parochial plant to preserve.

ST. DOMINIC (1889)
2905 Federal Boulevard

During Denver's bonanza days, the town of Highlands emerged in northwest Denver. Between its creation in 1875 and its annexation to Denver in 1896, Highlands ballyhooed its elevated site and elevated morals. Bounded by Zuni Street on the east, West 38th Avenue on the north, Sheridan Boulevard on the west, and West Colfax Avenue on the south, Highlands flourished, and Catholics in the area proposed a new parish.

This possibility also interested Joseph P. Carrigan, pastor of the overcrowded St. Patrick Church at West 33rd Avenue and Osage Street. When J. T. Murphy, OP (Order of Preachers), a Dominican, came West hoping that the sunshine would restore his health, Father Carrigan housed him at St. Patrick's and proposed splitting his huge parish to create a Dominican parish.

After Bishop Matz approved St. Dominic's formation, Father Murphy said the first mass on October 6, 1889, in the Rocky Mountain Seed Store (now a duplex apartment) at 2749 West 25th Avenue. Dry goods boxes served as both pews and altar in this dusty, makeshift chapel, yet parishioners proliferated, spilling out the front door on Sundays. This overflow inspired St. Dominic's to move services to the old Highlands Town Hall, which stood at the southwest corner of West 26th Avenue and Federal Boulevard.

Edward D. Donnelly, OP, was appointed the first pastor, with Father Murphy assisting. That summer of 1889, St. Dominic's raised $500 to buy three lots at the northwest corner of West 25th Avenue and Grove Street. A two-story brick, Romanesque church–school was dedicated by Bishop Matz in May 1890.

Five Dominican sisters from St. Clara Convent in Sinsinawa, Wisconsin, arrived on August 15, 1890. Sisters Evangelist, Lorenza, Dolora, Aqunin, and Zita converted the first floor of the church–school into four classrooms, where they welcomed young scholars a month later. By the end of the year, a convent was erected next to the school, at 3035 West 25th Avenue. The school overflowed with 180 students by 1898, when a two-story addition was added to the rear of the church with four more classrooms as well as an auditorium.

The vibrancy of the new parish was tested by a fire in February 1891. Undaunted, parishioners reconstructed immediately, using the charred ruins as a foundation. Father Donnelly's successors included several interim pastors and Dominican fathers B. F. Logan (1892–1894), M. P. O'Sullivan (1894–1896), S. R. Brockbank (1898–1902), Francis A. O'Neil (1902–1909), Philip J. Vallely (1909–1914), P. B. Doyle (1914–1918), and Roscoe F. Larpenteur, (1918–1927).

Father Larpenteur oversaw construction of the magnificent church that still graces Federal Boulevard. Father Vallely had acquired the eleven-lot site for $7,621.73 and started a building fund. In 1921, St. Dominic's hired Denver architect Robert Willison, the designer of the Denver Municipal Auditorium. Willison designed an English Gothic church of simple but grand appointments, eighty-five feet wide and 165 feet deep, seating 850. The Caen stone interior rose from the nave, transepts, and aisles in columns and groined arches to a ceiling soaring eighty feet overhead. Traditionally cruciform in floorplan, the church sported three rose windows, a red Spanish tile roof, and understated twin towers. The exterior facing of dark grey, light grey, and buff stone came from quarries in Monte Vista, Colorado, and Boise, Idaho.

St. Dominic's new home included a large basement housing the heating plant, a kitchen, large hall, store rooms, and restrooms. The main floor contained a spacious sanctuary, two sacristies, sexton's rooms, baptistry, and vestibule, with a choir gallery and grand organ loft overhead. After three years of construction, this $270,000 house of God was dedicated by Bishop Tihen on February 14, 1926, a snow-frosted but sunny Sunday. In their own snowy white garb, dozens of Dominican priests, brothers, and sisters gathered to celebrate the consecration of this home base for Rocky Mountain Dominicans.

A new $30,000 rectory, completed in 1923 at 2905 Federal, replaced the old house of Frank Goudy at 2431 Federal, which had been used for early-day services and then as a rectory. The old church was remodeled in 1933 as a little theater, where the Aquinas Players entertained. St. Dominic's also boasted the first parish credit union in the diocese, which opened its doors in 1933 to help parishioners cope with the Great Depression.

Following completion of the lovely new church, Father Larpenteur resigned in 1927 to do missionary work. He was succeeded by Patrick Robert Carroll, OP, who in 1933 was elected prior of St. Dominic's in Washington, D.C. Subsequent Dominican pastors included J. J. Reagan (1933–1939), Leo L. Farrell (1939–1942), Vincent R. Hughes (1943–1948), Peter O'Brien (1949–1951), Joseph G. Forquer (1952–1957), Willard P. Roney (1958–1963), Michael McNicholas (1963–1968), Willard H. Leuer (1968–1970), Robert J. Miller

At Denver's Dominican parish, which still lacks stained glass windows, Emma (Lombard) Donato filled the church with music. (Interior photo by C.W. Brown.)

(1970–1977), Kevin C. Thissen (1977–1984), and Albert G. Judy.

St. Dominic's dedicated a new, twelve-room school south of the church on October 21, 1951. This $350,000 red brick school soon registered as many as 475 students, taught by eleven Dominican sisters. The school closed in 1973 and was sold. The old church likewise was sold, to become remodeled as a one-story apartment house, while the old convent with its rooftop cross is now the AAA Guest Lodge. The new (1940s) convent is now the parish center. Across Federal Boulevard from the new church, the land was cleared in 1984, and landscaped as Viking Park, which provides a magnificent foreground for the grand, Gothic church.

"As in the days of our founder, St. Dominic," Father Judy stated in 1988:

> we Dominicans emphasize teaching and preaching. Our parish community houses a Dominican bishop, five priests, two brothers, and several sisters who work throughout the city in various ministries. For our 1989 centennial, we're tuckpointing and cleaning the stone façade of our church. We are also renewing ourselves spiritually

to continue the work begun in a feed store a century ago.

ST. ELIZABETH (1878)
1060 St. Francis Way (formerly 11th Street)

The lovely stone landmark crowning the Auraria Campus on the west bank of Cherry Creek has a vivid history, including ethnic rivalry, railroad circuit–riding Franciscan friars and Franciscan nuns who panhandled on Larimer Street—as well as a bizarre murder.

Germans—the largest foreign born group in nineteenth-century Colorado—petitioned Bishop Machebeuf for their own priest in the 1870s. Their prayers were answered in 1878, when the bishop established Denver's second parish, St. Elizabeth's. This new parish served Auraria and Southwest Denver, while St. Mary's continued to serve the northeast half of the Mile High City.

"I have a Prussian exile priest to whom I have given the care of the Germans of Denver," Bishop Machebeuf reported in 1879, "and I have applied to the Franciscans for two priests to establish a house of their order and a parish here." John Wagner, the "Prussian exile," raised money among the Germans to buy two lots at the corner of 11th and Curtis streets and began constructing a 30-by-100-foot brick church. Frederick Bender was transferred from Colorado Springs to complete St. Elizabeth Church, where he began saying Sunday masses in September 1879.

In 1887, the Franciscans responded to Bishop Machebeuf's appeals and sent Francis Koch, OFM (Order of Friars Minor), and Venatius Eder, OFM, to found a Franciscan House at St. Elizabeth's. These and subsequent Franciscans came to Denver from the Patterson, New Jersey, Monastery of the Franciscan Fathers of St. Elizabeth of Thuringia. With the Franciscans caring for the German-speaking parishioners, Bishop Machebeuf assigned Father Patrick Carr to establish another parish—St. Leo the Great—for English-speaking Catholics. John Kernan Mullen, a poor Irish immigrant on his way to becoming a millionaire flour miller, helped his fellow Irish at St. Elizabeth's to complete St. Leo the Great Church at 10th Street and West Colfax Avenue in 1889.

Despite the division of the Auraria parish, both churches flourished as Germans, Irish, and other Catholics streamed into the booming Queen City. Father Koch built a $20,000 two-story brick school (1890) and $18,000 rectory (1891). As the German national church for the entire city, St. Elizabeth's became so overcrowded that the old building was torn down to construct a new one in 1898. This $69,000 Romanesque church, designed by Father Adrian, OSF, was built of rusticated rhyolite (lava stone) from Castle Rock quarries. It measured 132 feet by sixty-nine feet with a single spire soaring 162 feet high.

The stately clock and bell tower enhanced Father Koch's reputation as a fund raiser whose exploits became the talk of the diocese. This Franciscan asked Philip Zang—who owned what was then the largest brewery in the Rockies—to help build the new church. Zang, a German Congregationalist, balked until Father Koch promised him that the biggest bell would be named St. Philip for him. Furthermore, the Franciscan promised the beer maker, the bells would advertise Zang's beer and embarrass the nearby Tivoli Brewery: They would be cast not to sound "Clang! Clang!" but "Zang! Zang!"

Father Koch's shabby brown habit embarrassed some parishioners. They showered him with clothing but would next encounter him in his tattered old garments. "I met a poor fellow suffering from the cold," Father Koch would explain. "What else could I do?"

One day this brown-robed Franciscan walked up Arapahoe Street to Denver's finest department store—the old Daniels & Fisher Stores Company—and began begging. After customers, clerks, and management became distressed, Father Koch told them softly, "Just give me $250 and I won't come back." As Father Declan Madden, OFM, wrote in his centennial history of St. Elizabeth's, "They did and he didn't."

The Franciscan sisters who opened St. Elizabeth Grade School in September 1890, and St. Rose Residence for Women next door, also refined their vow of poverty into artful begging. Daily, they patrolled the bakeries, taverns, and shops of Larimer Street, collecting funds and nourishment for themselves and the poor of the city.

Father Madden, who was pastor at St. Elizabeth's until the Franciscans turned the parish over to the Capuchins, continued the tradition. Every day at 11 A.M. he would orchestrate a bologna sandwich breadline behind the church. He also raised money for his "Senior Roadrunners," as he called the elderly he took on bus tours around Colorado.

Thanks to the polished pleas of the Franciscans and the generosity of Colorado's German Catholics, St. Elizabeth's became the first church in the diocese to retire its debt. In keeping with church policy, this enabled St. Elizabeth's to be consecrated on June 8, 1902, with Bishop Matz presiding.

In 1908, Bishop Matz had to reconsecrate the church because its pastor, Leo Heinrichs, OFM, was murdered while saying the 6 A.M. Sunday mass on February 23. Giuseppe Alia, an alleged anarchist, spat out the host at the communion rail and fired a bullet into the priest, who died while trying to return the sacred particles to his ciborium.

Colorado Catholics proposed that the martyred priest, who had been noted for his piety and spiritual leadership, be canonized. The lengthy, complex procedure for canonization was begun but never finished, to the disappointment of many who promoted a widespread devotion to the memory of Father Leo.

At the request of Bishop Matz, the Franciscans at St. Elizabeth's staffed missions in priestless towns of eastern Colorado. Franciscan friars spent one-month stints on the high plains, devoting a day to each small town for mass and the sacraments. The friars bummed rides on the Union Pacific out to its station stops at Watkins, Bennett, Strasburg, Byers, Deer Trail, Agate, River Bend, Limon, Hugo, Boyero, Aroya, Wild Horse, Kit Carson, and Cheyenne Wells. They would hop a ride back to Denver on the Rock Island line with stops at Burlington, Stratton, Flagler, Arriba, and Calhan.

In 1936, May Bonfils Berryman donated $150,000 to St. Elizabeth's to build the elegant monastary designed by Jacques Benedict for the Franciscans, with its fine arcade curving around the courtyard statue of St. Francis of Assisi—San Francisco to many of the Spanish surnamed parishioners moving into the neighborhood. Like the Irish before them, they teased the strict German Franciscans about their "Dutch Cleanser" confessions. Also like the Irish, these Hispanics wanted their own parish. Their prayers were answered in 1926 with the completion of St. Cajetan Church.

Auraria had three Catholic churches within a five-block area—an anomaly due to aspirations of three proud ethnic groups—until St. Leo's was demolished in 1965. Eight years later, Auraria Urban Renewal project proponents began demolishing the neighborhood. Preservationists and lovers of the two surviving Catholic churches struggled to convince the authority to spare these religious and ethnic monuments. Both churches were placed on the National Register of Historic Places. In recognition of their special architectural and historic merits, the Denver Landmark Preservation Commission likewise designated both structures.

Hispanic Catholics constructed a new St. Cajetan Church in 1975, and the old church became an auditorium for the Community College of Denver, Metropolitan State College, and the University of Colorado at Denver, the three schools sharing the 169-acre Auraria Higher Education Center campus.

St. Elizabeth's became the campus chapel. The old school and St. Rose Residence were demolished to build the St. Francis Interfaith Center. After a $250,000 restoration, St. Elizabeth's sparkles as it did in 1898. Once again, it is the only Catholic church in Denver's oldest neighborhood, named Auraria for the gold that first brought fortune seekers to Colorado. Now St. Elizabeth's offers a different reward to over 30,000 students, faculty, and staff on Colorado's largest campus.

ST. FRANCIS DE SALES (1892)
300 South Sherman Street

On Christmas day, 1911, Bishop Matz dedicated the church at South Sherman Street and East Alameda Avenue with its single, soaring spire and vestigial transepts framing large stained glass windows. The window along Alameda Avenue, "In memory of Monsignor John J. Donnelly," honors the fourth pastor, who led this working-class parish for thirty-seven years.

St. Francis was formed during Denver's bonanza days to relieve overcrowded St. Joseph Redemptorist Church and to care for Catholics east of the Platte River and south of First Avenue. James N. Brown, the first pastor, initially held services in the fire station at Center Avenue and Broadway. Before being reassigned to Annunciation parish in Lead-

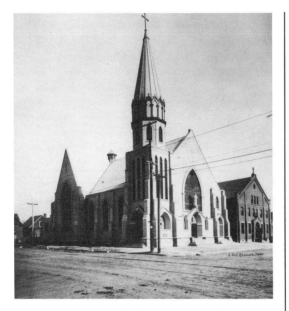

St. Francis de Sales Church in Denver. (Denver Public Library.)

ville, Father Brown acquired a site at East Alameda and South Lincoln for $4,000 and built a small, temporary chapel briefly called St. James.

James J. Gibbons, the celebrated historian priest of the San Juans, replaced Father Brown in 1893, when the silver crash postponed plans for a magnificent, permanent church. Father Gibbons and his flock did build a parish hall next to their chapel before he left in 1898 to succeed Father Brown, who had died in Leadville.

William Morrin, the third pastor, purchased the current site for his 300 parishioners. Like so many early priests, Father Morrin came to Colorado in poor health, hoping the climate would cure him. After rising from his own sick bed to comfort a dying parishioner, Father Morrin contracted a fatal case of pneumonia. Next came John J. Donnelly, an Irish-Canadian priest who took charge at St. Francis in 1903 after serving in Las Animas, Grand Junction, Georgetown, and Cripple Creek.

Under the guidance of Father Donnelly, the parish, in 1906, built an $8,000 grade school staffed by the Sisters of St. Joseph of Carondelet. The upper floor of this two-story building at 320 South Sherman served as the parish church until the current structure was completed. Father Donnelly, who had come to Colorado a sick man, regained his health

and made St. Francis a vigorous parish, rich in congregational activities that included a monthly magazine.

A $39,000 high school was completed in 1924 at 235 South Sherman with a convent at 301 South Grant Street. Father Donnelly, who had been a school teacher in Canada, developed the Donnelly method of teaching arithmetic, which introduced grade schoolers to mathematical feats usually not learned until high school or college. Father Donnelly, who was promoted to monsignor in 1935, grew ill in 1936, retired in 1940, and died four years later. Gregory Smith, who had briefly starred as assistant pastor at St. Francis after his graduation from St. Thomas Seminary in 1922, came back as pastor in 1940.

"When I returned to St. Francis," Monsignor Smith reminisced forty-seven years later, "over 1,000 families belonged to what we thought was one of the best organized parishes. Our high school attracted Catholic students from all over South Denver and pioneered courses such as applied aeronautics."

Monsignor Smith, who served as vicar general of the archdiocese, also taught in his parish high school. A $100,000 addition to the grade school was completed in 1948, and a gym and eight classrooms were added to the high school in 1960. During the 1950s and 1960s, as many as twenty-eight Sisters of St. Joseph taught 650 grade schoolers and 750 high schoolers. Among the high school's dedicated lay teachers was long-time speech coach Lenabell Sloan Martin, who helped St. Francis gain national forensic honors. A large home at 200 South Sherman was bought to house nuns, and the old convent was enlarged. St. Francis, according to Monsignor Smith, prided itself upon being one of the best high schools in the city before 1973, when it was closed and consolidated with Central Catholic High School.

Monsignor Smith retired in 1973, to be followed by Emmanuel Gabel and David P. Croak, VF. "We have a rich heritage of Catholic education at St. Francis de Sales," Father Croak observed in 1988, "which we are trying to continue not only with the grade school and kindergarten but also with after-school care, a book discussion club, and two Bible study programs."

ST. IGNATIUS LOYOLA (1924)
2301 York Street

Denver's first Jesuit parish, Sacred Heart, filled rapidly after its creation in 1879. To relieve crowding, Edward Barry, SJ, the pastor of Sacred Heart and an amateur architect, designed and constructed an $8,000 chapel at 2536 Ogden Street. It opened on Epiphany Sunday, January 6, 1910, as Loyola Chapel.

This little, double-gabled chapel soon overflowed with Sunday worshippers, leading Father Barry to propose building a much larger and grander church. This dream remained a dream until Charles A. McDonnell, SJ, became pastor of Sacred Heart and of Loyola Chapel in 1921. Finding crowds waiting outside to squeeze into the chapel, Father McDonnell plunged into a building campaign. He sold the chapel and purchased a prime block of land on the west side of City Park Golf Course.

The basement chapel of St. Ignatius Loyola Church was completed and opened for masses on October 1, 1923. A year later, on October 12, Bishop Tihen dedicated the church. Denver architects Frederick Mountjoy and Frank Frewen created the 192-foot-long and seventy-five-foot-wide perpendicular Gothic red brick structure with stone trim and red tile roof. Overhead, twin bell towers soared 110 feet skyward. Under the high domed ceiling, St. Ignatius seated 1,200. Carrara marble, exquisite stained glass, onyx and gold furnishings, and a new-fangled Celotex ceiling graced the columnless interior, which excelled accoustically and was bathed in morning and evening sunlight streaming through the immense front and rear windows.

Paying for this expensive church and coping with the Great Depression forced postponment of school building until 1938, when the basement was partitioned into four classrooms. The Sisters of Charity of Cincinnati commuted daily from Sacred Heart parish until 1943, when the Peter M. Peltier house at 2244 Vine Street was purchased and remodeled as a convent.

As the school overflowed with students, both sacristies of the church were converted to classrooms. By 1950, the enrollment had reached 292, and the parish undertook a $270,000 brick school, built in two stages between 1950 and 1954. By

The Gothic façade of St. Ignatius Loyola guards the west side of Denver's City Park. (Denver Public Library.)

1955, the school had 356 pupils taught by eight Sisters of Charity.

As the City Park neighborhood attracted black and Hispanic families, pastor Edward P. Murphy, SJ (1950–1970), welcomed them. During the 1970s and 1980s, Jesuit pastors Thomas J. Kelly, John Waters, James McMullen, and Donald Cunningham, assisted by associates and in-residence Jesuits including John F. Brady, Michael Delaney, Walter Harris, Vince Hovely, Tom Jost, and James C. Sunderland, made Loyola a model integrated parish. Small classes offering individual attention attracted many aspiring minority students who emerged as the majority in Loyola School by the 1970s. Sister Mary Ellen Roach, SC, the principal, and dedicated women such as sisters Sue Verbiscus, Janet Wehmhoff, and Jean Marie Amolsch, who served simultaneously as teacher, secretary, first aid specialist, bookstore manager, milk seller, bellringer, and after-school traffic coordinator, have kept Loyola open while other, better-financed parochial schools closed.

This monumental church built by a largely Irish and Italian flock in then thriving Northeast Denver is now a struggling core city parish. Although it never has found money to complete installation of its beautiful organ and stained glass windows, St. Ignatius has concentrated on a more important priority—providing a school and spiritual guidance in an integrated urban neighborhood.

ST. JAMES (1904)
1314 Newport Street

Every day since 1950, Tillie McBride has walked up Newport Street to the corner of East 13th Avenue to open St. James for mass. And every afternoon at 3 o'clock she goes back to clean the chalices, put out fresh purificators, change the altar cloths and priests' albs, and replace any candle less than an inch long.

"People like Tillie McBride," noted St. James's pastor, Michael W. Gass, "are what make a parish work. Such lay people are the salvation of the church with their commitment to parish life, to the lay ministry, and to the social concerns of the community."

Tillie McBride and the parishioners of St. James's have seen the parish grow with the East Denver neighborhood of Montclair. The Baron Walter B. von Richthofen, a German adventurer, founded Montclair in 1885 and promoted it as the "Beautiful Suburban Town of Denver." In this pioneer suburb four miles east of the city, only a few homes, farms, and ranches, as well as the Baron's Castle at East 12th Avenue and Olive Street, had sprouted on the prairie by 1900.

Nevertheless, Bishop Matz decided to establish a parish there, which would also serve Park Hill to the north, Aurora to the east, and the sparsely developed area around Fairmount Cemetery to the south. Initially, the boundaries were Colorado Boulevard on the west, Cherry Creek on the south, St. Augustine's parish in Brighton to the north, and St. John's in Yuma to the east. The only other congregation east of Colorado Boulevard at that time was the lovely little St. Luke Episcopal Chapel, East 13th Avenue and Poplar Street, which survives today as a designated Denver Landmark.

Bishop Matz sent the chaplain of Mercy Hospital, Hugh L. McMenamin, out to Montclair to organize the parish named for St. James the Lesser. Father McMenamin rounded up thirteen Catholic families

The original St. James was at the northeast corner of Newport Street and East 13th Avenue, now a parking lot for the low-slung new church next door, whose dramatic interior evokes the ancient catacomb churches of Rome.

and said mass for them in the Montclair Town Hall (demolished and replaced in 1936 by Denver Fire Station 14) at 1426 Oneida Street. Father Mac, who would become the best-known priest in the diocese, was transferred from St. James's on the prairie dog–infested eastern fringes of the city to the cathedral downtown. Before leaving, he purchased four lots for $360.

Father James M. Walsh, who succeeded to the pastorate in January 1905, initiated catechism classes taught by the Sisters of Mercy from Mercy Hospital, in the town hall. The sisters continued to offer religion classes there or in private homes in Montclair and Aurora until St. James School was built in 1948.

In 1909, Father Walsh resigned as chaplain of Mercy Hospital and moved in with the family who lived at 1205 Oneida Street. He began devoting his full time to building a modest, one-story stone church, which Bishop Matz dedicated on November 7, 1909. Father Walsh, in 1920, acquired a large frame house at 1284 Newport as a rectory. He also helped build and tend to a mission church established in 1910 in the Southeast Denver suburb of Sable.

Father Walsh stayed with the small parish until his death on March 9, 1937. Growth seemed to bypass Montclair and its little Catholic chapel. Park Hill to the north grew and launched its own parish, Blessed Sacrament, in 1912; Aurora established its own parish, St. Therese's, in 1926. Meanwhile, Montclair remained a sleepy suburb, with its one-priest parish headed by Mark W. Lappen (1937–1938), Charles M. Johnson (1938–1940), and William V. Powers (1940–1969).

Not until Denver's post–World War II boom did Montclair become the suburb that Baron von Richthofen had forseen sixty years earlier. With the help of GI and FHA loans, many families began building new homes. Suddenly, St. James's became one of the fastest growing parishes in the diocese. In the tiny stone church, children at Sunday mass had to sit on the altar steps.

Among the new families moving in were Charles and Matilda McBride. Sargeant McBride, like many of the neighborhood newcomers, had served at Lowry Air Force Base during World War II and had grown to like the quiet East Denver neighborhood with its beautiful parkways—Sixth Avenue, Monaco, Richthofen, and Montview.

"During the 1950s," Tillie McBride recalled in 1985, "large Catholic families lived in the areas around the church. Why, there were thirty-three children in the eight houses across Newport Street from the school."

> We sent all eight of our children to St. James. They learned discipline and got a good education. If kids didn't behave, Father Powers would head to the homes of parishioners, walk right in and ask, "How's everyone behaving today?" He knew most parishioners by name. And he really inspected his altar boys closely. First, he looked down at their feet to be sure their shoes were shined and tied. Hands had to be scrubbed clean, hair trimmed and combed. When my boys came out onto the altar they looked like little angels! If they slouched or mumbled their Latin, Father Powers would stop the mass and correct them: "Kneel up straight! Say that again, slowly!"

Father Powers and Archbishop Vehr asked the Civilian Production Administration, a World War II federal agency controlling building materials, for permission to build a $166,000 church and school. These requests were denied until August 26, 1946. John K. Monroe designed a three-story school building with a garden-level church, which seated 550 (the old church had accommodated only 180).

This school was completed in 1948 when the old house at 1205 Oneida Street, where Father Walsh had first lived, was purchased for $15,000 to serve as a convent for the Sisters of St. Joseph of Carondelet. With the help of a $25,000 remodeling and addition, it became home for as many as thirteen nuns. As the high tide of suburban growth swept through Montclair, the school bulged with over 800 students. There was a nun in practically every classroom, and classes with as many as fifty children. By 1955, the school was so crowded that Father Powers bought the bungalow at 1327 Oneida Street and converted it to additional classrooms.

St. James's bought the block of land between Oneida and Olive streets and East 8th and 9th avenues as a high school site. After its purchase in 1956, the block was converted to an athletic field. In 1958, a new garden-level church was constructed on the north wing of the school and a gymnasium added on top of the church in 1964. Father Powers started bingo in the 1960s, which made as much as $4,000 a night, to help support his parish of over 1,200 families. In recognition of his building efforts, Father Powers was promoted to monsignor before his retirement in 1969.

Father Clement DeWall was named pastor and carried through parish plans for a new church. The pioneer little stone church, which had been renamed Walsh Hall, was demolished in order to build the rectory. Next door, groundbreaking on January 15, 1974, began for a contemporary church. Architect Victor Langhart created a low-ceilinged composition of boxy rooms reminiscent of the catacombs. The new church could cozily seat a small weekday mass or accommodate as many as 600 for larger services. The confessionals accommodated either traditional anonymity or face-to-face reconciliation. Father DeWall, a promoter of Vatican II reforms, shocked some parishioners by introducing altar girls and by working closely with neighboring St. Luke's Episcopal, Montclair Methodist, and Montclair Lutheran churches.

Father DeWall resigned as pastor in 1976 and was replaced by Michael F. Kavanaugh, remembered by Tillie McBride:

Father Kavanaugh was a wonderful pastor. He was an old-fashioned, conservative priest, a pious man, and a real character. When the architect of the new St. James asked Father Kavanaugh how he liked it, Father replied, "Why didn't you build a church instead of a taco house?"

Father Kavanaugh also installed an electronic Angelus, which he played full blast at 6 A.M., noon, and 6 P.M. until a few late-sleeping Protestants raised a ruckus about the dawn call to rise and pray. Father Kavanaugh was followed in 1981 by Robert Harrington, whose untimely death in 1986 grieved the parish. "Father Harrington," recalls Tillie Mc-Bride, "was a people's priest. He would come to mass early to greet people individually and ask how they were. He also completed our wonderful stained glass windows. He was a strong supporter of the school, the twice-a-week bingo games, and he launched our annual fall carnival."

Despite the best efforts of its pastors, St. James experienced a fate common to Denver parishes. Young child-raising couples were increasingly concentrated in the suburban areas; new parishes such as Risen Christ on South Monaco as well as Queen of Peace and St. Pius X in Aurora boomed. Montclair saw its children grow up and move out. The land bought for a high school was sold to the city in 1978 and became Denison Park. After the last nuns left the convent, it was sold for $140,000 in 1975 to the University of Colorado Health Sciences Center, which established there the National Center for the Prevention and Treatment of Child Abuse and Neglect. This center, founded by Denver's famous Dr. Henry Kempe, has subsequently become a national leader in uncovering and treating child abuse.

Only slowly did the older couples die or move out of the neighborhood where they had raised families. As younger couples with children moved in, St. James School continued to attract pupils, retaining a healthy enrollment of 200–300 during the 1970s and 1980s. The parish population stabilized in the 1980s at about 1,000 registered families.

Michael W. Gass, a native of St. Paul, Minnesota, and a 1977 graduate of Denver's St. Thomas Seminary, became the tenth pastor of St. James's in

1987. Father Gass says he is most impressed by how "the parishioners deeply care about one another. Despite the ethnic, economic, and age diversity, the people of St. James make it an exemplary family of faith."

ST. JOSEPH POLISH (1902)
517 East 46th Avenue

St. Joseph Polish is the oldest continuous Polish parish in the Rockies. Always small and struggling, its pride and persistence are reflected in the strength and longevity of its four Polish-American pastors. They and sacrificing parishioners built not only a handsome brick church but a convent and school. They made St. Joseph's the heart and soul of Denver's Polish community, an achievement earning the building a place on the National Register of Historic Places in 1983.

Poles did not come to Denver in significant numbers until the 1880s, when they were recruited to labor in the smelters of Globeville, the working-class town that sprang up around the huge Globe Smelting and Refining Company. Globeville was platted in 1889, incorporated as a town in 1891, and annexed to Denver in 1902. It is bounded by 52nd Avenue on the north, the South Platte River on the east and south, and interstate highway 25 on the west. By 1900, roughly twenty-five Polish families lived in this industrial neighborhood that also attracted Scandinavians, Germans, and Austrians, as well as Slovenians, Croatians, Russians, and other Slavic peoples.

In Globeville's smelters, workers earned $2.50 for a ten-hour day of hot, dangerous, physically demanding labor separating gold, silver, and other valuable metals from Rocky Mountain ores. Families struggled to make ends meet by surrounding their shanties with pig pens, chicken coops, rabbit hutches, and vegetable patches. In spring, summer, and fall, many family members migrated to northeastern Colorado to plant, cultivate, and harvest sugar beets. Daughters worked in the Lindquist Cracker Company at 3520–3530 Walnut Street; sons sought work in the Globe and Grant smelters or at the Denver Union Stockyards across the South Platte River in the Swansea neighborhood.

For houses, many Globevillians bought second-hand lumber or old boxcars from the nearby rail-

yards of the Chicago, Burlington & Quincy and the
Union Pacific. Childhood in Globeville was a
scavenger hunt for survival, according to Frank
Makowski:

> We'd sneak under grain cars at the railyards and
> drill holes in them to fill up burlap bags with wheat.
> And we'd go over to the stockyards because if a
> new calf or lamb or pig was born in transit, the
> guys unloading railroad stock cars would give 'em
> to us. That way we could help our families put a
> meal on the table.

Life was grim, and Polish families in Globeville
longed for the comfort of their own national parish.
A neighborhood church would also save them the
two-mile walk on Sunday to the Annunciation
church. On September 27, Poles held a meeting
organized by St. Martin's Lodge, Group 134 of the
Polish National Lodge, and the St. Joseph's
Society, Group 62 of the Polish Union of North
America. These two pioneer Denver Polish lodges
spearheaded formation that day of the St. Joseph
Polish Roman Catholic Church and School Committee. Bishop Matz responded with a letter
authorizing the Polish community to raise money
for a national parish, an at-large, citywide parish for
all members of the ethnic group. The Germans had
St. Elizabeth's (1878), the Italians had Our Lady of
Mount Carmel (1894), and the Polish wanted St.
Joseph's.

Bishop Matz appointed Theodore Jarzynski, a
Polish born Holy Cross priest trained at Notre

A 1922 funeral at St. Joseph's, which remains a beautifully
maintained monument to Colorado's pioneer Poles. (Interior
photo by Rocky Mountain Photography, Denver Public Library.
Exterior photo by Roger Whitacre.)

Dame, the first pastor on July 14, 1902. James
Tynon, a Denver real estate man, donated four lots,
and Konstanty Klimowski, a teamster in the parish,
cleared the site. Another parishioner, Frank Wargin, had Father Jarzynski live with him and say
daily and Sunday masses at the Wargin home, 4698
Pennsylvania Street. The $2,000 church was con-
structed by the Frank Kirchoff Company of Denver.
This small brick church, thirty-two-by-sixty feet,
was completed in time for Christmas mass, 1902.
The tiny parish of about twenty-five families had
grown to over 100 families by 1920, when Father
Jarzynski persuaded the Colorado & Southern Railway to give him an old frame depot for a Sunday
school and meeting hall. It was dragged to the
northwest corner of East 46th Avenue and Pearl
Street, next to the church and called "the Green
School" because it was painted C&S green. Father
Jarr, as he was called, taught catechism classes,
punishing errant students with long-remembered
pencil raps on the nose.

Father Jarr helped organize the Polish Literary
Club and boasted that "Globeville people are read-

ing more, proportionally, than any other part of Denver and only one-third of this reading is fiction." He also perpetuated old country traditions such as the outdoor processions from the church with the monstrance carried under an embroiderd silk canopy. The paraders, decked out in flowers and their Sunday best, sang Polish songs as they visted the Polish National Alliance Hall on Washington, Globeville's main street, and stopped at the outdoor altars erected at the homes of parishioners.

Father Jarzynski died June 14, 1922, and was replaced by an American-born Polish diocesan priest, John Guzinski. Father Guzinski enlarged the church by knocking out the back wall for a $2,700 addition in 1923. The old Green School was replaced in 1926 by a $21,000 brick school designed by Sidney G. Frazier of Greeley. This two-story structure had four large classrooms on the second floor. The first floor had a 200 seat auditorium and a convent for the five Sisters of St. Joseph, an order of chiefly American-born nuns of Polish descent with a motherhouse in Stevens Point, Wisconsin, who came to the Denver diocese in 1926 to staff St. Joseph School.

The school, which charged no tuition and was open to nonparishioners, was supported by carnivals, such as the lavish mock Polish wedding staged on the parish grounds, August 18–19, 1935. Father Guzinski frowned on all the spoofing and gaiety but welcomed the $2,500 profit. After the parish debt was liquidated in 1959, St. Joseph's raised $56,000 to build a convent, in 1965, for their cherished teaching nuns. Henry Podzinski, a civil engineer and a parishioner, designed the convent at 4626 Pennsylvania Street. When the Sisters of St. Joseph left, the handsome,two-story brick building was converted to St. Joseph's Home, a senior residence, in 1977. The school closed in 1971 and became Ron Lyle's Boxing Gym, an academy of the pugilistic arts. After one of the longest pastorates in archdiocesan history, Father Guzinski died on April 4, 1969. He was replaced by his one-time assistant, Father Edward Fraczkowski, a graduate of St. Thomas Seminary. Father "Fraz," as he was affectionately known, guided the parish through some of its darkest days. Parishioners were displaced and separated from each other and from the church by construction of interstate highways

25 and 70, which intersected in Globeville at the notorious "mousetrap."

"Globeville is Denver's dumping ground," complained one parishioner:

> We get whatever other neighborhoods don't want: smelters; stockyards; public housing; rail yards; the city asphalt plant; the city sewage system; and the freeways. And whenever they excavate for a high-rise downtown, they dump the dirt on us. Huge trucks the size of boxcars are rumbling through here all the time, shaking our houses on the foundation and even moving the statues of the saints on their pedestals at St. Joseph's.

Many Polish parents saw their children prosper and move away from the Slavic neighborhood of tiny but tidy homes clustered around the church. "Our people," Father Fraz noted, "are spread all over town, but they still come back for marriages, baptisms, and funerals . . . to keep the old customs." They came back for Father Fraz's funeral after his death in 1973.

Jan Mucha, the assistant pastor, became the fourth shepherd of St. Joseph's. Born in Nowy Targ, Poland, he first worked as a priest in the Krakow diocese under the cardinal who became Pope John Paul II. Father Mucha had fallen in love with Colorado while vacationing in 1971, and St. Joseph's welcomed this stout, spirited priest, who showed the same drive as his three predecessors. Father Mucha refired Polish pride and the parish role as the center of Polish activities, from Solidarity rallies to neighborhood processions. The church has been restored, and the front entrance proudly bears the church's name in Polish, a striking sight to thousands who pass the church daily on interstate highway 70.

"Since I come here," Father Mucha reported in 1985 in his rich Polish accent, "we bury many of the pioneer parishioners. And we welcome ninety newcomers since martial law [was] declared in Poland in 1981. We have comforted them and they have rejuvenated St. Joseph's."

ST. JOSEPH REDEMPTORIST (1883)
605 West 6th Avenue

In the storefront bakery and home of the Stephen Wirtzes at 717 West 4th Avenue, on November 18,

1883, Percy A. Phillips, the chancellor of the diocese, gathered about twenty-five families to celebrate St. Joseph's first mass.

Bishop Machebeuf blessed the new parish in a predominantly working-class neighborhood. St. Joseph's, an offshoot of St. Elizabeth's to the north, would later be subdivided into St. Francis de Sales to the south and Presentation to the west. But in 1883, St. Joseph parish embraced all of Denver southwest of Cherry Creek and south of West Colfax Avenue.

St. Joseph Redemptorist Church in Denver. (Photo by James Baca.)

Father Percy, a Canadian who came to Denver in delicate health, turned over the arduous work of parish building in 1886 to Thomas H. Malone. Father Malone, an intellectual New Yorker come West as a health seeker, soon graduated from the small frame church Father Percy and his parishioners built on West 4th Avenue near Gallapago Street in 1884. Booming growth in the neighborhood and the church inspired Father Malone and his parishioners to undertake a grander church in 1886, at 600 Galapago Street. That Christmas they celebrated the first mass in a wooden structure that evolved, over the next three years, into a grand brick edifice, fifty-by-120 feet, containing a basement school with a large church upstairs.

After the dedication ceremony on November 10, 1889, the Sisters of Mercy moved their school from the old frame structure, where they had begun teaching that spring, into the basement. Partitions separated the subterranean school into four rooms where two nuns tackled classes of as many as ninety pupils. As in other schools of the "Mercies," Sister Mary Evangelist (who would later become the order's Colorado superior) used Reed's speller, David & Peck's arithmetic, Barnes' geography, Sadlier's history, Harvey's grammar, Ray's mental arithmetic, and Hutchinson's physiology.

Flush times for St. Joseph's—and for the city of Denver—ended abruptly with the crash of 1893. Parishioners, many of whom were thrown out of work, were hard put to finish paying for their $50,000 church–school. To make matters worse, Bishop Matz charged that Father Malone had sunk parish funds into his newspaper, *The Colorado Catholic*, an ancestor of the *Denver Catholic Register*.

Malone counter-attacked Bishop Matz, using his newspaper to publicize this embarrassing ecclesiastical squabble. According to the 1988 parish history by assistant pastor Stephen Rehrauer, CSsR, over 100 parishioners sued Father Malone for $12,000 missing from the building fund. Bishop Matz had asked them not to sue and became furious when they proceeded. On May 5, 1894, he angrily excommunicated both Father Malone and the parishioners who were suing him. The bishop then convoked the third synod of the Denver diocese and ousted Malone as pastor of St. Joseph's.

To the rescue came the Redemptorists, a European order that began missionary work in the United States in 1832. The Redemptorists assumed all parish debts and sent fathers Daniel Mullane and John McGough, CSsR (*Congregatio Sanctissimi Redemptoris*), out from St. Louis to take charge of St. Joseph's on November 19, 1894. At that time, it was legally renamed St. Joseph Redemptorist parish. Much to the relief of the bishop of Denver and the parishioners, the Redemptorists have operated the parish to this day. The order also began working as chaplains at nearby Denver General Hospital and making sick calls throughout the city.

Under a number of different Redemptorist pastors, St. Joseph's evolved into one of the largest parishes. A rectory (1895), a pipe organ (1902) for the choir loft, and two side altars (1906) beside the Gothic high altar indicated that this parish, born in a bakery and beset by poverty, chaos, and scandal, had finally found stability. In 1914, St. Joseph's completed the long-postponed steeple and bell tower at Sixth and Galapago, with a shorter north steeple. Three years later, the parish bought the Mormon mission across 6th Avenue for $6,200 and remodeled it as a convent for the Sisters of Mercy.

St. Joseph School, which had been squeezing kindergarten through ninth-grade pupils into the church basement, built a $29,000, brick, three-story facility at 601 Fox Street in 1908. A high school program initiated that fall featured a practical business curriculum designed to make its graduates employable. Students' morals and behavior were not overlooked: the parish *Annual* cautioned them that a "Saturday night dance is a pitiful preparation for the Lord's Day."

Many parishioners worked at the nearby railyards, particularly at the Burnham Shops of the Denver & Rio Grande. Fluctuating fortunes of the railroads and its workers led St. Joseph's, in 1918, to abolish pew rent. Better times in the 1920s enabled the parishioners to collaborate with the Redemptorist fathers in building a beautiful new rectory on the east side of the church. Jacques Benedict designed this exquisite medieval-style monastery with the elegant arcade along 6th Avenue.

The school overflowed in the 1920s when partitioned classrooms were reinstalled in the church basement. The parish also bought three cottages on 6th Avenue and converted them to classrooms. Despite the economic hardships of the Great Depression that began in 1929, parishioners continued to raise money for a new school at 6th and Fox—a $38,000, two-story pink brick structure, designed by John K. Monroe and dedicated by Bishop Vehr on March 21, 1937.

During World War II, St. Joseph parish more than proved its patriotism. The church made itself a center for USO activities to comfort and entertain the military. Nuns and parish women taught school children to knit, quilt, and make scrap books that were sent to fighting men overseas. The school's Genes Club, made up of future secretaries and stenographers, sent letters of encouragement to the many men of St. Joseph's at the front. Students also worked on scrap metal and war material drives as well as war bond sales.

Parishioners donated much of the labor and materials for the new gym completed in 1950, and the basketball team became the pride of the parish and the fear of the city. Three houses on the corners of 6th Avenue and Fox Street were purchased in a $20,000, 1957 expansion project; two were converted to additional convent space and the third into

a kitchen and cafeteria for the grade and high schools.

Spanish-surnamed families emerged as a parish majority during the 1950s. The Redemptorists responded with a Sunday mass and Bible lessons in Spanish and free English-language instruction. In 1957, Joseph Meunier, CSsR, launched a sign language mass that made St. Joseph's a center for the deaf and hard of hearing.

The parish fought archdiocesan plans to close its high school but surrendered in 1973. Afterwards, the basement of the school was remodeled as a practice area for St. Joseph's Boxing Club. The old Mormon mission, which had been converted to a convent, was recycled again in 1983, becoming an emergency shelter for the homeless operated by the St. Vincent de Paul Society. Declining elementary school enrollment led the parish to sell the grade school building and move classes into the remodeled former high school. In front of the handsomely rehabilitated school at 623 Fox Street, a 1987 sign read: "New St. Joseph's School now accepting students kindergarten to 8th grade. Negotiated Tuition. Christian values."

In 1982, on the eve of the church's centennial, its long and colorful history and architectural significance as a jewel of the historic Auraria and Baker neighborhoods were given national recognition, and it was placed on the National Register of Historic Places. For much of its life, St. Joseph's has been a poor, struggling urban parish. Brightly handpainted wooden flowers adorn the hardwood bannister of the creaky stairs leading into the antique church with its glorious stained glass Gothic windows shedding colored light on wooden altars painted to resemble marble.

LeRoy Burke, CSsR, an associate pastor, emceed St. Joseph's "grocery bingo" Friday afternoons after the free lunch provided daily by St. Joseph's and the Senior Citizens Nutrition Program. Besides feeding people, Father Burke used bingo as a way to "get folks out of their homes and apartments to meet people."

"In material terms, we have always been a poor parish," mused Robert Halter, CSsR, the pastor at St. Joseph's since 1981, adding:

> Our richness lies in a long history of serving the community, and in the courageous and generous

spirit of our congregation. They enable us to begin our second century with that same Christian hope that led to the formation of the parish long ago in a humble neighborhood bakery.

ST. MARY MAGDALENE (1907)
2817 Zenobia Street

Father Joseph M. Desaulniers, the French Canadian chaplain at St. Anthony Hospital, was asked by Bishop Matz to start a parish in Edgewater. This Jefferson County town on the west edge of Sloan's Lake had incorporated in 1901 and, according to the *Denver Catholic Register* of June 7, 1907, had 128 Catholic families plus the patients of six nearby sanitariums.

Lots north of West 26th Avenue on Depew Street were acquired, as well as large donations for the building fund. While awaiting construction of a church, Father Desaulniers said the first mass for fifty parishioners on June 2, 1907, at Sarah Berran's Edgewater home at 2537 Ames Street.

Frank Osborne, a carpenter–contractor in the parish, built and probably designed the brick church with its concrete foundation. Even before 900 people celebrated the laying of the cornerstone on June 30, 1907, the parish had celebrated its first wedding on June 24, 1907, for Frank Cody and Emily Negri.

The parish was formally organized July 9, 1907, and its modest church with a single alcove altar was finished on July 28, 1907. Father Desaulniers decorated the church with leaded and stained glass windows, an oak altar rail, and eight lightning rods. "Father D was terribly afraid of thunder and lightning," recalled long-time parishioner Albert G. Mariacher, but "he loved his snuff and always had his snuff box on the altar so he could have his sniff of snuff before the sermon. I served as an altar boy for Father D and he always reminded us to have his snuff box and a black handkerchief handy."

In 1918, Father Mark W. Lappen replaced Father Desaulniers and paid the parish debt with the help of fairs, festivals, and dances. Then he bought the old Methodist Episcopal church across the street and converted it into a hall for meetings and social gatherings, including popular performances of the parish's Dramatic Club.

St. Mary Magdalene's next sky pilot, following Father Lappen's assignment to Holy Family parish

in 1923, was Father William J. O'Malley, who had been the pastor of Annunciation Church in Leadville until the altitude threatened his frail health. KKK cross burnings in front of the rectory, parishioners said, aggravated his condition, contributing to his fatal heart attack on September 9, 1926. Father O'Malley also had served as director of Mt. Olivet Cemetery, where he was buried after being memorialized for his work with the poor, sick, and elderly.

James P. Flanagan assumed a forty-three-year pastorate in 1926, during which he enlarged the church with a new sanctuary and sacristies before stuccoing the exterior for a rededication by Bishop Vehr on October 15, 1933. In 1941, a third mass was added to the Sunday schedule with the help of the Jesuit fathers from Regis College, and in the next eight years a fourth and fifth mass were needed. Membership jumped from 400 families in 1938 to 1,400 in the 1950s, despite the creation of St. Bernadette's (1947) and Sts. Peter and Paul (1949). The baby boom in the parish led Father Flanagan and his parishioners to open a school savings fund.

Back in 1927, the parish had purchased property in the 2800 block of Sheridan Boulevard where, after more lots were bought in 1947–1948, a single story, four-classroom school became a reality in September 1950. Instead of the Sunday school that the Sisters of St. Joseph of Carondelet from St. Patrick parish had conducted since 1922, St. Mary Magdalene's finally had its own school, where two Franciscan nuns taught sixty-five students.

During the 1950s, more classrooms and a $165,000 auditorium were added to what soon became a school of eight grades. As the parish was outgrowing the old church, Sunday masses were moved to the new auditorium, which seated 400. The old church at 2601 Depew was used as a parish hall until it was sold to be recycled as the Templo Evangélico Bautista. Throughout the 1950s and early 1960s, there was continued growth in the parish school, with enrollment exceeding 500 students in 1961. Not until 1964, when Our Lady of Fatima opened its own school, did St. Mary Magdalene School drop in enrollment.

Although the school closed in 1979, the parish continued to stress education, providing an adult tutorial group to help refugees from Southeast Asia learn English. In 1979, Archbishop Casey officially designated St. Mary Magdalene's as the parish for ministry to the deaf community. St. Mary's also opened, thanks to generous support of the Knights of Columbus, a coffee house for developmentally disabled adults. In 1982, the parish worked with St. Anthony Hospital to open a child development center in the old school building and a playground north of the church at West 29th Avenue and Zenobia. For years, the Rustic Tavern next door had tried to rent the property to extend their building and open a nightclub. Father Flanagan, who consistently had fought this idea, felt it far better to use the site for a children's playground than for adult playboys and playgirls.

Father Flanagan, after forty-three years as pastor of St. Mary Magdalene parish and director of Mt. Olivet Cemetery, retired with the title of monsignor in 1969. He died December 21, 1980. Roy Figlino, VF, who was appointed pastor by Archbishop Casey, converted the spacious rectory to the Villa Madeleine, a home for retired priests. There, Father Figlino himself retired in 1986 when a layman, Gene Murray, was appointed administrator for St. Mary's. By this innovative arrangement, Father Roy tends to the spiritual needs of the parish while Gene Murray handles the day-to-day operations.

In guiding the parish through its seventy-fifth anniversary, Father Figlino noted in the 1982 jubilee booklet that St. Mary's had lost its school and many parishioners when three new parishes had been carved out of it. Despite these losses, he observed:

> Prophets of doom during the past 75 years have foretold a short history for our parish.... But like a Phoenix a new spirit was born more vibrant and beautiful, rising on the spirit of Community started by our forefathers at Saint Mary Magdalene. And today the spirit of loyalty and togetherness cannot be equaled anywhere.

ST. PATRICK (1881)
3325 Pecos Street

As North Denver's pioneer parish, St. Patrick's has an exotic history involving a bitter struggle between Bishop Matz and a pastor powerful enough to twist the 20th Street Viaduct—Joseph P. Carrigan, who also inaugurated festivities that have

Resembling an old Spanish mission, St. Patrick's in North Denver features an arcade, curvilinear parapets, and square towers. (Photo by Glenn Cuerden.)

evolved into Denver's popular St. Patrick's Day parade.

Bishop Machebeuf created St. Patrick parish in 1881. Michael J. Carmody, the first pastor, initially said mass in the fire station at 15th and Boulder streets while awaiting completion of a small brick church at 3233 Osage Street, in 1883. In 1884, the Sisters of Saint Joseph of Carondelet opened a parish school, living in the basement while using the first floor as a school and the second floor as a church.

St. Patrick's finally received a steady pastor with the 1885 appointment of Father Carrigan by Bishop Machebeuf. Carrigan, an Irishman born and trained in New York, had come to Colorado after his ordination. A capable and outspoken priest, he had served at St. Mary's in Breckenridge, St. Mary's in Denver, and as pastor of St. Ann (Annunciation) parish before coming to St. Patrick's.

This young priest proved to be an able and popular pastor. He paid off the parish debt and, in 1889, enlarged the church and school. Father Carrigan aggressively boosted church attendance by urging his flock to bring non-Catholic friends to mass each Sunday. Non-Catholics were also welcome in the church's public reading room.

North Denverites in those days were separated from the city by the South Platte River and a maze of railroad tracks, where trains killed and maimed people every year. Furthermore, the 15th Street bridge over the Platte was so rickety that the city posted a notice at either end: "No vehicles drawn by more than one horse are allowed to cross the bridge in opposite directions at the same time."

Father Carrigan and his parishioners joined the crusade to build a viaduct from downtown to North Denver as a safe crossing over the river and rail lines. Mayor Robert W. Speer cleverly persuaded the railroads to put up most of the cost of the viaduct. Completed in 1911 for $500,000, this three-quarter–mile-long trussed viaduct left Denver at 20th Street but landed in North Denver at 33rd Avenue—at the front door of St. Patrick's. Parishioners praised God for what is now the oldest and largest trussed viaduct in Colorado, and North Denverites still call its bend "Carrigan's Curve."

Father Carrigan could certainly bend the ears of City Hall. This powerful priest also took on Bishop Matz, criticizing his administration of the diocese publicly and repeatedly from the moment Bishop Matz succeeded Bishop Machebeuf in 1889. Carrigan had hoped for an Irish bishop, not another Frenchman.

In defiance of his bishop, Father Carrigan, in 1907, undertook the erection of a new church. After touring the Spanish missions of California founded by the Franscican friar, Junipero Serra, Father Carrigan became enamored with the mission revival style. With architects Harry James Manning and F. C. Wagner, he designed a beautiful stone church with asymmetrical front bell towers connected by a curvilinear parapet. An arcaded cloister along Pecos Street connected the church with a large courtyard and a rectory. Fund-raising difficulties and Father Carrigan's ongoing feud with the bishop prolonged construction for three years. Priest and parishioners finally celebrated completion of the new St. Patrick's, a block northwest of the old church, in May 1909. A year later, Bishop Matz reassigned Father Carrigan to St. Stephen parish in Glenwood Springs. This solution followed a rather uncivil civil court case, numerous appeals to Rome, and a scandalous public fight from the pulpits.

In 1911, David T. O'Dwyer assumed the pastorate at St. Patrick's and restored it to the good graces of the bishop. During Father O'Dwyer's long pastorate (1911–1928), the parish thrived, reaching a population of 775 families in 1917, when it was the third largest in Denver.

Father O'Dwyer, a native of County Cork ordained in Dublin, was noted for his calm judgment and quiet, scholarly temperament. "The gentleman priest," as he was called, restored serenity to a troubled parish. He was later appointed assistant chancellor of the Catholic University of America in Washington, D.C., where he became director of the National Shrine of the Immaculate Conception.

Father O'Dwyer was succeeded by his assistant, Italian-born Achille Sommaruga. "Father Sam" built a new $53,000 parish school, a one-story brick edifice, at 34th and Pecos. After years of crowded classes on the first floor of the old 1880s church, the Sisters of St. Joseph and their pupils moved into the new school in the fall of 1941. In 1949, a second story was added, and the curriculum was expanded to eight grades. Father Sam, who had paid for the new school by organizing students to collect "ten cents a brick," was awarded the rank of monsignor in 1949. To supplement all the dimes given for the school, Monsignor Sommaruga sold the old rectory, which became Mancinelli's Meat Market, and the old church–school, which became the Original Mexican Cafe, one of Denver's first Mexican restaurants. The cafe converted the upper-floor church to a dance hall, while the first-floor classrooms became dining rooms.

St. Patrick parish and its heavily Irish congregation helped launch Denver's St. Patrick's Day festivities. In 1885, Father Carrigan had initiated St. Pat's Day fund raising galas at the old Broadway Theater downtown. These festivals, complete with costumes, musical entertainments, and bagpipers, attracted celebrants from throughout the city. In collaboration with the Daughters of Erin and the Ancient Order of Hibernians, St. Patrick parish spearheaded festivities that celebrated the rich cultural and religious traditions of the Emerald Isle. A more militant approach was taken on March 17, 1902, according to the *Denver Times*, by Captain Stephen J. Donleavey, secretary of the Denver Fire and Police Board: He announced plans to recruit a volunteer army in Colorado in order to invade England and free Ireland.

In 1906, the Ancient Order of Hibernians organized what may have been Denver's first official

St. Patrick's Day parade. The parade was followed by high mass with Father William O'Ryan's sermon on "Ireland's Loyalty to Patrick's Faith," a grand reception, and an evening ball. St. Patrick's Day parades went out of style during the 1920s when anti-Catholic, anti-immigrant organizations such as the Ku Klux Klan frowned on any such displays of "un-American" ethnic groups.

Not until March 17, 1962 was Denver's parade revived when Red Fenwick, cowboy columist for The Denver Post, and some of his "Evil Companions Club" staged a mini-march. "Witnesses," reported The Denver Post, "claim it was a short march: the paraders walked out of Duffy's Shamrock Restaurant, went around the block, and back to the bar." Others claim that the inaugural modern St. Patrick's Day parade came a month later, April 17, 1962, when Lord Mayor Robert Briscoe of Dublin was visiting Denver. His Irish-American hosts took him to lunch at Duffy's; after a few hours of refreshments and lamentations about the parade deceased since World War I, these worthies took action. They proceeded to march around the block, proclaiming their procession a reinauguration of Denver's St. Patrick's Day parade. Furthermore, they established an official parade committee for 1963.

The 1963 St. Patrick's Day parade was a hit with thousands of marchers and spectators. By 1974, crowed the Denver Catholic Register, Denver's parade "drew a crowd estimated at over 120,000 people, making it the second largest parade in the U.S." Although this claim is contested by Boston, Chicago, Detroit, St. Paul, and other cities, Denver marchers continue to insist they are number two, if not number one.

While the parade was growing, St. Patrick's congregation was shrinking. The once overflowing parish had given birth to two others within six blocks—Our Lady of Mount Carmel (1894) and Our Lady of Guadalupe (1936). By the 1970s, six other North Denver parishes and a dozen suburban parishes in the northwest metro area competed with the struggling core parish. In May 1969, the Sisters of St. Joseph of Carondelet closed St. Patrick School and Convent, which they had operated since September 29, 1883. By 1980, St. Patrick's had dwindled to about 200 families.

Father Thomas M. Dowd, a Nebraskan trained at Denver's St. Thomas Seminary, became the seventeenth pastor in 1973. Father Tom, a personable Irishman, began restoring the church as well as its dwindling congregation. He oversaw restoration of the church, stripping off stucco and white paint to resurrect the original sandstone skin of Father Carrigan's day. The interior, with its heavy wooden ceiling beams, picturesque stained glass windows, and hand-carved Italian marble stations of the cross was spruced up to shine again as one of Denver's first and finest examples of mission revival architecture. In 1977, St. Patrick's was designated a Denver Landmark by the City Council. In 1979, the parish plant was put on the National Register of Historic Places.

Despite the honors, the congregation continued to dwindle. Father Dowd strove to enhance the parish by opening the first pastoral counseling center in the archdiocese with the help of Louis Barbato, a prominent psychiatrist. When Father Dowd left in 1983, Doctor Barbato and then Thomas Landgraff, OSFS, administered the parish.

On September 6, 1988, Archbishop Stafford reorganized St. Patrick's as a mission of St. Elizabeth parish, to be staffed by the Capuchins of the Mid-American Province. The spacious and elegant parish plant was given a $250,000 remodeling to become a cloister for ten Capuchin Poor Clare nuns from Mexico. These nuns, ranging in age from twenty-one to seventy, arrived wearing brown habits, rope belts, and sandals. Six hours of every day they spend in prayer. Other time they spend making sugar cookies for sale and vestments for the Capuchin friars.

In 1989, the Very Reverend Lorenzo Ruiz, OFM, episcopal vicar and secretary for Hispanic affairs, moved the Hispanic vicariate into the old St. Patrick School. Thus, what had been a center for Irish immigrants became a hub for the Hispanics who were becoming the dominant ethnic group in North Denver. In honor of the Mexican nuns who now live there, part of St. Patrick's was rechristened Our Lady of Light Monastery. The church and pastoral counseling center, renamed Old St. Patrick's mission, continue to reach out to the diverse economic and ethnic groups of North Denver.

ST. ROSE OF LIMA (1924)
1320 West Nevada Place

In 1923, the old Valverde Presbyterian Church became Denver's newest Catholic church. J.J. Gibbons, pastor of nearby Presentation Church, worked with fifteen families to launch the new parish in the secondhand church at 1310 West Nevada Place.

Bishop Tihen dedicated the little frame building to St. Rose of Lima on October 15, 1924. The first pastor was a young priest who also edited the *Denver Catholic Register*, Matthew J. Smith. A month later, Father Smith left the parish to devote full time to the *Register*, which he transformed into a prominent national newspaper.

Denver Mayor Federico Peña, the city's first Hispanic mayor, visited St. Rose of Lima School shortly after his 1982 election for a "can-do" pep talk. (Photo by James Kavet.)

John R. Mulroy, the next priest, moved into a rectory built for him and his mother, who kept house. Father Mulroy, who later became Monsignor Mulroy, was the founding director of Catholic Charities, which he developed into one of the major enterprises of the Church in Colorado.

Louis J. Grohman became the third pastor in 1930 and worked with volunteers to add a hall that doubled the size of the church. Three years later, the growing parish further remodeled and enlarged its home. To service the debt, St. Rose's staged bazaars with exotic themes, such as "A Night in Paris" and "A Night in Shanghai."

Following Father Grohman's resignation in 1949, Barry J. Wogan began a pastorate that lasted until his 1976 retirement. All the former pastors and Archbishop Vehr gathered on April 4, 1952, to dedicate a new basement church on West Dakota Avenue between Navajo and Pecos streets. Father Grohman delighted parishioners with his poem written for "the Rosebud fair that gave our Church its name."

Father Wogan oversaw the 1955 construction of a four-classroom school; the second floor of the structure was used as a church. This $172,000 project included a ten-bedroom convent at 375 South Navajo Street for the Sisters of Charity of Cincinnati. The original church was made into a parish hall.

By 1963, the parish had grown to about 900 families (over 3,500 persons), and Archbishop Vehr approved plans for a new 600-seat church on West Nevada Place. This $196,000 structure featured brick walls, exterior and interior, with the interior enhanced by laminated wood arches and a free standing altar canopy decorated with a white enameled dove.

"Flood Turns New Church Into Rubble," ran the headline in *The Denver Post* of June 20, 1965. After the June 16 flood caused $150,000 damage to St. Rose's parish plant, 150 parishioners spent the next Sunday cleaning out the water, mud, and debris to salvage what was left of the church, school, convent, and rectory, still under construction. With the help of $55,000 from the Archdiocesan Development Program, the parish rebuilt.

Upon Father Wogan's retirement in 1976, Bishop George R. Evans became pastor, reinstating the parish bazaar and helping develop a new sense of social activism. Bishop Evans remained in residence at St. Rose of Lima until the end of his life. He was followed as pastor by John F. Dold (1979–1983), John J. Loughran (1983–1988), and the current pastor, Lawrence B. Kaiser, a Denver native trained at St. Thomas Seminary.

ST. VINCENT DE PAUL (1926)
2375 East Arizona Avenue at South University Boulevard

During the 1920s, James J. Donnelly took a census of his South Denver parish, St. Francis de Sales. He found quite a few Catholics living east of Downing Street and south of Virgina Avenue were fulfilling their Sunday obligation at the chapel of St. Thomas Seminary.

Furthermore, Aksel Nielsen, George Olinger, Lawrence Phipps, and other wealthy developers

St. Vincent de Paul Church in Denver.

were eyeing the area for extensive, expensive new residential developments around Senator Phipps' country home, Belcaro. Bishop Tihen concurred with Father Donnelly that the area was ripe for a new parish but added the clarification that its purpose was "not to improve real estate, or to develop a certain section of the city, but to preach the gospel to every creature."

In honor of the Vincentian fathers who had accommodated area residents in their chapel at St. Thomas Seminary, the new parish was formed in March 1926 as St. Vincent de Paul. Bishop Tihen named Francis W. Walsh the first pastor. Father Walsh, a New Yorker come West for reasons of health, taught political science at Loretto Heights College. Working with a list of 175 potential parishioners, he raised money to purchase a sixteen-lot site at the northeast corner of East Arizona Avenue and South Josephine Street. This was in the Electric Heights subdivision, one of the first to be developed in the Belcaro area.

Ground was broken in May 1926 for a $50,000 church–hall–school building, designed in the collegiate Gothic style by Thomas MacLaran, a prominent Colorado Springs architect. Bishop Tihen officially dedicated the pressed blond brick edifice on November 14, 1926. The following autumn, the Sisters of Loretto from St. Mary's Academy opened St. Vincent's grade school on the second floor. The first floor was partitioned to provide a church and living quarters for the pastor, while the basement served as a school auditorium and parish hall. The

burgeoning parish population led to the conversion of the entire basement to a larger church.

St. Vincent's, according to the *Denver Catholic Register*, was known as "the radio church" after masses of the erudite, mellifluous Father Walsh were selected for transmission on radio station KFEL. By 1932, when Father Walsh returned to his native New York City and was replaced by Manus Boyle, the basement church was jammed at Sunday masses. Father Boyle, a jolly native of County Donegal, Ireland, soon became a regular of the parish Pinochle Club. These Wednesday night pinochle players also served as the parish development committee and put part of their pinochle pot into building a $16,500 rectory for Father Boyle in 1940.

Parish pinochle players purchased nineteen additional lots on the north side of Arizona Avenue between Josephine Street and University Boulevard for a new church. They also bought ten acres of land between Colorado Boulevard and Birch Street along Arizona Avenue. "The land had originally been intended as the site for a hospital to build up old bodies," as Father Boyle put it in 1947 when athletic fields were installed there, "but will now be used to build up young bodies." This $11,000 investment proved to be a real estate gold mine. When Southeast Denver began to boom after World War II, it was sold to launch a $650,000 building campaign.

Work began on the new church in 1951. Architect John K. Monroe designed the buff brick structure in the Norman Gottswald style, with a slender spire. Archbishop Vehr dedicated the 725-seat house of God on February 5, 1953. The elegantly understated neo-Gothic exterior sheltered an interior rich in dark wood and travertine marble, reminiscent of both the Californian mission and English Gothic styles. The Santa Fe Studios of Church Art created the stained glass windows, stations of the cross, and other furnishings.

Over the main entrance, a large statue of St. Vincent de Paul was donated by long-time parishioner Carl Dire. Dire, who opened the nearby Bonnie Brae Tavern in 1934, gave the statue after his sons returned safely from Marine Corps action in Korea. The sons now operate the tavern, a pizza lover's heaven and favorite place to go after bingo or to celebrate baptisms and weddings.

A new rectory was also built, allowing the old building to be converted, in 1951, to a convent for the Sisters of Loretto, whom the pastor had been daily chauffeuring from St. Mary's Academy. Upon Father Boyle's death in 1951, Eugene A. O'Sullivan became the third pastor of St. Vincent's.

Father O'Sullivan took a special interest in the school, whose eight grades hummed with as many as 700 pupils during the 1960s. Parishioner Betsy (Buchanan) Stapp, one of those students, recalled later that "at that time fashion dictated the wearing of so many petticoats that all the girls had difficulty fitting into a classroom at one time." To solve this problem, Father O'Sullivan started use of school uniforms and also did away with the minimum tuition requirement, two measures that made it easier for poorer children to attend one of the best parochial schools in the archdiocese.

Father O'Sullivan retired as a monsignor in 1969, to be followed as pastor by Francis J. Syrianey (1969–1979) and the current pastor, Melvin F. Thompson. Father Thompson presided over the remodeling of the church basement in 1984, when the new parish hall was renamed The Bishop George R. Evans Center, after a most illustrious St. Vincent's graduate.

With 845 parish families and over 400 students, St. Vincent's church and school are alive and well, Father Thompson reported in 1988. "It is our hope the parish family will continue to grow in love of God and neighbor in the future, always remembering its precious heritage."

Dillon

OUR LADY OF PEACE (1975)

Dillon, an 1880s mining town served by both the Denver, South Park & Pacific and the Denver & Rio Grande railroads, came back to life during the 1970s with construction of Lake Dillon, the Eisenhower Tunnel, and the Keystone ski and summer resort. Although the old town of Dillon lies under the lake, New Dillon town is thriving.

Our Lady of Peace opened on December 18, 1975, and a rectory was built across Lake Dillon in Frisco at 2 West Miners Creek Road. This humble church, made of plywood and cedar panels on a poured cement foundation, offers a Saturday evening and a Sunday morning mass. Thomas Mosher, Dillon's pastor since 1988, reports that:

> Because of the changing demographics in northern Summit County towns of Dillon, Frisco, Silverthorne, and Keystone, the number of parishioners in this "mission" has almost doubled in the period of one decade. We are looking into the possiblity of expanding or even replacing this humble church to meet the needs of a growing community.

Eagle

ST. MARY (1985)

Eagle's few, scattered Catholic clans have hung on to their often priestless parish ever since 1911, according to parish historian Eileen Randall. In 1911, Mrs. E. E. Glenn organized about twenty-two Catholic families under the guidance of Joseph P. Carrigan, pastor of St. Stephen's in Glenwood Springs.

Masses were said in the Glenn home until the old Eagle schoolhouse and lots were purchased in 1916 for $1,100. A donation from Denver and Colorado Springs mining man Verner Z. Reed helped the parish to pay for these transactions and fix up the old school with ten pews. The Catholic Church Extension Society of Chicago donated an altar and a tabernacle.

Father Carrigan offered the first mass in the present church in 1917. The tiny mission donated the rear of its building, in 1945, as a home for the Eagle Public Library. Having these books nearby was helpful to the Benedictine sisters from Canon City who came up in the summers to teach CCD classes.

Joseph J. Leberer became Eagle County's first resident pastor, based at Minturn but began offering regular Sunday masses at St. Mary's. As summer tourists squeezed into the little mission, Father Leberer expanded the church by moving the altar back into an adjacent room in 1953. The old homemade pews were replaced with elaborately carved oak pews from the old St. John Church at East 5th Avenue and Josephine Street in Denver.

Parishioners donated lumber and labor to remodel St. Mary's and painted the outside a soft desert rose. In 1985, the 185 members of St. Mary's became a full-fledged parish, with their own resident pastor for their historic church.

John E. Dold, the first resident pastor, worked with parishioners in 1986 to add a new nave and remodel the old building. Frank Deml, SVD, the second resident pastor, further remodeled the church, which is now adminstered by John F. O'-Shea, SJ. Archbishop Stafford dedicated the remodeled church on January 4, 1989.

Harold Koonce compiled a brief parish history, recalling the days when the congregation met in the old school house with

> an old-fashioned stove, which when ignited with wood and banked overnight with coal, would raise a mid-winter temperature from 20 below zero to a barely tolerable 50 degrees by morning, when a priest, who had travelled by train from Glenwood, would say Mass for us—once a month, if we were that fortunate.

Koonce noted proudly at the 1989 dedication that the

> fine new nave holds 200 plus persons, two classrooms, two offices, a big basement room outfitted with a full kitchen. When we are able, we plan to add more pews, to rebuild our old bell tower, to carpet our basement—all a tribute to Our Lord, and incidentally to our people.

Eaton

ST. MICHAEL (1930)

Eaton, a Weld County farm town ten miles north of Greeley, was named for the fourth governor of Colorado, Benjamin Eaton, who platted the town in 1889. After the Great Western Sugar Beet Company built a beet sugar refinery at Eaton in 1902, it became a thriving agricultural center.

To accommodate the many Hispanic Catholic workers in the area, Monsignor Bernard Froegel of St. Peter's in Greeley bought the Eaton Dance Hall in 1930 and converted it to St. Michael Chapel.

Gary Lauenstein, CSsR, pastor of Our Lady of Peace in Greeley, took charge in 1983, offering Saturday evening masses in the little frame cottage that used to house Saturday night fandangos.

Englewood

ALL SOULS (1954)
4950 South Logan Street

Omer V. Foxhoven was apppointed pastor of All Souls Church upon its founding, July 1, 1954. At that time, the parish consisted of some 200 families living east of Broadway and south of Quincy Avenue.

"The parish site was selected," according to Monsignor Thomas P. Barry,

> because Archbishop Vehr, standing on the steps of the cathedral, looked south down Logan and decided to build a church about every ten blocks so that older people would have the Blessed Sacrament within walking distance of their homes. And thus it is that we have the cathedral, Mother of God, St. Francis de Sales, Our Lady of Lourdes, St. Louis, and All Souls all along or near Logan Steet.

A house at 435 Pennwood Circle was purchased for $19,500 as a rectory where Father Foxhoven said daily masses in the basement, using the gym at St. Mary's Academy for Sunday services. Ground was broken for a church and parish hall on January 1, 1955.

After the church was dedicated on November 29, 1955, All Souls established a school fund, enabling the Sisters of Loretto to open, in September 1959, a nine-classroom school. By 1970, All Souls boasted a sixteen-classroom school with a full-sized gym, music room, cafeteria, and almost 600 students taught by six Sisters of Loretto, twelve lay teachers, and two physical education specialists. Although the sisters are now gone, a lay staff (including one teacher who was there on opening day in 1959) still taught over 300 kindergarteners through eighth graders in 1989. Among the school's many accomplishments are speech trophies, state science awards, sports trophies, and many spelling bee winners, including a state champion. Sheila Miyamoto, director of the parish's religious education program in 1989, and a staff of volunteer catechists instructed 350 Catholic children attending public schools, as well as conducting adult religious education classes.

Father Foxhoven transferred to another parish in 1962, to be followed by Francis J. Kappes. Father Kappes enriched the parish, encouraging the establishment of a seniors group, the "Saints of All Souls," and delighting children with his "Blessing of the Animals" on the feast of St. Francis of Assisi.

All Souls had become one of the largest parishes in the archdiocese before its eastern half was reorganized as Risen Christ parish in 1967. The southern half of what remained became part of St. Thomas More parish in 1972. As Father Kappes noted in the 1980 silver anniversary booklet, that though All Souls had shrunk "by reason of the dissection of our original terriory, none the less, we continue to carry the heaviest program."

Under Walter R. Jaeger, who became the third pastor of All Souls in 1985, the parish continues to carry this heavy program with its school and a full range of activities for more than 1,000 families.

HOLY NAME (1894)
3290 West Milan Avenue

The U.S. Army proudly arrived in Denver in 1887 to establish a new military base on Bear Creek north of Kenyon Avenue. Nine days later, a distressed ranch owner, Mason Howard, pointed out they were on his spread and steered the troops a mile south to the other side of Kenyon.

Once the army began building its fort in the right spot, towns quickly sprang up around the base—Sheridan, Fort Logan, and Englewood. Local Catholics bought a church site two blocks east of the Denver & Rio Grande passenger depot, from pioneer settler Issac E. McBroom. After this site was purchased for $130 in 1894, Bishop Matz created what he called St. Patrick parish.

Ignatius M. Grom, the pioneer pastor, oversaw construction of a strange-looking church with two-foot thick walls of Castle Rock rhyolite, a low, almost flat roof, and square windows. It looked like the basement of a bigger church-to-be or a military bunker. This thirty-one-by-sixty-foot subterranean

church seated about 130 parishioners, most of whom were Fort Logan personnel.

Fort Logan, a raunchy town of nine saloons, one general store, and a post office, needed a church. Yet St. Patrick's was not untouched by its surroundings and may have been the unnamed church described by Ralph Moody in his classic book about the Bear Creek Valley, *Little Britches*. Moody and his brother went to services there and picked up the army language used by children of Fort Logan personnel. When they brought this language home, their mother ordered them never to go to that church again.

Following several short-term missionary pastors, Father Richard Brady, the chaplain at Loretto Heights, was assigned to St. Patrick's in 1896. Father Brady, who was named a domestic prelate and vicar general in 1913, continued to minister until his death in 1940 to both the academy ladies and the army men.

Anthony A. Weinzapfel became chaplain at Loretto Heights and pastor of St. Patrick's in 1942. When Fort Logan closed as an army base in 1946, Father Weinzapfel jumped at the opportunity to improve his homey, one-building parish with some army surplus structures. For the bargain price of $1,000, he purchased a former barracks, had it placed on a new basement foundation next to the church, and remodeled it as a rectory.

Father Weinzapfel, who found himself rattling around in this 108-by-twenty-five-foot frame rectory, converted part of it into a school, doing much of the carpentry work himself. He and a lay teacher opened the first grade in 1952 and kept adding grades each year until reaching the sixth. Acquisition of another Fort Logan surplus barracks in 1954 enabled this prefab parish to boast six classrooms, three bedrooms, a dining room, kitchen, housekeeper's quarters, and a large parish hall. The elementary school also doubled as a summer religion school, conducted by the Sisters of Loretto from nearby Loretto Heights and later by the Victory Noll sisters from Holy Ghost Center in Denver.

Father Weinzapfel established a parish credit union in 1958 and also urged parishioners to donate to a building fund. The following year, the old stone basement church was demolished to begin a $200,000 replacement. Denver architects Victor D. Langhart and John F. McGuire planned a low-slung modern brick church, using gold and light woods inside and a six-foot crucifix over the main altar. To avoid confusion with the three other St. Patrick churches in Northern Colorado, the parish was officially renamed Holy Name on September 23, 1960. The new, 137-by-eighty-five-foot church, seating 800, was first used for Christmas midnight mass in 1960. Not until April 24, 1961 did Archbishop Vehr formally dedicate the new house of God with a solemn pontifical mass.

Father Weinzapfel retired in 1970, to be followed by Thomas McMahon (1971–1977) and Frank G. Morfeld, VF, (1978–present). Although Holy Name School closed in 1968, the parish thrived, claiming almost 500 families in the 1980s when it presented a far different scene than in the 1890s. Then, the homely stone dugout known as St. Patrick's perched on a bleak prairie hillside. Now, a modern church with an ultramodern steeple overlooks a sea of new suburban homes. Traffic rushes by on South Federal Boulevard and West Hampden Avenue to the east and north, but to the west lie the peaceful fields of Fort Logan National Cemetery, whose graves include those of some pioneer parishioners.

ST. LOUIS (1911)
3310 South Sherman Street

After Englewood incorporated in 1903, priests from St. Francis de Sales began offering mass there. "As a grocery delivery lad," Walter I. Pytlinski recalled sixty-nine years later, "I was asked to round up all the Catholics for the first mass, July 11, 1911."

For these early day masses, ladies of the parish tidied Bivens Hall at the northwest corner of Broadway and Cornell Avenue so that the remnants of Saturday night dances did not greet Sunday morning churchgoers. The aroma of cigars and whiskey clung to the hall, however, and the embryo parish soon shifted to the more dignfied chambers of William J. Broad's Undertaking Parlor at 3535 South Broadway.

Louis F. Hagus, whom Bishop Matz assigned to establish Englewood's first parish in 1911, was the first native Coloradan to join the diocesan clergy. Some say the parish was named for him, but officially it was for King Louis IX, the sole French monarch to be canonized. Father Hagus found about seventy Catholic families in Englewood and

Monsignor O'Heron helped to unload St. Louis's pioneer school bus. (Photo by Bill Smythe.)

began collecting for a church, a $12,000 white manganese brick building with Fort Collins sandstone trimming, which was dedicated on October 5, 1913.

Christopher V. Walsh became the second pastor of St. Louis's in 1918. Father Walsh bought a nearby house for use as a rectory and constructed Concordia Hall. Father Joseph P. O'Heron, pastor from 1929 until his death on August 18, 1956, transformed the little country parish into one of the diocesan powerhouses.

Father O'Heron quickly retired the parish debt, holding a summer fête at Englewood's Tuileries Gardens that cleared $1,200. He then transformed Concordia Hall into a school, which the Sisters of St. Joseph of Carondelet opened, in the fall of 1929, to ninety youngsters. As enrollment swelled, Father O'Heron bought neighboring houses and converted them to classrooms. A few years later, this ramshackle collection of classrooms was replaced by a $172,000, two-story school. Under one roof, the modern buff brick structure at 3301 South Sherman Street contained ten classrooms, a library, music room, cafeteria, offices, and kindergarten.

St. Louis School was blessed with a strong PTA, which provided nickel lunches (free to those who could not pay), conducted health clinics, and did anything and everything it could to bolster the school. The ladies of the PTA donated bookshelves as well as books to the library, contributed playground equipment and helped supervise the safety patrol and the parish Boy and Girl Scout Troops. Such staunch parish support enabled St. Louis's to operate for years without charging tuition.

Father O'Heron, a gregarious New Yorker educated at Denver's St. Thomas Seminary, proved to be an asset to Englewood as well as to his parish. He became chaplain at the University of Denver, a member of the Englewood Elks, Lions, and Chamber of Commerce, a director of the the Denver Area Community Chest (forerunner of the United Way), and he served on the Arapahoe County Child Welfare Committee.

For the Archdiocese of Denver, Father O'Heron directed the Newman Clubs and the St. Vincent de Paul Society. Named a monsignor for his efforts, O'Heron may have set the archdiocesan record for conversions—he brought 500 into the church, including one Presbyterian minister!

Notable St. Louis parishioners included James O'Brien, founder of the celebrated Cherrelyn Street Railway operating on South Broadway. Handsome, mustachioed Jim O'Brien became well known as the streetcar operator who would take your picture with Old Dobbin and the quaint wooden horsecar. He was elected alderman and then mayor of Englewood.

Nettie Steck, by pasting every parish-related clipping, photograph, and momento she could find in her scrapbooks, compiled a document that enriched St. Louis' 1936 jubilee booklet and the *Denver Catholic Register*'s special parish fiftieth-anniversary edition on September 28, 1961. Scrapbook memories of Monsignor O'Heron included that of Marie McRae: "He was a good, dear person. When we went to confession there under the curtain where he sat, a dog's tail was wagging. Was he petting the dog while he was listening to us? Also, his cat made visits to the altar while he said Mass."

Monsignor O'Heron undertook a $125,000 remodeling and expansion of the church in 1954. Under a new copper roof crowned with a copper Celtic cross, the church was enlarged from 260 to 500 seats. The Kernan Weckbaughs donated over $10,000 for the luxurious new pews and altar rail.

Following Monsignor O'Heron's death, Bernard J. Cullen took charge at St. Louis's. Father Cullen doubled the size of the convent at 3301 South Grant Street with a $135,000 addition. At its peak in the 1960s, St. Louis School had eleven sisters and six lay teachers instructing over 600 students.

Father Cullen, who became Monsignor Cullen in 1959, built a new parish hall in 1964 and remodeled the church interior in 1967. The William C. Cline parish hall was named for a parishioner who had served as an acolyte at St. Louis's from 1911 to 1983 and was alleged to have been "the world's oldest altar boy."

The Sisters of St. Joseph of Carondelet left the school in 1976, but lay teachers kept the kindergarten through eighth-grade school going. Following Monsignor Cullen's retirement in 1982, Robert I. Durrie, a native of Wyoming ordained at St. Thomas Seminary, became pastor. What was once a country church in a farm town in now a bustling parish of over 600 families.

ST. THOMAS MORE CENTER (1972)
8035 South Quebec Street

"We are not just a parish but a center for the life of this neighborhood," said Frederick D. McCallin, founding pastor of St. Thomas More Center. "And I chose the name of St. Thomas More because we wanted it to be a center for all seasons for all the community. We wanted a Vatican II parish to welcome people of all faiths and involve the lay people."

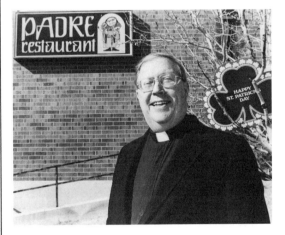

Father Michael Walsh, the second pastor at St. Thomas More's, offers an especially warm welcome to the parish restaurant on St. Paddy's Day. (Photo by James Baca.)

Father McCallin's dream materialized with the 1971 formation of St. Thomas More's, which was authorized by Archbishop Casey to serve the proliferating subdivisions south and east of Englewood. The first mass was said on February 13,

1971, in what soon became the largest parish in the archdiocese, with 4,371 families by 1987.

St. Thomas More's is also the only church in Colorado with a liquor license and a restaurant—The Padre. When Father McCallin applied in 1974 for the restaurant liquor license, it caused a great hubbub in the neighborhood and in the press. Since then, the restaurant's family atmosphere and tasty, inexpensive meals have pacified many one-time skeptics and opponents.

"Christ fed the masses, and so do we," explained Father McCallin.

> Jesus knew you had to feed people and make them comfortable before you could talk to them effectively. Through the Padre Restaurant, we have brought people closer to God, to the center and to each other. Nonbelievers, Jews, and Christians of many denominations have eaten together here and shared the social sacrament of humans reaching out to other humans.

The Padre's menu doubled as a quiz in Bible history: Adam's Pride (chef's salad); Eve's Pleasure (shrimp salad); the Apple (fruit salad); the Fig Leaf (spinach salad); the Prodigal Son (hamburger); Satan's Temptation (desserts); Heavenly Hops (beer); and Holy Spirits (cocktails). Customers of the Padre have frequently found a lively, small leprechan dressed as a priest there to greet them. "They are astonished to learn that this greeter is actually Father McCallin," reported a waitress. "And to find him such a lovable character!"

Father McCallin is the grandson of Andrew McCallin, an Irishman who came to Denver in 1883, going to work as a plasterer who helped build the Colorado State Capitol and the first building at Regis College. After growing up in South Denver's St. Francis de Sales parish and attending Regis College, Fred entered St. Thomas Seminary. Following ordination in 1942, his first assignment was to the Cathedral of the Immaculate Conception. There he learned how to manage and promote a parish from a master, Monsignor Hugh L. McMenamin.

From 1946 to 1967, Father McCallin headed St. Mary's in Littleton, spearheading that parish's move from a small downtown church to a twenty-acre site on Jackass Hill, where McCallin built a new church, parish center, grade school, junior high school, convent, and rectory. Father McCallin's reputation as a builder led Archbishop Casey to assign him to Colorado Springs in 1968 to build a new St. Mary High School and the beautiful new church of the Divine Redeemer.

After hernia surgery and severe complications, Father McCallin retired to All Souls parish in Denver. Some said he had come home to Denver to die, but he had other ideas. He began meeting with some old parishioners from St. Mary's in Littleton and new families moving to the fast growing areas of Arapahoe County near interstate highway 25. A 1971 census revealed that 590 Catholic families lived between Belleview Avenue on the north, County Line Road on the south, Colorado Boulevard on the west, and Parker Road on the east. On February 13, 1971, Father McCallin celebrated the first mass for this proposed parish in the gymnasium of the Walnut Hills Elementary School. A lunch table was used for the altar under a crucifix tied to a basketball hoop.

Soon Father McCallin was offering four masses a weekend in this makeshift church. He began driving around the fringe of fast growing suburbia, looking for a permanent site. He found the highest hill around on South Quebec Street, three blocks north of County Line Road, which separates Arapahoe and Douglas counties. From there, Father McCallin could see the full Front Range panorama framed between Pikes and Long's peaks. Downtown Denver's giant glass boxes looked like dwarf towers thirteen miles to the northwest beyond a sea of advancing subdivisions.

On that grassy prairie hilltop, Father McCallin buried a miraculous medal and prayed. The medal worked—later in 1971, he paid $200,000 for forty acres in the middle of nowhere, bounded by what would only later become Niagara Street on the west, Mineral Avenue on the north, Quebec Street on the east, and Otero Avenue on the south. Father McCallin later sold ten acres to the adjacent Fox Ridge subdivision for more than the cost of the original forty, making enough on the transaction to begin construction of St. Thomas More Center.

Architect Roland "Bud" Johnson designed a modular parish center as the first building, using the same low-slung glass and reddish-brown brick that he would employ for later additions. This pioneer $500,000 structure included a chapel, all-purpose hall, administrative offices, and the Padre Restaurant. The first mass was offered December 8,

1974, and the first meal served December 18 to what had become a parish of over 1,000 registered families.

In keeping with Father McCallin's hopes that St. Thomas would be a social and recreational center as well as a religious one, four tennis courts, seven softball fields, a football gridiron, and a soccer field were laid out on the west side of the center. Construction began on a 1,500-seat church-in-the-round in January 1982. Picture windows capitalize on the spectacular mountain views; the circular auditorium rises to a central skylight, above which a steel cross soars fifteen feet skyward. A vestigal apse serves as the tabernacle and as a solarium for some of Father McCallin's many potted plants.

Despite the huge size—eight weekend Masses serve as many as 15,000 people—St. Thomas More's remained a warm, personal place because of the efforts of Father McCallin, associate pastors Donald Willette and James Brennan, and several hundred committed lay volunteers. Besides the regular 6:30 Sunday morning silent mass, an 8:45 rock mass, a guitar mass, and traditional masses at 10:15 and 11:30, St. Thomas's has offered ethnic masses ranging from polka to Polynesian, from mariachi to bagpipe. Denver Symphony Orchestra musicians perform during Christmas and Easter services.

"A Mazzusah on the door of the Padre and kosher food service made Jews feel welcome here for meetings and Bar Mitzvahs," Father McCallin boasted in a 1986 interview. "We've also hosted Presbyterian and Episcopal services, political candidates nights, and we are the voting place for two precincts. We do everything we can to make St. Thomas More a center for everyone in this new suburban community of strangers."

St. Thomas More's is not content to be the largest parish and what some have called the "Catholic Country Club." To provide classrooms for over 3,000 parish children studying catechism in private homes, the parish built a new youth center in 1987. Father McCallin raised $10,000 toward this goal, selling $250 tickets on a Cadillac. "I'm in sales, not management," he quipped, but he had managed to build and maintain one of the most innovative parishes in the archdiocese.

On a typical weekend, 15,000 people flow through the center for mass, for meals, for athletics, and a full range of activities, from aerobics to Al-Anon meetings. At the time of his retirement in 1988, when he was replaced by another convivial Irishman, Michael A. Walsh, Father Fred was baptizing about twenty infants a week.

Father McCallin traced the inspiration for St. Thomas More Center to Vatican II: "Pope John XXIII went to the window and flung it open to allow fresh air to flow into the Catholic Church. At St. Thomas More we have tried to capture that fresh air and a fresh approach to Catholicism."

Erie

ST. SCHOLASTICA (1899)
600 Main Street

From all directions, horse drawn carriages converged on the little coal mining hamlet of Erie on Sunday morning, August 18, 1899, for the first visit of Bishop Nicholas C. Matz. Besides the bishop's carriage, others arrived from Longmont, Lafayette and Louisville.

Boulder sent its Sacred Heart of Mary choir to help the bishop celebrate solemn high mass. Benedictines joined their strong voices in Gregorian chant, celebrating the dedication of the little Erie chapel. One of them, Cornelius Enders, OSB, was the founding pastor. Using his own horse and wagon, Father Enders had hauled the lumber from the mountains and done much of the construction work on the little chapel of St. Scholastica. Theresa Kuemmert sang Millard's "Ave Maria," and all joined in the final chant, "Te Deum Laudamus." Then townsfolk treated the bishop and visitors to a banquet.

"I've only been a member of St. Scholastica's since 1931," Mary Miller reported in 1988, adding:

> Even though all the coal mines have closed, our parish has hung on. We're still in the little old white frame church and still a mission church, now tended from St. Theresa's in Frederick. This is the original church constructed in 1899. My husband, a coal miner from Lithuania, was only a little boy then but he helped put in the stone foundation. Not only Lithuanians, but French, Slavic and Italian coal miners built St. Scholastica's.

The church struggled to survive during the Great Depression. Then, Mrs. Miller recalls:

Bishop Vehr sent a nun up here who lived beside the church in a trailer and taught catechism lessons. The Imperial and Morrison coal mines donated coal for our furnace, to help us keep body and soul together.

Today 120 people squeeze in here for the Sunday mass, even filling the choir loft. We have a real keen parish that has built a parish hall on one side of the church and a rectory on the other. We've just started a St. Vincent de Paul Society and made a prayer tree to help us keep track of all our sick people. But we do more than pray. We visit the sick, drive them to the doctor and do whatever we can to help folks. Every Thursday Father McCormack and I take communion to the homebound. He's a keen priest who says a good mass, even when he found a fly floating in the altar wine. I was eucharistic minister that day and told him, "Don't worry, the fly won't drink much!"

Mrs. Miller reported that the parish still has its "leisure day" for ladies on the Sunday closest to St. Valentine's Day. "The men supposedly do all the work and serve us a sweetheart breakfast. But men come and go. You know how they are. So sometimes we ladies have to serve ourselves!"

Estes Park

OUR LADY OF THE MOUNTAINS (1915)
1000 Big Thompson Highway

William J. Howlett, the pioneer church builder and historian of Colorado Catholicism, started the parish in mountain-rimmed Estes Park. He found an angel in Patrick J. Walsh of Davenport, Iowa, who vacationed in Estes Park. When the Walshes' young son Walter died on one of these vacations, Walsh gave the money to erect a memorial church, St. Walter's.

Father Howlett, who as pastor of St. John the Evangelist's in Loveland had been saying missionary masses in Estes Park, accepted Walsh's offer and bought a site for $150. That summer of 1915, he completed a little chapel, with an additional gift

Our Lady of the Mountains Church in Estes Park. (Photo by Tom Noel.)

of $750 from a Chicago tourist, George J. Cooke, and $418.90 from Father Howlett's family. Father Howlett said the first mass in St. Walter's on August 29, 1915. With the end of the summer tourist season, he closed the church and turned over the keys to his successor as pastor of St. John's.

When Francis Kappes became pastor in Loveland in 1944, he took a special interest in St. Walter's. For the growing flock of all-year residents in Estes Park, Father Kappes began making winter visits. As St. Walter Church had no heating, he offered these off-season masses in the science room of the Estes Park High School.

With encouragement of his Estes Park congregation, Father Kappes broke ground for a larger, heated church on April 5, 1947. Justus Roehling designed a rustic structure of massive chunks of native granite and peeled logs. Raw beams and moss rock served as both exterior and interior of the church, which was dedicated in 1949 and renamed Our Lady of the Mountains. Beautifully sited amid ponderosa pines on a hilltop overlooking Lake Estes, it became a favorite with residents and tourists alike.

Membership climbed, leading Archbishop Vehr to assign Charles Sanger as the first full-time resident pastor in 1956. Upon Father Sanger's retirement in 1974, Daniel Bohte took charge and completed the fine two-story center attached to the side of the church. Daniel J. Flaherty and then Manuel Gabel guided this mountain parish, which by 1988 had grown to over 300 families, not to mention many summer tourists who patronize Our Lady of the Mountains.

Evergreen

CHRIST THE KING (1936)
4291 Colorado Highway 74

At first, Franciscan priests from St. Elizabeth's in Denver traveled up Bear Creek Canyon to offer masses in Evergreen's Episcopal chapel. Later, Monsignor John Moran of St. Joseph's in Golden tended to the Evergreen faithful, establishing Christ the King mission in 1924.

Shortly afterwards, George F. Cottrell donated a church site on the west side of the highway—a lovely, ponderosa pine–shaded site with the Evergreen Cemetery to the north and Dedisse Park to the south. With generous contributions from the John Vails, Edward Delehanty, Herbert Farrall, Joseph Little, Herbert White, and others, a rustic moss rock and log chapel was completed in 1935. John K. Monroe designed the structure, which was dedicated by Bishop Vehr in April 1936. Barry J. Wogan was assigned to Christ the King as its first pastor, followed in 1949 by John H. Kelly. Not until 1951, with the appointment of Joseph Bosch as the first resident pastor, did the little mountain town become independent of St. Joseph's in Golden.

George Greer and his family donated a rectory with a landscaped patio, while other parishioners helped construct a roadside shrine to St. Jude and an outdoor altar dedicated to Our Sorrowful Mother. Donald A. McMahon took a special interest, while serving as pastor, in gracing the picturesque church with fine art, including a life-sized Pieta fashioned of lead by Denver artist William Joseph. In 1956, Archbishop Vehr blessed a $75,000 parish hall, designed by architect-parishioner Frank W. Kullman, for the congregation of around 150 households.

Father Leo Blach, who became pastor in 1964, purchased seventeen acres of adjacent land in 1966. The following year, the parish sold its property across the road to the State Highway Department, which was widening Colorado 74 to accommodate the rapid growth transforming what had been a little town of 1,027 in 1950 to a city of 6,376 by 1980.

The first parish council, formed in 1968, hired John V. McCarthy Associates of Detroit to conduct a fund drive for a new church and education center.

After pledges reached the $88,000 mark in 1970, ground was broken for a new church and parish hall designed by Seracuse and Lawler, a Denver architectural firm.

Archbishop Casey blessed the new $247,000 church on May 24, 1971. It seated 500 and had five lower-level classrooms. The old stone church was razed, having been outgrown by a parish that had come to number over 500 households. To reach his far-flung flock, Monsignor Robert F. Hoffman experimented with monthly service in "little parishes" scattered around the foothills.

Nevertheless, the parish center remained in the multilevel, cantilevered complex built around the new rustic moss rock church. Surrounded by ponderosa trees, Christ the King's impressive parish plant is a beacon for high country Catholics.

John J. Murphy, the pastor, said in 1988 that Evergreen is now "a bedroom community, as the majority of its residents commute to Denver for work, shopping, and cultural events. But they find a hometown, full-service parish in Christ the King, which now cares for over 1,200 Catholic families in southwestern Jefferson County."

Fleming

ST. PETER (1913)
40027 County Road 18

In 1889, Bascom Fleming platted the railroad town named for him, and twenty-four years later Peter Lousberg held a parish organizational meeting at his house and donated four acres as a site for a church named for his patron saint.

Anthony C. Wagner, president of the local land company, financed church construction by asking his customers to pledge $50 for each quarter-section they bought. Church organizers paid J. W. Bentley $1,555 to construct "in good workmanlike manner . . . a perfect building . . . 26 x 40 feet, with 12 feet high ceiling."

Parishioners pitched in to help Bentley finish the handsome carpenter Gothic church in July 1913. St. Anthony parish in Sterling, of which St. Peter's had once been a mission, donated its old altar, which

For the May crowning of the Blessed Mother, St. Peter's school girls used wild prairie flowers as well as garden blossoms.

ladies decorated with sweet-smelling alfalfa for Bishop Matz's dedication mass.

A procession of different priests ministered to the newborn parish. Arriving on the Saturday train from Sterling, the priest was met at the depot by parishioners for a buggy ride to the church, which lay eight and a half miles south and one mile east of Fleming at a site known as Petersburg. After instructions and confessions, parishioners took their priest to Pete Lousberg's house for dinner and some sleep before the Sunday services. When priests could not come on Sundays, parishioners gathered in their little church for the rosary and catechism lessons anyway.

In 1919, when Peter P. Kluck moved to St. Peter's as resident pastor, the parish built the frame bungalow still in use as a rectory. By then, the flourishing Fleming flock had outgrown its 100-seat church, so parishioners sawed off the sacristy, then pulled it back forty feet to insert an addition, which enlarged the seating capacity to 320. During this

$3,500 remodeling, the old pot bellied stove was replaced by a basement furnace.

After the first death in the parish, a cemetery was opened a quarter-mile south of the church. In 1920, three Sisters of St. Francis from Milwaukee opened St. Peter Grade School in an $11,000 two-story frame structure, with eighty-eight students in eight grades.

Godfrey Guthausen, pastor from 1924 to 1929, sermonized in both German and English and, as an accomplished carpenter, made many improvements to the church, school, convent, and rectory. He built a choir loft and oak-stained it, the pews, the altar rail, and other fir woodwork. During the 1930s, St. Peter's was severely tested by declining population, dust storms, drought, and a church fire. Defying the depression, the parish added a ninth-grade class to its school in 1933 and a tenth grade in 1934. With the opening of an eleventh grade in 1935 and a twelfth in 1936, St. Peter's soon had a complete high school.

Father John H. Kelly, pastor from 1939 to 1948, began the practice of regularly praying for rain and prosperity. It worked! The drought ended during the 1940s, when World War II and the postwar boom also made wheat farming profitable again. Following the rich harvest of 1942, the congregation raised $7,321 in two weeks to liquidate the twenty-two-year-old parish debt.

Church members pitched in to build a parish hall in time for the Fall Festival in 1936. The parish hall doubled as the community hall, with its fine maple floor upstairs attracting gymnasts, dancers, and roller skaters. Downstairs housed meetings of the 4-H Club and Farmers Union, as well as the Altar and Rosary and the Holy Name societies.

To help keep the parish school open during thin times, Logan County agreed to pay the teachers and provide the schoolbooks. This unusual arrangement prompted a suit, ending with a 1952 decision that tax-supported public classes could not be conducted in St. Peter School.

Although St. Peter High School closed in 1946, the grade school remained open until 1967. The wonder is not that the school closed, but that this tiny congregation supported it so well and so long, fostering dozens of religious vocations among its sons and daughters, who now serve as priests and nuns around the world.

Father James R. Purfield became the eighth pastor of St. Peter's in 1959, when Logan County finally paved the road from Fleming to the church. Priest and parishioners also made progress, upgrading the parish plant and remodeling the church. With the help of Joseph and Aloys Lousberg and architect Lawrence Schaefer, the quaint frame building was transformed into a modern brick church.

In 1977, the tiny, proud parish lost its last full-time pastor, Father Dennis Grabrian, becoming a mission of St. Patrick's in Holyoke. By 1988, the parish still had sixty-one households, though Fleming, which once boasted a population of almost 600, had become a hamlet half that size. Undaunted, St. Peter's celebrated its seventy-fifth anniversary. Past trials and triumphs were recalled, inspiring the stouthearted congregation to rededicate themselves to St. Peter's journey of faith.

Fort Collins

HOLY FAMILY (1924)
326 North Whitcomb Street

Guillaume Joseph LaJeunesse, pastor of St. Joseph Church, realized that Fort Collins was ready for a second Catholic parish. So, in 1924, he bought the Second Presbyterian Church and helped recruit a Spanish-speaking Sulpician from Montreal, Canada—Father Joseph Peter Trudel, SS—as the first resident pastor of Holy Family parish.

With Father Trudel's encouragement, Margaret Murray opened a parish school in her home in 1928. After teaching alone for several years, she enlisted the help of Margaret Linden and Jovita Vallecillo. By the fall of 1934, the school had eight-five pupils, and four Sisters of St. Joseph of the Third Order of St. Francis from Stevens Point, Wisconsin, were recruited. Sister Quirine, the mother superior, and sisters Emanuelle, Ernestelle, and Matilda soon enrolled over 100 children in eight grades.

The old church–school at Whitcomb and Cherry streets, which was heated by pot-bellied stoves, was condemned in 1948. The school then moved into a new building on Whitcomb Street next to the parish rectory. A kindergarten class was opened in 1964, and the balcony of the gym was converted into a classroom for the fifth and sixth grades.

Although Holy Family School closed in 1969, the parish thrived. After Father Trudel's health failed in 1937, Juan Fullana, CR, took charge and undertook economic as well as spiritual uplift of his heavily Hispanic congregation. He and parishioners established a cooperative grocery and a mop factory. A recreation hall, auditorium, library, and kitchen were added to the parish plant with members of the congregation doing much of the construction themselves. Father Fullana's contribution to the community as well as to his parish is commemorated by Juan Fullana Elementary School, which Fort Collins named in his honor in 1975.

The cornerstone of a $12,000, ninety-six-by-forty-five-foot church was blessed in the spring of 1929 by Bishop Tihen. By the end of the year, a beautiful Romanesque church of wire-cut red brick had been completed. Architect Moresi of Denver designed a bricklayers' *tour de force*, with intricate window surrounds, corbelling, coursework, and gorgeous cathedral glass windows. The old church across the street was converted to classrooms for the school.

Father Anthony Homar, CR, served as pastor from 1951 to 1959, improving the parish plant and cutting his own salary to $80 a month to help reward the teaching nuns, who had been without a salary for twenty-two years. Bart Nadal, CR, pastor since 1973, further upgraded the Hispanic parish of Fort Collins. Father Nadal, an accomplished carpenter, remodeled and decorated the parish basement as a recreation hall and bingo parlor. To this day, Holy Family offers masses in both Spanish and English and stages an annual fiesta.

Eve Martínez, the first bride to be married in Holy Family Church in 1924, reported in her 1989 parish history:

> Holy Family has changed over the years from a Spanish language church to a bi-lingual church where all are welcome to a parish that has prospered spiritually and culturally.

JOHN XXIII (1967)
1220 University Avenue

A century after Colorado State Agricultural College was founded in 1878, the "Aggies" had evolved into Colorado State University (CSU) with 15,000 students pursuing practically every subject under the sun.

Among the academic possibilities at CSU were Catholic Inquiry, Christian Family Movement, and Theology classes offered by Leonard G. Urban. Father Urban transformed the CSU Newman Club into the Catholic Campus Ministry and became its first full-time director. Initially, he held Sunday services in the Engineering Building Auditorium, only to find all 400 seats filled; a house was acquired at 222 West Olive Street and converted to a center for activities and daily masses. The next step, taken with the help of Thomas J. Gleason, president of the First National Bank of Fort Collins, was acquistion of a large site at the west end of the campus.

As plans for a full-scale parish complex were drawn up, Archbishop Casey authorized creation of a new parish in 1967. At first, it was called St. Paul's but since an Episcopal Fort Collins church already had this name, it was changed in 1968 to honor Pope John XXIII. As the third parish in Fort Collins, it would serve primarily the students, staff, and faculty of CSU and spread the "Good News" of Vatican II.

The new center was completed and used for the first mass on September 15, 1969. When Father Urban transferred to another parish, Thomas L. McCormick took over at John XXIII in 1975, followed in 1979 by Reinhold B. Weissbeck, and in 1984 by Richard Ling.

Father Ling reported in 1986:

> John XXIII University parish is dedicated to its historical mandate to be the Catholic community in Ft. Collins serving the kingdom of God in and around Colorado State University. It has supported the Theologian-in-Residence program at CSU and has provided a full-time director of university ministry. It also provides traditional ministries to and with residential parishioners, while making the effort to bond both university and residential parishioners in a collaborative effort to foster the kingdom of God.

Father Leonard Urban returned as pastor in 1988 to the parish he had founded. "There's an interesting inscription on the bronze plaque of our parish center," he noted in 1988. "It's from Henry Cardinal Newman's *Idea of a University Defined* and ends with:

> 'Oh parting soul how has thou used thy gifts,
> Thy inspirations, the lights poured around thee.'

ST. ELIZABETH ANN SETON (1981)
5450 S. Lemay Avenue

In January 1981, Kenneth J. Koehler, VF, founded the fourth Catholic Church in Fort Collins. With a startup membership of 150 families, Father Koehler bought a house at 1200 Wheaton Drive and transformed it into a church, offices, and rectory.

Sunday masses were begun in the Fort Collins High School auditorium starting April 5, 1981. Our Savior Lutheran and St. Luke Episcopal churches offered their facilities for Saturday evening and Holy Day masses, two generous offers accepted by Father Koehler.

Father Ken was officially invested as pastor on October 18, 1981, and the parish was dedicated to Elizabeth Ann Bayley Seton, the first U.S.-born saint. Born in New York City in 1774, she was a wealthy and attractive debutante, a wife, mother and widow, then a nun who founded the Sisters of Charity. Appropriately, a Sister of Charity named Margaret Seton showed up in the summer of 1981 to help Father Ken start Seton parish.

Groundbreaking for phase one of a parish plant came on September 23, 1984. This parish hall was to be the first step in developing the thirteen-acre site, with an $850,000 building containing a chapel with adjacent multipurpose area seating 500, a nursery, classrooms, and kitchen. The multi-level, modern structure with Romanesque arch entries occupies a spacious suburban site with a fine view of the foothills.

"It is certainly a privilege," reflected Father Koehler, "to have the opportunity to build this parish in the 'Choice City of the Front Range.' I have made a commitment to the parishioners of this new parish to see this project completed, and with the support of everyone, we will see the fruits of our labor very soon."

Next, Father Koehler turned his attention, in 1988, to the homeless of Fort Collins, spearheading an ecumenical effort of nearly 100 Larimer County churches and synagogues to raise money for the Mission. Catholic Community Services purchased the site for the Mission in the spring of 1988 and made plans to include a Hostel of Hospitality, Hope Job Bank, the Hospitality Kitchen, and an Elderly Outreach Program. The $764,000, two-story, 8,600–square-foot Mission, designed by John Dengler & Associates of Fort Collins to look homey rather than institutional, opened in 1989 to sleep forty, feed 100, and provide employment and personal counseling.

"The Mission," Father Koehler told the *Denver Catholic Register* of November 11, 1987, does not serve

> primarily transient people as much as it helps neighbors and local citzens. They are 65% of the people helped. Many are persons who had good jobs, who want to work and who take pride in caring for themselves and their families. Because of conditions beyond their control, they are experiencing great difficulty doing this.

With completion of St. Elizabeth's parish plant and the Mission, Father Koehler's parish showed that it, like Mother Seton, could launch good works that snowballed into not only parish but also community assets.

ST. JOSEPH (1878)
308 West Mountain Avenue

Antoine Janis and other French Canadian fur traders and trappers first settled in the Fort Collins area, naming the Cache la Poudre River for several hundred pounds of gunpowder buried there by the American Fur Trade Company in 1836. Antoine's settlement at Laporte was later eclipsed by an Army post, Camp Collins, established five miles downriver in 1862.

Delighted at the prospect of visiting some fellow Frenchmen, Father Machebeuf ventured northward from Denver in 1866 to conduct the first non-Indian religious rites in Larimer County. After the Army abandoned Camp Collins in 1867, it became a

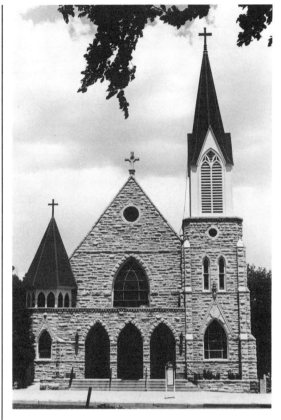

St. Joseph Church in Fort Collins. (Photo by Tom Noel.)

townsite, promoted by boosters as Fort Collins. Bishop Machebeuf and other missionary priests continued to visit Fort Collins, which replaced Laporte as the Larimer County seat in 1868. On an 1878 visit, Bishop Machebeuf said mass in the old Grout Building at Linden and Jefferson streets and helped organize a local parish. The bishop authorized Frank Michaud to pay $400, which was raised by subscription, to buy the first public schoolhouse in Fort Collins and convert it to St. Joseph Church. This little frame house built in 1870 still stands.

Father Anthony J. Abel, the pastor of Sacred Heart of Jesus in Boulder, was reassigned as the founding pastor of St. Joseph's in 1878. Father Abel was called elsewhere in 1880, and the tiny Fort Collins congregation was tended as a mission. The resident pastorate was reestablished in 1883 by J. J. LePage, who purchased lots next to the church and built a small brick rectory in 1883–1984. Between 1884 and 1898, fathers Gleason, Emblem, R. P.

Robinet, Edward Downey, and Volpe presided at St. Joseph's and tended missions at Greeley, Longmont, and Loveland.

Guillaume J. LaJeunesse, a French Canadian, became pastor in 1898 and purchased a more central site, catercorner from the Larimer County Courthouse at Mountain Avenue and Howes Street. In 1900, Father LaJeunesse and his parishioners started a $12,000 church of rusticated stone, which Bishop Matz dedicated on August 4, 1901. The buff and grey sandstone, according to parishioner Art Brookman who worked on the 1960 renovation, came from the Stout, Noney Frye, and Lamb quarries. Gothic portals and the single soaring spire distinguish this landmark at the beginning of the Mountain Avenue parkway. Father LaJeunesse lived in the sacristy with his cat, a feline famous for responding only to the French language.

Fort Collins, which did not grow past the 10,000 mark until the 1920s, lacked a Catholic school until the parishioners of St. Joseph's began building again in 1925. Denver architect Leo Desjardins designed a Spanish colonial revival edifice of wire-cut, rusticated tan-face brick with red sandstone trim and a red tile roof. This elegant school, with its concrete foundation and steel frame construction, is distinguished by its curvilinear parapets, balconettes, grand baroque double-staircase entry beneath an oriel window, and a colored tile bas relief of the lamp of learning.

St. Joseph School, a lesson in fine design, occupies spacious landscaped grounds north of the church on Howes Street. It is part of the historic block that includes the 1879 Victorian house of town founder Franklin C. Avery, a stone landmark now housing the Fort Collins Council for the Arts and Humanities. The 1985 revival of the Fort Collins Municipal Railway trolley on Mountain Avenue further enhanced the historical charm of St. Joseph's neighborhood.

Bishop Tihen, on August 26, 1926, blessed the $66,000 school, which the Sisters of Loretto opened that fall. When the Great Depression struck, both the church and school suffered financially. Card parties and other fund-raisers staged by the Altar and Rosary Society rescued both when even Easter Sunday collections brought in as little as $456.65. After guiding St. Joseph's through tough times, Father LaJeunesse died May 5, 1937, with the deathbed quip, "Someone just say three 'Hail Mary's' and mean them."

Monsignor Eugene O'Sullivan, the pastor from 1935 until 1948, supervised a 1948 renovation and enlargement of the church interior. In 1945, Monsignor O'Sullivan added a ninth grade to the school program, where he taught Latin and religion. He was followed by Monsignor Richard Duffy, a Denver native trained at St. Thomas Seminary, who helped the Sisters of Loretto construct a $100,000 convent between the church and the school in 1955. This showcase convent, complete with a sun deck and music rooms, was designed by Denver architect John K. Monroe.

In order to double the church's capacity, it was remodeled at a cost of $350,000 in 1960. Architect William V. Robb added 10,000 square feet to raise the seating from 300 to 700. The basement was excavated for an auditorium, rest rooms, kitchen, and furnace room. St. Joseph's stone exterior was repaired and restored, but the Gothic interior was modernized less faithfully. New stone crosses, carved by Art Brookman and Lon Ingram, were installed on the roof gables; the old steeple was repaired, and secondary steeples installed on the east and west sides of the addition.

New interior furnishings by the Santa Fe Studios of Church Art in New Mexico include a thirteen-foot high statue of St. Joseph. Bishop Hubert Newell of Cheyenne presided at the 1960 cornerstone laying, staging a reenactment of Bishop Matz's 1900 ceremony.

Monsignor Duffy was succeeded in 1967 by Monsignor John B. Cavanagh, former editor of the *Denver Catholic Register*. The new pastor, who enjoyed horseback riding and the great outdoors, opened a summer mission at Red Feather Lakes, a resort area thirty miles west of Fort Collins. In 1975, the church's diamond jubilee, Father Robert J. Reycraft, assistant pastor at St. Joseph's, compiled a parish history.

Monsignor Cavanagh was followed as pastor by Thomas J. Woerth (1981–1984), Anthony Bliss, who died shortly after becoming pastor, and by a priest who grew up in the parish, Father Thomas H. Coyte, the pastor since January 1985. Father Coyte focused on the elderly, launching such programs as "Young at Heart," monthly potluck dinners, a clinic, and tax preparation assistance.

Fort Collins has grown far faster in recent decades than Lieutenant Colonel William Collins, the namesake of the old military post, ever envisoned. By 1980, Fort Collins had 65,092 residents. St. Joseph's, with over 1,800 families, has also flourished. The parish school at 127 North Howes has well over 200 pupils, and the popular Sunday nursery program indicates that more students are on their way. Well into its second century, St. Joseph's is thriving. The French folk who founded the parish now share pews with Anglos, Hispanics, and Vietnamese in this elegantly restored stone church.

Fort Lupton

ST. WILLIAMS (1909)
1025 Fulton Avenue

Lancaster P. Lupton's 1836 fur trade fort was a crumbling adobe ruins by 1881, when the town was platted at the confluence of the South Platte River and Big Dry Creek.

Fort Lupton first received clerical attention in 1887 from William J. Howlett, pastor of St. Augustine's in Brighton. Masses were offered once a month or so in the home of James Gorman, a livery stable keeper, and in the meeting hall over Edward St. John's Dry Goods Store. Sister Loretta Clare, SC, then a little girl growing up in Fort Lupton, remembered riding bicycles with her friends to St. Augustine's in Brighton for Sunday services.

Fort Lupton's first mayor, Thomas Winbourn, the son of the town founder and a real estate dealer, was an Episcopalian. Yet, he donated land for a Catholic church, and a $10,000 gift from the Catholic Church Extension Society enabled Fort Lupton Catholics to build at 4th and Harrison in 1910. This traditional, front-gable, red brick church featured a Gothic entry, Gothic windows, and a rose window below the open bell tower. At the request of the Extension Society, the church was named Saints William and Juliana (her name was later dropped) in honor of the principal donors. Pastors from Brighton tended St. Williams as a mission

After completing their first church in 1910, St. Williams's parishioners donned their Sunday best for a flock photo. (Denver Archdiocesan Archives.)

church until 1920, when it became a mission of St. Nicholas's in Platteville.

After the Empson Packing Company (1898), the Silver State Canning, Creamery and Produce Company (1904), and the Great Western Sugar Company (1920) built plants in the area, Fort Lupton began to blossom. Many of the agricultural and food-processing plant workers were Hispanic Catholics.

Thomas Doran, who followed J. J. Shea as resident pastor at Platteville and missionary pastor at Fort Lupton in 1942, wrote to Archbishop Vehr that December:

There are about 400 Mexican people living in the [Fort Lupton] Spanish colony which is under government supervision. . . . Our church is so small that it couldn't begin to accommodate the numbers who should attend; also they have a very fine hall which the supervisor is willing to convert into a chapel. . . . I was told that the Pentecostals are quite zealous in their efforts to proselytize and Mr. Rud, the supervisor, feels that having Mass in the Colony would put an end to such activity.

Not until 1955 did Archbishop Vehr and Monsignor Mulroy, director of Catholic Charities, form a Special Committee on Migrant Labor Problems. It focused on the Fort Lupton Farm Labor Center, which over the course of a year housed as many as 17,000 men, some with families.

John W. Scannell, who succeeded Thomas Doran in 1955, established a mission station at the camp and recruited the Missionary Sisters of Our Lady of Victory in Brighton to establish a CCD program. Father Scannell also helped Hispanics set up a parish credit union in 1957.

"At my first mass in Fort Lupton," Father Scannell recalled later, "about 100 people jammed in with about 100 more standing outside in the July heat." Father Scannell began renting the Star Theater for Sunday services, while laying plans for a larger church.

Finding 500 Catholic families in Fort Lupton while there were only about 125 at St. Nicholas's in Platteville, Father Scannell moved his residence to Fort Lupton, where he purchased 7.5 acres from Joseph Witherow for $7,500. In one of the poorer parishes in the archdiocese, Father Scannell spent two years scraping together pledges, loans, and cash to build a $92,500 church and parish center. Although Archbishop Vehr suggested he not ask the poor Hispanics for money, they pledged $8,000.

Joseph P. Marlow, an architect and member of Denver's St. James parish, designed a modern, flat-roofed rectangular church, 192 by forty-two feet. Buff-colored Colorado sandstone was used for the exterior, while the interior featured lush carpeting and redwood walls. As the low-slung, flat-roofed structure did not look like a church, people had trouble finding it until a large sign was added. Besides the 450-seat church, the new parish plant had classrooms for 350 children.

Archbishop Vehr dedicated the church and school on October 22, 1959. *The Fort Lupton Press* of October 8, 1959, marveled that the congregation had donated $5,600 in labor and materials, including 105 tons of sandstone that they had hauled in their trucks from the Buckhorn Valley ninety miles away, to build one of the most dramatic, modern churches in Weld County.

The Fall Festival, begun in 1972, includes a tribute to an honored person for his or her contribution to the parish. Another tradition at St. William's is the weekly King's Table luncheon where parishioners and others provided a low-cost meal for the elderly and anyone else who wishes to attend. John P. Morton, CSsR, pastor since 1984, worked with the Fort Lupton Ministerial Alliance to establish a food and clothing bank.

"This vibrant Catholic community," Father Morton reported in 1988, "continues to respond to Christ's call to love God and to love one another—yesterday, today, and forever."

Fort Morgan

ST. HELENA (1910)
7th Avenue and Aurora Boulevard

A sod Civil War fort on the South Platte River, named for Colonel Christopher Morgan, evolved into a town during the 1880s. Subsequently, Fort Morgan became prominent as the seat of Morgan County and as a farming, ranching, sugar beet, and oil hub.

William J. Howlett reported in his *Recollections* that he said the town's first mass in a hotel parlor. Other priests from Brighton and then from Wray made mission stops in Fort Morgan until 1910. That year, St. Helena parish was founded after J. L. Juily, an energetic Frenchman, moved to town. Initially, Father Juily celebrated mass at the Elks Club, using the kitchen as a confessional and a dining room table as an altar.

To build a church, Father Juily and a handful of local Catholics acquired two lots, at the northwest corner of 7th Avenue and State Street, and constructed a simple, frame country church that was duly blessed by Bishop Matz on May 28, 1911. Non-Catholics joined in the ceremony after contributing much of the $3,000 cost of the 154-seat church, which had Gothic windows and an open bell tower.

The Great Western Sugar Company opened its Fort Morgan plant in 1906, sparking a boom; the town's population climbed from 634 to 2,800 in 1910. St. Helena's grew likewise, as Father Juily was followed by fathers Cornelius J. Vaughan (1920–1924), Peter U. Sasse (1924–1932), Harold Gleason (1932–1939), and Joseph C. Erger (1939–1952).

Herman J. Leite, who became the sixth pastor in 1952, wrote to Archibshop Vehr that the little frame church had become a "white elephant" and requested permission to build a larger church. "Due to the oil boom, and there is plenty of it around here," Father Leite added, "this town is growing by leaps and bounds." With over 200 families, the church overflowed at all three Sunday masses.

In 1955, St. Helena's bought seven acres in the Park-Lane subdivison on the western outskirts of Fort Morgan. The Boulder architectural firm of Langhart & McGuire planned a modern brick church with stone trim. A square, modernistic bell tower soared overhead while the full basement contained a large hall, kitchen, and restrooms. All 600 seats in the new church were filled on October 11, 1960, when Archbishop Vehr dedicated the $200,000 edifice. The old church was moved in pieces to the new site and used in the construction of an $18,000 convent.

Edward Dinan, a Denver-born St. Thomas Seminary graduate, became the next pastor in 1968. Father Dinan began the difficult task of implementing Vatican II changes by turning the 5,000-pound granite main altar around to face his congregation. Then, he recruited three Sisters of the Adorers of the Blood of Christ, who moved into the convent and opened a catechetical center. Until the nuns left the parish in 1981, sisters Amelia, Bernadine, and Loyola also taught religion classes in Brush, Keenesburg, Roggen, Weldona, and Wiggins.

Under Father Dinan's guidance, parish activities flourished. The Catholic Youth Organization, (CYO), for instance, started guitar masses and began visiting local senior citizens with "Hollyhock favor trays." By 1989, flourishing St. Helena's had loaned more than $300,000 to the Archdiocesan Revolving Fund to provide poorer parishes with low interest loans. By then, Fort Morgan had become a city of almost 9,000 and St. Helena's counted over 270 member families.

Pope Paul VI named Father Dinan a monsignor in 1976, when Archbishop Casey praised his "always cheerful, faithful and loving service." Celebrating twenty years at St. Helena's in 1988, Monsignor Dinan observed: "The history of St. Helena parish in not written in statistics or books; it is written in the hearts of people, and its faith is handed down from one generation to the next."

Frederick

ST. THERESA (1923)
436 5th Street

Coal miners crowded into the Frederick Union Hall for the monthly masses of Father Nicholas Seidl, OSB, pastor of St. John the Baptist's in Longmont. These well-attended services prompted Frederick residents to form St. Theresa parish in 1923. Doctor Paul L. Leyda donated two lots, and parishioners used socials, bazaars, local coal company contributions, and a $700 donation from the Catholic Extension Society of Chicago to build a church.

Catholics in the neighboring towns of Dacono and Firestone also pitched in to build a stucco Spanish-style church, with a graceful curvilinear parapet repeated in the doorway frame and the bell tower roof. After Raymond Layton, OSB, and his parishioners finished the $2,500 structure, Bishop Tihen dedicated it, on August 4, 1923, to St. Theresa of Lisieux.

By 1938, the Frederick–Dacono–Firestone congregation had outgrown its small church, whose walls were cracking and crumbling under a sagging roof. On Easter Monday, parishioners gathered to tear down the old church and begin work on a new one. This brown and buff brick church was designed and built under the supervision of Father James Maher, OSB, the pastor of St. John's in Longmont who handled the Frederick mission. Inside, Colorado alabaster was used for the altar and candlesticks.

The Farmer and Miner, the tritown newspaper, issued a special souvenir edition on September 21, 1939, to celebrate the grand opening of St. Theresa's. Bishop Vehr and the visiting clergy were treated, after the dedication, to a dinner in the domestic science room of the Frederick High School, followed by a dance in the gym with "Joe Cook and his well-known orchestra of Longmont." Besides the $10,000 church seating 250, the parish built a new rectory and a parish hall, where catechism classes were taught by Franciscan sisters from Longmont.

The many Italian parishioners sustained the parish during the depression years with spaghetti dinners that brought in as much as $300 a night.

During the next depression—the 1980s slump—the parish cosponsored "Esperanza para Comunidad." Sister Mary Regis Leahy, a local girl who had joined the Sisters of Mercy, administered this program to build low-income housing.

John D. McCormick had blessed several houses by the time he left St. Theresa's in 1988. "The Sisters of Mercy fund the project with a revolving fund," Father McCormick explained, "and low-income families use their labor—sweat equity—as a down payment."

Georgetown

OUR LADY OF LOURDES (1866)
9th and Taos Street

Genteel Georgetown was different from the beginning. Not only the heavenly setting in a spectacular 8,519-foot-high mountain valley but also the early presence of women and children led Father Machebeuf to select this silver town for his third parish.

George and David Griffith found gold and staked out a townsite in 1859, then went home to Kentucky to bring their families out to what was initially called George's Town. While other Colorado mining towns reveled in saloon halls, brothels, and gambling "hells," Georgetown prided itself on erecting Colorado's first opera house, the elegant Hotel de Paris, and prim homes, schools, and churches.

In 1864, Georgetowners built what is now the oldest Episcopal church in Colorado. Two years later, Father Machebeuf began offering Sunday mass in Brownell Hall and made Georgetown a mission tended by Father Raverdy of St. Mary's in Central City.

Georgetown's miners and their families prayed for their own parish, for which they donated a site on Main Street. In 1872, Bishop Machebeuf appointed John V. Foley the first resident pastor of Our Lady of Lourdes. After a few months, Father Foley was replaced by Thomas McGrath, who completed a small, frame, temporary church by the end of 1872. He then set to work on a permanent, $12,000 brick church with a large single bell tower

Our Lady of Lourdes, Georgetown. (Amon Carter Museum. Photo by Jacob Whitter.)

and spire over the entry. The new church was completed in time for Easter mass in 1875, and the whole town celebrated with hallelujahs.

William J. Howlett served as Georgetown's pastor from 1877 until 1880. Father Howlett found that many miners "seemed to have little time for the church except for funerals, and for grand services on St. Barbara's [the patron saint of miners] day."

Father Howlett was followed as pastor by Nicholas C. Matz, who went to work with the drive and ability that would make him Colorado's second Catholic bishop in 1889. He persuaded Georgetown's silver tycoon, Episcopalian William A. Hamill, to donate a 1,400-pound church bell. Father Matz also installed a hand-carved altar and pews for 400 people, making Our Lady of Lourdes the biggest and finest church in Georgetown.

Father Matz converted the old frame church into a rectory where he lived with his sister, who kept house for him. He constructed a new brick school in 1880 and moved in the Sisters of St. Joseph of Carondelet to staff it. By 1885, 140 boys and girls were reciting lessons there. The sisters also opened, in 1877, Georgetown's first and only hospital, initially using the Denim House, then building a two-story brick hospital on the north side of the church. Clear Creek County miners of all faiths gave a dollar a month to St. Joseph Hospital, which entitled them to free and tender care from Mother Theolinda and her eight nurse–nuns.

Churchgoers soon filled Our Lady of Lourdes to capacity, and Bishop Machebeuf consented to construction of another church two miles further up Clear Creek at Silver Plume. A small frame chapel, St. Patrick's, was constructed in 1876 with carved wooden front doors supposedly shipped from Italy. An aged Italian miner, after day labor in the Pelican

Mine, spent his nights in the church on a scaffold, painting wall and ceiling murals.

Thanks to the "Miracle of Silver Plume," St. Patrick's survived the fire of 1884 that destroyed the surrounding buildings. While men fought the fire, women and children knelt in front of the little church in prayer. Not a spark fell on St. Patrick's, which glistened a sparkling white against the blackened, smoking ruins of the town. In thanksgiving, devout miners enlarged St. Patrick's, turning the original structure to face east and west and serve as a transept for the new nave added to face south, where it still fronts Main Street.

Silver Plume's Buckley family, whose eight sons formed most of the town's crackerjack baseball team, were mainstays of St. Patrick's. They helped maintain the little church, closed after the 1893 silver crash. To this day, the altar of St. Patrick's, which for years was stored in the back of of the Buckley Brothers Livery and General Store, may be seen in the old schoolhouse now used as the Silver Plume Museum. Two blocks away, quaint St. Patrick Church, miraculous survivor of the 1884 fire, stands well-preserved, a cherished landmark.

Fire also struck Georgetown, where Our Lady of Lourdes was not as fortunate as St. Patrick's. A spark from a passing locomotive started the January 1917 blaze that destroyed both the church and the rectory. Only the stations of the cross, the statues, and the candlelabra were saved for use in the third, present church. This simple building, made from bricks salvaged from its predecessor, was erected on the site of a former Methodist church. Bishop Tihen dedicated it on February 23, 1919.

After Father Matz left in 1885, a long line of short term pastors guided the Georgetown parish, which included a church, rectory, school, hospital, and convent. Georgetown pastors tended to St. Patrick's mission at Silver Plume and a mission in Empire until both were closed, probably during the late 1890s.

Georgetown Catholics, like their brothers and sisters elsewhere, experienced some discrimination and snide remarks. For example, William D. Copeland's *One Man's Georgetown* ridiculed Catholics as "different" with their "strange statues and paintings" and because "they had to get up real early on Sunday mornings and go to Mass. Of course, this was compensated for by their being allowed to play ball on Sunday afternoon, and use strong drink, and be forgiven once a week by the priest for all they might have done amiss." Just as shocking to this Methodist was the "gambling" by which "the Catholic ladies raised considerable money with raffles" to benefit Our Lady of Lourdes. Such predjudice reflected a distasteful but real part of the Catholic experience in Colorado.

After the silver crash, Georgetown's population declined drastically. From 500, the parish shrank to less than 100 members. The school closed in 1913, followed in 1914 by the hospital. Christopher V. Walsh served as pastor from 1930 to 1945, keeping the church alive while Georgetown's population sank below 300. In 1945, Our Lady of Lourdes became a mission of St. Paul's in Idaho Springs.

Nowadays, Georgetown's tiny flock of Catholics gather at 5 o'clock every Saturday evening for a mass at Our Lady of Lourdes and pray for this small mountain parish, just as their predecessors did in the 1860s during the weekly visits of Father Machebeuf.

Gilcrest

SACRED HEART (1930)
Snowbird Avenue and Fourth Street

William K. Gilcrest organized the Gilcrest Town Company in 1906. By 1930, the farm town had enough Catholics to justify establishment of a mission, Sacred Heart. At first St. Peter's in Greeley and then Our Lady of Peace sent priests to the little dirt-streeted hamlet of Gilcrest, where the faithful erected a modern cinderblock church in 1967.

Parishioner Virginia Chacon, in a 1988 interview, explained:

> We built this church for about $20,000 on the site of the old white frame church. That old church, heated only by an old pot-bellied stove, was cold in the winter. Roughly fifty people go to our mass, which is at 5:30 on Saturday afternoons, although there are 100 families signed up who should be going. One of our special parish events is an annual blessing of the cars.

Glenwood Springs

ST. STEPHEN (1885)
1010 Grand Avenue

"For hundreds of years the Ute Indians availed themselves of the curative powers of the hot springs," Daniel J. O'Connell wrote in his brief 1935 history of St. Stephen's. "These healing waters that come gushing from the limestone cliffs at an average temperature of 127 degrees [demonstrate that] God, in his mercy, placed these springs here on earth in order to benefit the sick and the lame; and as an earthly sign that He is ever present."

The salubrious hot springs at the junction of the Colorado and Roaring Fork rivers soon attracted white settlers, too. Edward T. Downey, pastor of St. Mary's in Aspen, celebrated the first mass in 1879, in a tent of some troopers intent on driving the Utes from the mountains and hot springs they had known for centuries.

A few years after settlement began, Glenwood Springs was selected as the seat of Garfield County and formally incorporated as a town in 1885. Father Downey established St. Stephen's that year, saying the first mass on April 14 in the home of Mrs. James Lynch. After the Denver & Rio Grande Railroad arrived in 1887, the priest and his small flock built a chapel, which Father Downey named for his home church in New York. The first mass celebrated in this modest frame structure on November 14, 1886, attracted 138 churchgoers, including many non-Catholics.

Daniel P. Scannell, a healthseeker from Boston, became the first resident pastor in 1891. He was the first of many short-term pastors, most of whom were semi-invalids who stayed at the Hotel Colorado and tried to wash away their illness in Glenwood's famous bath, which still puffs itself as "the largest outdoor hot springs in the world." Not until the pastorate (1903–1910) of David T. O'-Dwyer was a $3,000 rectory built. Glenwood Springs Catholics helped open St. Joseph Sanatorium and Hotel (1899–1903), whose short life has been attributed to its location in the town's bar and brothel district.

St. Stephen Church of Glenwood Springs. (Photo by Tom Noel.)

Joseph P. Carrigan, who had headed St. Patrick parish in Denver until he began feuding with Bishop Matz, came to Glenwood as pastor in 1910. During his twenty-five-year pastorate, Father Carrigan spruced up the church and began a crusade to erect a shrine on Horn Silver Mountain facing the Mount of the Holy Cross. Today's Shrine Pass road between Vail Pass and Red Cliff is a relic of Carrigan's long and ambitious crusade to "make the Mount of the Holy Cross Pilgrimage the greatest annual religious event in the world."

One long-time St. Stephen's parishioner still remembers Father Carrigan as "a crusty old Irishman who insisted upon taking up the collection himself at mass, glaring at you until you had put enough in the basket. And he readily uncorked his views on politics and on the chancery in Denver." Father Carrigan, like his predecessors, was kept busy tending numerous missions, including, at various times, Basalt, Carbondale, Cardiff, Craig, Eagle, Gilman, Hayden, Marble, Meeker, Minturn, New Castle, Parachute, Red Cliff, and Rifle.

In 1935, Clarence E. Kessler took charge of St. Stephen's and began a campaign to build a new church. Lots were purchased in 1938, but construction did not begin until 1941. The eighty-two-by-thirty-two-foot church was designed by Denver architect John K. Monroe in the traditional cruciform with a basement parish hall. This $20,000 church, built of rusticated native red sandstone, was completed within the year. It has a modest Romanesque entry, rose window, and diminuitive buttresses; it seats 250 under an open beam mission-style ceiling. Before his retirement in 1965, Father Kessler bought land for a parish school at 414 South Hyland Park Drive.

Father Kessler's successors, after fumigating the rectory to get rid of all memories of his pet monkeys, continued his work. In 1981, Matthias J. Blenkush persuaded two hometown girls to return and open St. Stephen School, the only Catholic school to be opened in the archdiocese since the 1960s. Sisters of St. Joseph of Carondelet Marie R. Pretti and Ann Stevens were former Catholic school principals in Denver, whose abilities and experience enabled St. Stephen School to prosper at a time when many parochial schools were closing.

During a 1987 visit, my interview with the pastor, James V. Cuneo, VF, was interrupted by a young transient with a baby. After giving her "Lift Up" coupons good for food, gas, and lodging, Father Cuneo explained that St. Stephen's offers such assistance to as many as twelve indigents a day. "Night and day," he explained, "I give them sandwiches, pop, bananas, and yogurt. For families we give out the 'Lift Up' coupons which the charities and churches here have inaugurated." As in the days of the Utes, this hot springs resort attracts all sorts, and St. Stephen's opens its door to one and all.

Golden

ST. JOSEPH (1867)
969 Ulysses Street

"Our little church," Father Machebeuf wrote in 1867 of St. Joseph's in Golden, "is almost finished, although there are but two Catholic families in the town, and these represent four different nationalities."

Judge Jonas Johnson had donated a 300-by-600-foot church site on the north side of 14th Avenue near Ford Street. In 1874, he donated another twenty acres as a cemetery and possible church site. A white frame, $2,000 church was dedicated May 19, 1867, by Father Machebeuf, who brought out his choir from St. Mary's in Denver. "The church was thronged, mostly with non-Catholics," reported Father William Howlett, who was there, and the collection "amounted to only $26.15."

This tiny church at the base of South Table Mountain was the second church built in Golden, the 1859 gold-rush settlement on Clear Creek named for pioneer settler Tom Golden. "Golden City," as Father Machebeuf quipped in a letter to his brother in France, should be called "Iron City, for there is no gold here, but they have found rich iron mines." The gold lay fifteen miles up Clear Creek in the Central City area. The Baptist (1866), Calvary Episcopal (1869), Swedish Lutheran (1870), and First Presbyterian (1870, now the Foothills Art Center) churches also served pioneer Golden, a one-time territorial capital and urban rival of Denver.

Golden lost the territorial capital to Denver in 1867 and lost its hopes of becoming Colorado's rail hub in 1870 when the Denver Pacific and the Kansas Pacific steamed into Denver. Golden's golden hopes faded. After peaking at 2,730 in 1880, its population declined until 1940 when it finally climbed over the 3,000 mark.

Despite the dwindling population, St. Joseph's struggled to stay open. Thomas McGrath became the first resident pastor in 1871, followed by fathers L.B. Lebouc (1872–1873), S. Duroc (1873–1881), Anthony J. Abel (1881–1886), Martin P. O'Driscoll (1886–1888), George J. Morton (1888–1890), and Daniel Lyons (1891). In 1891, Bishop Matz, with some relief, turned over the poor, struggling parish to the Franciscans at St. Elizabeth parish in Denver. Briefly during the 1890s, the Franciscans turned over St. Joseph's to the Congregation of the Most Precious Blood, who also operated the nearby diocesan cemetery, Mt. Olivet.

Bernard Spiegelberg, OFM, began an ambitious pastorate in 1891, and in 1899 built a new, $8,000 brick church on the east side of the original frame structure. Lorraine Wagenbach, a long-time parishioner, described the 1899 church in "A Woman's Life in Golden":

> With only 25 to 50 families in the parish . . . we knew nearly all of them . . . [U]nder the stewardship of Father John P. Moran we thoroughly memorized the *Baltimore Catechism*. [The 1899 church] was a red brick traditional church with a high steeple and a large gold cross that glistened in the sun. It had beautiful stained glass windows. . . . The altar was wood, painted to look like marble, and there were a half-dozen lifesize statues. The communion rail and pews were carved oak. The

bell that pealed for over fifty years is now at the entrance of the new church.

Wagenbach's husband, Bill, recalls getting up at 3 A.M. on Sundays to start the old coal furnace to thaw the church out in time for the 8 A.M. mass. Both Lorraine and Bill remember the scary nights of the 1920s when the Ku Klux Klan burned crosses on South Table Mountain just behind the church.

The Franciscans worked to pay off the parish debt, enabling the church to be formally dedicated in June 1908. They returned a debt-free parish to the Denver diocese in 1913. Bishop Matz sent a French-born and trained priest, Robert Servant, as the pastor. Father Servant supported himself on the $15 a month he received as chaplain to the State Industrial School, which had been established in Golden in 1882 for juvenile delinquents aged ten to eighteen. A rectory had been built with the new church in 1899, but Father Servant used it as rental property to sustain his parish and lived with various parishioners.

After Father Servant's death, he was followed by Father John P. Moran, who built the mission of Christ the King (1936) in Evergreen. After the pastorate (1924–1940) of Father Moran, Barry Wogan guided St. Joseph's until 1949, adding a $19,959 hall north of the church on East Street. This hall, one of the largest in Golden, served Catholics and non-Catholics alike.

Andrew Warwick, pastor from 1952–1964, saw the fast growing parish double from 200 to 400 families. In addition, he ministered to many boys sentenced to the State Industrial School and to about 150 Catholics who each year wound up behind bars at the Jefferson County jail in Golden. Father Warwick also served the Newman Club at the Colorado School of Mines and provided spiritual services to National Guard and Highway Patrol trainees at Camp George West.

After World War II, Golden's growth finally began to match the golden hopes of its town founders. The town grew from 3,175 in 1940 to 7,118 in 1960 to 12,237 in 1980. St. Joseph's parishioners were overflowing the old 1899 church by October 3, 1958, when Archbishop Vehr dedicated a $135,000, 450-seat church. Located across 14th Street from the old church, it was designed by architect John K. Monroe as a basement church able to sustain a traditional ecclesiastical superstructure if future growth required it.

The old church, rectory, hall, and grounds were sold in 1965 for $130,749 to the Adolph Coors Company, which demolished the structures to expand its parking lot for tourists, who came in ever increasing numbers to inspect the huge brewery and sample its products. Proceeds were used to begin construction of a $227,870, eight-classroom school on the 10th Avenue and Ulysses Street site.

Richard Mershon (1964–1970), Monsignor Thomas P. Barry (1970–1976), Monsignor Edward A. Leyden (1976–1977), George V. Fagan (1977–1982), and several interim pastors guided St. Joseph's through years of rapid growth in Jefferson County, where it had once been the only parish. St. Joan of Arc parish (1967) in Arvada, and Our Lady of Fatima (1958), and Christ on the Mountain (1975) parishes in Lakewood were established to care for newly suburbanized areas once within the boundaries of St. Joseph's.

Even with these new parishes, St. Joseph's continued to grow. Angelo Ossino, who became pastor on July 1, 1982, began working with the council on plans for a new parish plant on the twenty-acre expansion site on the north side of the Golden Cemetery, which Judge Johnson had donated in 1874. The result is a $1.6-million church and rectory. For the October 19, 1986, dedication, a procession of parishioners carried the crucifix from the old church to the new. The old cornerstone and church bell of the 1867 church were also brought to the new site and placed at the outside entrance.

The church is pinned to a hillside by over 150 caissons and designed to be warm and welcoming, to have the earthy feeling of the nearby foothills. The pie-shaped structure seats over 500 with no one more than nine pews from the altar. Designed by architects Keith Ames and Associates of Longmont, the dramatic exterior of brick and raw wood rises to a central cone over the altar. The exterior features a solar wall and garden, with a baptismal font and pool just inside the main entrance. Custom handcrafted furnishings adorn the interior, including a suspended sculptural ceiling in the Eucharistic chapel and stations of the cross carved in glass. Under its huge conical roof, the complex contains a record vault, a reconciliation room, a chapel, offices, a library, and a kitchen.

Archbishop J. Francis Stafford anointed the altar with holy oil, sprinkled parishioners with holy water, and set off the smoke detectors with clouds of incense. Parishioners thanked the archbishop with a traditional western "Howdy!" by presenting him with a Stetson hat. Thus, St. Joseph's, the second church to be built outside Denver by Bishop Machebeuf, became the first new Colorado church to be dedicated by Archbishop Stafford.

Granby

OUR LADY OF THE SNOW (1969)
390 Garnet Avenue

This is the only Catholic church in Colorado with an Episcopal flag guarding the altar. Allen du Pont Breck explains why in *The Episcopal Church in Colorado*, which reports that St. John Episcopal Church started out in Granby in 1958 in a refitted building. In 1962, the Episcopalians replaced this secondhand chapel with a new $15,000 church whose nave and sanctuary were formed by "A-frame" beams covered with exposed knotty pine. A folding partition enabled the rear of the church to be used as a parish house.

This chapel also became home for Granby's Catholic parish, which since 1952 had been holding services in the Chuck Wagon Restaurant. The congregation gladly pays $200 a month to the Episcopalians in order to worship in a conventional church. Monsignor Thomas P. Barry, who helped establish the Granby parish, has his summer retirement home there. Summers, he offers the 7 A.M. Sunday mass, which allows him to spend the rest of the day fishing.

The current pastor of Our Lady of the Snow is H. Robert White, who travels from his resident parish, St. Anne's in Grand Lake, to offer year-round 10:30 Sunday masses (and coffee afterwards) in Granby's St. John Episcopal Church.

Grand Lake

ST. ANNE (1944)

The resort town of Grand Lake was founded in 1879 on the shores of Colorado's largest natural lake. What had been a haven for the Utes became a fashionable summering place, which boasted the world's highest yacht anchorage.

As early as 1906, circuit-riding priests celebrated masses in Grand County, usually at Kremmling, which was on the Denver & Rio Grande Railroad. Not until 1944 did Archbishop Vehr assign Father Thomas Patrick Barry to establish a parish in Grand County. Father Barry, an adventuresome, bold, and gregarious native of County Clare, welcomed the challenge. Besides, he reminisced in 1986, "I loved to fish—like the Apostles before me. I started out with worms, but moved up to flies, then daredevils, and since 1975 I've been trolling with triple teasers." (John McDermott of the Tripple Teaser Manufacturing Company of Kent, Washington, has named a triple teaser the "Monsignor Thomas Barry Kokanee Killer," the monsignor reports.)

On June 28, 1944, Father Barry became the founding pastor of what was initially called the Catholic parish of Kremmling–Grand Lake. While making St. Peter's in Kremmling his headquarters, Father Barry said mass in Grand Lake at the private chapel of Martin J. O'Fallon, the founder of O'Fallon Plumbing and Supply Company in Denver. O'Fallon named the chapel for his wife, Anne, and hired Franciscan priests to come up and say mass in the summer, putting them up at the Grand Lake Lodge. In 1945, Father Barry purchased the land for St. Anne's and moved the original building from the O'Fallon's private property on the shore of Grand Lake to the present site.

"Mr. O'Fallon was a fine Irish gentleman," recalls Monsignor Barry. "He never let on to anyone that he had donated that chapel, just felt it was part of his Christian duty."

State Senator Dennis Gallagher remembers visiting Grand Lake as a toddler and finding: "At the stop light in the middle of town, Monsignor Barry was standing there in his cassock selling raffle tickets to support the parish. We bought some, figuring that you couldn't get through the light otherwise."

Theodore Haas, who in 1954 became the second pastor of the Kremmling–Grand Lake parish, built the new St. Anne's in 1957. This beautiful church is an A-frame resting on sandstone walls. After the congregation moved into this rustic church surrounded by ponderosa pines, the old church was sold and moved to Grand Avenue across from the Town Park where it became the home of the Comic T Shirt Shop.

H. Robert White, who became pastor in 1986, oversaw establishment of St. Anne's as an independent parish and served as the first year-round resident pastor. In 1988, Father White completed an $8,000 remodeling of the interior, highlighted by modern stained glass windows depicting local lake and mountain scenes. Father White handles a vast and beautiful parish, sprawling over 4,000 mountainous acres in Grand, Jackson, and Summit counties, with missions in Granby and Winter Park.

Monsignor Barry still summers in Grand Lake, where he celebrated his fiftieth anniversary as a priest in 1988 and reminisced, "Grand Lake is a grand place, prayerful and uplifting, where I, like Our Lord and the Apostles and many priests before me, spend my time fishing—for fish and for human souls, Lord bless us."

Greeley

OUR LADY OF PEACE (1941)
1311 3rd Street

With Hispanics in mind, Archbishop Vehr established Our Lady of Peace on September 19, 1941. He entrusted the churchless parish to the Sons of the Holy Family, who assigned Dominic Morera, SF, to be the first pastor. With the help of Bernard J. Froegel of St. Peter's in Greeley, the parish purchased a block of land.

Our Lady of Peace Church, Greeley. (Photo by Tom Noel.)

Because of wartime rationing of construction materials, the church was not built and dedicated until July 8, 1948. In the meantime, Father Dominic held masses for Spanish-speaking people in St. Peter's, and parishioners cultivated the church site, raising vegetables for the poor and for the war effort. John K. Monroe designed the Romanesque church of brick with creamy terra cotta trim and a life-sized statue of Our Lady of Peace over the front entrance. Juan Menchaca, a Denver artist, hand painted the stations of the cross inside the church, which is illuminated by stained glass windows depicting Our Lady in her various roles.

Victory Noll sisters have been a part of the parish since 1944, when they moved into a little frame cottage, converting it to the Centro de Educación Católica for their work of teaching and caring for the poor. In 1988, the sisters, working with fathers Leonard and Peter Urban of St. Peter Church converted the former St. Peter's parish hall to the Guadalupe Center shelter.

This old church hall and a small wooden church attached to it had served the Spanish colony on Greeley's northwest side before Our Lady of Peace parish came onto the scene. Sister Mary Alice Murphy, OLVM, who spearheaded the Guadalupe Center shelter project, told the *Denver Catholic Register* of January 21, 1987:

When the migrants come into the Greeley area early in the spring they need a place to stay for two or three days until they can contact a farmer and arrange for a job. Many times these people go to the parks to sleep because they have no money, but the police roust them out and they often must spend all night walking around.

Father Francis Gonzales, SF, the last of eight Sons of the Holy Family to preside at the parish, left in 1983 when the Redemptorist order took charge. Gary Lauenstein, CSsR, the pastor since 1983, speaks both English and Spanish and has often gone to bat for his parishioners. He and other local clergy conducted a hearing on working conditions at Greeley's huge Monfort Beef Slaughterhouse. According to the *Colorado Labor Advocate* of November 11, 1987, Father Lauenstein hoped "to improve working conditions, and push management to be more responsive to worker grievances."

Pat Montoya, parish historian, reported in 1987 that "Father Gary and Our Lady of Peace tend three missions, St. Mary's in Ault, St. Michael's in Eaton, and Sacred Heart in Gilcrest."

ST. MARY (1965)
2200 23rd Avenue

Robert V. Nevans, pastor of St. Peter's in Greeley realized the need for another parish on the fast growing south side. Groundbreaking came April 29, 1964, for a unique church designed by the Colorado firm of Langhart, McGuire, and Barngrover. Using a network of beams like interlaced fingers, they capped a buff brick building, then roofed it with shake shingles. A raised rear dormer and a circular baptistry on the front of the church add architectural interest to this postmodern church built in a traditional spirit.

St. Mary's in Greeley. (Photo by Tom Noel.)

Father Nevans moved to the new church as its first pastor after it was dedicated on May 4, 1965.

The initial congregation of 500 families grew rapidly, reaching the 1,200 mark by 1986.

Father Nevans was followed as pastor by fathers Charles Jones, Michael Smith, Thomas P. Stone, Robert J. Greenslade, and Dorino DeLazzer, VF. In 1987, St. Mary's constructed a $1.5-million parish center next to the church. This 20,000–square foot postmodern structure contains a 550-seat meeting hall for, as Father DeLazzer put it, "everything from bingo to banquets."

The center, decorated with butcher-block wood squares and other modern art, contains eight classrooms, a library, kitchen, and offices. The complex is staffed by six full-time employees and includes a computer room. When Archbishop Stafford blessed this ultramodern parish center on November 1, 1987, Father DeLazzer reported that "parishioners were just bursting with pride."

ST. PETER (1903)
915 12th Street

Nathan C. Meeker, former agricultural editor of the *New York Tribune*, founded Greeley, the utopian dream of *Tribune* editor Horace Greeley. The Union Colony, formed in New York to recruit immigrants of means and morals, decided early that the Greeley colonists should worship together at a "Union Evangelical Church." Two Irish servant girls, however, had other ideas.

Maggie and Annie Flynn threatened to leave the household of James Freeman to find work in Denver where they could go to mass. Freeman, a prominent attorney and state senator, was not a Catholic, but he prized the services of these hard-working sisters, who cooked and cared for his family.

So Freeman arranged for Father Raverdy of Denver to celebrate Greeley's first mass in the living room of his home at 1202 7th Avenue. After Father LePage became pastor at Fort Collins, he regularly took the train to Greeley to conduct Sunday services at Senator Freeman's place.

Maggie and Annie Flynn saved their pennies to help Father LePage build, in 1884, at 12th Avenue and 6th Street, a tiny brick sacristy. David Boyd, a Greeley pioneer, reported in his 1890 *A History: Greeley and the Union Colony* that "this building, such as it is, was erected by a few, mostly servant girls."

Greeley did not count any known "cat lickers" among the "saints" who first settled at the junction of the South Platte and Cache la Poudre rivers for Colorado Territory's first great communal effort at irrigated farming. Indeed, the anti-Catholicism of many early residents was reflected in Boyd's history, where he explained that Greeley was a temperance town and wrote on page 294:

> Catholicism, at least Irish-Catholicism, and whisky go in harmony together. It is farther [*sic*] worthy of note that scarcely any Germans were among the original colonists. . . . We put them to too much trouble to get their lager beer.

Father G. Joseph LaJeunesse, after becoming pastor at Fort Collins, acquired a new Greeley church site at 9th Avenue and 10th Street for $500. He used the small five-room cottage as a rectory while constructing, next door on 10th Street, a $3,000 church that was dedicated in August 1899. Ten years later, this church was sold for around $13,000 as part of the site where the stately Weld County Courthouse was built in 1917.

Thirty years after its birth as a mission, St. Peter parish was formally organized in 1903 with the arrival of the first resident pastor, J.A. Bastien. After Father Bastien and another short-term, ailing pastor, St. Peter's received an energetic young Irish priest as a 1903 Christmas present. Andrew B. Casey formed an Altar and Rosary Society, a choir, a Young Ladies Sodality, a Sunday School, and a Newman Club to serve the State Normal School (now the University of Northern Colorado). Father Casey bought lots from the Union Pacific Railroad in the middle of Greeley's finest residential section. After a slow start, Catholics aspired to build a fine structure on a fine site. They succeeded— thanks to some unexpected help from nonCatholics. Father Casey, in a letter to Bishop Matz, reported that "the Protestants are all very kind to me and turn out for everything I have, otherwise, with the few Catholics here it would be impossible to do as well."

For Christmas mass in 1909, Father Casey used Newman Hall, as he christened the basement of the unfinished church. On May 8, 1910, Bishop Matz dedicated the monumental new St. Peter's. Standing on a nine-foot-high concrete foundation topped with eight feet of rusticated white stone, the gray manganese brick edifice featured a wealth of stone trim framing a variety of Gothic, rose, and roundel windows. Inside, under a soaring rib-vaulted ceiling, elegant furnishings were showcased by electric lights installed in graceful Gothic curves. The exterior rose seventy-four feet over the cruciform 118-by-fifty-foot nave. Although architects Ward and Patterson planned a 135-foot-high steeple atop the corner bell tower, it never materialized.

In 1914, Father Casey exchanged Dan, his nine-year-old sorrel horse, for a new Maxwell "gasoline burner" to speed him to the missions at Eaton, Keota, Kersey, Johnstown, Milliken, Nunn, Severance, and Windsor. In his horseless carriage, Father Casey visited even the remotest corners of Weld County to say masses at such places as the Kerchoff family's E-K Ranch. This hectic schedule, according to a sixty-one-page typed parish history in the archdiocesan archives, led to the death of the forty-one-year-old priest on May 16, 1916.

St. Peter School, a handsome two-story red brick structure across 12th Street from the church, was dedicated February 23, 1927, under the pastorate (1916–1929) of Raymond P. Hickey. This red-headed Irishman was the first priest to complete all of his seminary training at St. Thomas's in Denver. Father Hickey had bought a house, in 1922, to open the school and added grades each year until 1927, so St. Peter Grade School could send graduates on to Greeley Catholic High. Although the Sisters of Loretto had opened the school in September 1923, they withdrew and were replaced in 1927 by the Sisters of Mercy. The forty-three-year-old Father Hickey, like Father Casey before him, died young of overwork, expiring in the rectory on April 29, 1929.

Fortunately, the next pastor of St. Peter's enjoyed a much longer life. German-born, Regis College–educated Bernard J. Froegel became one of the first priests in the archdiocese to celebrate his golden jubilee of ordination. Father Froegel, who became Monsignor Froegel in 1949, is fondly remembered as "the priest with his pockets full of candy."

Not only children benefitted from Father Froegel's kindness. For German prisoners of war, held at agricultural camps in Greeley, Ault, Galeton, Kersey, and Pierce, Father Froegel procured German prayer books and ministered to the POWs in their own language. To the long list of Weld County missions served by St. Peter's, Father Froegel added not only the POW camps, but also

Ault, Gilcrist, and New Raymer. This handsome, square-jawed priest celebrated his golden jubilee five months before his death on October 31, 1953.

Father Froegel's assistant, Robert F. Hoffman, succeeded him. A native of Sterling and a graduate of St. Thomas Seminary, Father Hoffman retained architect Karl Schwartz for a $75,000 remodeling of the church. This young clergyman also built a new rectory behind the church and spent $12,000 to remodel the house at 12th Street and 9th Avenue as a convent for the Sisters of Mercy. A year after Archbishop Vehr awarded Father Hoffman the purple robes of a monsignor in 1959, he was reassigned to St. Mary's in Colorado Springs.

Even though St. Peter's seating had been enlarged from 320 to 400, the next pastor, Robert V. Nevans, a Denver native and St. Thomas's graduate, began work on another Greeley church. And after St. Mary's was completed in South Greeley in 1965, Father Nevans took charge there.

At St. Peter's, Father Nevans was followed by the Rev. Owen McHugh, a graduate of St. Thomas's and of Catholic University. Father McHugh and his constant companion, Sallie (a golden retriever), soon endeared themselves at St. Peter's. He took a special interest in Greeley Catholic High students and Newman Club students from the University of Northern Colorado, who fondly called him "Daddy-O."

In 1973, the Paulist fathers took over the parish, which closed its school in 1986. That year, the Paulists withdrew from the parish, which returned to archdiocesan priests and underwent "Urban Renewal." Fathers Leonard and Peter Urban had grown up in Wallace, Kansas, and gone to the seminary together. They shared a commitment that made Greeley's core city parish and university work attractive to them.

Father Leonard is a writer who contributes a column to the *Denver Catholic Register* and authored *Look What They've Done to My Church* (Chicago: Loyola Univeristy Press, 1965), a reflection on the post–Vatican II church in which he finds a broad historical continuity amid the changing approaches to Catholicism.

As Father Leonard told the *Greeley Tribune* of July 11, 1986, upon his arrival at St. Peter's, "We are very concerned and always have been about social injustice. We want to awaken people to the Gospel message, to help people both physically and spiritually poor." Pursuing that goal, they have opened parish properties to Right to Read, with its English language instruction, to the Mercy House that feeds and financially assists the poor, and to Guadalupe Center that provides room and board for the migrant and the indigent.

Haxtun

CHRIST THE KING (1933)

The Burlington railroad platted Haxtun in 1888 but not until 1907 was mass offered in the Odd Fellows Hall by Bernard J. Froegel, pastor of St. Augustine's in Brighton and caretaker of the Phillips County missions.

In 1933, Arthur R. Kerr, pastor at Holyoke, and the fourteen Catholic households in Haxtun procured the M.H. Keating home and converted it to a church, which was dedicated to Christ the King on November 27. Pews were installed and frosted windows added.

All the while they used this little frame house, Haxtun Catholics were saving and praying for a formal church structure. For these early-day faithful, some of whom lived in sod houses while scratching a living from the dry prairie, the dream finally came true in 1949. That year, they paid $5,000 for the Lutheran Church built in the 1920s and subsequently used as a Masonic Lodge. After selling the old church for $1,000, parishioners installed $1,400 worth of furnishings in their new home.

By 1952, the little parish had grown to thirty families, and the church was enlarged. At the same time, a basement parish hall was dug out. Parishioners donated much of the labor to keep the expansion expenses to $11,000. On October 8, 1952, Archbishop Vehr presided over the dedication of the rebuilt church.

Ongoing improvements included the 1963 purchase of a new electric organ and the 1985 remodeling of the basement hall during the pastorate of Terrance T. Kissel, when the upper floor was completely renovated, with improvements including cry and reconciliation rooms and a Eucharistic chapel.

"Everything was either painted, cleaned, or completely torn out and remodeled," parishioner Trilla Bornhoff noted, pointing out that the church received a new entrance and oak paneled walls. Two stained glass windows made by a local artist, Jessie Scott, highlight the oak altar and crucifix that were made by Larry Schaefer, the contractor for the remodeling project. In 1988, another of Scott's stained glass windows was installed to depict the parish's patron, Jesus Christ the King.

Gerald A. Young, pastor since 1987, wrote in 1989 of Christ the King:

> Always known as a church of loving, caring and close knit families, it remains so today. Only thru much donated labor, materials and energy and many helping hands did the new church become a reality. The pride of a job well done shines thru each parish family.

Holyoke

ST. PATRICK (1893)
535 Interocean Avenue

When Phillips County was formed from the eastern part of Logan County in 1889, Holyoke became the county seat. Both the town and the county owed their existence to the Burlington (now Burlington Northern) railroad, some of whose employees settled in Holyoke and asked Bishop Matz to send a priest.

William J. Howlett, then based in Brighton and trying to cover all of northeastern Colorado, answered the call. Father Howlett procured a railroad pass and steamed into the hamlet to celebrate the first mass in 1888. Apparently, this occurred at the home of Patrick Turley, but Matt Conlin and Michael Sheehan later also opened their homes to early missionary priests. Agnes Arens donated lots for a church, and her husband, John, spearheaded the volunteers who began putting up a frame meeting house in 1893. That same year, Bishop Matz authorized establishment of a new parish, which the Irish railroad workers dubbed St. Patrick's. For several years, masses were held in this unfinished shell of a church, which was not completed and capped with an open bell tower until 1904.

The integrated angels of St. Patrick's posed for this May 17, 1953, First Communion portrait. (Photo by Bill Smythe.)

St. Patrick's also doubled as the district courtroom for several years before a county courthouse was established in what had been the Burlington Hotel and Eating House. This quaint church with a pot-bellied stove near the communion rail had unplastered lumber walls that came together at the top to form a barrel-vault ceiling. The first resident pastor was M. Mennis, an Irishman who, in 1919, moved into a rectory at 309 East Furry Street. He was followed by fathers Joseph N. Oldenburg (1920–1925) and Leonard Meister (1925–1934).

A fire destroyed the church on July 4, 1934. Predawn Independence Day revelers throwing firecrackers at pigeons in the bell tower caused the blaze, according to St. Patrick's 1981 history booklet compiled by parish historian Laura Lindgren. Despite intense flames, smoke, and the 52,000 gallons of water poured on the church, some of the faithful bravely rescued the Blessed Sacrament and many of the furnishings. Mass was held in the Phillips County Courthouse, whose occupants remembered gratefully the days when parishioners had permitted their church to serve as the county courtroom.

The fire settled a debate as to whether a new church should be built, a debate made more difficult by Bishop Vehr's stipulation that the old church not be sold to a non-Catholic denomination. An $11,500 structure was erected on the old site and dedicated by Bishop Vehr on November 27, 1934. The ceremony took place during a blizzard, which the drought-stricken community regarded as a godsend.

After several short-term pastors, Francis J. Brady began an eighteen-year pastorate in 1935. During the time of John C. Walsh (1954–1968), St. Patrick's was remodeled and enlarged in 1963. Front and rear additions were made and the entire exterior was bricked, with a life-sized marble statue of St. Patrick placed in the front façade. Inside, the $50,000 renovation included a basement hall and a new marble altar with a bronze pelican (a symbol for Christ).

St. Patrick's has been continually improving its parish plant. Air conditioning was installed in 1973, and in 1984–1985, the church was repainted and remodeled. The cry room became the reconciliation room, with the new baby room featuring stained glass windows by Nancy Lynch, an Otis, Colorado, artist. An elevator was constructed to whisk folks to the church, the reconciliation room, or the basement library. A new furnace and ceiling fans were also installed by this lively parish that by 1988, had grown to embrace 153 families.

Idaho Springs

ST. PAUL (1881)
1632 Colorado Boulevard

"That bearded priest up in Idaho Springs, Father Henry R. McCabe, was a wild one," Father John V. Anderson recalled in 1986. "McCabe was a health seeker from Michigan who received special permission from the bishop to wear a full beard. He claimed he needed it to protect his delicate health. But when he came roaring into Denver he looked healthy enough, packing a pistol on one hip and a pint on the other."

Although Father McCabe may have scared the daylights out of his colleagues in Denver, he was beloved in rough-and-tumble Idaho Springs, where he stabilized a parish that had gone through ten priests and three churches in seventeen years.

Idaho Springs sprang up in a craggy mountain canyon in 1859, after George A. Jackson discovered gold near the junction of Chicago and Clear creeks. Despite nippy weather at 7,540 feet, the town's famous hot springs delighted miners and tourists, who helped sustain Idaho Springs during its long—and ongoing—cycle of mineral booms and busts.

After seventy years as St. Paul's, this Greek Revival cottage became a private residence in 1954. (Photo by Father Clement Green.)

After Bishop Machebeuf established St. Mary's in nearby Central City in 1861, its pastors tended Idaho Springs as a mission. By 1877, Bishop Machebeuf had purchased a small cottage northeast of "the castle," the stone mansion of Mayor Thomas B. Bryant at 1828 Illinois Street. This cottage was fitted up as a chapel and a residence for circuit-riding clergymen.

By 1881, Idaho Springs had become a town of 733, leading Bishop Machebeuf to establish St. Paul parish and appoint J.J. LePage as the first resident pastor. Father LePage constructed a small church, which was destroyed by fire in 1883. Afterwards, St. Paul's rented quarters over the offices of the local newspaper, the *Colorado Mining Gazette*. Father LePage was followed in 1884 by P. Sheridan, who immediately began work on a new church. Father Sheridan, another of the many priests come to Colorado in poor health, struggled mightily to complete the little frame church at the corner of Virginia Canyon Road and Virginia Street. While saying the first mass on Christmas Eve, 1884, in the still unfinished church, he contracted pneumonia and died shortly afterwards.

Michael Culkin, pastor from 1885 to 1886, completed the little frame church and also a small chapel, St. Michael's, five miles to the west in Lawson. After Father Culkin left, five short-term pastors struggled to keep both tiny churches open and pay off their debts.

Percy A. Phillips, chancellor of the diocese, had repeatedly to enlist new priests for the struggling

St. Paul parish. In a typical letter, written to a Father Brady in 1895, Phillips declared that "Idaho Springs is a lovely spot even in winter and I think the climate there is milder than Denver. . . . There is no necessity to worry about sick calls." Despite such propaganda, St. Paul's barely managed to remain open, thanks largely to the fund-raisers of the parish ladies. Annually the women of the Altar and Rosary Society (formerly the Ladies Aid Society) and the Servants of Mary staged a Catholic Fair in the now gone Opera House, entertaining the whole town with a bazaar, dinner, and dance.

Father McCabe came to the parish in 1898, and the town population reached its all-time peak in 1900—2,502. The population declined until the 1940s, when Idaho Springs bounced back to a relatively stable population of around 2,000. The nearby town of Lawson, however, dwindled, and in 1912, when only two Catholics lived there, St. Michael Chapel was closed.

Father McCabe guided St. Paul parish for forty-two years, retiring in 1940 and dying January 21, 1944. He was followed by fathers Forrest Allen (1941–1944), Francis P. Potempa (1944–1972), Edward H. Wintergalen, SJ (1972–1977), John J. Grabrian (1977–1984), John J. Murphy (1984–1987), and Francis Deml. During the 1940s, Father Potempa gained permission to build a larger church. Architect John K. Monroe designed a modern church and rectory on land donated by the D.J. Donnelly family, once the site of the Beebee House, the grandest hotel in Clear Creek County during the 1880s.

The quaint frame house that for sixty years was St. Paul's, with its front gable cross, plain frosted windows, and wooden altar and communion rail, still sits on James Dunn's placer mining claim at 338 Virginia Canyon Road. It is now a private residence, and the weathered white rooftop Celtic cross has been moved to the new buff brick church. Archbishop Vehr blessed the $75,000 church and rectory on March 1, 1955. The thirty-five parish families were joined by many non-Catholics who gathered that day for ceremonies. Among the celebrants were former pastor Allen, future pastor Wintergalen, and the widow of Cripple Creek mining magnate Spencer Penrose, who donated the organ.

For the 1981 centennial, St. Paul's recaptured the past in an eighteen-page parish history compiled by Mike Morris. Father Frank Deml, pastor since 1987, continues the circuit-riding traditions of his predecessors, ministering to St. Mary's in Central City and Our Lady of Lourdes in Georgetown, the two parishes that initally tended the Idaho Springs mission that became St. Paul's.

Iliff

ST. CATHERINE (1927)
111 South 5th Street

John Wesley Iliff, the king of Colorado cattleman, was the inspiration for the name of the South Platte River town on what was once part of his vast ranch. Father Peter U. Sasse, pastor of St. Anthony's in Sterling, said the first mass in the Iliff schoolhouse in 1911. Afterwards, masses were offered in various other schoolhouses and in the Glory Park Theater.

Proud parishioners of St. Catherine's assembled to dedicate their splendid new church on a hot July 31, 1927, when Bishop Tihen stood at the front door to deliver his famous oratorical masterpiece, "The Spirit of the West."

William Scherer, a German immigrant, became pastor at Peetz in 1924 and began parish building at the missions in Crook, Iliff, and Stoneham. Father Scherer persuaded one of his in-laws, a prominent Chicago architect and builder named Charles F. Roche (né Rochlitz), to design a church for Iliff. This Chicago big timer donated sixty days to supervising design and construction, while

Father Scherer served as concrete mixer and cement shoveler. Shortly after its completion, the church was gutted on August 18, 1926, by a fire of unknown origin. Undaunted, pastor and parishioners began rebuilding and celebrated Christmas in the brick, split-roof Gothic structure with a hardwood altar imported from Munich. After the sudden death of architect Roche in Sterling, the church settled for slightly less elegant elements, such as the cellophane saints on the plain glass windows.

Father Scherer, an artistic soul of musical abilities, composed "Greetings to the Bishop" for St. Catherine's debut. His composition, as well as "Ave Maria," "Veni Creator," and Bordesi's Mass in F were part of the dedicatory service led by Bishop Tihen on July 31, 1927. "Iliff had her largest crowd in recent years . . . only a third could find places inside the church," observed the *Sterling Advocate*. Afterwards, Bishop Tihen delighted the crowd of 1,800 with his oration, "The Spirit of the West."

A $14,000 rectory was built next to the church in 1930, and Godfrey Guthhausen became the first resident pastor, serving until his death in 1935. Herman J. Leite, the third pastor, often returned his meager salary to the parish to make ends meet. After strong winds sent the church chimney crashing through the rear ceiling in 1952, parishioners demolished their magnificent church and moved into the somewhat less grand parish hall.

With the help of a secondhand altar from Sacred Heart in Peetz, secondhand pews from Holy Family in Denver, and new cry and reconcilation rooms, the humble parish hall has been converted to a woodpaneled house of prayer, illuminated by Louis Rinaldo's stained glass windows.

The spirited little flock has supported itself ingeniously. When a Protestant church contemptuously refused an offer from the Coors Brewery to repair its roof as "beer money," parishioner Julia Dolan and Father John Stein of St. Catherine's wrote that they could use the money, and that "we of St. Catherine's Catholic Church have no objections to the manufacture, selling or drinking of beer. . . . In fact, at a recent parish picnic, Coors beer was the favorite beverage."

Shortly afterwards, St. Catherine's received a $500 check from the Adolph Coors Company. Although the 1980s flock of about seventy families is now a mission of Sacred Heart in Peetz, St. Catherine's spunky parishioners persist.

Johnstown

ST. JOHN THE BAPTIST (1937)
809 Charlotte Street

Johnstown was founded in 1902 by Harvey J. Parish, who named it for his seven-year-old son John. Hispanic laborers settled in the area after 1926, when the Great Western Sugar Company built an extraction plant there.

Juan Baca and Juan Trujillo—two of these farm workers—raised $400 in cash and promissory notes to finance a church. They helped persuade the sugar company to donate a site and in 1937 built a humble, $400 church with backless benches for pews. Bishop Vehr dedicated it on June 24, 1938, the feast of St. John the Baptist. The name also honored the two farm workers who spearheaded the project.

St. John the Baptist Church, Johnstown. (Photo by Tom Noel.)

Pastors from St. Joseph's in Fort Collins tended the little mission, which primarily served the Hispanic colony working at the sugar refinery and in the fields around Johnstown. In 1974, the growing parish bought the elegant old United Methodist Church, a Gothic gem built in 1884 at the urging of a pioneer Methodist circuit-riding minister, Cora M. Dilley. Originally located at Elwell, it had been moved into Johnstown in 1927. To commemorate the Methodist as well as the Catholic heritage of the church, Bishop George R. Evans concelebrated the dedication with Methodist minister H. Preston Childress.

Today, Thomas D. Kelly's flock at St. John the Baptist's keeps up the church beautifully. Behind two massive elm trees, the large belfry with its huge old black bell and gold cross on top summons the faithful to Tuesday, Thursday, Saturday, and Sunday masses. Father Kelly, an avid gardener, tends the lovely landscaping of both the white frame rectory and the handsome brick church.

Underneath the cool, high-ceilinged nave, a basement hall is used for parish gatherings and catechism classes. Johnstown's predominantly Hispanic congregation still remembers with fondness and appreciation the two dedicated founders named Juan.

Julesburg

ST. ANTHONY (1908)
606 West 3rd Street

One of the raunchiest towns in pioneer Colorado, Julesburg needed a church. Originating as Fort Sedgwick, it became a stagecoach town, then a Union Pacific railroad hell-on-wheels that harbored such criminals as Jack Slade, who murdered the town's eponym, Jules Beni, after cutting off his ear as a trophy.

Mark Twain, who passed through Julesburg, described it in *Roughing It* as "the strangest, quaintest, funniest frontier town" where Jack Slade was "more feared than the Almighty." Indians burned down Julesburg twice, but the town, tough as a thistle, always sprouted up again.

Two pioneer settlers were Catholic: the Belgian Adolph Eeckhout who settled into a sod-house farm with his family; and Uberto Gibello, an Italian homesteader who quarried the town's "Italian Caves" and built Julesburg's Brown Hotel. Upon his death in 1910, Gibello left his land and caves, by then a tourist attraction, to the sisters at Denver's Queen of Heaven Orphanage.

Not until 1906 did Bernard J. Froegel, resident pastor of St. Augustine's in Brighton, begin visiting Julesburg to offer masses. He used private homes,

the Sedgwick County court house, and the Union Pacific section house. Father Froegel and Adolph Eeckhout, chair of the collection committee, raised $2,700 to build a small church in 1908. At the request of A.A. Hirst of Philadelphia, who gave $1,000 to the Catholic Extension Society for the Julesburg church, it was named for St. Anthony of Padua.

Parishioners planted cottonwood trees on the lonesome prairie around the rusticated concrete-block church, which was constructed by contractor John Wren, a Julesburg resident and convert. Despite six inches of snow, St. Anthony's parishoners warmly welcomed Bishop Matz at the dedication on November 29, 1908. For the first decade, railroad-riding reverends from St. Anthony's in Sterling served Julesburg. Henry A. Geisert arrived as the first resident pastor in 1918, and parishioners helped him build a two-story rectory beside the church. Father Geisert was remembered for his scholarly work on criminology and for his "open air forum" street preaching.

Then there was Andrew C. Murphy, a most colorful pastor described in the 1983 parish diamond jubilee history:

> Father was a member of Teddy Roosevelt's "Roughriders" and periodically dressed up in his picturesque costumes. . . . To raise money Father Murphy bought a dozen or more piglets which he "farmed out" to various farmers to raise into marketable porkers. . . . Piqued when some of the farmers sold the animals "prematurely," he would walk on the opposite side of the street whenever he saw one of his disobedient flock. . . . During the fall fair in Julesburg, he set up his tent and made a few extra dollars for the church by telling fortunes.

Poor health forced Father Murphy to retire in 1941, when he was replaced by Andrew E. Warwick. Although extra pews had been squeezed into the front of the 1908 church, ushers still had to shoehorn the faithful into the Sunday services. To build a larger church, St. Anthony's parishioners, in the tradition of Father Murphy, went into show business, sponsoring bazaars, dinners, and carnivals with booths of chance—country store, bingo, and a baseball stand. With the proceeds, the congregation built a much larger church, designed by John K. Monroe and dedicated by Archbishop Vehr on June 21, 1949.

By 1989, the once wild town of Julesburg had become a peaceful agricultural center, and St. Anthony's a parish of almost 200 households. No startling episodes have marked the development of St. Anthony's, as Father Murphy put it fifty years ago, only slow and steady growth "like a little flower."

Keenesburg

HOLY FAMILY (1920)

"Keenesburg: The Home of 500 Happy People and a Few Soreheads," reads the highway sign in this Weld County farm town where about fifty families belong to Holy Family parish.

After 1904, when Monsignor Bernard J. Froegel was appointed dean of Brighton and northeastern Colorado, he began visiting Keenesburg. With his encouragement, local Catholic farmers dug out a basement and prepared the foundation for a church in 1918. Contractor John Dwyer completed a little brick church in the summer of 1919, when Bishop Tihen dedicated the structure.

Priests of St. Augustine's in Brighton cared for the Keenesburg mission until 1932, when Bernard Weakland became the first resident pastor, with responsibility for the missions of St. Isidore at Hudson and Sacred Heart at Roggen as well. He was followed by William J. Gallagher (1938–1944), who is remembered for his whistling parrot and beautiful sermons on the Blessed Virgin. Charles P. Sanger, the next pastor, stayed until 1949, when Holy Family was remanded to mission status, with the parish seat at Sacred Heart in Roggen.

During the 1950s, Keenesburg Catholics added a new tabernacle, padded kneelers, and an electric organ to the church. During the pastorate of Eugene Murphy, an Education Building was constructed for Confraternity of Christian Doctrine classes. Under the guidance of Robert L. Breunig since 1985, Holy Family parishioners have maintained their handsome, historic church and counted themselves among the town's happy folks.

Kremmling

ST. PETER (1944)

Where the Blue River and Muddy Creek flow into the Colorado River, Kare Kremmling established a general store that evolved into a town in 1905, when the Denver & Rio Grande Railroad decided to build through this remote stretch of Grand County.

Father Peter U. Sasse built a little white frame church in Kremmling, which was sporadically visited by missionary priests. Then came Thomas Patrick Barry in his 1939 Plymouth "with everything I owned in it" to establish a Grand County parish.

Father Barry tidied the little frame church and, as the first resident pastor at St. Peter's, built a rectory. "I put a big wooden cross on the rectory," Monsignor Barry recollected in 1988, "so that everyone—even the tramps and winos—would be able to find the priest. And I never encountered any anti-Catholicism. In fact, the Masons in Kremmling helped us stage our first bazaar for St. Peter's."

Father Barry soon distinguished himself not only as a devoted priest, but as a town character noted for his Irish wit, stories, and miraculous abilities as a fisherman. He showed compassion for everyone, even the German Prisoners of War at work camps in Kremmling, Gould, and Fraser. "I visited those Germans on Mondays," Monsignor Barry recalled. "They were very religious and we sang the Mass together, using Latin and their lovely German hymns at services in the POW mess halls."

With Kremmling's mayor, Carl Breeze, and Doctor A.C. Sudan, Father Barry helped found the Middle Park Community Hospital, using the former Sudan residence as its core building. He also tended missions at Grand Lake, Granby, Walden, and Winter Park until 1954, when Theodore Haas replaced him at the helm of the high country parish.

Since 1987, John G. Kauffman has been pastor at St. Peter's. Father Kauffman, who is noted for his book and lessons on gold panning, spruced up the charming, old-fashioned frame church in downtown Kremmling.

Lafayette

IMMACULATE CONCEPTION (1907)
110 West Simpson Street

Lafayette was founded in 1888 and incorporated in 1890 by Mary E. Miller. She named it for Lafayette Miller, her deceased husband, who had first homesteaded there in the 1870s. After the Millers found coal on their 640-acre spread, it evolved into the mining town of Lafayette.

Catholic miners in Lafayette persuaded Cyril Rettger, OSB, pastor of St. Louis's in nearby Louisville, to celebrate occasional masses in their homes in 1904. When attendance swelled, they resorted to the basement of the Lafayette bank and even to the Masonic lodge for Catholic services.

With the encouragement of Father Cyril, the Lafayette congregation proposed a new parish in 1906. "The first collection," Father Cyril announced the next Sunday, "will be for an altar stone and a chalice." Soon afterwards, Lafayette Catholics bought land at the northeast corner of Cannon Street and Roosevelt Road to construct a church they named for St. Ida. By Easter Sunday, 1907, the $7,000 church was far enough along to house its first mass. That August, Virgil Nisslein, OSB, became the first pastor of St. Ida's.

In this humble, white frame church with sheet-metal interior walls, Lafayette miners found strength during the bitter labor wars of the first two decades of the twentieth century. Half the congregation were forced to leave town during the 1910 coal strike. Nevertheless, Father Virgil and his tiny flock persisted and even helped tend missions in Superior, which had fifteen Catholic families, and Eastlake, which had an even smaller contingent.

The second pastor, Robert Murray, OSB, guided St. Ida's from 1914 to 1932. He was followed by another Benedictine, Urban Schnitzhofer, who purchased an unused building from the Columbine Mine Camp and converted it to a parish hall. After Father Schnitzhofer left in 1941, several pastors served briefly until the arrival of Rev. Joseph Hannan, OSB, in 1949.

Most of the coal mines had closed, but Lafayette began to grow during the 1950s as a bedroom community, a suburb of the flourishing Boulder–Denver metro area. This led Father Joseph in 1952 to purchase a new church site, which included a house that he converted to a rectory.

A modern, buff brick church with a red tile roof and life-sized Virgin over the entry was blessed by Archbishop Vehr in July 1954, when St. Ida's was rechristened Immaculate Conception in honor of the Marian Year. Father Martin Arno, the last Benedictine pastor, retired in 1968 because of failing health.

After losing the loyal and well-liked Benedictines, Immaculate Conception parishioners found new comfort in the Sisters of the Presentation. This Irish sisterhood moved to Louisville to teach at St. Louis School, then began visiting Immaculate Conception parish in 1971.

A Lafayette admirer donated a convent to another order, the Daughters of Charity. Sisters Patricia Ann Cleary and Carmen Ptacnik were the first to come, then Sister Hermine Regan, the first superior at Immaculate Conception. "Our work in Louisville is what our founder, St. Vincent de Paul, envisioned," Sister Mary Elizabeth Reed, superior of the order in Colorado, explained in 1987. "We work directly with the poor, visiting them in their homes, bringing them the Eucharist and sharing their losses. Besides directing the Religious Education Program in 1976, we worked with parishioners to open the Carmen Center three blocks from the church to provide food and clothing to the needy."

Since 1979, Michael Kerrigan, a Colorado native, has been pastor of Immaculate Conception parish. Father Kerrigan's flock grew in the 1980s to more than 500 families, including descendents of early-day coal miners who started St. Ida's and sustained Immaculate Conception.

Lakewood

CHRIST ON THE MOUNTAIN (1975)
13922 West Utah Avenue

As Jefferson County subdivisions began to climb the foothills during the 1970s, Archbishop Casey recognized the need for another parish in western Lakewood.

Richard B. Ling, appointed founding pastor on July 1, 1975, determined to make Christ on the Mountain an "open church," a post–Vatican II parish where the laity accepted full responsibilities. Parishioner Joyce Frink won the contest to name the church, which was planned and developed with lay input. Father Ling held the first mass in Green Mountain High School on July 19, 1975, while he and the membership began working on their dream parish.

Hoping to translate the aspiration of a post–Vatican II church into architectural reality, Father Ling and the Parish Profile Committee hired Denver architect Paul Foster, a graduate of Regis College and the University of California at Berkeley architectural school, to design a different kind of church. Speaking of the controversial result in 1987, Foster recollected:

> Father Ling, an outstanding liturgist, wanted to model Christ on the Mountain on the simpler earlier church. He asked me to simplify the symbolism in a "nonchurchy" church, which could serve many different functions. So we designed a box with poured-in-place concrete for a base and a wood frame and a textured, tawny-colored precast concrete panel superstructure. Inside, we used movable couches instead of pews. Harkening back to the early church, we designed a entry baptistry large enough for total immersion.

This boxy, brown church on the grassy eastern slope of Green Mountain greets visitors with the sound of running water. That happy splashing bubbles out of a copper tube fountain in its three-foot deep baptismal pool, which parish wits labeled Ling's Lagoon. Inside, the exposed redwood ceiling beams and the wrought iron sculptured stations of the cross are among the few embellishments. The movable altar platform and lectern are in the center of the hall, so parishioners look at each other as well as at the service. Underneath the church, a full basement contains a kitchen, a large multi-purpose hall, classrooms, and conference rooms.

After the church was dedicated October 28, 1978, on its seven-acre site, the parish bought a house at 12461 West Dakota Drive in September 1979, for use as a rectory and parish office. John F. X. Burton, SJ, who became the second pastor of Christ on the Mountain in 1982, reports:

The volunteerism of this parish is outstanding. Over 40 percent are active in one way or another. With over 500 parish families, we put this structure to many uses, ranging from our donut Sundays to parish dances, from our Family Life Ministry programs to religious ed[ucation] classes, from exercise classes to the Knights of Columbus Mothers' Day pancake breakfasts.

The future of the parish is bright with promise, as the number of families increases, as new responses to people's needs become reality, as the parish strives to remain faithful to being an "open church."

OUR LADY OF FATIMA (1958)
1985 Miller Street

Our Lady of Fatima parish was established by Archbishop Vehr on August 13, 1958, when Robert Syrianey was appointed the founding pastor. His parishioners were some 350 families who had previously been attending St. Bernadette, Sts. Peter and Paul, St. Mary Magdalene, or St. Joseph.

Our Lady of Fatima Altar and Rosary and Holy Name societies met at a local bank to organize parish activities, including the first social—a Christmas party in Sts. Peter and Paul's gymnasium. Father Syrianey moved into a house near the parish property and began offering daily masses in the remodeled carport. This carport–chapel also sheltered the first baptism and first wedding, while Sunday masses were held in the the Lakewood High School auditorium.

Meanwhile, the building committee worked with John K. Monroe to design a combination church, parish hall, and classroom building at 10530 West 20th Avenue. A gathering of white-surpliced, black-cassocked priests and altar boys joined Monsignor Delisle A. Lemieux on July 26, 1959, to break ground on a grassy field in suburban Lakewood. The first mass was celebrated June 26, 1960, when thirty youngsters received their first Holy Communion.

Archbishop Vehr dedicated the new complex on September 19, 1960. The annual Fall Fatima Festival that year, which included a dinner dance at the Brown Palace Hotel, raised $3,000, while other fund-raising campaigns and a tithing program enabled the parish to build eight classrooms that were opened in September 1964. The original rectory was converted to a convent for Benet Hill Benedictine sisters Irmina and Mary Giles, who began teaching with the help of two lay teachers. A new rectory was purchased across the avenue from the church.

By 1966, the parish included over 1,200 families, and a board of education was elected to help the fast-growing school. The board oversaw construction of a convent in 1966, and of a school addition for library, science, and audiovisual facilities in 1968.

Our Lady of Fatima became noted as the "partying parish" with its card parties, fashion shows, annual Mardi Gras and Fatima festivals, potluck suppers, bingo, square dancing, picnics, and ice cream socials. This active parish also conducted pilgrimages to Fatima, the tiny village in Portugal where "a Lady all of white, more brilliant than the sun and indescribably beautiful" appeared to three small children—Lucia, Francisco, and Jacinta—as they tended their sheep.

J. Harley Schmitt, a St. Thomas Seminary graduate who had also completed a doctorate in canon law at the Lateran University in Rome, became the second pastor of Our Lady of Fatima on July 15, 1970. Despite the inclusion of the southern part of Fatima parish in the 1967 formation of St. Jude parish, Father Schmitt's flock overflowed its meeting hall. In 1975, a building committee was formed to begin planning a new church. Four architects from within the parish—David E. Fritz, John F. Milan, Thomas E. Reck, and Ralph Santangelo—formed the Fatima Design Group. Together, they produced one of the finest pieces of modern church architecture in the archdiocese. Using textured precast concrete panels that echoed the huge entryway cross tower, the Fatima Group included graceful semicircular shapes to wrap a low-slung complex around a dramatic church, whose worship space is reminiscent of a theater. This state-of-the-art church even included special rooms for choir practice, altar boys, ushers, and brides. A band of stained glass windows, 3.5 feet high and ninety-two feet long, formed the clerestory light of the church. These windows, containing over 1,400 pieces of hand faceted Dalle glass, portray the miracle of "the dancing sun." Archbishop Casey and hundreds of parishioners dedicated the new edifice on August 13, 1978, the parish's twentieth anniversary.

After moving into the showcase church, the parish renewed its efforts to help others. Service committees tended to the sick in homes and in hospitals and to the elderly at home and in nursing homes, and distributed Christmas gifts and food to the needy. Our Lady of Fatima also contributed generously to the new St. Jude parish and to the maintenance of struggling core city parishes.

After eighteen years in which Benedictine sisters guided Our Lady of Fatima's kindergarten through eighth-grade school, Donald McMaster, who had been teaching there for twelve years, became the first lay principal in 1984. In 1987, Our Lady of Fatima's completed a $1,300,000 parish center and rectory, enabling it to celebrate its thirtieth birthday in a complete, modern parish plant serving 1,828 parish families. In the fall of 1988, parishioners rejoiced at the news that their long-time pastor, Harley Schmitt, had been elevated to the rank of monsignor.

ST. BERNADETTE (1947)
7240 West 12th Avenue

When St. Bernadette parish was created on July 2, 1947, Archbishop Vehr had already acquired a five-acre oat field near Wadsworth Boulevard, which houses the parish plant to this day.

John J. Doherty, a native of Killarney, County Kerry, was transferred from Cripple Creek to establish the first Catholic church in Lakewood. "We charge you in a special manner with the responsibility of seeking out all the lapsed Catholics," Archbishop Vehr wrote in his July 3, 1947, letter assigning Doherty to Lakewood, and "to have a special solicitude for all the non-Catholics."

While making plans for a church, Father Doherty began saying masses on August 17, 1947, at West 11th Avenue and Balsam Street in a small Veterans of Foreign Wars hall guarded by a huge howitzer. The veterans were glad to rent the hall for $15 on Sunday mornings provided no one moved the pool tables. This turned out to be a blessing in disguise as parishioners found the tables ideal for changing diapers and as cots for sleeping babies.

Architect John K. Monroe, a Lakewood resident, designed a brick rectory and stone church, which, in unfinished state, housed its first mass on

Christmas Eve, 1948. The twelve pews filled quickly at St. Bernadette's, whose parish boundaries—Sheridan Boulevard on the east, West Colfax Avenue on the north, Maple Grove Street on the west, and West Alameda Avenue on the south—embraced over 200 Catholic families.

After the church debt was retired in 1951, Father Doherty and Archbishop Vehr had architect James Johnson of Lakewood design a school. George Tollefson, a parishioner, served as the contractor for the one-story, eight-room, $150,000, brick school, which opened in September 1953. The four lay teachers who opened the school were followed in the fall of 1954 by five Sisters of Charity of Leavenworth, who commuted from Mount St. Vincent Orphanage.

The school always seemed crowded as St. Bernadette's was a parish of young people with rapidly growing families. Sister Mary Anysia, SCL, the principal, expanded it to six grades in 1955. Four additional acres of land were acquired as a playground and a possible future high school site; four more classrooms were added in 1956. Five years later, when enrollment had soared to 756 pupils, architect J. K. Monroe designed a second-story, eight-classroom addition.

A small house at 1120 Vance Street, purchased as a convent for the sisters, also became overcrowded. The nuns moved, in February 1960, to a modern, two-story, buff brick convent at the corner of West 10th Avenue and Upham Street. The old bungalow convent became the parish caretaker's home. After the Sisters of Charity left the parish in 1986, the Sisters of Our Lady of the Cenacle leased their old convent.

St. Bernadette church overflowed, despite a 1956 addition making room for 200 worshippers. Lakewood, which boomed during and after World War II, zoomed from a 1940 population of 1,701 to 19,338 in 1960. Our Lady of Fatima parish, created in 1958, served Lakewood Catholics living west of Garrison Street. Still, St. Bernadette's pews filled on Sundays, inspiring parishioners in 1964 to pledge $210,000 toward a new church.

Archbishop Vehr dedicated the new church, designed by architect Henry De Nicola, on May 16, 1966. While adhering to traditional church shape, it is modern in its clean lines and functional use of space. The church filled on Sundays even though St. Jude parish was created in 1967 for Lakewood

Catholics living south of Alameda and west of Wadsworth.

Father Doherty, who never lost his Irish brogue and sense of humor, retired at the age of seventy, after thirty-five years at the parish he had founded. He had come from Ireland to Denver, suffering from tuberculosis. He graduated from St. Thomas Seminary at age twenty-five in 1937, about the same time his medically predicted lifespan had expired. Hundreds of parishioners turned out for his 1982 retirement party, congratulating him on turning an oat field into a flourishing, debt-free parish.

The second pastor of St. Bernadette's is Father Edward T. Madden, a Denver native with three sisters who are all Sisters of Loretto. In a 1986 interview with parish historian Lou Duvall, Father Madden listed as one success an ecumenical effort with other Lakewood churches to establish In Jesus' Name Shelter, which provides food, clothing, and housing for the needy.

Among other parish coups, Father Madden included the Catholic Native Americans who meet every Sunday in Damien Hall, a chapel in the basement of the original church. Father John Quentin O'Connell, a Vincentian priest, organized this group in 1968, and it began meeting regularly at St. Bernadette's in 1985. Known as the Kateri Takakwitha Community, this Native American group welcomes all visitors to its masses and social events, which incorporate American Indian traditions. Among the regulars have been Charles Chaput, a Prairie Band Potowatamie who, in 1988, was ordained a bishop of Rapid City, South Dakota, a diocese of 35,000 including many Native Americans.

St. Bernadette's celebrated its fortieth anniversary in 1987. It had come a long way since 1947, when a few families gathered in the little VFW Hall for Father Doherty's first mass in what was then an unincorporated town of around 3,000 folks. Forty years later, Lakewood was an incorporated city of 112,860, the fourth largest in Colorado. And St. Bernadette parish, which as the pioneer Catholic church of Lakewood had given birth to three newer parishes, remains a prosperous community of 983 families with a thriving kindergarten through eighth-grade school.

St. Bernadette's in 1988 celebrated the opening of the Courtyard, 124 one- and two-bedroom apartments across the street from the church. Lakewood's Mayor Linda Shaw presided at the dedication of this senior housing effort, declaring, "Keeping our seniors here in Lakewood enriches our community, and we are delighted to welcome this very desirable and attractive addition to our city."

ST. JUDE (1967)
9405 West Florida Avenue

On August 22, 1967, St. Jude parish was created by Archbishop Casey to care for the fast growing area of southwest Lakewood, Green Mountain, and unincorporated southeastern Jefferson County. A census taker found 1,151 Catholic families in this area stretching from Wadsworth Boulevard to Hog Back Road, from Bear Creek to West Alameda Avenue. From three names recommended by a vote of the parishioners, Archbishop Casey chose St. Jude, patron of the hopeless.

Among those grateful for St. Jude's interest in difficult cases would be Lien Bui, then a one-year-old girl in Vietnam. After the Vietnamese war ended in 1975, Lien, her sister, two brothers, an aunt, an uncle, and her parents fled to America, where they were placed in a refugee camp at Fort Chaffee, Arkansas.

"We couldn't leave that camp," Lien explained in 1986, "until someone volunteered to help us make a new life in America. We had filled out many applications, but I was tired of hoping when Dad came home with the good news, 'We've been accepted by St. Jude Catholic Church in Lakewood, Colorado!' My Mom was overjoyed because we had been accepted by a Catholic church."

Jack and Karen Whittier headed the nine couples who had worked with Catholic Community Services to sponsor the Buis, welcoming them to a new house, filled with food, clothing, furniture, and toys. One couple enrolled Lien and her siblings in school. Another found her aunt a job sewing in a factory and showed her how to get to work, patiently driving behind the slow RTD bus to make sure she did not get lost. Another couple taught Mr. Bui how to drive to his job with Catholic Community Services, where he helped resettle other Southeast Asians.

"We soon learned to call our sponsors aunties and uncles," Lien wrote in a parish history for her Colorado history class at the University of Colorado at Denver. "They made us feel comfortable in a place where no other Vietnamese had resettled. They helped us with problems big or little. When my skin grew itchy and white and flaky all over, Karen reassured us it was caused by Colorado's dry atmosphere. She brought over some lotion."

Despite the fact that St. Jude's was the sixth largest parish in the archdiocese, with 2,138 registered families by 1986, it has been able to reach out to individual families like that of Lien Bui. When St. Jude's was created from the overflow of St. Bernadette, Notre Dame, St. Anthony of Padua, and Our Lady of Fatima parishes, William E. Sievers, the founding pastor, wrestled with the size factor. Like many other new suburban parishes, St. Jude's embraced many new subdivisons of strangers lacking the traditions and long-time neighborliness of older churches.

To strengthen parish bonds while St. Jude Church was in the planning and construction stages, Father Sievers held masses for his flock at "St. Alameda's," as Alameda High School auditorium was dubbed. For the convenience of all parts of his sprawling, eighteen–square mile parish, Father Sievers also held services and parish activites in the Notre Dame Parish Hall, in a Presbyterian church, and in the homes of parishioners. Father Sievers, a Denver native with a strong sense of community, came up with a novel solution to helping his parishioners get acquainted: He created twenty-six "little parishes."

Meanwhile, a ten-acre site, bounded on the north by Kendrick Lakes Elementary School and on the east by the lakes and a park, was bought on December 21, 1967. Denver architect Roland M. Johnson designed a church on the knoll with downtown Denver skyscrapers looming to the east, and Red Rocks Park and Mount Morrison commanding the western horizon.

A decidedly modern structure with nine irregular sides was begun on November 5, 1968. Huge steel arches served as the skeleton while burnt-orange brick was used as the skin beneath a rust-colored roof. The main entry is on the east, where churchgoers are welcomed by a life-sized linden wood statue of St. Jude, handcarved in Oberammergau, Germany. Three separate naves facing the altar seat 900 people. The fan-shaped clustering of the three banks of pews was designed so that no one is farther than seventy-five feet from the altar, a simple oak table symbolizing the humble furnishings of the Last Supper. The stained glass windows representing the eight beatitudes were crafted by Alice Alter of Denver's Watkins Stained Glass Company.

For the dedication on April 5, 1970, neighboring Protestant ministers and Jewish rabbis were welcomed among the hundreds who watched Archbishop Casey bless the new church. Some parishioners felt "consternation" about the contemporary architecture according to Ron Brockway, a Regis College history professor and founding member of the parish, who wrote "Saint Jude Church." Most, however, were delighted to have their own church at last.

This growing congregation in the booming suburbs of Jefferson County peaked at almost 3,000 registered households in 1975. That year 800 families in the area west of Union Boulevard became part of a new parish, Christ on the Mountain.

The young and lively families of St. Jude's did not stop with completion of their $359,000 church. In August 1974, they completed the St. Jude Youth Center—which claims to be the first in the Archdiocese of Denver. This $700,000 facility includes classrooms, meeting rooms, and offices for the Youth Ministry. Ten years later, on October 28, 1984, the St. Jude Community Center was dedicated. It houses administrative offices, a library, and a small chapel for weddings, funerals, and daily masses. This center hosts pancake breakfasts and spaghetti suppers, wedding receptions and Bible study classes, as well as the meetings of such parish groups as the Young Marrieds, the Singles, the Divorced and Separated, and the Prime Timers. Alienated Catholics, a unique St. Jude's effort, reaches out to ex-Catholics. "The idea is not so much to reconvert them," as Pastor Robert J. Kinkel explained in 1986, "as to listen to why they left the church."

St. Jude's contributes 15 percent of the regular Sunday offertory collection to help the needy around the parish, around the archdiocese, and around the world. Over the years, this relatively affluent suburban parish has provided both funds and volunteer workers for struggling inner city parishes. St. Jude's has also helped to build and maintain a church in Maracaibo, Venezuela, and reached out to Southeast Asian refugees.

Parishioners donate time, expertise, and money to the In Jesus' Name Shelter, an interdenominational bed, breakfast, and supper program for families and single women in Lakewood. Various Lakewood churches host the shelter on a three-month rotating basis. The Catholic Worker Soup Kitchen in downtown Denver, the Bread for the World organization fighting global hunger, and Birthright, Inc., a pregnancy counseling program, are among the twenty-seven outreach programs to which St. Jude's contributes over $50,000 a year.

Father Sievers left the parish in 1976; he was followed by John R. Slattery, and then by Robert J. Kinkel, pastor since 1981. "Father Sievers gave St. Jude's a vision of what a post–Vatican II parish should be," reflected Father Kinkel in 1986. "Our people have continued in that spirit of mutual ministry, saying yes to all that will be."

Littleton

LIGHT OF THE WORLD (1979)
10306 West Bowles Avenue

On one of the highest hills of Denver's southwestern outskirts looms a dramatic new church, Light of the World. The parish was created by Archbishop Casey in 1979, when 650 Catholic families lived in the area and twenty more subdivisons were under construction.

Francis Syrianey, the founding pastor, first held services in the gym of Colorow Elementary School at 6317 South Estes Street. He rented a house at 6295 South Flower Way as a rectory and used the full basement for parish meetings. All the while, Father Syrianey, a noted liturgist and church scholar, was planning a modern building that would be both functional and inspiring. He put together a design team that included Eugene Walsh, a liturgical consultant, John Buscemi, a liturgical artist, four parishioners, and Karl Berg of Denver's Hoover Berg Desmond architectural firm.

"The new building," Father Syrianey told the Denver Catholic Register of March 5, 1986, "was designed from the inside out. Berg did not put a line on paper until he had sat down together with the staff, the consultants, the building committee and myself to put down in writing who we are, what we are, where we are and what we wanted in a building."

The hilltop site, above the busy retail strip of Bowles Avenue and overlooking proliferating subdivisions, had been acquired by Archbishop Vehr. There, Father Syrianey and his team designed a church of modest materials—brick, drywall, laminated timber, and glass blocks. The ecclesiastical complex embraced the traditional forms of baptistry, cloister, colonnade, eucharistic chapel, gallery, worship space, and tower.

The tower rising above the baptistry is a geometric design of circles and squares, two conflicting shapes reconciled at the top to symbolize the guiding principle that the church community is a place for reconciling opposites. *Progressive Architecture* magazine, which made Light of the World its cover story for the February 1986 issue, praised the structure for "clarity, modesty, and the almost spiritual elegance of its organization."

The Colorado chapter of the American Institute of Architects concurred and presented one of its Honor Awards for Design Excellence to Hoover Berg Desmond for this edifice.

Archbishop Stafford blessed the new church on September 13, 1987, telling a standing-room-only crowd, "You are the light of the world, you dear brothers and sisters, as you sit on this high hill, silhouetted with those magnifcent mountains behind us." Father Syrianey was not there to see this dedication of the church he began, as he had passed away January 1, 1986.

John F. Dold, pastor since 1986, affirmed in 1988 that the fast growing parish of some 1,800 registered families had over sixty active parish and community organizations. Interviewed in *The Denver Post* of June 27, 1987, Father Dold said, "I have never been in a place where liturgy works so well, because of the simplicity and openness of the place and the openness of the people."

Light of the World with its spectacular tower—a square brick facade meeting a conical blonde brick one with a quarter cone skylight on top—has become a striking landmark of the southwest metro area. This tower catches light by day for the baptistry below and by night is an illuminated symbol of the Light of the World.

ST. FRANCES CABRINI (1973)
6673 West Chatfield Avenue

Archbishop Casey, who lived in the Columbine Country Club neighborhood, asked George L. Weibel to establish a parish in that fast growing Southwest metro Denver suburb. Initially, the new congregation was named for the area it served, Columbine Valley, which in turn was named for the Colorado state flower, the columbine. In Latin, the word means "of the dove," so that for Catholics the beautiful blossom also symbolizes the Holy Spirit. Not until November 13, 1988, was the parish name changed to honor the first American saint, Mother Frances Cabrini.

Father Weibel, former pastor of Denver's Holy Family parish, moved to Columbine to form a new parish in what had been the western part of St. Mary's in Littleton. Knocking on doors, he found families of the faithful and places to say home masses. The first parishwide mass was celebrated in Columbine Hills Elementary School on September 9, 1972. By Christmas, the parish had been formally established with boundaries of West Bowles Avenue on the north, South Sheridan Boulevard and South Platte Canyon Road on the east, Chatfield Reservoir State Park on the south, and the mountains on the west.

The "People of the Dove" built a house of the Lord that Archbishop Casey blessed and dedicated on September 21, 1974. Pioneer parishioners handmade the Good Samaritan mosaic on the altar, affirming the commitment of this relatively affluent flock to help poorer parishes and peoples.

A large addition to the original structure was completed in September 1977, for use as Sunday mass overflow seating, recreational activities, and other purposes. The addition included a nursery, a Renew room, religious education offices, classrooms and space for the Sunday children's liturgy.

With the 1977 addition, Columbine parish could accommodate 1,200 parishioners. Within two years, the number of registered families passed this limit, leading Archbishop Casey to establish a spiritual child of the Columbine congregation, Light of the World parish.

Even with the creation of the new parish for the folks living north of Ken Caryl Road, Columbine parish bounced back to 1,300 parishioners by 1981. Jesuit fathers and archdiocesan priests helped

Father Weibel with his burgeoning Mass and sacramental work load. In April 1981, a rectory was completed with much-needed office space, as well as living quarters for Father Weibel.

Roger W. Mollison became the second pastor of Columbine parish on September 8, 1984. "Father Weibel graciously and humbly chose to serve as associate pastor," according to the parish historian. By 1986, the parish had programs ranging from adult athletics to a blood bank, from Neighbors in Need to Bible study, as well as religious and special education for preschool through high school.

"Spirit of the Dove" continued to inspire parishioners in many ways. For example, after Father Mollison's sermon on child abuse, a couple offered to convert their house into the St. Joseph Home for Abused Children. It opened in October 1986, with the official sanction of Jefferson County Social Services. Another couple, who have five children of their own, volunteered to run the home with the help of dozens of other parishioners who have been trained by the county social services department. Columbine parishioners provisioned the house, and a physician in the parish agreed to be the *pro bono publico* doctor for the home.

This effort to deal with abused children is just one of the ways that members exemplify the work of the Good Samaritan, whose mural graces their altar. In 1988, Columbine worked with St. Gregory Episcopal Church next door to build an ecumenical prayer garden, which straddles their common boundary line. Father Mollison reported in 1988 that the congregation hopes to build new office and classroom space, which is desperately needed in this thriving community of 1,500 families. For its thirty community outreach programs, St. Frances Cabrini's was honored in 1988 as the "Archdiocesan Respect Life Parish of the Year."

ST. MARY'S (1901)
6843 South Prince Street

"Will you please hereafter take care of Littleton giving them Mass twice a month on Sundays?" With these words, on September 7, 1900, Bishop Matz assigned Richard Brady to the small Catholic community south of Loretto Heights College along the South Platte River.

"A little toy church" was pastor Gregory Smith's fond description of the first St. Mary's.

With his black buggy pulled by his horse, Jack, Father Brady drove the six miles from his home at Loretto Heights to Littleton to say mass for the families who gathered in the Masonic Hall on Main Street. Forty-five parishioners adopted the name St. Mary's Roman Catholic Church Society on December 9, 1900. They elected a committee of five, including Father Brady, to direct the building of the new church on the corner of Powers and Nevada. Land valued at $550 had been donated by Littleton pioneer Joseph W. Bowles.

The first St. Mary Church, a simple brick building fifty-by-thirty feet, seating 150 people, was blessed, and Father Brady celebrated the first mass on October 11, 1901. A pot-bellied stove in the back of the church warmed parishioners, who arrived in wagons and buggies from as far as twenty miles away.

Father Brady and his successor, Edward Clarke, who came in 1914, were both natives of Ireland who came to Colorado to improve their health. Father Brady was remembered for his catechism classes after mass on Sundays. Father Clarke, who loved music, often sang and played his violin at gatherings and, in 1917 started a choir.

Father Clarke acquired the parish house on South Nevada Street, a landmark in Littleton for the next sixty years. One staunch parishioner at St. Mary's was James Maloney, who as mayor of Littleton built the exquisite Beaux-Arts Littleton Public Library at the west end of Main Street. One of the Maloneys' seven children was David, who would become auxiliary bishop of Denver and, in 1967, bishop of Wichita, Kansas.

After the brief assignments of Charles Hagus and Joseph Oldenburg, the French Canadian Joseph Desaulnier served from 1920 to 1928, when young Gregory Smith arrived, full of hopes and plans for Littleton's Catholics.

"Littleton was then a little country town," Monsignor Smith recalled in a 1987 interview at the Mullen Home for the Aged. "Half my people were farmers. We had a little red brick 'toy' church." One of Father Smith's inspirations, the first vacation school for religious education, was begun at St. Mary's, when Bishop Tihen appointed Father Smith director for the Propagation of the Faith in 1927, a post he held until 1975.

Littleton, though the Arapahoe County seat, was a rural community of about 2,000 souls in the 1930s, when Father Smith served the fifty to sixty Catholic families, including a devoted group who came up from Louviers. Hubert Newell led St. Mary's from 1939 until he was named bishop of Cheyenne. The parish, with its youthful spirit, was ready for the young Father Frederick McCallin when he began a twenty-year love affair with St. Mary's in 1947. His vision, energy, and spirituality infused his people in those years of phenomenal growth.

By 1951, three Sisters of St. Joseph of Carondelet had arrived to open a school in the new parish hall. Ten years later, over 1,000 students filled eight grades, with another 1,000 students attending Confraternity of Christian Doctrine classes as the congregation mushroomed to 1,400 families. In the little church, over 3,000 people came to mass each Sunday. With the passing of the town's pioneer employer, the Rough and Ready Flour Mill, and the arrival of the Martin Marietta Aerospace Company, Littleton hit the "big time."

To accommodate all the newcomers, Father McCallin built St. Mary's new facilities south of town, on a hillside with a beautiful view of the foothills. The new church was dedicated on September 13, 1962, by Archbishop Vehr. "You're doing fine! Keep up the good work!"—Father McCallin's favorite phrase—was surely inscribed somewhere in the bricks and mortar of the beautiful new parish plant.

In 1968, Michael Kavanagh came to St. Mary's. During his five years, the people adapted to the many changes that Vatican II asked of Catholics. Through Parish Outreach, support was given to adopted causes and parishes in Denver's inner city, to the Interfaith Task Force, and to many clothing and housing needs.

Almost any occasion would be a cause for St. Mary's people to celebrate, be it at the annual Steer Roast or the Fall Festival, newcomers' parties or square dances. Father Kavanagh initiated home masses in small neighborhood "miniparishes," striving for more intimate, personal services that found their extension in the successful St. Mary's Renew program.

When Father Kavanagh moved to Colorado Springs in 1973, St. Mary's housekeeper for thirty-five years, Anna Brooks, retired to the Mullen Home. From 1973 to 1987, the pastor was Leonard Alimena, who portrayed St. Mary's as a "microcosm of community, where the people minister to the minister more than he ministers to them."

Social ministry is a priority of the parish, which now includes a director of pastoral care on the staff, as well as the Stephen ministers, who volunteer one-on-one, and the Marthas, on call each week to serve domestic needs in the community. Youth programs and study clubs, the popular Sunshine Club for seniors, the parish newsletter—*Reflections*—and a Justice and Peace Committee are all part of Parish Outreach.

The new parish center built in 1976–1977 increased gathering places for education and recreation. St. Mary School, in 1987, had 276 children in the primary grades at the Nevada Street complex and 197 older children at the Prince Street Middle School. In the summer of 1987, finding the number of their sisters living at St. Mary's reduced to three, the Sisters of St. Joseph of Carondelet established a new residence at 1821 West Briarwood Avenue. The building that had housed the sisters for twenty years was converted to a pastoral center.

During the 1970s, Sister Marianne Keene and Sister Barbara Dreher designed a religious education program and summer vacation school that made St. Mary's famous for preparing and supporting parents as the primary religious educators of their children. St. Mary's choir relishes not only sacred music both performed and recorded but also enjoys giving a yearly amateur variety show, which benefits the religious education of developmentally disabled persons. One of the favorite faces for many years—and very special to a small group of children —is Reverend Larry Freeman, whose special religious education classes were indeed special.

Joseph Monahan took over as pastor in 1987 to discover that the little "toy" church in a tiny farm town has evolved into a large parish plant serving 2,800 parishioners in a booming suburb of about 30,000 people.

Longmont

ST. JOHN THE BAPTIST (1882)
315 4th Avenue

Longmont, a Boulder County town founded at the junction of St. Vrain and Left Hand creeks in 1871, was named for Long's Peak, soaring in snowcapped splendor on the western horizon. The Chicago–Colorado Colony, an idealistic group of Chicagoans who dreamed of a better life in a rural utopia, purchased the 640-acre Longmont site after a super sales talk from *Rocky Mountain News* editor William N. Byers. The colony offered settlers of "industry, temperance, and morality" three town lots and outlying farmsteads in exchange for $155 memberships.

Approximately 500 colonists soon transformed Longmont into a model town with a communal irrigation system, tree-lined streets, and attractive homes, schools, and churches. Longmont grew slowly but steadily as an agricultural town, absorbing the nearby town of Burlington, a collection of log cabins begun in 1860.

Irish Catholics came to town in 1873 with the first railroad. Bishop Machebeuf said the first mass in the railroad section house of Longmont section boss Michael O'Connor. Before persuading priests to come to Longmont, O'Connor and his family had pumped their way to Boulder's Sacred Heart church in a railroad handcar. Priests from Denver and Boulder paid monthly visits to the section house until 1881, when services were moved to a second floor suite of the newly constructed Zweck (now Imperial) Hotel on Main Street.

Lawrence and William Mulligan donated two lots on the east side of Collyer Street between 3rd and 4th avenues, where this small parish of about

Catholics and non-Catholics gathered for the July 22, 1905, dedication of St. John the Baptist's new stone home, with Bishop Matz officiating. (Photo by Ed Tongon.)

twenty families, aided by generous contributions from many Longmont non-Catholics, completed a $1,117 twenty-by-forty-foot, frame church. As there were no pews, Michael O'Connor and his family donated chairs, and other parishioners helped complete the humble furnishings. This quaint, front-gable church with plain windows and a huge Celtic cross on top was consecrated by Bishop Machebeuf on June 24, 1882, the feast of St. John the Baptist.

Benedictines from Boulder and the pastor of St. Joseph's in Fort Collins tended the church, staying in a parsonage completed in 1891. Not until the spring of 1902 did Longmont receive a resident pastor, Father Nicholas Seidl, OSB (Order of St. Benedict). Father Seidl and his flock of about thirty families purchased two lots for $1,300 and engaged a Denver architect, Fred W. Paroth, to design and supervise construction of a new church. The old church was sold to Longmont's Norwegian Lutheran congregation for $4,150 to help pay for the new $14,000 Gothic church. Inside, it was forty-two feet by ninety-six feet; outside, it was dressed handsomely in alternating courses of smooth and rusticated red sandstone rising to a corner steeple height of 100 feet. Bishop Matz blessed the new church on July 22, 1905.

Over the years, parishioners used "Social Teas" and "Sacrifice Sunday Collections" to furnish their new church grandly. In 1910, artists from Pittsburg, Pennsylvania, were commissioned to paint a fresco in the vaulted interior, where a large chandelier was hung to illuminate the magnificent artwork. Three elaborate Gothic altars were installed a year later. Parishioners raised $1,000 in 1914, matching a grant from the Carnegie Organ Fund, to install a large pipe organ in the hanging wooden choir loft.

A large, brick, two-story rectory with a wrap-around verandah was completed in 1907 for $2,328 at the corner of 4th Avenue and Collyer Street. The community of Benedictines living there made missionary rounds throughout the area, tending congregations at Erie, Frederick, Lyons, and Mead, where in 1911 they established a new parish, Guardian Angels.

In 1907, St. John's helped give birth—accidentally—to a Franciscan school in Longmont. This episode began in 1906 when Mother Thecla and Sister Celestine of the Sisters of St. Francis of Milwaukee, Wisconsin, came to Colorado hoping to open an academy. Bishop Matz recommended Loveland as a good site. The nuns boarded the train for Loveland, but when the conductor called out the Longmont stop, these German-speaking sisters mistakenly got off. Thomas F. Mahoney, president of the Longmont Chamber of Commerce and a staunch St. John's parishioner, found them stranded, gave each a dollar, and began a conversation. Mahoney persuaded the grateful sisters to stay in Longmont, where he arranged for them to live at the home of David C. Donovan, another prominent Catholic, who presided over the First National Bank of Longmont.

Mahoney, Donovan, and Father Nicholas helped the Franciscan sisters purchase the old Presbyterian Academy, a handsome, four-story brick and stone building erected about 1884 at 6th Avenue and Atwood Street. Mother Thecla and Sister Celestine converted the former Protestant school to a convent and St. Joseph Academy. Sister Ermita opened a kindergarten and arranged for a horse-drawn school bus to bring in children, Catholics and non-Catholics alike, for lessons in "music, games, and politeness—but no religion." Tuition was fifty cents a week. By 1920, St. Joseph's bulged with 110 students, and St. John's parishioners and the sisters bought Cena Sampson's home, a large two-story house on four Atwood Street lots, for $10,350. They converted it to a boarding school and built a bungalow on the grounds for the upper grades. Although the Sampson house burned in 1922, it was replaced quickly, and in September 1926, St. John's constructed a $70,000, two and a half-story, red brick high school on the corner of 4th Avenue and Emery Street, next to the church. Although St. John High School closed in 1929, the grade school survived until 1982.

Thomas F. Mahoney, the parishioner who had persuaded the lost nuns to establish a Longmont school, also became a nationally noted champion of Spanish-speaking migrant workers. These poor seasonal workers, exploited by some farmers and the Great Western sugar beet plants of Loveland and other nearby towns, found a friend in Mahoney and comfort in the programs, including an annual fiesta, which he and St. John's began developing during the 1920s.

St. John the Baptist parish was guided by Father Nicholas until 1924, when he was transferred to Canton, Ohio, where he died on December 7, 1926. Various Benedictine priests briefly guided St. John's until 1940, when Father James Mahrer, OSB, began a nineteen-year stint as pastor. In 1958, he supervised construction of a $100,000 convent. Father Martin Arno, OSB, pastor from 1959–1966, converted the old high school into grade-school classrooms and renovated the old grade school. In 1962, the parish demolished its magnificent old stone church to build a large, modern $375,000 edifice completed for midnight Christmas mass in 1963. The modern, pyramidical brick church, with its tubular bell tower, seated 760, more than double the size of the old structure. Keith Ames, the architect, was a member of the parish and also designed the new Longmont Municipal Building.

The 1906 frame rectory is now gone; the nuns moved into a brick house at 337 Collyer in 1976 when their convent was converted to the Religious Education Center. The Hart house at 328 Emery was purchased in 1974 and remodeled as the parish Teen House. To provide food, clothing, second-hand goods, and counseling for the needy, St.

John's opened Samaritan House in 1971 in an antique cottage at 313 Collyer Street; the cottage was razed in 1978 and replaced by a new building, largely constructed by volunteer parish labor. Rechristened "OUR Center," it now serves hot lunches daily and distributes clothing to the needy as Longmont's ecumenical Outreach United Resource Center.

Fathers Gregory Hudson (1966–1970) and Patrick Noll (1970–1971) were the last Benedictine pastors at St. John the Baptist's. Archdiocesan priests subsequently served as pastors: fathers James Purfield (1971–1972), Thomas Stone (1973–1974), and Walter R. Jaeger (1974–1984). Michael W. Gass and Joseph E. Monahan, co-pastors of St. John's from 1984 to 1987, developed a notable program for elderly, homebound, and handicapped parishioners, commissioning almost 100 of these often neglected and unappreciated people as "Ministers of Praise." In ceremonies honoring their new role as special parishioners, Father Monahan gave each an olivewood cross from the Holy Land, a prayer book, and a certificate of membership.

James E. Fox, pastor since 1987, has focused on the Hispanic ministry in conjunction with Spirit of Peace parish. Father Fox also focused efforts on social action and the 1989 construction of a multipurpose parish center. Six sisters living in the Franciscan convent not only helped maintain the school, which offers kindergarten through ninth-grade classes, but also are engaged in a wide variety of parish and community ministries. St. John the Baptist parish, whose history is well documented in 1921, 1955, and 1982 booklets, is an old but thriving church in one of Colorado's fastest growing towns.

SPIRIT OF PEACE (1982)
1500 Hover Road

This small, nontraditional parish was the brain child of Father Daniel Flaherty, who suggested:

> Maybe, just maybe, if people shared facilities with another faith community, it would be possible to direct their resources principally to ministry and to outreach, while, at the same time, develop a deeper respect and understanding for those of a different faith.

In this spirit, Spirit of Peace parish was created and has shared quarters with Westview Presbyterian Church, rather than focusing parishioners' time, trouble, and money on parish building. "Without a debt or interest payments," Father Flaherty reports that the parish is able to give "80 percent of all funds to direct people ministry." Tom Brown, pastor of Westview Presbyterian, welcomed the Catholics and joined in the August 1, 1982, dedication mass of Archbishop Casey.

As Father Flaherty initially resided in Estes Park, where he served as pastor of Our Lady of the Mountain parish, day-to-day parish management and activities were placed in the hands of a five-person full-time parish team. Those on the team since the beginning have been Sister Dorothy Feehan, BVM, Rose Mullen, Margo Tiller, John Rejeske, and, since 1985, Jerry Jacobitz.

While providing complete parish ministry, this team continues to enable and nurture small Christian communities of which there are twenty in the parish, involving some 250 people who, in turn, help minister to the total community of Longmont. This team has overseen various "self-inventing" groups dedicated to diverse ministries, such as the Children's Liturgy of the Word with 150 youngsters participating, and the senior high school students' "Peace Gang."

By 1989, the Spirit of Peace community had grown to 530 households, suggesting that this experiment—this possible prototype for future parishes—was working. "Our parishioners are amazingly active," Father Flaherty concluded. "The parish is working so well after seven years that it scares me!"

Louisville

ST. LOUIS (1884)
902 Grant Street

Mass was first said in Louisville about 1879 in the home of David Kerr, who in 1864 became the area's first white settler. It was also on Kerr's farm that Louis Nawatny first found coal in 1877. Kerr and Nawatny arranged with C.C. Welch to sink a mine shaft. At 200 feet, Welch found a rich vein eight to thirteen feet wide, and Louisville began to blossom as a coal mining center.

Soon other mines were sunk, and Nawatny platted a townsite at the junction of Coal Creek and the Colorado Central Railroad tracks on October 24, 1878, naming the town after himself. By 1880, the fast growing coal town had 450 residents.

Anthony J. Abel, the pastor of Sacred Heart of Mary Church in South Boulder, continued to visit Louisville after saying the first mass in David Kerr's home. In 1881, he was succeeded as pastor of the South Boulder area by Godfrey A. Raber, a newly ordained Swiss priest who came to Colorado for the healthful climate.

Father Raber and Bishop Machebeuf strove to give Louisville its own church. After the bishop bought two lots at the corner of LaFarge Avenue and Walnut Street from coal mine owner C.C. Welch on October 9, 1883, Father Raber and his parishioners built a splendid little frame church, completed in 1884 and landscaped with trees and a white picket fence. Father Raber looked after the St. Louis mission until 1887, when the Benedictine fathers of St. Vincent Archabbey of Beatty, Pennsylvania, took over Boulder County at the request of Bishop Machebeuf.

Rhabanus M. Guttman, OSB, headed the tiny band of missionary Benedictines who headquartered at Sacred Heart of Mary and tended Louisville and other Boulder County missions. Typically, these circuit-riding Benedictines arrived Saturday afternoon to hear confessions, spent the night with a parish family, and said Sunday mass the next morning. In 1894, the Benedictines spent $564.40 on St. Louis Church, adding a choir loft and a sacristy with a sleeping nook. In 1899, Henry Hohman, OSB, became the first resident pastor, buying a small frame cottage that, with additions over the years, served as the rectory until 1953. The Benedictines sent Italian- or Slavic-speaking priests whenever possible, which delighted the two major immigrant groups of the parish. Although these miners could afford little or no salary for the priests, they rewarded them with ethnic feasts.

Father Cyril Rettger, OSB, pastor from 1903 to 1916, purchased twelve lots in the block west of the rectory and began work on a four-room, one-story frame school house. Four Benedictine sisters from Erie, Pennsylvania, opened the "St. Louis School and Business College" in the fall of 1905. Despite its proud name and fashionable bungalow architecture, the school could afford only one textbook, the *Baltimore Catechism*, which was also used as a reader and a speller. Over 200 students from Louisville and the nearby coal mining towns of Erie, Lafayette, Marshall, and Superior enrolled in the tiny, fifty-by-seventy-foot school. The Benedictines were succeeded in 1909 by the Franciscan sisters of St. Francis Convent from Milwaukee, Wisconsin, who ran the school until 1927. Subsequently, the Sisters of the Most Precious Blood and the Presentation Sisters from Ireland helped staff the school over the years. When the last sisters left in 1985, lay teachers took over all classes, kindergarten through sixth grade.

At the 1907 school dedication ceremony, Bishop Matz told the assembled parishioners that "the church would always defend the rights of the laboring man, and would come to his farms and mines with new churches and new schools." Father Rettger likewise sympathized with his working-class flock, who were trying to establish a local of the United Mine Workers. The struggle to unionize, gain safe working conditions, and secure a minimum wage of $3 for a maximum work day of eight hours led to bitter labor wars. Father Rettger's support of the miners apparently led to an attempt to assassinate him while he was saying mass, a near miss vividly commemorated by a bullet hole in the window nearest the altar.

Benedict Ingenito, OSB, took over in 1933 and began an annual bazaar to raise money for a new church near the school. This $40,000 brick church, designed in the Romanesque style with a red tile roof and an elegant rear bell tower, was dedicated on June 28, 1942, by Archbishop Vehr. Since that year, the parish complex in the 900 block of Grant Street has been growing. The parish spent $35,000 in 1950 to add two brick wings to the school, replace the old outhouses with indoor plumbing, reface the 1907 school in a brick veneer, and modernize the entire complex with glass brick windows, Celotex ceilings, and flourescent lighting. The old convent, a brick house where the sisters had been living since 1907, was replaced in 1953 with a new $33,000 structure now used as a preschool center. A new rectory was completed in 1961 for Harold Glentzer, OSB, the last Benedictine pastor, who served from 1959 to 1973, followed by John E. Casey, SJ, pastor from 1973 to 1980, and John J.

McGinn, an archdiocesan priest who has been pastor since 1980. Anticipating future expansion, Father McGinn has acquired eight acres near the church.

In 1984, Father McGinn lead St. Louis's parishioners in a centennial celebration. By that time, Louisville had become a town of over 5,000 with about 400 families in the parish and ninety-two children in the kindergarten and elementary school. Priest and parishioners met at the church, then marched in procession to Louisville's Memory Square Park for an open air centennial mass on Sunday, September 16, 1984.

Loveland

ST. JOHN THE EVANGELIST (1902)
1730 West 12th Street

William A.H. Loveland, president of the Colorado Central Railroad, gave his name to the town founded in 1877 where his railroad crossed the Big Thompson River. That year, the missionary priest of northeastern Colorado, William J. Howlett, apparently said the first mass in the railroad section house. Eight years later, J.J. LePage, pastor of St. Joseph's in Fort Collins, began saying masses regularly in the home of Daniel E. Mulvaney for Loveland's handful of Catholics.

In 1892, Reverend Edward Downey bought a little house at 8th and Cleveland to refit as a chapel. There, Fort Collins pastors continued to say mass until Father G. Joseph LaJeunesse purchased three lots at 5th and Grant. Father LaJeunesse sold the old chapel, using the proceeds and his own funds to build a splendid little brick church that he named for John the Evangelist. Four miniature bell towers and a grand large one topped this stately Romanesque landmark, completed in 1902.

Bishop Matz, in 1909, assigned William J. Howlett as Longmont's first resident pastor. Father Howlett, who had had said the first mass in Loveland thirty-two years earlier, lived in the sacristy where he cooked for himself. Eventually, he built a rectory, put a gallery in the church, and had the interior painted with frescoes before he retired in 1913 to the Sisters of Loretto Mother-

St. John the Evangelist Church in Loveland.

house in Kentucky, where he lived out his final years as chaplain.

George O. Ducharme, pastor from 1913 to 1944, was a French Canadian who came to Colorado in search of the climate cure. He never fully recovered but dutifully served the parish as well as St. Walter's mission in Estes Park until his retirement in 1944.

Francis J. Kappes, a German-American priest recruited from the archdiocese of Cincinnati, guided St. John's through the tremendous growth of the post–World War II era. Father Kappes raised a $10,000 school fund, recruited three Sisters of the Third Order of St. Francis from Joliet, Illinois, as teachers and hired a young Catholic architect, Victor D. Langhart, to design a school. On the west side of town, Father Kappes paid $21,000 for the 13.5 acre Prescott spread and arranged for its annexation to Longmont as St. John's Addition in order to secure utilities and other town services. Archbishop Vehr blessed the plans with kind words and checks totaling $3,000.

Financing and construction details for St. John the Evangelist School typify the finely tuned church and school construction operations of the Vehr era.

As usual, Bosworth, Sullivan & Company of Denver handled financing, arranging a $120,000, fourteen-year loan at 4 percent for a 1 and 1/2 percent commission. Young Father Kappes fretted over the delays and got fatherly advice from Archbishop Vehr in a June 26, 1956, letter: "Yours is the same story of building with its interminable delays. I think it might be best to delay the public dedication until the entire structure is completed."

The old Prescott farmhouse was converted to a convent. Nearby, architect Langhart designed a modern, $160,000 showcase school that attracted attention for its innovative engineering. A 250-ton single slab of precast concrete was lifted over the fifty-by-100-foot auditorium. Supported only by perimeter upright beams, this roof capped an auditorium without any middle-of-the-room supports to block views. Father Kappes put it into service as a new church for his rapidly growing parish when the building was finally finished and dedicated by Archbishop Vehr on May 1, 1957.

The lovely old downtown church briefly served as the Knights of Columbus Hall before being sold in 1957. Twenty years later, the old landmark was elegantly restored and recycled as roomy office space. Parishioners constructed a new rectory for Father Kappes on the spacious new church property. After completing the new, red brick, one-story church–school, Father Kappes was transferred to All Souls parish in Englewood. Omer Foxhoven, noted throughout the archdiocese as a "Church Builder," came to St. John's as pastor from 1965 to 1970. True to his reputation, he added four more classrooms to the school and built St. John's modern 1969 church, a striking Victor D. Langhart structure.

The high U-shaped ceiling gave the new church an airy feeling, and its lofty ceiling beams provided a winter home for sparrows. The post–Vatican II floor plan featured a central baptistry, raised choir area, and banks of pews huddled around a simple modern altar. In front of the church, a detached skeletal tower bears electric bells and a cross.

St. John the Evangelist School faced, in 1970, the same soaring costs that closed many parish schools. Parishioners, however, rallied to form a Save Our School (SOS) committee that raised enough money and pledges to keep the school open, though the seventh and eighth grades were dropped. Staffed by several nuns and lay teachers, it survives to this day.

Taking a tip from the Ecumenical Chapel adorning the main entry of their new church, St. John's joined All Saints Episcopal and First Congregational churches in sponsoring an ecumenical Bible School. Regis F. McGuire, the pastor since 1973, reported in 1988, "When I came here St. John's had about 850 families. Now that Hewlett Packard and Kodak have opened plants here we have around 2,300 families and are the largest congregation in 'the sweetheart city'."

Mead

GUARDIAN ANGELS (1911)
Weld County Highways 34 & 7

In 1911, the Benedictines of St. John the Baptist in Longmont established a new parish in Mead, which is ten miles northeast of Longmont and forty miles southeast of Greeley. This Weld County hamlet, named for Martin S. Mead, who first homesteaded there around 1886, became a town in 1905 when the Great Western Sugar Company built a railroad spur and sugar beet dump there. Paul Mead, son of Martin Mead, replatted forty acres of the old family homestead as the townsite.

Guardian Angels Church in Mead, February 15, 1938.

Beginning in the 1870s, Bishop Machebeuf and other circuit-riding priests said mass in what would become Mead, in the home of Thomas O'Donnell. By 1910, Mead claimed 114 residents, including twenty-five Catholic families living in and around the town, who bought the old Mt. Zion United

Brethren Church. They dragged this church a mile down county highway 7 to its present crossroads location, refitted and rechristened it as Guardian Angels Church, then celebrated their first mass there on January 1, 1911.

Vigorous growth characterized Mead and the church during the prosperous first two decades of the twentieth century. Standing-room-only masses led the parish to construct an addition to the rear of Guardian Angels in 1929, doubling its size.

Guardian Angels was tended by the Longmont Benedictines until 1945, when it became a mission of St. Theresa's in Frederick. In 1964, the congregation built a parish hall next to the church and, two years later, the little flock of about seventy-eight people moved their Sunday mass out of the tiny church and into the hall. The resident pastor of St. Theresa's in Frederick visits Mead every Sunday and reported in 1988 that his small but dedicated congregation in Mead is now hoping to raise $10,000 to restore and update the old church. This example of carpenter Gothic architecture is one of the most charming of the many white frame churches that grace the Colorado high plains.

Meeker

HOLY FAMILY (1905)
890 Park Street

The White River Ute Agency, where the Indians revolted and killed agent Nathan C. Meeker in 1879, evolved into the town of Meeker. Several Catholic families were among the early settlers, and Edward J. Downey, a circuit-riding pioneer priest, said the first mass in 1884, at the Delaney Ranch at White River City and, later on, in the old adobe Rio Blanco County courthouse.

Meeker remained a small ranching and farming (alfalfa, grain, and hay) town until the early 1900s, when oil discoveries, most notably the rich Rangely Field, pushed the population over the 1,000 mark by the 1920s. Although Holy Family parish was created by Bishop Matz in 1905, construction of a church did not begin until 1911, during the pastorship of Christopher Walsh. Denver architects Aaron M. Gove and Thomas F. Walsh, who were

Holy Family Church, Meeker. (Photo by James Baca.)

then finishing the Cathedral of the Immaculate Conception in Denver, were paid $125 to design Holy Family Church. Dedicated on July 6, 1913, this $15,000, red brick Romanesque edifice still sports its original Gothic entry and colored glass windows, with a rose window under the square, enclosed belfry.

Fathers Bernard Fajanelle (1919–1923), Emile J. Verschraeghen (1923–1929), Francis J. Brady (1930–1933), Paul Slattery (1935–1944), Paul Reed (1944–1949), and Edward J. Fraczkowski (1949–1958) were among the more memorable pastors. Among the prominent parishioners was Josephine Holland, superintendent of Rio Blanco county schools and president of the Holy Family Altar and Rosary Society. She and other members of the society regularly urged the bishop in Denver to send a resident priest to their parish, then a mission attended by the pastors of St. Mary's in Rifle.

Holy Family was removed from Rifle's mission list in 1959 to become a mission of St. Ignatius Church in Rangely. Leo M. Blach, the new pastor of the two towns, began offering some weekday services as well as Sunday masses. In what was becoming a busier parish, Father Blach successfully asked Archbishop Vehr for installation of a symbol of status and modernity—indoor plumbing.

John P. Schuneman served as pastor from 1978 to 1983 and worked with parishioners to build a parish hall, which included a kitchen, dining room, and two-bedroom apartment for clergymen. Thanks to the oil shale boom, Meeker's population climbed to 2,356 in 1980. When crude oil prices crashed from over $40 a barrel to under $10 in 1982, the oil boom burst. Rio Blanco County suffered a mass exodus, but Holy Family has clung to its resident priests.

Bert Chilson, who became the second resident pastor in 1983, found Meeker and Rangely, which are separated by sixty miles of townless highway, a challenge. "People are so spread out," Father Chilson reported. "And with lambing and ranching and tending the animals they can't get away to parish functions or to Mass all the time. When they can't come in, you have to go out."

Lawrence T. Solan, pastor since 1986, spent alternate weeks in the two parishes so that "parishioners always know where to find me and both parishes get equal attention."

Minturn

ST. PATRICK (1913)
482 Main Street

Ten miles northeast of the Mount of the Holy Cross lies Minturn, a lumber town founded on the Denver & Rio Grande line in 1889. Several Catholics settled in the community named for roadmaster Thomas Minturn (or for railroad director Robert G. Minturn).

James P. Carrigan, who was appointed pastor of St. Stephen's in Glenwood Springs in 1910, began making monthly visits to celebrate mass in Thomas Minturn's section house. With his encouragement, local Catholics formed St. Patrick parish on September 13, 1913. Thanks to a $500 gift from the Catholic Extension Society and funds raised by parish suppers and plays, a church was constructed in the fall of 1925. Howard G. Bayers built the one-story, frame, twenty-four-by-thirty-six-foot structure for $1,270.

Monthly masses were offered by the pastor of Glenwood Springs, and, in 1936, Benedictine sisters from Canon City launched a three-week summer vacation school at St. Patrick's. The sisters stayed with the families of various parishioners, including those of J.P. Doyle, J.A. Mack, William McBreen, and Charles A. Robbie.

St. Patrick's was enlarged in 1950 with an $875 donation from the Catholic Extension Society.

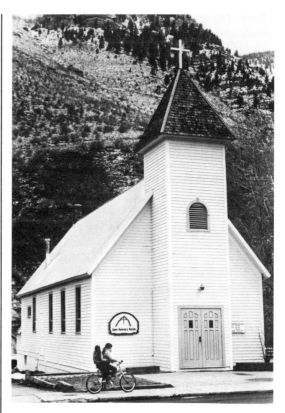

St. Patrick's in Minturn. (Photo by James Baca.)

After adding a basement, a choir loft, a confessional, and a new ceiling, members built a rectory and petitioned Archbishop Vehr for a resident priest. Joseph J. Leberer arrived in 1952 with responsibility for the missions of Mt. Carmel at Redcliff and St. Mary at Eagle, as well as St. Patrick's.

Edward J. Poehlmann (pronounced pail man), who took charge of the handsome, well-kept church at Minturn in 1987, said in a 1988 interview:

This parish has changed dramatically since 1913. What was a lumbering, mining, and railroading crossroads is now a fairly stable town of over 1,000. Most of them work at nearby ski resorts. We now have almost 500 households registered at St. Patrick's, an all-time high. We also have vibrant congregations at Redcliff, Vail, and Beaver Creek, where our new interdenominational chapel opened in 1988. And at St. Patrick's, we're building a parish center next year.

As to the name Minturn, last year Minturno, Italy, asked if we would like to be their sister city.

They say the name is Italian for a mine spur on a railroad.

Nederland

ST. RITA (1935)
326 East Colorado Highway 119

Nederland sprouted in the 1870s as a mining supply town, earning its name in 1874 when investors from the Netherlands bought Breed's Mill and Mine. Although founded because of rich silver deposits in nearby Caribou, Nederland did not thrive until the 1900s, when it became a major tungsten mining center. During the World War I tungsten boom, a Nederland mission was established by Regis Barrett, a Benedictine from Boulder. When the demand for tungsten collapsed in the 1920s, the mission closed.

Neither silver nor tungsten attracted James J. Regan, OP, a Dominican stationed at St. Dominic parish in Denver. He fell in love with the scenery, with jubilant Middle Boulder Creek gushing through the rustic mining town at the base of the snowcapped Indian Peaks. Father Regan, as chaplain of the Catholic Daughters of America, persuaded them to purchase Nederland's old Antlers Hotel, an 1897 frame lodge far less elegant than its Colorado Springs namesake. The Catholic Daughters and the Dominican converted the rambling two-story hotel to Mont Rita, a chapel and camp for Catholic girls, to complement the nearby boys' camp at St. Malo. In summers, Sunday mass was celebrated on the spacious open air hotel porch. This camp for girls aged ten to sixteen opened in 1932, closed from 1943 to 1946 because of the war, and closed permanently in 1954 when the Daughters bought another camp.

The Antlers Hotel has disappeared, but the chapel Father Regan began building on the site in 1932 still stands. "If you will put enough green stuff in the collection basket," Father Regan told his parishioners, "I'll build you a chapel." Over various summer vacations, Father Regan, the Hailey family of Nederland, the Zarlengo clan of Tolland, and Martha Logan of Rollinsville spearheaded construction of the rustic pine log chapel completed in

1935. Inside, it seated seventy-five and featured fine stained glass windows designed and built by parishioner Gilbert Postlewait. The tiny 1930s chapel was doubled in size in 1962 to seat 200, when it was winterized with the help of an old furnace donated by the Nederland Community Presbyterian Church.

Summer tourists, winter skiers at Eldora, and locals persuaded the Benedictines and other orders to keep St. Rita's open all year. In 1977, Gabor Cesh erected a bell tower on the quaint log church and hung an old locomotive bell, donated by the Order of the Christophers, a contingent of Catholic railroad men.

What began as a summer "chapel of convenience" for campers and tourists is now a year-round parish for about 130 households and many tourists. Since 1978, Thomas J. Sherlock, CPPS, has served as pastor, celebrating a 10 o'clock Sunday mass in the winter and a 9 o'clock service in summer. "Even in dead of winter, we have ninety people at mass," reported Father Sherlock of the Society of the Precious Blood in 1988, "and in the summer we have 180 to 200." He added that the Christmas Eve mass has become a cherished tradition in this small mountain town. And in summers, the rustic chapel standing alone above Barker Lake on a hill of wildflowers reminds tourists and locals of the Creator behind this heavenly setting.

Northglenn

IMMACULATE HEART OF MARY (1967)
11385 Grant Drive

Northglenn was laid out in 1959 by Perl-Mack Homes, Inc., on what had been the ranch of Thomas B. Croke, an Irish Catholic who pioneered irrigated farming and ranching and built the mansion at 1075 Pennsylvania Street in Denver.

This new Adams County suburb grew rapidly, reaching a population of 29,847 by 1980. As the area began to boom, interested Catholics were invited to a parish organizational meeting at Leroy School on September 1, 1967. Over 380 attended and organized a parish council to raise money for a new church. With the help of large dowries from

By August of 1969, the soaring skeleton of a church for Northglenn was in place. (Photo by James Baca.)

the neighboring parishes—Holy Cross in Thornton, Our Lady of Sorrows in Eastlake, and Holy Trinity in Westminster—groundbreaking took place in March 1969. By the time the altar was constructed of four large chunks of granite and consecrated on February 1, 1970, Immaculate Heart of Mary claimed 1,350 registered families.

Martin J. McNulty, the founding pastor, and Archbishop Casey blessed the modern, low-slung church with its conical roof on April 30, 1970. A new parish activity center was built in 1984, and the old one was remodeled into Our Lady of Guadalupe Chapel. In a symbolic move to tie this new ultramodern suburban church to the mother parish of the archdiocese, the statue of the Blessed Virgin that used to be on top of Cathedral High School before it closed in 1982 was moved to the Northglenn church.

Thomas S. Fryar, the current pastor, requested in 1988 that the faithful "in the name of Christ become involved and active in your parish and its works. The Lord has placed you within this faith family for a purpose!"

The 2,800 families of Immaculate Heart of Mary have fifty different ministries in which to become involved, ranging from a toddler care cooperative to funeral meals, from a prayer chain to joining the greeters who welcome newcomers to what the congregation, from the very beginning, strove to make the "Parish of Love."

Oak Creek

ST. MARTIN (1940)

Oak Creek is a coal mining town, founded in 1907, twenty miles southwest of Steamboat Springs. During the 1930s, J.J. Meyers of Holy Name parish in Steamboat Springs celebrated a monthly Sunday mass in Oak Creek's funeral home.

By 1940, more than 100 Catholics were squeezing into the mortuary for Sunday masses, and Edward Prinster, who took over at Steamboat and Oak Creek after Father Meyers' death in 1938, wrote to Bishop Vehr that "my parishioners, though poor, have nearly paid off the $400 debt for five lots." Bishop Vehr subsequently wrote to the Catholic Extension Society in Chicago that "recently we have purchased some lots in the central portion of the town. The parish . . . consists of Slavs, Italians and Mexicans working seasonally [in the coal mines]."

The Extension Society responded with a $1,500 donation that Bishop Vehr supplemented with $2,000 from Bishop Tihen's estate to build St. Martin Chapel in 1941. It was named for donors Mr. and Mrs. Martin Bieschke. J.K. Monroe, the Denver architect, designed the $4,978.40 frame chapel, which Archbishop Vehr dedicated late in 1941.

Oak Creek remains a blue-collar, coal mining town, which by the 1980s reached a population of 1,000. This Routt County town now has a 10:30 mass every Sunday offered by Monsignor Thomas T. Dentici of Holy Name parish in Steamboat Springs.

Peetz

SACRED HEART (1914)

Peter Peetz, a railroad section foreman, homesteaded in 1903 the future site of the Logan County town named for him. After a Burlington railroad subsidiary, the Lincoln Land Company, decided to plat a town in 1908, Peetz provided the townsite.

Initially, the Peetz family went to mass in nearby Sidney, Nebraska, then at St. Anthony's in Sterling. Mrs. Peetz persuaded Peter Sasse at Sterling to say mass once a month in the Peetz home. Twenty Catholic families gathered for these services, inspiring Father Sasse and Peter Peetz to think about building a parish. Peetz raised $300 and co-signed a loan from the Catholic Church Extension Society in Chicago to start a building fund.

Parishioners volunteered to construct the high-spired little frame church completed in 1914. It remained a mission tended by the pastor of St. Anthony's in Sterling until 1925. Then, after prodding from parishioner John Fehringer, Bishop Tihen assigned William Scherer to be the first resident pastor. The house across the street from the church was bought and converted to a rectory where the congregation stocked Father Scherer's larder with eggs, butter, milk, meat, and vegetables.

Philip Ryan, the fourth pastor, and parishioners dug out the basement by hand to create a parish hall and added sacristies to the little frame church in 1944–1945. Omer V. Foxhoven, pastor from 1962 to 1965, presided over the 1963 dismantling of the old frame church and construction of a modern, red brick church in 1964, the parish's fiftieth anniversary.

The new $68,000 parish home, designed by architect Henry De Nicola, showcased six stained glass windows by the noted Belgian artist, Bradi Barth. Miss Barth worked bits of local color into her stained glass compositions: The creation scene includes the cat who became her constant companion as she worked, while the Coronation window includes in the background the old frame church of Peetz.

Father Foxhoven wrote a golden anniversary history booklet, "Golden Yields Through 50 Years from Golden Fields," to record the history of this wheat-belt parish, concentrating on the farm families that have sustained this church, including the Bules, Davises, Elenzes, Fehringers, Fogales, Gertges, Goransons, Groegers, Hoffmans, Johnsons, LeBlancs, McRaes, Meyers, Nelsons, Peetzes, Roelles, Schilzes, Schumachers, Schweitzbergers, Steyaerts, Trujillos, Van Driels, Veiths, and Wiesers.

Platteville

ST. NICHOLAS (1889)
514 Marion Avenue

Platteville traces its origins to Fort Vasquez, an 1830s fur trade post now restored as a Colorado Historical Society museum on the south side of town. After the Denver Pacific Railroad reached this site on the Platte River, Platteville was founded in 1871.

St. Nicholas occupies the entry niche of his church in Platteville. (Photo by Tom Noel.)

Missionary priests from St. Joseph's in Fort Collins began saying masses in Platteville in 1885, and four years later, William J. Howlett erected a modest brick chapel, christened St. Nicholas of Myra. From 1889 to 1920, St. Nicholas's was a mission church tended by the pastor of St. Augustine's in Brighton.

St. Nicholas's received a resident pastor in 1920, when John Shea began a twenty-two-year stay. Father Shea remodeled the church and established Sacred Heart, a mission church for a heavily Hispanic flock in nearby Gilcrist. Thomas Doran, pastor from 1942 to 1955, strove to make Hispanics, particularly migrant workers, welcome at St. Nicholas's. The nuns who came from Denver to teach catechism every Sunday, he wrote to Archbishop Vehr in 1945, attracted "about 100 children." He added that "most of the Spanish children are working in the beet fields. . . . I have recently organized a society among the Spanish women and they have as one of their purposes the bringing of the children to catechism classes."

St. Nicholas, since 1958, has been a mission attended by the pastor of St. William in nearby Fort Lupton. Father Doran's efforts to reach out to migrant workers were continued in the 1970s by Reverend Joe Gamm and Sister Celestine Fiek, the parish's first resident nun. This Victory Noll sister established special Confraternity of Christian Doctrine education classes that enrolled as many as 160 children.

Father Doran built the present church a half block west of the original church in 1946. This stucco, Spanish-style structure occupies well-landscaped grounds, which it shares with a flower-bedecked Hispanic shrine, conveniently built next to an old hand water pump. A life-sized St. Nicholas in his niche over the church entry has three tiny children at his feet, presumably awaiting the blessings and gifts that have made the saint famous in the guise of Santa Claus.

"Now this is St. Nicholas," declared John P. Morton, CSsR, the pastor presiding over the parish's 1989 centennial. "And in the spirit of St. Nick our folks are friendly. They laugh easily, sing loudly and know how to celebrate!"

Rangely

ST. IGNATIUS (1931)
109 South Stanolind Avenue

Two Franciscan padres, Atanasio Dominguez and Silvestre Vélez de Escalante, passed through this area in September 1776, discovering the White River near which Rangely lies. In all probability, these Spanish priests said the first mass in what is now Rio Blanco County.

A trading post was established on the site in the 1880s but did not become a significant town until the Rangely oil and gas field was tapped in 1902. This subterranean "gold mine," still producing in the 1980s, has proved to be far and away the richest petroleum discovery in Colorado.

Not until 1931 did Francis J. Brady, the pastor at Holy Family in Meeker, open the St. Ignatius mission. During the 1940s, Blaise Schumacher, OSB, of Vernal, Utah—the famed "Flying Priest of the Rockies"—flew in two Sundays a month, buzzing

Archbishop Vehr and the faithful of St. Ignatius gathered together in 1951 for a parish snapshot in front of their storefront church.

the town upon his arrival so that everyone would know it was time for mass.

Services were held in the home of John Purdy, whose wife, Grace, was the cornerstone of the church. Besides making her home into the rectory, church, and catechetical center, she also took under her roof, at one time or another, the town funeral parlor, the Girl and Boy scouts, library, post office, Red Cross headquarters, and Women's Club.

With the post–World War II oil boom, Rangely began to grow. In 1950, St. Ignatius mission—with about 100 members—had outgrown the Purdy residence and purchased an abandoned grocery store for $1,500, which was paid for by the Catholic Extension Society of Chicago. Archbishop Vehr consecrated the hall on June 21, 1951. Six years later, members moved their church into a somewhat larger building, the Pan American Oil Patch Recreation Hall, and sold their old home to Trinity Lutheran Church.

St. Ignatius's received its first resident pastor, Leo Blach, in 1958. Two Sinsinawa, Wisconsin, Dominican sisters, Margaret Noll and Marlene Neuzerling, helped out, after moving into a trailer near the church in 1982. Since then, parish houses have been built in both Rangely and Meeker for the sisters as well as meetings of the congregation.

When the 1983 oil bust sent Rangely's population tumbling from a peak of about 3,000 to half that number, the sisters stayed on though the pastor, Elbert "Bert" Chilson, moved to Meeker. After Father Chilson left to serve in the Catholic missions in Colombia, South America, Lawrence T. Solan became pastor in 1986. Father Solan lives one week in Rangely and then a week in Meeker, splitting his time between the two parishes.

Redcliff

MOUNT CARMEL (1913)

Redcliff is the oldest town in Eagle County. After silver was discovered on Battle Mountain in 1879, the town sprang up where the Eagle River is joined by Turkey Creek. Above the red cliffs of the Eagle Valley soars the Mount of the Holy Cross. This cross, formed by snow lying in rock crevices, attracted Christian pilgrims after William Henry Jackson's famous photograph and Thomas Moran's celebrated paintings carried the inspirational scene to the four corners of the globe.

No one was more fascinated with the Mount of the Holy Cross than Joseph P. Carrigan, pastor of St. Stephen's in Glenwood Springs. He formed the Mount of the Holy Cross Trails Association and recruited interdenominational religious, civic, and political support to make it a shrine. Shrine Pass is a relic of this grand, unfulfilled scheme. Mount Carmel Church is another offshoot, having been established in 1913 with the hope of starting a monastery of the Carmelite fathers in Redcliff to welcome pilgrims.

Although the monastery never materialized, the little chapel—a frame structure with a bell tower and metal roof, has survived. St. Thomas Seminary donated the kneelers, and St. Mary's in Eagle gave the pews for what is, officially, Lady of Mount Carmel Catholic Church. Since the beginning, it has been a mission of St. Patrick parish in Minturn.

Red Feather Lakes

OUR LADY OF THE LAKES (1957)

The summer resort of Red Feather Lakes, developed during the 1920s on what had been called Mitchell Lakes, witnessed its first Catholic mass in 1956 in the Community Building. Norma Folda of the Red Feather Lakes Improvement Club, furniture dealer Edward E. Lilly of Greeley, and other Catholics worked with Archbishop Vehr to establish Our Lady of the Lakes as a summer mission the following year.

Parishioners persuaded various priests to offer summer Sunday masses until St. Peter's in Greeley accepted the parish as a mission in 1958. That year, a church site was purchased from R.V. Barker, and parishioners set about building a foundation onto which they placed an old chapel moved down from Fort Warren Air Force Base in Wyoming. In November 1959, a windstorm destroyed the church, which was rebuilt with slab log siding the following year and furnished with second hand pews from St. John Church in Longmont. Subsequently, this mission was transferred to St. Joseph parish in Fort Collins, which provides a priest for Saturday afternoon masses between Memorial and Labor days, when summer residents and vacationers flock to Red Feather Lakes.

Rifle

ST. MARY'S (1910)
440 White River Avenue

How did Rifle become the only town in the country with that name? The Rifle Reading Club, in their 1973 town history, *Rifle Shots*, reported that a lost gun led to the naming of Rifle Creek, which flows into the Colorado River at the spot where Rifle was founded in 1882.

Edward Downey, pastor of St. Mary's in Aspen, began making Rifle a mission stop in 1884, but it was Christopher V. Walsh who founded St. Mary parish in 1910 and became the first resident pastor. Father Walsh, a cowboy priest, earned the respect of parishioners by helping them with cattle roundups in exchange for their help with St. Mary's.

Charles H. Miller, a Rifle pioneer whose home had been used for the first masses, rounded up his two oldest sons to dig out a church basement with pick and shovel and a team and scraper. Then the Millers helped erect, in 1912, the $3,000 frame church on land donated by Judge Wall at the southwest corner of East 5th Street and Munro Avenue.

From his home parish in Rifle, Father Walsh rode his own horse or the Denver & Rio Grande's iron horse to mission stations at Buford, Grand Valley, Meeker, New Castle, Silt, and White River City.

The Irish pastor was followed by a Frenchman, Bernard Fajanelle, who headed St. Mary's from 1913 to 1918, and spruced up the church with five new pews, a confessional, a choir gallery, and an organ. A German, Henry Bernard Stern, became the third pastor in 1918. An accomplished pianist, he trained a choir and enlisted the aid of parishioners to build a $4,300 rectory in 1919.

Emile J. Verschraeghen became St. Mary's fourth resident pastor. Father Verschraeghen, according to R.J. Cook in his 1976 parish history, "fell in solidly with the cattlemen and cowboys, even more so than Father Walsh, for he was in the saddle much of the time with the McSweeney family at Rio Blanco and always participated in roundups.... He kept his horse and saddle ready at all times at a nearby friend's barn."

St. Mary's sponsored bridge parties and bingo games, but neither proved as popular with townsfolk as the St. Patrick's Day dances followed by a midnight supper. After Father Verschraeghen left in 1929, various pastors served at St. Mary's over the years. Father Edward J. Fraczkowski, pastor from 1949 to 1960, transformed one of Rifle's missions into a parish by converting the surplus Denver & Rio Grande section man's bunkhouse at Silt into Sacred Heart Church.

Father "Fraz," parishioners still remember, was "a teacher of the faith whose door was always open and whose coffee pot was always on." He regularly paid visits to Grand Valley (also known as Parachute), saying masses in a warehouse and in an abandoned garage before moving into a Methodist church. Grand Valley Catholics had built a little mission chapel, St. Brendan's, in 1889—making it the first Catholic church west of Glenwood Springs—but the building had deteriorated and was sold in 1929. Pastors at St. Mary's continued to make monthly mission calls at Grand Valley until 1969, when the mission was closed.

Most Precious Blood Church in New Castle was another mission tended from St. Mary's. This church, built in 1890 in the then booming coal town, was demolished in 1967 by a seventy-ton granite boulder. Although Robert I. Durrie built a church, which was dedicated by Archbishop Casey in July

1969, New Castle's dwindling population led to its closing in 1987.

Father Durrie guided St. Mary's from 1960 to 1969. He purchased the Nazarene Church a half block away from St. Mary's and converted it to a parish hall. This hall became headquarters of Lift-Up (Life's Interfaith Team Against Unemployment and Poverty) in 1982, when the oil shale boom failed on the Western Slope. Under James E. Fox, the new pastor, and Sister Barbara Piotrowski, SC, pastoral associate, Lift-Up was formed in conjunction with other Rifle churches to provide food, shelter, and employment guidance to Western Slopers.

Despite the economic disaster triggered by Exxon's abrupt 1982 closing of its giant Colony Oil Shale Plant, St. Mary's grew during the 1980s. With a 234-family parish in 1983, Father Fox undertook an $80,000 expansion that doubled the size of the old, 100-seat frame church. Philip P. Denig became pastor in 1987, two years after his ordination, with plans "to continue to improve the properties, reorganize the staff, reduce the parish debt, teach, and train parish members to face the reality of the priest shortage of the late 1980s."

Roggen

SACRED HEART (1924)
38044 Weld County Rd. # 16

Homesteader Tom Klausner arrived two years after Roggen was platted as a ranching and railroad town in 1908. The Klausners traveled by spring wagon to wherever the nearest mass was being offered.

In 1914, they rounded up enough Catholics to coax Bernard Froegel of Brighton to say mass in the Roggen School. In 1920, the growing band of Catholics purchased an abandoned schoolhouse in the sand hills five miles east of town. To get the building into Roggen, they used planks and teams of horses and mules. Not until March 1921 did they finish dragging the church to its present location. Then, planks were laid across bricks to create pews for the first services. Before Bishop Tihen arrived for the dedication on June 10, 1924, parishioners handcrafted permanent pews and plastered and decorated the interior of the frame structure.

M.C. Klausner, Tom Klausner's brother, conducted catechism classes, while his wife prepared the First Communion groups. Although some Protestants were scandalized, parishioners laid out a baseball diamond next to the church for after-mass games. Despite dust, debt, drought, and twenty-five-cents-a-bushel wheat during the depression, Sacred Heart parish endured, sharing a pastor with Holy Family Church in nearby Keenesburg. Sisters of Charity came from Denver to teach catechism in the summers, and an addition was attached to the rear of the church in 1930. Sacred Heart parish raised $7,346 in the winter of 1943 to build on land donated by the Charles Buchholzes a new church, a feat that Archbishop Vehr called "the miracle of the diocese."

The archbishop assigned architect John K. Monroe to help plan the new church and appointed Charles P. Sanger the first resident pastor. Archbishop Vehr dedicated the Romanesque church on June 10, 1947. As parishioners donated much of the labor and materials, this exquisite structure with its domed bell tower and coffered ceiling was built for only $29,000.

While undertaking their new church, this energetic congregation also bought a home for $2,480 and moved it a mile and a half to rest beside the old church. It was used as a convent, and the old church was divided into two classrooms where two sisters, Adorers of the Blood of Christ from Wichita, Kansas, opened Sacred Heart School in 1946. Enrollment reached sixty-five during the 1950s, but two decades later declining numbers and rising costs led the parish to close its school. Robert L. Breunig, pastor since 1985, reported in 1988 that Sacred Heart and its missions at Keenesburg and Wiggins are alive and well.

Silt

SACRED HEART (1948)
230 6th Street

The Rio Grande Railroad, which built through this part of Garfield County along the Colorado River

This one-time Denver & Rio Grande Railroad bunkhouse now serves as Silt's Sacred Heart Church. (Photo by Tom Noel.)

in 1889, named the town for its soil. Silt's Sacred Heart Church was established in 1948 as a mission tended by the pastor of St. Mary's in Rifle.

The diminutive chapel is a former Rio Grande section bunkhouse on a cinderblock foundation. A tiny bell tower and cross as well as a "swamp cooler" have been added to this one-room chapel, which sits in a grassy field next to the new Silt Branch Library.

Snowmass

ST. BENEDICT'S MONASTERY (1956)
1012 Monastery Road

Father Joseph Boyle, OCSO, the abbot, thought awhile when asked in 1988 how the Trappists came to pursue the cloistered, contemplative life next to one of the wealthiest and most fashionable resorts in this world.

> You could spend a long time meditating on that. Perhaps God wanted this monastery next to Aspen in order to bring people together who don't normally meet. Our community at Snowmass originated from St. Joseph's Abbey in Spencer, Massachusetts. An anonymous donor enabled us to purchase the LaMoy Ranch and parts of other ranches, including that of Aspen Mayor Harold "Shorty" Pabst.

"Shorty," a tall scion of the brewery clan, welcomed the Order of Cistercians of the Strict Obser-

St. Benedict's Monastery. (Photo by James Baca.)

vance, or Trappists. These followers of St. Benedict's Rule offered a spiritual counterpoint to the powder snow skiing, lavish resorts, and cultural life fostered by the Aspen Institute of Humanistic Studies.

"The Cistercians family decided this site near Mount Sopris was a place where we could support ourselves agriculturally and have the solitude necessary for the contemplative life," Father Joseph elaborated. The nineteen monks have raised sheep, cattle, and chickens, but perhaps their biggest source of income is their celebrated Snowmass cookies.

After acquiring the 3,800-acre site in 1955–1956, the monks built the sturdy, brick monastery and chapel in a mountain meadow on the headwaters of Capitol Creek. The public is welcome for morning lauds and mass and evening vespers, but otherwise, as the entry signpost announces, the monks ask to be left in solitude. St. Benedict's is not a parish but a special, spiritual retreat.

Snowmass Village, a resort and ski area, opened in the 1960s seven miles away. By the 1970s, hundreds of residents and thousands of tourists had flocked there. To provide for their spiritual needs, a mission was established in 1973. The pastor at St. Vincent's in Basalt offered mass in the Snowmass Village cinema on Sundays, after the ski runs closed. In 1989, the services were moved to the new Snowmass Interdenominational Chapel.

With both the Snowmass Village mission and St. Benedict's Monastery nearby, visitors seeking physical exercise and psychic renewal in the mag-

nificent Elk Mountains do not lack sacramental and spiritual guidance.

Steamboat Springs

HOLY NAME (1907)
504 Oak Street

Chugging, puffing steam from a hot springs led to the naming of Steamboat Springs, where James Harvey Crawford built the first cabin in 1875. A cluster of settlements followed along the Yampa River between Sod and Spring creeks.

Father William J. Howlett, who first visited Steamboat to say mass in 1880, reported:

> The vast district of Northwestern Colorado, comprising the counties of Jackson, Routt, Moffat and Grand, has been the slowest part of the state to receive settlers. Cut off by mountain ranges from railroads and markets, it has been left to herds of cattle and a few venturesome spirits who cared to brave solitude and privation.

Steamboat Springs did not flourish until the Denver, Salt Lake & Pacific Railroad arrived in 1909. Anticipating a railroad boom, Bishop Matz authorized creation of Holy Name parish. Early masses were held by John James Meyers, pastor of St. Peter's in Kremmling. He rode horseback to Steamboat to say mass in homes, the Masonic Lodge, and the newspaper office of the *Steamboat Springs Pilot.*

On June 5, 1911, Father Meyers bought a lot and house, nailed a giant cross atop the white frame cottage, and converted it to a house of God. He then moved to Steamboat, where he found a home with the large family of Frank M. Light. Light, in 1905, had opened F.M. Light & Sons (of whom there were seven), a Western clothing store. Light not only fed and housed Father Meyers, but presumably outfitted him in the best Western garb available.

First on horseback, then by rail and auto, Father Meyers traveled several hundred miles each Sunday to missions at Fraser, Kremmling, Oak Creek, and outlying ranches in his vast parish, which stretched from Walden and Kremmling to the Utah border. Father Paul D. Slattery visited Steamboat in

Monsignor Tom Dentici remodeled his Steamboat Springs parish plant, opened a hospitality center, and put out this welcome sign. (Photo by James Baca.)

1937 and reported to Bishop Vehr that Father Meyers' "fortune amounts to about $75," and "he is failing rapidly due to his advanced age." Father Meyers lived in a little room built onto the church until the Meunch family living next door took him in shortly before his fatal heart attack on December 31, 1938.

"The mountain priest," as people were reminded at the time of his death, had come to Colorado for his health and lived to be the oldest priest in the diocese. At his funeral, the crowd was too large to squeeze into the little Holy Name Church. "I know of no priest," said Archbishop Vehr, "more beloved by the people he served."

Father Edward Prinster, the second pastor, built a rectory in 1948 and established St. Martin Chapel in Oak Creek. He began planning a new Steamboat church but was killed in a fall from the roof of the rectory in 1956. Father Kenneth Funk, the next pastor, completed a new church on the old site. F. M. Light had donated an additional lot, and the congregation bought another for this spacious, modern brick church and rectory, a $100,000 project designed by J.K. Monroe and dedicated June 8, 1966.

Fathers Joseph Leberer, David Croak, Daniel Balzereit, Francis Ciaptacz, and Thomas Barry served as pastors until Monsignor Thomas Dentici arrived in 1983. By that time, Steamboat Springs had grown into a ski and summer resort as well as a ranching and mining center, boasting a 1980 population of 5,098. Holy Name parish had 250 registered families. Under Monsignor Dentici, Holy Name purchased the rest of its half-block site and began an active social ministry. A house next

to the church was acquired so that parish volunteers could renovate it as a hospitality center, which provided food, clothing, shelter, and pastoral care to anyone in need. The former rectory was converted to a retreat center.

"The symbol of the Oak Street church," as the *Steamboat Springs Pilot* noted upon Holy Name's seventy-fifth anniversary, are "the open hands, outstretched to cradle members of the parish family and extended to welcome visitors."

Monsignor Dentici added:

> It is one thing to preach about charity. We look upon our mission as an outward, tangible example of what charity should be. Our hospitality center is the only twenty-four-hour facility in Routt County. We consider it our way of paying back the community for what it had done for us. Our hands are not just outstretched but willing to get dirty.

Sterling

ST. ANTHONY (1908)
327 South 3rd Street

Founded in 1873, Sterling did not begin to grow until the Union Pacific arrived in 1887. Among other people and things, the railroad brought William J. Howlett to town. This pioneer missionary to northeastern Colorado reported in his *Recollections* that railroad workers flocked to the masses he held in a trackside tent: "From the graders on the road I collected enough money to buy a block of ground in Sterling, and in 1888 I built a frame church, which was dedicated by Bishop Matz, June 24, 1888, the feast of its patron, St. John the Baptist."

St. John's, Howlett added, was "hit three times by hurricanes and demolished the third time." Rather than rebuild this $1,000, 200-seat chapel after the August 1896 disaster, Father Howlett's successors said mass in the Logan County Courthouse. On their Sunday visits from St. Augustine's in Brighton, priests stayed with the families of Patrick Fleming or Anthony Giacomini.

Giacomini and Bernard Froegel, the missionary pastor, purchased the former Church of Christ at the corner of Chestnut and North 5th streets in 1902 for

St. Anthony's: in the garden grotto of Sterling's landmark church, Father Charles Hagus and some of his little lambs celebrated his May 1933 Silver Jubilee in traditional finery.

$600. Father Froegel fixed up the old brick church and frame parsonage next door. From Sterling, the Logan County seat, he also ministered to St. Peter's in Crook, St. Catherine's in Iliff, Sacred Heart in Peetz, and St. John's in Stoneham.

Meanwhile, the 1905 construction of the Great Western Sugar Company refinery sweetened life in Sterling, where the population swelled from 998 in 1900 to 3,044 in 1910. Catholics petitioned Bishop Matz to send them a resident priest, and in 1908, he answered their prayers by creating an independent parish and sending Peter U. Sasse, a native of Alsace-Lorraine. Although Father Sasse added on to the church, it remained inadequate.

Anthony Giacomini's son William, the town postmaster, worked with Father Sasse to purchase a site for a new church. This Romanesque structure used the traditional cruciform floorplan and con-

tained three altars, with the main altar front enhanced by a bas relief replica of Leonardo Da Vinci's painting, "The Last Supper." Frescoed walls sparkled in colorful shades cast by the imported stained glass windows. Over 500 people, half of them non-Catholics, gathered for the dedication by Bishop Matz on November 5, 1911, according to next day's *Sterling Evening Advocate*. Rather than use the old name—St. John's—the new church was named St. Anthony's in honor of Anthony Giacomini, the head of the pioneer Catholic clan who had for so long sustained the parish.

The German Congregational Zion Church bought old St. John's for $2,000, enabling Father Sasse to build a large two-story rectory north of the church in 1913. St. Anthony's, in 1917, purchased three adjacent houses to open a school. One was converted to a convent for nine Franciscan sisters from Milwaukee, Wisconsin, who opened a grade school in the former Frank H. Blair residence in the fall of 1918. The school soon swarmed with 400 students, inspiring the Sisters of St. Francis to start a high school in the house next door in 1922.

Following Father Sasse's transfer to Montrose in 1920, Charles H. Hagus took charge in Sterling. Father Hagus constructed a two-and-a-half-story, pressed red brick high school for $22,000 in 1934. A year earlier, both the parish and Father Hagus had celebrated silver jubilees, for which parishioners built Our Lady of Lourdes grotto.

St. Anthony's third pastor, Emile J. Verschraeghen, guided the parish from 1934 until his death in November 1962. Father Emile, who was fluent in English, French, German, and Italian, taught languages and religion in the high school. He delighted his many German-speaking parishioners by conducting a German school and preaching in German occasionally. Reflecting Father Verschraeghen's commitment to education, St. Anthony's replaced the two schoolhouses with a new brick grade school, gymnasium, and cafeteria, completed in 1951. This $200,000 expansion complemented the handsome high school and church. Although St. Anthony High School closed in 1970, the parish still offers preschool through sixth-grade education.

St. Anthony's rich history and elegant, well-preserved architecture led to its listing on the National Register of Historic Places in 1982. Eisenstraut, with the Black Hills Architects of

Deadwood, South Dakota, planned this $45,000 Romanesque revival gem, according to the *Sterling Advocate* of Febrary 17, 1913. Its reddish-orange pressed brick exterior is enhanced by cream-colored stone trim and foundations. The stocky, low façade is crowned by ornate gables with splendid corbelling and two mismatched crenelated towers.

Among the human landmarks of the parish is Sister Margaret Kohnen, OSF, who first came to teach at St. Anthony's in 1940 and was honored in 1976 as the Catholic Educator of the Year. St. Anthony's, which now occupies almost an entire block of downtown Sterling, provides some 800 families with spiritual, social, and scholastic opportunities.

Stoneham

ST. JOHN THE EVANGELIST (1910)

Like so many Colorado towns, Stoneham was a child of the railroad, platted in 1888 when the Burlington line reached its first section stop in eastern Weld County. In tiny Stoneham, the even tinier Catholic community built one of the loveliest of all the white churches on the Colorado high plains.

John Dugan, Alphonse Bethscheider, and Ernest Chockaert spearheaded organization of the parish in 1910, as a mission tended by Father Peter Stausse of Sterling, thirty miles to the east. Masses were held on the first Friday of every month in the home of John Dugan, proprietor of Dugan's Cash Grocer & General Merchandise, then moved to roomier quarters in the Stoneham School. Attendance exceeded all expectations, leading the congregation to build St. John the Evangelist Church in 1916.

Belgian, German, and Irish church members constructed a drop-sided frame church with Gothic windows and an enclosed bell tower. Inside, frosted glass windows shed soft light on plaster walls with plaster of Paris stations of the cross and a large statue of St. John the Evangelist (donated by John Dugan) over the altar tabernacle. According to the 1939 WPA church survey, other furnishings were wooden, with stained oak used for the pews and communion rail. The double sash windows could

be opened in summer in hopes of catching a cool breeze, while a pot-bellied coal stove warmed the congregation in winter.

After repeated requests from Dugan and other parishioners who offered to help buy the house next to the church for a rectory, Bishop Tihen assigned Leo Patrick as a resident pastor in 1926. Then the depression, drought, and dust storms struck. Grasshopper plagues and the shooting of John Dugan contributed to the plight of Stonehamites, who came to St. John's, where they could ponder the large painting by the altar—"The Agony in the Garden."

During the early 1930s, Bishop Vehr wrote to Father Patrick to point out that St. John's owed $183.93 to Will & Baumer Candle Company, America's oldest and largest church candlemaker. Furthermore, the diocese had received complaints that the priest was in arrears with others, ranging from a Stoneham shoe repairman to the church's insurance company. Father Patrick replied, in a letter dated November 17, 1931:

> The railroad has discharged all its help from this section. There is no organized charity here because we never needed it before, nor is there any possibility of raising funds hereabouts. There were three churches here and now only the Catholic Church remains. . . . Many of these people are in desperate shape, but their pride will not allow them to become county charges.

By 1950, Stoneham counted only 322 survivors, half the 1930 population. Despite the decline, St. John's had clung to its resident priest. Norbert J. Walsh, pastor from 1946 to 1951, reported that parishioners showered him with free coal and pheasant hunting possibilities.

During the 1980s, withering wheat and land prices left many farmers bankrupt. One frustrated fellow crashed through the front window of a Greeley bank on his tractor, which the bankers were repossessing.

In 1986, Archbishop Stafford, hoping to comfort farmers and get acquainted with the agricultural hinterlands of the archdiocese, visited the carpenter Gothic landmark in Stoneham, by then a mission tended from Brush. Kneeling with eight children at the altar of the seventy-year-old white clapboard church, the archbishop comforted Stoneham's flock with the prayer: "Dear Lord, we especially want to pray today for the farmers and their families in these hard times. May all their hopes and dreams be fulfilled."

Thornton

HOLY CROSS (1957)
9371 Wigham Street

Colorado Governor Dan Thornton was the namesake of the planned Adams County community of Thornton. Four years after the town's first show home opened in 1953, area Catholics convened in the historic Riverdale Grange Hall 187 to organize Holy Cross parish, which Archbishop Vehr formally created on August 15, 1957.

Charles T. Jones was selected as the founding pastor. When over 800 began squeezing into the grange hall for the four Sunday masses, he and members of the parish began "Operation Open House," with meetings in over 100 host homes to discuss church building.

Land was acquired on Eppinger Boulevard between York and Wigham streets, where a surplus Rocky Flats weapons plant structure was installed and remodeled as a church–school dedicated on October 13, 1957. The building was doubled in size and given a blond brick facing and a dramatic entryway wooden cross. Archbishop Vehr dedicated the new building on September 17, 1958. Franciscan nuns from nearby Marycrest Convent helped with religious instruction, to be followed in 1960 by the Sisters of Charity of Cincinnati; lay teachers taught secular subjects until the school closed in 1975.

To assist the many young families of the parish in buying new suburban homes in Thornton, Holy Cross established a parish credit union. Bake sales in Thornton Shopping Center, Mexican dinners, street dances, and St. Patrick's Day galas helped sustain the parish, whose membership soon climbed to over 1,000 families, with 125 children on the waiting list for the school.

Father Jones stepped down as pastor in 1967, to be followed by various pastors over the years, including Martin Lally, who has guided the parish of over 800 households since 1986. Charles J. Chaput,

a Native American Capuchin priest of the Prairie Band of the Potawatomis who served as pastor at Holy Cross during the 1970s, was appointed, in 1988, bishop of Rapid City, South Dakota.

A former parishioner, Pat Hillyer, became a prize winning reporter for the *Denver Catholic Register*, where she was appointed managing editor in 1988. In the parish's 1982 jubilee booklet, Pat reflected:

> Holy Cross'[s] humble beginning was an unpretentious grange hall, several miles outside the city. There was no polished wood, lovely furnishings, or golden ornaments. But, there was a nucleus of warm, loving people, on fire to become a united community and bear fruit for the Master. They, and those who followed, sacrificed countless amounts of time, talent and treasure to build what today stands as a unique parish, where people are the most important ingredient.

Vail

VAIL INTERFAITH CHAPEL (1965)
19 Vail Road

Vail, which was carved out of a mountain valley in 1962, has emerged as North America's premier ski resort. Many Catholic vacationers joined locals to establish a Catholic community in 1965.

Thomas Stone, the pastor of St. Patrick's in Minturn, offered mass for the Vail congregation in a restaurant and bar until the only church, the Interfaith Chapel, was constructed in 1966, an inspiring architectural monument designed by Pierce/Briner & Fitzhugh Scott, Inc. In 1978, the chapel was enlarged to accommodate 500 people.

Edward J. Poehlmann, resident pastor of St. Patrick's in Minturn, has tended Vail as a mission since 1987. "I've loved and skied Vail Mountain for years," Father Poehlmann reported in 1988. "Our ski masses at Vail are informal, with ski attire welcome as we pray to, among others, the patron saint of Alpinists, St. Bernard."

Roughly half the congregation, according to Father Poehlmann, consists of Spanish-speaking tourists from Mexico and Latin America, as well as U.S. celebrities such as Gregory Peck and tennis champion Jimmy Connors. For the crowded midnight mass on Christmas, the congregation has used the Vail skating rink and the Manor Vail Lodge.

Walden

ST. IGNATIUS (1960)

Walden, the seat of vast but sparsely settled Jackson County, has the county's only Catholic mission, tended from St. Peter's in Kremmling. Monsignor Thomas Patrick Barry, pastor of St. Peter's when the Walden mission was founded, told that parish's story in a 1987 interview:

> State Senator Charles P. Murphy of Walden picked a church site on the south side of the Jackson County Courthouse—two of the grandest lots in all of North Park—and gave them to me for a church. Archbishop Vehr and the Catholic Extension Society, a national outfit based in Chicago, gave us $5,000 to build a church provided we name it St. Ignatius after a donor wanting to honor his uncle.
>
> We built a cinderblock and stucco church with brick trim. Seated 100. Archbishop Vehr sent up an architect from J.K. Monroe's office to make sure we didn't build a barn, but a "churchy" church. We put in a wall of Lyons sandstone behind the altar, used golden oak pews and floors.
>
> After Archbishop Vehr dedicated the church in 1952, Senator Murphy quietly came to me and asked, "how much is the debt?" I told him we still owed $4,500 on what had turned out to be an $11,550 church. The next week I got seven checks from him, checks signed by him, his family, and his friends. So we never had a debt after the first week.
>
> Walden was a rugged little town with four saloons—all owned by my parishioners! I didn't get over to Walden in the winter—you couldn't—but showed up for Easter and about once a month during decent weather. And when I came into town in my 1949 green Ford, all four bars would stick up a sign—MASS—and give the time.

Wattenberg

OUR LADY OF GRACE (1978)

Wattenberg was established halfway between Brighton and Fort Lupton when the Denver, Laramie & Northwestern Railroad built to the site in 1909. Hispanic farm workers who settled there arranged to have Joseph P. Trudel offer mass.

Wattenbergers waited patiently for Father Trudell to roll into town in his old black Buick and ring the bell of the tiny chapel, which some whispered had been a Penitente *morada*. They met in this humble structure until the owner of an abandoned pea cannery donated his building. Parishioners contributed labor and materials, including two pot-bellied coal stoves, to convert the cannery to a church. The stations of the cross were donated by St. Leo's in Denver, while the pews came from Regis College, the statues of Joseph and Mary from St. Anthony's in Sterling, the altar from St. Benedict's Monastery in Snowmass, and the stained glass windows from St. Augustine's in Brighton.

Parishioners petitioned Archbishop Vehr for a priest but were told they would have to guarantee a Sunday collection of $30. This was no small goal for the poor flock, but Piedad and Toribio Tafoya undertook the task. When they had the money, they called Greeley, and St. Peter's or Our Lady of Peace sent a priest. In more recent years, this tiny but determined parish has been tended by the pastor of St. Williams in Fort Lupton.

Weldona

ST. FRANICS OF ASSISI (1919)

Reverend Bernard Froegel of Brighton stepped off the Union Pacific train in 1911 to say the first Weldona mass in Schafer's Hall. Theodora Arnold, who owned a nearby hotel, put up visitors, including First Communion and confirmation classes, which she helped prepare.

After Theodora and Henry Arnold donated a church site at Warner Avenue and Cottage Street, bricks were shipped out on the Union Pacific to the little South Platte River farm town. Members of the congregation hauled them to the site to build St. Francis of Assisi Church. Dedicated on November 1, 1919, the little Gothic church was tended first from Brighton, then from Fort Lupton (1920–1924), Stoneham (1925–1926), Brush (1927–1967), and, most recently, from Fort Morgan, which lies fourteen miles to the southeast.

Following its 1893 founding, Weldona attracted many Italian farm families who supported their church with dinners and dances. One of the pastors who cared for the St. Francis mission was wary of such fund-raisers. Father Peter U. Sasse wrote to Bishop Tihen on July 18, 1928, enclosing a newspaper clipping about the St. Francis Ladies Guild and Altar Society's dance hall permit from the Morgan County Commissioners, warning that "these road house dance halls have been the cause of untold scandal and agony to decent people." Several ladies of the parish, who have compiled more detailed histories for the archdiocesan archives, hasten to add that the dances were "always decent."

From 1948 until 1981, every man, woman, and child of the parish had been called upon to work the annual ravioli dinner, a fund-raiser that drew up to 1,000 guests. In 1961, the Union Pacific gave St. Francis's its twenty-two-by-fifty-foot frame depot, which was converted to a three-room parish hall. Once again, the congregation of two dozen families managed to raise enough—$600—to furnish their new facility, thanks to prayer, hard work, and a lot of ravioli.

Westminister

HOLY TRINITY (1948)
7595 Federal Boulevard

The Adams County town of Westminster grew up around Westminster College, a soaring castle-like building on the highest hill in what is now a thriving suburban community. Between 1940 and 1950, the town's population tripled from 534 to 1,619.

John Giambastiani, the Servite pastor of nearby Assumption parish in Welby, realized that mush-

Holy Trinity Church, Westminster, on its dedication day, September 24, 1959. (Photo by Ray DeAragon.)

rooming Westminster needed a parish of its own. He held a meeting in September 1948, in the home of Anthony Blatter, where eighty families opted to form a parish. A site was available as Archbishop Vehr had bought a four-acre tract on West 72nd Avenue between Hooker and Irving streets in December 1946.

For $6,000, an army barracks was moved to the tract and capped with a cross and steeple. Approximately 150 worshippers showed up for the first mass on Christmas Day, 1948. Archbishop Vehr formally dedicated the church to the Holy Trinity on April 7, 1949, and asked Forrest Allen of St. Anne's in Arvada to handle it on a mission basis. The Sisters of Saint Joseph of Carondelet from St. Catherine parish began teaching catechism classes in January 1949.

By August 28, 1957, when Holy Trinity Church had to offer four masses each Sunday to accommodate 1,100 parish households, Albert Puhl was appointed the first-full time pastor. He lived at St. Anne's in Arvada until the Frank Huber home at 7190 Julian Street was procured as a rectory. The fast growing parish soon had to offer additional masses in Westminster High School, and the building committee decided that the four-acre site was inadequate.

The old site was sold for $85,000, and a new 12.33-acre site was purchased for $68,000. The new location contained two old houses and some rickety outbuildings that were demolished before groundbreaking on September 7, 1958. To guide and inspire the parish through the construction process, Father Puhl placed a small roadside shrine to Christ Crucified in what was then a sheep field.

There, the shrine stood sentinel and remains to this day.

The new $250,000 building to house the growing worship community was dedicated on September 24, 1959. The Santa Fe Studios of Church Art designed and manufactured the interior furnishings for the modern, low-slung brick church. A $103,000 rectory was completed in 1962, and a convent in 1965. The $222,857 school opened in the fall of 1966, staffed by four lay teachers and four Dominicans from Great Bend, Kansas, until the sisters withdrew in 1985.

"From the Heart to the Head" is the motto of Holy Trinity School, 3050 West 76th Avenue, which offers education from preschool (age four) to eighth grade, as well as extended care before and after school. Father Puhl saw his booming parish through the changes inspired by Vatican II, including replacement of the traditional Latin Mass with an English service in 1964. After seventeen years at the parish he founded, Father Puhl stepped down in 1973, when the Servite order took charge. Since then, Mark Francescini, OSM, and Jude Herlihy, OSM, have guided Holy Trinity parish, which by 1988 served 1,800 registered households.

OUR LADY OF VISITATION (1950)
2531 West 65th Place

Back in 1949, the Spanish-speaking people of Goat Hill, a rural patch of unincorporated Adams County, prayed for a chapel of their own. They received a streetcar church.

After the Denver Tramway Company shifted to rubber-tired busses, Joseph Trudell asked them for a streetcar. They gave him two. Parishioners were overjoyed after years of meeting in the Penitente *morada* at the east end of West 65th Place for services with Father Trudel, the chaplain at Mercy Hospital. Benito García donated a lot next to his home for the old trolley cars. They were put on cinderblocks and the adjoining sides removed to make one large room. Parishioners donated labor and materials to refit the old streetcars with pews, an altar, and an altar rail. A small steeple bell was set on top in time to toll for Christmas mass in 1949.

Goat Hill residents lived mostly on the cattle, pigs, goats, chickens, rabbits, and vegetables they raised, and on paychecks from the Savory Mush-room plant at 100th Avenue and Federal Boulevard. But church members gave what they could to the streetcar church. Marcos Saiz contributed hogs and piglets for parish raffles—until the Pentecostal Church down the street won the Catholic porker.

The streetcar chapel served Goat Hill until 1954, when a concrete block church was built across the street. At that time, the name was changed from Chapel of the Good Shepherd to Our Lady of Visitation. Priests from various parishes, especially the Servite fathers, tended the tiny, poor Goat Hill flock. George R. Evans, before he became a bishop, asked for and received this parish and built a $9,800 hall for its legendary Mexican dinner fund-raisers.

Our Lady of Visitation Church became a mission of Holy Trinity, after that parish's creation in 1957. This humble mission has been more than a church over the years. The Adams County Welfare Department uses it as an outreach office, as has the Salvation Army's seniors program. Although never large or prosperous enough to merit a resident pastor, the streetcar parish has survived by offering much to its Spanish-speaking congregation.

ST. MARK (1973)
3141 West 96th Avenue

Although burgeoning Westminster already had two parishes, Albert Puhl, pastor of Holy Trinity, realized that the Catholic contingent in northern Westminster needed a church of its own. Fortunately, the far-sighted Archbishop Vehr had paid Thomas B. Croke $75,000 for a site back in 1960.

Father Puhl launched organizational meetings in 1972, and after the Servites took over Holy Trinity parish, he assured Archbishop Casey that he "found it a great privilege to be chosen for the challenge of forming a parish. It was a happy experience, but quite a challenge starting from scratch." Parishioners rejoiced, knowing that the parish building process would be much easier with their well-established, well-liked pastor.

Father Puhl continued to hold protoparish meetings at Holy Trinity while he and his parishioners had a chance "to think and thus to grow." Together, they planned what was tentatively called the Hollyhurst Catholic Community, as the sixty-five-acre Croke property had been subdivided in 1925 to create the residential area marketed as Hollyhurst.

Besides the Hollyhurst neighborhood, the new parish boundaries included what would become the Environs and various other new developments between Pecos Street on the east and Sheridan Boulevard on the west, between West 88th and 120th avenues.

Father Puhl offered the first mass for the Hollyhurst Catholic Community on April 2, 1973, in the gym of the Vista Grande Elementary School. After the Servites moved into his former rectory at Holy Trinity, he bought a residence at 3660 West 94th Avenue. Pastor and some 250 parish families looked forward to moving into a new parish plant. Ramón F. Martínez, a Denver architect, designed a $416,000 building for the five-lot site two blocks west of Federal Boulevard. The project was financed with the help of a $250,000 loan from the Bosworth Sullivan Investment Company.

The handsome church with clerestory windows was dedicated by Auxiliary Bishop George Evans on October 11, 1975. The 400-seat church included two interconnecting wings used as administration offices, rectory, and social hall (which had a folding wall so it could be converted to overflow church seating). The frugal simplicity of the new church struck opening day visitors as they entered on plywood panel walks and found folding chairs instead of pews inside.

Father Puhl was appointed pastor of Christ the King parish in Denver in March 1978 and was succeeded at St. Mark's by John A. Canjar, the present pastor. By 1986, when the parish had grown to 1,000 households, Father Canjar began a $608,000 expansion. Planned by Denver architect Ron Dougherty, the 3,961–square foot addition included seating for 200 more churchgoers, a Blessed Sacrament Chapel, a reconciliation room, an enlarged entry, and extensive landscaping, and expanded the parking lot.

"We would like to see the parish grow," Father Canjar noted in 1988, "not only in numbers, but as a stronger Christian community dedicated to the teachings of the Gospel." Evidence that the church was growing in this direction came in 1987, when parishioners adopted the Catholic Worker House Soup Kitchen in Denver's Five Points neighborhood. Empty soup kettles were placed at the entrances to St. Mark's and the money placed there— about $250 a month—as well as parish volunteers went into the inner city soup kitchen to nourish the poor. Since 1978, church members have sponsored one of the Westminster FISH food banks that gives baskets of food to the needy in the Westminster area Monday through Friday on a call-in basis.

Wheat Ridge

STS. PETER AND PAUL (1949)
3900 Pierce Street

Wheat Ridge, which once was wheat fields, has become a Jefferson County suburb of over 30,000. For Catholics in the prospering bedroom community, Archbishop Vehr, on June 1, 1948, bought from the Ricci family at a considerable discount— $1,600 an acre—a four-acre site .

Robert G. McMahon, the son of a prominent Denver clan and brother of Reverend Donald McMahon, was appointed the first pastor of Sts. Peter and Paul's on June 30, 1949. Many of the 120 Catholic families within the parish met for the first masses in Weakland Brothers Store before the $47,000 church–rectory–parish hall existed. Folding chairs and kneelers made of two-by-four-inch planks on cement blocks were used in the sparsely adorned basement church, which Archbishop Vehr dedicated on September 18, 1950. For the celebration, parishioners arose at 4 A.M. to plant 1,000 gladiolas in the bare earth surrounding the construction site.

Church members raised money with square dances, an annual Fall Fantasy Ball, bingo in the Wheat Ridge Grange Hall, and a "Ten for Ten Club" of supporters pledging ten dollars a month for ten months. In September 1955, Sts. Peter and Paul School opened as a two-story, $150,000, modern structure at 3920 Pierce Street on the north side of the church. The school, by architect John F. Connell, contained four classrooms, a gymnasium–auditorium, and a teachers' lounge. A home at 4040 Pierce Street was bought as a convent for the three Dominican sisters of Sinsinawa, Wisconsin, who opened the school for 138 children.

Father McMahon, who had gained some fame as the "skiing padre," took parishioners and their children to Arapahoe Basin to launch a parish ski program in 1956. He skied on Sundays with a Mass kit on his back for services on the snowy slopes. "Skiing is a wonderful sport," he told the *Denver Post*, "and skiers should have the same opportunity of assisting at Mass as those who have access to churches."

In 1957, church services were moved out of the overcrowded pioneer building into the school gym. A decade later, the parish celebrated Father McMahon's silver jubilee as a priest, and Archbishop Casey gave him a welcome gift—an assistant pastor, John Imesch, SMB, a Swiss-born member of the Bethlehem fathers. Two years later, the parish burned its mortgage at a party celebrating the achievement of a debt free million-dollar plant.

Time flew by for the young, energetic parish, which mourned the death of its first pastor on December 30, 1979. To that suburban community, Father McMahon's thirty-year pastorate had been a blessing—an unusual bit of stability in a rapidly changing suburban scene.

Omer V. Foxhoven, the second pastor of Sts. Peter and Paul, completed an impressive modern church dedicated on September 9, 1984. As Father Foxhoven explained at that time, the new church was "being erected on the foundation laid by Father McMahon, over the present basement structure, extending both to the east and the west. The present facilities will be dedicated to the memory of Father McMahon as the McMahon Parish Center."

Approximately 1,000 registered households sustain the large parish plant, where in 1988 the Dominicans, led by Sister Marie Janet Meis, OP, still operated the school for kindergarteners through eighth graders. Father Foxhoven's forty-four years as a priest in the archdiocese were rewarded in 1988 when, upon Archbishop Stafford's recommendation, Pope John Paul II appointed him a monsignor.

Wiggins

OUR LADY OF LOURDES (1916)

The Morgan County town of Wiggins started out in 1882 as the Burlington railroad depot of Corona. Around 1900, Corona was renamed in honor of Oliver P. Wiggins, a noted Indian scout who had a trading post there in the old days.

J.L. Juily, pastor at Fort Morgan, began celebrating mass in the apartment over Jacob Yegge's Wiggins Meat Market in 1916. That same year, Father Juily acquired two lots and permission from Bishop Matz to build a church. He designed the church and oversaw its construction; with the pastor and his eighteen parish families doing much of the work themselves, the little frame chapel was built for about $1,000, half of which was donated by the Catholic Extension Society, and dedicated in November 1916.

Father Juily, whose four brothers back in France were fighting in World War I, named the new parish for Our Lady of Lourdes with the prayer that she would protect them. After Father Juily was transferred in 1918, various other Fort Morgan priests offered monthly masses in the little mission church in Wiggins. In 1923, Our Lady of Lourdes became a mission of St. Mary's in Brush. After the Great Depression, the 1935 Memorial Day flood, and World War II took their toll, Our Lady of Lourdes dwindled to eight families and became inactive in 1953.

By 1959, when missionary priests resumed services in Wiggins, the church had fallen into such disrepair that masses were held in the music building of the Wiggins Grade School. The parish began growing again, particularly with the influx of migrant laborers, inspiring the congregation to purchase the old Wiggins Community Church building and five adjoining lots for $8,500. Volunteers remodeled the interior and converted the basement to a parish hall. The old church was sold, and parishioner Bob Franzel remodeled it into his residence.

James L. Ahern, pastor of St. Mary's in Brush, resumed weekly trips to Our Lady of Lourdes. The revived parish also began offering a summer school, conducted by students from St. Thomas Seminary in Denver. Missionary Sisters of Our Lady of Victory and Dominican sisters also visited the parish during the summer to help provide religious education.

In 1970, Wiggins became a mission of Sacred Heart parish in Roggen, whose pastor also attended Keenesburg. A May 7, 1973, flood of Kiowa Creek inundated the church, reconfirming parish sentiment to move and build a new church. On August 4, 1974, Archbishop Casey dedicated the new, $100,000 home of Our Lady of Lourdes. Although the small town of Wiggins remained a mission of Sacred Heart in Roggen, the fifty families of Our Lady of Lourdes demonstrated, with their impressive new church, their staunch commitment to Catholicism.

Windsor

OUR LADY OF THE VALLEY (1969)
129 Walnut Street

Windsor, a Weld County town first settled in the 1870s, was named for Reverend Samuel Asa Windsor, who founded the First Methodist Church. The railroad arrived in 1881, and in 1903 the Great Western Sugar Company opened its large plant. During the 1950s, priests from Greeley said masses in the homes of the Apodacas, the Velásquezes, and the Volges.

Windsor began to boom in 1968 when Eastman Kodak, the leading U.S. photography company, erected a giant plant there. The following year, area Catholics started a "little parish" and persuaded Kenneth Brin of St. Joseph's in Fort Collins to offer monthly masses in St. Alban Episcopal Church. Thomas L. McCormick, director of Catholic Community Services for Northern Colorado, was appointed the first pastor on March 16, 1973. Mildred Piñeda submitted the winning name for the new parish—Our Lady of the Valley.

In 1974, Our Lady of the Valley became a mission of St. John's in Loveland. By raising money with Mexican dinners, Christmas bazaars, and a Labor Day harvest festival booth at the town ball park, the faithful financed purchase of a 514–516 Main Street building. They converted it to a chapel, hall, offices, and rectory, which was blessed by Archbishop Casey on February 15, 1976.

Three years later, the fast growing parish sold its building and bought the old Zion Church, a handsome, white frame, carpenter Gothic church that has been extensively remodeled inside. Thomas D. Kelly, pastor of St. John the Baptist's in Johnstown, took charge in 1985 of this parish of about 180 households.

Winter Park

ST. BERNARD (1980)

After the City and County of Denver opened Winter Park as a ski area in 1940, a small town sprang up below the lifts at the west portal of the Moffat Railroad Tunnel.

Catholics found a little chapel nearby on the William Z. Cozens ranch. Cozens, the pioneer sheriff of Central City, had helped establish St. Mary Church there with his wife, Mary York Cozens. After the Cozenses became the first homesteaders in the Fraser River valley in 1872, they welcomed priests at their ranch where early-day masses were celebrated. Among the visitors to the ranch over the years were Jesuits from Regis College. William Cozens, Jr., continued his father's tradition of hosting Catholic masses and the Jesuits and, in 1931, gave that order the historic ranch and 400-acre spread. The Jesuits converted it to a retreat and recreation villa, which they called Maryvale.

Sheriff William Cozens' ranch house, thought to be the oldest structure in Grand County, was rechristened Maryvale by the Jesuits who offered Sunday masses in Winter Park.

The Jesuits at Maryvale offered a regular Sunday mass in the quaint cabin that still stands along U.S. highway 40. Winter Park became a full-blown resort town in the 1970s, Sunday worshippers soon outgrew the little church. In 1980, Archbishop Casey authorized establishment of St. Bernard parish. During the pastorate of Philip Meredith—a skier—the parish celebrated Christmas with a torchlight ski run followed by midnight mass.

H. Robert White, pastor of St. Anne's in Grand Lake, took charge of the St. Bernard mission in the 1980s. To accommodate the fast growing parish and many tourists, he began holding Saturday evening and Sunday morning masses in the Silver Screen Theater in Winter Park.

Wray

ST. ANDREW (1918)
504 South Ash

John Wray, a foreman on the nearby I.P. Olive ranch, gave his name to the town platted in 1886. As the seat of Yuma County, Wray has become a high plains hub noted for its cattle ranches, wheat farms, and prairie chicken preserves.

James J. Hickey, pastor at St. Augustine's in Brighton, rode the Burlington railroad to Wray for the first Catholic service. The Wray Public School, the nearby Eckley section house, and the residences of Andrew Hoy and Edward O'Donnell were used as mission stops.

The Lincoln Land Company, which developed many eastern Colorado railroad towns, donated a church site on the east side of Wray at the base of Flirtation Point. Hoy, a prominent town banker, started a building fund, promising to double the contribution of the next highest contributor. In his honor, the church was named for his patron saint. A carpenter–contractor named Moohat donated his labor in designing and building the twenty-four-by-twenty-four-foot frame church dedicated in 1891 by Bishop Matz.

A small rectory was completed in 1892 for Francis X. Schrafel, the first resident pastor. A year later, he was followed by John Brinker, who guided the small Wray congregation, as well as many outlying mission stations, through the drought and depression of the 1890s. During these crises, Wray once again became a mission, attended from Brighton, Fort Morgan, or Akron. A twelve-by-twenty-four-foot sacristy was added to the church in 1914 during a $410 remodeling, which included replacing the old coal stove with a basement furnace. During the 1926–1932 resident pastorate of James T. Cotter, the congregation spent approximately $6,500 on

St. Andrew's handsome carpenter Gothic chapel of 1891 was replaced in 1939 by this neat Romanesque house of worship in Wray. (Early photo from Denver Archdiocesan Archives; later photo by Tom Noel.)

expanding and enhancing the church. The little stick cross on front was replaced by a bell tower and the frame altar by a fine marble one.

The next pastor, Joseph A. Korb, stayed in Wray as its priest for thirty-seven years. When a fire destroyed the 1891 church, Father Korb moved his flock into a new church at the corner of Dexter and West 5th. Dedicated on October 12, 1939, by Bishop Vehr, the new structure was stuccoed cinderblock with a red tile roof, attractively trimmed in Spanish-southwestern style.

Father Korb retired in 1969, after celebrating the golden jubilee of his priesthood, but continued to make his home in Wray as pastor emeritus until his death in 1976. John Barone, pastor from 1981 to 1986, impressed parishioners with his loving attention to the elderly, to shut-ins and to children, all of whom he seemed to know by name. Father Barone also reroofed and repainted the church, mowed the large lawn, and minded the landscaping. St. Andrew's, blessed with caring pastors and a vigilant congregation that had grown to 110 families by the 1980s, has not only survived, but thrived.

Yuma

ST. JOHN (1888)
504 South Ash Street

Yuma was platted in 1885 and incorporated in 1887 as the Chicago, Burlington & Quincy Railroad laid tracks across the high plains of eastern Colorado. Yuma ("sons of the river") is the name of an Indian people on the lower Colorado River, one of whom supposedly worked on the railroad construction crew.

Yuma railroad workers, farmers, and ranchers welcomed the news that the Burlington was providing free passage for a priest, William J. Howlett. He arrived from Denver to celebrate the first mass on October 2, 1887, then organized a parish, secured lots and drew up plans for a church. Wenzel Blach, Sr., a native of Austria, led volunteers who began constructing a humble building. Not until 1906 did parishioners celebrate completion of their white frame church, graced with a Gothic door and windows and crowned by an open, two-story bell tower.

Even during winter blizzards, folks dressed up in their Sunday best, hitching up their spiffiest teams and wagons to head for church, where mass, the sacraments, and a tiny pot-bellied stove warmed both souls and bodies. Inside, parishioners prayed for rain, for an end to dust storms and grasshopper plagues, and for a resident priest.

Their prayers were answered when World War I drove grain and livestock prices to all-time highs, and prosperity came to Yuma, where the population reached 1,177 by 1920. In 1922, Wenzel Blach, Sr., finished the church interior—plastering the walls, installing floors and woodwork, and constructing an altar. In 1923, Bishop Tihen began assigning resident priests to minister to the fifty-two families of St. John's.

"The man who took our parish through the depression," recalled Perry Blach, grandson of Wenzel Blach, Sr.;

was Father William Coyne. Before he went into the priesthood, he had been a hat salesman. People had no money, but donated eggs, produce, and whatnot, which Father bartered for stuff the church needed. As a skilled businessman, he got us through until 1941 when the rains finally came. The grateful faithful in Yuma and Akron chipped in to buy him a new, $750, grey Ford. It was Father Coyne's first car.

Clement V. Gallagher arrived in 1947, donning overalls to join his parishioners in erecting a red brick parish hall and rectory in 1948. Townsfolk of all faiths came from miles around for St. John's annual Easter dances, a welcome respite from spring ranch and farm chores. Father Gallagher, a bibliophile, built up a large parish library and also donated generously to the Yuma Public Library.

A new church was built by the next pastor, John McGinn (1961–1966). Menfolk of the parish tore down the old frame church and rented the vacant Methodist Church at 3rd and Ash streets while construction began on a modern, $106,000 brick church. On June 11, 1964, the auxiliary bishop of Denver, David M. Maloney, presided as parishioners celebrated their diamond jubilee and dedication of their new spiritual home. Within three years, Father McGinn and his flock retired the debt on their new house of the Lord.

The new St. John's seated 300 and its sanctuary featured exquisite statues from Italy and a large crucifix from Germany. The basement contained two kitchens and a dining hall for 400.

Despite droughts and low farm prices that turned many neighboring towns into ghosts, Yuma flourished, reaching a population of 2,824 by 1980.

John L. Hilton, pastor since 1987, reported that St. John's eighty-two parish families observed their 1988 centennial with optimism and publication of a new parish history. "Cattle, corn, land, and wheat prices are finally going up again," Father Hilton said in 1988, "and St. John's, whose strength for a century has been its faithful and sturdy parishioners, is celebrating!"

SOURCES

As I was asked to write a popular history and keep it much shorter than this is, footnotes have been omitted. When quotes or statements seemed to cry out for documentation, I have tried to provide the source in the text.

History is only as accurate as its sources—which are fallible. In many cases I have relied on oral history, on wonderful sources like Monsignor Gregory Smith, who remembers Bishop Matz's burial and meeting William J. Howlett, the pioneer priest-historian of Colorado Catholicism. The best single source, to which I am deeply indebted, is Monsignor William Jones's meticulously documented book, *The History of Catholic Education in the State of Colorado*. Covering far more than its title claims, this book provides parish and institutional sketches as well as school history. Readers wanting fuller detail and documentation would be well advised to consult it.

The archdiocesan archives, organized in a most helpful fashion during the 1970s by Sister Elizabeth Skiff, are the major source for this book. They contain extensive file boxes for each bishop and archbishop as well as for each parish and agency of the church. Once again, Monsignor Jones's book, which has lengthy chapters on each bishop through Vehr, is also invaluable. William J. Howlett's *Life of Bishop Machebeuf*, recently revived in a third edition edited by Tomas Steele, SJ, and Ronald Brockway is the definitive source for Machebeuf, though copies of Machebeuf's letters (in the original French and in English translation) at the archives are irresistible.

The financial, personal, and personnel difficulties of Machebeuf and Matz, including the revelations that Machebeuf used a spittoon at mass and that several of his priests tried to assassinate Matz, are explored in documented detail in Thomas Francis Feely, *Leadership in the Early Colorado Catholic Church* (University of Denver, History Ph.D. Dissertation 1973), which presents the often overlooked darker side of church affairs. Such exposés are not available for later bishops, though rumors survive that Tihen was forced to resign.

For bishops Tihen and Vehr, Monsignor Jones's book is the best source, supplemented by the papers of these prelates at the archdiocesan archives. Robert A. Goldberg's first-rate *Hooded Empire: The Ku Klux Klan in Colorado* is enlightening on that spooky era, as were Monsignor Gregory Smith's transcribed memoirs and my interviews with him.

For the Casey and Stafford eras, the lack of published sources and a dearth of archival material led to a heavy reliance on the *Denver Catholic Register*, oral history interviews, and secular sources. Growing reliance on the telephone, alas, has left the historian at a loss for revealing letters, diaries, and written documents.

For the brief sketches of parishes, I am indebted to parishes for providing records and previously published histories, and for reviewing and correcting drafts sent to each pastor. Apologies to many a parish for the abbreviated treatment here, which generally precluded mention of assistant pastors, short-term pastors, sisters, donors, deacons, active parishioners, and other important people. Those wanting fuller histories should consult the parish or the archives.

Previously published histories, available for most of the parishes, range from lavish books with color photos to one-page typescripts. Besides these sources, I have relied on interviews and on files, arranged by parish, at the archdiocesan archives. At the Colorado Historical Society, archivist Stan Oliner kindly provided me with copies of the previously unused and most helpful 1930s WPA *State and Local Records Survey of Colorado Churches*. These architectural and historical reports on many of the Colorado parishes provided revealing descriptions of churches, their history, their record-keeping, and their staffs. Published county and community histories often yielded additional data.

Readers who wish to explore the history of Catholicism in a wider context are well-advised to look up Jay P. Dolan's books, including *The Immigrant Church* and *The American Catholic Experience*; James J. Hennesey's *American Catholics*; or John Tracy Ellis's *American Catholicism* and *A Guide to American Catholic History*.

ARCHIVAL SOURCES

Boulder. University of Colorado. Norlin Library. Western Historical Collections.
Westermeier, Clifford P. and Therese S. Collection.

Denver. Archdiocese of Denver Archives.
Archdiocese of Denver. *Mission and Ministry in Northern Colorado: Archdiocese of Denver Quinquennial Report to the Holy Father.* October, 1983.
Archdiocese of Denver. *Metropolitan Area Census Survey, November, 1967.* Washington, D.C.: Census Management, 1967.
Archdiocese of Denver. *Quinquennial Report for the Archdiocese of Denver.* 1978.
Archdiocese of Denver. *Review and Planning for the 1970s: A Study of the Catholic Charities Program.* New York: Ralph Whelan & Associates, 1970.

Archdiocese of Denver. Presbyteral Council Minutes.

Catholic Charities Files and Annual Reports. 1925–present.

Howlett, William J. *Diocese of Denver: History of Churches*. 131-page typescript. Undated.

——*Pioneer Priests of the Denver Diocese*. 183-page typescript. Undated.

——*Recollections of My Life and Reflections on Times and Events During It, 1847–1936*. 98-page typescript. Undated.

Machebeuf, Matz, Tihen, Vehr, Casey, and Stafford Collections.

Parish Records.

Smith, Gregory. *Taped and Typescript Memoirs*. A 1977–79 oral history project conducted by the Archdiocesan Archivist, Sister Elizabeth Skiff.

Smith, Matthew. *Memoirs*. Bound copy of articles serialized in the *Denver Catholic Register*, 1948–49.

Denver. Colorado Historical Society. Stephen Hart Library.

CWA Interviews. *Alamosa, Conejos and Costilla Counties*. 1934.

WPA Federal Writers Program Manuscripts. *Architecture of Denver Churches*. 1939.

Photo Collection.

Place Name Files.

Denver. Colorado State Archives.

WPA *Survey of State and Local Historical Records. Colorado. Church Records*. 1936–39.

Denver. Denver Catholic Register Library.

Clippings Files.

Photo Files.

Denver. Denver Public Library. Western History Department.

Clipping Files.

Photo Collection.

Place Name files.

Denver. Regis College. Jesuit History Library, Room 314, Carrol Hall.

Miscellaneous Documents.

Santa Fe. New Mexico State Records and Archives Center.
Archives of the Archdiocese of Santa Fe. Loose Documents, Letters to and from
    Bishops Lamy and Machebeuf, 1853–1860.

NEWSPAPERS AND PERIODICALS

The Catholic Periodical and Literature Index (formerly the *Guide To Catholic Litera-
    ture.* Bimonthly. Haverford, Penn.: The Catholic Library Association, 1930–1988.
The Colorado Catholic (Denver)
The Denver Catholic Register
The Denver Post
The Guild: Official Magazine of St. Thomas Seminary (Denver)
Rocky Mountain News (Denver)

BOOKS AND BOOKLETS

Archdiocese of Denver. *Official Directory.* Denver: Archdiocese of Denver, 1960–An-
    nual.
Arps, Louisa Ward. *Cemetery to Conservatory: A History of the Land Around Denver
    Botanic Gardens, 1859–1978.* Denver: Denver Botanic Gardens, 1980.
Arps, Louisa, ed. *Faith on the Frontier: Religion in Colorado Before 1876.* Denver:
    Colorado Council of Churches, 1976.
Bolton, Herbert E. *Pageant in the Wilderness: The Story of the Escalante Expedition
    to the Interior Basin, 1776.* Salt Lake City: Utah Historical Society, 1950.
Breck, Allen D. *The Episcopal Church in Colorado, 1860–1963.* Denver: Big Moun-
    tain Press, 1963.
Casey, M. Celestine, SL, and M. Edmond Fern, SL, *Loretto in the Rockies.* Denver:
    Loretto Heights College, 1943.
City Club of Denver and Denver Public Library. *Art in Denver.* Denver: 1928.
Cochran, Alice Cowan. *Miners, Merchants and Missionaries: The Roles of Mis-
    sionaries and Pioneer Churches in the Colorado Gold Rush and Its Aftermath,*

1858–1870. Metuchen, N.J.: Scarecrow Press and the American Theological Library Association, 1980.

Darley, Alex M. *The Passionists of the Southwest: Or, the Holy Brotherhood, A Revelation of the Penitentes*. Pueblo: 1893; reprint by Rio Grande Press, Glorietta, New Mexico, 1968.

Denver City Directories, 1873–1988 (various publishers). Annual.

Dyer, John L. *The Snow-Shoe Itinerant: An Autobiography*. Cincinnati: Cranston & Stowe, 1889; reprint by Father Dyer United Methodist Church, Breckenridge, 1975.

Eberhart, Perry. *Ghosts of the Colorado Plains*. Athens, Ohio: Swallow Press, 1986.

Gibbons, James Joseph. *In the San Juan, Colorado Sketches*. Chicago: Calumet Book and Engraving, 1898; reprint by St. Patrick's Parish, Telluride, 1972.

Hallett, Paul H. *Witness to Permanence: Reflections of a Catholic Journalist*. San Francisco, Calif.: Ignatius Press, 1987.

Hays, Alice Marie, OSB. *A Song in the Pines: The History of Benet Hill Community*. Colorado Springs: Benet Hill Benedictine Sisters, 1976.

Horgan, Paul. *Lamy of Santa Fe: His Life and Times*. New York: Farrar, Straus and Giroux, 1975.

Howlett, Willam J. *Life of Bishop Machebeuf*. Ed. with new foreword, endnotes and index by Thomas J. Steele, SJ, and Ronald S. Brockway. Pueblo: 1908; reprint by Regis College, Denver, 1987.

Jones, William H. *The History of Catholic Education in the State of Colorado*. Washington, D.C.: Catholic University of America Press, 1955.

Malone, T. A. *The Idea Persistent*. Denver: Smith-Brooks, 1916.

Manion, Patricia Jean, SL. *Only One Heart: The Story of a Pioneer Nun in America*. Garden City, N.Y.: Doubleday, 1963.

McMenamin, Hugh L., ed. *The Pinnacled Glory of the West: Cathedral of the Immaculate Conception*. Denver: Smith-Brooks Printing, 1912.

McNeill, Charles J. "The Catholic Church in Colorado." pp. 437–476. In LeRoy R. and Ann Hafen, *Colorado*. Denver: Old West, 1943.

Mulroy, John R. *Catholic Charities on the Wider Front, 1927–1951*. Denver: Archdiocese of Denver, 1951.

Noel, Thomas J. *Denver's Larimer Street: Main Street, Skid Row and Urban Renaissance*. Denver: Historic Denver, 1982.

——. *Denver: Rocky Mountain Gold*. Tulsa, Okla.: Continental Heritage, 1980.

Noel, Thomas J., and Barbara S. Norgren. *Denver: The City Beautiful and Its Architects*. Denver: Historic Denver, 1987.

Official Catholic Directory. Wilmette, Ill.: P.J. Kenedy & Sons, 1817– .

O'Ryan, William, and Thomas H. Malone. *History of the Catholic Church in Colorado*. Denver: C.J. Kelly, Art Printing, 1889; reprint by the Denver Catholic Register, 1961.

Rist, Martin. "History of Religion in Colorado." Vol 2. pp. 199–224. In LeRoy R. Hafen, ed., *Colorado and Its People*. N.Y.: Lewis Historical Publishing, 1948.

Salpointe, Jean Baptiste. *Soldiers of the Cross: Notes on the Ecclesiastical History of New Mexico, Arizona and Colorado*. Banning, Calif.: St. Boniface's Industrial School, 1898.

Segale, Blandina, SC. *At the End of the Santa Fe Trail*. Milwaukee, Wisconsin: Bruce Publishing, 1948.

Shaffer, Ray. *A Guide to Places on the Colorado Prairie, 1540–1975*. Boulder: Pruett Publishing, 1978.

Shikes, Robert H. *Rocky Mountain Medicine: Doctors, Drugs and Disease in Early Colorado*. Boulder: Johnson Books, 1986.

Skiff, Elizabeth, SC. "Roman Catholics." pp. 98–104. In Louisa Ward Arps, ed. *Faith on the Frontier: Religion in Colorado Before 1876*. Denver: Colorado Council of Churches, 1976.

Smiley, Jerome C. *History of the City of Denver*. Denver: Times Publishing, 1901; reprint with index by Western Americana, Denver, 1971.

Stansell, Harold L., SJ. *Regis: On the Crest of the West*. Denver: Regis Educational Corporation, 1977.

Stauter, Patrick C. *The Willging Years*. Chicago: Adams Press, 1986.

Vélez de Escalante, Silvestre. *The Dominguez-Esclante Journal: Their Expedition through Colorado, Utah, Arizona, and New Mexico in 1776*. Trans. by Fray Angelico Chávez and ed. by Ted J. Warner. Provo, Utah: Brigham Young University Press, 1976.

ARTICLES

Anthony, Brother Claudius, FSC. "Kit Carson, Catholic." *New Mexico Historical Review* 10 (December 1935): 331–36.

Casey, James V. "Another Holocaust: The Nuclear Arms Race." *Catholic Mind* 76 (October 1978): 2–5.

——. "Denver's Archdiocesan Investment Guidelines." *Catholic Mind* 77 (February 1979): 11–12.

Espinosa, J. Manuel. "The Neapolitan Jesuits on the Colorado Frontier, 1868–1919." *Colorado Magazine* 15 (March 1938):64–73.

Goodykoontz, Colin B. "Some Controversial Questions Before the Colorado Constitutional Convention of 1876." Colorado Magazine 17 (January 1940): 1–17.

McMenamy, Claire "Our Lady of Guadalupe at Conejos, Colorado." *Colorado Magazine* 17 (September 1940): 180–83.

Murphy, E.P. "Keeping the Record: Journal of Sister Blandina Segale." *Commonweal* 19 (November 17, 1933): 72–73.

Noel, Thomas J. "Spiritual Rebirth: Hispanic Denver's Annunciation Parish." *Colorado Heritage* 3 (1988): 42–47.

O'Conner, Thomas F. "Bishop Machebeuf." *Colorado Magazine* 12 (July 1935): 130–39.

——. "An Early Episcopal Visitation of Colorado: 1860 Letters of the Rt. Rev. John Baptiste Miege, S.J., D.D." *Mid-America Magazine* 18 (October 1936): 266–71.

O'Hayre, Paul, as told to Bernard Kelly. "Father Howlett—Colorado's Centennial Priest." *Empire Magazine* of *The Denver Post*, (November 14, 1976): 41–52.

Owens, M. Lilliana, SL. "Christ of the Rockies." *Colorado Magazine* 18 (May 1941): 110–13.

——. "Julia Greeley, 'Colorado Angel of Charity'." *Colorado Magazine* 20 (September 1943): 176–78.

——. "Coming of the Sisters of Loretto to Denver and the Founding of St. Mary's Acadamy." *Colorado Magazine* 16 (November 1939): 231–35.

——. "Denver's Pioneer Academy." *Colorado Magazine* 14 (May 1937): 85–92.

Singular, Stephen. "Archbishop James V. Casey: Cautious Shepherd to a Restless Flock." *Denver Magazine* (December 1981): 47–49.

Stafford, J. Francis. "On Being Catholic and American: This Home of Freedom." *Origins* 17 (June 11, 1987): 53–63.

Sweeney, Elizabeth Ann. "The Catholic Church at Central City." *Colorado Magazine* 17 (September 1941): 180–86.

INTERVIEWS

Anderson, John V. Denver. December 11 and 12, 1986.

Babbs, Dorothy. Cincinnati Historical Society. Telephone interview, July 23, 1987.

Barry, Thomas. Denver. March 18, 1987.

Benjamin, Julia, OSF. Denver. February 26, 1988.

Boggs, Julia. Denver. December 16, 1987.

Bowles, Richard J. Denver. December 3, 1987.

Chamberlain, Michael J., JCL. Denver. December 19, 1987.

Downey, Mary Lucy, SCL. Denver. November 24, 1986.

Hoffmann, Edward M. Denver. December 12, 1987.

Jones, William H. Denver. November 5, 11, 1987.

Keegan, Rosemary, SL. Denver. November 20, 1986.

Kraus, William, OFM, CAP. Denver. February 25, 1988.

Leonard, Dorothy. Denver. June 6, 1986.

Mauck, James H. Denver. February 18, 1987.

McCook, William J. Denver. February 11, 1988.

McGath, Marie Therese, OP. Denver. September 27, 1987

McGlone, Frank. Littleton. July 27, 1987.

McManus, Jarlath, CSJ. Denver January 28, 1988.

McNichols, Stephen L. R. Englewood. April 1, 27, 1987.

Newell, Hubert M. Denver. January 29, 1987.

Riedou, Alphonse. Denver. August 5, 1985.

St. Peter, Lawrence. Denver. December 29, 1987.

Smith, Gregory. Denver. March 23, 24; November 2, 1987; January 24, 1988.

Smythe, Pete. Estabrook. June 26, 1988.

Stafford, J. Francis. Denver. December 5, 1986; August 25, 1988.

Stansell, Harold L., SJ. Denver. October 29, 1987.

Woodrich, Charles B. Denver. December 29, 1987.

DISSERTATIONS

Courbois-Moore, Marie-Annick de. *The Stained Glass Windows of St. Thomas Seminary's Chapel*. Boulder: University of Colorado M.A. Thesis. Fine Arts, 1984.

Feely, Thomas Francis. *Leadership in the Early Colorado Catholic Church*. Denver: University of Denver Ph.D. Dissertation. History, 1973.

Fowle, Mary Peter, RSM. *The Beginnings of Catholic Education in Colorado before . . . 1887*. Denver: University of Denver M.A. Thesis. 1938.

Hastings, Martin F. *Parochial Beginnings in Colorado to 1889*. St. Louis: St. Louis University M.A. Thesis. 1941.

Leonard, Stephen J. *Denver's Foreign Born Immigrants, 1859–1900*. Claremont, California: Claremont Graduate School and University Center Ph.D. Thesis. History, 1971.

Linscome, Sanford A. *A History of Musical Development in Denver, Colorado, 1858–1908*. Austin: University of Texas Ph.D. Dissertation. Music, 1970.

Madden, Loretto Anne, SL. *The Social Apostolate of Joseph Projectus Machebeuf, First Bishop of Denver*. Washington, D.C.: Catholic University of America M.A. Thesis. 1956.

Rosen, Bernard. *Social Welfare in the History of Denver*. Boulder: University of Colorado Ph.D. Dissertation. History, 1976.